Special Edition

Using Java 2 Enterprise Edition

Mark Wutka

que®

201 W. 103rd Street

Indianapolis, Indiana 46290

Contents at a Glance

Special Edition Using Java™ 2 Enterprise Edition

International Standard Book Number: 0-7897-2503-7

Library of Congress Catalog Card Number: 00-111812

Printed in the United States of America

First Printing: May 2001

04 03 02 01 4 3 2 1

Trademarks

Warning and Disclaimer

Associate Publisher
Dean Miller

Acquisitions Editor
Todd Green

Development Editor
Sean Dixon

Managing Editor
Thomas F. Hayes

Senior Editor
Susan Ross Moore

Copy Editor
Julie McNamee

Indexer
Rebecca Salerno

Proofreader
Harvey Stanbrough

Technical Editors
Chuck Cavaness
Brian Keeton
Alan Moffet

Team Coordinator
Cindy Teeters

Media Developer
Michael Hunter

Interior Designer
Ruth Harvey

Cover Designers
Dan Armstrong
Ruth Harvey

Page Layout
Gloria Schurick

TABLE OF CONTENTS

About the Author

Mark Wutka has been programming since the Carter administration and considers programming a relaxing pastime. He managed to get a computer science degree while designing and developing networking software at Delta Air Lines. Although he has been known to delve into areas of system and application architecture, he isn't happy unless he's writing code—usually in Java.

As a consultant for Wutka Consulting, Mark enjoys solving interesting technical problems and helping his coworkers explore new technologies. He has taught classes, written articles and books, and given lectures. His first book, *Hacking Java*, outsold Stephen King at the local technical bookstore. He's also known for having a warped sense of humor.

Most recently, Mark wrote *Special Edition Using Java Server Pages and Servlets*.

He plays a mean game of Scrabble, a lousy game of chess, and is the bane of every greenskeeper east of Atlanta.

He can be reached via e-mail at `mark@wutka.com`. You can also visit his company Web site at `http://www.wutka.com`.

Dedication

To my wife, Ceal

Thank you for your patience and love.

Acknowledgments

Writing this book has been one of the toughest projects I've ever done. If it weren't for my family, friends, and the great folks at Que, I would never have made it.

If it weren't for my lovely wife Ceal, I don't know what I'd do. She put up with endless nights of clicking keys and some occasional yelps of distress. Sweetie, you're wonderful!

My family has been a great source of support and understanding. My mom, Dr. Patricia Graham, is a wonderful person and a role model that I could never live up to. Her husband, Dr. John Graham, is just as wonderful and just lives to teach. Next time I visit, Mom, I *promise* that we'll play Scrabble!

I'd also like to thank Mike Bates of the John H. Harland Company for good advice, plenty of patience, and the opportunity to try out some interesting ideas in enterprise development.

This book uses several third-party products, and the various software vendors have been quite helpful. I'd especially like to thank BEA for the assistance with its WebLogic product and WebGain for the assistance with TopLink. I would also like to thank the various open-source projects, such as jboss and Jakarta, for the wonderful work they do. I would also like to thank the vendors who have contributed evaluation versions of their products for inclusion on the CD-ROM that accompanies this book.

As an author, I am shocked when I read the list of people who work on a book. At most, I deal with only a handful of people at Que, yet the list of people who worked on the book is pretty large. I'd like to thank Todd Green, Sean Dixon, Susan Moore, Maureen McDaniel, Julie McNamee, Rebecca Salerno, and the other great folks at Que who got this book out the door. I couldn't ask for a better group of folks to work with.

I feel really lucky to have such excellent technical editors for this book. Chuck Cavaness and Brian Keeton have graciously taken time out of their own writing schedules to lend their technical expertise to this book. I look forward to reading their *Special Edition Using Enterprise JavaBeans*. These guys know their stuff. I'd also like to thank Alan Moffet, who is the most well-informed, thorough technical editor I've ever worked with.

Finally, I'd like to thank you, the reader. You're the one we're doing this for. I hope you enjoy the book!

Tell Us What You Think!

As the reader of this book, *you* are our most important critic and commentator. We value your opinion and want to know what we're doing right, what we could do better, what areas you'd like to see us publish in, and any other words of wisdom you're willing to pass our way.

As an associate publisher for Que, I welcome your comments. You can fax, e-mail, or write me directly to let me know what you did or didn't like about this book—as well as what we can do to make our books stronger.

Please note that I cannot help you with technical problems related to the topic of this book, and that due to the high volume of mail I receive, I might not be able to reply to every message.

When you write, please be sure to include this book's title and author as well as your name and phone or fax number. I will carefully review your comments and share them with the author and editors who worked on the book.

Fax: 317-581-4666

E-mail: `feedback@quepublishing.com`

Mail: Dean Miller
Associate Publisher
Que
201 West 103rd Street
Indianapolis, IN 46290 USA

INTRODUCTION

In this introduction

WHO SHOULD BUY THIS BOOK

Special Edition Using Java 2 Enterprise Edition is more than just a book about Java 2 Enterprise Edition—it's about developing enterprise-level applications in Java. It covers many of the aspects of enterprise-level development that aren't specific to J2EE, but are still very important. For example, this book discusses encryption and digital signatures. It's tough to do an Internet application these days without needing to know something about data security. This book also discusses some of the dynamic aspects of Java that really improve an application and allow you to make your application more configurable.

If you have never used Java before, this is not the book for you. It assumes that you are at least reasonably familiar with Java. *Special Edition Using Java 2 Standard Edition* is a good starting point for beginners.

If you are a Java developer who wants to do enterprise-level development, this book not only tells you how to use various parts of J2EE, it also explains application architecture so you know how the various technologies fit together.

If you are a system architect, this book tells you how Java solves many of the problems that you might have faced with other technologies. If you're studying for the Java 2 Enterprise Architect certification, this book covers almost all the material you need to know. All you need is a good tutorial on UML and you'll be ready for the test.

HOW THIS BOOK IS ORGANIZED

This book starts by giving you an overview of the core J2EE technologies. It then branches into some areas that aren't specifically part of J2EE, but are common in enterprise-level applications. Finally, the book finishes with some full-blown examples that show you how the various J2EE technologies work together.

PART I: ENTERPRISE JAVABEANS

This part covers JDBC and Enterprise JavaBeans, which is the core of J2EE server technologies. If you aren't too familiar with SQL, this section also includes a quick primer on SQL to get you up to speed.

PART II: JAVA SERVER PAGES AND SERVLETS

This part explains the J2EE Web technologies: Java Server Pages and servlets. It gives you a basic overview of these two technologies and shows you how to put them to good use.

PART III: ADDITIONAL J2EE TECHNOLOGIES

This part covers some of the other technologies that you might need when doing enterprise-level development and includes Java Naming and Directory Interface (JNDI), the Java Message Service (JMS), and CORBA.

Part IV: Using XML with J2EE

XML has become an integral part of many enterprise-level applications. This part explains the basics of XML and how to use XML in your applications.

Part V: Networking

This part not only gives you a basic overview of network programming, but it also goes into detail about many of the common networking protocols. This section also discusses firewalls and how they can affect your application. If you are developing an Internet application, you can bet that you'll have to deal with a firewall at some point.

Part VI: Security

As more people do business over the Internet, the need for security becomes more and more important. This part discusses the basic concepts of data security (encryption and digital signatures) and shows how to use the various Java APIs to protect your data.

Part VII: Dynamic Java

Java has the capability to load classes dynamically and access fields and methods at runtime using the Reflection API. This part discusses how you can use these dynamic capabilities to build flexible programs.

Part VIII: Applets

Although applets aren't used as frequently today as they once were, they still play a part in many Web applications. This part not only shows you how to use applets, but also how to digitally sign your applets to increase their capabilities.

Part IX: Problem Solving

Some aspects of a developer's job have nothing to do with programming. Many times you must figure out why a system isn't working like it should. This part gives you some practical advice on how to debug a system and how to fix things in an emergency.

Part X: J2EE in Practice

This part shows you how to build several applications using various J2EE technologies. You'll even see how to create an application for the wireless Web!

Appendixes

The final part of this book provides you with references to several APIs you will work with often as you develop enterprise-level Java applications. These appendixes are located on the CD-ROM that accompanies this book.

CONVENTIONS USED IN THIS BOOK

This book uses various stylistic and typographic conventions to make it easier to use:

Convention	Meaning
Italic	New terms and phrases when initially defined.
`Monospace`	Parts of code, Web addresses, and filenames.
`Bold Monospace`	Information that you type.
➥	Indicates the continuation of a long code line from the previous line.

Note When you see a note in this book, it indicates additional information that might help you avoid problems or that should be considered in using the described features.

Tip Tip paragraphs suggest easier or alternative methods of executing a procedure. Tips introduce techniques applied by seasoned developers to simplify a task or to make design and implementation decisions that produce robust and maintainable systems.

Caution Cautions warn you of hazardous procedures (for example, activities that delete files).

Each chapter contains either a "Troubleshooting" section that helps you solve common problems, or a "Case Study" that gives a real-life example of how the technology has been applied.

PART I

Enterprise JavaBeans

CHAPTER 1

Application Architecture Concepts

In this chapter

If you have little experience with system architecture, this chapter introduces basic concepts and explains how they affect you. You can use this information to make better decisions when you design your applications. Even if you aren't doing system design, just knowing the idea behind the organization of applications makes it easier to understand the design of the application you're working on. Although some people think of the system architect as the overall designer of the system (assuming there is one), developers usually end up asserting a large amount of their own design philosophy on the code. Of course, some projects give developers free reign, whereas others stick to meticulous code specifications. After you understand the basic styles of applications, you are able to see how the various parts of J2EE fit together.

THE THREE LAYERS OF AN APPLICATION

No matter how you slice it, a typical application consists of three layers:

- The *data* layer manages the data used by the application. An application that stores its data in data files is said to implement the data layer itself. Many applications use a database to manage the storage of the data. The database itself is considered the data layer for the application.
- The *business logic* layer contains the various business rules and operations that the application performs on its data. When you store an order, the data section stores the various parts of the order, whereas the business logic section calculates the price of the order, handles any credit card validation, and verifies that the order has all the required information.
- The *presentation* layer interacts with the user in one way or another. GUI screens and Web pages are typical examples of a presentation layer. A report generator is also considered part of the presentation layer.

These three parts of the application are referred to as "layers" because they build on each other. The data layer is the lowest level of the application and deals with raw data. The business layer sits on top of the data layer and gives life to the data by making it behave according to the business rules. The presentation layer sits on top of the business layer and makes the application useful to the user. Figure 1.1 shows the relationship between the layers.

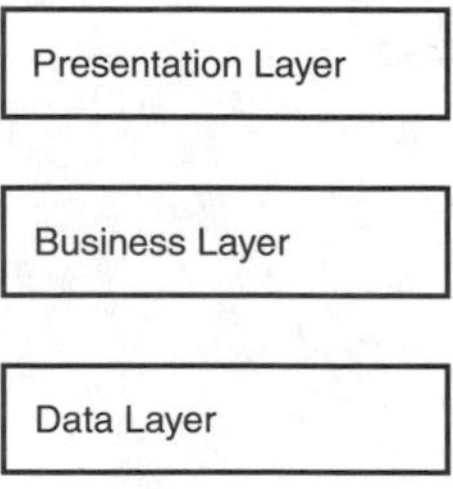

Figure 1.1
An application has three discernable layers.

Sun goes a step further when defining layers, splitting the presentation layer into a server-side presentation layer and a client-side presentation layer. Sun also refers to the data layer as the "Enterprise Information Layer." In addition to databases, the Enterprise Information Layer also contains legacy systems—existing systems that your application must access.

APPLICATION TIERS

Applications are frequently categorized by the number of tiers they have. A *tier* is a grouping of the three layers into a single component of the application. Although there are only three sections (data, business logic, and presentation), there are actually four categories for an application:

- *Single-tiered* applications combine all three sections into a single component (usually an executable program). Many programs that run on your PC and do their own data storage would be considered single-tiered applications.
- *Two-tiered* applications, in the traditional sense, combine the presentation and business logic layers into a single component and use a database program for the data layer. Although you could combine the data and business logic layers into a single unit and put the presentation layer in its own separate layer, most applications that separate presentation from the business logic also separate the business logic from the data layer.
- *Three-tiered* applications separate the three layers into separate components. These applications typically use distributed object middleware, such as CORBA, RMI, or DCOM. For example, you might have a GUI program that uses CORBA to communicate with a server containing the business logic. The CORBA objects on the server then communicate with a database.
- *N-tiered* applications are similar to three-tiered applications, but are more distributed than their three-tiered counterparts. An n-tiered application has many distributed objects spread across many machines, again using something such as CORBA, RMI, or DCOM. These objects might have their separate data layers. Many people still refer to n-tiered applications as three-tiered just to indicate that the three layers are separate from each other.

APPLICATIONS COME UNGLUED OVER TIME

If you look at the evolution of computer applications over the last 40 years, you see that applications have been coming unglued over time. Computer applications were originally just single-tiered applications running on a mainframe. Databases became popular in the 70s, and then exploded in the 80s when the PC entered the scene and hooked up with the local area network. The old single-tiered applications began to separate into two-tiered applications, with the database handling the data layer.

At the time, the concept of application "tiers" was not really used. As the local area network gained popularity, the term *client/server* caught on. Originally, a client/server system was a database server and an application client. Soon, applications began to make use of remote procedure calls (RPC), in which a client calls a procedure on a server. Unfortunately, RPC-based systems were also referred to as client/server. Because many RPC-based systems also used databases, the term client/server wasn't descriptive enough.

Eventually, the concept of tiers made its way into the lingo of system designers and it became easier to describe the overall structure of a system. These changes in terminology were necessary because the applications continued to split into different components—in other words, they came unglued.

Physical Versus Logical Tiers

The definition of a tier, unfortunately, is becoming more and more strained. First of all, people often refer to the number of tiers in an application as a count of the number of different machines the application runs on. For example, a "tier" can refer to a logical tier or a physical tier. Just because you can separate the business logic layer from the presentation layer doesn't mean you need to put those layers on separate machines, or even in separate programs. The benefit of working with separate tiers is that it is easy to organize and maintain your code. Some designers automatically assume that if you have separate tiers, those tiers must be physically separated.

If you have a three-tiered application in which each tier resides on a separate machine, that is referred to as a *physical three-tiered* model. When you separate your application tiers into three separate programs but run those programs on one or two machines (the business logic layer program running on the same machine as the database server, for example) that application is still, logically, a three-tiered application.

How Can You Have Half a Tier?

The Web has really thrown a monkey wrench into application design lingo (and application design in general). The problem is that the browser can be thought of as either a dumb terminal or smart platform on which you can execute programs. Remember that a mainframe application is considered a single-tiered application. Is a program that runs on a Web server, manages its own data and business logic, and generates the HTML it sends back to the browser a single-tiered application? Or is it a two-tiered application in which the business logic and data layers are on the Web server and the presentation layer is on the browser?

You could argue either way. From a physical standpoint, you could say that it's a two-tiered application. From a logical standpoint, however, you might say it's a single-tiered application because the code to manage all three layers is mingled together. It gets more confusing when you run JavaScript on the browser. You could consider HTML just static text like the characters a mainframe sends to a terminal. After you start executing code on the browser, it becomes more than just a dumb terminal.

One solution to this dilemma is to consider the browser a half-tier. You'll see an application described as a *two-and-a-half tiered* application. You have a database for the data layer, a servlet or JSP doing business logic and some presentation, and JavaScript on the browser for some of the presentation. Remember, Sun typically splits the presentation layer into a client side and a server side anyway. While you might see references to one-and-a-half or two-and-a-half tiers, you usually see *n*-tiered instead of three-and-a-half.

Combine the Web server with objects distributed around the network and you have more tiers than you can throw a stick at. You might see the "tier" notation change a little in the future. There will probably be a term distinguishing between the code that runs on a browser and the presentation code on the server. You might even see the use of the term "tier" diminish as more applications become just a conglomeration of distributed objects. After terms such as "three-tiered" or "n-tiered" describe almost all the applications you encounter, it will be time for a new term.

WHAT "TIER" MEANS IN THIS BOOK

As you can see, the use of the term "tier" is not so cut and dried. One person might call an application two-tiered, whereas another might call it single-tiered or one-and-a-half tiered. This book uses the term "tier" as a component-level tier. If you separate the data layer from the business logic and presentation layers, that's a two-tiered application. If you manage your data, perform business logic functions, and create the presentation output (including generating HTML) within the same components, that's a single-tiered application. If you separate the presentation layer, the business logic layer, and the data layer into separate components, that's a three-tiered application.

Note

The choice of terminology used here is somewhat arbitrary. If you would classify a particular application differently, you aren't wrong, you're just using a different point of view.

SINGLE-TIERED APPLICATIONS

Many Web applications are single-tiered, often out of necessity. Many Web providers don't provide database access, so applications have had to rely on local file storage. With the advent of small, cheap database engines such as MySQL, more Web providers are providing database access. There are still plenty of occasions where a single-tiered application is appropriate. Figure 1.2 shows the structure of a typical single-tiered application.

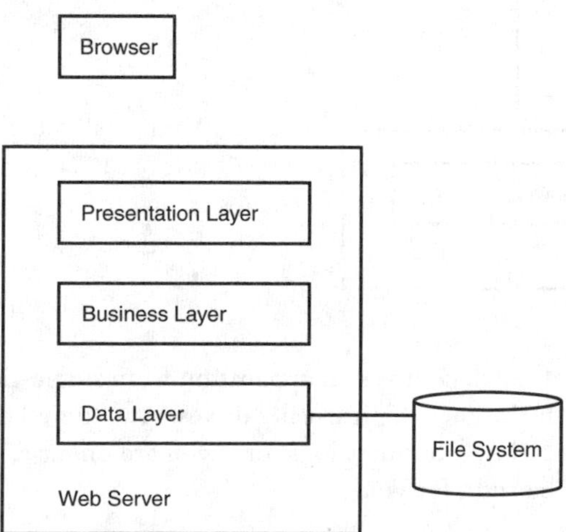

Figure 1.2
A single-tiered application manages presentation, business logic, and data from a single component.

Although single-tiered applications can have a fairly complex presentation layer, you will usually find that they have very simple business logic and data layers. After all, when a data layer becomes complex, you tend to use a database and turn the application into a two- or three-tiered design.

An online survey or poll would be a good candidate for a single-tier design because the data and business logic requirements are minimal. An online message board is another good candidate for single-tiered design, although you are probably better off separating the management of the messages from their presentation even if you store the messages in files rather than in a database.

TWO-TIERED APPLICATIONS

Two-tiered designs usually come about because the data layer is complex. If you must perform queries or maintain relationships between data items, you certainly don't want to write that code yourself. Figure 1.3 shows the structure of a typical two-tiered application.

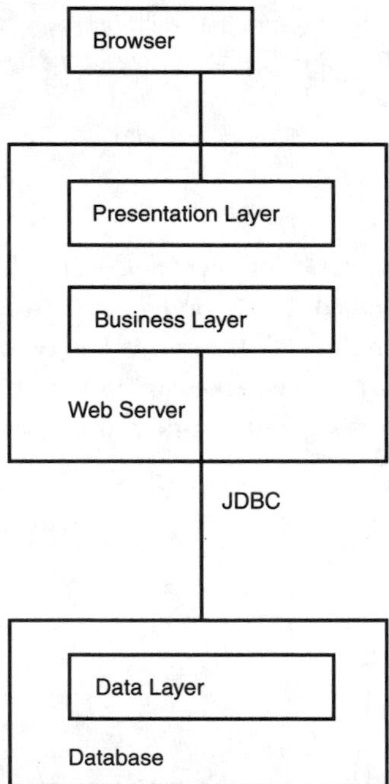

Figure 1.3
A two-tiered design usually puts the data layer into a separate component.

Although the complexity of the data drives an application from single-tiered to two-tiered design, the complexity of the business logic usually drives a two-tiered design into three tiers. If your application is light on business logic or if you are under extreme time pressure, a two-tiered design might be right for you.

One of the advantages that a two-tiered design still maintains over a three-tiered design is that there are many tools available for designing and accessing the data layer, but there are not many tools for designing and accessing the business logic layer. For example, you can find many object-to-relational mapping tools that help you create a database and map Java objects to database tables. These tools even let you design the database according to the structure of your Java object.

There are few tools that allow you to do the same kind of operation at a higher level. That is, when you need to package your business logic into separate components, there are few tools that help you decide how to perform the separation or how to make data available from these components. Hopefully, as Enterprise JavaBeans become more popular, you will find more tools that help you design the business logic layer. Until that time, given the presence of data layer tools combined with the lack of business logic layer tools, a two-tiered application is a better bet when you are short on time and are willing to make sacrifices in the extensibility and maintainability of your code.

THREE-TIERED APPLICATIONS

A three-tiered design is the most flexible and the most complicated to build. By separating presentation, business logic, and data layers into their own components, you can change the implementation of each layer without affecting the other layers. Figure 1.4 shows the structure of a typical three-tiered application.

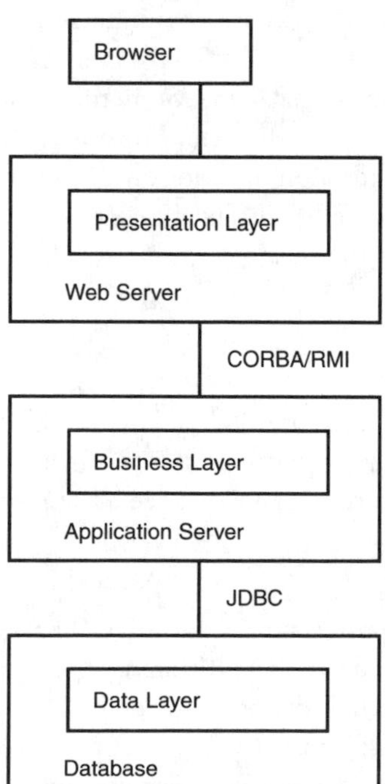

Figure 1.4
A three-tiered application has separate presentation, business logic, and data components.

When you separate the presentation, business logic, and data layers, you must determine how the layers interface with each other. The interface between the business logic and data layers is often determined by using a third-party database tool.

The interface between the presentation and the business logic layers is the difficult part to design, especially when it comes to Web programming. When you create a traditional three-tiered application with a graphical user interface, the coupling between the actual user interface and the business logic layer is a little tighter. The difference is that a graphical user interface can respond immediately to user requests and can perform more frequent interactions. In a Web application, the interaction between the user and the server is much slower.

Suppose, for example, that you have a data-entry system that must validate user input against a database. If you use a traditional graphical user interface, you can check the user input immediately and give instant feedback when the user's data isn't valid. With a Web application, you must wait until the user submits a form, making the feedback process much slower.

Note

If the amount of data you need to validate is small and you don't need any data from the server to perform the validation, you can always validate it with a JavaScript routine and still give immediate feedback.

You must also make sure that the business logic layer doesn't require a large number of short interactions with the user. In a traditional graphical user interface, you might get away with popping up a series of dialog boxes to ask questions. In a Web application, especially one that might be run over a slow connection, you want to minimize the number of times the user must submit a form to the server. If you need to make a series of business logic layer calls when the user submits a single form, that's fine. Sometimes, however, you just can't make multiple calls using the data from a single form. For example, you might make some sort of survey where the next survey question depends on the answer from the previous one. In these situations, you must either redesign the application or accept the fact that the user will need to make many short calls to the server.

THE TRADE-OFFS

There is no one-size-fits-all application architecture. When you choose a design, you must evaluate various aspects of the application, your development team, and your schedule to come up with the architecture that strikes a reasonable balance among various factors.

APPLICATION COMPLEXITY

The size and complexity of the application push toward more tiers. That is, the more complex the application, the more tiers you generally have. By partitioning your application into multiple tiers, it becomes easier to manage the complexity because you can focus on each layer individually and also parcel out the work to separate development teams. A single-tiered application is more difficult to split among various development teams because the same section of code might enable presentation, business logic, and data at the same time.

Maintainability

Some applications are quick, one-time shots that you need to get out quickly and then discard. For example, you might be switching over to a new backend system and you are writing an application to smooth the transition. After the transition is complete, your application goes away. In those cases, you don't care if it might be tough to make changes later on because the application won't be used. On the other hand, if you are writing an application that will be used for several years and needs to undergo periodic updates, you want to make it easy to modify parts of the system.

Application maintainability tends to push you toward more tiers, because the separation of the various layers allows you to change aspects of one layer without affecting the other layers.

Schedule Pressure

Schedule pressure tends to push you toward fewer tiers. It takes time to come up with a good three-tiered design that has a clean separation between the layers. It is often an iterative process where discoveries made about the presentation layer lead to changes in the interface between the presentation and business layers. Obviously, the more you know up-front, the easier it is to make design decisions. Unfortunately, with a short time schedule, you often don't have time to get all the information up front.

Note

> Although you can sometimes trim some time off the initial gathering of system requirements, you soon hit a point where the time you save up-front is lost when you need to rework code because of an incorrect assumption or an overlooked requirement.

Although you can gain some development speed by parceling out the work to various development teams, you might also lose some speed because developers of one layer are waiting for parts of another layer to be complete.

Development Team Skill

The skill of the development team tends to push toward fewer tiers. That is, the less skill a development team has, the less likely it is to be able to implement a three-tiered application. You must take this into account when deciding your application architecture. Although the addition of some key skill sets can enable the team to do the job, you must consider whether your team can handle the job with or without help, and whether you can get the help you need.

For a large, three-tiered application, you need architects and developers who know how to split the application logic into logical tiers. You need Web designers or GUI designers who know how to create a user interface that works well in a three-tiered environment. You also need developers who know how to debug three-tiered applications. When you have more tiers, you have more places where the application can break.

When the application is split across many machines, you need developers who know how to write code that can adapt to network outages.

Evaluating developer skill is a subjective process, of course. Try to find people with extensive experience in using the kind of architecture you want, and place these people in key positions (architecture and design). You can get by with junior-level developers doing actual implementation. Use design reviews and code reviews as a way to keep everyone going in the right direction, and also as a way to expose your inexperienced people to the potential pitfalls of your architecture.

MISCELLANEOUS FACTORS

There are miscellaneous factors involved with every project that tend to counteract some of the other factors. For example, if you have a large existing base of code that you can reuse, you might be drawn to use the same architecture as the existing code base. Your management might dictate that you are to use a specific kind of architecture. Don't laugh; it happens all the time.

Figure 1.5 shows the various trade-offs you must evaluate and how they push against each other.

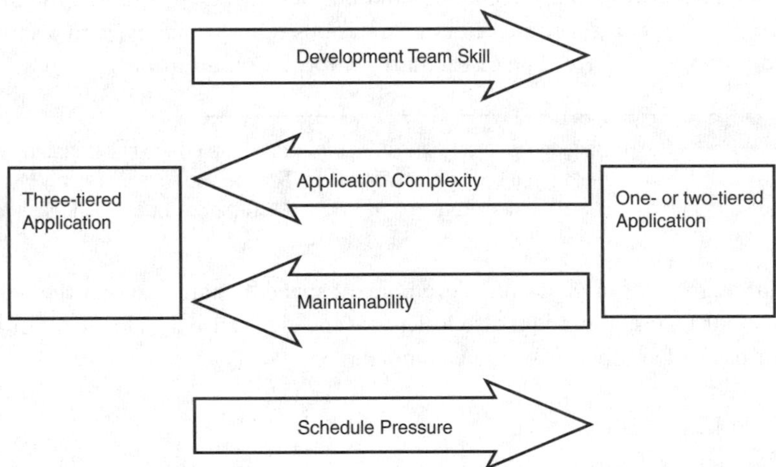

Figure 1.5 Various factors push you in different directions when you choose an architecture.

THE "ILITIES"

When you talk about the benefits of three-tiered and multitiered applications, you often talk in terms of "ilities"—scalability, maintainability, reliability, availability, extensibility, and manageability. The addition of multiple tiers affects each of these terms in different ways.

SCALABILITY

Scalability refers to the application's capability to support more and more users. In a two-tiered application, for example, each user might have a separate connection to the database. This is especially true for a two-tiered GUI application, because the GUI application typically connects directly to the database. If you have 10,000 users, you need 10,000 database connections. In a two-tiered Web application, you can support many users with a small number of database connections. You typically add more database connections when you can't handle enough simultaneous requests. For example, suppose your database transactions take an average of 50ms (milliseconds)—you can perform 20 in 1 second. Suppose, furthermore, that you can have 10,000 users that make, on average, one request every minute. That's just shy of 167 requests per second. If you can perform 20 transactions a second over one database connection, you should be able to perform 180 per second over nine connections (assuming the database is fast enough to handle 180 requests per second).

When you have fewer tiers, you have fewer places to add extra horsepower. In a three-tiered application, you can add extra computing resources to each layer—in fact, you can even spread the layers across multiple machines. You can have a cluster of servers doing Web presentation, another cluster handling business logic, and a third cluster of database machines.

MAINTAINABILITY

As you have already seen, *maintainability* indicates how easy it is to make changes to your code without breaking the rest of the system. You can write single-tiered applications that are easy to maintain if you take a little time up front to design the application well. As you add more tiers, however, you see an increase in maintainability. You can actually change a part of the application at runtime without affecting the rest of the system.

RELIABILITY

Although you typically think of *reliability* in terms of uptime, in this case it refers to the accuracy and integrity of the data. In single-tiered and two-tiered applications, where you have direct access to the data, you often see programs that perform a particular business operation in different sections of code. If you add a new business rule, it's possible that you might forget to add it in one section of code. You end up with situations in which you apply the rule one time and omit it the next time.

By separating the business logic into a separate module, you force the rest of the application to perform a particular business operation exactly the same way every time.

J2EE provides an extra level of reliability by allowing you to group business logic operations into transactions, giving you the same kind of reliability you normally expect from a database.

AVAILABILITY

Availability typically refers to system uptime. You always want the application to be available to the user. You might think that with more tiers, there are more things that can break, but actually, availability improves with more tiers. Your dependence on a particular machine decreases when you move parts of your application onto separate machines. You can recover from an outage faster because you don't need to restart everything, just the system that failed.

Availability really increases when you have the ability to create clusters of machines at each layer. A user may never see the effect of a particular machine failure.

EXTENSIBILITY

Extensibility refers to the ease at which you can add additional capabilities to the system. With fewer tiers, you are much more likely to break the existing application. For example, suppose you have a two-tiered application with some fairly complex business logic. You now want to create a second application that shares the same database. You must be careful that the business logic rules in the new application work the same way as the first application. When you split the business logic into its own tier, however, a new application can use the existing business logic tier—you have less code to write and the system will remain consistent.

MANAGEABILITY

Manageability refers to your ability to manage your system. When you split the application into several tiers, you can monitor each tier separately and make changes to a specific tier without affecting the rest of the system. Typically, it's easier to monitor separate parts of the system than to monitor a single system that does everything. It's also easier to make runtime changes (increase buffer sizes and connection pools) to a separate part of the system.

HYBRID ARCHITECTURES

You don't have to confine yourself to a single architecture for your entire application. Many applications use a mixture of two- and three-tiered designs. When you need to create a database maintenance application to modify the data used by your application, you can create a two-tiered application. The main application can still be three-tiered. You will often find that the amount of effort required to make a three-tiered database maintenance application is excessive, especially if your only goal is to use the same architecture for all parts of your application.

Likewise, you might have a two-tiered application that also needs to access some external data sources. You can create a component that accesses the external system and possibly the database along the way. Although the external system access resembles a three-tiered architecture, the core of your application is still two-tiered. Although there is something to be said for consistency, try to focus on the problems at hand first. Don't make huge sacrifices in time and effort just so you can say you used a specific architecture.

CASE STUDY: AN ONLINE ORDERING SYSTEM

A check printing company wanted to sell its checks online and needed a system reasonably quickly. Most of its previous applications had been on a mainframe and the company was fairly new to Java. For a simple ordering system and an inexperienced development staff, you would ordinarily consider a two-tiered application to start with. Unfortunately, this company had some complex business rules—banks could set up various purchasing plans that included free or discounted items. The company decided to go with a three-tiered application.

Not only was this company's business logic complex, but so was the data model. They created a separate application just for managing the data. The company opted for a hybrid approach, using a two-tiered GUI application to configure the database while the three-tiered ordering application used the data. The choice of the two-tiered GUI application was a difficult one, but it shortened the development time substantially. The GUI application didn't use the same business rules as the ordering application, so there was minimal duplication of code.

Because its staff didn't have much experience with Java development and even less experience with three-tiered application development, the company hired a few experienced Java developers to do the architecture and design. These developers helped mentor the junior developers and also kept the development on track.

Because the company opted for a three-tiered approach, they were able to add additional online ordering applications using the same business logic tier as the original application.

CHAPTER 2

A Quick Primer on SQL

In this chapter

INTRODUCTION TO RELATIONAL DATABASES

It's hard to do any significant enterprise-level development without using a relational database. This chapter gives you a quick overview of how to organize data in a database and how to use the *Structured Query Language* (SQL) to manipulate the database. If you already understand databases and SQL, you might want to skip to Chapter 3, "JDBC—The Java Database API."

When you use a relational database, you organize your data into two-dimensional tables. The columns of the table represent individual pieces of data: numbers, strings, dates, and so on. Within a particular table, each column must have a unique name, but you can use the same column names in different tables. All the column values in a single row in the table represent a single data entity. Figure 2.1 illustrates a simple table containing information about a person. Each row in the table represents a different person.

Figure 2.1
Rows in a table represent separate data entities.

First_Name	Middle_Name	Last_Name
Kaitlynn	Dawn	Tippin
Samantha	Lauren	Tippin
Edward	Alexander	Wutka
⋮	⋮	⋮

You might encounter the term *entity* frequently when you work with databases. An entity is basically an object—a thing—stored in the database. A person can be an entity, so can an order or an appointment. Although there is often a one-to-one correlation between entities and database rows, you will soon see that an entity can span multiple tables (but not multiple rows in the same table).

In a database table, there must be a set of columns (maybe just one, maybe several) that can uniquely identify a particular row. This set of columns is called the table's *primary key*. When you create the table, you designate which columns make up the primary key. The important thing to remember is that no two database rows can have the same primary key. If you specify `first_name` and `last_name` as the primary key columns for your `Person` table, you can't have two entries both with the same first and last names. Although there might be multiple sets of columns that uniquely identify a row, you must choose one set (which may be a single column) to represent the primary key.

The database usually creates an *index* based on the primary key. A database index is a lot like the index in a book—it's a condensed version of the data that helps you locate data quickly. If you perform a lot of queries on data items other than those in the primary key, you might consider creating a separate database index for the columns you are querying. For instance, if you find that you often search on a person's phone number, you can create an index on the phone_number column.

By definition, no two rows can have the same primary key value, and the database enforces this restriction. You can also force other columns to be unique by creating a *unique index* on the table. For example, if you have a social_security_number column in the Person table, you might want to create a unique index on the social_security_number column to make sure you can't accidentally create two people with the same SSN.

A column value can have a special value of null, which means there is no data there. In Java, null is used only in relation to object references. You can't have a null int or double variable. In fact, none of the primitive Java types can be null. In a relational database, however, any value can be null. The database keeps track of which values are null. Remember, too, that a null value is not a numeric or string value. In other words, there is no specific integer value that represents null in a numeric column. The database uses a special technique to tell whether a column's value is null or not. There is a difference between zero and null. You can also specify that a column value can't be null.

RELATIONSHIPS

Although tables are certainly the primary component of a relational database, it's the relationships between the tables that make the database so powerful. After all, if you couldn't establish relationships between tables, the database would be nothing but a simplified spreadsheet program. As it is, however, you can create relationships between tables by relating groups of keys together. There are three types of database relationships: *one-to-one*, *one-to-many*, and *many-to-many*.

The term *relationship* can refer to a relationship that the database knows about, or it can refer to a conceptual relationship that you might know about but the database does not. When you tell the database about a relationship, it automatically enforces *relational integrity*; that is, it prevents you from creating a faulty relationship. A relationship can exist without the database knowing about it. In other words, you might know the relationship between two tables, but the database doesn't have a clue. It thinks the two tables are totally unrelated. When you explicitly create a relationship in the database, you ensure relational integrity. Figure 2.2 shows two sample tables with a one-to-one relationship between them.

Figure 2.2
The Superhero table has a one-to-one relationship to the Alter_Ego table.

Superhero Table

Superhero_Name	Super_Power	Arch_Enemy
Particle Man	The things that a particle can	Triangle Man
The Cow	Moooves large objects	Burger Man

Alter_Ego Table

Superhero_Name	Real_Name	Occupation
The Cow	Fred Holstein	Chick-Fil-A Manager
Particle Man	Dot Speck	Diver

The `Superhero` table is related to the `Alter_Ego` table by the `Superhero_Name` column, which is present in both tables. Figure 2.3 shows the relationships between the rows in the two tables.

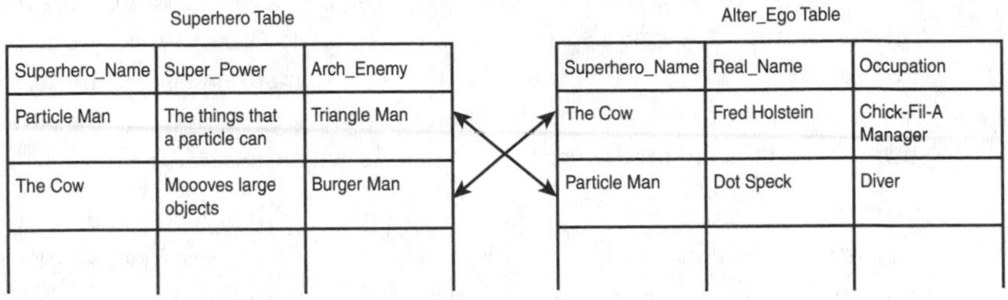

Superhero Table

Superhero_Name	Super_Power	Arch_Enemy
Particle Man	The things that a particle can	Triangle Man
The Cow	Moooves large objects	Burger Man

Alter_Ego Table

Superhero_Name	Real_Name	Occupation
The Cow	Fred Holstein	Chick-Fil-A Manager
Particle Man	Dot Speck	Diver

Figure 2.3
Rows in tables are related by matching column values.

Probably the most common type of relationship is the *foreign-key* relationship. In a foreign-key relationship, a column (or columns) in one table refers to a primary key in another table. For example, the relationship between the `Superhero` and `Alter_Ego` tables is a foreign-key relationship because the `Superhero_Name` in the `Alter_Ego` table refers to the `Superhero_Name` primary key field in the `Superhero` table.

Foreign-key relationships might have different cardinality (one-to-one, one-to-many, and so on); it all depends on how the relationships are set up.

A *one-to-many* relationship is the most common model—one-to-one is actually a special case of one-to-many, and many-to-many is a combination of two one-to-many relationships. In a one-to-many relationship, many rows in one table refer to a single row in another table. Figure 2.4 shows a common one-to-many model of an order and order items.

Order Table

Order_id	Buyer
1	Sam
2	Katie
3	Bunnie
4	Norton

Order Items

Item_Num	Order_id	Product
1	1	Barbie
2	1	Furby
3	1	Game Boy
4	2	Baby Doll
5	2	Toy Store
6	3	Food
7	3	Food
8	3	Food
9	4	Pillow

Figure 2.4
In a one-to-many relationship, many rows in one table relate to a single row in another table.

> **Note** In a *one-to-one* relationship, either table can contain the foreign key.

In the `Order_Items` table in Figure 2.4, the `Order_id` column is called a foreign-key column because it refers to a primary key in another table.

To turn a one-to-many relationship into a *one-to-one* relationship, put a unique index on the foreign-key column. When the foreign-key column is unique, you know that no two rows can refer to the same row in the other table. For example, suppose you put a unique index on the `order_id` column in the `Order_Items` table in Figure 2.4. You know that the `Order_id` column in the `Order` table must be unique, because it's the primary key. Now that the `Order_id` column in the `Order_Items` table is unique, there can be only one order item for any order. If there were two order items for the same order, they would have the same `Order_id`, which you have now forbidden because of the unique index.

A many-to-many relationship requires an additional table, usually called a *link table*. A link table has a one-to-many relationship with both tables. Figure 2.5 shows a many-to-many configuration relating students to classes. A student can attend many classes and a class has many students.

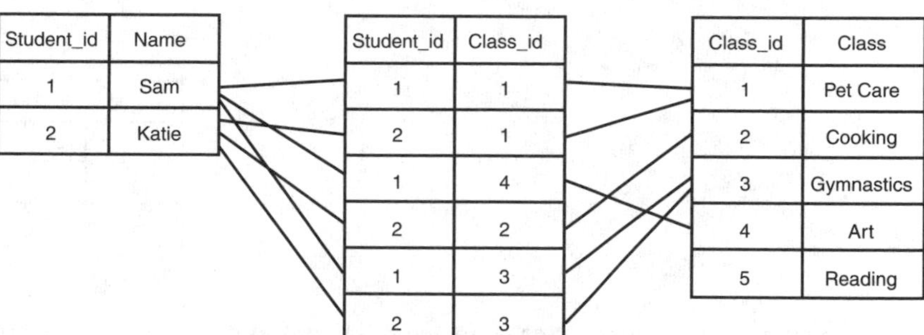

Figure 2.5
The `Student_Class` link table joins the `Student` and `Class` tables in a many-to-many relationship.

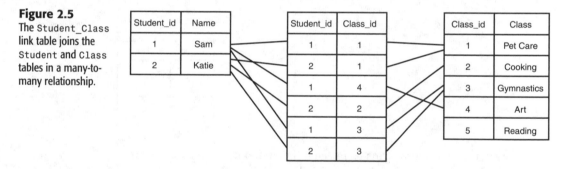

Sometimes, a link table contains additional data. This occurs when you need to keep data about the association itself. For example, an airline has aircraft and flight segments (a flight can go through several destinations; a segment is one hop along the entire flight path). A flight segment might have additional attributes, such as the amount of fuel it requires. The amount changes when the aircraft changes and when the flight changes. Your table structure might look like the tables shown in Figure 2.6.

A link table might also link more than two tables together. For example, when an aircraft is assigned to a flight, it also has a flight plan. This flight plan changes whenever the flight changes, and whenever the aircraft changes. Figure 2.7 illustrates the table structure when you introduce a `FlightPlan` table to the tables in Figure 2.6.

Figure 2.6
A link table might contain additional data.

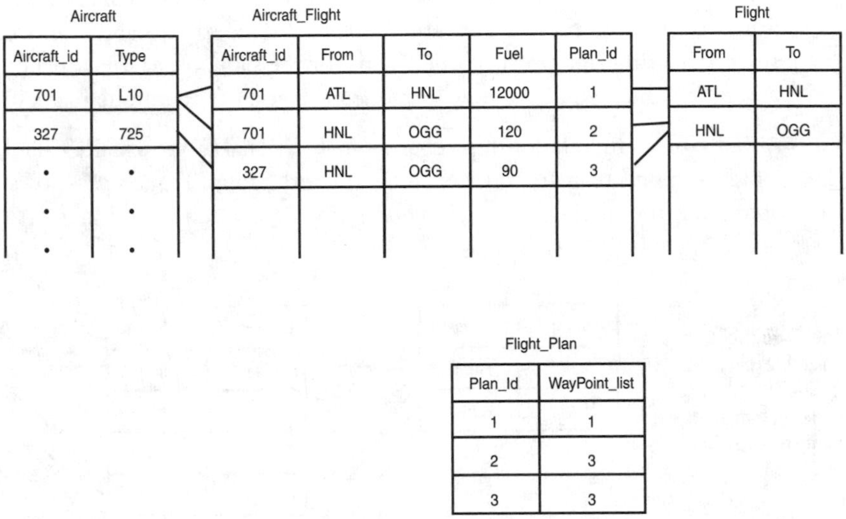

Figure 2.7
A link table might refer to additional tables.

Aircraft

Aircraft_id	Type
701	L10
327	725
•	•
•	•
•	•

Aircraft_Flight

Aircraft_id	From	To	Fuel	Plan_id
701	ATL	HNL	12000	1
701	HNL	OGG	120	2
327	HNL	OGG	90	3

Flight

From	To
ATL	HNL
HNL	OGG

Flight_Plan

Plan_Id	WayPoint_list
1	1
2	3
3	3

There are a few more terms you need to know about just in case you strike up a conversation with a database administrator. Database tables, indexes, and a few other resources are grouped together into *schemas*. You can think of a schema as a particular configuration of tables. You might make different schema versions for different versions of your software, or for testing purposes.

Schemas are grouped into *catalogs*. You might often find that there is only one catalog on your system, maybe two. You might have a catalog for all development schemas and a catalog for production schemas. When you log into the database, your username usually has a default catalog and schema, so when you try out SQL commands and write JDBC programs, you might never care about the schema and catalog.

THE STRUCTURED QUERY LANGUAGE (SQL)

The Structured Query Language (SQL) is a standard language for performing database operations. Although the language itself is a standard (and most database vendors support the standard fairly well), the way you access the database isn't standardized. Every database vendor has its own special API for sending SQL requests, although with the advent of the *Open Database Connectivity* (ODBC) API, you can write programs that can work with a variety of databases. As you'll see in Chapter 3, the Java database API—JDBC—lets you work with multiple databases easily.

Note JDBC is actually based on ODBC, as far as the kinds of objects you use.

Many database vendors supply you with a graphical query tool or a command-line query tool so you can enter SQL commands directly. These tools are handy for learning SQL.

One of the things you'll discover about SQL is that database vendors frequently add additional features and sometimes omit parts of the SQL standard. If you stick with simple data types and common operations, your database statements should work on most SQL databases.

DATA TYPES

Table 2.1 shows the common SQL data types. You should expect a database to support almost all of these, except that some databases don't support the `BLOB` or `CLOB` data types.

TABLE 2.1 THE COMMON SQL DATA TYPES

Type	Description
`CHARACTER(n)`	Fixed-length string of *n* characters
`VARCHAR(n)`	Variable-length string of at most *n* characters
`NUMERIC(t,r)`	Decimal number with exactly *t* digits of precision and *r* digits to the right of the decimal point
`DECIMAL(t,r)`	Decimal number with at least *t* digits of precision and *r* digits to the right of the decimal point
`INTEGER`	An integer number (precision is implementation-specific)
`SMALLINT`	A small integer number (precision is implementation-specific)
`FLOAT(t)`	Floating-point number with at least *t* digits of precision
`DATE`	A date containing year, month, and day
`TIME`	A time containing hours, minutes, and seconds
`TIMESTAMP`	A date/time combination containing year, month, day, hours, minutes, and seconds
`BLOB`	A binary large object for large noncharacter data (images, binary records, audio clips, and so on)
`CLOB`	A character large object—like a blob, but must contain printable characters

The DECIMAL and NUMERIC types can also represent integer values. You can specify 0 as the number of digits to the right of the decimal or you can use a shortcut. If you only specify a single number inside the parentheses, the database assumes that the second number is 0. In other words, DECIMAL(8) is the same as DECIMAL(8,0).

CREATING TABLES

The CREATE TABLE command creates a table. When you create the table, you must also specify the primary key. The general format for the CREATE TABLE command is

```
CREATE TABLE tablename (columndefs)
```

The *columndefs* part of the CREATE TABLE command is a list of column definitions and possibly a list of column constraints (indicating unique columns and primary key columns). Each column definition is of the form: *column-name data-type*. If there is only one column in the primary key, you can add PRIMARY KEY after that column's definition. Also, if a column can't contain a null value, add NOT NULL after the column definition.

Tip

SQL is case-insensitive, except for characters enclosed in quotes. The command CREATE TABLE is the same as Create table. It's best, however, to pick a standard and stick with it.

Listing 2.1 shows a CREATE TABLE command that creates a Person table.

LISTING 2.1 SOURCE CODE FOR create_person.sql

```
CREATE TABLE person
    (person_id decimal(10) not null primary key,
     first_name varchar(30),
     middle_name varchar(30),
     last_name varchar(30),
     address1 varchar(50),
     address2 varchar(50),
     city varchar(30),
     state varchar(2),
     zip decimal(5),
     age decimal(3),
     home_phone decimal(10),
     work_phone decimal(10),
     mobile_phone decimal(10));
```

Note

Notice that the CREATE TABLE command in Listing 2.1 ends with a semicolon. You normally use a semicolon to terminate commands in a command-line or graphical SQL tool, but not within a program. Some SQL tools don't require the semicolon at all.

In addition to defining columns, you can also define primary key and unique columns. In Listing 2.1, the primary key is defined as part of the column definition. When the primary key is made up of multiple columns, you must list the primary key columns in a separate part of the CREATE TABLE command. Listing 2.2 shows a CREATE TABLE command that defines a multicolumn primary key and also defines a particular column as being unique.

LISTING 2.2 SOURCE CODE FOR create_ssninfo.sql

```
CREATE TABLE SSN_Info
(
    first_name VARCHAR(30),
    middle_name VARCHAR(30),
    last_name VARCHAR(30),
    ssn DECIMAL(9),
    PRIMARY KEY(first_name, middle_name, last_name),
    UNIQUE(ssn)
);
```


In Listing 2.2, the primary key is made up of three columns: first_name, middle_name, and last_name. Furthermore, the values in the ssn column must be unique. No two rows can have the same ssn value.

Not only can you specify the PRIMARY KEY and UNIQUE constraints for the table, you can also declare any foreign keys. For example, suppose you want to restrict the Person table so that you can only insert a person who has a corresponding row in the SSN_Info table. You want to declare that the person table contains a foreign key that references the SSN_Info table.

Tip

Sometimes it's difficult to remember where to define the foreign key (that is, which table should contain the FOREIGN KEY) definition. Just remember that a FOREIGN KEY definition says "My table contains data values that are used as key values in another table."

To define a foreign key in the CREATE TABLE statement, add a FOREIGN KEY expression of the form

```
FOREIGN KEY (columns) REFERENCES table
```

Or

```
FOREIGN KEY (columns) REFERENCES table (columns)
```

If the column names in your table match the column names in the other table, you don't need to specify the column names in the REFERENCES section. If the column names are different, you must specify the matching columns. That is, if you call a column first_name in one table and fn in another table, your expression must look something like this:

```
FOREIGN KEY (first_name) REFERENCES other_table (fn)
```

Listing 2.3 shows an alternate definition of the Person table that contains a foreign key reference to the SSN_Info table. If you already have a table named Person, you'll need to delete it first with the DROP TABLE command:

```
DROP TABLE person
```

LISTING 2.3 SOURCE CODE FOR create_person2.sql

```
CREATE TABLE person
(
     person_id DECIMAL(10) NOT NULL PRIMARY KEY,
     first_name VARCHAR(30) NOT NULL,
     middle_name VARCHAR(30) NOT NULL,
     last_name VARCHAR(30) NOT NULL,
     address1 VARCHAR(50),
     address2 VARCHAR(50),
     city VARCHAR(30),
     state VARCHAR(2),
     zip DECIMAL(5),
     age DECIMAL(3),
     home_phone DECIMAL(10),
     work_phone DECIMAL(10),
     mobile_phone DECIMAL(10),
     FOREIGN KEY(first_name, middle_name, last_name)
         REFERENCES SSN_Info (first_name, middle_name, last_name)
);
```

Note

A table or column name in SQL can only contain letters, digits, and underscores. The first character in the name must be a letter, and you can't use any of the SQL reserved words (`PRIMARY`, `KEY`, `CREATE`, `TABLE`, and so on). A reserved word can appear in a name, of course. You can create a table named `PERSON_TABLE`, but you can't create one that is just called `TABLE`.

You can specify the default value for a column by using the `DEFAULT` keyword. The default value specification comes after the column definition and before any constraints (that is, `PRIMARY KEY`, `NOT NULL`).

To make the `city` column in the `Person` table default to `NULL` while the state defaults to `GA`, define the columns this way:

```
city VARCHAR(30) DEFAULT NULL,
state VARCHAR(2) DEFAULT 'GA',
```

DELETING A TABLE

If you want to remove a table from the database, use the `DROP TABLE` command. The syntax is

```
DROP TABLE tablename
```

For example, to remove the `Person` table, you can enter this command:

```
Drop table person
```

Remember, case doesn't matter. You don't have to capitalize any of the commands or names.

Querying the Database

When you work with databases, you typically spend most of your time performing queries, as opposed to inserting, updating, and deleting data. SQL has a fairly powerful query capability. You will occasionally find situations in which you can't perform a single query to get the data you need. These situations, however, are rare.

The simplest form of an SQL query is one in which you grab all the values from a table. The format of the query is


```
SELECT * FROM tablename
```

For example, to display the entire contents of the `Person` table, you use the query: `select * from person`. The `*` in the `SELECT` statement represents the columns you want to see. The `*` indicates that you want to see all the columns. If you only want to see certain columns, you can list them separated by commas in place of the `*`. For example, the following query displays the first and last names from the `Person` table:

```
SELECT first_name, last_name FROM Person
```

Most of the time, you don't want to get the whole table; you just want a subset of the data. The `SELECT` statement has an additional option called the `WHERE` clause that does the bulk of the query work. The `WHERE` clause lets you compare column values to specific data values or to other column values in various tables. For example, to select all people from the `Person` database who live in Georgia, you can use the following query:

```
SELECT * FROM Person where state = 'GA'
```

You can use the familiar =, <, >, >=, and <= operators to do comparisons. Unlike Java, SQL doesn't use `!=` for not-equal comparisons. Instead, it uses <>.

When comparing character values, you can use `LIKE` instead of `=` to perform wildcard searches. Use `%` as the wildcard character. For example, to select all people whose last names begin with W, use the following select statement:

```
SELECT * FROM Person WHERE last_name LIKE 'W%'
```

Note

Use single quotes whenever you must represent character data. If you need to put a quote in the character data, use two quotes. In other words, the string O'Brien would look like this `'O''Brien'`.

If you want to see whether a value is null or isn't null, use the `IS NULL` or `IS NOT NULL` keywords. For example

```
SELECT * FROM Person where first_name IS NOT NULL
```

You can also use the `BETWEEN` comparison to see whether a value lies between two values. For example

```
SELECT * FROM Person WHERE age BETWEEN 18 AND 65
```

The `BETWEEN` comparison includes the values, so the query would match on values equal to either 18 or 65 as well as any values between the two extremes.

QUERYING MULTIPLE TABLES

The real fun with SQL queries comes when you compare data values between tables. You can select values from one table that have column values in common with another table. This operation is called a *join*. Although you frequently hear the term *join*, you don't usually use the word `JOIN` in the `SELECT` operation.

When you perform a join operation, you must list all the tables involved in the join in the `FROM` clause of the `SELECT` statement. When you use multiple tables in a `SELECT` statement, you can specify column names with the table name as *`tablename.columnname`*. The following query locates the SSN numbers for people living in Georgia, using the `Person` and `SSN_Info` tables:

```
SELECT SSN_Info.SSN from SSN_Info, Person
    WHERE SSN_Info.first_name = Person.first_name
      AND SSN_Info.middle_name = Person.middle_name
      AND SSN_Info.last_name = Person.last_name
      AND Person.state = 'GA'
```

The `Person.state='GA'` part of the `WHERE` clause selects all people who live in Georgia. The other three comparisons in the `WHERE` clause perform the join; they locate `SSN_Info` rows with names that match the names in the `Person` table (but only the subset of items in `Person` that match the `Person.state='GA'` part of the clause).

Sometimes, it helps to draw out the tables and their relationships to figure out how your query should look. Figure 2.8 shows an `Aircraft` table, a `FlightSegment` table, and the link table between them.

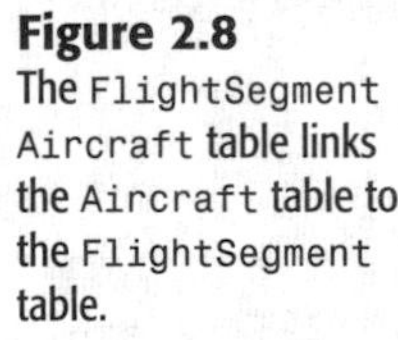

Figure 2.8
The `FlightSegmentAircraft` table links the `Aircraft` table to the `FlightSegment` table.

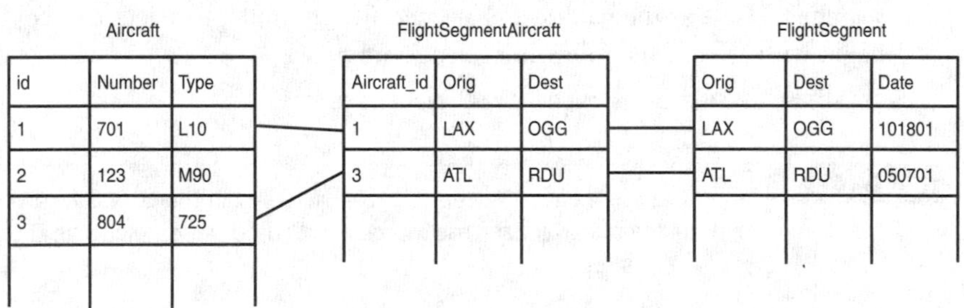

Aircraft

id	Number	Type
1	701	L10
2	123	M90
3	804	725

FlightSegmentAircraft

Aircraft_id	Orig	Dest
1	LAX	OGG
3	ATL	RDU

FlightSegment

Orig	Dest	Date
LAX	OGG	101801
ATL	RDU	050701

Now, suppose you want to find all the flight segments served by aircraft number 701. Start from the `Aircraft` table and trace your way over to the `FlightSegment` table. You obviously need to locate the aircraft with a number of 701, so you know you need `Aircraft.number=701` in your `WHERE` clause. Now, you need to get over to the link table. The link table has an `Aircraft_id` column that matches the `id` column in the `Aircraft` table, so you need `Aircraft.id=FlightSegmentAircraft.aircraft_id` in your `WHERE` clause.

Finally, you need to get from the link table over to the FlightSegment table. The Orig and Dest columns in the FlightSegment match the orig and dest columns in the FlightSegmentAircraft table. Your final query looks like this:

```
SELECT FlightSegment.*
    FROM Aircraft,FlightSegment,FlightSegmentAircraft
    WHERE Aircraft.number = 701
      AND Aircraft.id = FlightSegmentAircraft.aircraft_id
      AND FlightSegmentAircraft.flight_orig = FlightSegment.orig
      AND FlightSegmentAircraft.flight_dest = FlightSegment.dest
```


AGGREGATE FUNCTIONS

When you select values from the database, you can use certain built-in functions to operate on the values in the database. Although your database might offer many additional functions, you should at least be able to count on having SUM, AVG, MIN, MAX, and COUNT. These functions are called *aggregate* functions because they work on a set of data items as opposed to a single value.

If you want to see how many rows there are in the table, use the following query:

```
SELECT COUNT(*) from tablename
```

You use the COUNT function in conjunction with the WHERE clause to count the number of rows that match the WHERE clause. For instance, to count the number of people from New York, use the following query:

```
SELECT COUNT(*) FROM Person WHERE state='NY'
```

The AVG function calculates the average of a particular column across all the rows that match the WHERE clause. The MIN and MAX functions return the minimum and maximum values for a particular column in the rows that match the WHERE clause. For example, to compute the average, minimum, and maximum ages for all people in the database, use the following query:

```
SELECT AVG(age), MIN(age), MAX(age) FROM Person
```

The SUM function adds together all the values in a particular column for all rows that match the WHERE clause. For example, if you have an Order table that has a total_price column, you can compute the total price for all orders in the database with this query:

```
SELECT SUM(total_price) FROM Order
```

You can use the DISTINCT keyword to retrieve a distinct set of values from the table. For example, to get a list of all the distinct states from the Person database, use this query:

```
SELECT DISTINCT state FROM Person
```

You can also use DISTINCT with any of the aggregate functions, although you usually only use it with the COUNT function. In fact, DISTINCT doesn't affect the result of either the MIN or MAX functions. To count the number of unique state values in the database, use this query:

```
SELECT COUNT(DISTINCT state) FROM Person
```

SORTING DATA

The ORDER_BY clause lets you sort the results of your query. Simply list the columns you want to sort by, starting with the main column. For instance, when you display a sorted list of people, you usually sort on the last name, then for each set of values with the same last name, you sort on the first name. If there are any rows with the same first and last names, you sort by the middle name. To perform this kind of name sort, use the following query:

```
SELECT * FROM Person ORDER BY last_name, first_name, middle_name
```

GROUPING DATA

Normally, the aggregate functions operate over the entire set of rows matched by your query. You can group the rows, however, to apply the functions to a subset of the data. The GROUP BY clause takes a list of columns similar to the way ORDER BY works. For example, suppose you want to count the number of people by state in the Person table (how many people live in Georgia, how many live in Florida, and so on). Use the following query:

```
SELECT state, COUNT(*) FROM Person GROUP BY state ORDER BY STATE
```

The ORDER BY clause in the previous statement isn't necessary; it just causes the states to print out in alphabetical order.

If you use the GROUP BY clause, the items you select must either be aggregate functions or columns listed in the GROUP BY clause.

There is a special variation on the WHERE clause that can be used in conjunction with the normal WHERE clause. This alternate clause is called HAVING, and it lets you select groups matching specific criteria. The idea is that you can select groups based on the value of aggregate functions. An example HAVING clause would be HAVING AVG(age) > 35. For example, suppose you want to select all customers from your Order table who have ordered more than $10,000 worth of merchandise. The query would look like this:

```
SELECT customer FROM Order GROUP BY customer
    HAVING SUM(total_price) > 10000
```

INSERTING DATA

The INSERT statement inserts one or more rows of data into a single table. The general format for the INSERT statement is

```
INSERT INTO tablename (columns) VALUES (values)
```

The *columns* part of the insert statement is a comma-separated list of column names. The *values* part is a comma-separated list of values. To insert a row into the SSN_Info table, use the following statement:

```
INSERT INTO SSN_Info (first_name, middle_name, last_name, SSN)
    VALUES ('samantha', 'lauren', 'tippin', 123456789)
```

If you want to insert multiple values, you can add additional sets of values using this form:

```
INSERT INTO tablename (columns) VALUES (values),(values),(values)
```

For example, to insert multiple values into the SSN_Info class, use this statement:

```
insert into SSN_Info (first_name, middle_name, last_name, ssn)
values
    ('samantha', 'lauren', 'tippin', 123456789),
    ('kaitlynn', 'dawn', 'tippin', 234567890)
```

Note

Not all databases allow you to insert multiple values like this. If you get a syntax error when executing an insert with multiple values, you probably need to split the statement into multiple separate INSERT statements.

You can also insert data values from a select clause. Suppose you create a simple table containing first and last names. You can populate this table from the Person table by selecting first and last names from the Person table and inserting them into your new table:

```
INSERT INTO newtable (first_name, last_name)
    SELECT (first_name, last_name) FROM Person
```

UPDATING DATA

The UPDATE statement changes data values. The most common form of the update statement is

```
UPDATE tablename SET assignments WHERE whereclause
```

The *assignments* part of the UPDATE statement is a list of *column=value* assignments. The *whereclause* is similar to the WHERE clause for a SELECT statement except that it can't span multiple tables.

Suppose that instead of NULL, you want a person's city to be Unknown. You could use the following UPDATE statement:

```
UPDATE Person SET city = 'Unknown' WHERE city IS NULL
```

DELETING DATA

The DELETE statement deletes one or more rows from the database. The format for the DELETE statement is

```
DELETE FROM tablename WHERE whereclause
```

To delete all people with an age less than 18 from the database, use the following statement:

```
DELETE FROM Person WHERE age < 18
```

AUTO-GENERATED KEYS

One of the popular ways to design tables these days is to use sequence numbers as primary key values. Some databases let you define a column as being a sequenced value. Others include special sequencer objects. Even if the database doesn't support sequences, you can still create your own sequence table to generate the key value.

The advantage of the sequence numbers is that you don't have to worry about coming up with a unique set of keys. You can't rely on people having unique first, middle, and last names, so you must come up with an additional key to distinguish people. With a sequence number, however, you have a single key column.

> **Note**
>
> You can only use auto-generated keys when you have a single-column key. That is, if you use a composite key, you can't generate the key automatically.

TROUBLESHOOTING

CREATING TABLES

Why won't the database let me create a primary key using a column that allows null values?

Some databases require the primary-key column to have a non-null value at all times. Although some databases might permit null values, the fact that the column is a primary key means that you can have at most one null value for that column in the table, because the primary key must be unique.

Why does the database complain that my table already exists?

To create a new version of a table, you should first use the `DROP TABLE` command to delete the old version. Keep in mind, however, that `DROP TABLE` deletes all the data in the old table.

Why won't the database let me create a table?

Some databases have security settings that require special permissions to create a table. Contact your database administrator or your database documentation to see what you need to do to get permission.

CHAPTER 3

JDBC—The Java Database API

In this chapter

WHAT IS JDBC?

The *Java Database Connectivity* (JDBC) API is one of the most important APIs for enterprise-level development because you almost always need to access a database. JDBC gives you a standard API that is mostly database-independent, but still allows you to access specific features of your database if necessary.

There are actually two parts to the JDBC API. The core JDBC API (`java.sql.*`) comes with the standard Java Development Kit. J2EE includes the JDBC Optional Package (`javax.sql.*`) that includes some features more commonly used for J2EE development (especially in the area of Enterprise JavaBeans).

Most databases have very different APIs for communicating with the database. On the Windows platform and even some Unix platforms, the ODBC API (Open Database Connectivity) gives you a standard database API that works with many different databases. JDBC solves the same problem as ODBC because it also gives you a standard database API.

Like ODBC, the JDBC package itself doesn't know how to connect to any database. It is an API framework that relies on other packages to provide the implementation. You can go to `www.oracle.com` or `www.informix.com` and download JDBC drivers that work with the Oracle and Informix databases. No matter what database you use, there's a good chance that there's already a JDBC driver available for it.

There are four types of JDBC drivers, called Type 1, Type 2, Type 3, and Type 4. It's important to know the various types when you first choose a driver, and sometimes the driver choice might affect your application design—especially if you are developing Java applets.

The first distinction to draw among the four types is that Type 1 and Type 2 drivers involve native libraries—they aren't pure Java. This means it might be more difficult to find a driver for your hardware platform, and it also means you typically can't use the driver from a Java applet. Technically, you can't use the driver from an *unsigned* applet, but a *signed* applet might be able to use the driver. For more about signing applets, see Chapter 45, "Code Signing."

TYPE 1 JDBC DRIVERS

A Type 1 JDBC driver uses a native library with a common interface. That is, the native library isn't database specific. The most common example of a Type 1 driver is the JDBC-ODBC bridge that comes with the JDK. The bridge doesn't need to know about every kind of database; it only needs to know how to use the ODBC API.

Figure 3.1 illustrates a typical Type 1 driver configuration.

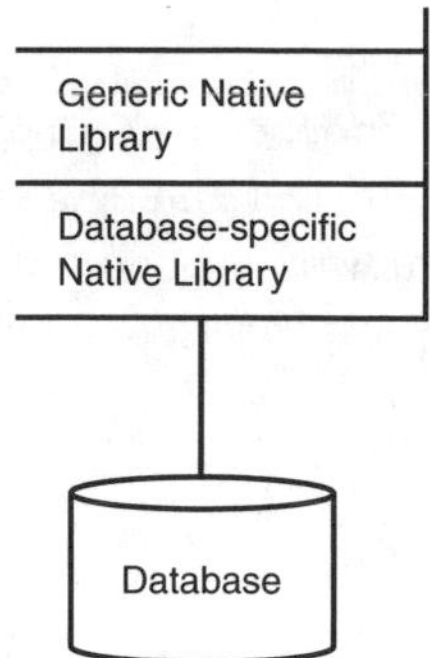

Figure 3.1
A Type 1 driver uses a native library to communicate with a database-independent API.

Although they use native code, Type 1 drivers still tend to be slow because the data must pass through so many layers. ODBC, for example, still needs a database-specific driver, so your data passes through the database-specific driver, the ODBC driver, and finally the JDBC driver before it reaches you.

Type 2 JDBC Drivers

A Type 2 driver accesses a database-specific driver through a native library. Because it uses a native library, a Type 2 driver is often fairly quick, although there is still some slowdown in the interface between Java and the native API. As with the Type 1 driver, the native library tends to limit your cross-platform options because you might not be able to find a driver for your hardware platform.

Figure 3.2 illustrates a typical Type 2 driver configuration.

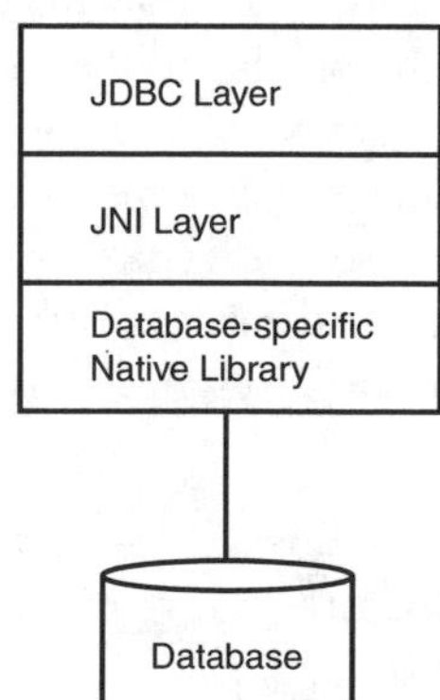

Figure 3.2
A Type 2 driver uses a database-specific native library.

TYPE 3 JDBC DRIVERS

A Type 3 JDBC driver is pure Java and uses a database-independent protocol to communicate with a database gateway. You typically use a Type 3 driver and database gateway when you develop Java applets because the gateway helps you work around some of the applet security restrictions. Figure 3.3 illustrates a typical Type 3 driver configuration.

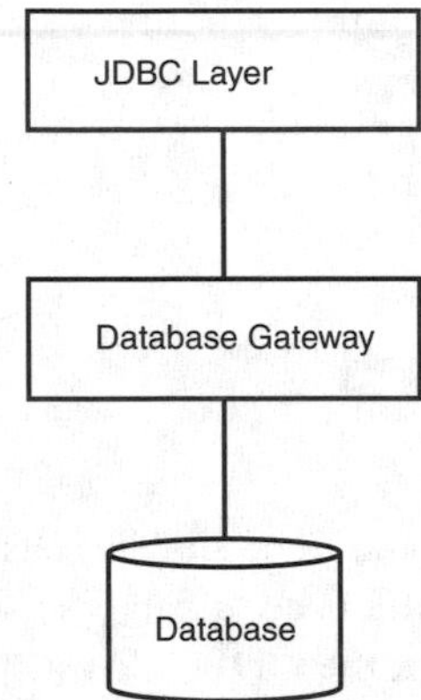

Figure 3.3
A Type 3 driver communicates with a database gateway.

Using a Type 3 driver can be one of the slowest ways to access data because of the presence of the database gateway. The gateway must read the data from the database and then send it to you. It doubles the amount of network traffic, and networking tends to be one of the slower parts of an application.

TYPE 4 JDBC DRIVERS

A Type 4 driver is pure Java and communicates directly with the database. In the very early days of Java, before Just-In-Time (JIT) compilers were available, Type 2 drivers were the most popular drivers because of their speed. Type 4 drivers are now the most popular because the JIT makes the driver perform at levels comparable to the native driver, and because the data doesn't pass through the JNI layer (that is, the driver doesn't need to translate data into Java objects), the Type 4 drivers typically outperform Type 2 drivers. Plus, the Type 4 drivers work on any Java platform. Of course, the Type 4 drivers are database-specific, so you need a different driver for each different database platform. A Type 4 driver for Oracle can't access an Informix database. Figure 3.4 illustrates a typical Type 4 driver configuration.

Keep in mind that your choice of driver doesn't change how you write your code. A large number of applications allow you to specify the JDBC driver at runtime. The API itself doesn't care about the type of driver.

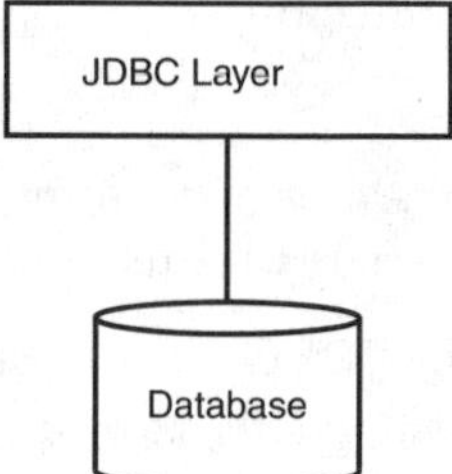

Figure 3.4
A Type 4 driver communicates directly with the database.

JDBC CORE COMPONENTS

Figure 3.5 illustrates the major classes of the JDBC API and how they relate to each other.

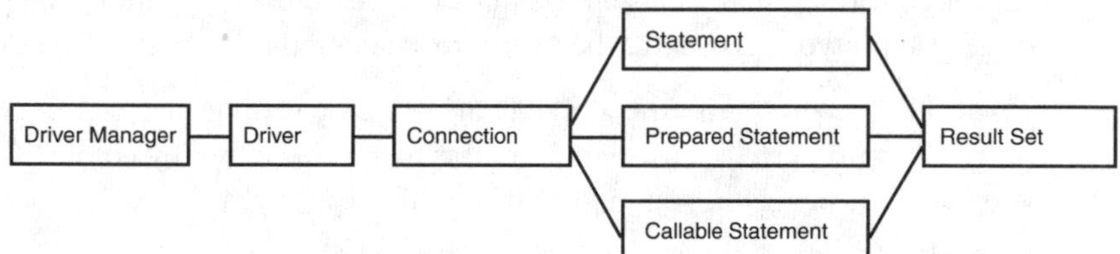

Figure 3.5
The major components of the JDBC API are shown here.

Of the major JDBC components, only `DriverManager` is a concrete Java class. The rest of the components are Java interfaces that are implemented by the various driver packages.

DriverManager

The `DriverManager` class keeps track of the available JDBC drivers and creates database connections for you. Although the JDBC driver itself creates the database connection, you usually go through the `DriverManager` to get the connection. That way you never need to deal with the actual driver class.

The `DriverManager` class has a number of useful static methods, the most popular of which is `getConnection`:

```
public static Connection getConnection(String url)
public static Connection getConnection(String url,
    String username, String password)
public static Connection getConnection(String url,
    Properties props)
```

The `url` parameter in the `getConnection` method is one of the key features of JDBC. It specifies what database you want to use. The general form of the JDBC URL is

`jdbc:`*`drivertype`*`:`*`driversubtype`*`://`*`params`*

The `:`*`driversubtype`* part of the URL is optional. You might just have a URL of the form

`jdbc:`*`drivertype`*`://`*`params`*

For an ODBC database connection, the URL takes the form

```
jdbc:odbc:datasourcename
```

Consult the documentation for your JDBC driver to see the exact format of the driver's URL. The only thing you can count on is that it will start with `jdbc:`.

The `DriverManager` class knows about all the available JDBC drivers—at least the ones available in your program. There are two ways to tell the `DriverManager` about a JDBC driver. The first is to load the driver class. Most JDBC drivers automatically register themselves with the `DriverManager` as soon as their class is loaded (they do the registration using a static initializer). For example, to register the JDBC-ODBC driver that comes with the JDK, you can use the statement:

```
Class.forName("sun.jdbc.odbc.JdbcOdbcDriver");
```

Although this method seems a little quirky, it's extremely common. Keep in mind that if the driver isn't in your classpath, the `Class.forName` method throws a `ClassNotFoundException`.

The other way to specify the available drivers is by setting the `jdbc.drivers` system property. This property is a list of driver class names separated by colons. For example, when you run your program, you might include the property

```
java -Djdbc.drivers=sun.jdbc.odbc.JdbcOdbcDriver:
[ccc]COM.cloudscape.core.JDBCDriver MyJDBCProgram
```

The `DriverManager` class also performs some other useful functions. Many database programs need to log data—especially database statements. Although you don't often log database statements in a production system, you frequently need to in a development environment. The `setLogWriter` method in the `DriverManager` class lets you specify a `PrintWriter` that will be used to log any JDBC-related information. The `DriverManager` class also supplies a `println` method for writing to the database log and a `getLogWriter` method to give you direct access to the log writer object.

DRIVER

The `Driver` interface is primarily responsible for creating database connections. The `connect` method returns a `Connection` object representing a database connection:

```
public Connection connect(String url, Properties props)
```

CONNECTION

The `Connection` interface represents the core of the JDBC API. You can group most of the methods in the `Connection` interface into three major categories:

- Getting database information
- Creating database statements
- Managing database transactions

GETTING DATABASE INFORMATION

The `getMetaData` method in the `Connection` interface returns a `DatabaseMetaData` object that describes the database. You can get a list of all the database tables and examine the definition of each table. You probably won't find the metadata too useful in a typical database application, but it's great for writing database explorer tools that gather information about the database.

CREATING DATABASE STATEMENTS

You use statements to execute database commands. There are three types of statements: `Statement`, `PreparedStatement`, and `CallableStatement`. Each of these statements works in a slightly different way, but the end result is always that you execute a database command.

The methods for creating a `Statement` are

```
public Statement createStatement()
public Statement createStatement(int resultSetType,
    int resultSetConcurrency)
```


When you create any kind of statement, you can specify a particular result set type and concurrency. These values determine how the connection handles the results returned by a query. Specifically, the `resultSetType` parameter lets you create a scrollable result set so you can move forward and backward through the results. By default, you can only move forward through the results. The `resultSetConcurrency` parameter lets you specify whether you can update the result set. By default, the result set is read-only.

The methods for creating a `PreparedStatement` are

```
public PreparedStatement prepareStatement(String sql)
public PreparedStatement prepareStatement(String sql,
    int resultSetType, int resultSetConcurrency)
```

The methods for creating a `CallableStatement` are

```
public CallableStatement prepareCall(String sql)
public CallableStatement prepareCall(String sql,
    int resultSetType, int resultSetConcurrency)
```

MANAGING TRANSACTIONS

Normally, every statement you execute is a separate database transaction. Sometimes, however, you want to group several statements into a single transaction. The `Connection` class has an auto-commit flag that indicates whether it should automatically commit transactions or not. If you want to define your own transaction boundaries, call

```
public void setAutoCommit(boolean autoCommitFlag)
```

After you turn off auto-commit, you can start executing your statements. When you reach the end of your transaction, call the `commit` method to commit the transaction (complete it):

```
public void commit()
```

If you decide that you don't want to complete the transaction, call the `rollback` method to undo the changes made in the current transaction:

```
public void rollback()
```

When you are done with a connection, make sure you close it by calling the `close` method:

```
public void close()
```

Statement

As you now know, there are three different kinds of JDBC statements: `Statement`, `PreparedStatement`, and `CallableStatement`.

The `Statement` interface defines methods that allow you to execute an SQL statement contained within a string. The `executeQuery` method executes an SQL string and returns a `ResultSet` object, while the `executeUpdate` executes an SQL string and returns the number of rows updated by the statement:

```
ResultSet executeQuery(String sqlQuery)
```

You usually use `executeQuery` when you execute an SQL `SELECT` statement, and you use `executeUpdate` when you execute an SQL `UPDATE`, `INSERT`, or `DELETE` statement:

```
int executeUpdate(String sqlUpdate)
```

When you are done with a statement, make sure you close it. If not, you might soon run out of available statements. A database connection usually allows a specific number of open statements. If the garbage collector hasn't destroyed the old connections you aren't using, you might exceed the maximum number of statements. To close a statement, just call the statement's `close` method:

```
public void close()
```

> **Note**
>
> When you close a `Connection`, it automatically closes any open statements or result sets.

Although the Statement interface contains a lot of methods for accessing results and setting various parameters, you will likely find that you only use the two execute methods and the close method in most of your applications.

Although the `Statement` interface is the simplest of the three statement interfaces, it can often cause you some programming headaches. Most of the time, you aren't executing exactly the same statement—you build a statement based on the data you are looking for or changing. In other words, you don't search for all people with a last name of Smith every time you do a query. You just search for all people with some specific last name.

If you just use the `Statement` interface, your query often looks something like this:

```
ResultSet results = stmt.executeQuery(
    "select * from Person where last_name = '"+
    lastNameParam+"'");
```

This code looks a little ugly because you've got the single quotes (for the SQL string) inside the double quotes for the Java string. Now, what happens if `lastNameParam` is O'Brien? Your SQL string would be

```
select * from Person where last_name = 'O'Brien'
```

The database would give you an error because you really need two single quotes in O'Brien (that is, O''Brien). You sometimes end up writing an `escapeQuotes` routine that looks for single quotes in a string and replaces then with two single quotes. Your `executeQuery` call would then look like this:

```
ResultSet results = stmt.executeQuery(escapeQuotes(
    "select * from Person where last_name = '"+
    lastNameParam+"'"));
```

You can handle this much better by using a prepared statement. A prepared statement is an SQL statement with parameters you can change at any time. For example, you would create a prepared statement with your last name search using the following call:

```
PreparedStatement pstmt = myConnection.prepareStatement(
    "select * from Person where last_name = ?");
```

Now, when you go to perform the query, you use one of the `set` methods in the `PreparedStatement` interface to store the value for the parameter (the `?` in the query string). You can have more than one parameter in a prepared statement. Now, to query for people whose last name is O'Brien, you use the following calls:

```
pstmt.setString(1, "O'Brien");
ResultSet results = pstmt.executeQuery();
```

The `PreparedStatement` interface has `set` methods for most Java data types and also allows you to store `BLOB`s and `CLOB`s using various data streams. The first parameter for each of the `set` methods is the parameter number. The first parameter is always 1 (not 0, as is the case with arrays and other data sequences). Also, to store a `NULL` value, you must indicate the data type of the column you are setting to `NULL`. For example, to set an integer value to `NULL`, use this call:

```
pstmt.setNull(1, Types.INTEGER);
```

The `Types` class contains constants that represent the various SQL data types supported by JDBC.

You can reuse a prepared statement. That is, after you have executed it, you can execute it again, or you can first change some of the parameter values and then execute it. Some applications create their prepared statements ahead of time, although many still create them when needed.

Usually, you can create the statements ahead of time only if you are using a single database connection, because statements are always associated with a specific connection. If you have a pool of database connections, you need to create the prepared statement when you actually need to use it, because you might get a different database connection from the pool each time.

The `CallableStatement` interface is used to access SQL stored procedures (SQL code stored on the database). The `CallableStatement` interface lets you invoke stored procedures and retrieve any results returned by the stored procedure. Stored procedures, incidentally, let you write queries that can run very quickly and are easy to invoke. It is often easier to update your application by changing a few stored procedures. The disadvantage, however, is that every database has a different syntax for stored procedures, so if you need to migrate from one database to another, you must rewrite all your stored procedures.

Tip

The Oracle database lets you write stored procedures in Java! You don't need to learn a new language to write Oracle stored procedures.

JDBC has a standard syntax for executing stored procedures, which takes one of two forms:

```
{call procedurename param1, param2, param3 … }
{?= call procedurename param1, param2, param3 … }
```

The parameters are optional. If your procedure doesn't take any parameters, the call might look like this:

```
{call myprocedure}
```

If your stored procedure returns a value, use the form that starts with `?=`. You can also use `?` for any of the parameter values in the stored procedure call and set them just like you set parameters in a `PreparedStatement`. In fact, the `CallableStatement` interface extends the `PreparedStatement` interface.

Some stored procedures have a notion of "out parameters," in which you pass a parameter in, the procedure changes the value of the parameter, and you need to examine the new value. If you need to retrieve the value of a parameter, you must tell the `CallableStatement` interface ahead of time by calling `registerOutParameter`:

```
public void registerOutParameter(int whichParameter, int sqlType)
public void registerOutParameter(int whichParameter, int sqlType,
    int scale)
public void registerOutParameter(int whichParameter, int sqlType,
    String typeName)
```

After you execute your stored procedure, you can retrieve the values of the out parameters by calling one of the many `get` methods. As with the `set` methods, the parameter numbers on the `get` methods are numbered starting from 1 and not 0. For example, suppose you have a stored procedure called `findPopularName` that searches the `Person` table for the most popular first name. Suppose, furthermore, that the stored procedure has a single out parameter that is the most popular name. You invoke the procedure this way:

```
CallableStatement cstmt = myConnection.prepareCall(
    "{call findPopularName ?}");
cstmt.registerOutParameter(1, Types.VARCHAR);
cstmt.execute();
System.out.println("The most popular name is "+
    cstmt.getString(1));
```

ResultSet

The ResultSet interface lets you access data returned from an SQL query. The most common use of the ResultSet interface is just to read data, although you can also update rows and delete rows as of JDBC version 2.0. If you just want to read results, use the next method to move to the next row and then use any of the numerous get methods to retrieve the data. For example

```
ResultSet results = stmt.executeQuery(
    "select last_name, age from Person);
while (results.next())
{
    String lastName = results.getString("last_name");
    int age = results.getInt("age");
}
```

Each of the get methods in the ResultSet interface lets you specify which item you want by the column name or by the position in the query. For example, when you query for last_name, age, the last_name column is in the first position and age is in the second position. You can retrieve the last_name value with

```
String lastName = results.getString(1);
```


Retrieving a result by index is faster than retrieving a result by column name. When you retrieve a result by column name, the result set must first determine the index that corresponds to the column name. The disadvantage of using the index is that your code is a little harder to maintain. If you change the order of the columns or insert new columns, you must remember to update the indexes. If you use column names, you don't need to change existing code if you add new columns to the query or change the order of the columns. Use the column names when possible, but switch to using an index when you need to improve performance.

Tip

You can use the findColumn method in the result set to determine the index for a particular column name. If you have a query that returns a large number of rows, you should consider using findColumn to determine the indexes first, then retrieve the values using the index instead of the column name. Your program will be faster, but you still will have the benefits of using column names.

A SIMPLE DATABASE QUERY PROGRAM

Listing 3.1 shows a simple JDBC query program. The database used for this example is the Cloudscape database, a 100% pure Java database available from www.cloudscape.com. The program puts together the various concepts you have already seen in this chapter.

LISTING 3.1 SOURCE CODE FOR `SimplyQuery.java`

```
package usingj2ee.jdbc;

import java.sql.*;

public class SimpleQuery
{
    public static void main(String[] args)
    {
        try
        {
// Make sure the DriverManager knows about the driver
            Class.forName("COM.cloudscape.core.JDBCDriver");

// Create a connection to the database
            Connection conn = DriverManager.getConnection(
                "jdbc:cloudscape:j2eebook");

// Create a statement
            Statement stmt = conn.createStatement();

// Execute the query
            ResultSet results = stmt.executeQuery(
                "select * from person");

// Loop through all the results
            while (results.next())
            {
// Get the values from the result set
                String firstName = results.getString("first_name");
                String middleName = results.getString("middle_name");
                String lastName = results.getString("last_name");
                int age = results.getInt("age");

// Print out the values
                System.out.println(firstName+" "+middleName+" "+lastName+
                    "    "+age);
            }

            conn.close();
        }
        catch (Exception exc)
        {
            exc.printStackTrace();
        }
    }
}
```

Tip

Don't forget to include the JDBC driver in your classpath before running the example. If you are using a database other than Cloudscape, you must also change both the driver name and the database URL.

INSERTING, UPDATING, AND DELETING DATA

After you know the SQL commands, it's not hard to make database updates. The pattern for performing inserts, updates, and deletions is basically the same. You can either use the `Statement` or the `PreparedStatement` interface, depending on whether you want to insert the data into the SQL string or use parameterized data.

Listing 3.2 shows a program that inserts, updates, and then deletes a row. The example uses the original definition of the Person table from Chapter 2, "A Quick Primer on SQL."

LISTING 3.2 SOURCE CODE FOR `InsUpdDel.java`

```
package usingj2ee.jdbc;

import java.sql.*;

public class InsUpdDel
{
    public static void main(String[] args)
    {
        try
        {
// Make sure the DriverManager knows about the driver
            Class.forName("COM.cloudscape.core.JDBCDriver");

// Create a connection to the database
            Connection conn = DriverManager.getConnection(
                "jdbc:cloudscape:j2eebook");

// Create a prepared statement for inserting data
// In case you are wondering about the efficiency of concatenating
// strings at runtime, if you just have a series of constant strings with
// no variables in between, the compiler automatically combines the
// strings
            PreparedStatement pstmt = conn.prepareStatement(
                "insert into SSN_Info (first_name, middle_name, last_name, "+
                "ssn) values (?,?,?,?)");

// Store the column values for the new table row
            pstmt.setString(1, "argle");
            pstmt.setString(2, "quinton");
            pstmt.setString(3, "bargle");
            pstmt.setInt(4, 1234567890);

// Execute the prepared statement
            if (pstmt.executeUpdate() == 1)
            {
                System.out.println("Row inserted into database");
            }
// Close the old prepared statement
            pstmt.close();

// Create another prepared statement
            pstmt = conn.prepareStatement(
                "update SSN_Info set ssn=ssn+1 where "+
                    "first_name=? and middle_name=? and last_name=?");
```

LISTING 3.2 CONTINUED

```
// Store the column values for the updated row
            pstmt.setString(1, "argle");
            pstmt.setString(2, "quinton");
            pstmt.setString(3, "bargle");

            if (pstmt.executeUpdate() == 1)
            {
                System.out.println("The entry has been updated");
            }

// Close the old prepared statement
            pstmt.close();

// Create another prepared statement
            pstmt = conn.prepareStatement(
                "delete from SSN_Info where "+
                    "first_name=? and middle_name=? and last_name=?");

// Store the column values for the updated row
            pstmt.setString(1, "argle");
            pstmt.setString(2, "quinton");
            pstmt.setString(3, "bargle");

            if (pstmt.executeUpdate() == 1)
            {
                System.out.println("The entry has been deleted");
            }

            conn.close();
        }
        catch (Exception exc)
        {
            exc.printStackTrace();
        }
    }
}
```

UPDATING DATA FROM A RESULT SET

There is another interesting way to update data. You can update items in the result set and then store the updates back into the database. The `ResultSet` interface contains methods for updating items of various data types. The format of the various update methods is similar to the `get` methods, in that the `update` methods take either a numeric column number or a string column name. The second parameter for each `update` method is the value you want to store in the column. For instance, to change the value of the `first_name` column, use the following statement:

```
results.updateString("first_name", "MyName");
```

When you create your query statement, you must specify a result set type to let the driver know you want to update result set values. The three statement creation methods—`createStatement`, `prepareStatement`, and `prepareCall`—allow you to specify a result set type and a result set concurrency. The result set type can be `TYPE_FORWARD_ONLY`, `TYPE_SCROLL_INSENSITIVE`, or `TYPE_SCROLL_SENSITIVE`. The `TYPE_FORWARD_ONLY` type indicates that you can only scroll forward through the result set, you can't jump back to a previous result set. For the other two types, you can move to any position in the result set. The sensitive/insensitive variation indicates whether or not the result set is sensitive to external changes to a row.

The options for the concurrency are `CONCUR_READ_ONLY` and `CONCUR_UPDATABLE`. If you plan to update rows, add new rows, or delete rows using the result set, you must set the concurrency to `CONCUR_UPDATABLE`.

Listing 3.3 shows a program that reads rows and updates them using the result set.

Note

The example in Listing 3.3 uses Oracle instead of Cloudscape to use some of the newer JDBC 2.0 features. You will find that not all servers and/or drivers support all the features of JDBC 2.0.

Listing 3.3 Source Code for `UpdateResultSet.java`

```
package usingj2ee.jdbc;

import java.sql.*;

public class UpdateResultSet
{
    public static void main(String[] args)
    {
        try
        {
// Make sure the DriverManager knows about the driver
            Class.forName("oracle.jdbc.driver.OracleDriver").newInstance();

// Create a connection to the database
            Connection conn = DriverManager.getConnection(
                "jdbc:oracle:thin:@flamingo:1521:j2eebook",
                    "j2eeuser", "j2eepass");

// Create a statement for retrieving and updating data
            Statement stmt = conn.createStatement(
                ResultSet.TYPE_SCROLL_SENSITIVE,
                ResultSet.CONCUR_UPDATABLE);

            stmt.executeQuery("select * from Person");

// Execute the query
            ResultSet results = stmt.getResultSet();

            while (results.next())
```

LISTING 3.3 CONTINUED

```
            {
// Get the name values
                String firstName = results.getString("first_name");
                String lastName = results.getString("last_name");

// Change the name values
                results.updateString("first_name", firstName.toUpperCase());
                results.updateString("last_name", lastName.toUpperCase());

// Update the row
                results.updateRow();
            }

            conn.close();
        }
        catch (Exception exc)
        {
            exc.printStackTrace();
        }
    }
}
```

To delete the current row, call the `deleteRow` method:

```
public void deleteRow()
```

To insert a new row, position the result set to a special row called the insert row by calling `moveToInsertRow`:

```
public void moveToInsertRow()
```

You still use the `update` methods to modify the contents for the new row, but when you need to save the changes, call `insertRow`:

```
public void insertRow()
```

THE JDBC OPTIONAL PACKAGE

The Core JDBC package is part of the standard Java Development Kit. There is also an additional JDBC package that is part of J2EE that addresses some of the enterprise-level uses of JDBC. These extensions belong to the `javax.sql` package as opposed to `java.sql`.

DATA SOURCES

One of the irritating parts of JDBC is the way to load drivers. It can be difficult to reconfigure an application to use a different database. Using the standard JDBC API, you must use a specific JDBC URL to access a database. The Optional JDBC package includes an alternative to the `DriverManager` class for creating database connections.

A `DataSource` object works like the `DriverManager` class, it has a `getConnection` method and also a `getLogWriter` method. The big difference is that a data source is typically stored in a naming service and accessed through the Java Naming API (JNDI). The naming service gives you an extra level of indirection—you don't code the JDBC URL into your application, and you don't need to reconfigure every application when you change the database URL. Instead, your application can always ask for a specific name in the naming service. When you configure your application server, you can change the database that a particular named `DataSource` object refers to. You need to change it in only one place instead of every place that uses the database.

Connection Pools

A *connection pool* is actually just a special data source that maintains a collection of database connections. In a typical application, you need to perform many database operations at once, so you usually need several database connections. The problem is, you don't know when you'll need a particular database connection, so your best bet is to put the connections into a common pool and pull out a connection when you need it.

In the past, programmers have solved the connection pooling problem by creating their own connection pool. One of the problems you often encounter with custom connection pools is that the users of the connections must be extremely polite to each other. If you use a connection from the pool, you can't close the connection, because someone else will need it. You must close all your open statements and result sets, however. Also, you must either commit or rollback any pending database transactions.

Connection pools wrap a special class around a physical database connection. This special class behaves just like a database connection, but you can close the connection and you don't have to worry about any pending transactions. The wrapper class performs any necessary cleanup.

RowSets

A `RowSet` object is similar to a `ResultSet`; in fact, the `RowSet` interface extends `ResultSet`. The `RowSet` interface includes `set` methods in addition to the `get` methods (remember, the `ResultSet` interface uses `update` methods instead of `set`). The `set` methods use only indexed, not column names. The end result is that the `RowSet` is a Java bean with readable and writable properties. The idea is that you can return a `RowSet` to a client object where it can be manipulated and sent back to the server. Also, because a `RowSet` is a bean, you can use it from a GUI design tool.

There isn't anything in the JDBC API that specifies how you get a `RowSet` from a `ResultSet`. Each implementation of `RowSet` must come up with its own way to copy `ResultSet` data into a `RowSet`. Of course, because a `RowSet` is a `ResultSet`, you can use a `RowSet` anywhere you would use a `ResultSet`.

TROUBLESHOOTING

USING JDBC

Why does the DriverManager tell me that no suitable driver exists?

This usually happens for one of three reasons:

- You mistyped the JDBC URL and the driver manager doesn't recognize the database type.
- You didnt load the JDBC driver class with `Class.forName`, and you didn't add it to the `jdbc.drivers` system property.
- The driver class isn't in the classpath.

My driver is in the classpath; why can't I connect to the database?

Your database URL may be incorrect, or you may be using the wrong driver.

Why do I get errors saying I can't allocate any more database statements after my program has been running for a few minutes?

If you don't explicitly close your `Statement` objects, they don't get closed until the garbage collector picks them up, which may not occur for a long time. Because a database statement takes up resources in the database as well, or at least in the driver, there is usually a limit to the number of open statements you can have. Under a heavy load, you might end up allocating more statements than the database can handle. The garbage collector only understands memory shortages; it isn't smart enough to clean up old statements when the database can't handle any more.

CHAPTER 4

Remote Method Invocation

In this chapter

WHAT IS RMI?

Remote Method Invocation (*RMI*) is one of the cornerstones of Enterprise JavaBeans and is an extremely handy way to make distributed Java applications. The idea is simple: Instead of invoking a method on another Java object running in the same Java Virtual Machine (that is, the same executing program), you invoke a method in a Java object in another JVM on the same computer or a different one. Figure 4.1 illustrates the difference between a normal method invocation and a remote method invocation.

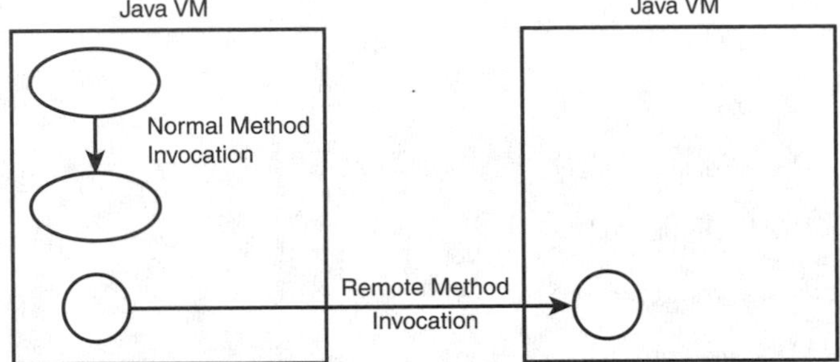

Figure 4.1
Remote method invocation takes place between separate Java Virtual Machines.

RMI is virtually seamless. You don't have to do much to enable a class for RMI, and invoking remote methods is also easy. RMI revolves around the use of `Remote` interfaces—interfaces that define all the remote methods for an object. Figure 4.2 shows a typical local method invocation using an interface.

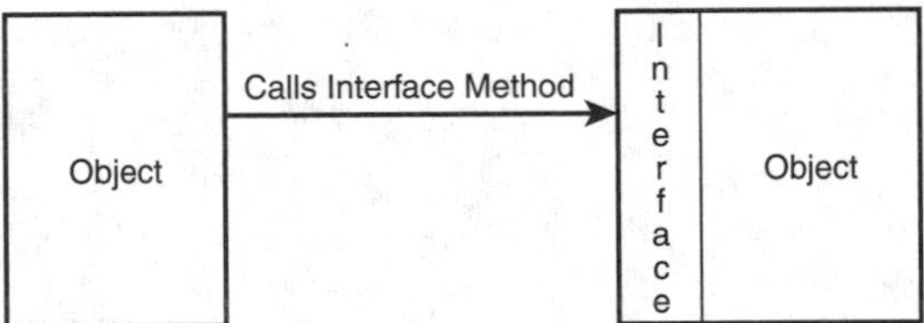

Figure 4.2
In a local invocation, the client invokes a method on an interface.

Now, when you use a `Remote` interface to invoke a remote method, RMI uses the interface to hide the fact that you are invoking a method remotely. The idea here is that RMI creates an object called a *stub* that implements the `Remote` interface and runs in the client's JVM. When the client invokes a remote method, the stub's implementation of the method transmits the method invocation over to the server's JVM where another special object called a *skeleton* interprets the request and invokes the correct method. When the server's method returns a value or throws an exception, the skeleton packages the resulting information and sends it back to the stub. The stub then returns the information to the client.

Note

In the original JDK 1.1 implementation of RMI, each specific interface had its own custom skeleton. As of JDK 1.2, RMI uses a generic skeleton class rather than separate interface-specific skeletons.

Figure 4.3 illustrates the relationship between the client, the stub, the skeleton and the server.

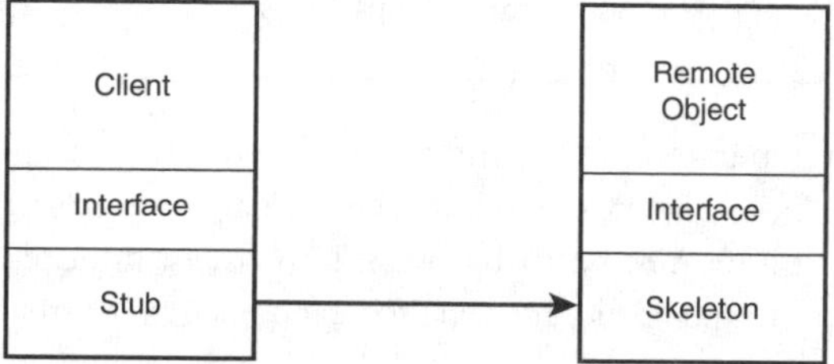

Figure 4.3
The stub and skeleton act as a bridge between the client and the server.

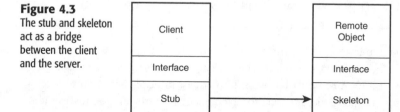

The neat thing about the stub is that the client doesn't know that it's talking to a stub. The client thinks it's just invoking a method through an interface, just like the object shown earlier in Figure 4.2. Likewise, the server doesn't know about the skeleton at all. As far as the server is concerned, the skeleton is just like any other class that uses the server class.

The stub and the skeleton communicate using a protocol called the Java Remote Method Protocol (JRMP). Actually, JRMP is just one of the protocols the stub and server can use. They might also use a protocol called IIOP (Internet Inter-ORB Protocol), which is a protocol from another remote method invocation architecture called CORBA. You'll learn more about CORBA, IIOP, and RMI-IIOP in Chapter 17, "CORBA." Before RMI got its IIOP support, no one bothered to mention JRMP by name. In fact, many veteran Java programmers might not recognize the term JRMP—it was just called the RMI wire protocol when it was discussed (you'll often hear the network referred to as "the wire").

You're probably wondering where the stub and skeleton come from. The good news is, you don't have to write them. You use a program called `rmic` (the RMI Compiler) to generate the stubs and skeletons from your `Remote` interface.

Obviously, before you can generate a stub and a skeleton, you must define the `Remote` interface. A `Remote` interface has two characteristics: It extends `java.rmi.Remote` and it contains some methods that can throw `java.rmi.RemoteException`. The `Remote` interface marks an object as being a *remote object*—that is, if an object implements an interface that extends `Remote`, RMI knows that you want to access the object remotely. `RemoteException` flags a specific method as being remote. You can define methods in a `Remote` interface that aren't actually remote methods, but you can't invoke them remotely, even though the interface is remote. The key is, if you want to invoke a method remotely, it *must* be able to throw `RemoteException`.

Listing 4.1 shows a simple `Remote` interface for a Message-of-the-Day (MOTD) service.

LISTING 4.1 SOURCE CODE FOR MOTD.java

```
package usingj2ee.motd;

import java.rmi.*;

/** Describes the Message-Of-The-Day (MOTD) interface */
public interface MOTD extends Remote
{
    public String getMOTD() throws RemoteException;
}
```

As it turns out, you can't generate the stub and skeleton yet. The `rmic` program uses the implementation of the remote object to generate the stub and skeleton, not the `Remote` interface. The reason is simple: A remote object can implement multiple `Remote` interfaces. You don't want to create multiple skeletons (one for each `Remote` interface). You just want a single skeleton.

CREATING AN RMI SERVER OBJECT

To implement a remote object, you must create a class that is a subclass of `java.rmi.server.UnicastRemoteObject` and implements one or more remote methods. You must write the implementation for the remote methods yourself, of course.

The `main` method of the server (the `main` doesn't need to be in the same class) must do one peculiar thing—it must set up a security manager like this:

```
if (System.getSecurityManager() == null)
{
    System.setSecurityManager(new RMISecurityManager());
}
```

Because of the way RMI can pass objects back and forth and perform dynamic class loading, you need a special security manager to make sure someone doesn't send you a bogus class file.

To activate your remote object (i.e. make it available for use), just publish it to the RMI Registry using the `java.rmi.Naming` class, like this:

```
Naming.rebind("//localhost/yourservicename", yourImplClass);
```

Listing 4.2 shows an example implementation of the Message-of-the-Day service.

LISTING 4.2 SOURCE CODE FOR MOTDImpl.java

```
package usingj2ee.motd;

import java.io.*;
import java.rmi.*;
import java.rmi.server.UnicastRemoteObject;

/** An implementation of the Message-Of-The-Day Remote interface. */
```

```
public class MOTDImpl extends UnicastRemoteObject
    implements MOTD
{
/** The name of the file containing the message */
    protected String motdFileName;

/** Creates a new instance of the MOTD server assigned to a
 *  specific filename.
 */
    public MOTDImpl(String aMotdFileName)
        throws RemoteException
    {
        motdFileName = aMotdFileName;
    }

/** Returns the Message-Of-The-Day */
    public String getMOTD()
    {
        try
        {
// Open the message file
            BufferedReader reader = new BufferedReader(
                new FileReader(motdFileName));

// Create a buffer to hold the resulting message
            StringBuffer buffer = new StringBuffer();

            String line;

// Read all the lines in the file
            while ((line = reader.readLine()) != null)
            {
// Put each line into the buffer separated by newlines
                buffer.append(line);
                buffer.append("\n");
            }

            reader.close();

// Return the message
            return buffer.toString();
        }
        catch (IOException exc)
        {
// If there's an error, just return an empty message
            return "";
        }
    }

/** Activates the MOTD service */
    public static void main(String[] args)
    {
        String motdFile = System.getProperty("file", "motd.txt");
        String motdService = System.getProperty("service",
            "MessageOfTheDay");

// Must assign an RMI security manager
        if (System.getSecurityManager() == null)
```

LISTING 4.2 CONTINUED

```
        {
            System.setSecurityManager(new RMISecurityManager());
        }

        try
        {
// Create an instance of the MOTD service
            MOTDImpl impl = new MOTDImpl(motdFile);

// Register the service with the RMI registry
            Naming.rebind("//localhost/"+motdService, impl);

        }
        catch (Exception exc)
        {
            exc.printStackTrace();
        }
    }
}
```

Note

Notice that the `MOTDImpl` constructor can throw `RemoteException`. Any object that is a subclass of `UnicastRemoteObject` must declare that the constructor throws `RemoteException`.

Next, you must use the `rmic` command to generate the stubs and skeletons (if necessary) for your implementation. For the `usingj2ee.motd.MOTDImpl` class, the `rmic` command looks like this:

```
rmic -d . usingj2ee.motd.MOTDImpl
```

The `-d` option specifies the directory where `rmic` will place the generated files, similar to the `-d` option on the `javac` command. You must also insure that `usingj2ee.motd.MOTDImpl` is in your classpath.

Before you run the `MOTDImpl` program, make sure you start the RMI Registry with the command:

```
rmiregistry
```

The RMI Registry is a directory service that allows clients to locate remote objects by name. The URL you use to bind to the naming service includes the hostname and possibly the port number for the RMI Registry. For example, if you run the RMI Registry on a host named `flamingo`, you would bind an RMI object named `TestObject` using the URL `//flamingo/TestObject`. The RMI Registry normally uses TCP port 1099 (if you don't understand TCP and UDP, Chapter 26, "Networks and Network Protocols," explains some of the common network protocols). When you start the `rmiregistry` program, you can provide an optional port number, like this:

```
rmiregistry 4321
```

Now, to register an object with an RMI Registry on a host named `flamingo` with a port number of 4321, use the URL `//flamingo:4321/TestObject`. Unless you already have a default security policy installed that permits RMI operations, you will get a security exception if you try to run `MOTDImpl` using this command:

```
java usingj2ee.motd.MOTDImpl
```

You must create a Java security policy file to override some of the security restrictions imposed by the RMI security manager. Listing 4.3 shows a security policy file that you can use *for testing only*.

Listing 4.3 Source Code for motd.policy

```
grant {
    // Allow everything for now
    permission java.security.AllPermission;
};
```

Caution

Make sure you don't use the `motd.policy` file in a production system. It disables all the security checking in the RMI security manager and opens your system to possible attack.

Use the `java.security.policy` system property to specify an alternate security policy. To run the `MOTDImpl` server in a test environment, use the following command:

```
java -Djava.security.policy=motd.policy usingj2ee.motd.MOTDImpl
```

Chapter 36, "Java Security Features," explains the Java security framework and the format of policy files, but in the meantime, you can use some simple policy files for running your server in a production environment.

Although it is still slightly unsafe, you can grant full permissions to files loaded using a certain classpath. Listing 4.4 shows a policy file that grants all permissions to classes loaded from a specific directory.

Listing 4.4 Source Code for motd2.policy

```
grant codebase "file:/C:/J2EEBOOK/ch04/examples/" {
    // Allow everything for now
    permission java.security.AllPermission;
};
```

The `MOTDImpl` program only needs permission for performing socket operations, so you can further restrict its operations with the policy file shown in Listing 4.5.

Listing 4.5 Source Code for motd3.policy

```
grant codebase "file:/C:/J2EEBOOK/ch04/examples/" {
    // Allow all socket operations
    permission java.net.SocketPermission "*", "accept,listen,connect";
};
```

CREATING AN RMI CLIENT

It's extremely easy to create an RMI client. You just need to use the `java.rmi.Naming` class to locate the remote object in the RMI Registry. Listing 4.6 shows a client that accesses the `MOTDImpl` server.

LISTING 4.6 SOURCE CODE FOR `MOTDClient.java`

```
package usingj2ee.motd;

import java.rmi.*;

public class MOTDClient
{
    public static void main(String[] args)
    {
        try
        {
// Locate the remote object
            MOTD motd = (MOTD) Naming.lookup("//localhost/MessageOfTheDay");

// Invoke the remote method and print the result
            System.out.println(motd.getMOTD());
        }
        catch (Exception exc)
        {
            exc.printStackTrace();
        }
    }
}
```

Unlike the server, an RMI client doesn't need to use any special security features. You don't need to see a policy file or install an RMI security manager.

REMOTE METHOD PARAMETERS

RMI imposes one significant restriction on the types of objects you can use in remote method invocations (either as parameters or return values). You can pass any of the native types (`int`, `float`, `double`, `boolean`, and so on) but any objects you pass must implement `java.io.Serializable` or `java.rmi.Remote`.

When you pass a serializable (local) object as an RMI parameter, the object is referred to as a *non-remote object*. That is, the entire object goes from the client to the server or from the server to the client. When you pass a remote object as an RMI parameter, on the other hand, RMI passes a remote reference. That is, instead of passing in an entire object, RMI passes what eventually becomes a stub. The remote object never moves. Figure 4.4 illustrates the difference between passing a remote and a non-remote object.

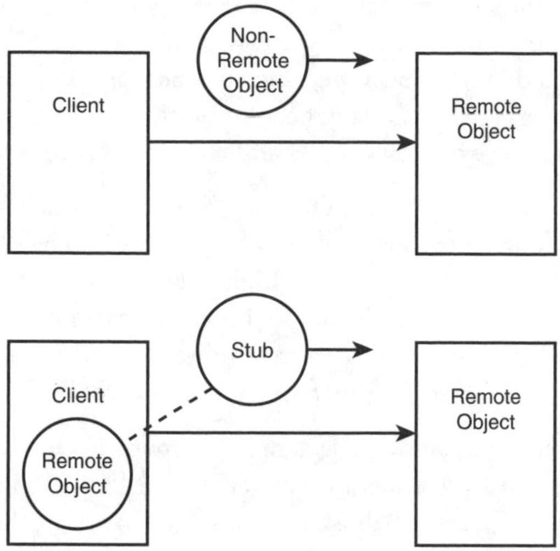

Figure 4.4
When you pass a remote object, RMI passes a stub instead of the entire object.

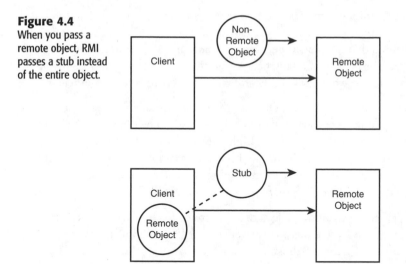

USING THE RMI REGISTRY

You've already seen the two most important methods in the `Naming` class (the interface to the RMI Registry). They are `rebind` and `lookup`. The `rebind` method, of course, associates a name with a remote object. The `Naming` class also includes a `bind` method that associates a name with an object. The difference between `bind` and `rebind` is that `bind` fails if the Registry already contains an object with the same name. Depending on the application, you might not want to overwrite an existing name, and in those cases, you use `bind` instead of `rebind`.

To remove an entry from the RMI Registry, use the `unbind` method. You specify the name you want to remove, like this:

```
Naming.unbind("//flamingo/TestObject");
```

You can get a list of the names already bound in the RMI Registry by calling `list`:

```
String[] names = Naming.list("//flamingo");
for (int i=0; i < names.length; i++)
{
    System.out.println(names[i]);
}
```

IMPLEMENTING A REMOTE OBJECT FACTORY

Distributed object systems often use a design pattern called the *factory pattern*, which is also used in a number of Java APIs, such as XML, security, and JDBC (the JDBC `DriverManager` class is a factory). The idea is that instead of calling a constructor to create an object, you use a separate factory class. In the case of the Java APIs, you use the factory to hide the actual implementation. You can use different XML parser implementations—the factory chooses one. For different JDBC URLs, you might need a different JDBC driver—the `DriverManager` picks one.

The reason you need a factory in some Java APIs is that a constructor can't pick a different implementation class. In other words, the `Driver` class constructor in JDBC can't look at a URL string and determine that it needs to become an `OracleDriver` instance. At the time the constructor is called, the class has already been instantiated—it's too late to change it. The factory lets you figure out what class you need before you create a new instance.

In a distributed object system, you have a slightly more complex problem: Most distributed object systems don't let you use a constructor to locate an object. The object must already exist. Suppose you're writing a program to track flights for a particular airline. On a given day, you'll have several thousand flights (Delta Air Lines, for example, flies well over 5,000 flights a day). You don't necessarily want to create remote objects ahead of time for every flight. Instead, you create a factory object that creates flight objects when you need them.

To create an RMI object factory, you must declare an interface for the factory. A typical RMI factory interface has at least one method that creates or locates an instance of another remote object and returns it. Figure 4.5 illustrates how the factory works.

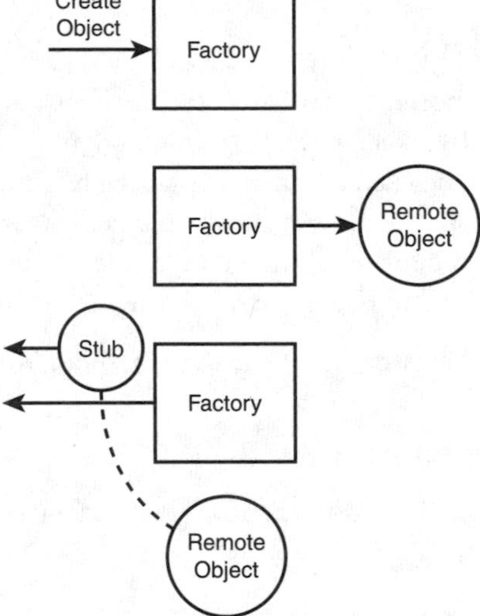

Figure 4.5
A factory creates a remote object and hands the client a reference to the remote object.

Listing 4.7 shows a simple factory class for creating `Flight` objects.

LISTING 4.7 SOURCE CODE FOR `FlightFactory.java`

```
package usingj2ee.rmi;
import java.rmi.*;

public interface FlightFactory extends Remote
{
    public Flight getFlight(String flightNumber)
        throws RemoteException;
}
```

Listing 4.8 shows the implementation for the flight factory. The `FlightFactoryImpl` caches flights in a hash table to avoid creating multiple copies of the same flight.

LISTING 4.8 SOURCE CODE FOR `FlightFactoryImpl.java`

```
package usingj2ee.rmi;

import java.rmi.*;
import java.rmi.server.*;
import java.util.*;

public class FlightFactoryImpl extends UnicastRemoteObject
    implements FlightFactory
{
    protected Hashtable flights;

    public FlightFactoryImpl()
        throws RemoteException
    {
        flights = new Hashtable();
    }

    public Flight getFlight(String flightNumber)
        throws RemoteException
    {
// See if the flight has already been created
        Flight flight = (Flight) flights.get(flightNumber);

        if (flight != null) return flight;

// You would normally look up the flight in a database or get
// it from a mainframe. For this example, just create a dummy flight
        flight = new FlightImpl(flightNumber, null, null, null, null);

// Add the flight to the current table of flights
        flights.put(flightNumber, flight);

        return flight;
    }

    public static void main(String[] args)
    {
        try
        {
            if (System.getSecurityManager() == null)
            {
                System.setSecurityManager(new RMISecurityManager());
            }

            FlightFactoryImpl impl = new FlightFactoryImpl();

            Naming.rebind("FlightFactory", impl);
        }
        catch (Exception exc)
        {
```

LISTING 4.8 CONTINUED

```
        }
    }
}
```

Listing 4.9 shows a client program that uses the factory to create a new object instance.

LISTING 4.9 SOURCE CODE FOR `FlightClient.java`

```
package usingj2ee.rmi;

import java.rmi.*;

public class FlightClient
{
    public static void main(String[] args)
    {
        try
        {
            FlightFactory fact =
                (FlightFactory) Naming.lookup("//localhost/FlightFactory");

            Flight flight = fact.getFlight("795");

            System.out.println("Flight "+flight.getFlightNumber()+":");
            System.out.println("From "+flight.getOrigin()+" to "+
                flight.getDestination());
        }
        catch (Exception exc)
        {
            exc.printStackTrace();
        }
    }
}
```

Notice that you use the `FlightFactory` class to get a reference to a `Flight` object.

If you keep a `HashMap` or a `Hashtable` of RMI objects, you should consider using a `WeakHashMap` instead. A `WeakHashMap` uses weak references to refer to items, making it a great class for caching data. The idea behind a weak reference is that the garbage collector ignores weak references. If the only references to an object are weak references, the garbage collector can get rid of the object. If you store an object in a `WeakHashMap` and later the object is reclaimed by the garbage collector, the `WeakHashMap` returns `null`, just as it does for items that were never there to begin with.

If you use a regular `HashMap` or a `Hashtable`, you keep a reference to every object you have ever created, even if that object doesn't have any clients and might not have any for a long time.

PERFORMING CALLBACKS

In most RMI applications, a client makes a call to a server object. In some cases, however, the server needs to make a call back to the client. For example, in a stock quote system, you might set up the server to call the client every time a stock price changes. A client registers with the server by invoking a remote method and passing a remote object reference to the server. From the client's standpoint, it's really passing a remote object, but RMI converts the remote object to a remote reference (that is, stub) when it sends the request to the server.

Figure 4.6 illustrates how the callback generally works.

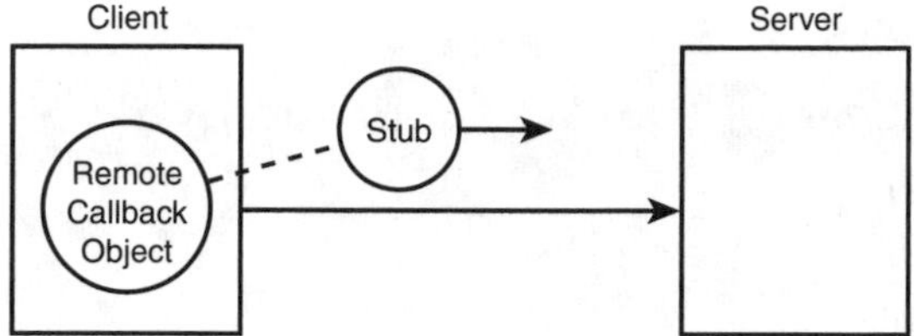

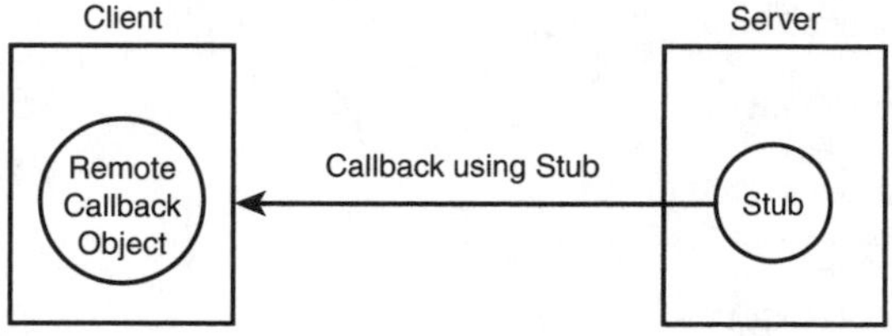

Figure 4.6 With a callback architecture, the server can invoke methods on a client.

Listing 4.10 shows a simple callback interface for receiving stock quotes.

LISTING 4.10 SOURCE CODE FOR `StockQuote.java`

```
package usingj2ee.rmi;

import java.rmi.*;

public interface StockQuote extends Remote
{
    public void quote(String stockSymbol, double price)
        throws RemoteException;
}
```

Listing 4.11 shows the stock quote server's interface for registering and unregistering clients.

LISTING 4.11 SOURCE CODE FOR `StockQuoteServer.java`

```
package usingj2ee.rmi;

import java.rmi.*;
```

LISTING 4.11 CONTINUED

```
public interface StockQuoteServer extends Remote
{
    public void registerClient(StockQuote client)
        throws RemoteException;

    public void unregisterClient(StockQuote client)
        throws RemoteException;
}
```

Listing 4.12 shows the stock quote server. As you can see, it's not much different from any other RMI server.

LISTING 4.12 SOURCE CODE FOR `StockQuoteServerImpl.java`

```
package usingj2ee.rmi;

import java.rmi.*;
import java.rmi.server.*;
import java.util.*;

public class StockQuoteServerImpl extends UnicastRemoteObject
    implements StockQuoteServer, Runnable
{
    protected HashSet clients;

    public StockQuoteServerImpl()
        throws RemoteException
    {
        clients = new HashSet();
    }

    public void run()
    {
// Create some stock symbols
        String[] symbols = new String[] {
            "SUNW", "MSFT", "DAL", "WUTK", "SAMY", "KATY"
        };

        Random rand = new Random();

        double values[] = new double[symbols.length];

// Assign random values to each stock
        for (int i=0; i < values.length; i++)
        {
            values[i] = 25.0 + rand.nextInt(100);
        }

        for (;;)
        {
// Pick a random stock
            int sym = rand.nextInt(symbols.length);
```

```
// Allow the stock to change by $1.00 in either direction
            int change = 100 - rand.nextInt(201);

            values[sym] = values[sym] + ((double) change) / 100.0;

// Don't allow zero or negative values
            if (values[sym] < 0) values[sym] = 0.01;

            Iterator iter = clients.iterator();

            while (iter.hasNext())
            {
                StockQuote client = (StockQuote) iter.next();

                try
                {
// Publish the quote to the client
                    client.quote(symbols[sym], values[sym]);
                }
                catch (Exception exc)
                {
// If there's an error while publishing, remove the client
                    System.out.println("Removing invalid client");
                    iter.remove();
                }
            }

            try { Thread.sleep(1000); } catch (Exception ignore) {}
        }
    }

    public void registerClient(StockQuote client)
        throws RemoteException
    {
        System.out.println("Adding client");

        clients.add(client);
    }

    public void unregisterClient(StockQuote client)
        throws RemoteException
    {
        System.out.println("Removing client");

        clients.remove(client);
    }

    public static void main(String[] args)
    {
        try
        {
            if (System.getSecurityManager() == null)
            {
                System.setSecurityManager(new RMISecurityManager());
            }

            StockQuoteServerImpl impl = new StockQuoteServerImpl();
```

LISTING 4.12 CONTINUED

```
            Naming.rebind("//localhost/StockQuotes", impl);

// Start the quote publisher
            (new Thread(impl)).start();
        }
        catch (Exception exc)
        {
            exc.printStackTrace();
        }
    }
}
```

Finally, Listing 4.13 shows the stock quote client. Notice that the client is a subclass of `UnicastRemoteObject` because it is a remote object. When it registers itself with the server, it passes an instance of `StockQuoteClient`, which the RMI library converts to a remote object reference when calling the server.

LISTING 4.13 SOURCE CODE FOR `StockQuoteClient.java`

```
package usingj2ee.rmi;

import java.rmi.*;
import java.rmi.server.*;

public class StockQuoteClient extends UnicastRemoteObject
    implements StockQuote
{
    public StockQuoteClient()
        throws RemoteException
    {
    }

    public void quote(String symbol, double value)
        throws RemoteException
    {
        System.out.println(symbol+": "+value);
    }

    public static void main(String[] args)
    {
        try
        {
            if (System.getSecurityManager() == null)
            {
                System.setSecurityManager(new RMISecurityManager());
            }

            StockQuote quote = new StockQuoteClient();

            StockQuoteServer server =
                (StockQuoteServer) Naming.lookup("//localhost/StockQuotes");

            server.registerClient(quote);
```

```
        }
        catch (Exception exc)
        {
            exc.printStackTrace();
        }
    }
}
```

REMOTE ACTIVATION

One of the problems with RMI is that you must start your servers manually. A client can't use a server object until a server program registers the server object with the RMI Registry. The RMI activation framework gives you an alternative way to access server objects, however. Using a special setup program, you tell the activation framework how to start your server object.

Now, instead of insuring that your various servers are running, you just make sure that the activation server—`rmid`—is running.

The activation server takes the place of custom RMI servers. It starts a Java VM and sets up a security policy. This allows you to focus on creating the RMI objects instead of worrying about the server program that creates the RMI object.

Note

For more information about the activation framework, see the RMI section of the Javasoft Web site at `http://java.sun.com/products/jdk/rmi/index.html`.

To use the activation framework, you must make a few changes to your normal implementation class. Instead of subclassing `UnicastRemoteObject`, you subclass `java.rmi.activation.Activatable`. Your constructor must accept an activation ID and a marshalled object, like this:

```
public MyObject(ActivationID id, MarshalledObject object)
```

The marshalled object contains the initialization data for the object. Because the activation service must instantiate the server object, it needs a way to pass the initialization data to the object. The `MarshalledObject` class holds a serialized object that you can retrieve with the `get` method.

Listing 4.14 shows an activatable version of the MOTD server implementation.

LISTING 4.14 SOURCE CODE FOR `MOTDImplActivate.java`

```
package usingj2ee.motd;

import java.io.*;
import java.rmi.*;
import java.rmi.activation.*;
import java.rmi.server.UnicastRemoteObject;
```

LISTING 4.14 CONTINUED

```
/** An activatable implementation of the Message-Of-The-Day remote
 *  interface.
 */

public class MOTDImplActivate extends Activatable
    implements MOTD
{
/** The name of the file containing the message */
    protected String motdFileName;

/** Creates a new instance of the MOTD server assigned to a
 *  specific filename.
 */
    public MOTDImplActivate(ActivationID id, MarshalledObject data)
        throws RemoteException
    {
        super(id, 0);

// Fetch the MOTD filename from the marshalled data
        try
        {
            motdFileName = (String) data.get();
        }
        catch (ClassNotFoundException exc)
        {
            throw new RemoteException(exc.toString());
        }
        catch (IOException exc)
        {
            throw new RemoteException(exc.toString());
        }
    }

/** Returns the Message-Of-The-Day */
    public String getMOTD()
        throws RemoteException
    {
        try
        {
// Open the message file
            BufferedReader reader = new BufferedReader(
                new FileReader(motdFileName));

// Create a buffer to hold the resulting message
            StringBuffer buffer = new StringBuffer();

            String line;

// Read all the lines in the file
            while ((line = reader.readLine()) != null)
            {
// Put each line into the buffer separated by newlines
                buffer.append(line);
                buffer.append("\n");
            }

            reader.close();
```

```
// Return the message
            return buffer.toString();
        }
        catch (IOException exc)
        {
// If there's an error, just return an empty message
            return "";
        }
    }
}
```

Notice that the `MOTDImplActivate` class doesn't have a `main` method. You don't run the class; the only service you need to run is `rmid`.

To register an object with the activation service, you need to write a small setup class. Although you must create several interim classes, after you have the procedure down, it's easy to create new setup programs.

The basic setup sequence is

1. Install the `RMISecurityManager` just like you do in a server program.
2. Create a properties file containing the `java.security.policy` setting for the activated object and any other JVM properties you need to set.
3. If necessary, specify the pathname and command-line arguments for the Java Virtual Machine needed to run your object (you can use separate JVMs for different objects).
4. Create an activation group description containing the JVM description and the properties.
5. Generate an activation group ID from the description.
6. Create an activation group.
7. Create an activation description containing the initialization data, the class you want to register, and the code base for the registered class (the URL for the registered class and its associated classes).
8. Register the activation description with the activation server and generate an activation reference.
9. Register the activation reference with the RMI register just as if it was a regular remote object.

One of the nice things about the activation framework is that the client programs can't tell the difference between a normally registered remote object and an activated object. You only need to change the server side of things to support activation.

Listing 4.15 shows the setup program for the `MOTDImplActivate` class.

LISTING 4.15 SOURCE CODE FOR `MOTDSetup.java`

```
package usingj2ee.motd;

import java.rmi.*;
import java.rmi.activation.*;

import java.util.*;

public class MOTDSetup
{
    public static void main(String[] args)
    {
        try
        {
// Create a security manager
            if (System.getSecurityManager() == null)
            {
                System.setSecurityManager(new RMISecurityManager());
            }

// Create a property set containing the name of the policy file
// for the activated object
            Properties secProps = new Properties();
            secProps.put("java.security.policy",
                "c:\\j2eebook\\ch04\\examples\\motd.policy");

// Use the default java command and environment variables
            ActivationGroupDesc.CommandEnvironment env = null;

// Create an activation group description
            ActivationGroupDesc group = new ActivationGroupDesc(
                secProps, env);

// Generate an activation group ID
            ActivationGroupID groupID =
                ActivationGroup.getSystem().registerGroup(group);

// Register the activation group
            ActivationGroup.createGroup(groupID, group, 0);

            String codeLocation = "file:/c:/j2eebook/ch04/examples/";

            MarshalledObject initData =
                new MarshalledObject("c:\\j2eebook\\ch04\\examples\\motd.txt");

// Create a class indicating the name of the class to load, the path for
// loading the classes, and the initialization data for the activated
// object.
            ActivationDesc desc = new ActivationDesc(
                "usingj2ee.motd.MOTDImplActivate", codeLocation, initData);

// Register the object with the activation service
            MOTD motdRef = (MOTD) Activatable.register(desc);

// Register the activation under the same name as the old MOTD service
// so the MOTDClient can access it the same way as usual
```

```
            Naming.rebind("//localhost/MessageOfTheDay", motdRef);

            System.exit(0);
        }
        catch (Exception exc)
        {
            exc.printStackTrace();
        }
    }
}
```

To run the activation service, first make sure you have started the RMI Registry. Then, run `rmid`, specifying a policy file, like this:

```
rmid -J-Djava.security.policy=motd.policy
```

When you run the setup program, you must also specify a policy file, like this:

```
java -Djava.security.policy usingj2ee.motd.Setup
```

After you have registered the object with the activation service, you can use the original `MOTDClient` program to activate and use the object.

TROUBLESHOOTING

RUNNING `rmic`

Why does `rmic` complain that my class doesn't implement a Remote interface?

Most likely, you either forgot to declare that your Remote interface extends `Remote` or you forgot to declare that your implementation class implements the Remote interface.

RUNNING THE SERVER

Why do I get an error about a missing `RemoteObject_Stub` class when I run the server?

You forgot to use `rmic` to generate the stub and skeleton for the server class.

Why do I get a security exception when I run the server?

You probably forgot to specify a security policy with the `-Djava.security.policy` option. Remember, because you set up a special security manager, you must use a policy file to grant special permissions to your RMI server object.

CHAPTER

Overview of Enterprise JavaBeans

In this chapter

THE NEED FOR EJB

People have been writing three-tiered database applications for years now and they usually end up trying to solve the same problems over and over. As you saw back in Chapter 1, "Application Architecture Concepts," the basic structure of a three-tiered application consists of a presentation layer, a business logic layer, and a data layer. In a typical business application, you use a database for the data layer and either a GUI front-end or a Web server for the presentation layer.

The business logic layer is traditionally the most difficult to design. You must figure out how your code will interact with the database and with the clients. How you interact with the clients often dictates how you will interact with the database.

You must figure out how clients will access remote business objects. Will each client have its own remote object or will a single remote object handle multiple clients? You must also decide whether an object remembers anything between successive method invocations—that is, whether the object keeps any state data between method invocations. Things become even more difficult when a client needs to interact with multiple objects as part of a single operation.

When you write a typical database application, you make changes to the database as part of a transaction. The database either performs all the operations in a transaction or performs none of them. A withdrawal from an automatic teller machine is a classic example of a transactional operation. The teller must dispense money to you and it must also subtract the amount from your bank account. If either one of these operations fails, both of them must fail. After all, you wouldn't want the teller to subtract money from your account if you didn't receive the cash, and the bank certainly doesn't want you to get free cash.

In the past, it was difficult to group operations on distributed objects into a single transaction. Transaction Processing Monitor (TPMon) programs such as Tuxedo and CICS made it easier to create distributed transactions, but they didn't always integrate well with distributed object systems. With Java's growing popularity for server-side programming and its great networking capabilities, Java needed a mechanism for performing distributed transactions. In creating the J2EE specification, Sun included support for distributed transactions to make an ideal platform for distributed objects.

Transactions are typically associated with database operations, although the concept can be applied to objects in general. To extend transactions to Java objects, Sun defined a class of Java objects called Enterprise JavaBeans, which are beans that might or might not be stored in a database and can participate in transactions.

When you look at the development of the Java environment since 1995, you can't help but notice several areas in which Java seems to mimic various Microsoft technologies. JavaBeans appear to be modeled after COM/ActiveX objects in the way that they support properties, methods, and events. Although COM/ActiveX is one of the most well-known component technologies, it isn't the first. Although it might look like Sun is borrowing Microsoft's ideas, many of the technologies that they share have been around for a while in some form or another. When two companies develop competing products (in this case, the Windows Platform versus the Java Platform), you are likely to see them learn from each other's successes and failures. For instance, the new Microsoft .Net platform is similar to Java in its use of a virtual machine and a more Net-centric approach.

Microsoft has Active Server Pages, and Java has Java Server Pages. Microsoft also makes the Microsoft Transaction Server (MTS), which is a distributed transaction server that supports distributed objects. EJB appears to be a direct response to MTS, but it offers many capabilities beyond those offered in MTS.

One of the shortfalls of MTS is that it only supports stateless objects—that is, objects that don't keep any data between method invocations. Stateless objects are easier for a server to manage because it can keep a pool of objects to handle requests in which any object can handle any request. Because the objects don't remember anything about the clients, one object is just as good as the next. Unfortunately, this restriction places a bigger burden on developers, who must come up with alternative ways to keep track of data between method calls. Although EJB allows for stateless objects, it also allows objects to hold onto state data. You can even mix stateless beans with stateful beans as you need to.

Another area in which MTS is deficient is in object persistence. MTS objects usually don't represent items in the database. Instead, they typically represent business processes. These business processes frequently operate on database information directly. Although this technique is good for many applications, it is often easier to encapsulate your data into objects. For example, jumping back to the automatic teller example, it's usually easier to ask an Account object to subtract $20 from your bank account than it is to access the Account table in the database and update the balance column. The Account object, of course, would access the Account table and update the balance column, but you only have to write that code once.

When you operate directly on database tables, you tend to duplicate operations in various parts of your programs. For example, your automatic teller code updates the balance, and so do your online banking application and your automated bill-paying system. Would you rather write database code in each of these applications or just use the Account object?

Enterprise JavaBeans can represent data stored in the database. In fact, you can even get an EJB server to read database data into a bean automatically and write bean data back to the database automatically! For a large database application, this can be a huge time saver.

Jumping back to the communications between the client and server for a moment, you must decide how a client actually sends a message to a remote object. In the Java world, the three most popular solutions are the Common Object Request Broker Architecture (CORBA), Remote Method Invocation (RMI), and custom sockets.

The advantage of CORBA is that it defines a number of services that you frequently need in a distributed object system. CORBA has standards for security, naming, events, persistence, and several other important services. CORBA is language-neutral—it doesn't care which language you use to create your objects. A client written in Java can communicate with a remote object written in C++. Unfortunately, because CORBA works across multiple languages, it doesn't always use all the available features of the implementation language. In particular, CORBA only recently gained the capability to pass objects by value.

Custom socket solutions are popular because systems such as CORBA are often overkill for small applications. You also have more control over the interactions between the client and server. If you have specific networking requirements, a custom socket solution is often your best choice.

RMI is a Java-only solution that is extremely simple to use. Because it is a Java-only solution, RMI can take advantage of all Java's features and you don't need to learn a new way of performing common tasks as you often must with CORBA. Because RMI is such a good choice for Java developers, it has gradually been edging out CORBA as the preferred framework for distributed object development. There is even a way to allow CORBA objects to invoke remote methods in RMI objects. Because of the simplicity and popularity of RMI, Sun chose RMI as the framework for communicating with Enterprise JavaBeans.

RMI gives EJB yet another advantage over Microsoft Transaction Server (MTS). MTS uses Distributed COM (DCOM) for communications. DCOM basically extends COM to work over a network (COM by itself just provides communication within a single machine).

DCOM isn't very friendly when it comes to passing objects back and forth. MTS developers usually end up passing record sets (similar to JDBC result sets) back and forth. To support more dynamic data, Microsoft allows results sets to be nested. Unfortunately, this is not an optimal solution.

CONTAINERS, COMPONENTS, AND CONNECTORS

As you work with various parts of J2EE, you'll encounter the term "container" from time to time, and it might confuse you at first. Many developers tend to think of a container as a data structure like an array, a linked list, or a vector. In the J2EE world, however, a container is almost like a mini-server—it provides the runtime support for the items it contains. An EJB container contains Enterprise JavaBeans and provides connection pooling and transaction processing, whereas a Servlet container contains servlets and Java Server Pages. A server can have multiple containers and objects in each container are somewhat isolated from each other, although objects in one container can communicate with objects in another container. For instance, a servlet in one container might access an EJB in another container.

Enterprise JavaBeans are referred to as components. The distinction between a component and an object is sometimes fuzzy, but in general, a *component* is a software module designed to be used in many applications without being modified. Back in the 1980s, developers dreamed of *Software ICs*—software libraries that were as reusable as IC chips. When you design a circuit board, you don't need to crack open an IC or understand how all its wiring works. You just need to conform to its interface specification. Software components are the closest thing you have to a software IC. An object can be a component, but you usually think of components as being larger than objects. In a distributed system, the distributed objects are closer to being components than objects.

Note

The concept of software components actually dates back far beyond the 1980s. In 1968, NATO held a conference on "Software Engineering," which was a new term at the time. The conference addressed the growing "software crisis" of unreliable, unmaintainable code. In that conference, M.D. McIlroy presented a paper arguing that the software industry should focus on creating software components.

Enterprise JavaBeans, being distributed objects, are more like components. In fact, an EJB is defined not by a single object but by a group of objects. Regardless of whether you understand or care about the difference between a component and an object, the important thing is that you concentrate on reuse when you design your EJBs. Try to anticipate the various ways the EJB might be used so that future applications can use it without requiring additional changes.

EJB is a new technology and most companies are unlikely to rewrite all their applications to support EJB anytime soon. More likely, they will continue to use existing systems and use EJB for new development. You can create connectors to access external systems from your J2EE applications. These connectors can even participate in transactions, allowing you to keep data synchronized between multiple systems. In the past, synchronizing data between multiple systems could be a nightmare. Imagine, for instance, that you are writing a new reservations program for an airline. You must store the reservation in a local database and also send the reservation to the mainframe. You insert the reservation in the database, but then there's an error storing the reservation in the mainframe so you must now delete the reservation from the database. Suppose you try adding the reservation to the mainframe first? Now when there's an error inserting the reservation into your database, you must send a message to the mainframe to delete the reservation. What happens if there's an error deleting the reservation? You have an ugly synchronization problem. By creating a transaction-aware connector, you can synchronize the database operation with the mainframe communication and insure that the reservation is either inserted in both places or neither place.

Figure 5.1 shows the various parts of an EJB server and how it interacts with various parts of an application.

Figure 5.1
An EJB server is made up of containers, components, and connectors.

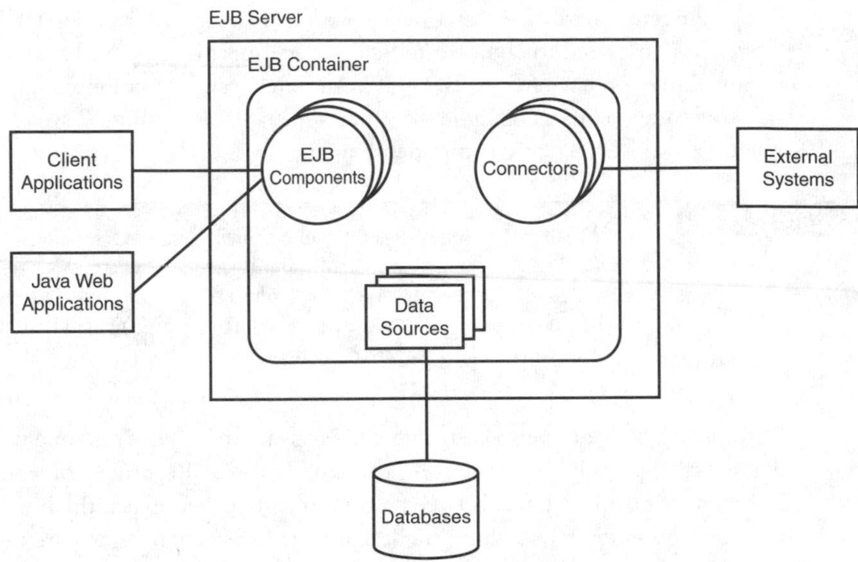

ENTERPRISE JAVABEANS

An Enterprise JavaBean is a special kind of JavaBean made for performing server-side business logic operations. When you create a regular JavaBean, you only need to create `get/set` methods for each property you want to define, maybe add some public methods and define `addXXXListener` and `removeXXXListener` methods to define any events. You might also want to create a `BeanInfo` object to describe your bean.

There are three kinds of Enterprise JavaBeans:

- A session bean, which represents a conversation between a client and a server. There is usually one session bean per client and the session beans aren't persistent data objects—you don't store a session in the database.
- An entity bean, which represents a persistent data object. Although you often store entity beans in a relational database, the only requirement is that the entity bean be stored persistently. An entity bean can be used by many clients, but typically, you hide the entity beans from the clients, letting the session beans interact with the entity beans.
- A message bean, which listens for incoming messages from the Java Message Service (JMS). A message bean doesn't have "clients." The only way you can interact with a message bean is by sending it JMS messages. Message beans are a recent addition to EJB and might not be available in all EJB containers.

You will learn more about these types of beans shortly.

An Enterprise JavaBean has a minimum of three required Java classes:

- The Remote interface defines the methods that a client program can invoke on the bean.
- The Home interface defines methods for creating and locating an EJB.
- A Java class implements both the Home and Remote interfaces. This class is what you would normally think of as the EJB itself.

Figure 5.2 shows how a client interacts with both the Home and Remote interfaces of an EJB. It is a subtle point, but keep in mind that a client never interacts directly with the EJB. A client must only use the Home and Remote interfaces when referring to an EJB.

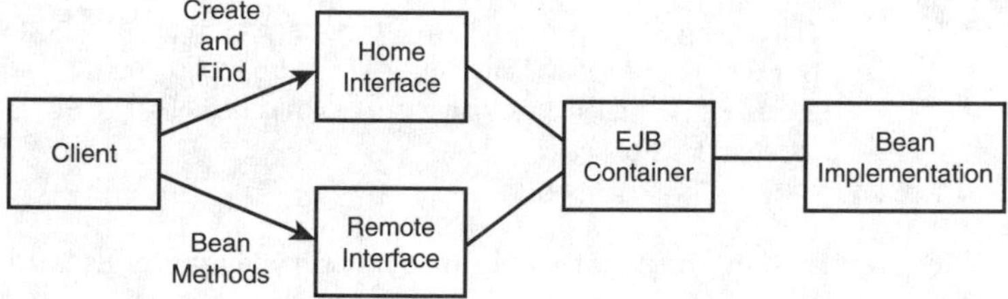

Figure 5.2
A client uses the Home interface to create an EJB and then communicates using the Remote interface.

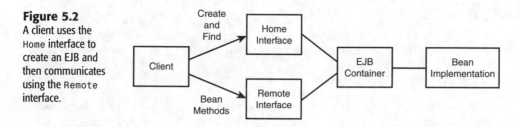

THE Home INTERFACE

Both session beans and entity beans have Home interfaces, although the entity bean typically defines more methods in its Home interface. The two main functions of Home interface methods are creating beans and locating beans.

Both session and entity beans define methods to create beans, but only entity beans need to define methods to locate beans. Listing 5.1 shows an example Home interface for a session bean.

LISTING 5.1 SOURCE CODE FOR MySessionHome.java

```
import java.rmi.*;
import javax.ejb.*;

public interface MySessionHome extends EJBHome
{
    public MySession create() throws RemoteException, CreateException;
}
```

Listing 5.2 shows an example Home interface for an entity bean. An entity bean needs at least a findByPrimaryKey method and usually methods to locate the bean by other criteria.

LISTING 5.2 SOURCE CODE FOR MyEntityHome.java

```
import java.rmi.*;
import java.util.*;
import javax.ejb.*;

public interface MyEntityHome extends EJBHome
 {
```

LISTING 5.2 CONTINUED

```
    MyEntity create() throws RemoteException, CreateException;

    MyEntity findByPrimaryKey(String myEntityPK)
            throws RemoteException, FinderException;

    Enumeration findByCountry(String aCountry)
        throws RemoteException, FinderException;
}
```

Note

Although `MyEntityHome` returns an `Enumeration` of entity beans, it is better to return a `Collection` of beans. In the original EJB 1.0 specification, you could only return enumerations. EJB 1.1 added the capability to return collections, and that is now the preferred way to return a set of beans.

The object returned by the `create` and `findByPrimaryKey` methods is an object that implements the bean's `Remote` interface. It is not the actual class that implements the bean.

THE `Remote` INTERFACE

A bean's `Remote` interface consists of the remote methods you can call on a bean after you have located or created the bean using the `Home` interface. The remote methods are usually called "business methods" because they implement your business logic.

Listing 5.3 shows a simple `Remote` interface for a bean that contains a first and last name.

LISTING 5.3 SOURCE CODE FOR `MyEntity.java`

```
import java.rmi.*;

public interface MyEntity
{
    public String getFirstName() throws RemoteException;
    public void setFirstName(String aFirstName) throws RemoteException;

    public String getLastName() throws RemoteException;
    public void setLastName(String aLastName) throws RemoteException;
}
```

PROGRAMMING RESTRICTIONS

Unless you are writing a Java applet, you usually don't expect Java to place any restrictions on what you do.

When you write an EJB, however, there are a number of things that your EJB can't do. The reason for these restrictions is that an EJB must be managed by an EJB container. The programming restrictions keep the EJB from making too many assumptions about its environment or interfering with its environment. They also give the container more flexibility in handling the beans.

An Enterprise JavaBean cannot

- Create or manage threads
- Access files using the `java.io` package
- Create a `ServerSocket` or change the socket and stream handler factories
- Load a native library
- Use the AWT to interact with a user

There are other minor restrictions dealing with return types and method parameters. You'll learn more about these additional restrictions in the next few chapters.

SESSION BEANS

Session beans typically represent business logic functions and are not stored in the database. A session bean can still access the database, however.

A session bean might or might not hold onto data between method invocations. If a session bean keeps data, it is referred to as a *stateful session bean*. If the bean doesn't keep any data, it is referred to as a *stateless session bean*.

Each client has its own separate session bean, which is one reason the bean is called a session bean. You can think of the bean as representing a client's session with the EJB container. For example, many online shopping sites have the concept of a shopping cart. You click an item to add it to your shopping cart and when you're ready to check out, the cart lists the items you want to buy.

A shopping cart is often implemented using a stateful session bean. You don't necessarily want to store the shopping cart items in a database, although you can if you want to. The shopping cart must be stateful, because it remembers what items you have placed in the cart.

Although each client has its own session bean, when session beans are stateless, there might be a different session bean handling each method invocation from the client. Because the bean doesn't remember anything between method invocations, it doesn't matter if the session bean received a request from a different client the last time. It can't tell the difference.

ENTITY BEANS

Entity beans are Enterprise JavaBeans that represent data objects in your application and are typically stored in a database. A client can invoke methods on an entity bean just as it can on a session bean, although in some applications, the entity beans might only be accessed by session beans.

Unlike session beans, entity are always stateful, that's the whole idea behind an entity bean. Also unlike session beans, the same entity bean can be accessed by multiple clients at the same time. The EJB container takes care of any transaction conflicts that might arise from the entity beans being shared.

The EJB container decides when it should load and store entity beans. Depending on the persistence model the bean uses, the container might even handle the task of writing the bean out to the database.

Entity beans can either manage their own persistence (loading and saving to the database) or they can ask the container to handle their persistence. When a bean manages its own persistence, it is using Bean Managed Persistence (BMP). When the container manages the bean's persistence, the bean is using Container Managed Persistence (CMP). You'll learn more about these two persistence models in Chapter 7, "Creating an Entity Bean."

TRANSACTIONS

One of the features of EJB that distinguishes it from typical distributed object systems is that it has integrated support for transactions. Although you do find transaction support in CORBA and MTS, the support provided in EJB is easier to use and more flexible.

As with the persistence model, you can choose whether you want the container or the bean to manage a transaction.

A transaction can be in effect for a single remote method invocation or it can span method invocations. By default, each remote method invocation takes place within a separate transaction.

One of the more interesting features of Enterprise JavaBeans is that a transaction can include more than just a database operation. The Java Message Service allows you to send messages to other application objects as part of a single transaction. You could, for example, store an order in your database and send a message to your order fulfillment application. If something goes wrong with the database part of the operation, the message isn't sent because it's part of the whole transaction. Likewise, if there's a problem sending the message, the database operation is rolled back. Without transactions, this kind of application is much harder to write. You could end up sending a message to the fulfillment service for an order that isn't in the database, or you could store an order that the fulfillment service would never know about.

Connectors can also participate in transactions, but only in certain circumstances. Some connector operations might not support transactions that also involve database operations. You will learn more about this in Chapter 20, "Connecting to Existing Systems."

CORE TECHNOLOGIES

Enterprise JavaBeans use several key technologies. Many of these technologies are used behind the scenes—invisible to most developers. The three technologies that are in the forefront of EJB development are RMI, JDBC, and JNDI.

The `Remote` and `Home` interfaces for an EJB must be RMI interfaces. Every remote method must be declared as throwing `java.rmi.RemoteException`. In addition, your remote methods must have return types and parameters that are compatible with RMI. The main thing to remember when you pass objects back and forth with RMI is that the objects must implement the `java.io.Serializable` interface.

If you use Container Managed Persistence (CMP), there's a chance you won't need to use JDBC at all. Odds are, however, that you'll need to use JDBC here and there. There are still cases in which CMP doesn't handle all the different ways that you can access data, although with version 2.0 of the EJB specification, there are fewer cases.

If you use BMP, of course, you use JDBC to load and store your entity beans. Furthermore, if you need to access the database from a session bean, you'll need to use JDBC.

Finally, you use the JNDI naming API to locate objects in the system. For example, when a client program needs to access a bean's `Home` interface, it uses JNDI to locate the `Home` interface. After you locate an object, you communicate directly with it instead of going through JNDI. Aside from a few setup method calls, you don't need to know much about JNDI to create and use Enterprise JavaBeans.

Figure 5.3 shows how the various core technologies fit into your EJB application.

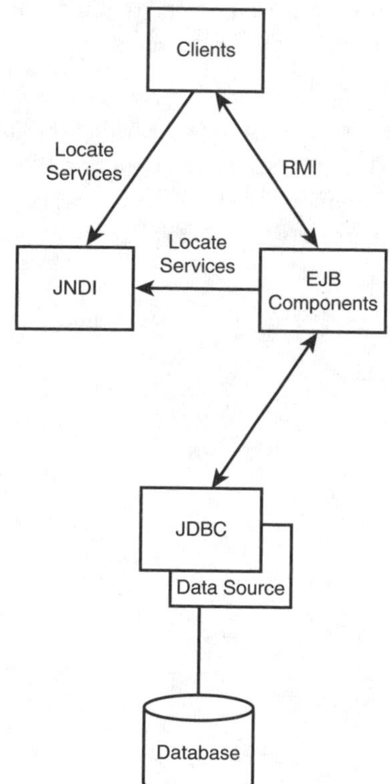

Figure 5.3
JDBC, RMI, and JNDI are the primary technologies you use when implementing and using EJBs.

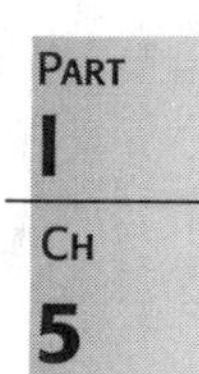

CASE STUDY

An e-commerce company wanted to develop an ordering system that allowed customers to place orders from the Internet, and also allow call center operators to enter and view orders. Because of the large number of call center users, the company realized that a typical two-tiered application would not work well with the number of database connections required to support so many users.

The company already had a reasonable relational database model, so the company needed to decide how to implement and design a three-tiered application. A Windows-only solution was initially considered that used Visual Basic to design the call-center application, MTS for the application server, and Active Server Pages for the Web technology. The company decided, however, that it didn't feel comfortable locking into a Windows-only solution. The company already had server Unix servers that they could use for the application.

The company then considered using CORBA, possible with a Visual Basic front end (using a special package called a COM-CORBA bridge that lets Visual Basic applications talk to CORBA objects). While prototyping a CORBA solution, the company realized that the intricacies of its data model would require a lot of careful coding to insure transactional integrity. The company finally settled on Enterprise JavaBeans. This platform-independent solution handled much of the unpleasant transaction overhead and also handled the database interaction automatically.

The biggest gripe about the decision was that the GUI developers didn't like creating GUIs in Java. They preferred a Visual Basic solution. They ended up doing the call center front end in Java. Sun is addressing the lack of EJB connectivity from Visual Basic. You will soon be able to use a special EJB-COM bridge to create VB and Delphi applications that access EJB.

CHAPTER 6

Creating a Session Bean

In this chapter

WHAT DOES A SESSION BEAN DO?

A session bean represents a conversation between a client application and an EJB container. Session beans typically implement business logic and often interact with a number of entity beans to perform an operation. A session bean isn't required to use entity beans, however. It communicates directly with the database if it needs to.

A "HELLO WORLD" SESSION BEAN

The structure of Enterprise JavaBeans can be a little awkward to work with at first, but after you get a feel for the structure, EJBs aren't too bad. Fortunately, you can become familiar with the basic EJB structure without worrying about database connections or transactions. To do this, start with a good old-fashioned "Hello World" bean.

When you design EJB applications, you might wonder whether you should start with the bean and then create the interfaces, or start with the interfaces and then create the bean. Your best bet here is to start with the interfaces. If you can't describe how a client is going to use the bean, you aren't ready to write it.

CREATING THE `Remote` INTERFACE

Listing 6.1 shows the `HelloWorldSession` interface, which is the `Remote` interface for the "Hello World" session bean.

LISTING 6.1 SOURCE CODE FOR `HelloWorldSession.java`

```
package usingj2ee.hello;

import java.rmi.*;
import javax.ejb.*;

/** Defines the methods you can call on a HelloWorldSession object */

public interface HelloWorldSession extends EJBObject
{

/** Returns the session's greeting */
    public String getGreeting() throws RemoteException;

/** Changes the session's greeting */
    public void setGreeting(String aGreeting) throws RemoteException;

}
```

CREATING THE `Home` INTERFACE

You might recall from Chapter 5, "Overview of Enterprise JavaBeans," that the `Home` interface for a session bean contains methods for creating a new session. For the "Hello World" example, there are two different create methods, one that takes no parameters and a second that allows you to provide your own greeting. Listing 6.2 shows the HelloWorldSessionHome interface.

LISTING 6.2 SOURCE CODE FOR HelloWorldSessionHome.java

```
package usingj2ee.hello;

import java.rmi.*;
import javax.ejb.*;

/** Defines the methods for creating a HelloWorldSession */

public interface HelloWorldSessionHome extends EJBHome
{

/** Creates a HelloWorldSession bean with default settings */
    public HelloWorldSession create() throws RemoteException, CreateException;

/** Creates a HelloWorldSession bean with a specific initial greeting */
    public HelloWorldSession create(String aGreeting)
        throws RemoteException, CreateException;

}
```

CREATING THE IMPLEMENTATION CLASS

The interfaces are the easy part of EJB development. The session bean requires a bit more work. When you write a session bean, there are a few methods that you must include in the bean to satisfy the EJB container. These extra methods are setSessionContext, ejbRemove, ejbActivate, and ejbPassivate. In addition, when you implement your create methods, you must name them ejbCreate instead of just create.

Note

Keep in mind that the container calls these methods. When you use a method in the Home interface to create a new EJB, the container ends up invoking your ejbCreate method. Likewise, when you remove a bean, the container invokes the ejbRemove method to tell the bean it has been removed.

Listing 6.3, the implementation for the HelloWorldSession and HelloWorldSessionHome interfaces, should make things clearer.

LISTING 6.3 SOURCE CODE FOR HelloWorldSessionImpl.java

```
package usingj2ee.hello;

import java.rmi.*;
import java.util.*;
import javax.ejb.*;

/** The implementation class for the HelloWorldSession bean */
```

LISTING 6.3 CONTINUED

```
public class HelloWorldSessionImpl implements SessionBean
{
/** Holds the session's greeting */
    protected String greeting;

/** The session context provided by the EJB container. A session bean must
    hold on to the context it is given. */

    private SessionContext context;

/** An EJB must have a public, parameterless constructor */

    public HelloWorldSessionImpl()
    {
    }

/** Called by the EJB container to set this session's context */

    public void setSessionContext(SessionContext aContext)
    {
        context = aContext;
    }

/** Called by the EJB container when a client calls the create() method in
    the Home interface */

    public void ejbCreate()
        throws CreateException
    {
        greeting = "Hello World!";
    }

/** Called by the EJB container when a client calls the
    create(String) method in the Home interface */

    public void ejbCreate(String aGreeting)
        throws CreateException
    {
        greeting = aGreeting;
    }

/** Called by the EJB container to wake this session bean up after it
    has been put to sleep with the ejbPassivate method. */

    public void ejbActivate()
    {
    }

/** Called by the EJB container to tell this session bean that it is being
    suspended from use (it's being put to sleep). */

    public void ejbPassivate()
    {
    }
```

```
/** Called by the EJB container to tell this session bean that it has been
    removed, either because the client invoked the remove() method or the
    container has timed the session out. */

    public void ejbRemove()
    {
    }

/** Returns the session's greeting */

    public String getGreeting()
    {
        return greeting;
    }

/** Changes the session's greeting */

    public void setGreeting(String aGreeting)
    {
        greeting = aGreeting;
    }
}
```

All you wanted to do was make a bean with `getGreeting` and `setGreeting` methods and you ended up with two Java interfaces and an implementation class with eight methods. Enterprise JavaBeans obviously involve a lot of extra work, and for small projects, it might seem like you're doing almost as much work creating EJB methods as you are implementing your business logic. As your application grows, however, you'll find that the amount of work you're putting into your EJBs will begin to pay off as it becomes easier to mix objects together to implement new features.

Some Integrated Development Environments (IDEs) provide some support for creating Enterprise JavaBeans. Mostly, these IDEs generate the required methods and some helper methods. Unfortunately, most of the tools that provide these utilities are the expensive "Enterprise versions." The `Kawa Enterprise` IDE from Allaire (`www.allaire.com`) is reasonable inexpensive and has good EJB support. Hopefully, you will soon find some free tools for creating EJBs as well.

Tip

Because you end up with so many files when writing EJB applications, it is important to have a consistent naming convention for your classes. The `Remote` and `Home` interfaces are usually named `XXX` and `XXXHome` where `XXX` is the name of the bean. The implementation class is usually named `XXXBean` or `XXXImpl`. You might also consider naming the implementation class `XXXEB` or `XXXSB` depending on whether the bean is a session bean or an entity bean. No matter how you decide to name your classes, be consistent. It makes it easier when there are multiple developers.

Note

This book uses the `XXX` for the `Remote` interface, `XXXHome` for the `Home` interface and `XXXImpl` for the implementation. It also refers to the bean using the `Remote` interface name. If the `Remote` interface is called `ShoppingCart`, the `Home` interface is `ShoppingCartHome`, the implementation is in `ShoppingCartImpl`, and the bean is referred to as the `ShoppingCart` bean.

DEPLOYING THE BEAN

One of the other aspects of Enterprise JavaBeans that might be difficult to get used to is that you don't run EJBs, you deploy them. You use a packaging tool of some kind to create a JAR file containing the EJB classes, some XML deployment descriptor files, and some helper classes that are specific to the container you're using.

Although you'll get a more thorough introduction to EJB deployment in Chapter 10, "Mapping Objects to a Relational Database," you really can't go on learning about EJBs without writing your own beans and trying them out.

Each EJB vendor supplies its own custom deployment tool. Although some tools are easier to use than others, most of them follow the same general pattern. In this chapter, you'll see how to package the bean and deploy it using the Java 2 Enterprise Edition SDK (J2EE SDK) from Sun. The deployment tool for the J2EE SDK is called `deploytool` and in the `bin` directory of the SDK.

After starting `deploytool`, select New Application from the File menu. In the New Application dialog box, enter the name of the EAR (Enterprise Archive) file you want to create. An EAR file is a JAR file for J2EE applications. Figure 6.1 shows the dialog box with the information for the Hello World session bean filled in.

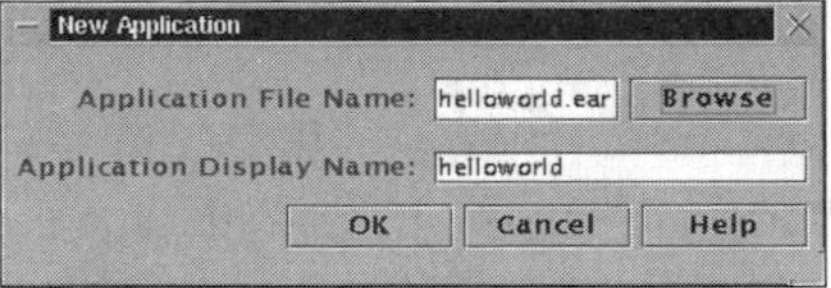

Figure 6.1
Enter the name of the EAR file you want to create.

Next, from the File menu, select New Enterprise Bean. You can also change the display name for the JAR if you like.

In the New Enterprise Bean Wizard, click the Add button on the lower-right section next to the Contents area. You should see a dialog box like the one in Figure 6.2. The dialog box allows you to select the class files that make up your EJB. In this case, select the `HelloWorldSession.class`, `HelloWorldSessionHome.class`, and `HelloWorldSessionImpl.class` files and click the Add button.

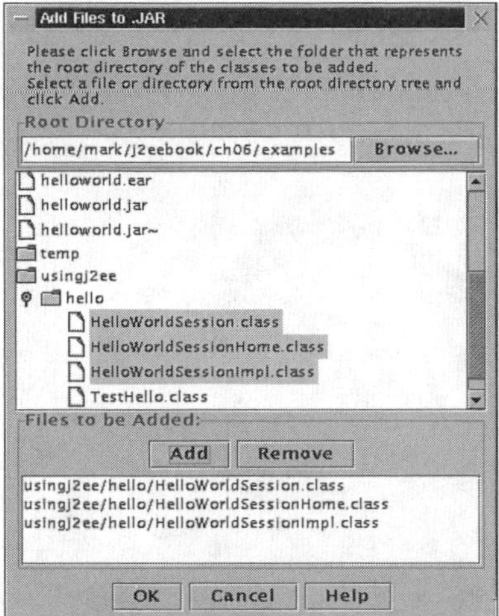

Figure 6.2
Select the files that make up the Enterprise JavaBean.

Next, tell `deploytool` what classes to use for the Enterprise Bean class, the `Home` interface, and the `Remote` interface. You can also give the bean a display name, which is only used within `deploytool`. You must also tell the tool whether the bean is a session bean or an entity bean, and if it is a session bean, whether it is stateless or stateful. Figure 6.3 shows the configuration entries for the Hello World bean.

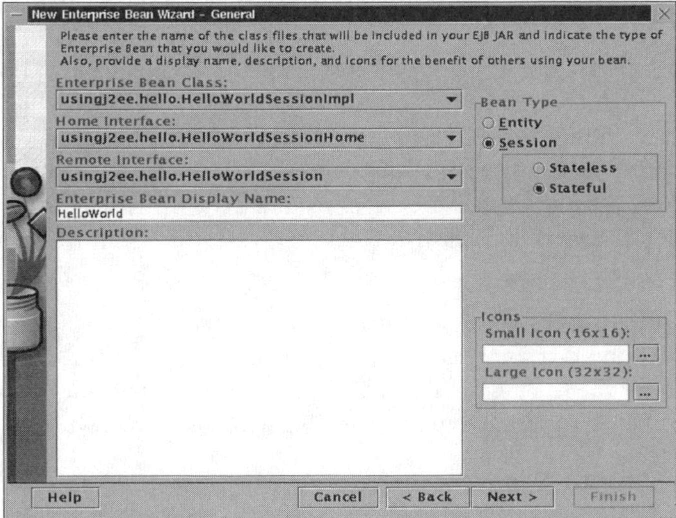

Figure 6.3
Specify which classes implement which parts of the EJB.

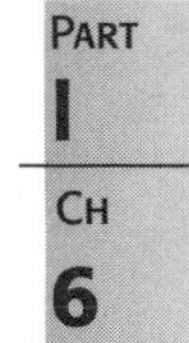

Because the Hello World example is a simple session bean that doesn't have any other configuration requirements, you can continue to click Next and then click Finish when you have the opportunity. You should now be ready to deploy the bean.

Make sure the EJB server is running before you deploy to it. You might also need to tell `deploytool` which server to use by selecting Add from the Server menu option. After the server is running, select Deploy Application from the Tools menu. You should see a dialog box like the one shown in Figure 6.4.

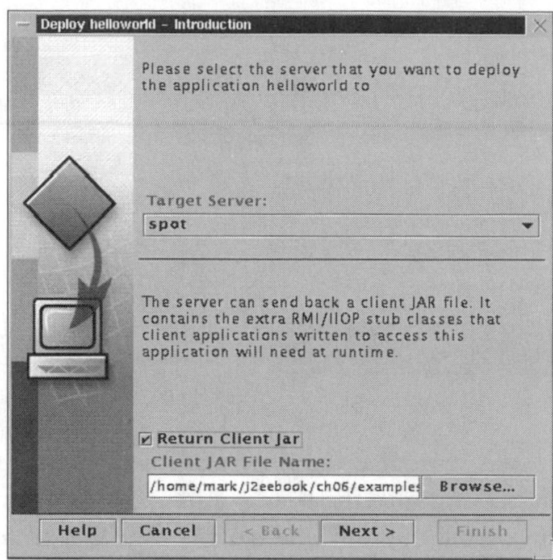

Figure 6.4
Select the server where you want to deploy and generate a client JAR file.

When you deploy an EAR file or a JAR file, you usually end up generating a number of additional classes that the server needs to handle network access to the bean. For servers such as BEA's WebLogic server, you generate these classes when you create the JAR file. For the J2EE SDK, you generate the classes when you deploy the JAR file. Many EJB servers also generate a client JAR file, which contains classes that a client needs to access the EJB. Not all servers need to generate a client JAR file, however. WebLogic, for example, manages to load important classes dynamically at runtime without needing a special JAR file. The J2EE SDK, however, does require a client JAR file. Make sure you tell `deploytool` to generate a client JAR file. In this case, the client JAR is called `helloClient.jar`.

Finally, tell `deploytool` what JNDI name you want the EJB to be known by. Again, this setting is something that some servers let you configure into the JAR file. The J2EE SDK doesn't ask for the name until deploy time, however, allowing you to deploy the same bean to different servers under different names. Figure 6.5 shows the dialog box that allows you to set the name for the bean.

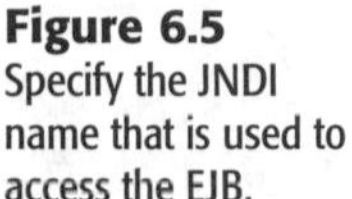

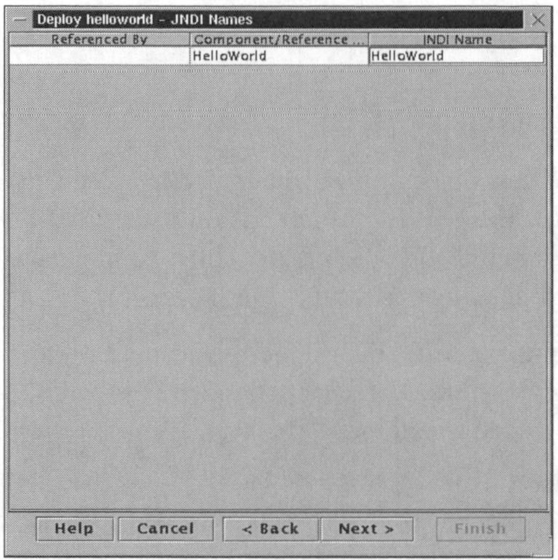

Figure 6.5 Specify the JNDI name that is used to access the EJB.

Creating a Client to Access the Session Bean

After all the work you had to do to implement and deploy a session bean, you might expect that writing a client is equally painful. Fortunately, that's not the case. It's easy to write a client program to use an Enterprise JavaBean.

The only tricky part about using an EJB is getting a reference to the EJB's `Home` interface. After you have a reference to the `Home` interface, you just use one of the `create` methods to create an instance of the bean and then invoke methods on the bean's `Remote` interface.

The first thing you need to do, of course, is get a reference to the JNDI naming context, which is your interface to the naming system. You use the naming system to locate EJBs and other objects. The easiest way to get a reference to the naming context is just to create an `InitialContext` object, like this:

```
Context namingContext = new InitialContext();
```

Depending on your application server, you might need to either provide a `Properties` object with additional information or define a system property when you run your client. The reason for the extra information is that the JNDI API (the Java Naming API) provides an interface into a naming system but doesn't provide the naming service itself. If you are running WebLogic, for example, you use the WebLogic naming service. Likewise, if you're running JRun, you use the JRun naming service. JNDI uses something called a context factory to create a `Context` object. You just need to tell it what class to use as the context factory.

If you're running WebLogic, the context factory is called `weblogic.jndi.WLInitialContextFactory`. You can specify it on the command line, like this:

```
java -Dnaming.factory.initial=weblogic.jndi.WLInitialContextFactory
```

You can also specify the context factory via a `Properties` object, like this:

```
Properties p = new Properties();
```

```
p.put(Context.INITIAL_CONTEXT_FACTORY,
    "weblogic.jndi.WLInitialContextFactory");

Context context = new InitialContext(p);
```

The advantage of the `Properties` object is that you don't need to do anything special on the command line. The disadvantage is that your code only works with a WebLogic server. Although you might only use one brand of server, it's still a good idea to keep vendor-specific information out of your source code whenever possible.

Now that you have the naming context, you use the `lookup` method to locate the EJB you want. For example, if you deployed the `HelloWorldSession` bean with a JNDI name of "HelloWorld", the following code would locate the bean's `Home` interface for you:

```
HelloWorldSessionHome home = (HelloWorldSessionHome)
    PortableRemoteObject.narrow(
        context.lookup("HelloWorld"),
        HelloWorldSessionHome.class);
```

When you use EJB, you can't cast remote references using the standard Java cast operator. Instead, you must use `PortableRemoteObject.narrow`. EJB uses a special form of RMI called RMI-IIOP that requires this special syntax for casting.

Remember, too, that you never locate EJB `Remote` interfaces, only `Home` interfaces. You then use the `create` and `find` methods in the `Home` interface to get the `Remote` interface.

You will learn much more about JNDI in Chapter 18, "JNDI—Java Naming and Directory Interface."

Listing 6.4 shows a complete client program that creates a `HelloWorldSession` bean first using the default `create` method, and then again by using the `create(String)` version.

LISTING 6.4 SOURCE CODE FOR `TestHello.java`

```
package usingj2ee.hello;

import java.util.*;
import javax.naming.*;
import javax.rmi.*;

public class TestHello
{
    public static void main(String[] args)
    {
        try
        {

/** Creates a JNDI naming context for location objects */
            Context context = new InitialContext();

/** Asks the context to locate an object named "HelloWorld" and expects the
    object to implement the HelloWorldSessionHome interface */
```

```
            HelloWorldSessionHome home = (HelloWorldSessionHome)
                PortableRemoteObject.narrow(
                    context.lookup("HelloWorld"),
                    HelloWorldSessionHome.class);
/** Asks the Home interface to create a new session bean */
            HelloWorldSession session = (HelloWorldSession) home.create();

            System.out.println("The default greeting is: "+
                session.getGreeting());

            session.setGreeting("Howdy!");

            System.out.println("The greeting is now: "+session.getGreeting());

/** Destroy this session */
            session.remove();

/** Now create a session with a different greeting */
            session = (HelloWorldSession) home.create("Guten Tag!");

            System.out.println("Created a new session with a greeting of: "+
                session.getGreeting());

/** Destroy this session */
            session.remove();

        }
        catch (Exception exc)
        {
            exc.printStackTrace();
        }
    }
}
```

Figure 6.6 shows the output from the `TestHello` program.

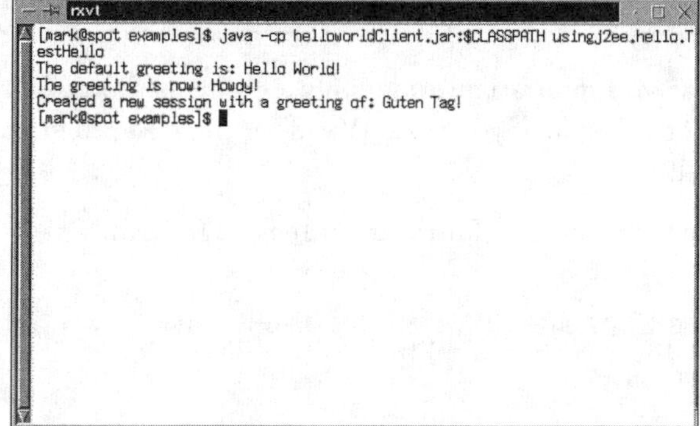

Figure 6.6
The `TestHello` class exercises the capabilities of the `HelloWorldSession` bean.

CREATING A STATELESS SESSION BEAN

From a programming standpoint, it's just as easy to create a stateless session bean as it is to create a stateful one. The only real difference, other than changing a setting in the deployment tool, is in the initial design of the bean. A stateless session bean doesn't remember anything from one method invocation to the next, so any information the bean requires must be passed in from the client. Although it's true that a stateless session bean doesn't remember session-oriented data, you can store data in a stateless session bean. You just can't store client-specific data.

In the `HelloWorldSession` example bean, the bean had a greeting string that it remembered between method invocations. For instance, you called the `setGreeting` method to change the greeting, and then when you called `getGreeting`, the session remembered the greeting you had saved.

Listing 6.5 shows the `Remote` interfaces for a stateless version of the "Hello World" session bean.

LISTING 6.5 SOURCE CODE FOR `StatelessHello.java`

```
package usingj2ee.hello;

import java.rmi.*;
import javax.ejb.*;

/** Defines the methods you can call on a StatelessHello object */

public interface StatelessHello extends EJBObject
{

/** Returns a greeting for the named object */
    public String greet(String thingToGreet) throws RemoteException;

}
```

In this example, the `Remote` interface provides only a `greet` method that takes an item and returns a greeting. For example, if you pass "World" as the thing to greet, the `greet` method returns "Hello World!".

Listing 6.6 shows the `Home` interface for the `StatelessHello` bean.

LISTING 6.6 SOURCE CODE FOR `StatelessHelloHome.java`

```
package usingj2ee.hello;

import java.rmi.*;
import javax.ejb.*;

/** Defines the methods for creating a StatelessHelloWorld */

public interface StatelessHelloHome extends EJBHome
```

```
{

/** Creates a StatelessHello session bean. A stateless session bean
    can't have a create method that takes parameters. */
    public StatelessHello create() throws RemoteException, CreateException;

}
```

A stateless session bean can only have one `create` method and it can't take any parameters. Although it might seem strange to not allow parameters to the `create` method, it makes sense when you think about what it means for the session bean to be stateless. The bean must not remember anything about a particular client. In fact, the container might, for performance reasons, let a different session handle a particular client's method invocations from time to time. Because the session isn't supposed to remember anything about a particular client, there shouldn't be any problem in letting another bean handle the load.

Now, if the bean's `create` method took any parameters, that would be saying that one instance of the session bean might behave differently than another because you've supplied a different value to the `create` method.

It's as easy to implement a stateless session bean as it is to implement a stateful bean. Listing 6.7 shows the `StatelessHelloImpl` class, which implements the `Remote` and `Home` interfaces.

LISTING 6.7 SOURCE CODE FOR `StatelessHelloImpl.java`

```
package usingj2ee.hello;

import java.rmi.*;
import java.util.*;
import javax.ejb.*;

/** The implementation class for the StatelessHello bean */

public class StatelessHelloImpl implements SessionBean
{
/** The session context provided by the EJB container. A session bean must
    hold on to the context it is given. */
    private SessionContext context;

/** An EJB must have a public, parameterless constructor */

    public StatelessHelloImpl()
    {
    }

/** Called by the EJB container to set this session's context */

    public void setSessionContext(SessionContext aContext)
    {
        context = aContext;
    }

/** Called by the EJB container when a client calls the create() method in
    the Home interface */
```

LISTING 6.7 CONTINUED

```
    public void ejbCreate()
        throws CreateException
    {
    }

/** Called by the EJB container to wake this session bean up after it
    has been put to sleep with the ejbPassivate method. */

    public void ejbActivate()
    {
    }

/** Called by the EJB container to tell this session bean that it is being
    suspended from use (it's being put to sleep). */

    public void ejbPassivate()
    {
    }

/** Called by the EJB container to tell this session bean that it has been
    removed, either because the client invoked the remove() method or the
    container has timed the session out. */

    public void ejbRemove()
    {
    }

/** Returns a greeting for the named object */

    public String greet(String thingToGreet)
    {
        return "Hello "+thingToGreet+"!";
    }
}
```

Note

The deployment procedure for the stateless session bean is almost identical to the deployment procedure for the stateful bean. Just make sure you indicate that the bean is stateless. You might need to check a box such as Stateless or make sure a box such as Manages Conversational State is unchecked.

Finally, Listing 6.8 shows a client that tests the stateless session bean.

LISTING 6.8 SOURCE CODE FOR `TestStatelessHello.java`

```
package usingj2ee.hello;

import java.util.*;
import javax.naming.*;
import javax.rmi.*;
```

```
public class TestStatelessHello
{
    public static void main(String[] args)
    {
        try
        {

/** Creates a JNDI naming context for location objects */
            Context context = new InitialContext();

/** Asks the context to locate an object named "HelloWorld" and expects the
    object to implement the HelloWorldSessionHome interface */

            StatelessHelloHome home = (StatelessHelloHome)
                PortableRemoteObject.narrow(
                    context.lookup("StatelessHello"),
                    StatelessHelloHome.class);
/** Asks the Home interface to create a new session bean */
            StatelessHello session = (StatelessHello) home.create();

            System.out.println(session.greet("World"));
            System.out.println(session.greet("Solar System"));
            System.out.println(session.greet("Universe"));

/** Destroy this session */
            session.remove();
        }
        catch (Exception exc)
        {
            exc.printStackTrace();
        }
    }
}
```

Figure 6.7 shows the output from the `TestStatelessHello` program.

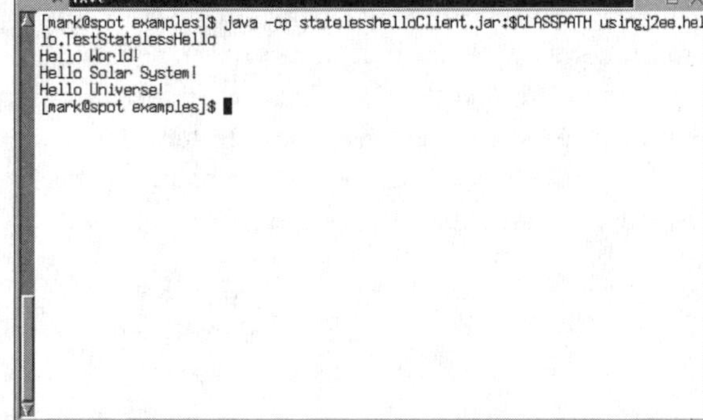

Figure 6.7
The `TestStatelessHello` class exercises the capabilities of the `StatelessHello` bean.

MORE DETAILS ABOUT SESSION BEANS

Now that you have a feel for the structure of session beans and what it takes to implement them, there are a few more details you need to know to be more effective when designing and developing session beans.

THE SessionBean INTERFACE

Every session bean must implement the `SessionBean` interface, which contains four methods. The EJB container uses these methods to manage the session bean.

setSessionContext

A `SessionContext` object contains information about the environment the session bean is running in. It contains a reference to the bean's `Home` interface, a reference to the bean itself, transaction information, and the identity of the caller who invoked a specific method.

The `setSessionContext` method is called once for each session bean and is part of the initialization of the bean. The bean is an active part of the EJB container after `setSessionContext` and remains active until the `ejbRemove` method is called.

Tip

The `setSessionContext` method is a great place to put initialization code. You might, for instance, want to create a database connection or locate another bean's `Home` interface in `setSessionContext`.

Of the methods in the `SessionContext` interface, `getEJBObject` is the one that you'll probably call the most. Sometimes, an EJB must pass itself to another method call. For example, suppose you have a `ShoppingCart` session bean that contains items that a user wants to order. Furthermore, suppose that you have an `OrderPlacement` session bean that takes the contents of a shopping cart and enters it into your ordering system. You often find situations like this when a company has an existing ordering system, possibly even on a mainframe. If you ever plan to migrate the ordering system to another platform, maybe from the mainframe to an EJB server, you want to design the `ShoppingCart` bean so it doesn't care how the order is entered—its only task is to manage the items you want to buy. The `OrderPlacement` bean takes care of placing the order. When you change over to a new ordering system, just change the `OrderPlacement` bean and leave the shopping cart alone.

Now, when the `ShoppingCart` bean needs to call the `OrderPlacement` bean, you would think it could just pass itself using the `this` keyword. In other words, it might do something like this:

```
orderPlacementBean.submitOrder(this);
```

The problem here is that the `submitOrder` method is probably declared something like this:

```
public void submitOrder(ShoppingCart cart) throws RemoteException;
```

This is a problem because `ShoppingCart` is a `Remote` interface for a session bean (for this example, at least). The `this` variable would refer to a `ShoppingCartImpl` object, however, which doesn't implement the `ShoppingCart` interface. When you first start working with EJBs, these distinctions can be a little confusing. An EJB really has two parts: the `Remote` interface and the implementation. The implementation is *not* a remote object. That is, it does not implement the `Remote` interface. In fact, in many EJB implementations, the `Remote` interface invokes a method in the container, and the container invokes a method in the implementation, just as it does for the standard methods, such as `ejbCreate` and `ejbRemove`.

The correct way to call the `submitOrder` would be

```
orderPlacementBean.submitOrder((ShoppingCart)
    sessionContext.getEJBObject());
```

This code assumes, of course, that your `setSessionContext` method does this:

```
public void setSessionContext(SessionContext aContext)
{
    sessionContext = aContext;
}
```

Even if you don't need the session context in your bean, it's still a good idea to keep track of it. It only takes a few lines of code and you can always count on it being there.

Tip

If you decide to make it a standard practice to keep the session context, make sure you also standardize the access to the context. In other words, either pick a standard variable name for the context that every developer can count on, or create a standard method name, such as `getSessionContext`.

`ejbRemove`

The EJB container calls a session bean's `ejbRemove` method to tell the bean it is going out of service. The bean should clean up any resources it is holding on to.

Tip

If your bean establishes a database connection in the `setSessionContext` method, close down the connection in the `ejbRemove` method. If you create any session beans, `remove` them in the `ejbRemove` method, and if you locate any `Home` interfaces, set them to `null`.

`ejbPassivate` AND `ejbActivate`

One of the interesting aspects of the Enterprise JavaBeans specification is that it provides various ways for EJB containers to do load balancing and various other kinds of performance-related operations. Passivation/activation is one such operation, and it is similar to the way your computer manages memory.

Most modern operating systems use a concept called *virtual memory*, where instead of keeping everything in RAM memory, the operating system writes some information out to disk.

Over time, the least-recently used memory areas are written to disk (this technique is called "swapping"). You might notice sometimes that if you start up an application and then minimize or iconify it (depending on what windowing environment you are using) and run a lot of things, it takes a while to display the application when you finally try to access it again. This happens because application's memory areas were written out to disk to free up space for the other stuff you were running. The delay is caused by the computer reading the information back off the disk.

The `ejbPassivate` and `ejbActivate` methods allow an EJB container to perform swapping. If, at some point, the EJB container realizes that it has a lot of beans in memory that haven't been accessed in a while, it might choose to store some of those beans to disk. The idea is that the EJB container uses object serialization to store infrequently used beans to a file somewhere. This process, in EJB, is called *passivation*. When a client tries to access a passivated bean, the EJB container activates the bean again by reading it back from the disk.

The `ejbPassivate` and `ejbActivate` methods help the EJB container solve a messy problem—you can't serialize certain "live" operating system resources such as network connections. Because most database connections involve a network connection, this means you can't serialize database connections, either.

If you establish a database connection in your `setSessionContext` method, you must do something with that connection when the EJB container needs to passivate the session bean. Specifically, you should close the connection and set the connection variable to `null`. When the EJB container calls your `ejbActivate` method, re-establish the connection.

Tip

Don't be fooled into thinking that `ejbActivate` is called when the session bean is first created. The `ejbActivate` method is only called sometime after the `ejbPassivate` method has been called.

SESSION BEAN REQUIREMENTS, RESTRICTIONS, AND PERMISSIONS

The EJB specification places some specific restrictions and requirements on session beans. Some of these requirements indicate things that a bean must do, others indicate things a bean must not do, and others specify methods and interfaces that a bean must implement. There are also things that the specification specifically allows, just in case you might get the impression that they were forbidden by other restrictions.

IMPLEMENT THE `SessionBean` INTERFACE

You probably wouldn't think of creating a session bean that doesn't implement `javax.ejb.SessionBean`, but just in case the thought crosses your mind, forget it!

DECLARE THE CLASS AS PUBLIC, AND NOT FINAL OR ABSTRACT

Remember that the EJB container needs to create instances of the bean, so the class must be public and concrete (non-abstract).

CREATE A PUBLIC, PARAMETERLESS CONSTRUCTOR

Again, the EJB container must create instances of the bean. If the constructor is protected or private, the container can't create the instance.

DON'T IMPLEMENT A `finalize` METHOD

Although you rarely need to define a `finalize` method in the first place, the EJB specification explicitly forbids `finalize` in both session and entity beans. If your bean needs to do any cleanup, it should do it in the `ejbRemove` method or in `ejbPassivate`.

IMPLEMENT THE `create` METHOD AND ANY `remote` METHODS

A session bean must implement any `create` methods specified in the `Home` interface, and all methods specified in the `Remote` interface. In implementing these methods, there are several additional requirements:

- The methods must be public and cannot be static or final.
- The parameters and return types must be valid RMI/IIOP return types. In general, this means that they must either be native types (`int`, `char`, `double`, and so on), serializable objects, or `Remote` interfaces.
- The method name can't start with `ejb` (this might confuse an EJB deploy tool and possibly create conflicts).

OPTIONALLY IMPLEMENT THE `Remote` INTERFACE

It might sound strange to say that a bean can implement the `Remote` interface, but is not required to. The distinction is subtle but extremely important. The methods in the implementation class must have the same method signatures as those in the `Remote` interface, except that the methods in the implementation class are not required to throw `RemoteException`. In other words, although every method in the `Remote` interface must have a corresponding method in the implementation class, the implementation isn't required to implement the `Remote` interface with a declaration like this:

```
public class ShoppingCartImpl implements SessionBean, ShoppingCart
```

The reason you might be tempted to implement the `Remote` interface is that the compiler will then tell you when you miss a method. In other words, if your implementation class doesn't implement a method in the `Remote` interface, the compiler generates an error. Otherwise, you won't know about the missing method until you run a deployment tool or a packaging tool. The longer it takes you to learn about an error, the longer it takes to fix it because you must repeat more steps.

The problem with implementing the `Remote` interface is that you might accidentally try to pass the object using the `this` keyword when you should really be using the `getEJBObject` method in the session context. Normally, when you accidentally use `this` instead of `getEJBObject`, the compiler generates an error because it is expecting an object that implements the `Remote` interface, and the implementation class doesn't. By implementing the

Remote interface, you get around the compiler error, but you end up with a runtime error because the implementation is not really a proper reference to a Remote interface as the EJB container expects.

Tip

Although implementing the Remote interface can point out errors at compile time, it can also cause errors that might not be discovered until runtime, which can be much costlier to fix. You are better off not implementing the Remote interface and discovering some errors at deployment time.

OPTIONALLY IMPLEMENT THE SessionSynchronization INTERFACE

The SessionSynchronization interface gives a session bean better control over how a transaction takes place. You will learn more about this interface and how to use it in Chapter 8, "Using Container-Managed Persistence."

SUBCLASS ANOTHER CLASS WHEN NECESSARY

Just in case you were worried about it, your implementation class might be a subclass of another class. In fact, that superclass could even be the implementation class for another kind of bean.

IMPLEMENT HELPER METHODS AS NECESSARY

An implementation class might have additional helper methods that are not part of the Remote or Home interfaces. There are no restrictions on the kinds of parameters, the return type, or the visibility (public, protected, private) of the method.

DON'T THROW RemoteException

If you need to throw an EJB-related exception, throw javax.ejb.EJBException instead.

Remote AND Home INTERFACE RESTRICTIONS

In addition to the restrictions on the implementation class, there are some restrictions on the Remote and Home interfaces. Most of these restrictions are similar to ones you have already seen for the implementation class.

REMOTE INTERFACES MUST EXTEND javax.ejb.EJBObject

When you use some deployment tools, such as the one provided by WebLogic, you'll notice that it automatically knows which class contains the Remote interface. It looks for the EJBObject interface to detect a Remote interface. Furthermore, the EJBObject interface contains some additional methods that every EJB must implement.

HOME INTERFACES MUST EXTEND javax.ejb.EJBHome

As with the Remote interfaces an EJBObject, the EJBHome interface helps identify Home interfaces and defines some methods that you can invoke on every Home interface.

PARAMETERS AND RETURN TYPES MUST BE VALID FOR RMI/IIOP

Again, this generally means the types must either be native types, serializable objects, or `Remote` interfaces.

ALL METHODS MUST THROW `java.rmi.RemoteException`

Because the `Home` and `Remote` interfaces extend the `java.rmi.Remote` interfaces, all the methods in the interfaces must throw `java.rmi.RemoteException`. The RMI specification explicitly requires all methods in a remote interface to throw `RemoteException`.

ALL METHODS MUST HAVE CORRESPONDING IMPLEMENTATIONS

Normally, in a typical RMI implementation, this would go without saying because the implementation class would implement the `Remote` interface. In the case of EJB, however, because the implementation class isn't required to implement the `Home` and `Remote` interfaces, the compiler can't enforce the relationship between the implementation class and the `Home` and `Remote` interfaces.

Each `create` method in the `Home` interface must have a corresponding `ejbCreate` method in the implementation class. Also, the `create` method must throw `CreateException`.

INTERFACES CAN EXTEND OTHER INTERFACES

To support subclassing of Enterprise JavaBeans, the `Home` and `Remote` interfaces can extend other interfaces, as long as the parent interfaces are descendants of `EJBObject` (for `Remote` interfaces) or `EJBHome` (for `Home` interfaces).

CREATING A SESSION BEAN THAT DOES SOME WORK

The main purpose of the `HelloWorldSession` example was to get you familiar with the overall structure of a session bean. Writing three different Java files for a single component seems overwhelming at first, but after you're used to it, it doesn't seem like such a big deal.

Now that you're familiar with the structure of a session bean, you can write a bean that does some work. Specifically, you can write a bean that retrieves data from a database. For this example, assume that you have an SQL table containing product codes and prices, created using the following SQL statement:

```
create table price
    (product_code varchar(10) not null primary key,
     price decimal(10,2) not null)
```

The `Pricing` session bean gives you a list of all valid product codes and can return the price for a specific code, as specified by the `Remote` interface shown in Listing 6.9.

LISTING 6.9 SOURCE CODE FOR Pricing.java

```
package usingj2ee.pricing;

import java.rmi.*;
import javax.ejb.*;

/** Defines the methods you can call on a Pricing session */

public interface Pricing extends EJBObject
{

/** Returns all the available product codes */
    public String[] getProductCodes() throws RemoteException;

/** Returns the price for a specific product code */
    public double getPrice(String productCode)
        throws RemoteException, InvalidProductCodeException;

}
```

The `Pricing` session bean doesn't need to remember anything about a particular client, so it can be implemented as a stateless session bean. Thus, the `PricingHome` interface, shown in Listing 6.10, only needs a single `create` method.

LISTING 6.10 SOURCE CODE FOR PricingHome.java

```
package usingj2ee.pricing;

import java.rmi.*;
import javax.ejb.*;

/** Defines the methods for creating a Pricing session */

public interface PricingHome extends EJBHome
{

/** Creates a Pricing session bean */
    public Pricing create() throws RemoteException, CreateException;

}
```

When a session bean needs to access a database connection, it usually allocates the connection in the `setSessionContext` method and releases the connection in the `ejbRemove` method. Of course, if you are holding onto a database connection, you must also be prepared to close it if the container calls `ejbPassivate` and make the connection again when the container calls `ejbActivate`.

You'll find that most EJB developers create a method to return a connection; that way you can change the way you get connections without affecting the various places where you need to create one. You should also use a `DataSource` object to create your connections. A `DataSource` makes it easy to change database drivers and to use a connection pool when necessary.

Listing 6.11 shows the `PricingImpl` implementation class for the `Pricing` session bean.

LISTING 6.11 SOURCE CODE FOR `PricingImpl.java`

```
package usingj2ee.pricing;

import java.rmi.*;
import java.util.*;
import javax.ejb.*;
import java.sql.*;
import javax.sql.*;
import javax.naming.*;

/** The implementation class for the Pricing bean */

public class PricingImpl implements SessionBean
{
/** The session context provided by the EJB container. A session bean must
    hold on to the context it is given. */

    private SessionContext context;

/** The database connection used by this session */

    private Connection conn;

/** An EJB must have a public, parameterless constructor */

    public PricingImpl()
    {
    }

/** Called by the EJB container to set this session's context */

    public void setSessionContext(SessionContext aContext)
    {
        context = aContext;
    }

/** Called by the EJB container when a client calls the create() method in
    the Home interface */

    public void ejbCreate()
        throws CreateException
    {
        try
        {
// Allocate a database connection
            conn = getConnection();
        }
        catch (Exception exc)
        {
            throw new CreateException(
                "Unable to access database: "+exc.toString());
        }
    }
```

LISTING 6.11 CONTINUED

```
/** Called by the EJB container to tell this session bean that it is being
    suspended from use (it's being put to sleep). */

    public void ejbPassivate()
        throws EJBException
    {
        try
        {
// Shut down the current database connection
            conn.close();
            conn = null;
        }
        catch (Exception exc)
        {
            throw new EJBException("Unable to close database connection: "+
                exc.toString());
        }
    }

/** Called by the EJB container to wake this session bean up after it
    has been put to sleep with the ejbPassivate method. */

    public void ejbActivate()
        throws EJBException
    {
        try
        {
// When the bean wakes back up, get a database connection again
            conn = getConnection();
        }
        catch (Exception exc)
        {
            throw new EJBException(
                "Unable to access database: "+exc.toString());
        }
    }

/** Called by the EJB container to tell this session bean that it has been
    removed, either because the client invoked the remove() method or the
    container has timed the session out. */

    public void ejbRemove()
        throws EJBException
    {
        try
        {
// Shut down the current database connection
            conn.close();
            conn = null;
        }
        catch (Exception exc)
        {
            throw new EJBException("Unable to close database connection: "+
                exc.toString());
        }
```

```
    }

/** Returns a list of the available product codes */

    public String[] getProductCodes()
        throws EJBException
    {
        Statement s = null;

        try
        {
            s = conn.createStatement();

            ResultSet results = s.executeQuery(
                "select product_code from price");

            Vector v = new Vector();

// Copy the results into a temporary vector
            while (results.next())
            {
                v.addElement(results.getString("product_code"));
            }

// Copy the vector into a string array
            String[] productCodes = new String[v.size()];
            v.copyInto(productCodes);

            return productCodes;
        }
        catch (Exception exc)
        {
            throw new EJBException("Unable to get product codes: "+
                exc.toString());
        }
        finally
        {
// Close down the statement in a finally block to guarantee that it gets
// closed, whether an exception occurred or not
            try
            {
                s.close();
            }
            catch (Exception ignore)
            {
            }
        }
    }

/** Gets the price for a particular product code */

    public double getPrice(String productCode)
        throws EJBException, InvalidProductCodeException
    {
        PreparedStatement ps = null;

        try
```

LISTING 6.11 CONTINUED

```
        {
// It's always better to use a prepared statement than to try to insert
// a string directly into the query string. This way you don't have to
// worry if there's a quote in the product code

            ps = conn.prepareStatement(
                "select price from price where product_code = ?");

// Store the product code in the prepared statement
            ps.setString(1, productCode);

            ResultSet results = ps.executeQuery();

// If there are any results, get the first one (there should only be one)
            if (results.next())
            {
                return results.getDouble("price");
            }
            else
            {
// Otherwise, if there were no results, this product code doesn't exist
                throw new InvalidProductCodeException(productCode);
            }
        }
        catch (SQLException exc)
        {
            throw new EJBException("Unable to get price: "+
                exc.toString());
        }
        finally
        {
// Close down the statement in a finally block to guarantee that it gets
// closed, whether an exception occurred or not
            try
            {
                ps.close();
            }
            catch (Exception ignore)
            {
            }
        }
    }

    protected Connection getConnection()
        throws SQLException, NamingException
    {
// Get a reference to the naming service
        InitialContext context = new InitialContext();

// Get the data source for the pricing database
        DataSource ds = (DataSource) context.lookup(
            "java:comp/env/jdbc/PriceDB");
```

```
// Ask the data source to allocate a database connection
        return ds.getConnection();
    }
}
```

The getConnection method in PricingImpl deserves some special attention. Notice that it uses JNDI (the naming service) to locate a data source named java:comp/env/jdbc/PriceDB. The prefix java:comp/env refers to the JNDI naming context for your session bean. When the session bean is deployed in an EJB container, the container sets up a naming context for the bean with various entries that are set up when you deploy the bean. The java:comp/env naming context lets you associate logical names with various resources. The idea is that when you write the bean, you don't need to know the exact name of a data source or Home interface to use it. When you deploy the bean into a container, you set up associations that link the names used by the bean to the actual resource name. This substantially improves the portability of the bean because it isn't tied to specific resource names.

When you deploy the Pricing bean, you must specify an alias name for jdbc/PriceDB. If you're using the Cloudscape database that comes with the J2EE SDK, this alias must be jdbc/Cloudscape. Otherwise, you must set up a data source in the EJB server that points to the database you want to work with. When you deploy the Pricing bean, you specify the name of the data source that jdbc/PriceDB refers to. Again, jdbc/PriceDB is a logical name. You can use the Pricing bean with many different databases just by changing the naming association when you deploy the bean.

If you are using a different data source, you can change it at deployment time. You can also set up a default.properties file containing information about various drivers and databases you want to use. For example, you can use the following default.properties file for an Oracle database:

```
jdbc.drivers=oracle.jdbc.driver.OracleDriver
jdbc.datasources=jdbc/Oracle|jdbc:oracle:thin:@localhost:1521:orcl
```

After you set up this alternate data source, which is called jdbc/Oracle, you can change the association for jdbc/PriceDB to make it use the Oracle data source. Once again, you don't change the Pricing bean, just its deployment properties.

Assuming you're running the J2EE SDK deploy tool, you set up the jdbc/PriceDB naming entry in the Resource References section of the deploy tool, as shown here in Figure 6.8.

The only other difference between the deployment of the Pricing bean and the HelloWorldSession bean is that you must specify the alias for the jdbc/PriceDB in the JNDI Names tab panel, as shown in Figure 6.9.

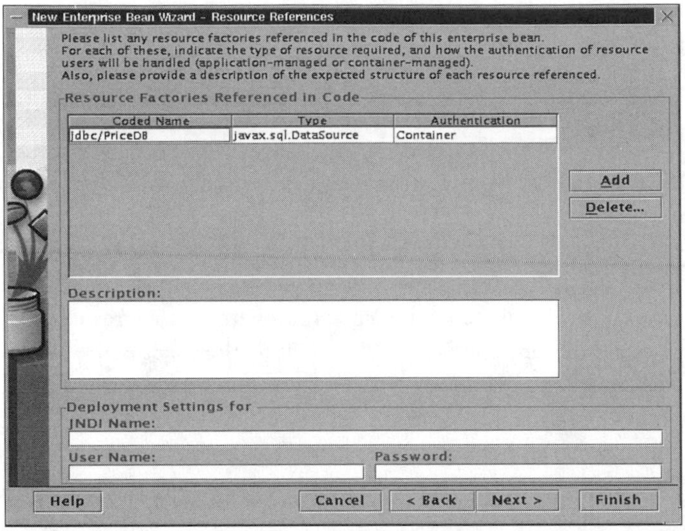

Figure 6.8
The Resource References dialog box lets you configure a session bean's naming context.

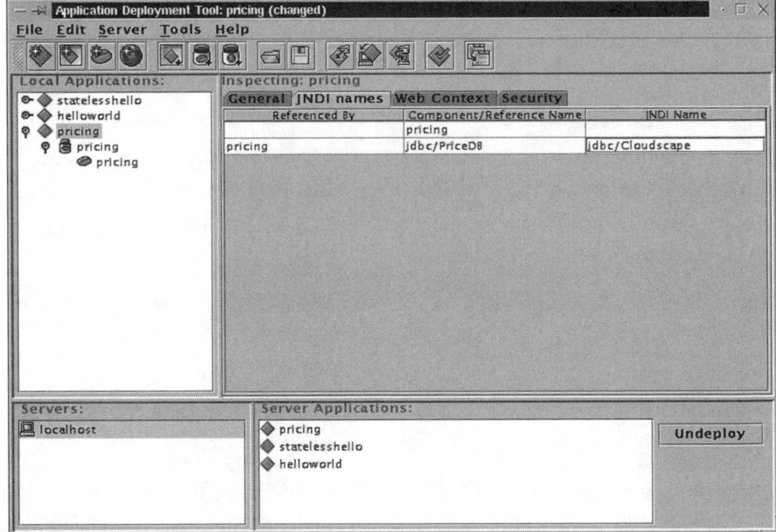

Figure 6.9
The JNDI names panel lets you set up JNDI aliases for various names your bean uses.

Writing a client to test the `Pricing` bean is simple and the program looks similar to the other client programs you have seen. Listing 6.12 shows the pricing test client.

LISTING 6.12 SOURCE CODE FOR `TestPricing.java`

```
package usingj2ee.pricing;

import java.util.*;
import javax.naming.*;
```

```
import javax.rmi.*;

public class TestPricing
{
    public static void main(String[] args)
    {
        try
        {

/** Creates a JNDI naming context for location objects */
            Context context = new InitialContext();

/** Asks the context to locate an object named "Pricing" and expects the
    object to implement the PricingHome interface */

            PricingHome home = (PricingHome)
                PortableRemoteObject.narrow(
                    context.lookup("Pricing"),
                    PricingHome.class);
/** Asks the Home interface to create a new session bean */
            Pricing session = (Pricing) home.create();

/** Get a list of valid product codes */
            String[] codes = session.getProductCodes();

            for (int i=0; i < codes.length; i++)
            {
                System.out.println(codes[i]+":  "+
                    session.getPrice(codes[i]));
            }

            try
            {
                session.getPrice("f00b4r");
            }
            catch (InvalidProductCodeException exc)
            {
                System.out.println("Got invalid product code exception: "+
                    exc.toString());
            }

/** Destroy this session */
            session.remove();

        }
        catch (Exception exc)
        {
            exc.printStackTrace();
        }
    }
}
```

Finally, Figure 6.10 shows the output from the pricing test client. Notice that nowhere in the source code or the output does the client have any idea that the bean is getting its data from a database.

Note

The `makeprices.sql` script included on the CD-ROM contains insert commands to populate the pricing database.

```
INSERT INTO price (product_code, price) VALUES ('A1', 1.59);
```

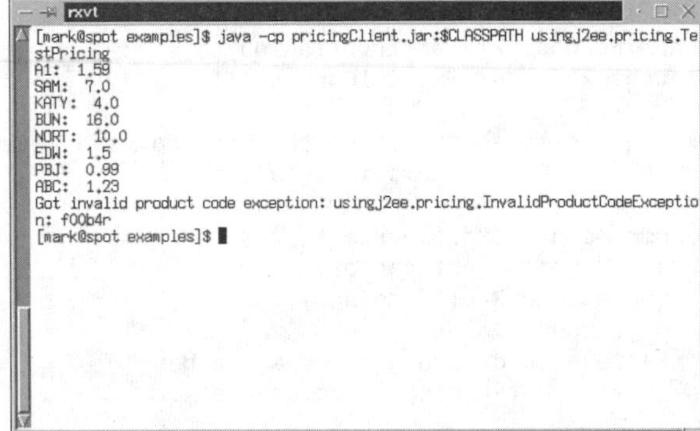

rxvt
[mark@spot examples]$ java -cp pricingClient.jar:$CLASSPATH usingj2ee.pricing.TestPricing
A1: 1.59
SAM: 7.0
KATY: 4.0
BUN: 16.0
NORT: 10.0
EDW: 1.5
PBJ: 0.99
ABC: 1.23
Got invalid product code exception: usingj2ee.pricing.InvalidProductCodeException: f00b4r
[mark@spot examples]$

Figure 6.10
The client doesn't know that the session bean gets its data from a database.

Now that you've started with session beans, Chapter 7, "Creating an Entity Bean," introduces you to the other important EJB: the entity bean. Chapter 8 then shows you how transactions fit in to the EJB world.

TROUBLESHOOTING

DEPLOYMENT PROBLEMS

Why won't the deployment tool generate my EAR or JAR file?

You probably forgot to implement a method in your implementation class. It's also possible that you might have violated one of the other EJB restrictions or requirements. Most deployment tools have an option to test your items for compliance. For instance, in the J2EE SDK, the option is called Verifier; in the WebLogic deployment tool, it's called Check Compliance. Also, check for windows that might contain error messages. Some tools don't always pop up a nice window telling you what's wrong. You can also check the various log files that are in the `logs` subdirectory of the J2EE SDK.

Why doesn't the tool generate a client JAR file?

You probably don't need anything special other than your `Remote` and `Home` interface classes, so there's no need for the tool to create the JAR for you. Most of the time, the client JAR file is necessary because the deployment tool generates a number of utility classes needed for client development.

RUNTIME PROBLEMS

Why can't my client program locate the JNDI naming service?

First, make sure your EJB server is running. Next, you might need to define the initial naming context factory class on the command line. Check the documentation for your EJB server to see if you need additional command-line options. Also, make sure your bean is deployed. If you deployed the bean with a deployment tool and you have restarted the server since then, the server might have forgotten about the bean. Try deploying it again. Also, check to make sure the name your client program is asking for is actually the JNDI name you configured for the bean. The names must match exactly, including any capitalization.

Why do I get an error accessing the data source?

You probably didn't set up the data source correctly for your EJB server. Also, you might not have set up the association properly to go from the logical name your EJB uses to the actual data source name in the JNDI directory.

CHAPTER 7

Creating an Entity Bean

In this chapter

WHAT IS AN ENTITY BEAN?

On the surface, an entity bean is similar to a session bean. They both have `Home` and `Remote` interfaces and an implementation class. They are both subject to many of the same restrictions. The big difference between entity beans and session beans is in the area of persistence and the implications stemming from it.

An *entity bean* represents persistent data—that is, data stored in some kind of database. Various client classes, which can be session beans, entity beans, or application programs, manipulate entity beans and save them back to the database. These operations always take place within the scope of a transaction.

Because an entity bean represents a piece of data that is accessible to multiple users, the entity beans themselves are available to multiple users at the same time. In other words, unlike the session bean, in which each client has its own session bean, an entity bean is shared between different clients. The EJB container manages any potential conflicts caused by two clients updating the same bean.

Each entity bean must have a primary key value that is unique among all entity beans of the same type. Two beans of different types might have the same primary key, of course. A `Person` entity bean might have a primary key of "Della Street" and a `Street` entity might also have a primary key of "Della Street" without any conflicts, but you can't have two `Person` entity beans with a primary key of "Della Street".

The entity bean's `Home` interface takes on an extra role not found in the session bean home. When you obtain access to a session bean, it's always a new session bean—that is, you can only create session beans. An entity bean, on the other hand, might already exist. For example, when you access a shopping site, you create a new shopping cart, but the catalog of items you're allowed to order already exists. In addition to the `create` methods that allow you to create new entity beans, an entity bean's `Home` interface defines various finder methods that allow you to locate existing entity beans. These finders might return a single bean or a collection of beans. For instance, a `PersonHome` interface might have a method called `findByLastName` that would return a collection of `Person` entity beans all matching a specific last name.

Note

Remember that clients can't access EJBs directly, but instead must use a remote reference to the EJB. When you return a collection of entity beans, you're really returning a collection of remote references to those beans.

The `Home` interface also includes a `remove` method that allows you to delete an entity bean (which removes the bean from use by its clients). Although the `Home` interface for session beans also contains a `remove` method (because the method is defined in the common `EJBHome` interface), you can't call the `remove` method on the `Home` interface of a session bean—if you do, you'll get a `RemoveException`.

Note

You don't need to define the `remove` methods in your `Home` interface because they are inherited from the `EJBHome` interface. Technically, a session bean `Home` interface also has `remove` methods, but you usually just remove the session bean by invoking `remove` on the `Remote` interface. Because entity beans can be shared by multiple clients, it makes sense to have a `remove` shortcut for entity beans. With session beans, you almost always have a reference to the `Remote` interface to begin with.

Lastly, a `Home` interface can contain methods that perform functions that are related to the entity beans, but not a specific entity bean. These are methods that you might otherwise consider placing in a stateless session bean. For example, you might create a `computeAverageAge` method to compute the average age of all the `Person` objects stored in the database. These special methods are referred to as *Home methods*.

HOW AN ENTITY BEAN INTERACTS WITH THE DATABASE

In a traditional database application, you might use stored procedures to perform various database operations, or you might have specific database statements to make a change. You might, for example, use an `update` statement to change all rows matching a specific set of criteria.

In an EJB application, however, the database is just a place where you store entity bean data. The beans themselves aren't stored in the database; that is, the class definition for the bean isn't stored in the database, just the persistent state data for the bean. Also, keep in mind that you don't need to store entity beans in a traditional relational database; you can use object database and other kinds of persistent storage, as long as your EJB container supports your storage mechanism.

Working with entity beans is not quite like working with rows in a database. In a database, you can perform updates and delete rows based on a `where` clause. In other words, you can operate over a large number of items at one time. With an entity bean, however, you must update each entity bean manually. If you want to delete all beans matching a particular `where` clause, you can create a `find` method to locate the matching beans, but you must then manually invoke the `remove` method in each bean. Likewise, if you want to perform a mass update, you must locate the beans with a finder method and make the update to each bean. When you work with entity beans, you are working with objects—not database rows. It doesn't matter that the bean's data may be stored in a database.

The first time an entity bean is accessed during a transaction, the container loads the bean's data from the database by calling the bean's `ejbLoad` method. When the transaction completes, the container calls the bean's `ejbStore` method. In between the `ejbLoad` and `ejbStore` calls, you can change the entity bean as much as you like. The thing to keep in mind is that the EJB container decides when to load and when to store the bean.

In Chapter 9, "EJB Transactions," you'll learn more about how to define transaction boundaries so you can have better control over when you load and store a bean. For the moment, however, don't worry about when the container loads and stores beans. It's better to learn *how* to load and store the beans before you worry about *when* to load and store.

There are two styles of entity bean persistence—bean-managed persistence (BMP) and container-managed persistence (CMP). You'll see the terms BMP and CMP frequently, because persistence is such an important aspect of entity bean operations. Different types of entity beans can have different styles of persistence, but all instances of the same type of entity bean all have the same kind of persistence. All `Person` entity beans might use BMP whereas all `Address` entity beans might use CMP.

BEAN-MANAGED PERSISTENCE

Bean-managed persistence means that the bean's implementation class performs all the SQL operations required to load the bean's data from the database, store the data for a new bean, and update the data for an existing bean.

BMP gives the bean the ultimate control over its database access, but with this control comes a lot of extra responsibility. The bean must keep track of any database connections it uses and must make sure it allocates connections efficiently.

The bean must also figure out when to access associated data items and how to save and update the associated items. For instance, an `Order` entity bean might have a number of associated items that are stored in different database tables. When you delete the order, you must remember to delete the items as well.

CONTAINER-MANAGED PERSISTENCE

Container-managed persistence means that the EJB container knows how to load and store the bean, including any associated data items. The beauty of CMP is that you can focus on implementing business logic without spending a lot of time writing database access code.

When you deploy a bean that uses CMP, you tell the container where to store the bean (the name of the table where the bean is stored and the column names where each field is stored). You also describe the queries used for each finder method.

The quality of CMP is directly dependent on the persistence manager implementation. That is, the EJB container has a persistence manager that performs CMP, and how well the CMP works depends on how well the persistence manager works. The EJB specification doesn't say how a persistence manager should work, or even how you actually map a bean's fields to a database. That is left up to each persistence manager to decide. Chapter 8, "Using Container-Managed Persistence," tells you how to create an entity bean with CMP, deploy the bean, and create the database mapping for the bean.

CREATING AN ENTITY BEAN WITH BEAN-MANAGED PERSISTENCE

An entity bean looks just like a session bean in that you still create `Home` and `Remote` interfaces as well as an implementation class. One of the differences is that the `Home` interface can have finder methods, `remove` methods, and other utility methods. The other difference is that the implementation class must have several methods that a session bean doesn't need.

As with the session bean, it's best to start by creating the `Home` and `Remote` interfaces, because if you can't define these, you don't know yet what the bean is supposed to do. Suppose you want to create a simple address book application. You can store the name, address, and phone number of each person by creating a `Person` entity bean. You should also be able to search for people with a specific name, or for names beginning with a certain prefix (such as all names beginning with "t").

Assume that the `Person` beans are stored in a `person` database table that is defined using SQL statement shown in Listing 7.1.

LISTING 7.1 SOURCE CODE FOR `create_person.sql`

```
create table person
    (person_id decimal(10) not null primary key,
     first_name varchar(30),
     middle_name varchar(30),
     last_name varchar(30),
     address1 varchar(50),
     address2 varchar(50),
     city varchar(30),
     state varchar(2),
     zip varchar(10),
     home_phone varchar(20),
     work_phone varchar(20),
     mobile_phone varchar(20))
```

The primary key for the `person` table is a simple integer sequence number. Unfortunately, some databases don't support sequence numbers or auto-increment keys. For this example, the `Person` bean implements the sequence number manually using a `person_id_seq` table defined like this:

```
create table person_id_seq
    (next_person_id decimal(10) not null primary key)
```

Note

You can use the `create_person.sql`, `create_person_id_seq.sql`, and `insert_people.sql` scripts included on the CD-ROM to create your tables and insert data.

CREATING THE Remote INTERFACE

For a minimal entity bean, one that does nothing more than represent data, the `Remote` interface just contains `get` and `set` methods for the various data members. In more complex beans, you might have different operations you can perform on the bean.

Listing 7.2 shows the `Remote` interface for the `Person` entity bean.

LISTING 7.2 SOURCE CODE FOR Person.java

```
package usingj2ee.addressbook;

import java.rmi.*;
import javax.ejb.*;

/** Defines the methods you can call on a Person object */

public interface Person extends EJBObject
{
    public String getFirstName() throws RemoteException;
    public void setFirstName(String aFirstName) throws RemoteException;

    public String getMiddleName() throws RemoteException;
    public void setMiddleName(String aMiddleName) throws RemoteException;

    public String getLastName() throws RemoteException;
    public void setLastName(String aLastName) throws RemoteException;

    public String getAddress1() throws RemoteException;
    public void setAddress1(String anAddress1) throws RemoteException;

    public String getAddress2() throws RemoteException;
    public void setAddress2(String anAddress2) throws RemoteException;

    public String getCity() throws RemoteException;
    public void setCity(String aCity) throws RemoteException;

    public String getState() throws RemoteException;
    public void setState(String aState) throws RemoteException;

    public String getZip() throws RemoteException;
    public void setZip(String aZip) throws RemoteException;

    public String getHomePhone() throws RemoteException;
    public void setHomePhone(String aHomePhone) throws RemoteException;

    public String getWorkPhone() throws RemoteException;
    public void setWorkPhone(String aWorkPhone) throws RemoteException;

    public String getMobilePhone() throws RemoteException;
    public void setMobilePhone(String aMobilePhone) throws RemoteException;
}
```

CREATING THE Home INTERFACE

The `Home` interface for the `Person` bean should allow you to create a new bean and search for existing beans by various search criteria. You've already seen the `create` method, which works the same in session beans and entity beans. The `Home` interface also has finder methods, which must start with the word `find` and must throw `FinderException`. Although all the finder methods in `PersonHome` start with `findBy`, you aren't required to have the word "By" in there. You could have a method such as `findAllGeorgians`. Don't forget to include the `findByPrimaryKey` method, which is the only finder method that is required.

Listing 7.3 shows the `Home` interface for the `Person` bean.

LISTING 7.3 SOURCE CODE FOR PersonHome.java

```
package usingj2ee.addressbook;

import java.rmi.*;
import javax.ejb.*;
import java.util.Collection;

public interface PersonHome extends EJBHome
{

/** Creates a Person bean */
    public Person create() throws RemoteException, CreateException;

/** Locates a Person by the primary key */
    public Person findByPrimaryKey(PersonPK primaryKey)
        throws RemoteException, FinderException;

/** Locates all Person beans with a specific last name */
    public Collection findByLastName(String aLastName)
        throws RemoteException, FinderException;

/** Locates all Person beans with a specific first and last name */
    public Collection findByFirstAndLastName(String aFirstName,
        String aLastName)
        throws RemoteException, FinderException;
}
```

CREATING THE ENTITY BEAN IMPLEMENTATION

The implementation part of an entity bean is much more complex than that of a session bean. There are more methods to implement, and you typically have to do more database work.

An entity bean has a complex lifecycle. The EJB container creates an entity bean and places it in a pool of beans. The pool concept is pretty interesting. Think of the pool as a group of faceless beans, and for this example, assume that these are `Person` beans. At some point, the container grabs a bean from the pool and says "Here, you are now Bob Smith." When the client or clients are through with the Bob Smith `Person` bean, the container throws it back in the pool. Next time, the container might grab the bean instance that was Bob Smith a minute ago and say "Okay, now you're Fred Farkle."

Figure 7.1 illustrates the lifecycle of a bean and how it changes from being in a pool to being active and vice-versa.

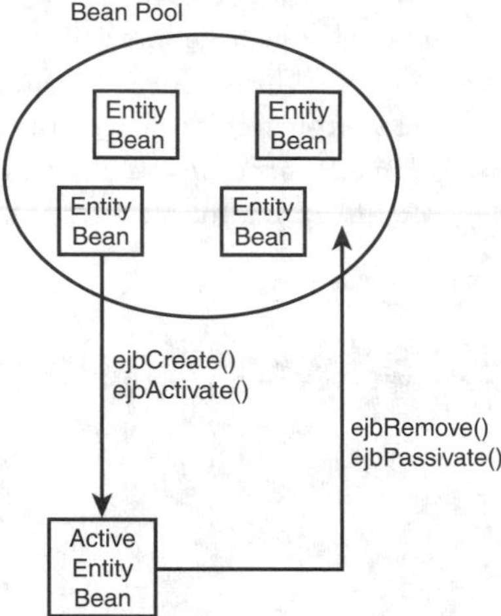

Figure 7.1
An entity bean goes from a pool to an active state and back again.

The container creates a new entity bean instance and gives it a context with `setEntityContext`. After its entity context has been set, the bean goes into the pool.

The container might use any pooled bean to perform a find operation or one of the special methods defined in the `Home` interface (`Home` methods). The only way a bean comes out of the pool and into an active status is by the `ejbActivate` or `ejbCreate` methods.

The EJB container calls the `ejbCreate` method to create a brand new entity bean—that is, to create some data that isn't already in the database. After the `ejbCreate` method has executed, the EJB container calls `ejbPostCreate` to let the entity bean do any additional initialization that it might need to do after the bean has been created. After `ejbPostCreate` executes, the EJB container puts the bean in an active, or ready state.

When the entity bean instance must represent data that already exists, the EJB container uses the `ejbActivate` method to tell the bean that it is now active. The bean must query its context object to find out its primary key. The *primary key* tells an entity bean instance about its current identity. When the EJB container grabs a bean from the pool and says "You are now Bob Smith," it really just calls the bean's `ejbActivate` method. The bean then looks at its context and gets its primary key, which is now magically set to the primary key for Bob Smith.

Note

In an entity bean, the `ejbActivate` method is called to put the bean into active mode. This is different from the session bean, in which `ejbActivate` is only called after `ejbPassivate` has been called. In an entity bean, `ejbActivate` indicates that the bean is now active and `ejbPassivate` indicates that the bean is moving back into the pool.

After the bean is in active mode, the EJB container can call entity bean's `ejbLoad` and `ejbStore` methods to tell the bean to read the database or to write data to the database. The bean is in active mode when a client invokes any of the methods in the bean's `Remote` interface, as well.

Figure 7.2 shows the sequence of method invocations performed on the bean that result in the client loading an existing `Person` bean and reading the person's first name.

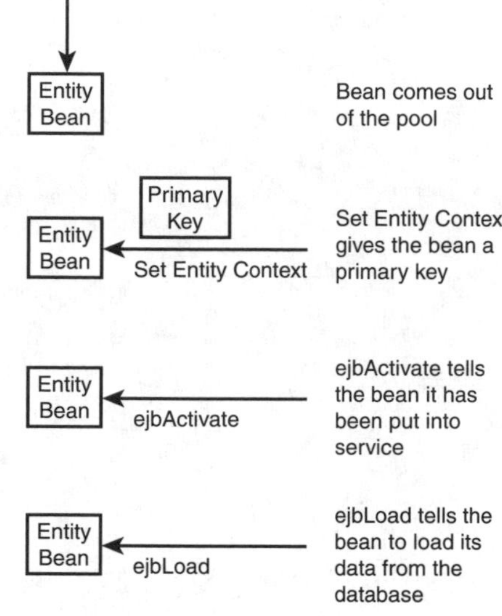

Figure 7.2
The container takes a bean from the pool, sets the bean's context, activates it, and then populates its data.

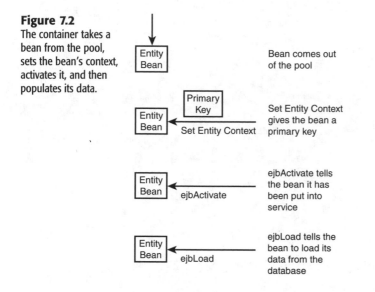

Listing 7.4 shows the implementation class for the `Person` bean.

LISTING 7.4 SOURCE CODE FOR `PersonImpl.java`

```
package usingj2ee.addressbook;

import java.rmi.*;
import java.util.*;
import javax.ejb.*;
import java.sql.*;
import javax.sql.*;
import javax.naming.*;

public class PersonImpl implements EntityBean
{
/** The entity context provided by the EJB container. An entity bean must
    hold on to the context it is given. */

    private EntityContext context;

/** The database connection used by this entity bean */

    private Connection conn;
```

LISTING 7.4 CONTINUED

```
/** The entity bean fields that represent data from the database */
    protected PersonPK primaryKey;
    protected String firstName;
    protected String middleName;
    protected String lastName;
    protected String address1;
    protected String address2;
    protected String city;
    protected String state;
    protected String zip;
    protected String homePhone;
    protected String workPhone;
    protected String mobilePhone;

/** An EJB must have a public, parameterless constructor */

    public PersonImpl()
    {
    }

/** Called by the EJB container to set this entity's context */

    public void setEntityContext(EntityContext aContext)
    {
        context = aContext;
    }

/** Called by the EJB container to clear this entity's context */

    public void unsetEntityContext()
    {
        context = null;
    }

/** Called by the EJB container when a client calls the create() method in
    the home interface */

    public PersonPK ejbCreate()
        throws CreateException
    {
        PreparedStatement ps = null;

        try
        {
// Allocate a database connection
            conn = getConnection();

// Compute the new primary key for this object
            primaryKey = new PersonPK(getNextId());

// Create a new, empty person object in the database
            ps = conn.prepareStatement(
                "insert into person (person_id) values (?)");
            ps.setInt(1, primaryKey.personID);
```

```
            if (ps.executeUpdate() != 1)
            {
                throw new CreateException(
                    "Unable to insert new person with ID "+
                    primaryKey.personID+" into the database");
            }

            return primaryKey;
        }
        catch (SQLException exc)
        {
            throw new CreateException(
                "Unable to access database: "+exc.toString());
        }
        catch (NamingException exc)
        {
            throw new CreateException(
                "Unable to access database: "+exc.toString());
        }
    }

/** Called by the EJB container after ejbCreate to allow the bean to do
    any additional setup that may be required. */
    public void ejbPostCreate()
        throws CreateException
    {
    }

/** Called by the EJB container to put the bean into active mode
    */

    public void ejbActivate()
        throws EJBException
    {
        try
        {
// When the bean becomes active, get a database connection
            conn = getConnection();
        }
        catch (Exception exc)
        {
            throw new EJBException(
                "Unable to access database: "+exc.toString());
        }

// The bean needs to know its primary key, go ask the context what it is
        primaryKey = (PersonPK) context.getPrimaryKey();
    }

/** Called by the EJB container to tell this bean that it is being
    deactivated and placed back into the pool */

    public void ejbPassivate()
        throws EJBException
    {
        try
        {
```

LISTING 7.4 CONTINUED

```
// Shut down the current database connection
            conn.close();
            conn = null;
        }
        catch (Exception exc)
        {
            throw new EJBException("Unable to close database connection: "+
                exc.toString());
        }
        primaryKey = null;
    }

/** Called by the container to tell the entity bean to read its data from
    the database */

    public void ejbLoad()
        throws EJBException
    {
        PreparedStatement ps = null;

        try
        {

// Technical tip: If you add a bunch of constant strings together with
// no variables in-between, the compiler puts them together at compile-time,
// so the following statement does not result in a bunch of string
// concatenations at runtime.

            ps = conn.prepareStatement(
                "select first_name, middle_name, last_name, "+
                "address1, address2, city, state, zip, "+
                "home_phone, work_phone, mobile_phone "+
                "from person where person_id = ?");

            ps.setInt(1, primaryKey.personID);

            ResultSet rs = ps.executeQuery();

            if (!rs.next())
            {
                throw new EJBException(
                    "Unable to locate entity bean!");
            }

            firstName = rs.getString("first_name");
            middleName = rs.getString("middle_name");
            lastName = rs.getString("last_name");
            address1 = rs.getString("address1");
            address2 = rs.getString("address2");
            city = rs.getString("city");
            state = rs.getString("state");
            zip = rs.getString("zip");
            homePhone = rs.getString("home_phone");
            workPhone = rs.getString("work_phone");
            mobilePhone = rs.getString("mobile_phone");
        }
```

```
        catch (SQLException exc)
        {
            throw new EJBException(
                "Unable to load person from database: "+exc.toString());
        }
        finally
        {
// It's best to close statements and connections in a finally block
            try
            {
                ps.close();
            }
            catch (Exception ignore) {}
        }
    }

/** Called by the EJB container to tell the entity bean to
    write its data out to the database */
    public void ejbStore()
        throws EJBException
    {
        PreparedStatement ps = null;

        try
        {

// Technical tip: If you add a bunch of constant strings together with
// no variables in-between, the compiler puts them together at compile-time,
// so the following statement does not result in a bunch of string
// concatenations at runtime.

            ps = conn.prepareStatement(
                "update person set "+
                "first_name=?, middle_name=?, last_name=?, "+
                "address1=?, address2=?, city=?, state=?, zip=?, "+
                "home_phone=?, work_phone=?, mobile_phone=? "+
                "where person_id = ?");

            ps.setString(1, firstName);
            ps.setString(2, middleName);
            ps.setString(3, lastName);
            ps.setString(4, address1);
            ps.setString(5, address2);
            ps.setString(6, city);
            ps.setString(7, state);
            ps.setString(8, zip);
            ps.setString(9, homePhone);
            ps.setString(10, workPhone);
            ps.setString(11, mobilePhone);
            ps.setInt(12, primaryKey.personID);

            if (ps.executeUpdate() != 1)
            {
                throw new EJBException(
                    "Unable to save entity bean!");
            }
        }
        catch (SQLException exc)
```

LISTING 7.4 CONTINUED

```
        {
            throw new EJBException(
                "Unable to load person from database: "+exc.toString());
        }
        finally
        {
// It's best to close statements and connections in a finally block
            try
            {
                ps.close();
            }
            catch (Exception ignore) {}
        }
    }

/** Called by the EJB container to tell this bean that it has been
    removed. */

    public void ejbRemove()
        throws EJBException
    {
        try
        {
            PreparedStatement ps = conn.prepareStatement(
                "delete from person where person_id = ?");
            ps.setInt(1, primaryKey.personID);

            if (ps.executeUpdate() != 1)
            {
                throw new EJBException(
                    "Unable to remove person from the database");
            }

// Shut down the current database connection
            conn.close();
            conn = null;
        }
        catch (SQLException exc)
        {
            throw new EJBException(
                "Unable to remove person from the database: "+
                    exc.toString());
        }
    }

/** Locates a person by the primary key. It looks odd to simply return
    the primary key back again, but this does verify that the bean
    exists in the database. */

    public PersonPK ejbFindByPrimaryKey(PersonPK primaryKey)
        throws FinderException
    {
        Connection conn = null;

        try
```

```
        {
            conn = getConnection();

// Make sure the person_id actually exists
            PreparedStatement ps = conn.prepareStatement(
                "select person_id from person where person_id = ?");
            ps.setInt(1, primaryKey.personID);

            ResultSet rs = ps.executeQuery();

// If the person_id exists, return a new PersonPK for the person_id
            if (rs.next())
            {
                return new PersonPK(rs.getInt("person_id"));
            }
            else
            {
                throw new FinderException("Unable to locate person");
            }
        }
        catch (SQLException exc)
        {
            throw new FinderException("Unable to locate person: "+
                exc.toString());
        }
        catch (NamingException exc)
        {
            throw new FinderException("Unable to locate person: "+
                exc.toString());
        }
        finally
        {
            try
            {
                conn.close();
            }
            catch (Exception ignore) {}
        }
    }

/** Returns collection of persons whose last names start with
    the string in lastName */

    public Collection ejbFindByLastName(String lastName)
        throws FinderException
    {
        Connection conn = null;

        try
        {
            conn = getConnection();

// Use a 'like' instead of '=' to do the comparison, the % on the end
// of the name is a wildcard, so last_name like 'j%' would match
// jones, johnson, jefferson, and so on.
```

LISTING 7.4 CONTINUED

```
            PreparedStatement ps = conn.prepareStatement(
                "select person_id from person where last_name like ?");
            ps.setString(1, lastName+"%");

            ResultSet rs = ps.executeQuery();

            ArrayList retval = new ArrayList();

            while (rs.next())
            {
// The ejbFind implementation must return a collection of
// primary key objects, not actual entity beans
                retval.add(new PersonPK(rs.getInt("person_id")));
            }

            return retval;
        }
        catch (SQLException exc)
        {
            throw new FinderException("Unable to locate person(s): "+
                exc.toString());
        }
        catch (NamingException exc)
        {
            throw new FinderException("Unable to locate person(s): "+
                exc.toString());
        }
        finally
        {
            try
            {
                conn.close();
            }
            catch (Exception ignore) {}
        }
    }

/** Returns collection of persons whose first and last names start with
    the strings in firstName and lastName */
    public Collection ejbFindByFirstAndLastName(String firstName,
        String lastName)
        throws FinderException
    {
        Connection conn = null;

        try
        {
            conn = getConnection();

// Use a 'like' instead of '=' to do the comparison, the % on the end
// of the name is a wildcard, so last_name like 'j%' would match
// jones, johnson, jefferson, and so on.

            PreparedStatement ps = conn.prepareStatement(
                "select person_id from person where first_name like ?"+
                " and last_name like ?");
```

```
            ps.setString(1, firstName+"%");
            ps.setString(2, lastName+"%");

            ResultSet rs = ps.executeQuery();

            ArrayList retval = new ArrayList();

            while (rs.next())
            {
// The ejbFind implementation must return a collection of
// primary key objects, not actual entity beans
                retval.add(new PersonPK(rs.getInt("person_id")));
            }

            return retval;
        }
        catch (SQLException exc)
        {
            throw new FinderException("Unable to locate person(s): "+
                exc.toString());
        }
        catch (NamingException exc)
        {
            throw new FinderException("Unable to locate person(s): "+
                exc.toString());
        }
        finally
        {
            try
            {
                conn.close();
            }
            catch (Exception ignore) {}
        }
    }

    protected Connection getConnection()
        throws SQLException, NamingException
    {
// Get a reference to the naming service
        InitialContext context = new InitialContext();

// Get the data source for the person database
        DataSource ds = (DataSource) context.lookup(
            "java:comp/env/jdbc/PersonDB");

// Ask the data source to allocate a database connection
        return ds.getConnection();
    }

/** Uses a separate database table to generate a unique ID number for
    a person. You should perform the update before you read the value
    to make sure you don't have any locking problems.
    */
    protected int getNextId()
        throws SQLException
    {
        Connection conn = null;
```

LISTING 7.4 CONTINUED

```
        try
        {
            conn = getConnection();

// Increment the next person ID number
            PreparedStatement ps = conn.prepareStatement(
                "update person_id_seq set next_person_id = next_person_id + 1");

            if (ps.executeUpdate() != 1)
            {
                throw new SQLException("Unable to generate person id");
            }

            ps.close();

// Read the next person ID number
            ps = conn.prepareStatement(
                "select next_person_id from person_id_seq");

            ResultSet rs = ps.executeQuery();

            if (rs.next())
            {
                return rs.getInt("next_person_id");
            }
            else
            {
                throw new SQLException("Unable to generate person id");
            }
        }
        catch (NamingException exc)
        {
            throw new SQLException("Unable to generate person id: "+
                exc.toString());
        }
        finally
        {
            try
            {
                conn.close();
            }
            catch (Exception ignore) {}
        }
    }

// Implement the get/set methods for all the data elements

    public String getFirstName() { return firstName; }
    public void setFirstName(String aFirstName) { firstName = aFirstName; }

    public String getMiddleName() { return middleName; }
    public void setMiddleName(String aMiddleName) { middleName = aMiddleName; }

    public String getLastName() { return lastName; }
    public void setLastName(String aLastName) { lastName = aLastName; }
```

```
    public String getAddress1() { return address1; }
    public void setAddress1(String anAddress1) { address1 = anAddress1; }

    public String getAddress2() { return address2; }
    public void setAddress2(String anAddress2) { address2 = anAddress2; }

    public String getCity() { return city; }
    public void setCity(String aCity) { city = aCity; }

    public String getState() { return state; }
    public void setState(String aState) { state = aState; }

    public String getZip() { return zip; }
    public void setZip(String aZip) { zip = aZip; }

    public String getHomePhone() { return homePhone; }
    public void setHomePhone(String aHomePhone) { homePhone = aHomePhone; }

    public String getWorkPhone() { return workPhone; }
    public void setWorkPhone(String aWorkPhone) { workPhone = aWorkPhone; }

    public String getMobilePhone() { return mobilePhone; }
    public void setMobilePhone(String aMobilePhone)
    {
        mobilePhone = aMobilePhone;
    }
}
```

Note

Notice that the `ejbFind` methods return either a primary key or a collection of primary keys, even though the `Home` interface declares that the `find` method returns a `Remote` interface or a collection of `Remote` interfaces. The EJB container handles the translation between the primary key and the remote reference.

The `Person` bean uses a special class to represent its primary key. A primary key object must be serializable and must have working `hashCode` and `equals` methods. Listing 7.5 shows the primary key class for the `Person` bean.

LISTING 7.5 SOURCE CODE FOR PersonPK.java

```
package usingj2ee.addressbook;

public class PersonPK implements java.io.Serializable
{
    protected int personID;

    public PersonPK()
    {
    }

    public PersonPK(int aPersonID)
    {
        personID = aPersonID;
```

LISTING 7.5 CONTINUED

```
    }

    public int hashCode()
    {
        return personID;
    }

    public boolean equals(Object ob)
    {
        if (ob == this) return true;
        if (!(ob instanceof PersonPK)) return false;

        PersonPK other = (PersonPK) ob;
        if (personID != other.personID) return false;

        return true;
    }
}
```

DEPLOYING THE ENTITY BEAN

You've already seen how to deploy a session bean, and deploying the entity bean is exactly the same. Depending on the EJB server you're using, you might need to take an extra step. You must define the transaction characteristics of each remote method. Even though you aren't dealing with transactions yet, this is one case in which you need to do something transaction-oriented. You just need to specify that a transaction is required for each remote method. You shouldn't need to do this if you're using WebLogic, but if you're using the J2EE SDK from Sun, you'll need to specify that each method requires a transaction.

When you deploy the bean, don't forget to specify the primary key class for the bean. You usually specify the primary key class where you specify the classnames for the `Home`, `Remote`, and implementation classes.You must also remember to specify the data source name. Remember, the name that the bean uses to access the data source is not necessarily the same as the actual data source. EJB separates the coded name from the deployment name to increase portability. You can use the same bean with different data sources just by changing the data source at deployment time.

Figure 7.3 shows the panel where you set the transaction requirements for each method.

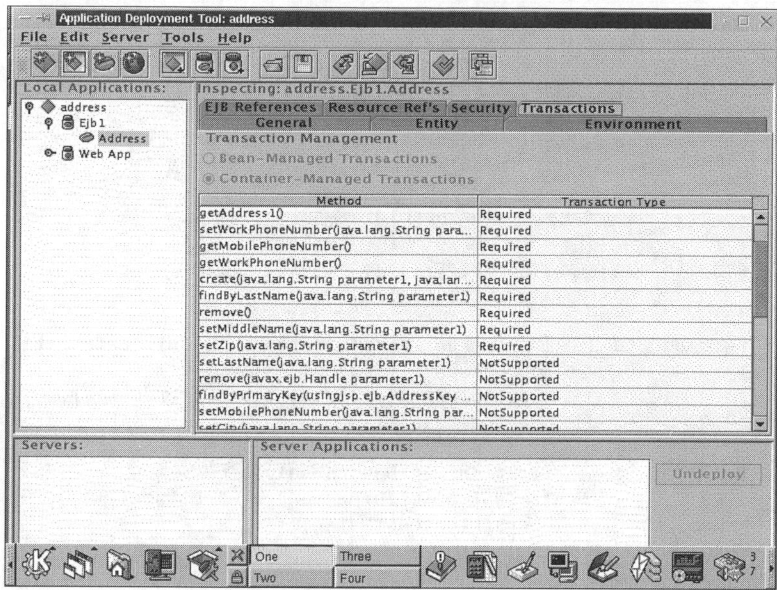

Figure 7.3
You can specify the transactional requirements for each entity bean method.

TESTING THE ENTITY BEAN

Writing a test client for the `Person` entity bean is just as easy as writing a test client for a session bean. You just need to get the initial naming context, locate the `Home` interface, and then either create a new bean or locate one or more existing beans.

Listing 7.6 shows a test client that searches for all `Person` beans with a last name starting with "t" and then prints out the first and last names.

LISTING 7.6 SOURCE CODE FOR `TestGetPeople.java`

```
package usingj2ee.addressbook;

import java.util.*;
import javax.naming.*;
import javax.rmi.PortableRemoteObject;

public class TestGetPeople
{
    public static void main(String[] args)
    {
        try
        {

// Creates a JNDI naming context for location objects
            Context context = new InitialContext();

/* Asks the context to locate an object named "Person" and expects the
    object to implement the PersonHome interface */

            PersonHome home = (PersonHome)
```

LISTING 7.6 CONTINUED

```
                PortableRemoteObject.narrow(context.lookup("Person"),
                    PersonHome.class);

// Looks for all people whose last names begin with t
            Collection people = home.findByLastName("t");

            Iterator iter = people.iterator();

// Loop through all the entity beans in the collection
            while (iter.hasNext())
            {
// Remember to use the narrow method instead of just casting the value
                Person person = (Person)
                    PortableRemoteObject.narrow(iter.next(),
                    Person.class);

// Print out some of the entity bean's values
                System.out.println(person.getFirstName()+" "+
                    person.getLastName());
            }
        }
        catch (Exception exc)
        {
            exc.printStackTrace();
        }
    }
}
```

USING CONNECTION POOLS TO IMPROVE PERFORMANCE

Connecting to the database is usually a time-consuming task, and for the database, maintaining multiple connections often requires a lot of memory. Tuning your system usually requires striking the right balance between keeping database connections open and limiting the total number of connections.

When each entity bean requires its own connection, or at least each active entity bean, you often make a lot of database connections that spend most of their time idle even when there are other classes that might need the connection. Ideally, you want to request a connection when you need one, perform some database operations, and then close the connection. Because database connections take so long to set up, however, your system ends up running slowly because it spends a huge amount of time making connections.

Connection pools solve this problem. A *connection pool* keeps a number of open database connections and when you ask for a connection, it just pulls one out of the pool. If there are no connections available in the pool, the pool might wait for a connection to become free or allocate additional connections. This behavior, of course, is implementation dependent.

The true beauty of connection pools is that they are implemented as data sources, so you allocate a connection from a connection pool exactly the same way you do from a normal data source. The connection pool creates a special connection wrapper class that looks and acts like a normal database connection. The reason for the wrapper is that normally when you're through with a connection, you close it. With a connection pool, however, you don't want to close the physical connection to the database, you just want to return the connection to the pool. This special wrapper class has a special `close` method that still closes any open statements and result sets, but instead of closing the physical database connection, it just returns the connection to the pool.

Configuring a connection pool is an implementation-specific task, so you'll need to consult the EJB server documentation to see whether it includes connection pools and if so, how to configure a connection pool.

Note

> If your EJB server doesn't support connection pools you might be able to use PoolMan, available from `http://poolman.sourceforge.net`.

You can, however, code your entity bean so it works best with a connection pool.

Rather than allocating a database connection when the bean becomes active—that is, allocating the connection in `ejbActivate` or `ejbCreate`, postpone the connection creation until you actually need to use it. Of course, in `ejbCreate` you usually need to use a connection, but you should release it as soon as you're done. In your `ejbLoad` method, allocate a connection, use it, and then release it. Do the same in your `ejbRemove` and `ejbStore` methods.

The other important thing is to make sure you release the connection from a `finally` block. This insures that you release the connection even if the method throws an exception. Otherwise, you run the risk of allocating connections and not returning them to the pool. For example, you might expect that a section of code can only throw a `SQLException`, so you just catch that exception and close the connection both the try block and the catch block. What you might not realize is that a runtime exception such as `NullPointerException` might sneak through and your connection would never be returned to the pool. The `finally` block keeps you from having to worry about catching exceptions just to clean up your connections.

More Details About Entity Beans

Although you have seen what it takes to implement an entity bean, some of the aspects of the entity bean might not seem so obvious. Some of the things you have already seen are important enough to bear repeating. After you understand the major parts of an entity bean, you begin to see how the EJB container uses the bean to load and store database information.

The `EntityBean` Interface

Every entity bean must implement the `EntityBean` interface. This interface controls the lifecycle of the bean—creation, updates, and removal. The EJB container uses these methods to tell the entity bean what is going on, and the entity bean must respond appropriately.

setEntityContext

An EntityContext object contains information about the environment the entity bean is running in, and more specifically, about the database information the current entity bean represents. When an entity bean is activated, it might have a different primary key than it did the last time it was active. After all, the EJB container might keep a pool of objects that can represent different data items at different times. The EntityContext always contains the current primary key for the entity bean. The getPrimaryKey method returns the current primary key.

Tip

Hang on to the EntityContext object, in an entity bean it's a necessity because the ejbActivate method needs to discover its primary key.

The EntityContext also has a reference to the entity bean's Remote interface, in case the bean needs to pass an instance of itself to another bean. The getEJBObject returns a remote reference to the entity bean. As with the session bean, you can't pass the implementation object to a method that expects a Remote interface; you must use getEJBObject instead.

Tip

If you want to perform initialization on an entity bean instance that you only need to do once during the life of the bean, you should perform the initialization in the setEntityContext method. Some developers allocate a database connection in this method, which cuts down on the number of times you need to create a connection, but doesn't work well with connection pools and might waste database connections. If you allocate any resources in the setEntityContext method, you can release them from the unsetEntityContext method.

unsetEntityContext

The unsetEntityContext method tells the entity bean that it is about to be taken out of service for good and it should release any resources it allocated in its setEntityContext method. You might wonder why the SessionContext class doesn't also define such a method. The reason is that in a session bean, the ejbRemove method indicates that the bean is being taken out of service. In an entity bean, the ejbRemove method only indicates that the data the bean currently represents is being deleted from the database.

ejbRemove

The EJB container calls an entity bean's ejbRemove method to tell the bean to delete its data from the database. Because an entity bean might represent different data at different times (a different person, for example), this method doesn't indicate that the entity bean itself is going away.

`ejbActivate` AND `ejbPassivate`

It's somewhat unfortunate that session beans and entity beans have different semantics for the same method names. The `ejbActivate` and `ejbPassivate` methods are particularly confusing. In a session bean, the container will never call `ejbActivate` unless it has first called `ejbPassivate` because a bean starts out being "awake" and `ejbPassivate` puts it to sleep. The `ejbActivate` method in the session bean then wakes the bean back up.

In an entity bean, on the other hand, the `ejbActivate` method tells the bean that it is going into active service, after it has been sitting around in the entity bean pool. The `ejbPassivate` method tells the bean that it is no longer active and is going back into the pool.

Tip

> When the EJB container calls `ejbActivate`, your entity bean should update its primary key variable using the value stored in the `EntityContext`. It will need the value when it attempts to load or store database data.

With a session bean, there is a one-to-one relationship between invocations of `ejbPassivate` and `ejbActivate`. The same cannot be said for entity beans. Figure 7.4 shows you the entity bean lifecycle diagram that you first saw in Figure 7.1.

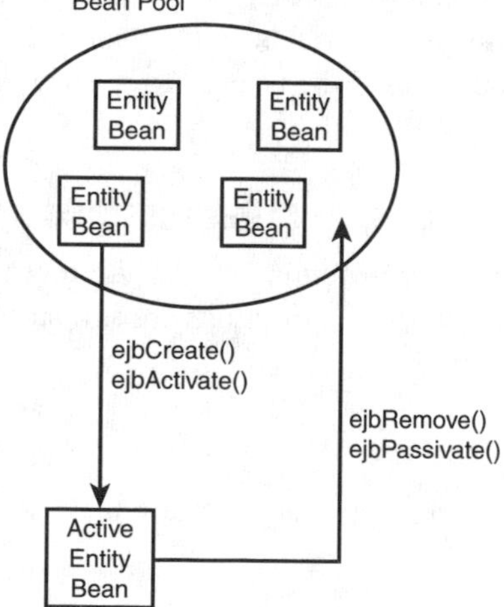

Figure 7.4 An entity bean goes from a pool to an active state and back again.

Notice that the bean can become active when the EJB container calls the `ejbCreate` method. The container might activate the bean through `ejbCreate` but send it back to the pool with `ejbPassivate`. Likewise, it might activate a bean with `ejbActivate` but return it to the pool by calling `ejbRemove`. If you create a bean, manipulate it, and then remove it, it's possible that the container might never call either `ejbActivate` or `ejbPassivate`. Remember that you have no control over when the container calls `ejbActivate` and `ejbPassivate`. Although you never call `ejbCreate` and `ejbRemove` directly, you do prompt the container to call these methods when you call `create` or `remove`.

`ejbLoad` AND `ejbStore`

When you first access an entity bean as part of a transaction, the EJB container invokes the bean's `ejbLoad` method. The bean should then load its data from the database. When the transaction completes, the container invokes `ejbStore` to tell the bean to store its data back to the database.

Suppose, for example, you locate a `Person` bean and then set the first and last name for the bean. If you do this within the scope of a single transaction (you'll learn how to do this in Chapter 9), the EJB container would perform the following sequence:

1. Activate the bean by calling `ejbActivate`.
2. Tell the bean to load its data from the database with `ejbLoad`.
3. Invoke `setFirstName`.
4. Invoke `setLastName`.
5. Tell the bean to save its data to the database with `ejbStore`.
6. Send the bean back to the pool by calling `ejbPassivate`.

If you don't perform the `setFirstName` and `setLastName` within the scope of a single transaction, the EJB container will perform the `ejbLoad` and `ejbStore` for each method invocation. If you invoke a lot of methods, that's a lot of unnecessary loading and storing. Again, after you see how to define transaction boundaries, you'll be able to control the frequency of loading and storing. The container must reread the bean during a new transaction to pick up any changes that might have been made by other clients.

ENTITY BEAN REQUIREMENTS, RESTRICTIONS, AND PERMISSIONS

The EJB specification places some specific restrictions and requirements on entity beans, just as it does with session beans. Most of these restrictions are similar to the ones you saw in the last chapter.

IMPLEMENT THE `EntityBean` INTERFACE

Just implementing the methods isn't enough; you must declare that the class implements the interface.

DECLARE THE CLASS AS PUBLIC, AND NOT FINAL OR ABSTRACT

The EJB container needs to create instances of the bean, so the class must be public and concrete (non-abstract).

CREATE A PUBLIC, PARAMETERLESS CONSTRUCTOR

Again, the EJB container must create instances of the bean. If the constructor is protected or private, the container can't create the instance.

DON'T IMPLEMENT A finalize METHOD

Although you rarely need to define a finalize method in the first place, the EJB specification explicitly forbids finalize in both session and entity beans. If your entity bean needs to do any cleanup, it should do it in ejbPassivate.

IMPLEMENT THE create METHODS, THE finder METHODS, THE Home METHODS, AND ANY Remote METHODS

An entity bean must implement any create methods, finder methods, and Home methods specified in the Home interface, and all methods specified in the Remote interface. In implementing these methods, there are several additional requirements:

- The methods must be public and cannot be static or final.
- The parameters and return types must be valid RMI/IIOP return types. In general, this means that they must either be native types (int, char, double, and so on), serializable objects, or Remote interfaces.
- The name of the implementation of a create method must start with ejbCreate. If a create method is called createSpecial, the implementation method is called ejbCreateSpecial.
- The name of the implementation of a finder method must start with ejbFind. If the finder method is called findByLastName, the implementation method is called ejbFindByLastName.
- There are no restrictions on the name of a Home method in the Home interface, except that it can't start with create, find, or remove. In the implementation class, a Home method must start with ejbHome. If the Home method is called computeAverageAge, the implementation method is called ejbHomeComputeAverageAge.
- The remote method name can't start with ejb (this might confuse an EJB deploy tool and possibly create conflicts). That is, the remote methods can't start with ejb.

OPTIONALLY IMPLEMENT THE Remote INTERFACE

In the last chapter, you saw how you could implement the Remote interface in your implementation class so the compiler would tell you when you forgot to implement a remote method. The problem is that the compiler no longer warns you when you try to pass this as a parameter to another remote method when you should be passing a proper remote reference. You are better off not implementing the Remote interface.

SUBCLASS ANOTHER CLASS WHEN NECESSARY

If your Remote or Home interfaces need to be subclasses of other interfaces, or if the implementation class needs to be a subclass of another class, there's no problem. The EJB specification specifically states that subclassing is permitted.

IMPLEMENT HELPER METHODS AS NECESSARY

An implementation class might have additional helper methods that are not part of the `Remote` or `Home` interfaces. There are no restrictions on the kinds of parameters, the return type, or the visibility (`public`, `protected`, `private`) of the method.

DON'T THROW `RemoteException`

If you need to throw an EJB-related exception, throw `javax.ejb.EJBException` instead.

`Remote` AND `Home` INTERFACE RESTRICTIONS

In addition to the restrictions on the implementation class, there are some restrictions on the `Remote` and `Home` interfaces. Most of these restrictions are similar to ones you have already seen for the implementation class.

`Remote` INTERFACES MUST EXTEND `javax.ejb.EJBObject`

When you use some deployment tools, such as the one provided by WebLogic, you'll notice that it automatically knows which class contains the `Remote` interface. It looks for the `EJBObject` interface to detect a `Remote` interface. Furthermore, the `EJBObject` interface contains some additional methods that every EJB must implement.

`Home` INTERFACES MUST EXTEND `javax.ejb.EJBHome`

As with the `Remote` and `EJBObject interfaces`, the `EJBHome` interface helps identify `Home` interfaces and defines some methods that you can invoke on every home interface.

PARAMETERS AND RETURN TYPES MUST BE VALID FOR RMI/IIOP

Again, this generally means the types must either be native types, serializable objects, or `Remote` interfaces.

ALL METHODS MUST THROW `java.rmi.RemoteException`

As you saw in Chapter 4, "Remote Method Invocation," `RemoteException` tells RMI that a method can be called remotely. Because the `Home` and `Remote` interface methods must all be remotely callable, they must all throw `RemoteException`.

ALL METHODS MUST HAVE CORRESPONDING IMPLEMENTATIONS

Normally, in a typical RMI implementation, this would go without saying because the implementation class would implement the `Remote` interface. In the case of EJB, however, because the implementation class isn't required to implement the `Home` and `Remote` interfaces, the compiler can't enforce the relationship between the implementation class and the `Home` and `Remote` interfaces.

Each `create` method in the `Home` interface must have a corresponding `ejbCreate` method in the implementation class. Also, the `create` method must throw `CreateException`. Each finder method must have a corresponding ejbFind method and the finder method must throw FinderException. Each Home method must have a corresponding ejbHome method.

INTERFACES CAN EXTEND OTHER INTERFACES

To support subclassing of Enterprise JavaBeans, the Home and Remote interfaces can extend other interfaces, as long as the parent interfaces are descendants of EJBObject (for Remote interfaces) or EJBHome (for Home interfaces).

USING AN ENTITY BEAN FROM A SESSION BEAN

Although an entity bean can use a session bean, it makes more sense for a session bean to use an entity bean. The entity bean might be shared by multiple sessions, so what session bean would an entity bean use? Would it have its own session bean? That's possible, and in situations where an entity bean does use a session bean, it's likely that the bean would have its own session. It's much more common for a session bean to use an entity bean, however.

Many developers choose not to expose the entity beans to the client at all. The client must always go through a session bean to get things done. Of course, some developers go so far as to not use entity beans at all and do all the database work in the session. Entity beans, however, let you encapsulate your data entities into a nice, clean framework and provide clear transaction boundaries for operations on the data entities.

The important thing to remember when you need to reference another EJB from your bean is that you should not directly ask for the name of the other bean's Home interface. Instead, you should look for java:comp/env/ejb/*someEJBName*. For example, instead of looking for Person, you should look for java:comp/env/ejb/Person. When you deploy your bean, you can specify the name that java:comp/env/ejb/Person refers to. This is useful for two reasons. First, the EJB container can tell that you are trying to locate another EJB and can manage your application better knowing that it is using other beans.

Second, because you choose at deployment time what bean name the java:com/env/ejb refers to, you can change what bean you use when testing your bean. For example, on a large development project, you might have different implementations of the same bean. You might have one called PersonDev that is the development version of the Person bean, as well as PersonQA and PersonProd for the QA and production versions. When testing a new bean, you might want to make sure it works with the QA version of Person. You can choose this at deployment time.

Listing 7.7 shows a method from a session bean that uses an entity bean.

LISTING 7.7 getHomePhone METHOD FROM AddressBookImpl.java

```
/** Returns the home phone number for the specified person */

    public String getHomePhone(String firstName, String lastName)
        throws EJBException
    {
```

LISTING 7.7 CONTINUED

```
        try
        {
// Get a naming context to lookup the PersonHome interface
            Context context = new InitialContext();

// Locate the PersonHome interface
            Object personHomeRef = context.lookup(
                "java:comp/env/ejb/Person");

// Use the narrow method to cast the reference to type PersonHome
            PersonHome home = (PersonHome)
                PortableRemoteObject.narrow(personHomeRef, PersonHome.class);

// Get the list of people with the specified first and last names
            Collection people = home.findByFirstAndLastName(
                firstName, lastName);

            Iterator peopleIter = people.iterator();

// Just get the first person in the list
            if (peopleIter.hasNext())
            {

// Get the person object from the collection
                Person person = (Person)
                    PortableRemoteObject.narrow(peopleIter.next(),
                    Person.class);

// Get the person's home phone number
                return person.getHomePhone();
            }

// If there's no person, just return null
            return null;
        }
        catch (NamingException exc)
        {
            throw new EJBException(
                "Unable to perform lookup: "+exc.toString());
        }
        catch (FinderException exc)
        {
            return null;
        }
        catch (RemoteException exc)
        {
            throw new EJBException(
                "Unable to perform lookup: "+exc.toString());
        }
    }
```

Note

Each EJB server has a different way to deploy beans, and the mapping between a coded bean name and the actual bean name is often difficult to configure. The coded name is usually called a Component Reference. In the J2EE reference implementation, you configure the name of the referenced bean on the JNDI Names tab.

PASSING REFERENCES FROM ONE ENTITY BEAN TO ANOTHER

There are cases when an entity bean needs to pass a reference to itself to another entity bean. In a non-EJB program, you occasionally need to pass `this` as a parameter to a method. In the EJB world, however, a remote method usually expects a `Remote` interface as a parameter, and the `this` reference for an implementation class is not a proper remote reference, even if the implementation class implements the `Remote` interface.

When you need to pass the equivalent of `this`—that is, when you need a remote reference to the current bean, whether it be a session bean or an entity bean—use the `getEJBObject` method in the `EntityContext` (or `SessionContext`) object. Don't forget to use the `PortableRemoteObject.narrow` method instead of just performing a cast.

For example, if the `PersonImpl` class needs to pass itself via a `Remote` interface that requires an object of type `Person` (the `Person` Remote interface), it uses `getEJBObject` and `PortableRemoteObject.narrow` like this:

```
otherBean.examinePerson(
    (Person) PortableRemoteObject.narrow(
    context.getEJBObject(), Person.class);
```

Now that you can create session and entity beans, you need to be able to define transaction boundaries so you can control what operations should be grouped together into a particular transaction. Chapter 9 shows you how to define transaction boundaries. First, however, Chapter 8 shows you how to use container-managed persistence.

TROUBLESHOOTING

DEPLOYMENT PROBLEMS

Why does the deployment tool complain that my primary key is invalid?

There are any number of reasons why this might happen. First, make sure that you actually specify the name of the primary key class in the deployment tool, including the package name. If you omit the package name, the deployment tool won't recognize the class. Next, make sure that the primary key is serializable, has a public constructor, and has valid `hashCode` and `equals` methods.

Why does the deployment tool complain that there are no transactions defined for some of my methods?

Some deployment tools don't make any assumptions about the transactional requirements for your bean's methods. When using one of these deployment tools, you must manually specify what kind of transactional requirements each method has. "Required" is a good default option.

RUNTIME PROBLEMS

Why do I get a `NullPointerException` in my `ejbLoad` method?

Obviously, there are the usual things to look for, like uninitialized variables, or failing to check for a `null` being returned from a method invocation. One of the subtle causes of this problem, however, is failing to get the primary key during the `ejbActivate` or the `ejbLoad` method. It's safest to grab the primary key during the `ejbActivate` method to make sure you have it whenever you need it.

CHAPTER 8

Using Container-Managed Persistence

In this chapter

WHY USE CONTAINER-MANAGED PERSISTENCE (CMP)?

In Chapter 7, "Creating an Entity Bean," you saw how to create an entity bean that uses BMP (bean-managed persistence) to store the bean in the database. BMP gives you direct control over the storage of the bean and you can handle any odd database relationships just by writing additional SQL code. If you create a lot of entity beans, it doesn't take long for you to get tired of writing SQL code. It's boring, repetitive, and error-prone.

Container-managed persistence (CMP) eliminates a lot of the unpleasantness of entity bean coding by handling the database operations for you. You don't need to write any SQL code (with the possible exception of the `WHERE` clauses for the finder methods). Aside from freeing you of the burden of SQL, CMP can bring additional advantages, depending on your EJB server.

One of the unfortunate aspects of CMP is that it is still fairly new and has undergone a major change between version 1.1 and version 2.0 of the EJB specification. Although the CMP specification covers a lot of features, some items are still left up to the individual CMP implementations. One of the most notable omissions is in the area of automatically generated keys.

Many large applications rely on the database to generate the keys for new database rows. It's not always easy to identify database columns that could uniquely identify a row. If you create a single ID column, you must create unique values for each ID. Some databases can generate the ID values automatically, sometimes by the use of a separate data item called a *sequence*. When the database can't generate the values automatically, you can create a table with a single row and single column holding the next value for the unique ID. Of course, you might need to create one of these tables for each different table that has a unique ID. Some applications use a single ID generation table for all the IDs in the database. The end result is that you run out of IDs faster and you rarely have consecutive ID values in a single table.

Although the CMP specification doesn't specifically support automatically generated keys, a specific CMP implementation might. For example, the TOPLink object-relational mapping library supports automatically generated keys and can act as the CMP provider for several different brands of EJB server.

A good CMP implementation can make your application run much faster than a typical BMP application with a lot less work. One of the biggest improvements you can see from a CMP implementation is the addition of caching. If a CMP engine has the capability to cache objects, it can drastically reduce the number of times you interact with the database. You see more benefits from caching for objects that you read a lot, especially when those objects are used frequently.

Imagine that you have `Company` objects that have related `Employee` objects. From a `Company`, you can get a list of employees and from an `Employee` you can access the `Company`. Without any caching, you must read a `Company` every time you call `getCompany` from an `Employee`. Even if an `Employee` object keeps a local reference to the `Company` after you call `getCompany`, two different Employee objects that have the same Company must each read the Company from the database.

If your CMP implementation uses caching, a Company object goes into the cache the first time you read it. If you call getCompany again from the same Employee or even another Employee with the same Company, the CMP implementation uses the cached version instead of hitting the database.

Two of the top-notch CMP implementations are TOPLink (www.webgain.com) and Persistence Powertier for EJB (www.persistence.com). Both of these implementations support caching and use a nonintrusive mechanism to map the entity beans to database tables.

Creating a CMP Entity Bean Under EJB 1.1

Although version 1.1 of the EJB specification allows you to map entity beans to database tables automatically, it might not provide all the capabilities you need. The specification itself leaves a lot of implementation details up to the CMP provider. Although this gives the providers plenty of flexibility to choose how they provide CMP services, it doesn't require enough from the providers. In other words, although version 1.1 of the EJB specification allows CMP providers to give you tremendous capabilities without violating the specification, it also allows the providers to give you limited capabilities and still remain true to the specification.

Regarding CMP, EJB 1.1 is particularly weak in the area of relationships. When one object has a relationship with another—as when an order has a relationship to its line items—you would expect CMP to understand the relationship and fetch related items. Unfortunately, CMP in EJB 1.1 ignores relationships.

To create a CMP entity bean under EJB 1.1, you follow the same procedure you use for BMP beans. The only real difference is that most of the required methods are dummy methods. For example, your ejbLoad and ejbStore methods in a BMP bean must load the object from the database and store the object in the database. In a CMP bean, however, these methods do nothing. The container performs the load and store for you.

The one method you might still need to do a little work in is the ejbCreate method. You must still copy the method parameters to their corresponding attribute values. For example, suppose your ejbCreate method looks like this:

```
public PersonKey ejbCreate(String aFirstName, String aLastName)
```

You still need to initialize the firstName and lastName fields in the bean:

```
firstName = aFirstName;
lastName = aLastName;
```

Normally, the ejbCreate method returns the key value for the created object. When you use CMP, however, you must return null. The container generates the new key value and returns it to the client.

In Chapter 7, you saw a technique for automatically generating key values that involves a separate sequence table. You can still use the technique with CMP. You fetch the new key value in your `ejbCreate` method and store the value in the appropriate field. Even if you automatically generate the key, your `ejbCreate` method *still* must return `null`. The container picks up the automatically generated key when it examines the bean's fields.

Listing 8.1 shows the EJB 1.1 CMP version of the `PersonImpl` class from Chapter 7. One of the beauties of EJB is that the implementation doesn't affect the Home and Remote interfaces. You can change the `Person` bean to use CMP instead of BMP and you leave the `Person.java` and `PersonHome.java` classes alone. Not only that, you don't need to change the clients because the interfaces remain the same!

LISTING 8.1 SOURCE CODE FOR `PersonImpl11.java`

```
package usingj2ee.addressbook;

import java.rmi.*;
import java.util.*;
import javax.ejb.*;
import java.sql.*;
import javax.sql.*;
import javax.naming.*;

public class PersonImpl11 implements EntityBean
{
/** The entity context provided by the EJB container. An entity bean must
    hold on to the context it is given. */

    private EntityContext context;

/** The database connection used by this entity bean */

    private Connection conn;

/** The entity bean fields that represent data from the database */
    public int personId;
    public String firstName;
    public String middleName;
    public String lastName;
    public String address1;
    public String address2;
    public String city;
    public String state;
    public String zip;
    public String homePhone;
    public String workPhone;
    public String mobilePhone;

/** An EJB must have a public, parameterless constructor */

    public PersonImpl11()
    {
    }

/** Called by the EJB container to set this entity's context */
```

```
    public void setEntityContext(EntityContext aContext)
    {
        context = aContext;
    }

/** Called by the EJB container to clear this entity's context */

    public void unsetEntityContext()
    {
        context = null;
    }

/** Called by the EJB container when a client calls the create() method in
    the Home interface */

    public PersonPK ejbCreate()
        throws CreateException
    {
        try
        {
// Compute the new primary key for this object
            personId = getNextId();

            return null;
        }
        catch (SQLException exc)
        {
            throw new CreateException(
                "Unable to access database: "+exc.toString());
        }
    }

/** Called by the EJB container after ejbCreate to allow the bean to do
    any additional setup that may be required. */
    public void ejbPostCreate()
        throws CreateException
    {
    }

/** Called by the EJB container to put the bean into active mode */

    public void ejbActivate()
        throws EJBException
    {
    }

/** Called by the EJB container to tell this bean that it is being
    deactivated and placed back into the pool */

    public void ejbPassivate()
        throws EJBException
    {
    }

/** Called by the container to tell the entity bean to read its data from
    the database */
```

LISTING 8.1 CONTINUED

```
    public void ejbLoad()
        throws EJBException
    {
    }

/** Called by the EJB container to tell the entity bean to
    write its data out to the database */
    public void ejbStore()
        throws EJBException
    {
    }

/** Called by the EJB container to tell this bean that it has been
    removed. */

    public void ejbRemove()
        throws EJBException
    {
    }

/** Although this class uses CMP, you still need to locate a connection
 *  in order to generate the primary key (Person generates its own unique
 *  id automatically using the person_id_seq table.
 */
    protected Connection getConnection()
        throws SQLException, NamingException
    {
// Get a reference to the naming service
        InitialContext context = new InitialContext();

// Get the data source for the person database
        DataSource ds = (DataSource) context.lookup(
            "java:comp/env/jdbc/PersonDB");

// Ask the data source to allocate a database connection
        return ds.getConnection();
    }

/** Uses a separate database table to generate a unique ID number for
    a person. You should perform the update before you read the value
    to make sure you don't have any locking problems.
    */
    protected int getNextId()
        throws SQLException
    {
        Connection conn = null;

        try
        {
            conn = getConnection();

// Increment the next person ID number
            PreparedStatement ps = conn.prepareStatement(
                "update person_id_seq set next_person_id = next_person_id + 1");
```

```
            if (ps.executeUpdate() != 1)
            {
                throw new SQLException("Unable to generate person id");
            }

            ps.close();

// Read the next person ID number
            ps = conn.prepareStatement(
                "select next_person_id from person_id_seq");

            ResultSet rs = ps.executeQuery();

            if (rs.next())
            {
                return rs.getInt("next_person_id");
            }
            else
            {
                throw new SQLException("Unable to generate person id");
            }
        }
        catch (NamingException exc)
        {
            throw new SQLException("Unable to generate person id: "+
                exc.toString());
        }
        finally
        {
            try
            {
                conn.close();
            }
            catch (Exception ignore) {}
        }
    }

// Implement the get/set methods for all the data elements

    public String getFirstName() { return firstName; }
    public void setFirstName(String aFirstName) { firstName = aFirstName; }

    public String getMiddleName() { return middleName; }
    public void setMiddleName(String aMiddleName) { middleName = aMiddleName; }

    public String getLastName() { return lastName; }
    public void setLastName(String aLastName) { lastName = aLastName; }

    public String getAddress1() { return address1; }
    public void setAddress1(String anAddress1) { address1 = anAddress1; }

    public String getAddress2() { return address2; }
    public void setAddress2(String anAddress2) { address2 = anAddress2; }

    public String getCity() { return city; }
    public void setCity(String aCity) { city = aCity; }
```

LISTING 8.1 CONTINUED

```
    public String getState() { return state; }
    public void setState(String aState) { state = aState; }

    public String getZip() { return zip; }
    public void setZip(String aZip) { zip = aZip; }

    public String getHomePhone() { return homePhone; }
    public void setHomePhone(String aHomePhone) { homePhone = aHomePhone; }

    public String getWorkPhone() { return workPhone; }
    public void setWorkPhone(String aWorkPhone) { workPhone = aWorkPhone; }

    public String getMobilePhone() { return mobilePhone; }
    public void setMobilePhone(String aMobilePhone)
    {
        mobilePhone = aMobilePhone;
    }
}
```

Not much has changed between the BMP version and the CMP version. The main difference is that a lot of code has been removed for the CMP version. Notice that `ejbLoad`, `ejbStore`, `ejbRemove`, `ejbActivate`, and `ejbPassivate` are all empty. Also notice that `PersonImpl11` still uses the automatic key generation.

The `PersonHome` interface expects the `Person` object to have a primary key of type `PersonPK`. When you write a CMP bean with its own key class, the field values in the key class *must match* the field names in the CMP object. Specifically, when you create the deployment descriptor for the bean, you specify a list of `<cmp-field>` items that list the field names for the bean. The primary key class field names must match items in the `<cmp-field>` list. The container can then figure out how to create the key value.

Note

Don't forget that for classes with a single-field primary key, you don't need to create a primary key class. You can use a standard class, such as `Integer` or `String`, to represent the key value.

Listing 8.2 shows the primary key class for the person object.

LISTING 8.2 SOURCE CODE FOR `PersonPK.java`

```
package usingj2ee.addressbook;

public class PersonPK implements java.io.Serializable
{
    public int personId;

    public PersonPK()
    {
    }
```

```
    public PersonPK(int aPersonId)
    {
        personId = aPersonId;
    }

    public int hashCode()
    {
        return personId;
    }

    public boolean equals(Object ob)
    {
        if (ob == this) return true;
        if (!(ob instanceof PersonPK)) return false;

        PersonPK other = (PersonPK) ob;
        if (personId != other.personId) return false;

        return true;
    }

    public String toString()
    {
        return ""+personId;
    }
}
```

When you use CMP, you must do a little extra work when you create the deployment descriptor for the bean (the XML file that describes the bean). If you use a deployment tool, your job will be a lot easier. Listing 8.3 shows the `ejb-jar.xml` deployment descriptor file for the `Person` bean, using `PersonImpl11` as the implementation class.

LISTING 8.3 SOURCE CODE FOR `ejb-jar.xml` FOR EJB 1.1 CMP

```
<?xml version="1.0"?>

<!DOCTYPE ejb-jar PUBLIC '-//Sun Microsystems, Inc.//DTD Enterprise JavaBeans 1.1//EN'
'http://java.sun.com/j2ee/dtds/ejb-jar_1_1.dtd'>

<ejb-jar>
    <description></description>
    <enterprise-beans>
        <session>
            <display-name>AddressBook</display-name>
            <ejb-name>AddressBook</ejb-name>
            <home>usingj2ee.addressbook.AddressBookHome</home>
            <remote>usingj2ee.addressbook.AddressBook</remote>
            <ejb-class>usingj2ee.addressbook.AddressBookImpl</ejb-class>
            <session-type>Stateful</session-type>
            <transaction-type>Container</transaction-type>
            <ejb-ref>
                <ejb-ref-name>ejb/PersonHome</ejb-ref-name>
                <ejb-ref-type>Entity</ejb-ref-type>
```

LISTING 8.3 CONTINUED

```
            <home>usingj2ee.addressbook.PersonHome</home>
            <remote>usingj2ee.addressbook.Person</remote>
        </ejb-ref>
    </session>
    <entity>
        <description></description>
        <display-name>Person</display-name>
        <ejb-name>Person</ejb-name>
        <home>usingj2ee.addressbook.PersonHome</home>
        <remote>usingj2ee.addressbook.Person</remote>
        <ejb-class>usingj2ee.addressbook.PersonImpl11</ejb-class>
        <persistence-type>Container</persistence-type>
        <prim-key-class>usingj2ee.addressbook.PersonPK</prim-key-class>
        <reentrant>False</reentrant>
        <cmp-field>
            <description></description>
            <field-name>personId</field-name>
        </cmp-field>
        <cmp-field>
            <description></description>
            <field-name>address2</field-name>
        </cmp-field>
        <cmp-field>
            <description></description>
            <field-name>mobilePhone</field-name>
        </cmp-field>
        <cmp-field>
            <description></description>
            <field-name>firstName</field-name>
        </cmp-field>
        <cmp-field>
            <description></description>
            <field-name>lastName</field-name>
        </cmp-field>
        <cmp-field>
            <description></description>
            <field-name>workPhone</field-name>
        </cmp-field>
        <cmp-field>
            <description></description>
            <field-name>city</field-name>
        </cmp-field>
        <cmp-field>
            <description></description>
            <field-name>middleName</field-name>
        </cmp-field>
        <cmp-field>
            <description></description>
            <field-name>zip</field-name>
        </cmp-field>
        <cmp-field>
            <description></description>
            <field-name>state</field-name>
        </cmp-field>
        <cmp-field>
```

```
            <description></description>
            <field-name>homePhone</field-name>
        </cmp-field>
        <cmp-field>
            <description></description>
            <field-name>address1</field-name>
        </cmp-field>
    </entity>
  </enterprise-beans>
</ejb-jar>
```

The `ejb-jar` file in Listing 8.3 includes the deployment information for the `AddressBook` bean that uses the `Person` bean. The `<cmp-field>` entries tell the container which fields in the bean need to be persisted to the database. Also, of course, you must set the `<persistence-type>` value to `Container` for CMP.

The format of the `ejb-jar` file is standard for all EJB containers. One of the things you should notice immediately is that the file doesn't tell you the name of the database table in which the bean is stored or the names of the columns for the various fields. There are two main reasons for this omission:

- Each container might have a different way to associate fields with columns that might not match the way you specify information in the `ejb-jar` file.
- A container might not use a relational database at all. It might use an object database or some other persistence mechanism that doesn't even have the concept of table and column names.

If you're using the WebLogic Application Server, for example, you must include two additional deployment descriptors when deploying a CMP entity bean. First, you must create a `weblogic-ejb-jar` file containing some miscellaneous information about the bean, including its JNDI name. Listing 8.4 shows the `weblogic-ejb-jar.xml` file for the `Person` bean (along with the `AddressBook` bean).

LISTING 8.4 SOURCE CODE FOR `weblogic-ejb-jar.xml` FOR EJB 1.1 CMP

```
<?xml version="1.0"?>

<!DOCTYPE weblogic-ejb-jar PUBLIC '-//BEA Systems, Inc.//DTD WebLogic 5.1.0 EJB//EN'
'http://www.bea.com/servers/wls510/dtd/weblogic-ejb-jar.dtd'>

<weblogic-ejb-jar>
    <weblogic-enterprise-bean>
        <ejb-name>AddressBook</ejb-name>
        <caching-descriptor>
            <max-beans-in-cache>100</max-beans-in-cache>
        </caching-descriptor>
        <reference-descriptor>
            <ejb-reference-description>
                <ejb-ref-name>ejb/PersonHome</ejb-ref-name>
                <jndi-name>PersonHome</jndi-name>
            </ejb-reference-description>
```

LISTING 8.4 CONTINUED

```
        </reference-descriptor>
        <jndi-name>AddressBookHome</jndi-name>
    </weblogic-enterprise-bean>

    <weblogic-enterprise-bean>
        <ejb-name>Person</ejb-name>
        <caching-descriptor>
            <max-beans-in-cache>1000</max-beans-in-cache>
        </caching-descriptor>
        <persistence-descriptor>
            <persistence-type>
                <type-identifier>WebLogic_CMP_RDBMS</type-identifier>
                <type-version>5.1.0</type-version>
                <type-storage>META-INF/weblogic-cmp-rdbms-jar.xml</type-storage>
            </persistence-type>
            <persistence-use>
                <type-identifier>WebLogic_CMP_RDBMS</type-identifier>
                <type-version>5.1.0</type-version>
            </persistence-use>
        </persistence-descriptor>
        <jndi-name>PersonHome</jndi-name>
    </weblogic-enterprise-bean>
</weblogic-ejb-jar>
```

Notice that the `weblogic-ejb-jar.xml` file doesn't contain any database information, other than a link to the persistence descriptor file, which *does* contain the database information.

The real database mapping work takes place in the `weblogic-cmp-rdbms-jar.xml` file, which you can see here in Listing 8.5.

LISTING 8.5 SOURCE CODE FOR `weblogic-cmp-rdbms-jar.xml` FOR EJB 1.1 CMP

```
<?xml version="1.0"?>
<!DOCTYPE weblogic-rdbms-bean PUBLIC
 '-//BEA Systems, Inc.//DTD WebLogic 5.1.0 EJB RDBMS Persistence//EN'
 'http://www.bea.com/servers/wls510/dtd/weblogic-rdbms-persistence.dtd'>
<weblogic-rdbms-bean>
    <pool-name>personPool</pool-name>
    <table-name>Person</table-name>
    <attribute-map>
        <object-link>
            <bean-field>personId</bean-field>
            <dbms-column>person_id</dbms-column>
        </object-link>
        <object-link>
            <bean-field>firstName</bean-field>
            <dbms-column>first_name</dbms-column>
        </object-link>
        <object-link>
            <bean-field>middleName</bean-field>
            <dbms-column>middle_name</dbms-column>
        </object-link>
        <object-link>
            <bean-field>lastName</bean-field>
```

```
            <dbms-column>last_name</dbms-column>
        </object-link>
        <object-link>
            <bean-field>address1</bean-field>
            <dbms-column>address1</dbms-column>
        </object-link>
        <object-link>
            <bean-field>address2</bean-field>
            <dbms-column>address2</dbms-column>
        </object-link>
        <object-link>
            <bean-field>city</bean-field>
            <dbms-column>city</dbms-column>
        </object-link>
        <object-link>
            <bean-field>state</bean-field>
            <dbms-column>state</dbms-column>
        </object-link>
        <object-link>
            <bean-field>zip</bean-field>
            <dbms-column>zip</dbms-column>
        </object-link>
        <object-link>
            <bean-field>homePhone</bean-field>
            <dbms-column>home_phone</dbms-column>
        </object-link>
        <object-link>
            <bean-field>workPhone</bean-field>
            <dbms-column>work_phone</dbms-column>
        </object-link>
        <object-link>
            <bean-field>mobilePhone</bean-field>
            <dbms-column>mobile_phone</dbms-column>
        </object-link>
    </attribute-map>
    <finder-list>
        <finder>
            <method-name>findByLastName</method-name>
            <method-params>
                <method-param>java.lang.String</method-param>
            </method-params>
            <finder-query><![CDATA[(like lastName $0)]]></finder-query>
        </finder>
        <finder>
            <method-name>findByFirstAndLastName</method-name>
            <method-params>
                <method-param>java.lang.String</method-param>
                <method-param>java.lang.String</method-param>
            </method-params>
            <finder-query><![CDATA[(& (like firstName $0)
                (like lastName $1))]]></finder-query>
        </finder>
    </finder-list>
    <options>
        <use-quoted-names>false</use-quoted-names>
    </options>
</weblogic-rdbms-bean>
```

The `weblogic-cmp-rdbms-jar` file contains several noteworthy items. First, notice that in addition to specifying the table name, you also specify the name of a connection pool. WebLogic lets you configure connection pools separately from data sources. When you use the newer EJB 2.0 CMP model, you specify a data source instead of a connection pool (WebLogic uses another configuration file to map connection pools to data sources).

Next, the `<object-link>` tags associate bean fields with database columns. WebLogic can only store a bean in a single table—you can't split the bean across multiple tables.

Finally, WebLogic has its own query language for writing the finder methods. Other EJB containers actually make you write an SQL statement. As you'll soon see, EJB 2.0 has a standard query language. The WebLogic query language uses operators of the form (*operation param1 param2*), and uses $0, $1, $2, and so on to represent the first, second, third, and so on finder parameters. For example, to compare the `firstName` field in a bean with the first parameter in a finder method, use this comparison:

```
(like firstName $0)
```

You can also use the = operator for equality comparisons:

```
(= firstName $0)
```

To combine operations, use the `&` (AND) and `|` (OR) operators like this:

```
(& (= firstName $0) (= lastName $1))
```

Notice that the AND expression is of the form (*operation param1 param2*); it's just that the two parameters are expressions themselves.

After you deploy the CMP bean, your client program can access the bean just like it would a BMP bean. In fact, the client can't tell what kind of persistence mechanism the bean uses.

CREATING A CMP ENTITY BEAN UNDER EJB 2.0

Although container-managed persistence in EJB 1.1 provided a good starting point for developers, it leaves a lot of things up to the container providers. This omission gives the container providers a lot of flexibility; however, it also means that the container providers can skimp on some of the features.

When you move an EJB 1.1 CMP bean from one application server platform to another, you must go through the pain of mapping the bean to the database all over again because each vendor does it differently. Queries can be especially painful because of the variety in query languages. EJB 2.0 addresses some of these problems by creating a standard query language (EJBQL). It also changes the format of the implementation class to give the container providers more flexibility.

If you have a substantial number of beans that use the EJB 1.1 form of CMP, don't worry. The EJB 2.0 specification requires the containers to support the EJB 1.1 version as well. You don't need to rewrite all your CMP beans yet.

As with EJB 1.1, your `ejbLoad`, `ejbStore`, `ejbRemove`, `ejbActivate`, and `ejbPassivate` methods don't need to do anything. Again, your `ejbCreate` method needs to populate the fields from the method parameters, but it doesn't do any database operations.

The big difference between an EJB 1.1 CMP bean and an EJB 2.0 CMP bean is that the EJB 2.0 CMP bean class must be abstract. Not only that, it doesn't declare member variables for any of the persistent fields—just abstract accessor methods. Whereas the conversion from a BMP bean to an EJB 1.1 CMP bean takes a matter of minutes and mostly involves removing code, converting to EJB 2.0 CMP is a bit more involved.

Listing 8.6 shows the EJB 2.0 CMP version of the `Person` bean implementation. Notice that the various field values are now gone and that the accessor methods are abstract.

LISTING 8.6 SOURCE CODE FOR PersonImpl20.java

```
package usingj2ee.addressbook;

import java.rmi.*;
import java.util.*;
import javax.ejb.*;
import java.sql.*;
import javax.sql.*;
import javax.naming.*;

public abstract class PersonImpl20 implements EntityBean
{
/** The entity context provided by the EJB container. An entity bean must
    hold on to the context it is given. */

    private EntityContext context;

/** The database connection used by this entity bean */

    private Connection conn;

/** An EJB must have a public, parameterless constructor */

    public PersonImpl20()
    {
    }

/** Called by the EJB container to set this entity's context */

    public void setEntityContext(EntityContext aContext)
    {
        context = aContext;
    }

/** Called by the EJB container to clear this entity's context */

    public void unsetEntityContext()
    {
        context = null;
    }
```

LISTING 8.6 CONTINUED

```
/** Called by the EJB container when a client calls the create() method in
    the Home interface */

    public PersonPK ejbCreate()
        throws CreateException
    {
        try
        {
// Compute the new primary key for this object
            setPersonId(getNextId());

            return null;
        }
        catch (SQLException exc)
        {
            throw new CreateException(
                "Unable to access database: "+exc.toString());
        }
    }

/** Called by the EJB container after ejbCreate to allow the bean to do
    any additional setup that may be required. */
    public void ejbPostCreate()
        throws CreateException
    {
    }

/** Called by the EJB container to put the bean into active mode */

    public void ejbActivate()
        throws EJBException
    {
    }

/** Called by the EJB container to tell this bean that it is being
    deactivated and placed back into the pool */

    public void ejbPassivate()
        throws EJBException
    {
    }

/** Called by the container to tell the entity bean to read its data from
    the database */

    public void ejbLoad()
        throws EJBException
    {
    }

/** Called by the EJB container to tell the entity bean to
    write its data out to the database */
    public void ejbStore()
        throws EJBException
    {
    }
```

```
/** Called by the EJB container to tell this bean that it has been
    removed. */

    public void ejbRemove()
        throws EJBException
    {
    }

/** Although this class uses CMP, you still need to locate a connection
 *  in order to generate the primary key (Person generates its own unique
 *  id automatically using the person_id_seq table.
 */
    protected Connection getConnection()
        throws SQLException, NamingException
    {
// Get a reference to the naming service
        InitialContext context = new InitialContext();

// Get the data source for the person database
        DataSource ds = (DataSource) context.lookup(
            "java:comp/env/jdbc/PersonDB");

// Ask the data source to allocate a database connection
        return ds.getConnection();
    }

/** Uses a separate database table to generate a unique ID number for
    a person. You should perform the update before you read the value
    to make sure you don't have any locking problems.
    */
    protected int getNextId()
        throws SQLException
    {
        Connection conn = null;

        try
        {
            conn = getConnection();

// Increment the next person ID number
            PreparedStatement ps = conn.prepareStatement(
                "update person_id_seq set next_person_id = next_person_id + 1");

            if (ps.executeUpdate() != 1)
            {
                throw new SQLException("Unable to generate person id");
            }

            ps.close();

// Read the next person ID number
            ps = conn.prepareStatement(
                "select next_person_id from person_id_seq");

            ResultSet rs = ps.executeQuery();
```

LISTING 8.6 CONTINUED

```
            if (rs.next())
            {
                return rs.getInt("next_person_id");
            }
            else
            {
                throw new SQLException("Unable to generate person id");
            }
        }
        catch (NamingException exc)
        {
            throw new SQLException("Unable to generate person id: "+
                exc.toString());
        }
        finally
        {
            try
            {
                conn.close();
            }
            catch (Exception ignore) {}
        }
    }

// Implement the get/set methods for all the data elements

    public abstract int getPersonId();
    public abstract void setPersonId(int aPersonId);

    public abstract String getFirstName();
    public abstract void setFirstName(String aFirstName);

    public abstract String getMiddleName();
    public abstract void setMiddleName(String aMiddleName);

    public abstract String getLastName();
    public abstract void setLastName(String aLastName);

    public abstract String getAddress1();
    public abstract void setAddress1(String anAddress1);

    public abstract String getAddress2();
    public abstract void setAddress2(String anAddress2);

    public abstract String getCity();
    public abstract void setCity(String aCity);

    public abstract String getState();
    public abstract void setState(String aState);

    public abstract String getZip();
    public abstract void setZip(String aZip);

    public abstract String getHomePhone();
    public abstract void setHomePhone(String aHomePhone);
```

```
    public abstract String getWorkPhone();
    public abstract void setWorkPhone(String aWorkPhone);

    public abstract String getMobilePhone();
    public abstract void setMobilePhone(String aMobilePhone);
}
```

The `PersonImpl20` class must contain accessor methods for *all* the fields that are stored in the database, including the `personId` primary key field. Although some of the accessor methods can be exposed to the client through the Remote interface, that's not a requirement. You can create accessor methods that aren't visible via the Remote interface.

Although the `ejb-jar.xml` file for EJB 2.0 CMP is similar to the one for EJB 1.1, you now include the queries for the finder methods in the `ejb-jar.xml` file instead of the vendor-specific configuration file(s). You specify the finder using a special query language called EJBQL (EJB Query Language).

USING THE EJB QUERY LANGUAGE

If you already know SQL, EJBQL should be a snap because it uses a similar syntax. The only major difference is that EJBQL is object-aware. You can select objects and examine field values. When you write a query for a finder method, you supply a `WHERE` clause, using `?1`, `?2`, and so on for the various finder parameters.

For example, to locate all objects whose `lastName` field is the same as the first parameter to the finder method (that is, `findByLastName(String lastName)`), use this EJBQL query:

```
WHERE lastName = ?1
```

To compare both the first and last names, use a query like this:

```
WHERE lastName = ?1 and firstName = ?2
```

As with SQL, you can use the `like` operator instead of `=` to perform wildcard comparisons (using `%` as the wildcard character). For example, to locate all objects whose last name starts with X, use

```
WHERE lastName like 'X%'
```

You can also use the `SELECT` and `FROM` keywords to perform more complex queries. For example, suppose you want to create a finder method to find instructors who have students with a 4.0 grade point average. You can do a select like this:

```
SELECT instr FROM instructors as instr,
    cl in instr.classes, student in cl.students
WHERE student.gpa = 4.0
```

Unraveling this query, you see that you look at all the instructors and use an identifier called `instr` to represent a particular instructor in the query. Next, you look at all the instructor's classes, using `cl` to identify a class. Now you look at all the students in the class, using `student` to identify a particular one, and you examine that student's grade point average (GPA).

You can also include finder methods in your query, using this form: `EJBName >> finderMethod(finder params)`. For example, suppose you write a finder method to locate instructors by degree, and you want to find all classes taught by instructors with a Ph.D. Use the following query:

```
SELECT cl from classes as cl
WHERE cl.instructor in Instructors >> findByDegree('Ph.D')
```

In other words, for every class, see if the class instructor is in the set of instructors returned by the `findByDegree` finder method.

Note

The `FROM` clause in an EJBQL query refers to abstract schemas, not bean names. In other words, when you select "FROM classes", `classes` is the name of an abstract schema, which is simply a name you assign in your `ejb-jar.xml` file.

Listing 8.7 shows the `ejb-jar.xml` file for the EJB 2.0 CMP version of the `Person` bean.

LISTING 8.7 `ejb-jar.xml` FILE FOR THE PERSON BEAN

```
<?xml version="1.0"?>

<!DOCTYPE ejb-jar PUBLIC '-//Sun Microsystems, Inc.//DTD Enterprise JavaBeans 2.0//EN'
'http://java.sun.com/j2ee/dtds/ejb-jar_2_0.dtd'>

<ejb-jar>
    <description></description>
    <enterprise-beans>
        <session>
            <display-name>AddressBook</display-name>
            <ejb-name>AddressBook</ejb-name>
            <home>usingj2ee.addressbook.AddressBookHome</home>
            <remote>usingj2ee.addressbook.AddressBook</remote>
            <ejb-class>usingj2ee.addressbook.AddressBookImpl</ejb-class>
            <session-type>Stateful</session-type>
            <transaction-type>Container</transaction-type>
            <ejb-ref>
                <ejb-ref-name>ejb/PersonHome</ejb-ref-name>
                <ejb-ref-type>Entity</ejb-ref-type>
                <home>usingj2ee.addressbook.PersonHome</home>
                <remote>usingj2ee.addressbook.Person</remote>
            </ejb-ref>
        </session>
        <entity>
            <description></description>
            <display-name>Person</display-name>
            <ejb-name>Person</ejb-name>
            <home>usingj2ee.addressbook.PersonHome</home>
            <remote>usingj2ee.addressbook.Person</remote>
            <ejb-class>usingj2ee.addressbook.PersonImpl20</ejb-class>
            <persistence-type>Container</persistence-type>
            <prim-key-class>usingj2ee.addressbook.PersonPK</prim-key-class>
            <reentrant>False</reentrant>
```

```
<cmp-version>2.x</cmp-version>
<abstract-schema-name>Person</abstract-schema-name>
<cmp-field>
    <description></description>
    <field-name>personId</field-name>
</cmp-field>
<cmp-field>
    <description></description>
    <field-name>address2</field-name>
</cmp-field>
<cmp-field>
    <description></description>
    <field-name>mobilePhone</field-name>
</cmp-field>
<cmp-field>
    <description></description>
    <field-name>firstName</field-name>
</cmp-field>
<cmp-field>
    <description></description>
    <field-name>lastName</field-name>
</cmp-field>
<cmp-field>
    <description></description>
    <field-name>workPhone</field-name>
</cmp-field>
<cmp-field>
    <description></description>
    <field-name>city</field-name>
</cmp-field>
<cmp-field>
    <description></description>
    <field-name>middleName</field-name>
</cmp-field>
<cmp-field>
    <description></description>
    <field-name>zip</field-name>
</cmp-field>
<cmp-field>
    <description></description>
    <field-name>state</field-name>
</cmp-field>
<cmp-field>
    <description></description>
    <field-name>homePhone</field-name>
</cmp-field>
<cmp-field>
    <description></description>
    <field-name>address1</field-name>
</cmp-field>
<resource-ref>
    <res-ref-name>jdbc/PersonDB</res-ref-name>
    <res-type>javax.sql.DataSource</res-type>
    <res-auth>Container</res-auth>
</resource-ref>
<query>
    <query-method>
```

LISTING 8.7 CONTINUED

```
                    <method-name>findByLastName</method-name>
                    <method-params>
                        <method-param>java.lang.String</method-param>
                    </method-params>
                </query-method>
                <ejb-ql>
                    <![CDATA[WHERE lastName like ?1]]>
                </ejb-ql>
            </query>
            <query>
                <query-method>
                    <method-name>findByFirstAndLastName</method-name>
                    <method-params>
                        <method-param>java.lang.String</method-param>
                        <method-param>java.lang.String</method-param>
                    </method-params>
                </query-method>
                <ejb-ql>
                    <![CDATA[WHERE firstName like ?1 and lastName like ?2]]>
                </ejb-ql>
            </query>
        </entity>
    </enterprise-beans>
</ejb-jar>
```

The format of the file is similar to the one for EJB 1.1, except that you must specify the `<cmp-version>` and the `<abstract-schema-name>`. Remember, the abstract schema name represents the name you use in a `FROM` clause to select beans of this type.

The only other difference is that you include `<query>` tags containing EJBQL statements for the various finder methods you have defined.

Listing 8.8 shows the `weblogic-ejb-jar.xml` file for the EJB 2.0 CMP version of the `Person` bean.

LISTING 8.8 SOURCE CODE FOR `weblogic-ejb-jar.xml` FOR EJB 2.0 CMP

```
<?xml version="1.0"?>

<!DOCTYPE weblogic-ejb-jar PUBLIC '-//BEA Systems, Inc.//DTD WebLogic 6.0.0 EJB//EN'
'http://www.bea.com/servers/wls600/dtd/weblogic-ejb-jar.dtd'>

<weblogic-ejb-jar>
    <weblogic-enterprise-bean>
        <ejb-name>AddressBook</ejb-name>
        <stateful-session-descriptor>
            <stateful-session-cache>
                <max-beans-in-cache>100</max-beans-in-cache>
            </stateful-session-cache>
        </stateful-session-descriptor>
        <reference-descriptor>
            <ejb-reference-description>
```

```
                <ejb-ref-name>ejb/PersonHome</ejb-ref-name>
                <jndi-name>PersonHome</jndi-name>
            </ejb-reference-description>
        </reference-descriptor>
        <jndi-name>AddressBookHome</jndi-name>
    </weblogic-enterprise-bean>

    <weblogic-enterprise-bean>
        <ejb-name>Person</ejb-name>
        <entity-descriptor>
            <entity-cache>
                <max-beans-in-cache>1000</max-beans-in-cache>
            </entity-cache>
            <persistence>
                <persistence-type>
                    <type-identifier>WebLogic_CMP_RDBMS</type-identifier>
                    <type-version>6.0</type-version>
                    <type-storage>META-INF/weblogic-cmp-rdbms-jar.xml
                        </type-storage>
                </persistence-type>
                <persistence-use>
                    <type-identifier>WebLogic_CMP_RDBMS</type-identifier>
                    <type-version>6.0</type-version>
                </persistence-use>
            </persistence>
        </entity-descriptor>
        <reference-descriptor>
            <resource-description>
                <res-ref-name>jdbc/PersonDB</res-ref-name>
                <jndi-name>PersonDB</jndi-name>
            </resource-description>
        </reference-descriptor>
        <jndi-name>PersonHome</jndi-name>
    </weblogic-enterprise-bean>
</weblogic-ejb-jar>
```

Once again, the differences between the EJB 1.1 and EJB 2.0 versions of this file are fairly minimal—basically version differences. Listing 8.9 shows the `weblogic-cmp-rdbms-jar.xml` file for the EJB 2.0 CMP version of the `Person` bean.

LISTING 8.9 SOURCE CODE FOR `weblogic-cmp-rdbms-jar.xml` FOR EJB 2.0 CMP

```
<?xml version="1.0"?>
<!DOCTYPE weblogic-rdbms-jar PUBLIC
 '-//BEA Systems, Inc.//DTD WebLogic 6.0.0 EJB RDBMS Persistence//EN'
 'http://www.bea.com/servers/wls600/dtd/weblogic-rdbms20-persistence-600.dtd'>
<weblogic-rdbms-jar>
    <weblogic-rdbms-bean>
        <ejb-name>Person</ejb-name>
        <data-source-name>PersonDB</data-source-name>
        <table-name>Person</table-name>
        <field-map>
            <cmp-field>personId</cmp-field>
            <dbms-column>person_id</dbms-column>
        </field-map>
        <field-map>
```

LISTING 8.9 SOURCE CODE FOR `weblogic-cmp-rdbms-jar.xml` FOR EJB 2.0 CMP

```
            <cmp-field>firstName</cmp-field>
            <dbms-column>first_name</dbms-column>
        </field-map>
        <field-map>
            <cmp-field>middleName</cmp-field>
            <dbms-column>middle_name</dbms-column>
        </field-map>
        <field-map>
            <cmp-field>lastName</cmp-field>
            <dbms-column>last_name</dbms-column>
        </field-map>
        <field-map>
            <cmp-field>address1</cmp-field>
            <dbms-column>address1</dbms-column>
        </field-map>
        <field-map>
            <cmp-field>address2</cmp-field>
            <dbms-column>address2</dbms-column>
        </field-map>
        <field-map>
            <cmp-field>city</cmp-field>
            <dbms-column>city</dbms-column>
        </field-map>
        <field-map>
            <cmp-field>state</cmp-field>
            <dbms-column>state</dbms-column>
        </field-map>
        <field-map>
            <cmp-field>zip</cmp-field>
            <dbms-column>zip</dbms-column>
        </field-map>
        <field-map>
            <cmp-field>homePhone</cmp-field>
            <dbms-column>home_phone</dbms-column>
        </field-map>
        <field-map>
            <cmp-field>workPhone</cmp-field>
            <dbms-column>work_phone</dbms-column>
        </field-map>
        <field-map>
            <cmp-field>mobilePhone</cmp-field>
            <dbms-column>mobile_phone</dbms-column>
        </field-map>
    </weblogic-rdbms-bean>
</weblogic-rdbms-jar>
```

Although the tag names have changed, the format of the file is almost identical to the one for EJB 1.1. Instead of specifying a connection pool, however, you must specify a data source.

RELATIONSHIPS

EJB 2.0 lets you define relationships between beans. In other words, you can indicate that one bean can contain (or refer to) one or more other beans. For example, an order can contain any number of line items but it has only one customer. A customer, however, can have multiple orders.

When a bean has a relationship to another bean, you typically have get and set methods to make the association. For example, to get the customer for a particular order, you might have a `getCustomer` method in the `Order` object. Likewise, to get the line items for an order, you might have a `getLineItems` method that returns a collection of line items.

As it turns out, these get and set methods are all you need to put into your entity beans to indicate the presence of a relationship. Of course, you must still add some extra information to the `ejb-jar.xml` file.

Listing 8.10 shows a `FlightSeg` Remote interface, which represents a flight between two cities on a particular date. A `FlightSeg` can have a single aircraft assigned to it.

LISTING 8.10 SOURCE CODE FOR `FlightSeg.java`

```
package usingj2ee.flightops;

import java.rmi.*;
import javax.ejb.*;
import java.util.Date;

/** Defines the methods you can call on a FlightSeg object */

public interface FlightSeg extends EJBObject
{
    public String getFlightNumber() throws RemoteException;
    public String getOrigin() throws RemoteException;
    public String getDestination() throws RemoteException;
    public Date getLeaves() throws RemoteException;

    public Date getArrives() throws RemoteException;
    public void setArrives(Date anArrivalTime) throws RemoteException;

    public int getFirstBookings() throws RemoteException;
    public void setFirstBookings(int firstBookings)
        throws RemoteException;

    public int getBusinessBookings() throws RemoteException;
    public void setBusinessBookings(int firstBookings)
        throws RemoteException;

    public int getCoachBookings() throws RemoteException;
    public void setCoachBookings(int firstBookings)
        throws RemoteException;

    public Aircraft getAircraft() throws RemoteException;
    public void setAircraft(Aircraft aircraft)
        throws RemoteException;
}
```

Listing 8.11 shows the Remote interface for the `Aircraft` bean. An aircraft can be associated with any number of flight segments.

LISTING 8.11 SOURCE CODE FOR Aircraft.java

```
package usingj2ee.flightops;

import java.rmi.*;
import javax.ejb.*;
import java.util.*;

/** Defines the methods you can call on an Aircraft object */

public interface Aircraft extends EJBObject
{
    public String getAircraftType() throws RemoteException;
    public void setAircraftType(String anAircraftType)
        throws RemoteException;

    public int getFirstCapacity() throws RemoteException;
    public void setFirstCapacity(int newCapacity) throws RemoteException;

    public int getBusinessCapacity() throws RemoteException;
    public void setBusinessCapacity(int newCapacity) throws RemoteException;

    public int getCoachCapacity() throws RemoteException;
    public void setCoachCapacity(int newCapacity) throws RemoteException;

    public Collection getFlightSegments() throws RemoteException;
    public void setFlightSegments(Collection flightSegs)
        throws RemoteException;
}
```

As with the accessor methods for fields, you don't define any member variables to represent associations in your entity bean implementation, just abstract methods. You establish the presence of the relationships by adding a `<relationships>` section to your `ejb-jar.xml` file. Listing 8.12 shows an excerpt from the `ejb-jar.xml` file for the `Aircraft` and `FlightSeg` beans.

LISTING 8.12 RELATIONSHIP DECLARATIONS FROM ejb-xml.jar

```
<relationships>
    <ejb-relation>
        <ejb-relation-name>Aircraft-FlightSeg</ejb-relation-name>
        <ejb-relationship-role>
            <ejb-relationship-role-name>aircraft-has-flightsegs
            </ejb-relationship-role-name>
            <multiplicity>one</multiplicity>
            <role-source><ejb-name>Aircraft</ejb-name></role-source>
            <cmr-field>
                <cmr-field-name>flightSegments</cmr-field-name>
                <cmr-field-type>java.util.Collection</cmr-field-type>
            </cmr-field>
        </ejb-relationship-role>
        <ejb-relationship-role>
            <ejb-relationship-role-name>flightseg-has-one-aircraft
            </ejb-relationship-role-name>
            <multiplicity>many</multiplicity>
```

```
            <role-source><ejb-name>FlightSeg</ejb-name></role-source>
            <cmr-field>
                <cmr-field-name>aircraft</cmr-field-name>
            </cmr-field>
        </ejb-relationship-role>
    </ejb-relation>
</relationships>
```

Basically, you create an `<ejb-relation>` that specifies the relationship between two objects. Then, you create `<ejb-relationship-role>` declarations for each item involved in the relationship. When you define the relationships, keep in mind that the `<multiplicity>` tag indicates how many of the current item there are in the relationship.

For example, a single aircraft has many flight segments. In the relationship role for the aircraft (where the `<role-source>` tag refers to an `Aircraft` EJB), the multiplicity is one, because there is one aircraft in the relationship. In the role for flight segment, however, the multiplicity is many, because there can be many flight segments for a particular aircraft.

DEPENDENT OBJECTS

Sometimes you want to split an object across multiple tables, but you don't want to expose the various parts of the object as separate entity beans. For example, you might create an order that has line items, but you don't want to create a `LineItem` entity bean. Instead, you want to create a data class that contains the line item data, but is only used on the server. This object is called a dependent object. It's an object that is necessary for storing persistent data, but isn't used by a client.

Note

The EJB specification keeps clients from accessing dependent objects by restricting an entity bean's remote methods. An entity bean's `Remote` interface can't include dependent objects, so there is no way for a client to ever obtain a reference to a dependent object.

An address is another good candidate for a dependent object. A person can have multiple addresses, but an address is hardly the kind of object you want to use as a full-blown EJB. Sun suggests that a good rule of thumb for determining whether an object is a dependent object is whether that object can exist on its own. Certainly, a line item can't exist without an order. An address doesn't exist without a person. A flight segment, on the other hand, *can* exist without an aircraft, so it is not a dependent object.

EJB 2.0 has special support for these dependent objects. Basically, you create an object just like you were writing an EJB, except that you only create the implementation—no Home or Remote interfaces. As with the entity bean implementation, you create abstract accessor methods for the various dependent object fields and relationships, but you don't create any of the `ejbXXX` methods.

Because there is no Home interface for dependent objects, you must define a standard way to create them. You do so by writing a `createXXXX` method in any of the entity beans that can contain the dependent object.

You declare a dependent object in the `ejb-jar.xml` file just like you declare an entity bean. In other words, a dependent object exists in the file as a separate object from an entity bean. In the `ejb-jar.xml` file, the `<enterprise-beans>` tag contains all the EJB declarations. Likewise, the `<dependents>` tag contains the declarations for all the dependent objects. Listing 8.13 shows the declaration for a dependent object.

LISTING 8.13 EXAMPLE DEPENDENT OBJECT DECLARATION

```
<dependents>
    <dependent>
        <dependent-class>usingj2ee.orders.LineItem</dependent--class>
        <dependent-name>LineItem</dependent-name>
        <cmp-field>
            <field-name>productCode</fieldName>
        </cmp-field>
        <cmp-field>
            <field-name>description</fieldName>
        </cmp-field>
        <cmp-field>
            <field-name>quantity</fieldName>
        </cmp-field>
        <cmp-field>
            <field-name>price</fieldName>
        </cmp-field>
    </dependent>
</dependents>
```

You can declare dependent objects to be members of relationships just as you can with entity beans. Of course, the dependent objects are also managed by the container.

The EJBQL language lets you query for dependent objects, just as it does for other objects. For example, you might want to search for all orders with unshipped items. Assuming that you have an `Order` entity bean that contains a number of `OrderLineItem` dependent objects, your query might look something like this:

```
FROM order o, item in o.orderLineItems
WHERE item.shippedDate is null
```

TROUBLESHOOTING

IMPLEMENTATION PROBLEMS

Why do I get errors saying that I don't have an `ejbCreate` method or that the method signature of `ejbCreate` is invalid?

You may have accidentally declared the `ejbCreate` method to have a void type. Because CMP entity beans don't return their primary key but return `null` instead, you might often find yourself declaring the method as `void`, thinking that there is no return value. There *is* a return value, but it should always be `null`.

Why do I get errors complaining about my field variables?

Remember, under EJB 2.0, you don't declare the field variables as part of the class. You just create the accessor methods (which must be abstract), and let the EJB container worry about the fields.

DEPLOYMENT PROBLEMS

Why can't the container find the database columns I'm using?

Some containers, such as WebLogic, require you to map column names to field names in a separate configuration file. Other containers require the field names to have the same name as the column names. Consult the documentation for your EJB container to see what special requirements it has.

Why does the WebLogic server complain about not finding keys for my relationships?

Check the multiplicity settings for your relationships. It's easy to get the values backward. The multiplicity applies to the current object, not the related object. For example, when you create a relationship between one order and many items, you specify the multiplicity for the order to be `one`, and the multiplicity for the items to be `many`.

CHAPTER 9

EJB Transactions

In this chapter

WHY TRANSACTIONS ARE IMPORTANT

When you write a database application, you often take transactions for granted. Transactions are an integral part of database applications, although in simple applications you might not notice transactions taking place because your database connection can be automatically committing the transactions without your knowledge.

A transaction lets you group a set of operations into an all-or-nothing operation. In other words, either the operations all succeed or they all fail. Going back to the example in Chapter 5, "Overview of Enterprise JavaBeans," imagine that you're using an automatic teller machine. The dispensing of the cash and the debiting of your account should be accomplished as a single transaction. You don't want the bank to debit the money from your account if the machine doesn't dispense the cash, and the bank doesn't want you getting cash without your account being debited.

In a simple database application, it's easy to define and control transactions, but when you start dealing with distributed object systems and the possibility of multiple databases, transactions become much more complicated. Suppose you are writing an equipment-scheduling application for an airline. You have flight segments (a flight from one city to the next) and aircraft. In case you're wondering, a flight has a single flight number, but can be made up of several flight segments, which can even be served by different aircraft. An aircraft can only fly on one flight segment at a time, and only one aircraft can serve a particular flight segment. Also, assume that you can get an aircraft from a pool of free aircraft, or grab one from another flight. Now, when you remove an aircraft from the free pool and assign it to a flight, you want both operations to either succeed or fail. Otherwise, if you remove the aircraft from the pool successfully but you fail to assign it to a flight, you've lost track of the aircraft.

If your application is a simple database operation, you can start a transaction, update the free pool, update the flight, and then commit the transaction, as shown in Figure 9.1.

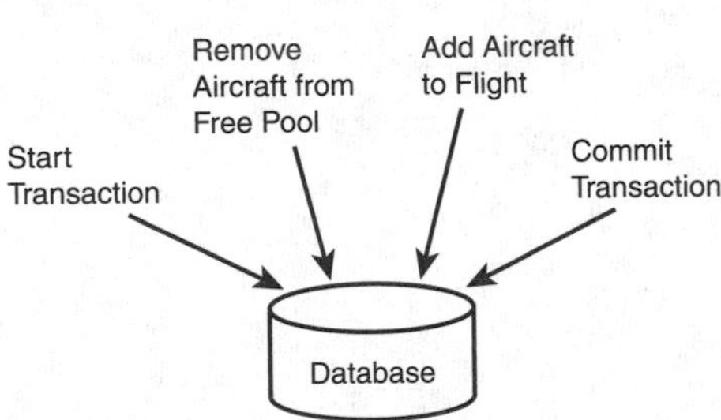

Figure 9.1
In a simple two-tiered application, it's easy to manage database transactions.

Things get more complicated when you start working with distributed objects, however. For the moment, imagine that you don't have an EJB server and instead have a server program managing the pool of free aircraft and another program managing the flight segments. Figure 9.2 shows how the programs interact with the database. Notice that each program has its own connection to the database.

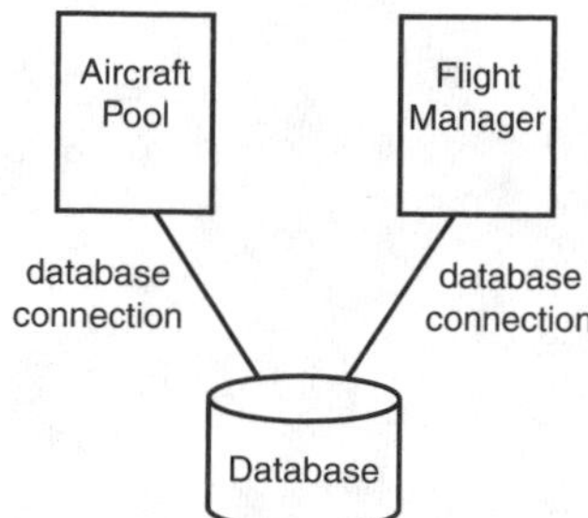

Figure 9.2
In a basic distributed object system, different sets of objects have their own database connections.

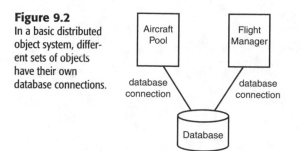

The problem here is, how can you insure that the removal of the flight from the pool and the assignment of the flight to a flight segment take place as a single operation? Obviously, you could back out the first change if the second change fails—that is, return the aircraft to the free pool if you can't assign it to a flight segment. The problem is, you are now talking about separate database transactions. As Figure 9.3 shows, removing the aircraft from the pool is one database transaction, assigning it to a flight segment is another database transaction.

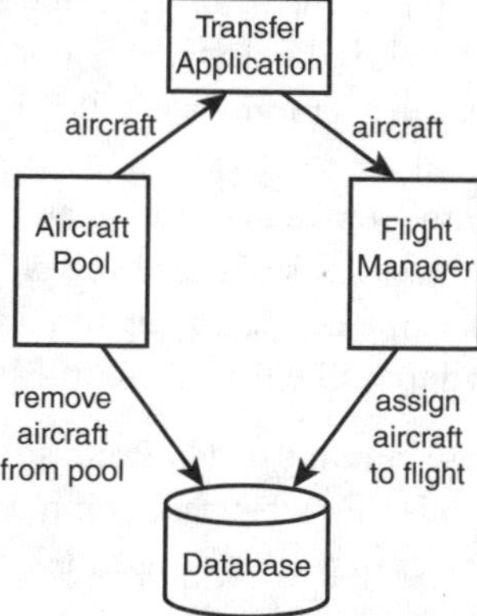

Figure 9.3
Without a transaction coordinator, each operation is a different transaction.

Suppose the second transaction fails. The first transaction has already taken place, so now you must start a third transaction to undo the changes you made in the first one. What happens if that third transaction fails? You are holding onto an aircraft and you have nowhere to put it. The key to transactions in a distributed system is a technique called a *two-phase commit*. A transaction coordinator manages separate database transactions and adds an extra step to the process. For a two-phase commit to work, both the database and the JDBC driver must support two-phase commit.

Now when you try to commit the transaction, the coordinator asks each database connection to prepare to commit. The connections make sure that they can perform the operation and that there would be no errors or locking problems if the transaction was committed. Figure 9.4 illustrates the interaction between the coordinator and the database connections.

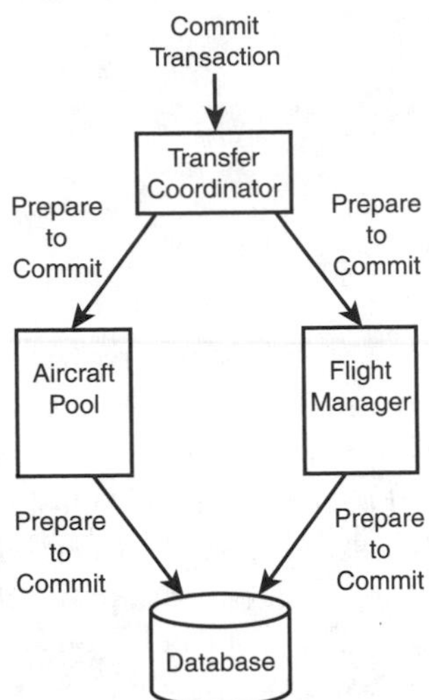

Figure 9.4
The database connection prepares to commit a transaction but doesn't make any changes.

The important thing about the preparation step is that the database promises to commit the transaction if asked no matter what happens. That is, if the database crashes just after it prepares to commit, the database will still carry out the operation when it comes back up, assuming that the transaction coordinator asks it to. After all the database connections involved in the transaction have agreed to commit their part of the transaction, the transaction coordinator tells them to commit the data. If any one of the databases refuses during the preparation step, the transaction coordinator tells them all to abort the operation. It's important to remember that the database doesn't actually make any changes during the first phase (the preparation phase).

The other important thing about the two-phase commit is that it doesn't just apply to database operations. As long as an object understands the two-phase commit protocol, the object can participate in a distributed transaction. For example, you might use the Java Message Service to send a message as part of a database operation. For example, you might want to send a message to the flight planner when you change an assignment. The planner needs to create a new flight plan, after all. Figure 9.5 illustrates the operation, which now has three steps: removing the aircraft from the pool, assigning it to a flight segment, and notifying the flight planner.

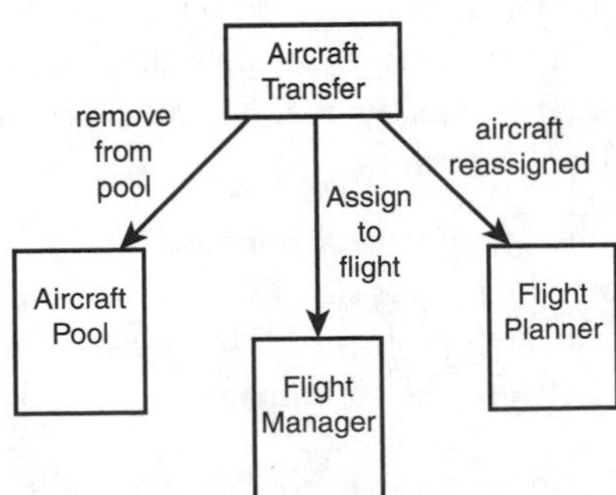

Figure 9.5
You can send a message as part of a distributed transaction.

Again, if any part of the transaction fails, the entire operation fails. If there is a database error assigning an aircraft to a flight segment, the aircraft isn't removed from the pool and the message isn't sent to the flight dispatcher. If there is an error sending a message to the dispatcher, the flight is never removed from the pool or added to the flight segment.

In the world of Enterprise JavaBeans, you can perform both single-phase and two-phase transactions. If a transaction takes place in a single EJB container with a single database, you might end up just doing a single-phase commit (which is considerably faster than a two-phase commit). Sometimes, the objects you operate on can only support a single-phase commit and you must take the risk that part of the transaction might fail. Although you might think this is an extreme disadvantage, it's better than the alternative of not being able to do anything at all!

THE ACID TEST

Transactional operations are usually judged by whether they meet the ACID test, which is a simple set of four criteria that describes the desired properties of a transaction. These properties are atomicity, consistency, isolation, and durability.

ATOMICITY

Atomicity means that all operations in the transaction succeed or they all fail. As you have already seen, if only part of a transaction can succeed, it becomes extremely difficult to maintain data integrity.

CONSISTENCY

No matter what happens, during the transaction, the data is still in a consistent state. Some aspects of consistency are dependent on the program itself and not specifically the transaction coordinator or the database. For example, if a transaction could allow you to remove an aircraft from the free pool and not assign it to a flight, but instead just lose it, that wouldn't leave the data in a consistent state.

ISOLATION

Each transaction appears to be isolated from all other applications. Although two transactions might execute simultaneously, one transaction can't see changes made by another while the transactions are in progress. Another way to look at this is that it appears that transactions always happen serially—one after the other, even if they really occur at the same time.

DURABILITY

When you commit a transaction, the change is durable—it sticks around. You wouldn't get far if your transactions could randomly not stay around. It wouldn't be so bad if you used an automatic teller machine and the debit against your bank account didn't stick around and your balance went back up. The bank, of course, wouldn't be too happy.

WHO STARTS AND ENDS A TRANSACTION?

In the EJB world, a transaction is typically associated with a session and not an entity bean. That is, entity beans don't have any control over when a transaction begins or ends, although an entity bean can signal that the transaction must be rolled back.

Session beans might or might not begin transactions on their own. You can specify that a session bean controls transactions on its own, in which case you must explicitly begin and end a transaction from within the various methods in your bean. When a session bean starts and ends transactions on its own, it's using Bean-Managed Transactions, or BMT.

A session bean can also let the container choose when to begin and end a transaction. You probably already guess this, but when a session bean lets the container handle the initiation and termination of transactions, it is using Container-Managed Transactions, or CMT. When you deploy the session bean, you specify for each session a transaction type value that can be one of the values shown in Table 9.1.

TABLE 9.1 CMT TRANSACTION TYPES

Transaction Type	Meaning
`NotSupported`	If the method is called from within an existing transaction, the transaction is suspended until the method completes.
`Required`	If the method is called from outside a transaction, the container begins a new transaction. If the method is called from within a transaction, the container doesn't need to do anything else.
`RequiresNew`	If the method is called from outside a transaction, the container begins a new transaction. If the method is called from within a transaction, the container suspends the original transaction and begins a new one. The container resumes the old transaction when this method completes.
`Mandatory`	The method must be called from within an existing transaction, otherwise the container throws a `TransactionRequiredException`.
`Supports`	This type indicates that the method doesn't care if it is called from within a transaction or not. The container won't start a new transaction and won't do anything with the current transaction if there is one.
`Never`	This method can never be called from within a transaction. If it is called from within a transaction, the container throws a `RemoteException`.

You might wonder how the container knows whether a method is being called within an existing transaction or not. The transaction manager associates transactions with execution threads. When you think about it, associating transactions with the execution thread makes perfect sense. Each client usually performs a separate transaction and each client has its own thread of execution (even in a distributed object system, each request from a remote client has its own separate thread). A client calls different methods in different beans, but the one thing that remains constant is the execution thread, so why not associate the transaction with the thread?

Transactions don't have to start within the EJB container. A client program can begin a transaction before calling any EJB methods. In fact, a client can start a transaction and then invoke methods on several different EJB servers that are all executed as a single transaction.

Using Container-Managed Transactions

Container-managed transactions are a painless way to define transactions and should be good enough for most situations. The easiest way to use container-managed transactions is to define the transaction types for each method. Each deployment tool has a different way of specifying these types. Figure 9.6 shows how you configure the transaction types in the J2EE SDK `deploytool`.

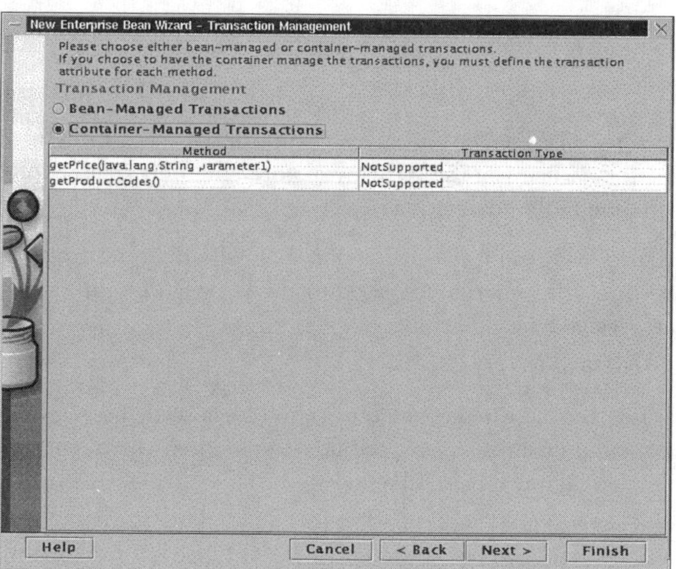

Figure 9.6
The J2EE SDK `deploytool` lets you set the transaction attributes for each session bean method.

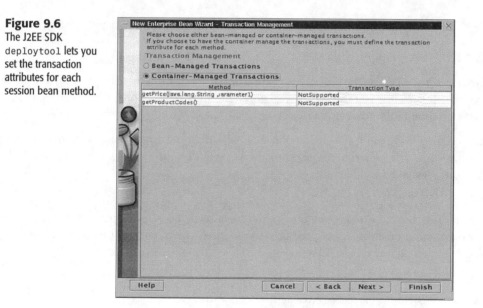

The WebLogic deployment tool takes a similar approach, but you can create multiple groups of transaction permissions. After you select the Method Transactions option for your JAR file and click Add, the deployment tool creates a new transaction group. When you click the transaction group, you see a dialog box like the one shown in Figure 9.7.

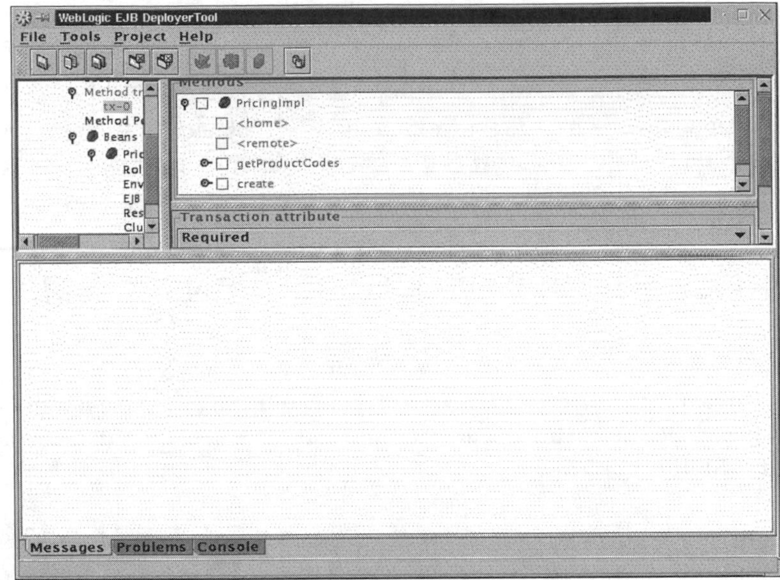

Figure 9.7
After you create a transaction group, setting the transaction types for a method is similar to the J2EE SDK `deploytool`.

Whether you use CMT or BMT, you can't control the transaction by manipulating a database connection. When you use JDBC, you normally roll a transaction back by calling the `rollback` method in the transaction object.

When you use CMT, you roll a transaction back by calling the `setRollbackOnly` method on the session context (another good reason to always hang on to the session context!) In other words, you just make a call like this:

```
context.setRollbackOnly();
```

You can also determine whether the transaction has already been rolled back. For instance, if your transaction involves a time-consuming operation, you might want to skip it if the transaction must be rolled back, like this:

```
if (!context.getRollbackOnly())
{
// Do the time-consuming operation here
}
```

Note

You can only roll a transaction back from a method with a transaction type of `Required`, `RequiresNew`, or `Mandatory`. If the method's transaction type is `Supports`, `NotSupported`, or `Never`, you'll get an `IllegalStateException` when you invoke either `getRollbackOnly` or `setRollbackOnly`.

USING THE SessionSynchronization INTERFACE

The `SessionSynchronization` interface gives your session bean an extra measure of control over its transactions. The interface contains three methods and is defined as shown in Listing 9.1.

LISTING 9.1 INTERFACE DEFINITION FOR SessionSynchronization

```
public interface SessionSynchronization
{
    public void afterBegin();
    public void beforeCompletion();
    public void afterCompletion();
}
```


A session bean can optionally implement the `SessionSynchronization` interface to learn about when a transaction starts and ends. When a session becomes part of a transaction, the container invokes the session's `afterBegin` method. Before the transaction is committed, the container invokes the `beforeCompletion`. All business methods for a particular session bean executed between the call of `afterBegin` and `beforeCompletion` are part of the same transaction context. The container calls `afterCompletion` after the transaction has been committed. You can call `setRollbackOnly` on the `SessionContext` object from within both `afterBegin` and `beforeCompletion`, but because the transaction has already completed when `afterCompletion` is called, you can't roll the transaction from within `afterCompletion`.

Note

Some of the methods in a session bean are called with an unspecified transaction context, meaning you can't count on being able to do any transaction-related operations from within these methods. For example, you shouldn't try to access the database within these methods. The methods that have an unspecified transaction context are `setSessionContext`, `ejbCreate`, `ejbRemove`, `ejbPassivate`, `ejbActivate`, and `afterCompletion`. The session's constructor is also called with an unspecified transaction context.

USING THE JAVA TRANSACTION API (JTA) FOR BEAN-MANAGED TRANSACTIONS

The Java Transaction API (JTA) is a simple API for defining transaction boundaries. The architecture of JTA is similar to JDBC in that it defines an abstract interface, which then accesses an underlying implementation. In this case, you use JTA to control transactions and the JTA classes access the Java Transaction Service (JTS) implementation. You never access the JTS directly, you always use the JTA. The main class you need to know about is the `UserTransaction` class. Keep in mind that an entity bean is not allowed to control its transaction scope at all, so you can only use the `UserTransaction` class from a session bean.

Note

When you create a session bean, you can choose whether the container manages the bean's transactions (that is, CMT) or the bean manages its own transactions (BMT). An entity bean always uses CMT–it never manages its own transactions.

To get a `UserTransaction` object, a session bean can call the `getUserTransaction` method in the `SessionContext` object.

After you have the `UserTransaction` object, you might begin a new transaction by calling the `begin` method, like this:

```
context.getUserTransaction().begin();
```

To explicitly commit the transaction, call the `commit` method:

```
context.getUserTransaction().commit();
```

There are two different ways to roll a transaction back. You can either roll it back immediately by calling `rollback` or you can keep the transaction open but insure that the transaction must roll back by calling `setRollbackOnly`.

Note

When using BMT, you must use the `UserTransaction` object to roll a transaction back. Don't call the `setRollbackOnly` method in the `SessionContext` object. Instead, call `context.getUserTransaction().setRollbackOnly()`.

If you are using EJB 2.0, you can access the `UserTransaction` through JNDI using the name `jta/usertransaction`.

TROUBLESHOOTING

CMT PROBLEMS

Why do I get an error when I call `setRollbackOnly`*?*

Your method probably has a transaction type of `Supports`, `Never`, or `NotSupported`. You can only roll back a transaction when the method's transaction type is `Required`, `RequiresNew`, or `Mandatory`.

Why can't I call `getUserTransaction` *when I use CMT?*

By using CMT you have agreed that you don't want to manage your bean's transaction scope. You shouldn't be using the `UserTransaction` object anyway.

BMT PROBLEMS

Why do I get an error when I call `setRollbackOnly` on the `SessionContext` object?

When using BMT, you should use the `setRollbackOnly` in the `UserTransaction` object (which you get by calling `getUserTransaction` on the `SessionObject`).

Isn't the BMT a subway?

Yes, the Brooklyn-Manhattan Transit Corp. in New York City.

CHAPTER 10

Mapping Objects to a Relational Database

In this chapter

RELATIONAL MODELS VERSUS OBJECT MODELS

When it comes to application development in the business world, the conflict between relational models and object models is one of the biggest headaches. Relational databases are firmly entrenched in most companies. Even startup companies tend to prefer relational databases to some of the less-common alternatives, such as object databases.

You can generally find more tools available for relational databases—from schema managers to report generators. Relational databases are more language-independent. You can usually store data with a Perl script and read it back out with a Visual Basic program. Object databases and other object persistence mechanisms aren't as language-independent. You might be able to use C++ to write an object and Java to read it back out, but you're probably not going to be hitting the database with a Visual Basic client any time soon.

From Chapter 2, "A Quick Primer on SQL," you already know that you organize relational data into tables. You create relationships between tables using various key values. For instance, an address might have a `person_id` column that refers to the primary key for a row in the `person` table. These column values are called *foreign keys* because the value refers to a primary key in another table.

A database can have three types of relationships: one-to-one, one-to-many, and many-to-many. In a *one-to-one* relationship, a row in one table can be associated with a single row in another table. In a *one-to-many* relationship, a row in one table can be associated with several rows in another table, but the each row in the second table can only be associated with a single row in the first table. In a *many-to-many* relationship, a row in one table can be associated with several rows in another table, and a row in the second table can be associated with several rows in the first table. In the relational world, you create a many-to-many relationship using a third table called a *link table*. Each table has a one-to-many relationship with the link table.

Figure 10.1 illustrates the three kinds of relationships.

In the object world, you have many more options for creating relationships. Obviously, you still have one-to-one, one-to-many, and many-to-many relationships. You also have various data structures—stacks, lists, queues, trees, and maps. Although you can represent these structures in a relational database, it's not always easy. For example, in Java, you can have a vector containing objects of several different types. How do you represent that in a relational database? You don't know ahead of time what different types are in the vector, so how do you know what tables to query? You might end up representing the vector as a table whose elements are a table name and some kind of key value for the table. In any case, there's no pretty solution.

You have a similar problem when it comes to inheritance. Recently, several databases have begun to support table-level inheritance, but generally, relational databases don't support inheritance directly. The problem, then, is how to map a hierarchy of classes to one or more relational tables. You have three choices when it comes to modeling inheritance: using a single table, using one main table and smaller subclass tables, or using one full table per subclass.

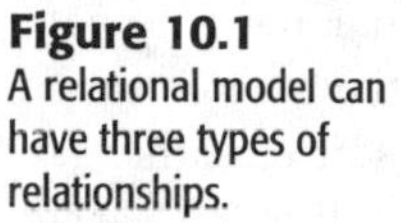

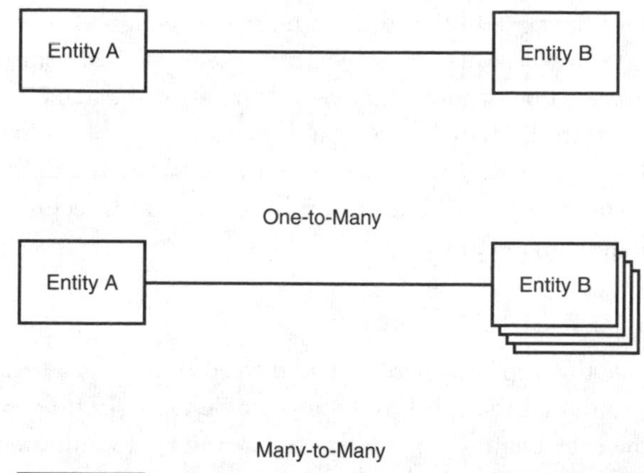

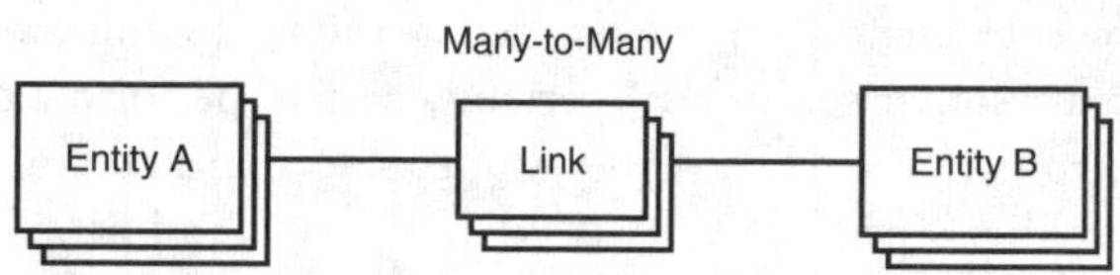

Figure 10.1
A relational model can have three types of relationships.

Using Separate Tables for Subclasses

One of the most intuitive ways you can store subclasses is to store each subclass in a separate table. For instance, you might have a `Person` class that maps to a `person` table with `first_name`, `middle_name`, and `last_name` columns. If you create a subclass called `Soldier` with an additional `rank` attribute, you create a separate `soldier` table with `first_name`, `middle_name`, `last_name`, and `rank` columns. The advantage of this arrangement is that you can grab all the data for a soldier from the `soldier` table by making a single query.

Figure 10.2 illustrates the single-class-per-table architecture.

Person

First Name	Middle Name	Last Name
•	•	•
•	•	•
•	•	•

Soldier

First Name	Middle Name	Last Name	Rank
•	•	•	•
•	•	•	•
•	•	•	•

Figure 10.2
You can store each subclass in a completely separate table.

The problem with using totally separate tables is that it's difficult to perform a query to get every person. You must now get all the rows from the `person` table and all the rows from the `soldier` table. Things get even worse when you try to set up relationships. For example, suppose a person can have one or more addresses. In relational database terminology, `person` has a one-to-many relationship with `address`, and the `address` table contains a foreign key to the `person` table. Now that `person` and `soldier` are two separate tables, how can `address` have a relationship to both of them? The answer is, it can't. This technique breaks down when it comes to foreign key relationships.

Mapping Subclasses to a Single Table

Now, suppose you take the opposite extreme and instead of having separate tables for each subclass, you decide to put all the subclasses into a single table. In other words, the `person` table also includes the `rank` column for soldiers and a column to indicate what kind of object is in a particular row (person or soldier). It's certainly easy to perform a query for all people, you just select all the rows in the table. If you want to select all soldiers, just select all rows whose object type is soldier. Speed-wise, it's easier to query for all people because you only need to query a single table. It might take the database longer to fetch all soldiers because it must weed out the person objects that aren't soldiers, but on the whole, this table structure should be more efficient than using separate tables.

Figure 10.3 illustrates the single table for all subclasses architecture.

Figure 10.3
You can group all the subclasses into a single table.

Person

Person Type	First Name	Middle Name	Last Name	Rank
•	•	•	•	•
•	•	•	•	•
•	•	•	•	•

From a relationship standpoint, because all the data is in the same table, the `address` table just needs a foreign key in the `person` table and the relationship works.

Although everything looks rosy so far with the single-table approach, there are a few unfortunate holes. First of all, you can't specify that a subclass column is not null. In other words, you might want to specify that a soldier must have a rank, so you want to declare the column as NOT NULL. Unfortunately, because the table can contain persons and soldiers, and only soldiers can have a rank, the `rank` column must allow nulls.

Although you can easily create relationships from other tables to the `person` table, you can't define relationships between other tables and soldiers. In other words, any time you define a relationship between another table and the `person` table, the relationship must apply to all members of the table. After all, the database only keeps track of the foreign key columns; you can't tell it to create a foreign key only to rows in the `person` table with a specific object type.

The other issue that comes up with the single-table model is that you might end up with a lot of wasted space. If you have a number of subclasses with many fields, you find that the majority of columns in the table are unused. For example, if your base class has 5 columns and you create 5 subclasses each with 4 columns, then a given row in the table uses 9 columns—the 5 base columns and its 4 subclass columns. That leaves 16 columns unused—4 subclasses with 4 subclass columns each.

Neither of these problems are show-stoppers, however. They only mean that you sacrifice some storage space and relational integrity checking in the name of performance. If your objects manage the relationships properly, you can use the single-table model quite well.

Splitting Subclass Data into Separate Tables

Your other choice in splitting the data is to put the common data in one table and the individual subclass data into another table. For example, the `person` table might have `first_name`, `middle_name`, `last_name`, and `object_type`. The `soldier` table has fields that make up a foreign key into the `person` table (which might very well be `first_name`, `middle_name`, and `last_name`) and the `rank` column.

Figure 10.4 illustrates the table-splitting architecture.

Figure 10.4
You can split an object to span multiple tables.

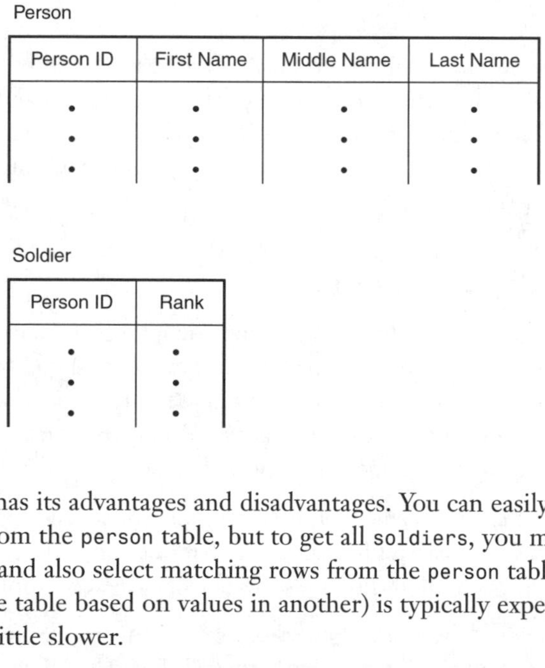

Person

Person ID	First Name	Middle Name	Last Name
⋮	⋮	⋮	⋮

Soldier

Person ID	Rank
⋮	⋮

This method has its advantages and disadvantages. You can easily locate all people by selecting all rows from the `person` table, but to get all `soldiers`, you must select all rows from the `soldier` table and also select matching rows from the `person` table. A join operation (selecting data in one table based on values in another) is typically expensive, so this technique tends to be a little slower.

You do get some nice benefits in exchange for your sacrifice in performance. You don't waste space with columns that have nothing to do with the object. You only have rows in the `soldier` table for soldiers. You can create relationships to subclasses by defining foreign keys into the subclass table (you can't accidentally relate something to a person that should only be related to a soldier). You can also define subclass fields as being NOT NULL. That is, you can define the `rank` column as NOT NULL because you know only soldier data is stored in the `soldier` table.

Although splitting the objects across multiple tables seems like the best approach from a relational-integrity standpoint, it's the slowest of the three approaches. Your best bet is to try to group the data into a single table. If the table becomes unwieldy, try splitting some of the subclasses into a separate table. You can actually mix the single-table and split-object techniques together, where some subclasses have their own tables for the subclass fields, and others reside only in the main table.

PERFORMANCE ISSUES

One of the biggest problems with using objects and a relational database is that you access data differently with objects. For example, suppose you want to make a list of all people who live in Georgia. In the object world, you loop through your container of people, call `getAddress` on each person and then call `getState` on the address object to see whether it's 'GA'.

In the relational world, you do a query like this:

```
SELECT person.* from person, address
where address.person_id = person.person_id
    and address.state = 'GA'
```

Both of these techniques are reasonably efficient. Now, when you use an object-to-relational mapping, things get ugly. Once again, you fetch a container of people and you call `getAddress`. This time, however, every time you call `getAddress`, you make a call to the database to get the address for the person, resulting in a huge number of calls to the database.

The problem here is that in the object world, you tend to skip from object to object. In the relational world, you tend to deal with large groups of rows, and you tend to look for relationships between various groups all at once.

One thing that helps speeds up an object-to-relational mapping is the use of caching. After you read an address object, it's in the cache. The next time you call `getAddress` on a person and the address is in the cache, you don't hit the database. Of course, if the address isn't already in the cache, you must go out to the database. When you use a cache, your programs tend to speed up over time as more and more data gets cached.

Caching can be tricky, of course. When you have multiple threads performing separate transactions, you must be very careful to make sure that one thread doesn't affect another's transaction. Typically, you end up having the same object cached multiple times.

The other thing that helps is the ability to perform custom queries. Some object-to-relational mapping tools let you specify a query in terms of object, but then query the database using an optimized SQL query. In other words, rather than looping through a container of people, grabbing the address, and checking the value, you create a query similar to the SQL query, only working with the object values. In other words, something like this:

```
select person where person.address.state = 'GA'
```

Using an Object Database

Object databases are a nice alternative to relational databases. You might have trouble finding third-party tools to work with the databases (Access, Visual Basic, and Crystal Reports might not work), but with the addition of ODBC bridges to some of these databases, you might find everything you need.

An object database isn't constrained by the relational way of doing things. It doesn't need to keep data in tables. It can arrange the data in many interesting combinations and still give you the power to search. Just as relational databases have a standard query language called SQL, object databases have a standard query language called OQL, which is similar to SQL.

Some of the popular object databases are Gemstone (`www.gemstone.com`), Versant (`www.versant.com`), and Poet (`www.poet.com`). Some of these vendors make a plug-in CMP engine for various J2EE application servers; others, such as Gemstone, provide their own J2EE environment.

Using the TopLink Object-to-Relational Mapper

TopLink for Java is one of a small set of industrial-strength Object-to-Relational mapping libraries for Java. It is available from WebGain (`www.webgain.com`). TopLink provides caching capabilities, support for inheritance, and a wide variety of mapping capabilities for attributes and relationships.

In addition to the standard TopLink for Java library, which is typically used in non-EJB applications, TopLink makes a CMP engine for both WebLogic and WebSphere (with the possibility of more to come). You can also use TopLink for bean-managed persistence if you aren't using WebLogic or WebSphere. Keep in mind that TopLink for WebLogic is a separate product from TopLink for Java and is also separate from the built-in CMP that comes with WebLogic.

TopLink for Java consists of two main parts: the Mapping Workbench (a graphical tool for setting up the object-to-relational mapping) and the TopLink for Java Foundation Library (the runtime library). Both of these parts share one main piece of information: the project file. The project file contains the complete description of the mapping between the objects and the database, including the type of database and possibly even the login information.

After you start the Mapping Workbench and ask it to start a new project, you select the database you want to map. The window on the right lets you enter the information about the type and location of the database as well as the login information. Figure 10.5 shows an example database setup.

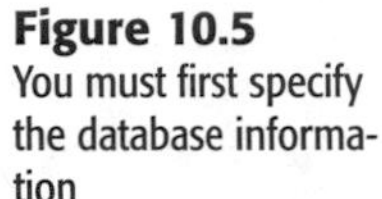

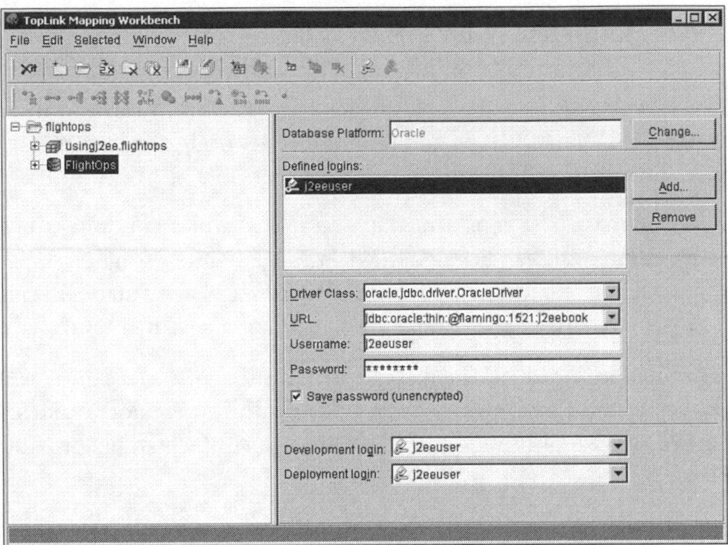

Figure 10.5
You must first specify the database information

After you specify the database information, you can login to the database by highlighting the database icon and then choosing Selected, Log In from the main menu bar. After you login, you can choose Selected, Add Existing Tables, From Database to import existing table definitions, or create your own table. TopLink is flexible enough to create table definitions and even class definitions for you!

After you select some database tables, you can map the tables to Java classes (or let the Mapping Workbench generate the classes for you). Listing 10.1 shows an example `Aircraft` class that uses the same table as the example in Chapter 8, "Using Container-Managed Persistence."

> **Note**
>
> To generate a class automatically, just right-click a table, select the Generate Descriptors and Classes menu, and then choose the Selected Tables option.

LISTING 10.1 SOURCE CODE FOR `Aircraft.java`

```
package usingj2ee.flightops;

import java.rmi.*;
import java.util.*;

import TOPLink.Public.Indirection.*;

public class Aircraft
{
    public String aircraftId;
    public String aircraftType;
    public int firstCapacity;
    public int businessCapacity;
    public int coachCapacity;
```

```
public ValueHolderInterface flightSegments;

public String getAircraftId()
{
    return aircraftId;
}

public String getAircraftType()
{
    return aircraftType;
}

public void setAircraftType(String anAircraftType)
{
    aircraftType = anAircraftType;
}

public int getFirstCapacity()
{
    return firstCapacity;
}

public void setFirstCapacity(int newCapacity)
{
    firstCapacity = newCapacity;
}

public int getBusinessCapacity()
{
    return businessCapacity;
}

public void setBusinessCapacity(int newCapacity)
{
    businessCapacity = newCapacity;
}

public int getCoachCapacity()
{
    return coachCapacity;
}

public void setCoachCapacity(int newCapacity)
{
    coachCapacity = newCapacity;
}

public void addFlightSegment(FlightSegment flightSeg)
{
    getFlightSegments().addElement(flightSeg);
    flightSeg.setAircraft(this);
}

public void removeFlightSegment(FlightSegment flightSeg)
{
    getFlightSegments().removeElement(flightSeg);
```

LISTING 10.1 CONTINUED

```
            flightSeg.setAircraft(null);
        }

        public Vector getFlightSegments()
        {
            return (Vector) flightSegments.getValue();
        }

        public void setFlightSegments(Vector newSegments)
        {
            flightSegments.setValue(newSegments);
        }
}
```

The `Aircraft` class in Listing 10.1 does little more than manage its own attributes. The only part of it that has any connection to TopLink is the `ValueHolderInterface` class that contains the related flight segments. TopLink uses a lazy-fetch algorithm for related objects. It doesn't fetch the object until you try to access it. In other words, when you read in an `Aircraft`, you don't read in all the related flight segments until you try to access them. To support a lazy fetch, TopLink needs a way to find out when you ask for a related object, hence the `ValueHolderInterface`.

Listing 10.2 shows the `FlightSegment` class that is the partner class for the `Aircraft` class. Notice that it too only uses the `ValueHolderInterface` and nothing else related to TopLink.

LISTING 10.2 SOURCE CODE FOR `FlightSegment.java`

```
package usingj2ee.flightops;

import java.rmi.*;
import java.util.Date;

import TOPLink.Public.Indirection.*;

/** Defines the methods you can call on a FlightSeg object */

public class FlightSegment
{
    public String flightNumber;
    public String origin;
    public String destination;
    public Date leaves;
    public Date arrives;
    public int firstBookings;
    public int businessBookings;
    public int coachBookings;
    public ValueHolderInterface aircraftHolder;

    public String getFlightNumber()
    {
        return flightNumber;
    }
```

```
public void setFlightNumber(String aFlightNumber)
{
    flightNumber = aFlightNumber;
}

public String getOrigin()
{
    return origin;
}

public void setOrigin(String anOrigin)
{
    origin = anOrigin;
}

public String getDestination()
{
    return destination;
}

public void setDestination(String aDestination)
{
    destination = aDestination;
}

public Date getLeaves()
{
    return leaves;
}

public void setLeaves(Date leavesDate)
{
    leaves = leavesDate;
}

public Date getArrives()
{
    return arrives;
}

public void setArrives(Date arrivesDate)
{
    arrives = arrivesDate;
}

public int getFirstBookings()
{
    return firstBookings;
}

public void setFirstBookings(int newBookings)
{
    firstBookings = newBookings;
}
```

LISTING 10.2 CONTINUED

```
    public int getBusinessBookings()
    {
        return businessBookings;
    }

    public void setBusinessBookings(int newBookings)
    {
        businessBookings = newBookings;
    }

    public int getCoachBookings()
    {
        return coachBookings;
    }

    public void setCoachBookings(int newBookings)
    {
        coachBookings = newBookings;
    }

    public Aircraft getAircraft()
    {
        return (Aircraft) aircraftHolder.getValue();
    }

    public void setAircraft(Aircraft aircraft)
    {
        aircraftHolder.setValue(aircraft);
    }
}
```

So far, so good. You have two classes that are very simple and contain no database access code whatsoever. You can now use the Mapping Workbench class to create the mapping between these classes and the database. You might need to add the classpath for these classes to the TopLink project. When you do, you should see the package show up on the left side of the screen just above your database.

Note

The tables used in this example are the same as the tables in Chapter 8. You must also configure a reference to the database. TopLink must be able to read the table definitions from the database.

When you right-click the package name, you have the option to add classes. Figure 10.6 shows the screen where you specify which classes you want to add to the project.

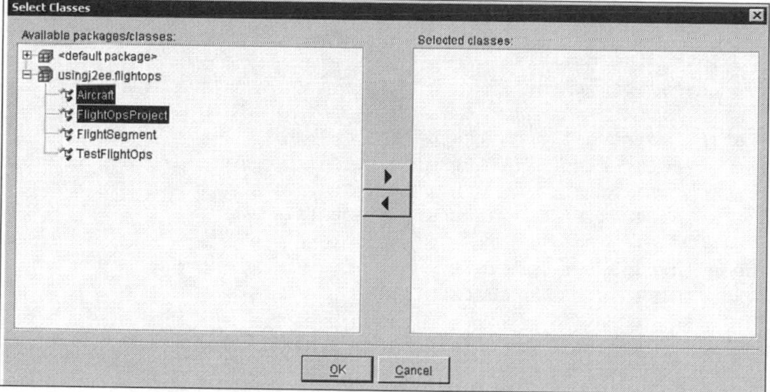

Figure 10.6 Tell TopLink which classes you want to map.

After you add the classes, you can expand the class definition in the tree on the left. You can then create attribute mappings (right-click an attribute and select Map As or use one of the toolbar icons).

After you have created your mappings and saved the project, ask the Mapping Workbench to create a Java class representing the project. Choose File, Export Project to Java Source. This creates a class that you can use in your program to read-in the configuration information. The Java class is the easiest way to manage the information because you can just put it in a JAR file with the rest of your classes.

Listing 10.3 shows a Java program that uses TopLink to read values from the database.

LISTING 10.3 SOURCE CODE FOR `TestFlightOps.java`

```
package usingj2ee.flightops;

import java.util.*;

import TOPLink.Public.Sessions.*;
import TOPLink.Public.Expressions.*;
import TOPLink.Public.QueryFramework.*;

public class TestFlightOps
{
    public static void main(String[] args)
    {
// The directory where the TopLink license is stored (you must have this)
        String licenseFilePath = "f:\\TOPLink";

// Load the project information from the generated Project class file
        Project project = new FlightOpsProject();

// Create a new database session
        DatabaseSession session = project.createDatabaseSession();

// Tell the session where to locate the license file
        session.getProject().getLogin().setLicensePath(licenseFilePath);
```

LISTING 10.3 CONTINUED

```
// Login to the database
        session.login();

// Get all aircraft from the database
        Vector aircraft = session.readAllObjects(Aircraft.class);

        Enumeration e = aircraft.elements();

// Loop through the aircraft
        while (e.hasMoreElements())
        {
            Aircraft ac = (Aircraft) e.nextElement();

// Get all the flight segments
            Vector flightSegs = ac.getFlightSegments();

            System.out.println(ac.getAircraftId()+" ("+ac.getAircraftType()+
                ")");

            Enumeration fs = flightSegs.elements();

// Loop through the flight segments
            while (fs.hasMoreElements())
            {
                FlightSegment seg = (FlightSegment) fs.nextElement();

                System.out.println(seg.getFlightNumber()+" From: "+
                    seg.getOrigin()+" To: "+seg.getDestination()+" on "+
                    seg.getLeaves());
            }
            System.out.println();
        }
    }
}
```

Notice that you haven't seen any SQL code in any of the Java classes. In fact, you hardly do any work at all to access database objects. TopLink really makes things easy for you.

TROUBLESHOOTING

MAPPING WORKBENCH PROBLEMS

Why can't the Mapping Workbench find my database tables?

You probably haven't told Mapping Workbench where to locate the database, or TopLink can't find the JDBC driver for your database.

Why can't I see any of my classes in the Mapping Workbench?

Your classes probably aren't in the classpath. Just add them to the system classpath.

EXECUTION PROBLEMS

Why does TopLink complain that there isn't a valid license?

Apart from having an invalid or expired license file, you might have provided the wrong pathname when you specified the license file path. Remember that you only specify the directory name and not the name of the license file itself.

CHAPTER 11

Debugging an EJB

In this chapter

WHY DEBUGGING IS TOUGH

Server-side programs are often tougher to debug than GUI programs. Although a GUI application can be more complex in terms of code structure and callbacks, server-side applications that are hosted by an application server are more difficult to debug because they are being hosted by another program.

If you want to debug a standalone Java program, you can usually start it up in a debugger and start tracing right from the start. When you need to debug a J2EE server component (EJB, servlet, or JSP), you must find a way to use a debugger with your J2EE environment. It gets even tougher when you want to debug a JSP because you must first locate the servlet that was generated from the JSP and then debug it.

Server-side programs tend to have more threading problems and more database locking problems because they usually perform multiple services simultaneously. One person running an application is unlikely to try to edit the same record in two different windows, but two people might try to use the same server to edit the same record.

USING LOG FILES TO DEBUG AN APPLICATION

At one time, there were no symbolic debuggers. You couldn't bring up the source code and step through one line at a time, printing out variable values as the program changed them. The only thing you could do was write out debugging statements to indicate what the program was doing.

Believe it or not, logging is still one of the most common ways to debug a program. Debuggers, although useful, often interfere with the debugging process in a number of ways. With other languages, such as C++, programs could behave significantly differently when running a debugger. It is not uncommon for a C++ program to run fine under a debugger and crash without the debugger.

Logging lets you display information at different points in the program without interfering too much with the overall running of the program. Obviously, if you spend too much time writing to log files, your program will slow down, but overall, logging is an excellent way to locate bugs.

> **Note**
>
> The log4j package, available at `http://jakarta.apache.org` is a nice logging package that is easy to use. You can also find a simple logging package on the download page at `http://www.wutka.com`.

USING `System.out` AND `System.err`

In a standalone Java program, you frequently write debugging information to `System.out` and `System.err`. When you call the `printStackTrace` method in a `Throwable`, for example, the stack trace goes to `System.err` unless you specify otherwise.

Because server-side J2EE components run inside a container, messages you write to `System.out` and `System.err` won't necessarily appear on your screen. Exactly where the messages appear depends on the application server.

Not all application servers support the use of `System.out` and `System.err`, so don't be surprised if you're using one that doesn't.

Logging to a File

When all else fails, you can always open a file and write log messages to it. Remember, if you close the file after writing, make sure you open it again with the append option set to true. That is, make sure that you don't overwrite the existing file, otherwise you'll lose the previous log message every time you write a new one.

Note

You can't write to a file from an Enterprise JavaBean; that's forbidden by the EJB specification. Of course, if you're just debugging, and your EJB container doesn't stop you from writing to a file, go ahead and do it. Just don't forget to take out the debugging code when you're done.

Using Exceptions to Trace Execution

Sometimes when you're debugging, you want to find out what routine called a particular method. You could throw an exception, but you don't want to stop executing the method; you just want to write a log message indicating who called the method. For instance, one class might be calling a method with bad values and you want to locate the offending class.

You can throw an exception and catch it immediately to get an instant snapshot of the current thread's call stack, like this:

```
try
{
    throw new Exception("dummy");
}
catch (Exception exc)
{
    System.out.println("This method was called from:");
    exc.printStackTrace(System.out);
}
```

This technique isn't the prettiest or fastest thing in the world, but sometimes it's the only choice you have.

Tip

Using a Just-In-Time (JIT) compiler keeps the `printStackTrace` method from determining the exact line number where an exception occurred. You can turn off the JIT with either `-nojit` for the Java 1.1 JRE, or `-Djava.compiler=NONE` under Java 1.2. Other Java implementations might have similar options.

USING A DEBUGGER

Many kinds of debuggers exist for Java. The JDK comes with a command-line debugger called `jdb`. Many people find `jdb` painful to use, because it isn't a graphical debugger like you find in a Java Development Environment.

Many times, however, you're working on a server where you might not have access to a graphical environment anyway. When you have a lot of machines stored away in a machine room somewhere and you can't use X-Windows because of firewall restrictions, you might need to resort to using telnet to access the machines. If you're using telnet, `jdb` is probably your best bet.

Tip

If you can't use X-Windows because of firewall restrictions, you might try Virtual Network Computing (VNC) from `http://www.uk.research.att.com/vnc`. VNC often lets you go through firewalls that don't allow X traffic. It can also let you access a Windows NT machine the same way PCAnywhere does.

In general, there are two ways to debug a Java program: Start the program from a debugger, or run the Java program with remote debugging enabled and attach a debugger to the program. The advantage of remote debugging is that you don't need to figure out what class to run at startup. You let the server go through its normal startup and then attach the debugger and start running.

DEBUGGING AN ENTERPRISE JAVABEAN

Debugging an EJB can be a simple task, or it can be a nightmare. Some EJB containers allow you to use a debugger easily, while others require you to jump through hoops. Some containers even come with their own debuggers that can plug right into the beans almost effortlessly. For most containers, however, you must use a fairly standard debugging technique. Basically, you put the Java Virtual Machine into debugging mode and then attach a remote debugger to the program.

DEBUGGING UNDER JDK 1.2

To use remote debugging with any Java program, you must include the `-debug` flag in the `java` command. Most Java 1.1 Virtual Machines automatically turn off the Just-In-Time compiler when they see `-debug`, but the standard Java2 JVM does not. When you use Java2, you must include the `-Djava.compiler=NONE` flag before the `-debug` flag.

Also, turning on debug mode seems to mess up the built-in classpaths for the JVM, so you must specify a special boot classpath with `-Xbootclasspath`. The boot classpath must include the `rt.jar` file from Java's `jre/lib` directory and `tools.jar` from Java's `lib` directory.

If you're using the J2EE Reference Implementation from Sun, you can just make a copy of the `j2ee.bat` file and insert the debugging options into the Java command line (the line that starts with `%JAVACMD%`). I call my copy `j2eedebug.bat`. Whenever I want to debug, I start the server with `j2eedebug` instead of `j2ee`.

When the J2EE server starts, you should see a line giving you an agent password, as shown in Figure 11.1.

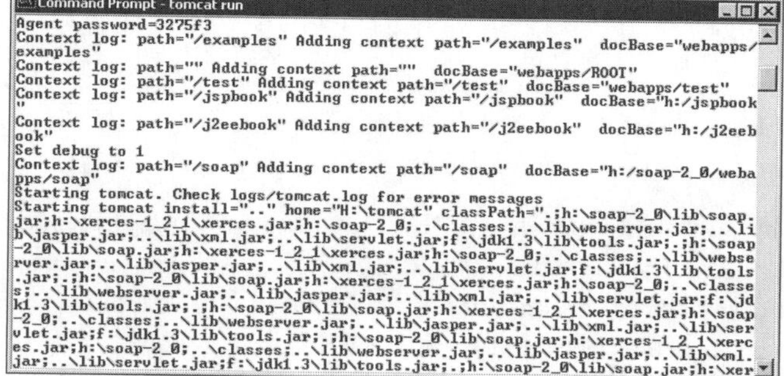

Figure 11.1
The agent password is a code that debuggers can use to access the Java Virtual Machine.

Now, to run `jdb`, just type

```
jdb -host localhost -password xxxx
```

Use the agent password from the JVM startup instead of *xxxx*, of course. You should now see a screen like the one shown in Figure 11.2.

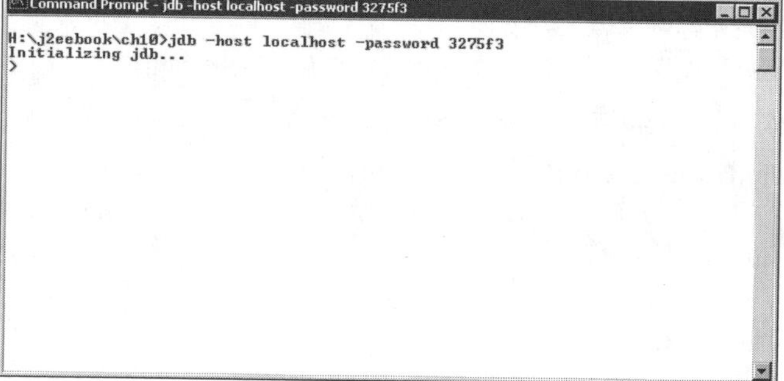

Figure 11.2
The Java Debugger can connect to a JVM running in debug mode.

PART I

CH 11

DEBUGGING UNDER JDK 1.3

JDK 1.3 introduces a new debugging architecture and requires slightly different parameters. Instead of using the `-debug` and `-Xbootclasspath` options, you use the following list of options: `-Xdebug -Xnoagent -Djava.compiler=NONE -Xrunjdwp:transport=dt_shmem,address=`*`debugname`*`,server=y,suspend=n`.

The `address=`*`debugname`* option gives the name of the debugging session that you specify when you run JDB.

Unlike the JDK 1.2 version of the debugger, you don't need to wait for the agent password before you begin debugging. You just type

```
jdb -attach debugname
```

For example, if you specify `j2ee` for the `debugname`, you start the debugger with the command

```
jdb -attach j2ee
```

Although `jdb` is a reasonably functional debugger, it is still a reflection of Sun's Unix heritage; it's not a graphically-oriented debugger. You can find other debugging tools for remote debugging that are much easier to use.

If you use IBM's implementation of JDK 1.3, you can use a graphical debugger called iCat. Kawa, the excellent Java IDE from Allaire (`www.allaire.com`), supports remote debugging, as does the Forte IDE from Sun and the Forte-based NetBeans IDE (`www.netbeans.org`). You can also use a debugger called Jswat, available at `http://www.bluemarch.com/java/jswat`.

TROUBLESHOOTING

STARTING A DEBUGGING VM

Why does my JDK 1.2 implementation complain when I try to use the `-debug` *flag?*

You probably didn't turn off the Just-In-Time (JIT) compiler. Most Java implementations can't run the debugger when the JIT is active. Not only must you disable the JIT, but you must usually disable it on the command-line before the `-debug` options.

Why does JDK 1.2 complain about not being able to find tools when I use the `-debug` *flag?*

You must include the `-Xbootclasspath` on the command line when you use the `-debug` flag. Make sure you include the `lib\tools.jar` and the `jre\lib\rt.jar` files (including the complete path name, such as `c:\jdk1.2.2\lib\tools.jar`).

ATTACHING A DEBUGGER

I started my Java Virtual Machine in debug mode; why does my debugger complain that the VM isn't in debug mode?

Some of the newer debuggers require JPDA (Java Platform Debugger Architecture), which doesn't come with JDK 1.2, although it is standard with JDK 1.3. You can download the JPDA extension for JDK 1.2 from `http://java.sun.com`.

Why doesn't the Java VM recognize my agent password?

Although this is a rare occurrence, it usually happens because the debugger is trying to connect to the wrong host. If you're trying to connect to the local host, either using the name `localhost` or the address 127.0.0.1, then you probably just entered the password incorrectly.

CHAPTER 12

EJB Design

In this chapter

CLIENT ACCESS TO ENTERPRISE JAVABEANS

Like it or not, how your clients access your Enterprise JavaBeans has some effect on the design of your EJB. Ideally, you want to design your enterprise beans to be immune to changing client designs. That is, if you decide to write a new client that accesses data in a drastically different way, you don't want to change any EJBs. It's the same way in the database world. After you set up your database schema, you don't want to rearrange the data just because you must access it differently.

You can take steps to make your EJBs as flexible as possible, but don't be disappointed if you eventually find yourself redesigning some of the beans or adding new beans. As you often find with applications, the act of developing the software reveals new and different ways to use the data that no one had ever thought about.

The biggest thing to keep in mind when you design your Enterprise JavaBean interfaces is that remote method calls are very expensive in terms of time. You want to limit the number of times a client must invoke a method on an EJB. For example, if you have a `Person` EJB that has `getFirstName`, `getMiddleName`, and `getLastName` methods, a client that displays these names must make three separate remote method calls.

If you manage transactions from the client, you're really asking for trouble. The transaction manager must make several remote method calls to coordinate the transaction with the EJB container. Now you aren't just incurring expensive overhead for the calls to your remote methods—you're also losing a lot of time coordinating the transaction.

The problem here is, you seem to be stuck either way. If you call the methods individually and let the container manage the transaction, then every time you invoke a remote method, you start a new transaction. Starting a transaction involves some additional overhead. If you manage the transaction yourself, of course, you have the overhead of distributed transaction management. It seems like you can't win.

This is one of the reasons for having session beans. Rather than accessing an entity bean directly, you go through a session bean. The session bean invokes the methods you want and then returns the data you want. All the transaction management happens in the container, and the transaction begins when you invoke the method on the session bean. You minimize the overhead for remote method calls and also for transaction management.

One of the subtler points of EJB is that method calls between Enterprise beans are more expensive than normal method calls, even if both beans are running in the same Java Virtual Machine. Many EJB containers "marshall" parameters even for local method invocation. *Marshalling* is a process in which you put the data into a form where it can be transmitted over a connection (usually a network connection). For example, when you invoke a remote method, the stub marshalls your parameters and sends them to the skeleton, which unmarshalls them. When the server returns a value, the skeleton marshalls the results and sends them to the stub, which unmarshalls them. When you use CORBA, the process is the same, only the format of the marshalled data changes.

The reason the marshalling happens, even within the same JVM, is that EJBs always communicate with each other through Remote interfaces, which usually use the marshalling routine no matter what. Because marshalling imposes such a big performance cost, some EJB containers have code to optimize the method invocations. These optimizations usually involve copying parameters instead of marshalling them. In other words, when the container detects that both classes are running in the same JVM, it makes a simple copy of the parameters and performs a normal method invocation rather than using marshalling.

Copying is still a little more expensive than just invoking the method with the original parameters. The container can't just pass the parameters as they are because two beans might end up with references to the same object while they participate in separate transactions. The EJB specification specifically requires the containers to pass all parameters by value—and when it comes to objects, make a copy of the object. Remember, Java normally passes parameters by value, but when it comes to objects, the "value" is the reference to the object. You can't change the reference itself, but you can change the contents. The EJB specification, however, requires the container to pass the entire object by value, not just the object reference. That being said, keep in mind that even local method calls between EJBs are more expensive than a typical method call.

So the things you need to minimize are client-managed transactions, remote method calls, and EJB-to-EJB method calls.

SESSION BEANS VERSUS ENTITY BEANS

By now, you already have a good concept of the difference between a session bean and an entity bean. The question now is, how do you go about using them from a client? Furthermore, do you even need both types of beans?

Typically, your clients don't access entity beans directly. Some EJB architects make this a hard and fast rule; others aren't as restrictive. The main reason you don't access entity beans directly is that you generally need to invoke several methods on an entity bean to perform an operation. This would require you to manage the transaction from the client, which is not very efficient.

Another reason you don't want to use entity beans directly is that the entity beans typically represent data objects but might not contain all the necessary business rules. Going back to the standard three-tier architecture model, you might consider entity beans to be part of the data layer instead of the business layer, as shown in Figure 12.1.

Figure 12.1
Entity beans can, in some situations, be part of the data layer.

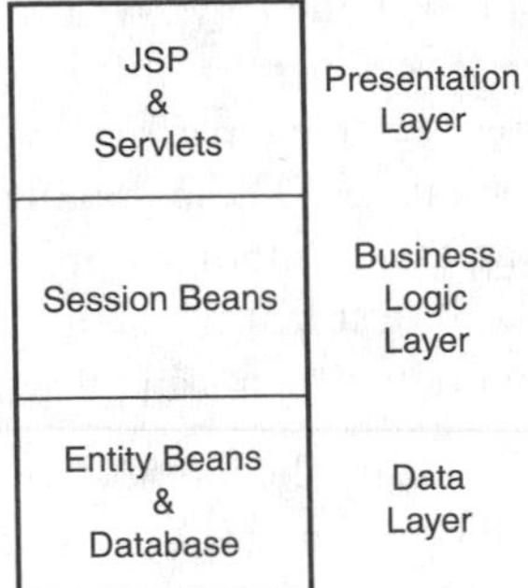

Although you normally think of the database as the data layer, if the entity beans don't contain any business logic, the entity beans appear to your session beans and clients as a simple data layer, almost as if you're using an object database.

Now, if your entity beans are essentially data-only and your clients access the entity beans directly, you are creating essentially a two-tiered application. Figure 12.2 shows this kind of configuration. Because the business logic isn't in the entity beans and there are no session beans, the client must have both the presentation and the business logic layers.

Figure 12.2
A client accessing entity beans directly might be a two-tiered application.

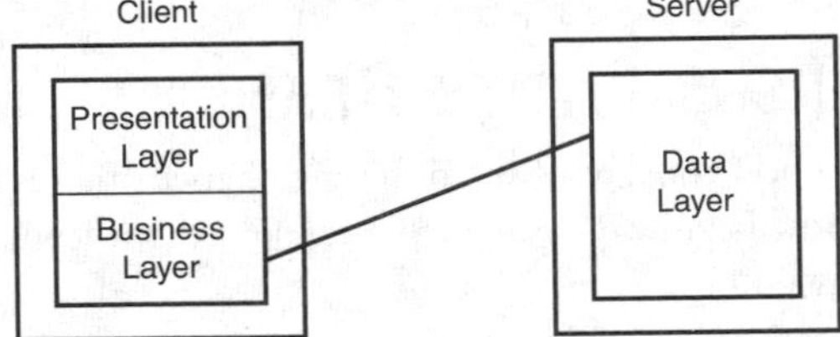

Although you can debate all day long whether this would be a two-tiered or three-tiered application, the important point is that you end up with business logic in the client, which makes the application harder to maintain.

In a typical EJB application, the business logic is in the session beans and the entity beans. Entity beans typically have methods to maintain their relationships with other entity beans and to validate their data. Session beans have methods that implement common business operations.

Sometimes, you want to create a method that operates on a set of entity beans but doesn't seem to fit in well with any of your session beans. You often find yourself writing session beans just to perform certain maintenance functions on your entity beans. For example, suppose you design an online shopping application that stores pending orders in the database. Periodically, you want to clear out orders that haven't been accessed in a long time. Before EJB 2.0, your only real choice was to create a session bean to clear out the pending orders. The Home methods introduced in the EJB 2.0 specification give you another choice. You can write the cleanup method as a Home method.

As the EJB specification gets progressively better, and as container-managed persistence gets better, both in capabilities and performance, you should see more applications going toward the ideal configuration of clients interacting with session beans and session beans using the entity beans. Unfortunately, for some applications, EJB isn't quite there yet.

One of the most common knocks against EJB has been its performance. Certainly, if you try to access an entity bean directly or make many calls to session beans, you will get slow performance. Even if you work to minimize your remote calls, however, EJB still tends to be slow. Early developers went with bean-managed persistence because CMP under EJB 1.1 wasn't very useful and there were few good implementations.

You should use CMP entity beans if possible. EJB was designed with the idea of CMP entity beans containing your data and the session beans implementing your business logic. Although CMP might not do everything you need it to, it is a good starting point. You can often get your application up and working by first using CMP. Then, if you identify any performance bottlenecks caused by CMP, you can always use BMP for beans that have special performance requirements. As CMP improves, you should eventually find that you rarely need to use BMP, but while EJB is still maturing, you might often find that CMP doesn't handle everything you need it to. For example, if you use automatically generated keys in your tables, you must write code to read the new key—CMP doesn't recognize these keys on its own. Also, CMP might not handle some fairly complex relationships.

Because entity beans haven't always been a very fast, some developers have opted to use only session beans. You end up with an architecture similar to traditional CORBA and RMI solutions. Even though you aren't using the full capabilities of EJB in this kind of configuration, there are benefits over using straight RMI and CORBA. First, EJB still provides you with transaction management so you can define transactions across multiple databases and other resources. Most EJB servers also supply connection pools and good server-management utilities. These are all things you normally must write if you just use CORBA and RMI.

CREATING VIEW OBJECTS

One of the most common patterns you see in three-tiered applications is the use of view objects. Remember, you want to reduce the number of calls you make from the client to the EJB container. If you need to retrieve a large number of fields from an EJB, either a session bean or an entity bean, you want to retrieve the values with a single method call.

You package all the values you want into a view class, which contains all the data items you want to retrieve. For example, Listing 12.1 shows a `PersonView` class holding all the data for a `Person` bean.

LISTING 12.1 SOURCE CODE FOR `PersonView.java`

```
package usingj2ee.addressbook;

public class PersonView implements java.io.Serializable
{
```

LISTING 12.1 CONTINUED

```
    public String firstName;
    public String middleName;
    public String lastName;
    public String address1;
    public String address2;
    public String city;
    public String state;
    public String zip;
    public String homePhone;
    public String workPhone;
    public String mobilePhone;

    public PersonView()
    {
    }
}
```

Now, you add two methods to the `Person` interface to allow a client to get and set the data in the bean using a view instead of the individual methods, like this:

```
public PersonView getAsView() throws RemoteException;
public void setFromView(PersonView aView) throws RemoteException;
```

Then, you just update the bean implementation class, as Listing 12.2 shows.

LISTING 12.2 VIEW UPDATES FOR `PersonImpl20.java`

```
public PersonView getAsView()
{
    PersonView view = new PersonView();
    view.firstName = getFirstName();
    view.middleName = getMiddleName();
    view.lastName = getLastName();
    view.address1 = getAddress1();
    view.address2 = getAddress2();
    view.city = getCity();
    view.state = getState();
    view.zip = getZip();
    view.homePhone = getHomePhone();
    view.workPhone = getWorkPhone();
    view.mobilePhone = getMobilePhone();
    return view;
}

public void setFromView(PersonView aView)
{
    setFirstName(aView.firstName);
    setMiddleName(aView.middleName);
    setLastName(aView.lastName);
    setAddress1(aView.address1);
    setAddress2(aView.address2);
    setCity(aView.city);
    setState(aView.state);
    setZip(aView.zip);
```

```
        setHomePhone(aView.homePhone);
        setWorkPhone(aView.workPhone);
        setMobilePhone(aView.mobilePhone);
    }
```

Listing 12.3 shows a sample client that uses the `Person` entity bean directly.

Listing 12.3 Source Code for TestPerson.java

```
package usingj2ee.addressbook;

import java.util.*;
import javax.naming.*;
import javax.rmi.PortableRemoteObject;

public class TestPerson
{
    public static void main(String[] args)
    {
        try
        {
// Set up properties for WebLogic so you don't have to do
// this on the command-line
            Properties props = new Properties();
            props.put(Context.INITIAL_CONTEXT_FACTORY,
                "weblogic.jndi.WLInitialContextFactory");

/** Creates a JNDI naming context for location objects */
            Context context = new InitialContext(props);

/** Asks the context to locate an object named "Person" and expects the
    object to implement the PersonHome interface */

            PersonHome home = (PersonHome)
                PortableRemoteObject.narrow(context.lookup("PersonHome"),
                    PersonHome.class);

// Locate edward
            Collection people = home.findByFirstAndLastName(
                "edward", "wutka");

            Iterator iter = people.iterator();

            if (!iter.hasNext())
            {
                System.out.println("Edward's not in the database");
                System.exit(0);
            }

            Person person = (Person) iter.next();

// Get a view of edward's data
            PersonView view = person.getAsView();

// Print some of the data
            System.out.println(view.firstName+" "+view.middleName+" "+
                view.lastName+": "+view.homePhone);
```

LISTING 12.3 CONTINUED

```
// Update edward's mobile phone number to 1-555-228-2255 (555-CAT-CALL)
            view.mobilePhone = "1-555-228-2255";

// Save the new data
            person.setFromView(view);

// Retrieve the data again
            view = person.getAsView();

// Print out the mobile number
            System.out.println(view.firstName+" "+view.middleName+" "+
                view.lastName+": "+view.mobilePhone);
        }
        catch (Exception exc)
        {
            exc.printStackTrace();
        }
    }
}
```

Although this view mechanism helps reduce the interaction between the client and server, it's still not the best solution. First of all, from an overall architecture standpoint, it's not necessarily a good idea to take a copy of the data over to the client, change it outside the scope of a transaction and then send it back. This is another issue that you could probably debate for a while. At some point, you will have a copy of the data that isn't part of a transaction and you will make changes to the object based on that data. There's just a danger of creating inconsistent data (if you don't check for updates). This gets back to a pessimistic versus optimistic locking issue.

If you plan to make updates to the object and you want to use pessimistic locking, you must begin a transaction before you first read the data. You can do this even while using the view mechanism. Then, when you update the data and commit the transaction, you know that either the change will go through or the EJB container will detect that the object has changed and reject your transaction.

If you want to use optimistic locking, you might consider sending the optimistic locking field along with the view, perhaps as a private member variable. When you send the view back to the server, the entity bean can check the locking field in the view against the current value in the bean and tell whether the view is still in sync with the entity bean.

Besides the transaction implications of using views, there's the problem that one view just doesn't suit everyone. One application might want to see a small portion of a bean, whereas another might want all the data. The problem is, when you write your session beans and entity beans, you don't necessarily know how they will be used.

Early on, when Java was first making its way onto the scene, people got the idea that Java would make a good language for implementing agents. The idea is that it's tough to transfer a lot of data over the network just so you can sift through it, so why not send some code over to where the data is and sift through it right there? There were even suggestions that agents could venture from machine to machine collecting data. IBM even created a framework called Aglets for creating agents. In fact, the Aglets framework is now an open-source project and is available at www.aglets.org. (Incidentally, an aglet is also the plastic tip on the end of a shoelace.)

You can use a concept similar to agents to create a more flexible view architecture. Figure 12.3 illustrates how this might happen. Basically, the entity bean presents an interface that a viewer can use to store and retrieve data. The interface is a local interface. The entity bean loads an instance of a particular viewer and asks it to either store or retrieve data.

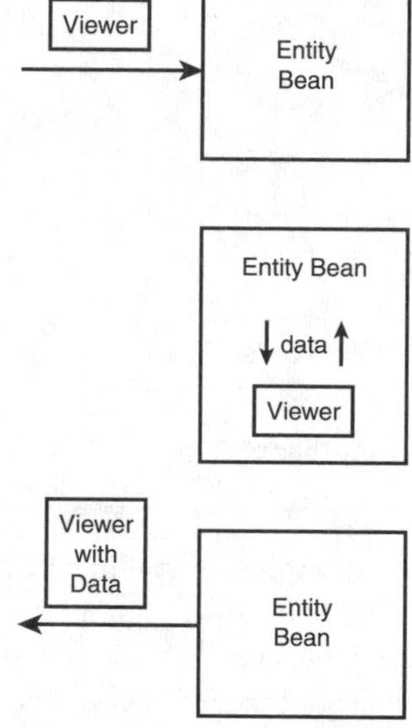

Figure 12.3
You can use a concept similar to agents for implementing views.

Listing 12.4 shows an example data interface for the `Person` bean. The data interface is how the viewer (view agent) retrieves data from the entity bean and also stores data in the entity bean.

Listing 12.4 Source Code for `PersonData.java`

```
package usingj2ee.addressbook;

/** Defines the local methods you can call to get a Person object's data */

public interface PersonData
{
    public String getFirstName();
    public void setFirstName(String aFirstName);

    public String getMiddleName();
    public void setMiddleName(String aMiddleName);
```

LISTING 12.4 CONTINUED

```
    public String getLastName();
    public void setLastName(String aLastName);

    public String getAddress1();
    public void setAddress1(String anAddress1);

    public String getAddress2();
    public void setAddress2(String anAddress2);

    public String getCity();
    public void setCity(String aCity);

    public String getState();
    public void setState(String aState);

    public String getZip();
    public void setZip(String aZip);

    public String getHomePhone();
    public void setHomePhone(String aHomePhone);

    public String getWorkPhone();
    public void setWorkPhone(String aWorkPhone);

    public String getMobilePhone();
    public void setMobilePhone(String aMobilePhone);
}
```

You change the `getAsView` and `setAsView` methods in the `Person` interface to work with viewers. To retrieve a view, it would be easier from a code standpoint to pass an empty viewer to the entity bean and ask it to populate the viewer, but that might result in extra network traffic. Instead, you simply pass the name of the viewer class and let the entity bean create the viewer instance.

Listing 12.5 shows the changed methods in the `Person` interface.

LISTING 12.5 CHANGES TO `Person.java` TO SUPPORT A VIEWER

```
public PersonViewer getAsView(String viewerClassName)
        throws RemoteException;
public void setFromView(PersonViewer viewer) throws RemoteException;
```

Listing 12.6 shows the implementation of the `getAsView` and `setFromView` method. You must also make sure that the bean implementation class implements the `PersonData` interface.

LISTING 12.6 IMPLEMENTATION OF THE `getAsView` AND `setFromView` METHODS

```
public PersonViewer getAsView(String viewerClassName)
    throws EJBException
{
    try
```

```
    {
// Locate the class for this viewer
        Class viewerClass = Class.forName(viewerClassName);

// Create a new instance of the viewer
        Object viewer = viewerClass.newInstance();

// Make sure the class implements PersonViewer
        if (!(viewer instanceof PersonViewer))
        {
            throw new EJBException("Class doesn't implement PersonViewer");
        }

// Tell the viewer to look at the bean's data
        ((PersonViewer) viewer).dataToView(this);

// Return the viewer
        return (PersonViewer) viewer;
    }
    catch (Exception exc)
    {
        throw new EJBException(exc.toString());
    }
}

public void setFromView(PersonViewer viewer)
{
// Tell the viewer to copy its data to the bean
    viewer.viewToData(this);
}
```

Figure 12.4 illustrates how the viewer mechanism works for retrieving data. Basically, the entity bean creates an instance of a viewer based on a classname. It then asks the viewer to retrieve whatever data is necessary, passing it the `PersonData` reference that the viewer uses to fetch data. All the method calls done during data retrieval are local calls; they don't even require parameter copying. After the viewer has the data it needs, the entity bean returns the viewer to the client.

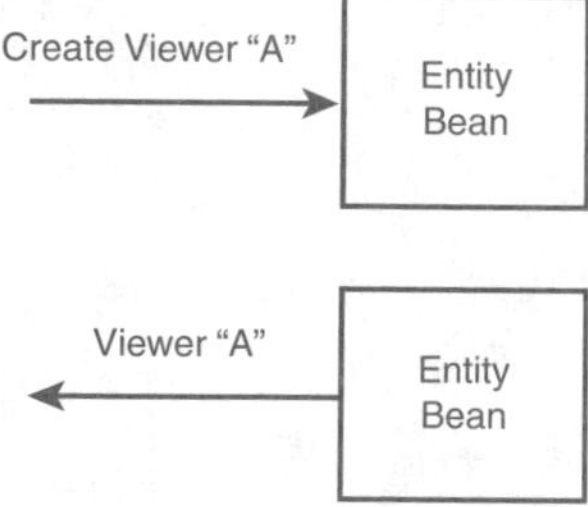

Figure 12.4 To retrieve data, you tell the entity bean what viewer class to instantiate.

Figure 12.5 illustrates the sequence for saving data. You send a viewer to the entity bean, and the entity bean passes the viewer a `PersonData` reference that the viewer can use to store data.

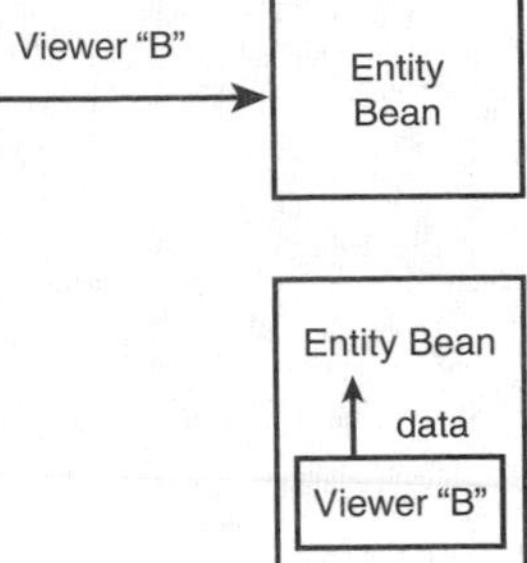

Figure 12.5
To store data, you send the viewer to the entity bean.

Keep in mind that because the entity bean must dynamically load the viewer class, the viewer class must be visible in the EJB container's class path. The idea behind the viewer framework is that you can create many different types of viewers to fetch data different ways. You don't change the entity bean at all because it always uses the same interface to communicate with the viewers.

Listing 12.7 shows an example viewer.

LISTING 12.7 SOURCE CODE FOR FullPersonViewer.java

```
package usingj2ee.addressbook;

public class FullPersonViewer implements java.io.Serializable, PersonViewer
{
    public String firstName;
    public String middleName;
    public String lastName;
    public String address1;
    public String address2;
    public String city;
    public String state;
    public String zip;
    public String homePhone;
    public String workPhone;
    public String mobilePhone;

    public FullPersonViewer()
    {
    }

    public void dataToView(PersonData data)
    {
        firstName = data.getFirstName();
        middleName = data.getMiddleName();
        lastName = data.getLastName();
        address1 = data.getAddress1();
        address2 = data.getAddress2();
        city = data.getCity();
        state = data.getState();
        zip = data.getZip();
        homePhone = data.getHomePhone();
```

```
            workPhone = data.getWorkPhone();
            mobilePhone = data.getMobilePhone();
        }

        public void viewToData(PersonData data)
        {
            data.setFirstName(firstName);
            data.setMiddleName(middleName);
            data.setLastName(lastName);
            data.setAddress1(address1);
            data.setAddress2(address2);
            data.setCity(city);
            data.setState(state);
            data.setZip(zip);
            data.setHomePhone(homePhone);
            data.setWorkPhone(workPhone);
            data.setMobilePhone(mobilePhone);
        }
    }
```

Listing 12.8 shows a client that uses the new viewer architecture to load and store data.

LISTING 12.8 SOURCE CODE FOR TestPerson2.java

```
package usingj2ee.addressbook;

import java.util.*;
import javax.naming.*;
import javax.rmi.PortableRemoteObject;

public class TestPerson2
{
    public static void main(String[] args)
    {
        try
        {
// Set up properties for WebLogic so you don't have to do
// this on the command-line
            Properties props = new Properties();
            props.put(Context.INITIAL_CONTEXT_FACTORY,
                "weblogic.jndi.WLInitialContextFactory");

/** Creates a JNDI naming context for location objects */
            Context context = new InitialContext(props);

/** Asks the context to locate an object named "Person" and expects the
    object to implement the PersonHome interface */

            PersonHome home = (PersonHome)
                PortableRemoteObject.narrow(context.lookup("PersonHome"),
                    PersonHome.class);

// Locate edward
            Collection people = home.findByFirstAndLastName(
                "edward", "wutka");
```

LISTING 12.8 CONTINUED

```
            Iterator iter = people.iterator();

            if (!iter.hasNext())
            {
                System.out.println("Edward's not in the database");
                System.exit(0);
            }

            Person person = (Person) iter.next();

// Get a view of edward's data
            FullPersonViewer view = (FullPersonViewer) person.getAsView(
                FullPersonViewer.class.getName());

// Print some of the data
            System.out.println(view.firstName+" "+view.middleName+" "+
                view.lastName+": "+view.homePhone);

// Update edward's mobile phone number to 1-555-228-2255 (555-CAT-CALL)
            view.mobilePhone = "1-555-228-2255";

// Save the new data
            person.setFromView(view);

// Retrieve the data again
            view = (FullPersonViewer) person.getAsView(
                FullPersonViewer.class.getName());

// Print out the mobile number
            System.out.println(view.firstName+" "+view.middleName+" "+
                view.lastName+": "+view.mobilePhone);
        }
        catch (Exception exc)
        {
            exc.printStackTrace();
        }
    }
}
```

IMPROVING EJB PERFORMANCE

You have already seen some of the important techniques for improving EJB performance. If you reduce the number of interactions between the client and the server, your application should speed up a great deal.

Some of the other areas where you can improve performance are

- Increased entity bean and session bean caching
- Database connection pooling
- Faster database interface libraries

- An optimized local call mechanism (one that doesn't use marshalling)
- Data caching

Most of these features should be available in a commercial EJB container (and in several excellent open-source ones, for that matter). One of the most important features, one that isn't as common in EJB containers, is data caching.

You might need a commercial CMP engine like the ones provided by WebGain (TOPLink), Versant, or Persistence. These products keep data cached in memory so that the next time you access a bean, the container doesn't go out to the database to get the bean data; it's already loaded. This kind of caching can give you absolutely huge performance boosts—maybe 10 times or 100 times faster if you spend most of your time reading data as opposed to writing it.

Although you should keep some of the performance issues in mind, like the minimal interaction between the client and the server, you should first work on getting the application to work. As my good friend Cliff McCartney always told us during development, "Rule 1: Get the right answer. Only then do you worry about performance".

CASE STUDY

A company was implementing an online-ordering system using EJB 1.1. The database architecture was inherited from a previous version of the application and used automatically generated keys. The implementation of CMP wasn't very efficient and didn't deal with many of the complex relationships in the database.

The company opted for using BMP with views for many of the database tables. The entity beans had methods to return views of its data and to change its data from the contents of a view. Because some of the relationships were too complex to represent with single entity beans, the company also decided to use session beans to do some of the database work. For example, some views contained data spread across different database tables. The session beans used SQL statements to manipulate these tables directly rather than using entity beans that might require too much extra work.

The company also created caches for commonly used tables of data: vendor name and products, pricing plans, and so on. Although these caches weren't portable across different EJB implementations (they violated some of the EJB restrictions), they made the application run at a reasonable speed.

PART II

Java Server Pages and Servlets

CHAPTER 13

Servlets

In this chapter

WHAT IS A SERVLET?

Although Enterprise JavaBeans perform many of the data-oriented tasks in an application server, you also need a way to generate Web pages containing dynamic data. *Servlets* are Java classes that handle Web requests and generate responses. Most of the time, servlets receive requests from Web browsers and generate HTML output.

A "HELLO WORLD" SERVLET

A servlet contains a `service` method that handles incoming requests. A single servlet can handle many different requests. Listing 13.1 shows you the "Hello World" program in servlet form.

LISTING 13.1 SOURCE CODE FOR `HelloWorldServlet.java`

```
package usingj2ee;

import javax.servlet.*;
import java.io.*;

public class HelloWorldServlet extends GenericServlet
{
    public void service(ServletRequest request,
        ServletResponse response)
        throws IOException
    {
// Tell the Web server that the response is HTML

        response.setContentType("text/html");

// Get the PrintWriter for writing out the response
        PrintWriter out = response.getWriter();

// Write the HTML back to the browser
        out.println("<HTML>");
        out.println("<BODY>");
        out.println("<H1>Hello World!</H1>");
        out.println("</BODY>");
        out.println("</HTML>");
    }
}
```

The HTML portion of the `HelloWorldServlet` is probably the most recognizable part. For the sake of completeness, the browser's view of the `HelloWorldServlet` is shown in Figure 13.1.

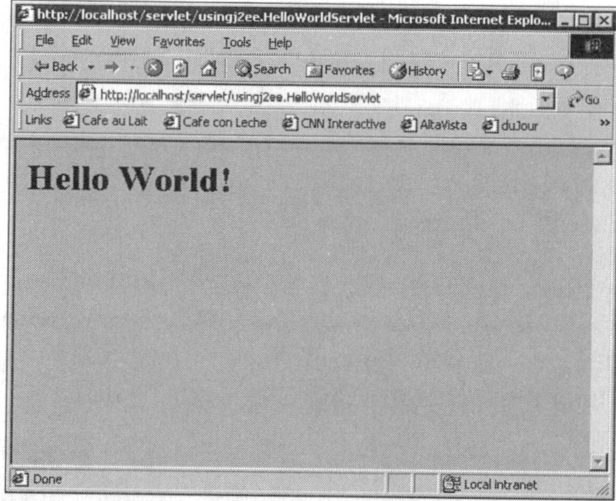

Figure 13.1
A servlet can generate HTML code.

Compiling the Servlet

Before you compile the servlet, make sure the servlet classes are in your classpath. The location of the servlet classes varies depending on which servlet engine you are using, but typically they are in a file called `servlet.jar`. The servlet API is also included in the `j2ee.jar` file that comes with most EJB containers. The location of the JAR file also varies, but you usually find it in the `lib` directory.

If you are having trouble compiling your servlet, see "Can't Compile the Servlet" in the "Troubleshooting" section at the end of this chapter.

Runtime Classpath

Servlets must be in the servlet engine's classpath. Most servlet engines enable you to modify the classpath for the purpose of loading servlets, so you won't have to add all your servlet directories to the system classpath.

Listing 13.1 showed that you can put your servlet into a package. The name of the servlet becomes the fully qualified classname of the servlet. The URL used to load the servlet specifies the pathname for the servlet as `/servlet/usingj2ee.HelloWorldServlet` (refer to Figure 13.1). Most servlet engines contain a special URL mapping for the `/servlet` directory, which signals that you want to run a servlet. When the Web server sees this special URL, it passes it on to the servlet engine. This `/servlet` directory usually picks up servlets from the classpath, so you can easily run any servlet that is in your system classpath just by appending the classname to `/servlet/`.

Note

You almost always have to set up a specific URL pattern for running servlets (such as `/servlet/`) or you need to set up a full URL that points to a servlet.

If you are having trouble running your servlet, see "The Servlet Won't Run" in the "Troubleshooting" section at the end of this chapter.

THE `HelloWorldServlet` IN DEPTH

The first thing your servlet must do is implement the `Servlet` interface. There are two ways to do it: subclass from a class that implements the `Servlet` interface or implement the `Servlet` interface directly in the servlet. The `HelloWorldServlet` takes the easier approach by subclassing an existing class that implements `Servlet`. Other classes also implement the `Servlet` interface and they will be discussed shortly.

When a request comes in for a particular servlet, the servlet engine loads the servlet (if it has not yet been loaded) and invokes the servlet's `service` method. The method takes two arguments: an object containing information about the request from the browser and an object containing information about the response going back to the browser.

Tip

Currently, most servlet engines don't automatically reload a servlet after it has been loaded. If you make changes to a servlet and recompile it, you usually need to restart the servlet engine to pick up the changes. This problem should slowly disappear over time as vendors create special class loaders to reload servlets when needed.

Next, the servlet must tell the Web browser what kind of content is being returned. Most of the time, you will be returning HTML content, so set the content type to `text/html`. As you will see in Chapter 22, "XML—The Extensible Markup Language," you can set the content type to `text/xml` and return XML data back to the browser. Earlier in this chapter, Listing 13.1 showed that you set the content type of the response by invoking `setContentType` in the response object.

After you set the content type, you are ready to start sending text back to the browser. Of course, you need some sort of output object to send the text back. Again, the response object has the methods necessary to get an output stream for writing a response. Because the "Hello World" servlet is writing out text, it only needs a `PrintWriter` object, so it calls the `getWriter` method in the response object. If you need to send binary data back to the browser, you should use the `getOutputStream` method in the response object.

The final part of the "Hello World" servlet should be the most obvious. The "Hello World" servlet uses the `println` method in the `PrintWriter` to send HTML back to the browser.

THE ANATOMY OF A SERVLET

As you just saw in the `HelloWorldServlet`, a servlet is a Java class that implements a few important methods. You can choose to implement these methods yourself or create a subclass of an existing servlet class that already implements these methods. The `Servlet` interface defines the methods that are required for a Java class to become a servlet. The interface definition is shown in Listing 13.2.

LISTING 13.2 THE DEFINITION OF THE `Servlet` INTERFACE

```
package javax.servlet;

public interface Servlet
{
    public void destroy();
    public ServletConfig getServletConfig();
    public String getServletInfo();
    public void init(ServletConfig config)
        throws ServletException;
    public void service(ServletRequest request,
        ServletResponse response)
        throws ServletException, java.io.IOException;
}
```

Most of the time, you will create a servlet by subclassing either `GenericServlet` or `HttpServlet`. Both of these classes implement the `Servlet` interface, but they provide a few handy features that make them preferable to implementing the `Servlet` interface yourself.

THE `service` METHOD

The heart of any servlet is the `service` method. As you just learned, the servlet engine calls the `service` method to handle each request from a browser, passing in an object containing information about the request that invoked the servlet and information about sending back a response. The `service` method is the only method that a servlet is actually required to implement. The service method is declared this way:

```
public void service(ServletRequest request,
    ServletResponse response)
    throws java.io.IOException
```

THE `init` METHOD

Many times, a servlet needs to perform some initialization one time, before it begins to handle requests. The `init` method in a servlet is called just after the servlet is first loaded, but before it begins to handle requests. Listing 13.3 shows a simple `init` method that initializes a database connection.

LISTING 13.3 `init` METHOD FROM `JDBCServlet.java`

```
protected Connection conn;

public void init()
{
    try
    {
// Make sure the JdbcOdbcDriver class is loaded
        Class.forName("sun.jdbc.odbc.JdbcOdbcDriver");

// Try to connect to a database via ODBC
        conn = DriverManager.getConnection(
            "jdbc:odbc:usingjsp");
```

LISTING 13.3 CONTINUED

```
    }
    catch (Exception exc)
    {
// If there's an error, use the servlet logging API
        getServletContext().log(
            "Error making JDBC connection: ", exc);
    }
}
```

Notice that the `init` method in Listing 13.3 does not take a parameter like the `init` method in the `Servlet` interface. One of the convenient features of the `GenericServlet` and `HttpServlet` classes is that they have an alternate version of `init` that doesn't take any parameters. In case you're wondering why it even matters, the `init` method in the `Servlet` interface takes a `ServletConfig` object as a parameter. The servlet is then responsible for keeping track of the `ServletConfig` object. The `GenericServlet` and `HttpServlet` classes perform this housekeeping chore and then provide the parameterless `init` method for you to do any servlet-specific initialization.

Caution

If you override the `init(ServletConfig config)` method of `GenericServlet` or `HttpServlet`, make sure you call `super.init(config)` as the first statement in your `init` method so that the housekeeping will still be performed.

THE destroy METHOD

Sometimes, the servlet engine decides that it doesn't need to keep your servlet loaded anymore. This could happen automatically, or as the result of you deactivating the servlet from an administration tool. Before the servlet engine unloads your servlet, it calls the `destroy` method to enable the servlet to perform any necessary cleanup. The cleanup usually involves closing database connections, open files, and network connections. Listing 13.4 shows the `destroy` method that is a companion to the `init` method in Listing 13.3.

LISTING 13.4 destroy METHOD FROM JDBCServlet.java

```
public void destroy()
{
    try
    {
// Only try to close the connection if it's non-null
        if (conn != null)
        {
            conn.close();
        }
    }
    catch (SQLException exc)
    {
// If there's an error, use the servlet logging API
        getServletContext().log(
```

```
                "Error closing JDBC connection: ", exc);
        }
    }
```

THE getServletInfo AND getServletConfig METHODS

If you are subclassing GenericServlet or HttpServlet, you probably won't need to override the getServletInfo or getServletConfig methods. The Servlet API documentation recommends that you return information such as the author, version, and copyright from the getServletInfo method. Although there is no specific format for the string returned by the method, you should return only plain text without any HTML or XML tags embedded within it.

The getServletConfig method returns the ServletConfig object that was passed to the servlet in the init method. Unless you are keeping track of the config object yourself, your best bet is to leave this method alone and let the superclass handle it.

SENDING A RESPONSE TO THE BROWSER

Probably the biggest difference between Java Server Pages and servlets is in the way responses are sent back to the browser. In a JSP, most of the response is embedded in the JSP in the form of static text. In the servlet, however, the response is usually in the form of code—mostly calls to out.print and out.println.

A minimal servlet needs to do two things to send a response: set the content type and write the response. If you are new to Web programming, you are probably unfamiliar with the notion of *content type*. Even though every request you make to a Web server involves a content type, it has probably been invisible to you. Whenever a browser asks the server for a file, the server sends back a content type along with the file. The content type tells the Web browser how it should display the file. A content type is simply a name consisting of a general category and a specific type, separated by a slash. For instance, if the file is an HTML file, the content type is text/html, whereas a JPEG image file has a content type of image/jpeg.

Most Web servers determine the content type by looking at the extension on the filename (for example, .htm and .html indicate HTML files, whereas .jpg indicates a JPEG image). In the case of a servlet, however, the Web server can't guess what the servlet is going to send back. It could be sending back HTML, XML, WML, or even a JPEG image. Instead, the Web server relies on the servlet to tell it what is being returned.

As you saw earlier in Listing 13.1, you set the content type by calling the setContentType method in the ServletResponse object. If you already know the exact length of the response, you can also call the setContentLength method. If you are just sending an HTML response, you don't need to send the content length. The browser can figure it out.

After you have set the content type, you are ready to send the response. If you are sending a text response, as is the case with HTML and XML, you should use the PrintWriter object returned by response.getWriter(). If you are sending a binary file, such as a JPEG image, an audio file, or an animation file, you should use the `ServletOutputStream` returned by `response.getOutputStream()`.

Note

Although the `ServletOutputStream` class also contains print and `println` methods such as the `PrintWriter` class, you should use the `PrintWriter` object when sending text output. Some content types require a slightly different character set and the `PrintWriter` object automatically adjusts the character set based on the content type. In fact, the general rule of thumb with Java I/O is that you should always use a `Writer` object when writing out character data.

You don't need to worry about closing the output stream when you are done writing out the response, the servlet engine knows you are through when the `service` method has finished executing. In addition to giving you the output streams, the response object performs other interesting tasks. You can control the amount of buffering, flush the output stream, and even clear the output stream.

Caution

Make sure you set the content type before you call `getWriter`. Because the servlet engine modifies the character set mapping depending on the content type, it needs to know the content type before it creates the `Writer`.

THE `HttpServlet` CLASS

You've seen that two prebuilt servlet classes are available for you to subclass, but so far, you don't know why you would choose `HttpServlet` instead of `GenericServlet`. The main difference between the two is that `HttpServlet` has extra methods and special request and response objects that are geared toward the HTTP protocol. The `HttpServlet` provides separate methods for handling the different types of HTTP requests (`GET`, `POST`, `PUT`, and so on). The two most common types of HTTP requests are `GET` and `POST`, which are handled by the `doGet` and `doPost` methods:

```
protected void doGet(HttpServletRequest request,
    HttpServletResponse response)
    throws ServletException, java.io.IOException;

protected void doPost(HttpServletRequest request,
    HttpServletResponse response)
    throws ServletException, java.io.IOException;
```

As you can see, the `doGet` and `doPost` methods are of the same general form as the `service` method. The `service` method of `HttpServlet` looks at the type of the HTTP request and then calls the appropriate handler methods. The `HttpServletRequest` and `HttpServletResponse` classes contain extra methods for dealing with the HTTP protocol.

TROUBLESHOOTING

CAN'T COMPILE THE SERVLET

Why won't my servlet compile? The compiler reports that it can't find the `javax.servlet` *package.*

Your classpath isn't set up correctly. You need to locate the `servlet.jar` file (it might have a different name) and add it to your classpath. You can also use the `j2ee.jar` file that comes with the J2EE SDK. If you can't find a file with either of these names, consult the documentation for your servlet engine to locate the correct filename.

THE SERVLET WON'T RUN

Why does the Web server gives me a `404 (File Not Found)` *error or a* `500 (Internal Server Error)`*?*

This is usually either an installation problem or a classpath issue. One way to check the installation is to run one of the default servlets that comes with the servlet engine. If you can't run one of the defaults, you need to check the configuration of your servlet engine and possibly reinstall it. If you can run the default servlet, but not your own, your classpath probably doesn't point to your servlet. Also, if you change the classpath after you have started the servlet engine, you need to restart the servlet engine to pick up the changes.

CHAPTER 14

JAVA SERVER PAGES

In this chapter

A "HELLO WORLD" JAVA SERVER PAGE

Java Server Pages are, in the most basic sense, Web pages with embedded Java code. The embedded Java code is executed on the server before the page is returned to the browser. If a picture is worth a thousand words, in this case an example is worth a thousand explanations. Listing 14.1 shows a basic Java Server Page.

LISTING 14.1 HelloWorld.jsp

```
<HTML>
<BODY>
<%
    out.println("<H1>Hello World!</H1>");
%>
</BODY>
</HTML>
```

Although you can probably guess what the browser will display when this page runs, Figure 14.1 shows the output from this page.

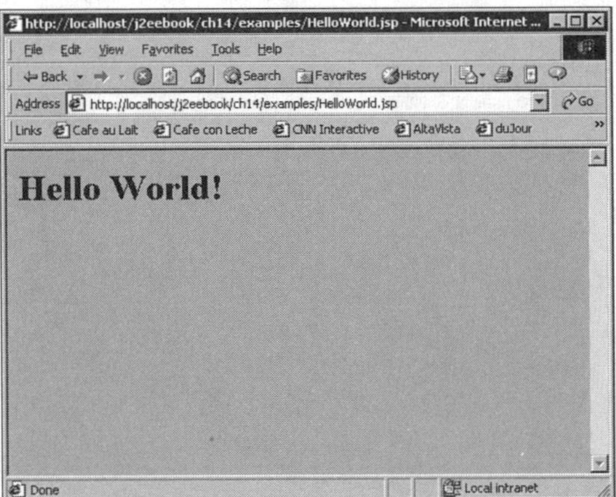

Figure 14.1
A Java Server Page can generate HTML output.

Note

If you want to try out the "Hello World" Java Server Page, treat it like an HTML page. Put it in the same place that you would put an HTML page and point your browser to it. You will also need to install a JSP engine, such as Tomcat or Resin. Many EJB containers also include a JSP engine as well.

If you are having trouble displaying the "Hello World" JSP, refer to the "Troubleshooting" section at the end of this chapter.

When the browser asks the Web server for a Java Server Page, the Web server invokes the JSP engine. This JSP engine converts the Java Server Page into a servlet that displays the HTML code in your JSP file and executes any of the Java code embedded in the JSP file. After the code has been translated, the JSP engine compiles the servlet, loads it automatically, and then executes it. Typically, the JSP engine checks to see whether there is already a servlet for a JSP file and whether the modification date on the JSP is older than the servlet. If the JSP is older than its generated servlet, the JSP engine assumes that the JSP hasn't changed and that the generated servlet still matches the contents of the JSP. Because it takes some time to generate a servlet and compile it, the JSP engine wants to minimize the number of compiles it has to perform, so it tries to avoid unnecessary compiles.

The other interesting piece of this equation is the actual HTML code that was sent to the browser. Most browsers enable you to view the HTML source for the Web page you are viewing. Listing 14.2 shows you the HTML code generated by the JSP in Listing 14.1.

LISTING 14.2 HTML SOURCE CODE FOR `HelloWorld.jsp`

```
<HTML>
<BODY>
<H1>Hello World!</H1>

</BODY>
</HTML>
```

As you can see, the text from the `out.println` statement in the JSP file is inserted directly into the HTML output. Of course, printing out a text string is not a practical use for JSP. Typically, you want to print out things that might change every time you run the JSP. The current time and date are trivial examples of items more suited for a JSP.

The `out` object used to write the "Hello World" string is an object of type `JspWriter`. For now, you just need to know that this `out` object has approximately the same methods as `PrintWriter`, which is similar to the older `PrintStream` class. There are `print` and `println` methods for writing out various types of data. One word of caution, however, `JspWriter` is neither a `PrintStream` nor a `PrintWriter`, so you cannot pass the `out` object to methods that expect either of those two classes.

When the browser asks the Web server for `HelloWorld.jsp`, the JSP engine (the software responsible for handling Java Server Pages) first checks to see whether `HelloWorld.jsp` has already been compiled into a servlet. If not, it creates a servlet that prints out the HTML in your JSP file and executes the code contained within the JSP file. Listing 14.3 shows the portion of the generated servlet that produces the HTML code in Listing 14.2.

LISTING 14.3 JAVA CODE TO PRODUCE THE HTML FROM LISTING 14.2

```
// begin
out.write("<HTML>\r\n<BODY>\r\n");
// end
// begin
[file="D:\\ch14\\examples\\HelloWorld.jsp";from=(2,2);to=(4,0)]
out.println("<H1>Hello World!</H1>");
// end
// begin
out.write("\r\n</BODY>\r\n</HTML>\r\n");
// end
```

Typically, you won't need to look at the generated servlet; however, sometimes it is useful. If your JSP throws an exception and you print out the Java stack trace from the exception, the line numbers displayed in the stack trace will be line numbers from the generated servlet. There is no standard indicating where the generated servlets must be placed. It varies from JSP engine to JSP engine.

USING THE <% %> TAGS IN A JAVA SERVER PAGE

As you saw in the `HelloWorld.jsp` example, the `<%` and `%>` tags in a JSP file are used to indicate the presence of Java code within the HTML. The JSP specification allows for languages other than Java to be used for scripting. At the present time, few servers support languages other than Java; however, eventually there will be more support for other scripting languages. Until that time, and certainly for the rest of this book, the focus is on Java as the JSP scripting language.

Note

The Resin JSP engine from Caucho (`www.caucho.com`) has support for using JavaScript in a JSP instead of Java.

You can intermix the `<%` and `%>` tags with other HTML tags in just about any combination you can think of. The rules are simple. Any text outside the `<%` and `%>` tags is rendered verbatim. Any Java code within the `<%` and `%>` tags is executed. If you want to generate HTML from the Java code between the `<%` and `%>` tags, use the `out` variable, which is a `JspWriter` object. Listing 14.4 shows a simple, yet hard to follow example of mixing the `<%` and `%>` tags with regular HTML.

LISTING 14.4 SOURCE CODE FOR `Greeting.jsp`

```
<HTML>
<BODY>
Good
<%
    java.util.Calendar currTime = new java.util.GregorianCalendar();

    if (currTime.get(currTime.HOUR_OF_DAY) < 12)
    {
%>
        Morning!
<%
    }
    else if (currTime.get(currTime.HOUR_OF_DAY) < 18)
    {
%>
        Afternoon!
<%
    }
    else
    {
%>
        Evening!
```

```
<%
    }
%>
</BODY>
</HTML>
```

If you are unfamiliar with either Active Server Pages or Java Server Pages, the code in Listing 14.4 probably looks bizarre to you. First, remember that the code outside the `<% %>` tag pair is sent verbatim. Of course, that might lead you to conclude that the three strings `Morning!`, `Afternoon!`, and `Evening!` should all be sent in the response. What really happens is that items outside of the `<% %>` tag pair are converted into Java statements that print out the HTML verbatim. Because the `Morning!`, `Afternoon!`, and `Evening!` strings occur within an `if` statement, they are only printed when their section of the `if` block is true.

Note

Listing 14.4 avoids importing `java.util.*` just to keep the example simple. If you need to import a package, the syntax for importing `java.util.*` is `<%@ page language="java" import="java.util.*" %>`.

Listing 14.5 shows you a portion of the Java code generated by the JSP in Listing 14.4. Don't worry, you won't have to look at the Java code for every JSP in this book, or even in this chapter.

LISTING 14.5 JAVA CODE GENERATED BY LISTING 14.4

```
// begin
    out.write("<HTML>\r\n<BODY>\r\nGood\r\n");
// end
// begin
[file="D:\\ch14\\examples\\Greeting.jsp";from=(3,2);to=(8,0)]
    java.util.Calendar currTime = new java.util.GregorianCalendar();
    if (currTime.get(currTime.HOUR_OF_DAY) < 12)
    {
// end
// begin
        out.write("\r\n\t\tMorning!\r\n");
// end
// begin
[file="D:\\ch14\\examples\\Greeting.jsp";from=(10,2);to=(14,0)]
    }
    else if (currTime.get(currTime.HOUR_OF_DAY) < 18)
    {
// end
// begin
        out.write("\r\n\t\tAfternoon!\r\n");
// end
// begin
[file="D:\\ch14\\examples\\Greeting.jsp";from=(16,2);to=(20,0)]
    }
    else
    {
// end
```

LISTING 14.5 CONTINUED

```
// begin
        out.write("\r\n\t\tEvening!\r\n");
// end
// begin
[file="D:\\ch14\\examples\\Greeting.jsp";from=(22,2);to=(24,0)]
    }
// end
// begin
    out.write("\r\n</BODY>\r\n</HTML>\r\n\r\n\r\n");
// end
```

The Java code in Listing 14.5 looks ugly, and those `//begin` and `//end` comments make it tough to read. After you start comparing it to Listing 14.4, you should begin to get the idea of how the `<% %>` tags relate to the rest of the file.

> **Tip**
>
> It's easier to read through a JSP if you remember that any text outside the `<%` and `%>` tags is really just shorthand for an `out.write` statement containing that text.

DISPLAYING A VALUE WITH <%= %>

The earlier example in Listing 14.4 could have been written in a much more compact way that determined the time of day first and printed out its greeting near the end of the file. Listing 14.6 shows a much more compact version.

LISTING 14.6 SOURCE CODE FOR `Greeting2.jsp`

```
<HTML>
<BODY>
<%
    java.util.Calendar currTime = new java.util.GregorianCalendar();

    String timeOfDay = "";

    if (currTime.get(currTime.HOUR_OF_DAY) < 12)
    {
        timeOfDay = "Morning!";
    }
    else if (currTime.get(currTime.HOUR_OF_DAY) < 18)
    {
        timeOfDay = "Afternoon!";
    }
    else
    {
        timeOfDay = "Evening!";
    }
%>
Good <% out.write(timeOfDay); %>
</BODY>
</HTML>
```

As you can see, Listing 14.6 is much easier to read because it doesn't jump back and forth between Java and HTML so rapidly. Down at the bottom of the listing, you can see where the `timeOfDay` variable is written out as part of the display. Notice that even though it is a single statement on the same line as some HTML text, `out.write(timeOfDay)` must still end with a semicolon because it must be a legal Java statement.

JSP provides a shorthand for printing out variables to save you from having to put `out.write()` all over the place. The line that prints out the greeting in Listing 14.6 can be replaced with the following line:

```
Good <%= timeOfDay %>
```

The <%= tag indicates that you want to write out a Java expression as part of the output sent back to the browser. Notice that you still close the tag with %> and not =%>. You can include any Java expression; just make sure you don't put a semicolon after the expression. The following line shows you a more complex expression:

```
<%= 2*3+4-5*6+7*8-9 %>
```

As you can see, it's just as valid to print out a numerical expression as it is to print out a string. In fact, you can also print out an entire object. For example, you can print out the string representation of a calendar object using the following line:

```
<%= new java.util.GregorianCalendar() %>
```

Of course, the result of printing out an object might not be what you expect. Figure 14.2 shows how the `GregorianCalendar` object looks when displayed using the <%= tag.

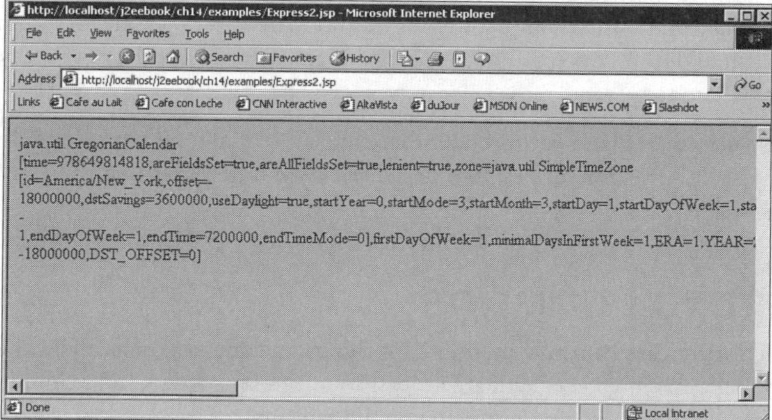

Figure 14.2
The <%= tag can print out an entire object.

> **Note**
>
> Make sure you don't put any space between the <% and the = sign.

When you display an object using the <%= tag, the result is the same kind of output you would see if you wrote out the object to `System.out` in a regular program. Basically, the output routine calls the `toString` method in the object and displays the results of the method call.

Tip

Anything you put between the <%= and %> ends up inside an `out.write()` expression. In other words, think of <%= as shorthand for `out.write(` and its closing %> as shorthand for `);`.

Listing 14.7 shows a somewhat more practical combination of <% and <%= to display the current date.

LISTING 14.7 SOURCE CODE FOR `ShowDate.jsp`

```
<HTML>
<BODY>
<% java.util.Calendar currDate = new java.util.GregorianCalendar();
   // add 1 to month because Calendar's months start at 0, not 1
   int month = currDate.get(currDate.MONTH)+1;
   int day = currDate.get(currDate.DAY_OF_MONTH);
   int year = currDate.get(currDate.YEAR);
%>
The current date is: <%= month %>/<%= day %>/<%= year %>
</BODY>
</HTML>
```

The <%= tag is often useful when graphics designers are creating the Web page and Web programmers are adding the server-side Java code. Typically, the Web programmers encase their code in <% %> tags somewhere near the beginning of the JSP file. They put all the interesting data (the data interesting to the graphics designers) into Java variables. Then, the graphics designers can lay out the page the way they want it and use the <%= %> tags to insert the data where they want without having to write any Java code. Listing 14.7 is a basic example of this concept. The graphics designers can insert the `month`, `day`, and `year` variables anywhere they want.

As you will see later in this book, there are additional ways that the Web programmers can supply information for graphics designers when different groups must maintain the same JSP page.

INSERTING COMMENTS

Comments are generally used for two things: making notations about the code, and removing sections of code. There are at least four different ways to add comments to a Java server page, each with its own advantages and disadvantages. If your JSP is generating HTML, you can use HTML comments, which use the <!-- and --> tags, like this:

```
<!-- This is an HTML comment -->
```

In general, only use HTML comments in a JSP if you want the comment to be visible on the browser. Most of the time, you don't care if the user can see any of your comments, so the HTML comments are usually not used in a Java Server Page. You might find yourself using the HTML comments if you have a large section of HTML in your JSP and you want to remove a section temporarily. Although you could remove it with the JSP comment tags (which you will learn about in a moment), it's nicer to keep the block pure HTML rather than turn it into a mixture of HTML and JSP tags.

Because any code you place inside the <% %> tags is Java code, you can use both of Java's commenting mechanisms. For example, you can do a one-liner comment like this:

```
<% // This is a one-line JSP comment %>
```

You can also use the /* */ comment tags within separate <% %> tag pairs. This method is difficult to follow; fortunately, there is a better way. Here is an example of using the /* and */ comment tags:

```
<% /* %>
  This is actually commented out
<% */ %>
```

Not only is the commenting method confusing, it's also wasteful. When the JSP is compiled into a servlet, the text within the /* */ tags is still converted into Java statements that emit the text. Because the Java statements are surrounded by /* */, they are ignored by the compiler.

Java Server Pages have a special comment tag pair recognized by the JSP compiler. You can surround your comments with <%-- --%> to place a comment in your JSP code. The <%-- --%> prevents text from even being placed into the Java servlet generated by the JSP compiler. Here is an example of a JSP comment:

```
<%-- This comment will not appear in the servlet --%>
```

If you need to remove a section of code from a Java Server Page, the <%-- --%> tags are the best way to do it. They take priority over the other tags. In other words, if a <% %> tag pair occurs within the comment tags, the <% %> tag pair is ignored, as the following example shows:

```
<%--
<%
    out.println("You will never see this.");
%>
--%>
```

Declaring Methods and Variables with <%! %>

So far, you have seen how to insert Java statements and Java expressions into your code. In case you haven't realized it yet, all the code within the <% %> tags and all the expressions within the <%= %> tags belong to one big Java method in the generated servlet. That is why you can use the <%= %> tags to display a variable that was declared inside the <% %> tags.

You might want to put an entire Java method into a JSP. If you try to declare a method within the <% %> tags, the Java compiler reports an error. It won't let you declare a method within another method.

Use the <%! %> tags to enclose any declarations that belong outside the big method that generates the page. Listing 14.8 shows a JSP file that declares a separate method and then uses the <%= %> tags to display the result of calling the method.

LISTING 14.8 SOURCE CODE FOR `DeclareMethod.jsp`

```
<HTML>
<BODY>
<%!
    public String myMethod(String someParameter)
    {
        return "You sent me: "+someParameter;
    }
%>
<%= myMethod("Hi there") %>
</BODY>
</HTML>
```

Figure 14.3 shows the results of the `DeclareMethod.jsp` as they are displayed on the browser.

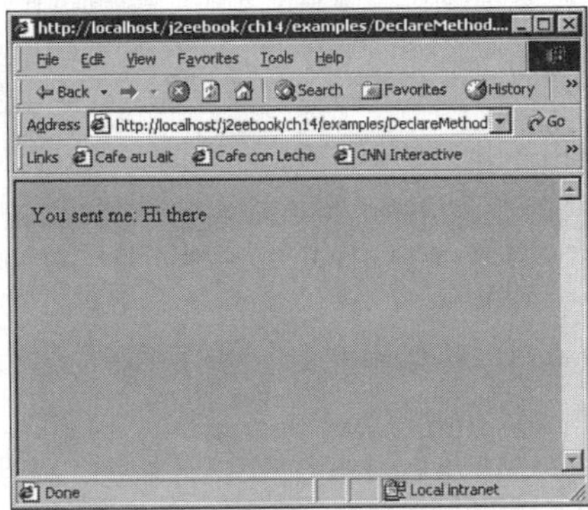

Figure 14.3
You can declare Java methods in a JSP and display results returned by those methods.

Tip

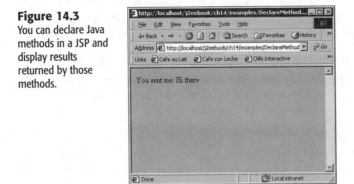

The `out` variable is not available inside any methods you declare using the `<%!` tag. If you need to send data back to the browser from within a method, you must pass the `out` variable in as a parameter of type `JspWriter`.

In addition to declaring methods, you can also use the `<%! %>` tags to declare instance variables. These instance variables are visible to any methods you declare, and also to the code within the `<% %>` tags. Declaring an instance variable is as simple as this:

```
<%! int myInstanceVariable = 10; %>
```

After this variable has been declared, you can use it in other methods declared with `<%! %>` or within the `<% %>` and `<%= %>` tags. For example, you could display the value of `myInstanceVariable` this way:

```
<%
    out.println("myInstanceVariable is "+myInstanceVariable);
%>
```

Likewise, you can display the variable using the `<%= %>` tags this way:

```
MyInstanceVariable is <%= myInstanceVariable %>
```

Note

Several implementations of Java Server Pages still use the older Java Server Pages specification version 0.92. In the older specification, the `<%! %>` tags did not exist. Instead, you had to start the embedded methods and declarations with `<SCRIPT RUNAT=SERVER>` and close them with `</SCRIPT>`.

HANDLING MULTIPLE THREADS IN A JSP

Even though Java is a fairly thread-friendly language, many Java developers are not comfortable dealing with a threaded application. If you are developing Java Server Pages for a production system, you need to become comfortable with threading. By default, the JSP engine assumes that your Java Server Pages are thread-safe and might invoke the same page from multiple threads.

If all your Java code is enclosed within the `<% %>` tags and you don't use any external objects, your code is probably already safe. Remember, because each Java thread has its own execution stack (where local variables are stored), any method that only uses local variables should already be thread-safe. If you do use external variables, or if you declare instance variables with the `<%! %>` tags, you might run into threading issues.

Note

Just in case you're worried, the `JspWriter` class (that is, the `out` variable) is properly synchronized. You don't have to worry that your `out.print` and `out.println` statements will fail when multiple threads try to call them at the same time.

Listing 14.9 shows an abbreviated example of a real-life situation in which threading issues became a problem. In the real-life program, the error was not discovered until the program was being tested with multiple users. In this example, the Java Server Page is formatting name and address information for a customer.

LISTING 14.9 SOURCE CODE FOR `Address.jsp`

```
<HTML>
<BODY>

<%!
// Holders for the various portions of the address
    String firstName;
    String middleName;
    String lastName;
    String address1;
    String address2;
    String city;
    String state;
    String zip;
%>

<%
```

```
// Copy the information passed into the JSP
    firstName = request.getParameter("firstName");
    middleName = request.getParameter("middleName");
    lastName = request.getParameter("lastName");
    address1 = request.getParameter("address1");
    address2 = request.getParameter("address2");
    city = request.getParameter("city");
    state = request.getParameter("state");
    zip = request.getParameter("zip");

// Call the formatting routine
    formatNameAndAddress(out);
%>
</BODY>
</HTML>

<%!
// Print out the name address
    void formatNameAndAddress(JspWriter out)
        throws java.io.IOException
    {
        out.println("<PRE>");
        out.print(firstName);
// Only print the middle name if it contains data
        if ((middleName != null) && (middleName.length() > 0))
        {
            out.print(" "+middleName);
        }
        out.println(" "+lastName);
        out.println(address1);

// Only print the second address line if it contains data
        if ((address2 != null) && (address2.length() > 0))
        {
            out.println(address2);
        }
        out.println(city+", "+state+" "+zip);
        out.println("</PRE>");
    }
%>
```

The problem is that the variables holding the name and address information are instance variables. Typically, only one instance of a JSP class is loaded at one time. Each time a browser asks a Java Server Page, the Web server spawns another thread to handle the request. It's possible to have multiple threads executing the same Java Server Page at the same time.

In the case of Listing 14.9, the problem is that the instance variables are shared across all the threads. One thread could set all the variables, and then before it has a chance to call the formatting routine, another thread comes along and changes the values. Figure 14.4 illustrates how this happens.

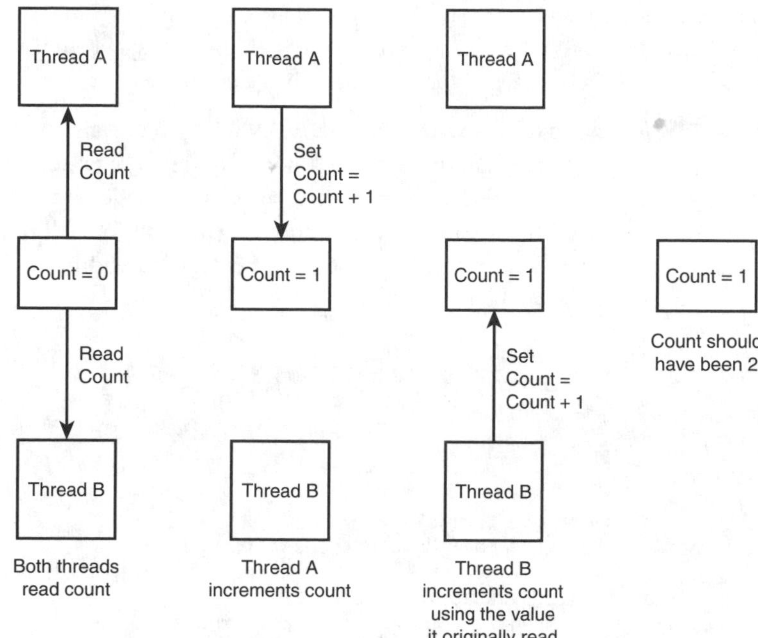

Figure 14.4
Multiple threads can modify the same member variable in a JSP.

The root of the problem is that the data is being passed to `formatNameAndAddress` via instance variables instead of as parameters to the method. Although it seems like an obvious thing to just pass parameters, in the real-life program this example was pulled from, the formatting routine needed around 30 different values. It would have been more than a little cumbersome to pass 30 parameters around, especially if they must be passed to several different methods. One solution for this problem is to synchronize the variable assignments and the method call, like this:

```
// Copy the information passed into the JSP
    synchronized (this)
    {
        firstName = request.getParameter("firstName");
        middleName = request.getParameter("middleName");
        lastName = request.getParameter("lastName");
        address1 = request.getParameter("address1");
        address2 = request.getParameter("address2");
        city = request.getParameter("city");
        state = request.getParameter("state");
        zip = request.getParameter("zip");

// Call the formatting routine
        formatNameAndAddress(out);
    }
```

Although synchronization can prevent threading problems, it does so at the cost of performance. The reason the server tries to use multiple threads to call a JSP is to try to service as many requests as possible in a short amount of time. If you suddenly create a bottleneck in which a large amount of work can only be done by one thread at a time, you are defeating the performance enhancements of threading. There is nothing wrong with using the `synchronized` keyword here and there to prevent errors, but synchronizing all or more of the work in one large block is usually not a good idea.

The solution for the problem posed in Listing 14.9 involves passing the data as method parameters rather than through instance variables. Although the example could be rewritten to pass each data item as 8 separate parameters, the original code from which this example was taken had 30 separate parameters and a more elegant solution. All the parameters can be encapsulated in a Java class, and the Java class can be declared within the JSP as a nested class. Listing 14.10 shows the thread-safe solution.

LISTING 14.10 SOURCE CODE FOR `AddressGood.jsp`

```
<HTML>
<BODY>

<%
// Allocate a holder for the data
    NameAndAddress data = new NameAndAddress();

// Copy the information passed into the JSP
    data.firstName = request.getParameter("firstName");
    data.middleName = request.getParameter("middleName");
    data.lastName = request.getParameter("lastName");
    data.address1 = request.getParameter("address1");
    data.address2 = request.getParameter("address2");
    data.city = request.getParameter("city");
    data.state = request.getParameter("state");
    data.zip = request.getParameter("zip");

// Call the formatting routine
    formatNameAndAddress(data, out);
%>
</BODY>
</HTML>

<%!
// The holder for the formatting data
    class NameAndAddress
    {
        public String firstName;
        public String middleName;
        public String lastName;
        public String address1;
        public String address2;
        public String city;
        public String state;
        public String zip;
    }

// Print out the name address
    void formatNameAndAddress(NameAndAddress data, JspWriter out)
        throws java.io.IOException
    {
        out.println("<PRE>");
```

```
            out.print(data.firstName);
    // Only print the middle name if it contains data
            if ((data.middleName != null) &&
                (data.middleName.length() > 0))
            {
                out.print(" "+data.middleName);
            }
            out.println(" "+data.lastName);
            out.println(data.address1);

    // Only print the second address line if it contains data
            if ((data.address2 != null) &&
                (data.address2.length() > 0))
            {
                out.println(data.address2);
            }
            out.println(data.city+", "+data.state+" "+data.zip);
            out.println("</PRE>");
        }
%>
```

The example in Listing 14.10 avoids thread collisions by allocating an object to hold the data it passes to another routine. Because each thread allocates its own copy of the data object, the threads cannot overwrite one another's data.

CHOOSING BETWEEN SERVLETS AND JAVA SERVER PAGES

Although you've just barely scratched the surface of JSP and servlets, now is a good time to talk about when to use servlets, when to use JSP, and when to use both. To make such decisions, you need to weigh the advantages and disadvantages of each. Remember, too, that because Java Server Pages are translated into servlets, they can't be all that different when you get right down to it.

THE ADVANTAGES AND DISADVANTAGES OF JSP

The biggest strength of JSP is that it looks like HTML (or XML or whatever kind of content you are generating). You can give a JSP to someone who is familiar with HTML and expect that person to be able to make changes in a fairly short amount of time. It is also obvious what the HTML will look like when it is sent to the browser. It is not always so obvious when the HTML is generated by Java code.

An add-on to this strength is the fact that people who are weaker with Java can use Java Server Pages. You don't need to know too much Java to do at least basic things with JSP. You don't even need to know how to declare a Java class. As vendors begin to support other languages with JSP (some already support JavaScript), you will have people writing Java Server Pages that don't even know Java!

A much more subtle advantage of JSP, one that you have not encountered yet, is that when the JSP is turned into a servlet, that servlet is automatically loaded into the servlet engine.

When the JSP changes, its corresponding servlet is automatically regenerated and reloaded. When you are doing rapid development, it's great to be able to make quick changes and see them without having to restart the server. If you make a lot of changes to a lot of files, you don't have to worry about reloading all the changed files, because the JSP engine picks them up automatically.

Because Java Server Pages eventually become servlets, it's difficult to point to any technical disadvantages of a JSP that aren't also present in servlets. The greatest disadvantage noted in practice is related to the greatest strength of JSP: the capability to mix Java code with HTML. If you aren't careful in organizing your code, you can end up with an ugly mess: huge JSP files with HTML interspersed between huge blocks of Java code. Things only get worse if you do a lot of JavaScript in the page, too. It can be terribly confusing to look at a page and not know whether you are looking at server-side Java code or client-side JavaScript. Fortunately, you will learn ways around this in the next few chapters.

THE ADVANTAGES AND DISADVANTAGES OF SERVLETS

For the most part, the advantages of servlets are the disadvantages of JSP and vice versa. Because servlets are Java classes, you don't end up with a huge mess of Java, HTML, and JavaScript. Everything in your servlet is Java. Of course, when the servlet is generating HTML or XML, you might find that you still have a huge mess in the form of ugly `out.print` and `out.println` statements.

Servlets are not always automatically reloaded by the servlet engine, although that situation will hopefully change in the future. You also need to specify a special URL or at least a URL pattern (such as "/servlet/") for executing a servlet, although for a JSP you only need to have a filename that ends with `.jsp`. This makes your site configuration a little more tedious to maintain.

If this discussion seems biased in favor of JSP, it's because a JSP eventually becomes a servlet and you have the entire servlet API available to you from within the JSP. There is an interesting combination of servlets and JSP that has been used by many people around the world. When the initial request comes in, it is handled by a servlet. The servlet performs any business logic (fetching data from the database, doing computations, pulling data in from other sources). When it's time to send a response back to the browser, the servlet calls a JSP to render the output. This uses the strength of each of these technologies: The servlet is a simple Java class, whereas the JSP is a template geared towards generating output.

If you take a little extra time, you can create a JSP that doesn't contain any Java code at all. It might seem a little strange to make a JSP with no Java code, but throughout the rest of this book you will learn about built-in JSP tags that let you access Java objects, and also a tag-extension mechanism that lets you create new JSP tags. Using these features, you can easily eliminate embedded Java code, which some would argue is the best way to use JSP.

It probably sounds a little too simplistic, but you should use the technology that best fits your requirements, or at least your comfort level. If you have a lot of static HTML, XML, WML, or other textual markup language, use a JSP. If you are sending back binary data, such as an image or an audio file, a servlet is probably a better bet (not from a technical standpoint, just an aesthetic one). If you aren't comfortable with your Java skills, start playing with JSP to get your feet wet.

TROUBLESHOOTING

ERRORS WHEN ACCESSING THE PAGE

Why do I get a `404 (File Not Found)` error when I access the Java Server Page?

You are probably putting the JSP in a directory that the Web server can't get to. If you have an HTML page that you can access from the Web server, put the JSP in the same directory and see if you can get to it. Also try using the default directory for your Web server (for Microsoft Web servers it's usually `c:\InetPub\WWWRoot`).

Why do I get a `500 (Internal Server Error)` error when I access the Java Server Page?

Usually a 500 error is caused by a miscommunication between the Web server and the JSP engine, or an error in the JSP engine. First, check to make sure that you have configured your JSP engine properly. Many JSP engines come with a pure-Java Web server as well as an interface to an existing Web server. Usually these pure-Java servers run on port 8000 or 8080. Try hitting the JSP using the pure-Java server (if you type `http://localhost/HelloWorld.jsp`, try `http://localhost:8000/HelloWorld.jsp`). If the JSP displays correctly, the interface between the JSP engine and your regular Web server is broken. Try reconfiguring it. Another possibility is that you don't have a Java compiler set up correctly. See the next troubleshooting tip to see how to solve that problem.

Why do I get an error saying `No Compiler Available` or `unable to locate com.sun.tools.javac.Main`?

The JSP engine converts your Java Server Pages into Java classes and then compiles them. To compile them, it needs a Java compiler. You need to install either a full JDK or at least get the `tools.jar` file from an existing JDK installation and put it in your classpath. This error occurs mostly when you have only installed the JRE (Java Runtime Environment), which does not come with a Java compiler.

COMPILER ERRORS

Why do I see bizarre compiler errors like `expected }` or `no catch/finally clause`?

You probably forgot an opening `<%` or a closing `%>`.

DOESN'T SHOW HTML

Instead of seeing an HTML page, why do I see the source code for my JSP?

You don't have the JSP engine set up correctly. The Web server doesn't understand that the JSP engine is supposed to handle filenames ending in `.jsp`. You might need to reinstall your JSP engine.

CHAPTER 15

Common JSP Tasks

In this chapter

A SIMPLE HTML FORM

Up to this point, you have only learned how to send output back to the browser. One of the key points of the Web is the fact that you can create forms to send data from the browser to the server. You are ready to begin creating forms with JSP and servlets, and that's where the fun really begins!

To begin exploring HTML forms, it's best to start with a small form and expand from there. Also, it's better to start with a Java Server Page rather than a servlet, because it is easier to write out the HTML. Most of the form handling for JSP and servlets is identical, so after you know how to retrieve form information from a JSP, you know how to do it from a servlet as well. Listing 15.1 shows an HTML file containing a simple input form that calls a JSP to handle the form.

LISTING 15.1 SOURCE CODE FOR `SimpleForm.html`

```
<HTML>
<BODY>

<H1>Please tell me about yourself</H1>

<FORM action="SimpleFormHandler.jsp" method="get">

Name:  <INPUT type="text" name="firstName">
       <INPUT type="text" name="lastName"><BR>
Sex:
       <INPUT type="radio" checked name="sex" value="male">Male
       <INPUT type="radio" name="sex" value="female">Female
       <INPUT type="radio" name="sex" value="alien">Alien<BR>
<P>
What Java primitive type best describes your personality:
<SELECT name="javaType">
       <OPTION value="boolean">boolean</OPTION>
       <OPTION value="byte">byte</OPTION>
       <OPTION value="char" selected>char</OPTION>
       <OPTION value="double">double</OPTION>
       <OPTION value="float">float</OPTION>
       <OPTION value="int">int</OPTION>
       <OPTION value="long">long</OPTION>
</SELECT>
<BR>
<INPUT type="submit">
</FORM>
</BODY>
</HTML>
```

The `<FORM>` tag in Listing 15.1 sends the input from the form to a JSP called `SimpleFormHandler.jsp`. Figure 15.1 shows this form running in a browser.

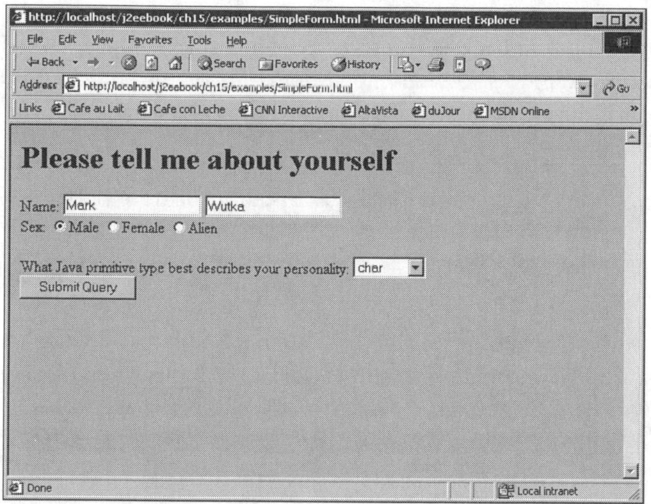

Figure 15.1
HTML forms frequently serve as the front end for a JSP.

The `SimpleFormHandler.jsp` does little more than retrieve the form variables and print out their values. Listing 15.2 shows the contents of `SimpleFormHandler.jsp`, which you can see is pretty short.

Listing 15.2 Source Code for `SimpleFormHandler.jsp`

```
<HTML>
<BODY>

<%

// Grab the variables from the form
       String firstName = request.getParameter("firstName");
       String lastName = request.getParameter("lastName");
       String sex = request.getParameter("sex");
       String javaType = request.getParameter("javaType");
%>
<%-- Print out the variables --%>
<H1>Hello, <%=firstName%> <%=lastName%>!</H1>
I see that you are <%=sex%>. You know, you remind me of a
<%=javaType%> variable I once knew.

</BODY>
</HTML>
```

If you are having trouble displaying the form, or some of the form results, see "Form and Form Variable Names" in the "Troubleshooting" section at the end of this chapter.

Most of `SimpleFormHandler.jsp` should seem familiar to you. It is similar to an example in Chapter 14, "Java Server Pages," that assigned some variables and printed out their values using the `<%= %>` tags. The only new thing introduced in Listing 15.2 is the built-in `request` object. Every Java Server Page has a few built-in objects. The most common ones are `out` and `request`.

The out object was introduced in Chapter 2, "A Quick Primer on SQL," and is the output stream used to send data back to the browser. The request object contains information about the request from the browser and although it contains quite a bit of information, the request object is most commonly used for retrieving the values of form variables.

Tip

The request object is really just an instance of HttpServletRequest. After you know how to use the request object in a JSP, you are ready to use the HttpServletRequest object in a servlet.

As you look at the SimpleFormHandler JSP, it should be fairly obvious what the output would look like. Figure 15.2 shows how SimpleFormHandler looks when displayed in a browser.

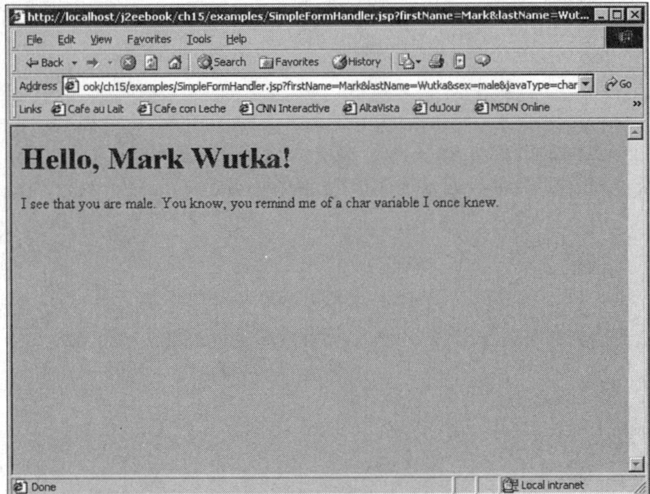

Figure 15.2
A JSP can read form input and embed the form data in its output.

USING THE request OBJECT

As you saw in Listing 15.2, the getParameter method in the request object retrieves the values of form variable. The lone argument to getParameter is the name of the form variable as it was defined in the HTML form, and must match the case exactly. In other words, if you called a form variable firstName in the HTML file, you must pass "firstName" to getParameter and not "firstname" or "FIRSTNAME."

If you ask the request object for the value of a form variable that does not exist, it returns null. Note that getParameter always returns a string. If you are expecting a number, you have to convert it yourself.

Note

There's a difference between a form variable that is empty and a form variable that does not exist. The value of an empty text box is `""` (a string with a length of 0). The `getParameter` method should only return `null` if a form variable does not exist at all.

Although the term "form variable" has been used to describe the parameters passed to the JSP, these parameters technically have nothing to do with forms. When you click the "Submit" button on an HTML form, the browser encodes the form variables and passes them one of two ways: using an HTTP GET command or an HTTP POST command. Without getting down into the nitty-gritty of the HTTP protocol, parameters in a GET command are passed in the actual URL, and in a POST command they are passed in a different part of the request.

You might notice while surfing the Web that the URL displayed by the browser has a ? and some values of the form "name=value" separated by "&" characters. In fact, if you look back at Figure 15.2, you can see exactly that. If you wanted to, you could run `SimpleFormHandler.jsp` directly without going through the initial HTML form. All you need to do is add the parameters to the end of the URL.

Note

URLs have a special encoding for many characters. For example, a space is represented by "+". Many characters are represented by "%" followed by the character's ASCII value in hex. The "=" sign, for instance, is represented by %3D because its ASCII value is 61 decimal or 3D hex. You might want to stick to characters and numbers when entering parameters by hand.

Why is this important? Well, you will often need to test a form handler and rather than typing in the form values every time, you will find that manually passing the parameters straight to the form handler is a big timesaver. Also, because all the form variables are encoded directly into the URL, you can bookmark the JSP in your browser and display the form output whenever you select that bookmark.

Bookmarking a Java Server Page is not always useful, especially when the JSP is just accepting form input. When the JSP is displaying updated information, such as sports scores, weather, stock quotes, or other frequently changing data, bookmarking the page is useful. Unfortunately, if the data is sent to the server via an HTTP POST request, bookmarking doesn't work. The bookmark only contains the URL, and when form data is sent via POST, the URL does not include the form data.

Tip

Because form data in an HTTP POST request isn't bookmarked, you should always use a POST request when you pass private data that shouldn't be bookmarked.

HANDLING MULTIPLE FORM VALUES

The browser passes parameters to the server as a series of name-value pairs, such as "firstname=Sam" or "lastname=Tippin". When there are multiple values for the same form variable name, the browser sends multiple name-value pairs. Listing 15.3 shows a simple input form with several text-input fields.

LISTING 15.3 SOURCE CODE FOR `MultiForm.html`

```
<HTML>
<BODY>

<H1>Please enter a list of names</H1>

<FORM action="MultiFormHandler.jsp" method="get">
        <INPUT type="text" name="names"><BR>
        <INPUT type="text" name="names"><BR>
        <INPUT type="text" name="names"><BR>
        <INPUT type="text" name="names"><BR>
        <INPUT type="text" name="names"><BR>

        <INPUT type="submit">
</FORM>
</BODY>
</HTML>
```

Figure 15.3 shows the form running inside a browser.

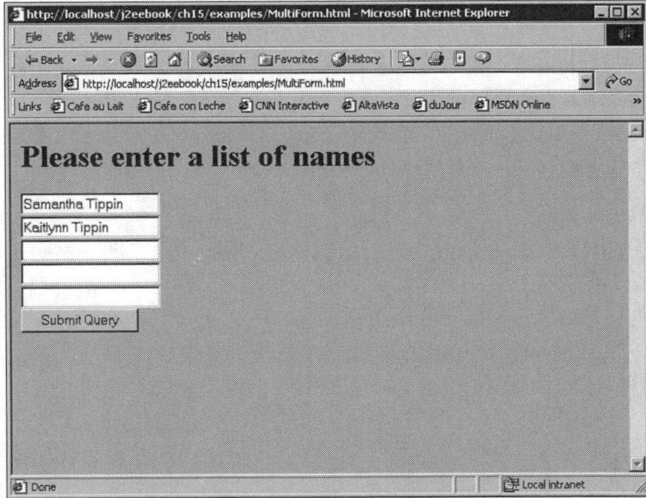

Figure 15.3
You can prompt the user with multiple values for the same form variable.

Notice that in Listing 15.3 the names of each of the fields are the same. If you were to use the `getParameter` method to fetch the names, you would only get the first one. When you need to fetch multiple parameters, use the `getParameterValues` method. Listing 15.4 shows a Java Server Page that retrieves the values from the page in Listing 15.3.

LISTING 15.4 SOURCE CODE FOR MultiFormHandler.jsp

```
<HTML>
<BODY>
The names you entered are:
<PRE>
<%
// Fetch the name values
       String names[] = request.getParameterValues("names");

       for (int i=0; i < names.length; i++)
       {
                out.println(names[i]);
       }
%>
</PRE>

</BODY>
</HTML>
```

There are two things you need to know about the getParameterValues method:

- If the parameter value doesn't exist at all (that is, there was no form variable with that name), then getParameterValues returns null.
- If there is exactly one parameter value, you still get back an array. The length of this array will be 1.

You usually know the names of all the parameters you are expecting, but when you need to discover the names of all the parameters passed in, you can use the getParameterNames method. The method signature for getParameterNames in the request object is

```
java.util.Enumeration getParameterNames()
```

The getParameterNames method returns an enumeration of String objects. Each of these strings is the name of a parameter and can be used as an argument to getParameter or getParameterValues. Listing 15.5 shows a Java Server Page that dumps out the names and values of all the parameters passed to it, including multiple values.

LISTING 15.5 SOURCE CODE FOR ShowParameters.jsp

```
<HTML>
<BODY>
You passed me the following parameters:
<PRE>
<%

// Find out the names of all the parameters
        java.util.Enumeration params = request.getParameterNames();

        while (params.hasMoreElements())
        {
// Get the next parameter name
              String paramName = (String) params.nextElement();
```

LISTING 15.5 CONTINUED

```
// Use getParameterValues in case there are multiple values
                String paramValues[] =
                          request.getParameterValues(paramName);

// If there is only one value, print it out
                if (paramValues.length == 1)
                {
                          out.println(paramName+"="+paramValues[0]);
                }
                else
                {
// For multiple values, loop through them
                          out.print(paramName+"=");

                          for (int i=0; i < paramValues.length; i++)
                          {
// If this isn't the first value, print a comma to separate values
                                    if (i > 0) out.print(',');

                                    out.print(paramValues[i]);
                          }
                          out.println();
                }
        }
%>
</PRE>
</BODY>
</HTML>
```

Figure 15.4 shows the output from the JSP shown in listing 15.5. You can easily play around with the `ShowParameters` JSP by passing parameters directly in the browser. One such set of parameters is shown at the top of Figure 15.4.

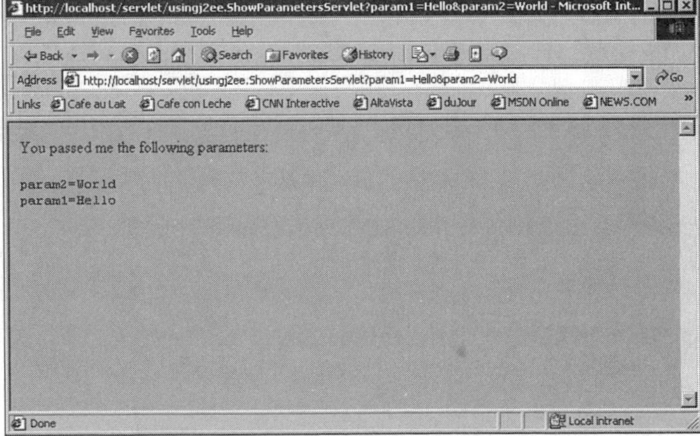

Figure 15.4
You can pass parameters to the JSP manually by adding them to the end of the URL.

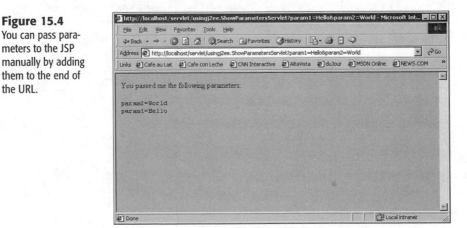

RETRIEVING FORM VARIABLES IN A SERVLET

Up to this point, the discussion has centered around the `request` object in Java Server Pages. In case you missed it, the `request` object in a JSP is an instance of `HttpServletRequest`. If you recall from Chapter 13, "Servlets," an HTTP servlet receives an instance of `HttpServletRequest` when its `service` method is invoked. This means, of course, that you already know how to retrieve form variables in a servlet because you do it the same way you do in a Java Server Page.

Listing 15.6 shows a servlet version of the `ShowParameters` Java Server Page you saw in Listing 15.5. Again, you can test it out by passing parameters directly in the URL.

LISTING 15.6 SOURCE CODE FOR `ShowParametersServlet.java`

```
package usingj2ee;

import javax.servlet.*;
import javax.servlet.http.*;
import java.io.*;
import java.util.*;

public class ShowParametersServlet extends HttpServlet
{
    public void service(HttpServletRequest request,
        HttpServletResponse response)
        throws IOException
    {
// Tell the Web server that the response is HTML
        response.setContentType("text/html");

        PrintWriter out = response.getWriter();

        out.println("<HTML>");
        out.println("<BODY>");
        out.println("You passed me the following parameters:");
        out.println("<PRE>");

// Find out the names of all the parameters
        Enumeration params = request.getParameterNames();

        while (params.hasMoreElements())
        {
// Get the next parameter name
            String paramName = (String) params.nextElement();

// Use getParameterValues in case there are multiple values
            String paramValues[] =
                request.getParameterValues(paramName);

// If there is only one value, print it out
            if (paramValues.length == 1)
            {
                out.println(paramName+
                    "="+paramValues[0]);
            }
```

LISTING 15.6 CONTINUED

```
            else
            {
// For multiple values, loop through them
                out.print(paramName+"=");

                for (int i=0; i < paramValues.length; i++)
                {
// If this isn't the first value, print a comma to separate values
                    if (i > 0) out.print(',');

                    out.print(paramValues[i]);
                }
                out.println();
            }
        }

        out.println("</PRE>");
        out.println("</BODY>");
        out.println("</HTML>");
    }
}
```

The output from `ShowParametersServlet` is identical to the output from the `ShowParameters` JSP. In fact, the core part of both programs is the same. The only difference is the code to print out the beginning and ending HTML tags.

STORING DATA IN A `session` OBJECT

One thing you need to realize when dealing with the Web is that there is no permanent connection between the browser and the Web server. If you have done database programming or socket programming, you are familiar with the concept of a *session*—an active connection between two participants.

The HTTP protocol used by the browser and the Web server is not session-oriented. When the browser needs a page from the Web server, it opens a connection, retrieves the page, and then closes the connection. Because there is no active connection, the Web server has no idea what is happening on the browser. The browser could crash or the entire client computer could be turned off and the Web server would be oblivious.

That being said, servlets and Java Server Pages do have a notion of a session, and it comes in the form of the `HttpSession` object. The beauty of the `HttpSession` object is that it does not rely on form variables and will work even if a servlet or JSP is accessed via a hyperlink. `HttpSession` is able to work without hidden form variables because it uses a cookie to store the user's session key. The only thing you need to know about cookies at this point is that a *cookie* contains a piece of data that the server sends to the browser and that the browser sends back to the server with each request.

USING THE session OBJECT IN A JSP

The Java Server Pages API has several built-in objects. You have already seen two of them—request and out. The next important one is called session, an instance of HttpSession. The three methods that you use the most in the session object are getAttribute, setAttribute, and removeAttribute. The declarations for these methods are

```
public void setAttribute(String name, Object value)
    throws IllegalStateException
public Object getAttribute(String name)
    throws IllegalStateException
public void removeAttribute(String name, Object value)
    throws IllegalStateException
```

These methods act much like the get and put methods in the Hashtable class. That is, setAttribute associates a name with a value, and getAttribute returns the value associated with a name or null if there is no value associated. For example, to store some data in a session, you would do something like this:

```
session.setAttribute("someKey", "here is my data");
```

To retrieve the data back out of the session, you would do something like this:

```
String myData = (String) session.getAttribute("someKey");
```

Note

The getAttribute, setAttribute, and removeAttribute methods were added to the servlet API in version 2.2. Prior to version 2.2, these methods were called getValue, putValue, and removeValue (with the same parameters). Although getValue, putValue, and removeValue are supported under version 2.2 of the servlet API, they are deprecated. Only use them if your servlets must run under servlet API version 2.1 or earlier.

IllegalStateException is thrown when you try to get or set an attribute on an invalid session. A session becomes invalid either when you call its invalidate method or after the session has timed out. The servlet engine keeps track of how long it has been since a session has been accessed and, after a certain period of inactivity, the session is marked as invalid. You can configure the amount of time it takes to time out a session, either on a per-session basis or for all sessions.

Note

The servlet API specifies a way for you to control the timeout period on a per-session basis. Most servlet engines also provide a way for you to specify a default timeout length, but they are not required to by the servlet API.

Listing 15.7 shows a login page that calls a JSP to handle the login.

LISTING 15.7 SOURCE CODE FOR Login.html

```
<HTML>
<BODY bgcolor="#ffffff">
<H1>Login</H1>
```

Listing 15.7 Continued

```
Please log in

<FORM action="Login.jsp" method="POST">

<TABLE>
<TR><TD>User Name:<TD><INPUT type="text" name="username">
<TR><TD>Password:<TD><INPUT type="password" name="password">
</TABLE>
<P>
<INPUT type="submit" value="Login!">
</FORM>
</BODY>
</HTML>
```

Listing 15.8 shows the `Login.jsp` page that stores the user information in a session.

Listing 15.8 Source Code for `Login.jsp`

```
<%@ page language="java" import="java.util.*,usingj2ee.*" %>


<HTML>
<BODY bgcolor="#ffffff">

<%
// Get the login information
    String userName = request.getParameter("username");
    String password = request.getParameter("password");

// Store the username in the session
    session.setAttribute("username", userName);
%>
Welcome, <%=userName%>!
<FORM action="/servlet/usingj2ee.ColorServlet" method="POST">

<P>
Please enter your favorite color:
<SELECT name="color">
    <OPTION value="blue" SELECTED>Blue</OPTION>
    <OPTION value="red">Red</OPTION>
    <OPTION value="green">Green</OPTION>
    <OPTION value="yellow">Yellow</OPTION>
    <OPTION value="mauve">Mauve</OPTION>
</SELECT>
<P>
<INPUT type="submit" value="Choose color!">
</FORM>
</BODY>
</HTML>
```

USING THE session OBJECT IN A SERVLET

You have probably guessed this already, but the session object that you use in a servlet is identical to the one you use in a Java Server Page. The only difference is that it isn't already conveniently sitting around in a variable named session. Instead, you must get the session object from the request object.

To get the session object from the request object, just call the getSession method:

```
HttpSession session = request.getSession();
```

Inside a servlet, you use the same getAttribute and setAttribute methods to update session variables as you do in a Java Server Page. After all, the session object is an instance of HttpSession in both a servlet and a JSP.

Caution

Because the servlet engine needs to send a session cookie back to the browser, make sure you get the session before you start sending a response back to the browser. Otherwise, it might be too late for the servlet engine to send back the cookie, because the cookie must be sent back in the header portion of the response. In a JSP, the session is usually available immediately. You really only need to worry about this inside a servlet.

Listing 15.9 shows a servlet that reads the session information stored by Login.jsp.

LISTING 15.9 SOURCE CODE FOR ColorServlet.java

```
package usingj2ee;

import javax.servlet.*;
import javax.servlet.http.*;
import java.io.*;
import java.util.*;

public class ColorServlet extends HttpServlet
{
    public void service(HttpServletRequest request,
        HttpServletResponse response)
        throws IOException
    {
// Tell the Web server that the response is HTML
        response.setContentType("text/html");

// Get the PrintWriter for writing out the response
        PrintWriter out = response.getWriter();

// Fetch the color parameter
        String color = request.getParameter("color");

// Get the username from the session
        HttpSession session = request.getSession();
```

LISTING 15.9 CONTINUED

```
        String userName = (String) session.getAttribute("username");

// Write the HTML back to the browser
        out.println("<HTML>");
        out.println("<BODY bgcolor=\"#ffffff\">");
        out.println("Well, I see that "+userName+
            "'s favorite color is "+color+".");
        out.println("</BODY>");
        out.println("</HTML>");
    }
}
```

Note

Because the `HttpSession` object relies specifically on features of the HTTP protocol, you can only use it in servlets that are subclasses of `HttpServlet`.

HOW SESSIONS WORK

Now that you see that servlets and Java Server Pages can support sessions, you can take a step back and look at how the sessions work. When the servlet engine creates a session, it sends a session identifier (also referred to as a session key earlier in this chapter) back to the browser in the form of a cookie. Again, the cookie is just a piece of information that the browser sends back to the server whenever it asks the server for a page.

Usually, for a session, the cookie disappears when the Web browser is shut down.

A browser can, however, save cookies to disk, so that when the browser starts up again it still knows about the cookies it had when it was shut down. Because sessions are typically short-lived, and because shutting the browser down is an action that would warrant the termination of a session, the session cookie is usually not saved to disk. Remember, the server has no idea when the Web browser shuts down. Figure 15.5 illustrates the interaction between the browser and the servlet engine as it relates to cookies and sessions.

When the browser asks the server for a page, the server looks at the session cookie, and then finds the session corresponding to that session identifier. Occasionally, the servlet engine will look through its sessions and get rid of those that haven't been accessed in a long time. If it didn't do this, the servlet engine would eventually be wasting a lot of memory holding onto sessions that could never be accessed again because the cookies associated with those sessions are long gone (people shut down their browsers eventually, and that would kill the session cookies).

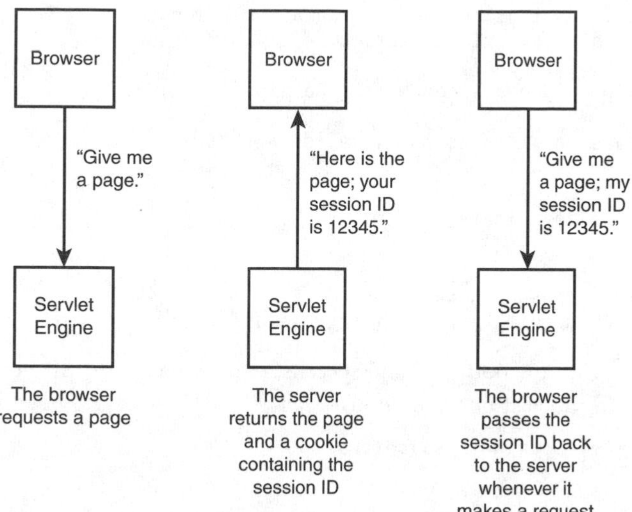

Figure 15.5
The server sends the session identifier in a cookie, which the browser passes back.

FORCING A NEW SESSION

When you call the `getSession` method to retrieve the current session, the `request` object automatically creates a session if one doesn't already exist. In some JSP implementations, the session is created automatically even if you never use it. Most of the time, you don't really care when the session has been created. Other times, however, you need to explicitly reset the existing session and start over.

Suppose, for example, that you have implemented an online shopping site. A user logs on, visits a few pages, and selects several items to buy. You store these items in the user's session as they travel from page to page. Now, suppose that the user decides that she doesn't want any of these items, and rather than go through the trouble of removing them from her shopping cart, she decides to just log in to your site again.

If a user comes back into your login page, you probably want to start her over with a clean slate. Although you could design a site that is smart enough to figure out what you were last doing and send you back to where you left off, most people assume that when they come in through the "front door," they are starting over fresh.

Note

> A user might go back to the login screen and walk away from the computer, thinking that his order is now gone. Imagine his surprise if another user could walk up to the computer, log back in, and have the previous user's order complete with credit card number.

The `getSession` method in the `request` object allows you to control the creation of new sessions. When you ask for a session, you can ask that the `request` object not create a new session if one doesn't already exist. The following segment of code automatically invalidates the previous session and then creates a new one:

```
// Get the old session, but don't create a session if
// one didn't already exist (passing true would allow
// creation of a new one).
    HttpSession oldSess = request.getSession(false);

// If there was an old session, invalidate it
    if (oldSess != null)
    {
        oldSess.invalidate();
    }

// Now create a fresh new session
    HttpSession session = request.getSession(true);
```

This code will work for both JSP and servlets, except that for a JSP, you shouldn't redeclare `session`. Instead, the last line should just read

```
session = request.getSession(true);
```

HANDLING SESSION TERMINATION

There are two ways a session can be terminated: You force the termination by calling the `invalidate` method on the session, or the servlet engine times the session out. Depending on what kind of data you store in the session, you might need to perform some kind of cleanup of the session data. For example, you might have a database connection stored in the session, or a connection to an RMI or CORBA service on another machine. Although these resources would eventually be eliminated by Java's garbage collector, you shouldn't keep them open any longer than you need to.

A `session` object has a callback mechanism to notify an object when it has been associated with a session and when it is no longer associated with a session. That is, when you call `session.setAttribute("someName", someObject)`, the `session` object can notify the object that it is being associated with a session. When the session terminates, the `session` object can notify the object that it is no longer associated with the session.

This notification is on an object-by-object basis. Although it might seem strange at first, the notification technique is actually very flexible. You can write objects that are session aware and can perform their own cleanup. If you are using standard objects, such as a JDBC `Connection` object, you can create a special `session` cleanup object that releases your database connection.

THE `HttpSessionBindingListener` INTERFACE

The `HttpSessionBindingListener` interface defines notification methods that the `session` object uses to notify objects when they are added to or removed from a session. There are two methods in the interface:

```
public void valueBound(HttpSessionBindingEvent event);
public void valueUnbound(HttpSessionBindingEvent event);
```

As you might have guessed, `valueBound` is called when an object is added to a session, whereas `valueUnbound` is called when the object is removed from a session. Listing 15.10 shows an example class that listens for `valueBound` and `valueUnbound` messages and counts the number of sessions that are bound to it.

LISTING 15.10 SOURCE CODE FOR `BindListener.java`

```
package usingj2ee;

import javax.servlet.http.*;

/** Counts the number of sessions that are bound to this object. */

public class BindListener implements HttpSessionBindingListener
{
// The current session count
    protected int numSessions;

    public BindListener()
    {
        numSessions = 0;
    }

// Every time this object is added to a session,
// valueBound is called
    public synchronized void valueBound(HttpSessionBindingEvent event)
    {
        numSessions++;
    }

// Every time this object is removed from a session,
// valueUnbound is called
    public synchronized void valueUnbound(HttpSessionBindingEvent event)
    {
        numSessions--;
    }

// Returns the current number of bound sessions
    public int getNumSessions()
    {
        return numSessions;
    }
}
```

To test the `BindListener` class, you need to observe what happens when you access it from multiple sessions, and also what happens when you invalidate a session containing a `BindListener` object. You should expect to see the session count go up whenever the object is added to a session, and you should see the count go down when the object is removed from a session, or when the session it belongs to is invalidated.

Listing 15.11 shows a test harness JSP that exercises the `BindListener` class. By selecting various hyperlinks, you can remove the `BindListener` object from the session or invalidate the session.

LISTING 15.11 SOURCE CODE FOR BindTest.jsp

```
<%@ page language="java" import="usingj2ee.BindListener" %>

<HTML>
<BODY bgcolor="#ffffff">

<%-- Set up a static BindListener shared by all instances of this JSP.

     There is probably only one instance, but just in case the server creates

     multiple instances, this page can handle it. --%>
<%!
    protected static BindListener listener = new BindListener();
%>

<%

    BindListener l = null;

// Allow the browser to pass a "removeListener" parameter to remove
// a listener from the session

    if (request.getParameter("removeListener") != null)
    {
        session.removeAttribute("listener");
    }

// Allow the browser to pass a "resetSession" parameter to clear out
// the session
    else if (request.getParameter("resetSession") != null)
    {
// See if there is already a session
        HttpSession oldSession = request.getSession(false);

// If there was already a session, invalidate
        if (oldSession != null)
        {
            l = (BindListener)
                oldSession.getAttribute("listener");
            oldSession.invalidate();

// Tell the user that the session was reset and show that the
// bind counts have been updated. Make sure there was a
// listener on the old session, too.

            if (l != null)
            {
%>
Your current session was reset. The listener now has <%=l.getNumSessions()%>
active sessions.<P>
<%
            } else {
%>
Your old session didn't have a listener.<P>
<%
            }
```

```
            l = null;
        }
    }
    else
    {
// See if the listener is already in the session
        l = (BindListener)
            session.getAttribute("listener");

// If not, add the global copy of the listener to the session
        if (l == null)
        {
// Put the global listener variable into the session
            session.setAttribute("listener", listener);
            l = listener;
        }
    }
%>
<%
    if (l != null)
    {
%>
You have a listener bound to your session.
<%
    } else {
%>
You do not have a listener bound to your session.
<%
    }
%>
There are currently <%=listener.getNumSessions()%> sessions holding onto the
bind listener.
<P>
<TABLE>
<TR>
<TD>
<A href="BindTest.jsp">Refresh Form</A>
<TD>
<A href="BindTest.jsp?removeListener">Remove Listener</A>
<TD>
<A href="BindTest.jsp?resetSession">Reset Session</A>
</TABLE>
</BODY>
</HTML>
```

Caution

The Tomcat JSP engine may not run the `BindTest.jsp` example correctly. The Tomcat 3.1 implementation had a problem with managing the listeners that might not be fixed in the current implementation.

Figure 15.6 shows several browser sessions running `BindTest.jsp`.

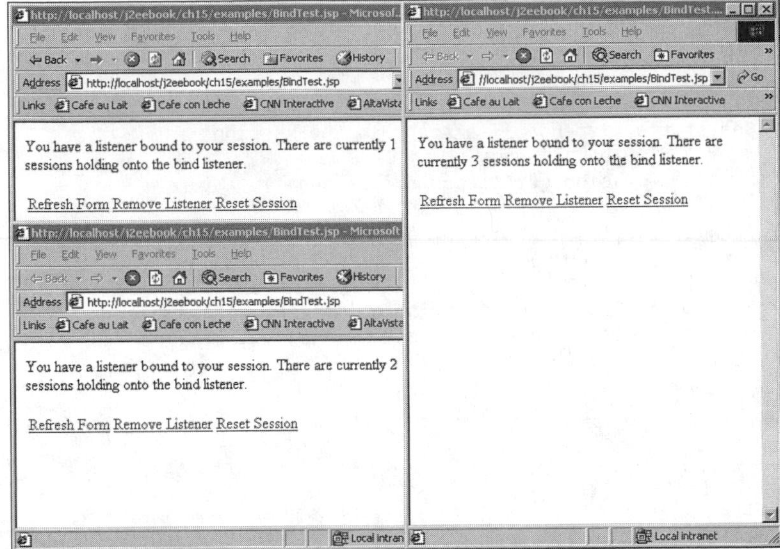

Figure 15.6
The `BindListener` object keeps track of how many sessions it belongs to.

HANDLING SESSIONS WITHOUT COOKIES

Normally, JSP and servlet sessions rely on the HTTP cookie mechanism to preserve the session identifier between requests. Cookies are really nice for doing things like sessions, and even for online ordering. Unfortunately, cookies have also been abused. Many Web sites store personal information in cookies, and many Web users don't like their personal information being sent to another Web server without their knowledge. To put it simply, cookie abuse has given cookies a bad name.

Many users now disable cookies within their browser. You might think that with cookies disabled, there is no way to keep track of session information.

Fortunately, there is another solution.

If you knew the session ID, you could pass it as a parameter to all your servlets and Java Server Pages. The `HttpSession` object contains a `getId` method, so you could pass it around. Now all you need is a way to take a session ID and find the session with that ID. In version 2.1 of the servlet API, there was a way to locate a session by ID (the `getSession` method in the `HttpSessionContext` object). Unfortunately, the `HttpSessionContext` class has been deprecated for version 2.2 of the servlet API, meaning the class might be removed from future versions of the servlet API.

You don't need to go through the trouble of tracking the session ID, however. The servlet API provides a way for you to insert a session ID into a URL. The idea is, for every URL in your Web application that refers to a servlet or a JSP, you insert the session ID as a parameter to that servlet or JSP. Because the session ID is normally stored in a cookie, you only need to pass the session ID as a parameter when cookies are disabled.

Note

Many Web sites that do session-oriented work require you to enable cookies. Although it is nice to be able to support sessions without cookies, users generally find them acceptable for applications such as online shopping. If you decide to require cookies, you might need to put a note on your Web site explaining the necessity of cookies.

The `HttpServletResponse` object (the `response` object in a JSP) contains two methods to help you pass the session ID around to different pages:

```
public String encodeURL(String url);
public String encodeRedirectURL(String url);
```

If you need to do session tracking but the browser doesn't support cookies, `encodeURL` and `encodeRedirectURL` will return a modified URL containing the session ID as a parameter for that URL. If the browser supports cookies, the URL is returned unmodified. Listing 15.12 shows a JSP that presents a form, handles the submission of the form, and puts the form results into a session. It calls `encodeURL` and `encodeRedirectURL` to make sure that sessions are supported even with cookies turned off.

LISTING 15.12 SOURCE CODE FOR RewriteDemo.jsp

```
<HTML>
<BODY>

<H1>URL Rewriting Demo</H1>

<%-- See if the session already contains the name.
    If so, say "Hello" to the user --%>

<%
    String name = (String) session.getAttribute("name");


    if (name != null)
    {
// This user already has a session, show the name and show the list of
// items they have entered

        out.println("Hello, "+name+"!");
%>
        <A href="<%=response.encodeURL("RewriteDemo2.jsp")%>">
            Click here to continue</A>
<%

    }
// If name is passed in as a parameter, it must be as a response to
// the form input. Put it in the session and redirect it to the second
// page.
    else if (request.getParameter("name") != null)
    {
        session.setAttribute("name",
            request.getParameter("name"));
        response.sendRedirect(response.encodeRedirectURL(
            "RewriteDemo2.jsp"));
```

LISTING 15.12 CONTINUED

```
    }
    else
    {
%>
<FORM ACTION="<%=response.encodeURL("RewriteDemo.jsp")%>">
Please enter your name: <INPUT type=text name="name">
<P>
<INPUT type="submit" value="Login!">
</FORM>
<%
    }
%>

</BODY>
</HTML>
```

Figure 15.7 shows the results from `RewriteDemo2.jsp`, which `RewriteDemo.jsp` redirects the user to. Notice that the address line contains an embedded session ID. The session ID appears because the browser in this situation has cookies turned off.

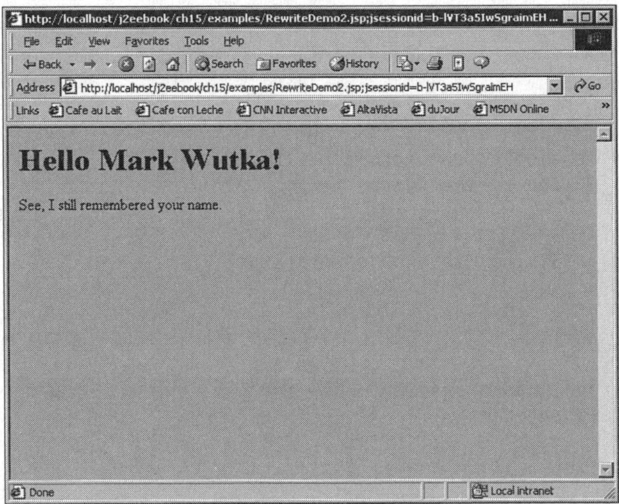

Figure 15.7
The session ID can be embedded in a URL.

Tip

To turn cookies off in Internet Explorer, change the security setting for your security zone to High. If you are accessing pages on your local machine or a machine on your local network, change the Local Intranet Zone security setting. Otherwise, change the setting for Internet Zone.

Listing 15.13 shows the `RewriteDemo2.jsp` file.

LISTING 15.13 SOURCE CODE FOR RewriteDemo2.jsp

```
<HTML>
<BODY>
<H1>Hello <%=session.getAttribute("name")%>!</H1>
<P>
See, I still remembered your name.
</BODY>
<HTML>
```

Unfortunately, to make full use of URL rewriting, you must pass all your pages through the URL rewriting process. In other words, if you have a static HTML page with links to Java Server Pages or servlets that need session information, you must turn these static HTML pages into Java Server Pages that use `encodeURL` to rewrite the HREF values for all the hyperlinks. In other words, in your HTML file where you have a line such as this

```
<a href="CallMe.jsp">
```

the JSP file would read like this:

```
<a href="<%=response.encodeURL("CallMe.jsp")%>">
```

You would also need to change the action attributes in each of your `<FORM>` tags. A `<FORM>` tag with an action of `"HandleForm.jsp"` would appear in the JSP, like this:

```
<form action="<%=response.encodeURL("HandleForm.jsp")%>">
```

Note Modifying your Web site to rewrite all your forms and hyperlinks is a difficult task. Try to design your site to minimize the amount of rewriting necessary.

STORING APPLICATION-WIDE DATA

The `HttpSession` class stores data items on a per-user basis. Sometimes, however, you have data that you need to share between various servlets and Java Server Pages that doesn't need to be stored for each user. For example, if you are writing a database application, you might need to share a database connection. From a Java Server Page, you can store data in the `application` object. The methods for storing data in the `application` object are identical to the ones for the `session` object:

```
public void setAttribute(String name, Object value)
public Object getAttribute(String name)
public void removeAttribute(String name, Object value)
```

From a JSP, if you want to store information in the application object with a name of `myInformation`, you would make a call, like this:

```
application.setAttribute("myInformation", "Here is the info");
```

To get the information back out of the application object, you would call `getAttribute`:

```
String theInfo = (String) application.getAttribute("myInformation");
```

The application object is really an object that implements the ServletContext interface. The servlet context is also available from within servlet. If your servlet is a subclass of GenericServlet or HttpServlet, as most are, you can call the getServletContext method:

```
ServletContext context = getServletContext();

context.setAttribute("myInformation", "Here is the info");
```

Remember, your servlet doesn't have to be a subclass of GenericServlet or HttpServlet. You could choose to write your own class that implements the Servlet interface. If you need to get the servlet context in these cases, it is contained in the ServletConfig object that is passed to your servlet's init method. You can always call getServletConfig().getServletContext() to get the servlet context.

WHY DO YOU NEED THE application OBJECT?

From all appearances, the application object seems like overkill. What is the difference between storing something in the application object and storing it in a static variable somewhere? You will see in Chapter 21, "Packaging and Installing a J2EE Application," that it is possible to group a set of Java Server Pages and servlets into an application. The servlet engine knows which application a particular JSP or servlet belongs to. You could, for example, have a set of Java Server Pages deployed in a server under an application called "QA" and an identical set of JSPs under an application called "Beta". These two applications, although running in the same server and the same Java Virtual Machine, would have different application objects (that is, different ServletContext objects).

Now you can see how this differs from a static variable. If you tried to store a data item in a static variable, you would circumvent the notion of separate applications. There is only one copy of a static variable within a single Java Virtual Machine. You can't say that the "QA" application gets its own copy of a static variable while the "Beta" application gets another unless you are somehow able to run each application in a separate virtual machine. Because you can't count on a servlet engine to support multiple JVMs, you shouldn't rely on static variables for application-level data sharing.

TROUBLESHOOTING

FORM AND FORM VARIABLE NAMES

I clicked the Submit button, but the form won't load.

Aside from the obvious spelling errors in the action attribute of the <FORM>, you must also make sure that the capitalization action attribute matches the name of the form JSP. Even if you are running under Windows, Java is case sensitive, so you can run into problems if you try to invoke a JSP using capitalization that is different from the actual filename.

My form variable values are null.

Usually the reason you can't get the value of a form variable is because the name of the variable in the form doesn't exactly match the name you use in the getParameter method, either because of a spelling difference or a capitalization difference.

CHAPTER 16

Extending JSP with New Tags

In this chapter

Up to this point, you have only seen the basic syntax and core features of Java Server Pages and servlets. Many of the examples you have seen are difficult to read because they frequently shift between Java and HTML. In fact, one of the biggest complaints about JSP is that the pages end up looking messy and become difficult maintain. In this chapter, you will see how to organize your Java Server Pages and servlets to make them much easier to read and maintain.

INCLUDING OTHER FILES

Splitting your code is one of the first techniques you can use to organize it. Many sites have a consistent header on every page. You can put the header into a separate file and include it in every page. When you need to change the header, you only need to change one file.

Within a Java Server Page, you can choose to include another file at page compile time or at runtime. The advantage of including a file at compilation time is performance. At runtime, the JSP engine doesn't need to do any work because the file has already been included. Unfortunately, the servlet engine can only include files at runtime. After all, you are the one who compiles the server—how could the servlet engine include something at compile time?

To include another file at compile time, use the include directive, like this:

```
<%@ include file="includedFileName" flush="true"%>
```

Note

The path for the included file is relative to the path of the original JSP. That is, if the included file is in the same directory as the including file, you don't need to specify a directory name.

Listing 16.1 shows a JSP file that includes another file. Because the file is included at compile time, you can look at the generated servlet and see that the included code is there.

LISTING 16.1 SOURCE CODE FOR `CrazyWorld.jsp`

```
<HTML>
<BODY>
<%@ include file="Header.html" %>
<p>
Welcome to <i>It's a Crazy World</i>
<p>
</BODY>
</HTML>
```

By putting all your header code in a single file, you can make sure that all your pages have an identical header. When you change the header, you only need to change one file.

Listing 16.2 shows the `Header.html` file included by `CrazyWorld.jsp`.

Listing 16.2 Source Code for `Header.html`

```
<table bgcolor="#0000ff">
<tr><td><img src="face.jpg" align=left></td>
<td><h1><font color="#ffff00">It's a Crazy World</font></h1></td>
<td><img src="face.jpg" align=right></td></tr>
</table>
```

Figure 16.1 shows `CrazyWorld.jsp` as it appears in a browser. The image and header come from `Header.html`, and the welcome message comes from `CrazyWorld.jsp` itself.

Figure 16.1 You can include header information at compile time using `<%@ include %>`.

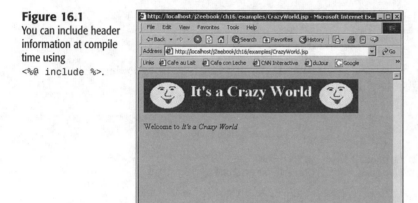

When you include a file with the include directive, the JSP compiler processes the included file as if it were part of the JSP. You can use any JSP directives within the included file, and even include another file. Any variables and methods defined in the main JSP are available to included files.

Caution

The JSP specification does not provide a standard way for a JSP engine to learn that an included file has changed. Many JSP engines can detect that an included file has changed, but some cannot. You should test your JSP engine to see whether it can detect changes in included files and recompile automatically.

Although there is a potential speed gain by including files at compile time, you give up a lot of flexibility. When you include files at runtime, you are able to freely mix servlets and Java Server Pages.

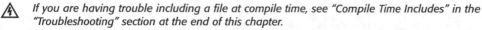

If you are having trouble including a file at compile time, see "Compile Time Includes" in the "Troubleshooting" section at the end of this chapter.

INCLUDING FILES IN A JSP AT RUNTIME

When you want to include a servlet or another JSP into your JSP, use the `<jsp:include>` directive, like this:

```
<jsp:include page="includedFileName" flush="true"/>
```

The `flush` attribute indicates whether the output buffer should be flushed before the file is included. According to version 1.1 of the JSP specification, this attribute is required but can only have a value of True.

Caution

> Make sure you always include `flush="true"` in your include tags. At least one JSP engine—ServletExec—will report an error if you omit `flush="true"`.

Listing 16.3 shows a menu Java Server Page that displays a tab-style menu, highlighting a specific menu item according to a parameter that is passed to it.

LISTING 16.3 SOURCE CODE FOR Menu.jsp

```
<%
// See which menu item should be highlighted
    String highlighted = request.getParameter("highlighted");

// Set the names for the individual menu items

    String welcome = "welcome.jpg";
    if (highlighted.equalsIgnoreCase("welcome"))
        welcome = "welcomeS.jpg";

    String products = "products.jpg";
    if (highlighted.equalsIgnoreCase("products"))
        products = "productsS.jpg";

    String services = "services.jpg";
    if (highlighted.equalsIgnoreCase("services"))
        services = "servicesS.jpg";

    String support = "support.jpg";
    if (highlighted.equalsIgnoreCase("support"))
        support = "supportS.jpg";

    String aboutUs = "aboutUs.jpg";
    if (highlighted.equalsIgnoreCase("aboutUs"))
        aboutUs = "aboutUsS.jpg";
%>
<table cellpadding="0" cellspacing="0">
<tr>
<td><a href="welcome.jsp"><img src="<%=welcome%>" border="0"></a></td>
<td><a href="products.jsp"><img src="<%=products%>" border="0"></a></td>
<td><a href="services.jsp"><img src="<%=services%>" border="0"></a></td>
<td><a href="support.jsp"><img src="<%=support%>" border="0"></a></td>
<td><a href="aboutUs.jsp"><img src="<%=aboutUs%>" border="0"></a></td></tr>
</table>
```

Listing 16.4 shows a JSP that includes the Menu.jsp file using the <jsp:include> tag.

LISTING 16.4 SOURCE CODE TO support.jsp

```
<HTML>
<BODY bgcolor="#ffffff">
<%@ include file="Header2.html"%>

<jsp:include page="Menu.jsp" flush="true">
    <jsp:param name="highlighted" value="support"/>
</jsp:include>
<p>
<h1>Frequently Asked Questions</h1>
<p>
<i>What in the world is a Zither?</i>
<br>
A zither is a stringed instrument that has between 30 and 40 strings.
<p>
<i>How do you expect to earn money if all you sell is zithers?</i>
<br>
We don't. This business is a tax write-off for our highly successful
Amalgamated Golf Tees, Inc.

</BODY>
</HTML>
```


Note

Listing 16.4 uses the <jsp:param> tag (discussed later in this chapter) to tell the Menu.jsp file which item to highlight. It also uses the <%@ include %> tag to include a standard header.

Figure 16.2 shows the output of support.jsp. The menu items are generated by the Menu.jsp file.

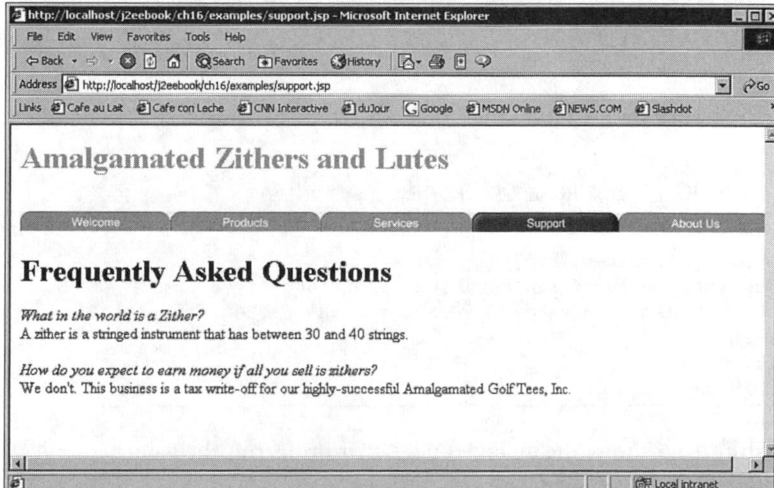

Figure 16.2
You can use the <jsp:include> tag to implement a menu.

A few restrictions are imposed on files when they are included at runtime. These restrictions are not imposed on files that are included at compile time. An included file cannot change any header information sent back to the browser. You cannot set any cookie information from within an included file.

If you are having trouble including a file at runtime, see "Runtime Includes" in the "Troubleshooting" section at the end of this chapter.

PASSING PARAMETERS TO AN INCLUDED FILE

Included files can access all the information in the `request` object, so they have access to any form variables passed from the browser. In addition, you can pass parameters to the included file using the `<jsp:param>` directive:

```
<jsp:include page="someIncludedPage" flush="true">
    <jsp:param name="myParamName" value="paramData"/>
</jsp:include>
```

Note

The `<jsp:include>` tag follows the XML standard of ending a tag with /> when there is no closing tag. When you include a file and don't pass any parameters, end the `<jsp:include>` tag with />. When you pass parameters with `<jsp:param>`, you include a closing `</jsp:include>` tag. Notice too, that the `<jsp:param>` tag closes with a />.

The included file fetches the parameters using `request.getParameter` and `request.getParameterValues` just as if the parameters were passed from the browser as form variables. Values from `<jsp:param>` take precedence over parameters already in the request. In other words, if you use `getParameter` to retrieve the parameter value, you will get the value specified in `<jsp:param>`. If you use `getParameterValues`, you will get both the value specified by `<jsp:param>` and the value passed from the browser.

Note

The parameters added with the `<jsp:param>` tag are only visible to the included page. They are not visible to the original page; that is, they don't affect the original set of parameters.

Listing 16.5 shows a page that includes another page while passing it a parameter value.

LISTING 16.5 SOURCE CODE FOR `MainForm.jsp`

```
<HTML>
<BODY bgcolor="#ffffff">
<jsp:include page="IncludedForm.jsp" flush="true">
    <jsp:param name="myVar" value="I was passed from main"/>
</jsp:include>
</BODY>
</HTML>
```

Listing 16.6 shows the included page that prints out the values for `myVar` using `getParameter` and `getParameter` values.

LISTING 16.6 SOURCE CODE FOR IncludedForm.jsp

```
<PRE>
<%
    String myVar = request.getParameter("myVar");
    String myVars[] = request.getParameterValues("myVar");

    out.println("myVar = "+myVar);
    out.println("The values for myVar are:");
    for (int i=0; i < myVars.length; i++)
    {
        out.println(myVars[i]);
    }
%>
</PRE>
```

Notice that the included form doesn't contain `<HTML>` or `<BODY>` tags. It always assumes that it is included from another page and that the surrounding page contains those tags. Figure 16.3 shows the output from `MainForm.jsp`. The original value for `MainForm.jsp` is passed as part of the URL, as you can see in the address line on the browser.

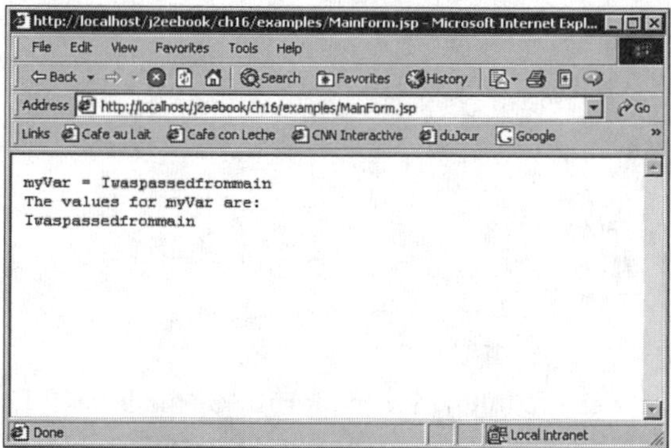

Figure 16.3 Included pages usually assume that they are included and don't contain `<HTML>` or `<BODY>` tags.

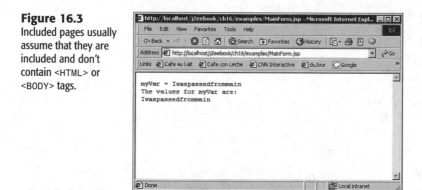

INCLUDING FILES FROM A SERVLET

The servlet API has a peculiar way to include files. Although you might expect either the request or response objects to provide a method to include a file, it's not that simple. To include another servlet, JSP, or text file, you must obtain a request dispatcher for the resource you want to include.

Fortunately, you can obtain a request dispatcher easily. The fastest way to get a request dispatcher is to call `request.getRequestDispatcher` and pass it through the URL of the resource you want to include, like this:

```
RequestDispatcher d =
            request.getRequestDispatcher("destinationURL");
d.include(request, response);
```

Listing 16.7 shows a servlet that includes the `IncludedForm.jsp` from Listing 16.6.

LISTING 16.7 SOURCE CODE FOR MainFormServlet.java

```
package usingj2ee;

import javax.servlet.*;
import java.io.*;

public class MainFormServlet extends GenericServlet
{
    public void service(ServletRequest request,
        ServletResponse response)
        throws IOException, ServletException
    {
// Tell the Web server that the response is HTML
        response.setContentType("text/html");

// Get the PrintWriter for writing out the response
        PrintWriter out = response.getWriter();

// Write the HTML back to the browser
        out.println("<HTML>");
        out.println("<BODY>");

// Get the request dispatcher for the JSP to include
        RequestDispatcher dispatcher =
            request.getRequestDispatcher(
                "/j2eebook/ch16/examples/IncludedForm.jsp");

        dispatcher.include(request, response);

        out.println("</BODY>");
        out.println("</HTML>");
    }
}
```

Notice that Listing 16.7 uses the full pathname for the included JSP. The servlet is not in the same directory as the JSP it is including. The `getRequestDispatcher` method takes a relative URL, so if you include another servlet that is in the same directory as your servlet, you don't have to specify the full pathname.

Tip

To pass parameters to a resource you are including, add the parameters to the URL when you call `getRequestDispatcher`. For example: `getRequestDispatcher("MyForm.jsp?param1=blah")`.

FORWARDING TO ANOTHER PAGE

In addition to including another page, you can transfer to another page without returning to the original. This technique is called *forwarding*. When you forward the request on to another page (or servlet), the forwarding page is no longer involved in handling the request. You typically would use forwarding to handle an error, or if you need several different response pages that depend on the data in the request. In the latter case, you would use a JSP or a servlet to look at the incoming request, decide which response page to use, and forward the request on to that page.

FORWARDING TO ANOTHER PAGE FROM A JSP

The JSP syntax for forwarding is very similar to the syntax for including. You use the `<jsp:forward>` tag like this:

```
<jsp:forward page="destinationPage"/>
```

When you forward to another page or servlet, your original page is replaced with the new page. That is, any output you might have sent is cleared.

Tip

If you get an `IllegalStateException` when forwarding to another page, you might not be buffering the page. Make sure you turn on the buffering.

Listing 16.8 shows a simple JSP that forwards itself to another page.

LISTING 16.8 SOURCE CODE FOR `MainForwarder.jsp`

```
<HTML>
<BODY>

You should never see me because my output is erased before forwarding.

<jsp:forward page="ForwardedPage.jsp"/>
</BODY>
</HTML>
```

As you can see in Figure 16.4, the text in the `MainForwarder.jsp` file doesn't show in the browser because it is erased before the `ForwardedPage.jsp` page executes.

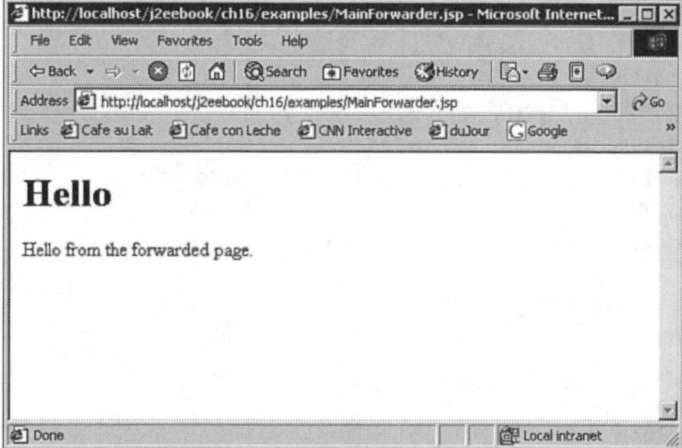

Figure 16.4 When a JSP forwards to another JSP, the output from the original JSP is lost.

FORWARDING TO ANOTHER PAGE FROM A SERVLET

Just as the syntax for forwarding from a JSP is similar to the syntax for including, the syntax for forwarding from a servlet is also very similar. You again use the `RequestDispatcher` object, only this time instead of calling it `include` method, you call it `forward` method:

```
RequestDispatcher d =
        request.getRequestDispatcher("destinationURL");
d.forward(request, response);
```

Listing 16.9 shows an example servlet that forwards to the same `ForwardedPage.jsp` page used by the JSP in Listing 16.8. Again, the output from the servlet is erased before the forwarded page runs.

LISTING 16.9 SOURCE CODE FOR `ForwarderServlet.java`

```
package usingj2ee;

import javax.servlet.*;
import java.io.*;

public class ForwarderServlet extends GenericServlet
{
    public void service(ServletRequest request,
        ServletResponse response)
        throws IOException, ServletException
    {
// Tell the Web server that the response is HTML
        response.setContentType("text/html");

// Get the PrintWriter for writing out the response
        PrintWriter out = response.getWriter();

// Write the HTML back to the browser
        out.println("<HTML>");
        out.println("<BODY>");

        out.println("You should never see this");
        out.println("because my output buffer gets erased");

// Get the request dispatcher for the JSP to include
        RequestDispatcher dispatcher =
            request.getRequestDispatcher(
                "/j2eebook/ch16/examples/ForwardedPage.jsp");

        dispatcher.forward(request, response);

        out.println("</BODY>");
        out.println("</HTML>");
    }
}
```

PASSING PARAMETERS TO THE FORWARDED PAGE

As you might have already guessed, passing parameters to a forwarded page works exactly like it does when you include another page. From a Java Server Page, you use the `<jsp:param>` tag, and from a servlet, you add the parameters to the end of the URL when you call `getRequestDispatcher`.

THE <jsp:useBean> TAG

When you want to use a Java bean within a Java Server Page, use the `<jsp:useBean>` tag to either create a new instance of the bean or use an existing bean. The idea behind the `<jsp:useBean>` tag and its associated helper tags is that you should try to move as much of your application logic as possible out of your JSP so all that remains is code to display the output.

When you encapsulate business objects or business logic into a Java class, you should make that Java class a bean. Many of Sun's Java APIs and tools revolve around the idea that you put your logic into beans and then use tools to help you create applications that use those beans. JSP is one of those tools.

ADDING THE BEAN TO THE PAGE

When you add a bean to a JSP, you can either create a new bean or use an existing one. The JSP engine determines whether it needs to create a new bean for you based on the bean's `id`.

When you add a bean to a page, you must at least give the bean an `id`, which is just a name, and the bean's class, like this:

```
<jsp:useBean id="myBean" class="usingjsp.TestBean"/>
```

The JSP engine first searches for an existing bean with the same `id` (`myBean` in this case). If it doesn't find an existing bean, the JSP engine creates a new instance of the class you specified. Where the JSP engine looks to find existing beans depends on the bean's scope.

Note

The JSP compiler creates a variable with the same name as the `id` in the `<jsp:useBean>` tag. You can use this `id` in any Java code you put in your JSP. For instance, if you instantiated a bean with an `id` of `myBean`, you could write an expression like `<%= myBean.getFirstName() %>`.

One of the other options you can use in the `<jsp:useBean>` tag is `scope`. The `scope` determines where the JSP engine stores a created bean and also where it looks to see whether a particular bean `id` already exists. A bean can have a `scope` of `page`, `request`, `session`, or `application`. A bean with a `scope` of `page` is only visible on the current Java Server Page and disappears when the page finishes executing or forwards itself to another JSP or a servlet.

Note If you do not specify a scope, the default scope is page.

A bean with request scope is visible to other Java Server Pages and servlets and is stored in the request object. You can use the bean's id to get it out of the request with the getAttribute method. For example, suppose you set up the following bean in a JSP:

```
<jsp:useBean id="myBean" scope="request" class="usingjsp.TestBean"/>
```

Now, suppose you want to include a servlet or forward the request on to a servlet, and the servlet needs to access your bean. The servlet would access the bean like this:

```
    usingjsp.TestBean theBean = request.getAttribute("myBean");
```

Because the request object disappears when the request completes, it should be obvious that a bean stored in the request is no longer visible.

Beans with session scope are stored in the session object. Suppose you created the following bean:

```
<jsp:useBean id="mySessionBean" scope="session" class="usingjsp.TestBean"/>
```

You could access this bean from a servlet, like this:

```
    HttpSession session = request.getSession();
    Usingjsp.TestBean theBean =
            session.getAttribute("mySessionBean");
```

Finally, beans with application scope are stored in the application object, which is actually a ServletContext object. Like anything else stored in the application object, a bean with application scope is visible to any other JSP or servlet within the same "application."

Note There is no servlet equivalent for accessing a bean stored with page scope because the page scope implies that the bean is only visible within the page. After you leave the page, you can't access the bean. If you need to access the bean within Java code in the JSP, use pageContext.getAttribute("theBeanName").

 *If you are having trouble locating existing bean objects, see "Scope Problems" in the "Troubleshooting" section at the end of this chapter.*

Getting Bean Properties

So far, you know how to put a bean on a page. Now you need to do something with it. Obviously, you must either put data into the bean, get data out of the bean, or both. Use the <jsp:getProperty> tag to get information from a bean. The syntax of <jsp:getProperty> is simple:

```
<jsp:getProperty name="beanId" property="propertyName"/>
```

The <jsp:getProperty> tag automatically inserts the property value into the output of the Java Server Page. It works like the <%= tag in that respect. In fact, for a bean stored in the request object, here are two identical ways to display one of the bean's properties:

```
<jsp:getPropery name="myBean" property="firstName"/>
<%= ((usingjsp.TestBean) request.getAttribute("myBean")).
   getFirstName() %>
```

As you can see, the <jsp:getProperty> tag takes care of fetching the bean from wherever it is stored, casting it to the appropriate type, and invoking the property's get method.

Because the <jsp:useBean> tag also creates a variable with the same name as the bean, you could also use the following expression:

```
<%= myBean.getFirstName() %>
```


The main reason you would choose the <jsp:getProperty> tag over the <%= tag is that the <jsp:getProperty> tag is language independent. Although the focus of this book is on using Java as the JSP scripting language, the JSP specification allows for other scripting languages such as JavaScript. Although the expression <%= myBean.getFirstName() %> works for JavaScript, it probably wouldn't work for other scripting languages. If you used Smalltalk as a scripting language, the expression would be something like <%= myBean firstName %>. You can be sure that <jsp:getProperty> will work no matter what scripting language you are using.

SETTING BEAN PROPERTIES

Obviously, if you can get bean properties from a JSP, you need to set them, too. The <jsp:setProperty> enables you to set bean properties and provides some useful shortcuts for copying parameter values into a bean.

The basic syntax for setting a bean property is

```
<jsp:setProperty name="beanName" property="propertyName"
   value="propertyValue"/>
```

You can even use the <%= tag inside the <jsp:setProperty> tag like this:

```
<jsp:setProperty name="myBean" property="name"
   value="<%=myName%>"/>
```

You can only use <jsp:setProperty> to set the value of string properties and certain data types that can be converted from a string. Table 9.1 lists the data types that are automatically converted and the method used to convert them.

TABLE 16.1 AUTOMATIC TYPE CONVERSIONS PERFORMED BY <jsp:setProperty>

Java Type	Conversion Method
boolean or Boolean	Boolean.valueOf
byte or Byte	Byte.valueOf
char or Character	Character.valueOf
double or Double	Double.valueOf
float or Float	Float.valueOf

TABLE 16.1 CONTINUED

Java Type	Conversion Method
`int` or `Integer`	`Integer.valueOf`
`long` or `Long`	`Long.valueOf`

For example, if your bean includes the following `set` method:

```
public void setAge(int age)
```

You can safely set the age like this:

```
<jsp:setProperty name="myBean" property="age" value="35"/>
```

The string `"35"` is automatically converted to an integer when the JSP engine sets the property.

SETTING PROPERTIES DIRECTLY FROM PARAMETERS

One of the great features of `<jsp:setProperty>` is that it recognizes the frequent need to copy values out of form variables and into beans. You can automatically copy a parameter into a bean property, like this:

```
<jsp:setProperty name="myBean" param="paramName"
    property="propertyName"/>
```

If the property name is the same as the parameter name, you can omit the parameter name, like this:

```
<jsp:setProperty name="myBean" property="propertyName"/>
```

The presence or absence of the `value` keyword in `<jsp:setProperty>` determines whether the JSP engine uses a specific value or gets the value from a parameter. You can't have both a `value` and a `param` attribute in a single `<jsp:setProperty>`.

Note

If the value of a parameter is `null` or if it's an empty string, the `<jsp:setProperty>` method won't attempt to set the value. Although this behavior is normally good, it could trip you up if you expect to be able to clear out an entry by sending a blank value.

If your property is an indexed property (that is, an array of values), `<jsp:setProperty>` can handle it as long as it's an array of strings or one of the types previously listed in Table 16.1. To see how this works, imagine you have a class like the one shown in Listing 16.10.

LISTING 16.10 SOURCE CODE FOR `Group.java`

```
package usingj2ee;
public class Group implements java.io.Serializable
{
  protected java.util.Vector members;

  public Group()
  {
```

```
            members = new java.util.Vector();
        }

        public String getMember(int which)
        {
            return (String) members.elementAt(which);
        }

        public void setMember(int which, String member)
        {
            members.setElementAt(member, which);
        }

        public String[] getMembers()
        {
// Convert the members vector into an array of strings
            String[] memberArray = new String[members.size()];
            members.copyInto(memberArray);

            return memberArray;
        }

        public void setMembers(String[] memberArray)
        {
// If there are no members, just clear out the vector
            if (memberArray == null)
            {
                members.setSize(0);
                return;
            }
// Copy the contents of the member array into the members vector
            members.setSize(memberArray.length);
            for (int i=0; i < memberArray.length; i++)
            {
                members.setElementAt(memberArray[i], i);
            }
        }
}
```


The Java Server Page shown in Listing 16.11 copies any `member` parameters it receives into the `Group` object, and then displays the contents of the object. Notice how easy it is to copy the values into the bean compared to the difficulty of getting the values out. The `<jsp:getProperty>` tag doesn't handle indexed properties well, so stick to single-value properties when using that tag.

LISTING 16.11 SOURCE CODE FOR `ShowGroup.jsp`

```
<HTML><BODY><%-- Create the bean --%>
<jsp:useBean id="group" class="usingj2ee.Group"/>
<%-- Copy any member parameters into the bean --%>
<jsp:setProperty name="group" property="members" param="member"/>
<P>Group members:<br>

<%-- Display the contents of the bean --%>
<%
```

LISTING 16.11 CONTINUED

```
    usingj2ee.Group theGroup = (usingj2ee.Group) pageContext.
        getAttribute("group");

    String[] members = theGroup.getMembers();

    for (int i=0; i < members.length; i++)
    {
        out.println(members[i]+"<BR>");
    }
%>
</BODY>
</HTML>
```

Figure 16.5 shows the ShowGroup Java Server Page in action, using values passed directly into the URL (look at the address line).

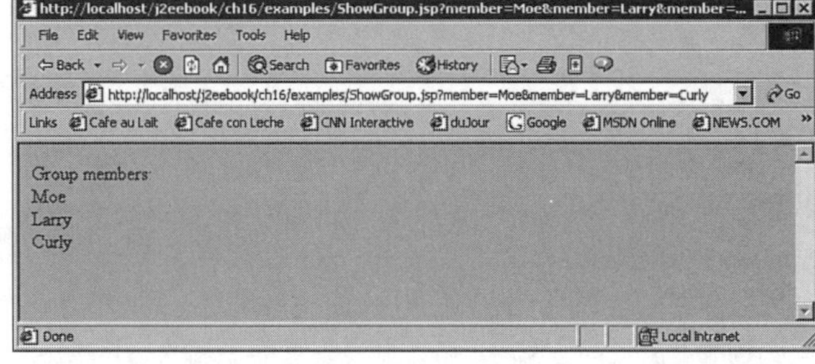

Figure 16.5 You can set multi-valued properties easily with `<jsp:setProperty>`.

In addition to the convenience of setting multiple values, the `<jsp:setProperty>` tag can also scan for matches between property names and parameter names. All you need to do is specify `*` for the parameter name, like this:

```
<jsp:setProperty name="myBean" property="*"/>
```

Listing 16.12 shows a simple test bean with a few properties.

LISTING 16.12 SOURCE CODE FOR TestBean.java

```
package usingj2ee;

public class TestBean implements java.io.Serializable
{
  protected String firstName;
  protected String lastName;
  protected int age;

    public TestBean() { }

    public String getFirstName() { return firstName; }
    public void setFirstName(String aFirstName)
        { firstName = aFirstName; }

    public String getLastName() { return lastName; }
    public void setLastName(String aLastName)
        { lastName = aLastName; }
```

```
    public int getAge() { return age; }
    public void setAge(int anAge) { age = anAge; }
}
```

Listing 16.13 shows a Java Server Page that inserts values into a `TestBean` object and then displays the values again. One of the striking things about this JSP is that it does a fairly good bit of work but doesn't contain any explicit Java code.

LISTING 16.13 SOURCE CODE FOR `ShowTestBean.jsp`

```
<HTML><BODY><%-- Create an instance of the bean --%>
<jsp:useBean id="myBean" class="usingj2ee.TestBean"/>

<%-- Copy the parameters into the bean --%>
<jsp:setProperty name="myBean" property="*"/>

The bean values are:<br>
First Name: <jsp:getProperty name="myBean" property="firstName"/><BR>
Last Name: <jsp:getProperty name="myBean" property="lastName"/><BR>
Age: <jsp:getProperty name="myBean" property="age"/><BR>

</BODY>
</HTML>
```

Figure 16.6 shows the output of `ShowTestBean.jsp` with parameters passed in directly in the URL.

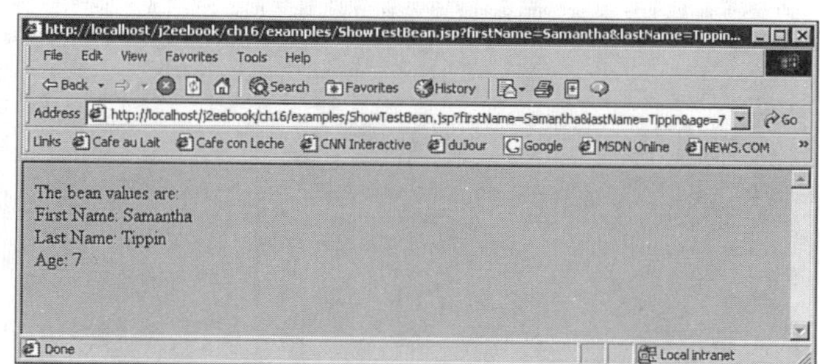

Figure 16.6 The `<jsp:setProperty>` tag makes it easy to set several bean properties from `request` parameters.

If you are having trouble accessing bean properties, see "Bean Property Problems" in the "Troubleshooting" section at the end of this chapter.

INITIALIZING A NEW BEAN

Frequently, you'll only want to set certain properties on a bean the first time it is created, but after that, you want to leave those properties alone. Rather than putting a `/>` at the end of `<jsp:useBean>`, you can use a closing `</jsp:useBean>` tag and put your initialization tags between the opening and closing tags for `<jsp:useBean>`. In other words, any code, HTML, or JSP tags between the `<jsp:useBean>` and `</jsp:useBean>` are only executed if the bean is created. If the bean already exists, any content between the opening and closing tags is skipped.

Listing 16.14 shows a variant of the JSP in Listing 16.4. This variant JSP changes the scope of the bean from `page` (the default) to `session` and executes some code when the bean is created.

LISTING 16.14 SOURCE CODE FOR `TestInit.jsp`

```
<HTML><BODY><%-- Create an instance of the bean --%>
<jsp:useBean id="myBean" class="usingjsp.TestBean" scope="session">
    I initialized the bean.<BR>
    <jsp:setProperty name="myBean" property="firstName"
        value="blah"/>
    <% out.println("I ran some Java code during the init, too<P>"); %>
</jsp:useBean>

<%-- Copy the parameters into the bean --%>
<jsp:setProperty name="myBean" property="*"/>

The bean values are:<br>
First Name: <jsp:getProperty name="myBean" property="firstName"/><BR>
Last Name: <jsp:getProperty name="myBean" property="lastName"/><BR>
Age: <jsp:getProperty name="myBean" property="age"/><BR>

</BODY>
</HTML>
```

Figure 16.7 shows the output from the `TestInit.jsp` page when it is run for the first time from a browser.

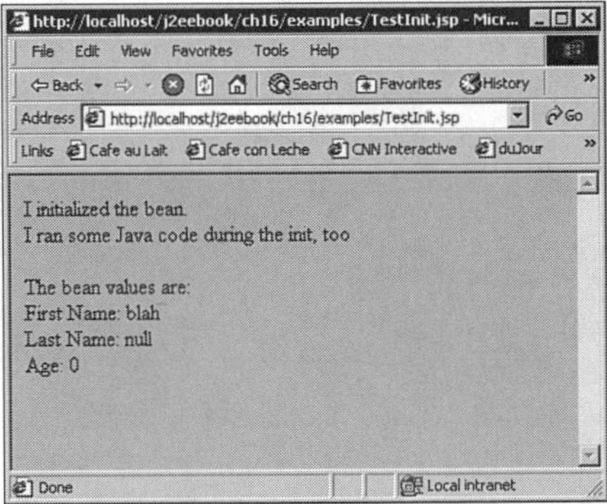

Figure 16.7
You can place initialization code between `<jsp:useBean>` and `</jsp:useBean>`.

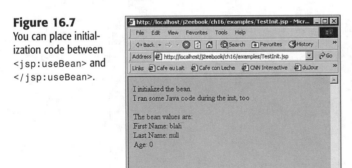

Figure 16.8 shows the output from the `TestInit.jsp` page when you click the Refresh button on the browser after seeing the output from Figure 16.7. Notice that the initialization code isn't executed because the bean already exists and is stored in the `session` object.

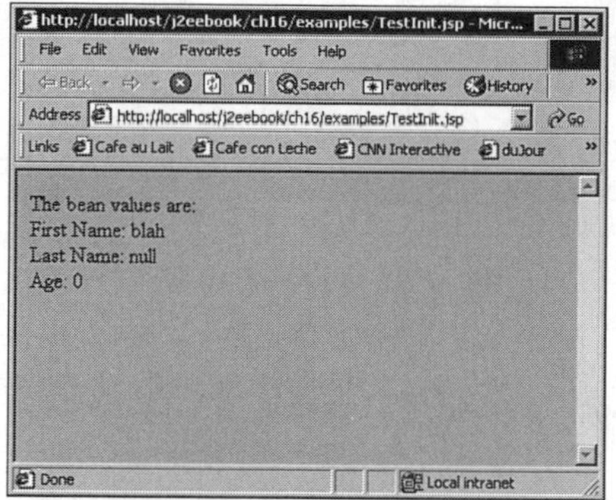

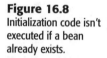

Figure 16.8 Initialization code isn't executed if a bean already exists.

THE TYPE OF AN EXISTING BEAN

Suppose you have a bean that implements a particular Java interface or is a subclass of some abstract Java class. Furthermore, suppose you want to refer to that bean using the interface or the abstract Java class. After all, you might be able to choose between several different subclasses of the abstract class when you first create the bean. Should all the following Java Server Pages have to figure out which subclass they are using and create separate `<jsp:useBean>` tags for each one?

When you need to refer to a bean using an abstract base class or an interface, you can use the `type` attribute instead of a `class` attribute in the `<jsp:useBean>` tag. For example, suppose you created a `Nameable` interface with a `getFirstName` and a `getLastName` like the one shown in Listing 16.15.

LISTING 16.15 SOURCE CODE FOR `Nameable.java`

```
package usingj2ee;

public interface Nameable
{
  public StringgetFirstName();
  public String getLastName();
}
```

You want to write a JSP that prints out the first name and the last name stored in a bean, but you don't care about the actual classname of the bean. All you really care about is that it implements the `Nameable` interface. By specifying `type=usingjsp.Nameable` as opposed to `class= usingjsp.SomeBeanClass`, you can use any bean that implements `Nameable`. Listing 16.16 shows an example page:

LISTING 16.16 SOURCE CODE FOR `ShowNameable.jsp`

```
<HTML><BODY><%-- Locate an instance of the bean --%>
<jsp:useBean id="myBean" type="usingj2ee.Nameable" scope="session"/>

The bean values are:<br>
First Name: <jsp:getProperty name="myBean" property="firstName"/><BR>
Last Name: <jsp:getProperty name="myBean" property="lastName"/><BR>
```

LISTING 16.16 CONTINUED

```
</BODY>
</HTML>
```

If you need to create a bean, you must supply a classname. If you try to use the `type` attribute without a `class` attribute and the bean does not exist, the bean will be null. In other words, the JSP won't try to create a bean.

If you make changes to a bean and they don't appear to have any effect, see the "Making Changes" section in the "Troubleshooting" section at the end of this chapter.

CUSTOM TAG EXTENSIONS

Many times, you need a Web designer to design your Java Server Pages. The designer might be an expert with HTML but might not know anything about Java. The `<jsp:useBean>`, `<jsp:setProperty>`, and `<jsp:getProperty>` tags allow you to make parts of your application accessible through tags, but you can't invoke bean methods without using either the `<%` or `<%=` tags. You can also provide some additional flexibility with the `<jsp:include>` and `<jsp:forward>` tags, but these tags are often overkill. You need a way to allow a Web designer to perform a specific operation without knowing any Java.

JSP Tag Extensions let you create new tags that a Web designer can insert directly into a Java Server Page. Through Tag Extensions, you can define tags that let you insert data into the output stream, include sections of a page only if certain conditions are met, and even modify the contents of the page itself before it is sent back to the browser.

A "HELLO WORLD" TAG

To create a custom JSP tag, you must first create a Java class that acts as a tag handler. Whenever your custom tag appears in a Java Server Page, the JSP engine invokes your tag handler. If your custom tag doesn't care about the body text between its opening and closing tags, you can use the simple `TagSupport` class, which implements the `Tag` interface. If you need to access and possibly change the body text within the opening and closing tags, you must subclass the `BodyTagSupport` class instead. The `BodyTagSupport` class implements the `BodyTag` interface, which allows you to access body text.

For example, suppose you define a custom tag named `<mytags:DoSomething>` and use it this way:

```
<mytags:DoSomething>
   Here is some text
</mytags:DoSomething>
```

If your tag handler only implements the `Tag` interface, it can't see the body text (that is, "Here is some text"). All it can do is decide whether you can see the body text or not. Your custom tag can also generate its own output.

Listing 16.17 shows the HelloWorldTagHandler class that inserts the familiar "Hello World!" message into the JSP response. Because it doesn't need to access its body text, it subclasses TagSupport.

LISTING 16.17 SOURCE CODE FOR HelloWorldTag.java

```
import javax.servlet.jsp.tagext.*;
import javax.servlet.jsp.*;
import java.io.*;

public class HelloWorldTag extends TagSupport
{
    public int doStartTag()
        throws JspException
    {
        try
        {
            JspWriter out = pageContext.getOut();

            out.println("<h1>Hello World!</h1>");
        }
        catch (IOException ioExc)
        {
            throw new JspException(ioExc.toString());
        }

        return SKIP_BODY;
    }

public int doEndTag()
    {
        return EVAL_PAGE;
    }
}
```

PART II CH 16

Note

Don't worry about the SKIP_BODY and EVAL_PAGE return values just yet. You'll see what they mean shortly.

Listing 16.18 shows a JSP that calls HelloWorldTag via a tag named <mytag:hello>. At this point, you don't yet know how to relate HelloWorldTag to <mytag:hello>. You will see that in the next section.

LISTING 16.18 SOURCE CODE FOR TestHello.jsp

```
<%@ taglib uri="/hello" prefix="mytag" %>
<html>
<body>
<mytag:hello/>
</body>
</html>
```

Figure 16.9 shows the output from TestHello.jsp.

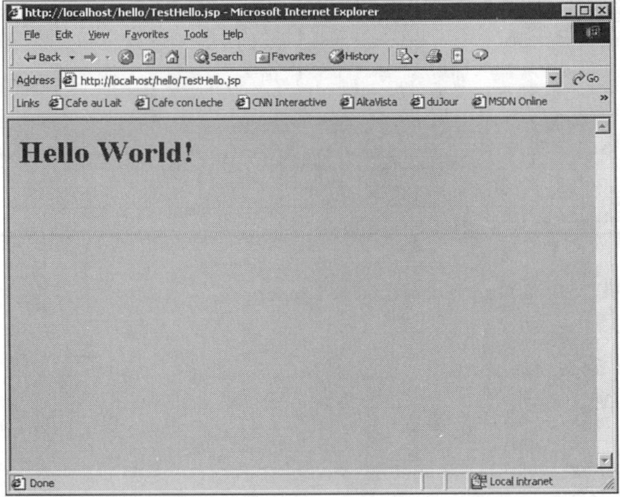

Figure 16.9
Custom tags can insert text into the response.

PACKAGING AND INSTALLING A TAG

When you create a custom tag library you must also create a Tag Library Descriptor (TLD) that describes each tag in your tag library. Listing 16.19 shows the TLD for the `HelloWorldTag` Java class.

LISTING 16.19 SOURCE CODE FOR `hello.tld`

```
<?xml version="1.0"?>
<!DOCTYPE taglib
    PUBLIC "-//Sun Microsystems, Inc.//DTD JSP Tag Library 1.1//EN"
    "http://java.sun.com/j2ee/dtds/web-jsptaglibrary_1_1.dtd">

<taglib>
    <tlibversion>1.0</tlibversion>
    <jspversion>1.1</jspversion>
    <shortname>hello</shortname>
    <uri></uri>
    <info>
        An example Hello World tag
    </info>

    <tag>
        <name>hello</name>
        <tagclass>HelloWorldTag</tagclass>
    </tag>
</taglib>
```

The first few lines of `hello.tld` are pretty standard for an XML file. You must start with the `<?xml?>` tag, of course. The next line defines the location of the Document Type Definition for this kind of document. The `<!DOCTYPE` tag should be the same for all your TLDs.

<taglib> is the root tag for a TLD and encloses all the other tags. Remember an XML document has a single root tag that encloses everything else in the document. The next few tags describe the tag library.

The <tlibversion> tag describes the version number of the tag library, while the <jspversion> tag indicates which version of JSP the tag library requires. The <shortname> tag gives a short name for the tag library that can be used within a JSP page-authoring tool. The idea is that you would load various tag libraries and see a list of the available libraries. The short name is the name you would see in the list. The <info> tag gives the long description of the tag library. Finally, the <uri> tag gives the normal URI for this tag library. Again, the URI is handy for a page-authoring tool in which you might have a local copy of the library, but when you build a JSP that uses the tag library, you might want to put the normal URI into the library. In other words, the page-authoring tool might see the tag library on the hard drive with a path like `c:\taglibs\hello.tld`. You don't want the JSP to refer to the tag library with a URI of `file:///c/taglibs/hello.tlb`, because the JSP might be deployed on a machine that doesn't have a `c:\taglibs` directory. You want a URI that works no matter where the JSP is deployed.

Part II Ch 16

After the initial information describing the tag library, you can list the tags contained in the library. This tag library contains a single tag with a name of `hello` (as indicated by the <name> tag). The tag name, along with the prefix for the tag library, make up the full tag that you put in the JSP. In other words, you take the tag name `hello` and combine it with the prefix specified in the JSP (`mytag` in Listing 16.1) to get the full name of the tag, which is <mytag:hello>.

Note

The reason for splitting the naming into two parts is that several people might make a tag named `hello` in their tag libraries. You need a way to specify which tag you mean, so you must use a prefix to indicate which library you are referring to.

Finally, the <tagclass> tag indicates the fully qualified pathname of the class that implements this tag.

Now that you have created the TLD file, you must deploy the tag library and your test Web page as a Web application. Create a directory called `WEB-INF` and in the `WEB-INF` directory, create a file called `web.xml` that looks like the file in Listing 16.20.

Listing 16.20 Source Code for web.xml

```
<?xml version="1.0"?><!DOCTYPE web-app    PUBLIC
    ➥"-//Sun Microsystems, Inc.//DTD Web Application 2.2//EN"
    "http://java.sun.com/j2ee/dtds/web-app_2.2.dtd">

<web-app>
    <display-name>Tag Demo</display-name>
    <description>An application for testing custom tags</description>
    <taglib>
        <taglib-uri>/hello</taglib-uri>
```

LISTING 16.20 CONTINUED

```
        <taglib-location>/WEB-INF/tld/hello.tld</taglib-location>
    </taglib>
</web-app>
```

The web.xml file describes the contents of a Web application. To deploy a Web application, like a custom tag, you create a special JAR file called a WAR file (Web ARchive) containing the web.xml file and any files required by your application.

Although you'll learn much more about WAR files in Chapter 21, "Packaging and Installing a J2EE Application," you need to know a little bit about them now to install a custom tag.

The <web-app> tag is the main tag for all web.xml files. The <display-name> and <description> tags provide general descriptive information about the Web application. As with all XML files, the web.xml file must start with the <?xml?> processing directive, and should also contain the <!DOCTYPE> tag to identify the set of XML tags that the file uses. The <web-app>, <display-name>, and <description> tags are valid for any Web application. The other tags are specific to custom tags.

The <taglib> tag defines a tag library that the Web application uses. The <taglib-uri> tag defines the name that a JSP would use as the URI for this tag library. Look back at Listing 16.18 and you can see that TestHello.jsp specifies /hello as the URI for the tag library, which matches what you see in web.xml. The <taglib-location> tag specifies the location of the hello.tld file, which is the file from Listing 16.19. According to the web.xml file, hello.tld should be stored in a directory called tld that is below the WEB-INF directory.

Now, under the WEB-INF directory, create a classes directory and copy the HelloWorldTag.class file to the classes directory. Make sure that TestHello.jsp is in the same directory as the WEB-INF directory. Now, create a file called tagdemo.war by going to the directory where WEB-INF and TestHello.jsp are located and entering the following command:

```
jar cvf tagdemo.war WEB-INF TestHello.jsp
```

The jar command should respond with something like this:

```
added manifest
adding: WEB-INF/(in = 0) (out= 0)(stored 0%)
adding: WEB-INF/classes/(in = 0) (out= 0)(stored 0%)
adding: WEB-INF/classes/HelloWorldTag.class(in = 839) (out= 486)(deflated 42%)
adding: WEB-INF/tld/(in = 0) (out= 0)(stored 0%)
adding: WEB-INF/tld/hello.tld(in = 457) (out= 268)(deflated 41%)
adding: WEB-INF/web.xml(in = 441) (out= 262)(deflated 40%)
adding: TestHello.jsp(in = 87) (out= 68)(deflated 21%)
```

The J2EE standard doesn't specify how you should install a WAR file in a J2EE server, so different servers take different approaches. Some servers, such as WebLogic and Apache's Tomcat JSP & Servlet engine, automatically unpack WAR files when you place them in the main application directory of the server. Other servers, such as JRun, provide a management console that lets you install the WAR file by filling out a form. Still others, such as the Resin JSP & servlet engine, require you to manually unpack the WAR file in the application directory. Consult the documentation for your server to see how it wants you to install WAR files.

After the file is installed, you should be able to access TestHello.jsp and see the output shown previously in Figure 16.7.

If you are having trouble installing your custom tag library, see "Install Problems" in the "Troubleshooting" section at the end of this chapter.

CONDITIONAL INCLUDES USING CUSTOM TAGS

Back in Listing 16.17, you saw that the doStartTag method in the custom tag returns a value of SKIP_BODY and the doEndTag method returns a value of EVAL_PAGE. These values tell the JSP engine how to handle the content between the start and end of the custom tag, and also whether to continue evaluating the rest of the page after the custom closing tag. When doStartTag returns SKIP_BODY, it tells the JSP engine to ignore the content between the start and end of the custom tag. If the doStartTag returns EVAL_BODY_INCLUDE, the data between the start and end tags is copied to the response and any nested tags are evaluated.

When doEndTag returns EVAL_PAGE, it tells the JSP engine to continue evaluating the rest of the page. If doEndTag returns SKIP_PAGE, the JSP engine ignores everything else in the JSP after the closing tag and returns the response to the browser.

Because you can control whether the JSP engine includes body text between the start and end of a tag, you can create tags that include text only if certain conditions are met.

Listing 16.21 shows a custom tag that only includes its content when the time of day is between 6 a.m. and 6 p.m.

LISTING 16.21 SOURCE CODE FOR DayTag.java

```
import javax.servlet.jsp.tagext.*;
import javax.servlet.jsp.*;
import java.util.*;

public class DayTag extends TagSupport
{
    public int doStartTag()
        throws JspException
    {
// Get the time of day
        GregorianCalendar currTime = new GregorianCalendar();

// Get the hour of day
        int hour = currTime.get(Calendar.HOUR_OF_DAY);

// If the time is between 6 a.m. and 6 p.m., tell the JSP engine to
// include the text between the start and end tag
        if ((hour >= 6) && (hour <= 18))
        {
            return EVAL_BODY_INCLUDE;
        }
        else
        {
// Otherwise, ignore the body text
            return SKIP_BODY;
        }
```

LISTING 16.21 CONTINUED

```
    }

    public int doEndTag()
    {
        return EVAL_PAGE;
    }
}
```

You can easily make a `NightTag` class that does the same test except that it only includes the body content when the hour is less than 6 or greater than 18. Listing 16.22 shows the `daynight.tld` file describing the `DayTag` class and its companion `NightTag` class.

LISTING 16.22 SOURCE CODE FOR `daynight.tld`

```
<?xml version="1.0"?>
<!DOCTYPE taglib
    PUBLIC "-//Sun Microsystems, Inc.//DTD JSP Tag Library 1.1//EN"
    "http://java.sun.com/j2ee/dtds/web-jsptaglibrary_1_1.dtd">

<taglib>
    <tlibversion>1.0</tlibversion>
    <jspversion>1.1</jspversion>
    <shortname>daynight</shortname>
    <uri></uri>
    <info>
        day tag to include text between 6am and 6pm, night to include
        text otherwise
    </info>

    <tag>
        <name>day</name>
        <tagclass>DayTag</tagclass>
    </tag>

    <tag>
        <name>night</name>
        <tagclass>NightTag</tagclass>
    </tag>
</taglib>
```

The `daynight.tld` file should seem pretty familiar now. It doesn't contain any tags that you haven't already seen from the `hello.tld` file, it just defines two tags instead of one. Listing 16.23 shows a JSP that tests the day and night tags to make sure they work.

LISTING 16.23 SOURCE CODE FOR `TestDayNight.jsp`

```
<%@ taglib uri="/daynight" prefix="dn" %>
<html>
<body>

<dn:day>
<h1>My, what a beautiful day it is!</h1>
```

```
</dn:day>

<dn:night>
<h1>I hate night, it's too dark for golf!</h1>
</dn:night>

</body>
</html>
```

Figure 16.10 shows the output from `TestDayNight.jsp` when run during the day.

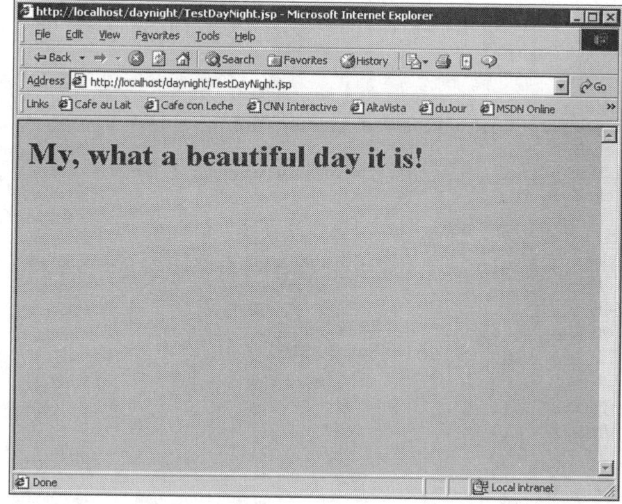

Figure 16.8
A custom tag can choose whether to include its body content or not.

Figure 16.11 shows the output from `TestDayNight.jsp` when run at night. Notice that the text between the `<dn:day>` and `</dn:day>` doesn't show up.

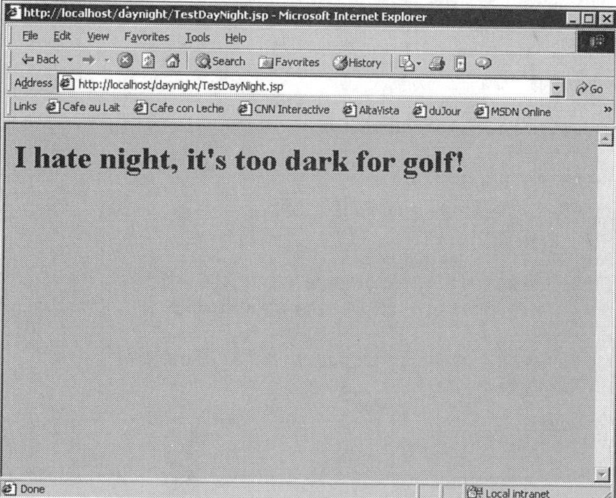

Figure 16.8
The `<xx:night>` tag only shows up at night time.

ACCESSING TAG ATTRIBUTES

Just like regular tags, custom tags can have attribute values. You just need to provide get and set methods for each attribute. Although you enclose each attribute in quotes, you can have numeric attributes in your custom tag. The JSP engine performs the conversion automatically. Listing 16.24 shows a custom tag to display a checkerboard. The board has several options that can be changed by various attributes in the `<xx:checkerboard>` tag.

LISTING 16.24 SOURCE CODE FOR CheckerboardTag.java

```
import javax.servlet.jsp.tagext.*;
import javax.servlet.jsp.*;
import java.io.*;

public class CheckerboardTag extends TagSupport
{
// Variables to hold the attributes for the checkerboard

    protected int width = 40;
    protected int height = 40;
    protected int rows = 8;
    protected int cols = 8;
    protected String darkColor = "#000040";
    protected String lightColor = "#FFFFC0";

    public int doStartTag()
        throws JspException
    {
        try
        {
            JspWriter out = pageContext.getOut();

            out.println("<table>");

// Count down so the bottom row is row 0 (it helps for
// calculating the colors, the bottom left should be dark)

            for (int i=rows-1; i >= 0; i--)
            {
// Start a new row with the specified height
                out.print("<tr height=\""+height+"\">");

// Loop through the columns
                for (int j=0; j < cols; j++)
                {

// Start making the cell for this square
                    out.print("<td width=\""+width+"\" bgcolor=\"");

// If row+column is even, make the square dark. The lower-left
// corner should always be dark

                    if ((i + j) % 2 == 0)
                    {
                        out.print(darkColor);
                    }
```

```
                    else
                    {
                        out.print(lightColor);
                    }
                    out.print("\"> </td>");
                }
                out.println("</tr>");
            }
            out.println("</table>");
        }
        catch (IOException ioExc)
        {
            throw new JspException(ioExc.toString());
        }

        return SKIP_BODY;
    }

    public int doEndTag()
    {
        return EVAL_PAGE;
    }

// Get/set methods, just like in a bean

    public int getHeight() { return height; }
    public void setHeight(int aHeight) { height = aHeight; }

    public int getWidth() { return width; }
    public void setWidth(int aWidth) { width = aWidth; }

    public int getRows() { return rows; }
    public void setRows(int aRows) { rows = aRows; }

    public int getCols() { return cols; }
    public void setCols(int aCols) { cols = aCols; }

    public String getDarkColor() { return darkColor; }
    public void setDarkColor(String aDarkColor)
    {
        darkColor = aDarkColor;
    }

    public String getLightColor() { return lightColor; }
    public void setLightColor(String aLightColor)
    {
        lightColor = aLightColor;
    }
}
```

Now, just putting the attributes in the tag is not enough. You must also configure the attributes in the TLD file. Each attribute is defined using an `<attribute>` tag. Within the `<attribute>` tag, there is a `<name>` tag defining the name of the attribute, a `<required>` tag indicating whether the attribute is required, and a tag called `<rtexprvalue>`. You might have noticed other JSP examples where the value of a tag attribute was specified using a JSP expression (the `<%=` tag). Evaluating custom tags in which the attribute value can be generated at runtime is a difficult task for the JSP engine. Rather than allow all attribute expressions to be computed at runtime, the JSP engine wants you to explicitly mark the attributes whose values might be generated at runtime. Set the value of `<rtexprvalue>` to `yes` or `true` if you need the attribute to be evaluated at runtime. The value is `false` by default.

For the `<required>` tag, you can use values of `yes`, `no`, `true`, or `false`. The `<required>` tag is `false` by default, meaning that if you don't explicitly say otherwise, an attribute is optional.

Listing 16.25 shows the TLD file for the `CheckerboardTag` class.

LISTING 16.25 SOURCE CODE FOR `checkerboard.tld`

```
<?xml version="1.0"?>
<!DOCTYPE taglib
    PUBLIC "-//Sun Microsystems, Inc.//DTD JSP Tag Library 1.1//EN"
    "http://java.sun.com/j2ee/dtds/web-jsptaglibrary_1_1.dtd">

<taglib>
    <tlibversion>1.0</tlibversion>
    <jspversion>1.1</jspversion>
    <shortname>checkerboard</shortname>
    <uri></uri>
    <info>
        A tag that prints out a checkerboard pattern
    </info>

    <tag>
        <name>checkerboard</name>
        <tagclass>CheckerboardTag</tagclass>
        <attribute>
            <name>width</name>
            <required>no</required>
        </attribute>
        <attribute>
            <name>height</name>
            <required>no</required>
        </attribute>
        <attribute>
            <name>rows</name>
            <required>no</required>
        </attribute>
        <attribute>
            <name>cols</name>
            <required>no</required>
        </attribute>
        <attribute>
            <name>darkColor</name>
            <required>no</required>
        </attribute>
        <attribute>
            <name>lightColor</name>
            <required>no</required>
        </attribute>
    </tag>
</taglib>
```

The `checkerboard.tld` file is similar to the other TLD files you have seen except that it defines attributes for its tag. You'll also need to create a `web.xml` file similar to the one you used for the other tags. In fact, you can just copy one of the existing files and change the `<taglib-uri>`, `<taglib-location>`, `<display-name>`, and `<description>` tags. Listing 16.26 shows a JSP that tests out the `CheckerboardTag` class.

LISTING 16.26 SOURCE CODE FOR `TestCheckerboard.jsp`

```
<%@ taglib uri="/checkerboard" prefix="cb" %>
<html>
<body>

<cb:checkerboard width="50" height="50" rows="8" cols="8"
    darkColor="#000000" lightColor="#ffffff"/>

</body>
</html>
```

Figure 16.12 shows the output from `TestCheckerboard.jsp`.

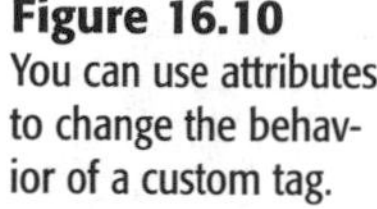

Figure 16.10
You can use attributes to change the behavior of a custom tag.

If you are having trouble setting attribute values in a custom tag, see "Attribute Values" in the "Troubleshooting" section at the end of this chapter.

PROCESSING BODY CONTENT WITH A CUSTOM TAG

One of the most interesting features of the JSP tag extension mechanism is that the tags can access their own body content. That is, a tag can see the text contained between its begin and end tags and even modify that text.

Processing body text is a little more involved and requires a specialized tag interface. A basic tag implements an interface called `Tag` and usually inherits from the `TagSupport` class. A tag that processes its body text must implement the `BodyTag` interface and usually inherits from `BodyTagSupport`.

Because the `BodyTag` interface extends the `Tag` interface, it includes the `doStartTag` and `doEndTag` methods. A tag implementing the `BodyTag` interface can still return `SKIP_BODY` from the `doStartTag` method to indicate that the JSP engine should not evaluate the text between the beginning and end of the tag. Instead of returning `EVAL_BODY_INCLUDE`, however, a body tag must return `EVAL_BODY_TAG` to include its body text.

> **Note**
>
> A custom tag that implements the `BodyTag` must not return `EVAL_BODY_INCLUDE`, otherwise the JSP engine reports an error. If a custom tag that only implements the `Tag` interface returns `EVAL_BODY_TAG`, the JSP engine also reports an error. In other words, `EVAL_BODY_INCLUDE` can only be used with nonbody tags and `EVAL_BODY_TAG` can only be used with a body tag.

Body tags have a peculiar way of operating on body text. When the JSP engine starts evaluating the body text, it calls the `doInitBody` method in the custom tag. There is no return value for `doInitBody`, and it is intended for you to perform initialization in this method. After the JSP engine evaluates the body content, it calls `doAfterBody` in the custom tag. Whenever `doAfterBody` is called, the custom tag can access the current body content by calling `getBodyContent`. The peculiar thing is that if `doAfterBody` returns `EVAL_BODY_TAG`, the JSP engine re-evaluates the current body content and calls `doAfterBody` again! The JSP engine finally accepts the content after `doAfterBody` returns `SKIP_BODY`.

That sounds counter-intuitive and it is. Before delving into some of the complexities, take a look at a minimal body tag. Listing 16.11 shows a body tag that prints its body text to the response (in other words, it shows the text between its begin and end tags as if the tags weren't there).

LISTING 16.27 SOURCE CODE FOR `TestBodyTag.java`

```
import javax.servlet.jsp.tagext.*;
import javax.servlet.jsp.*;
import java.io.*;

public class TestBodyTag extends BodyTagSupport
{
    public int doStartTag()
        throws JspException
    {
        return EVAL_BODY_TAG;
    }

    public int doEndTag()
    {
        return EVAL_PAGE;
```

```
    }

    public void doInitTag()
    {
    }

    public int doAfterBody()
        throws JspException
    {
// Get the current body content
        BodyContent body = getBodyContent();

        try
        {
// Ask the body content to write itself out to the response
            body.writeOut(body.getEnclosingWriter());
        }
        catch (IOException exc)
        {
            throw new JspException(exc.toString());
        }
// Tell the JSP engine that the body content has been evaluated
        return SKIP_BODY;
    }
}
```

If you are having trouble getting a body tag to work, see "Body Tags" in the "Troubleshooting" section at the end of this chapter.

In Listing 16.27, you see that you can write the body content into the response by calling `body.writeOut(body.getEnclosingWriter())`. The `body.writeOut` method writes the contents of the body to any `Writer` object. The `getEnclosingWriter` method returns the writer for the section of the response that this body tag is contained in. You can use `body.getReader` to get a `Reader` object that lets you read the contents of the body, or just call `body.getString` to get the contents as a string. In fact, an alternate way to write out the contents of a body is

```
body.getEnclosingWriter().println(body.getString());
```

Caution

Make sure you always have a case in which your `doAfterBody` method returns `SKIP_BODY`. If you only return `EVAL_TAG_BODY`, the JSP engine will get stuck in an infinite loop calling your `doAfterBody` method over and over.

The odd looping behavior with `doAfterBody` gets even more confusing with the fact that the JSP engine does not re-parse the body content after each call to `doAfterBody`. In other words, if you write out some additional text or tags, those do not get added to the current body content. Why have this looping structure at all, then? Why can't you just use a `for` loop? The reason for the looping behavior is that you might have a body tag with some nested custom tags that change the values of some variables, like this:

```
<xx:bodyTag>
   Some HTML text
```

```
    <xx:computeNewValue/>
    Some more text
</xx:bodyTag>
```

In this example, the `<xx:computeNewValue>` tag calculates some value that helps determine when the `<xx:bodyTag>` tag should stop looping. It doesn't really matter what the values are, the important point is that the tag handler for `<xx:computeNewValue>` is called every time the body text is re-evaluated. If you tried to do a `for` loop to print out the body text, you wouldn't have a way to call the tag handler for `<xx:computeNewValue>`.

ADDING SCRIPTING VARIABLES

Your custom tags can define scripting variables that are accessible to your Java Server Pages. In fact, you can even get the JSP engine to add a Java variable to the generated servlet to hold the value of your script variable. All you need to do is create a special `TagExtraInfo` class that describes the scripting variables your tag can define.

Listing 16.28 shows a subclass of `TagExtraInfo` that defines a scripting variable called `scriptVar`.

LISTING 16.28 SOURCE CODE FOR ScriptExtraInfo.java

```
import javax.servlet.jsp.tagext.*;

public class ScriptExtraInfo extends TagExtraInfo
{
    public VariableInfo[] getVariableInfo(TagData data)
    {
        return new VariableInfo[] {
                new VariableInfo("scriptVar", "java.lang.String",
                true, VariableInfo.AT_END) };
    }
}
```

The `getVariableInfo` method returns a list of the variables defined by a tag. The `VariableInfo` class describes a single variable, and contains a variable name, a classname, a declaration flag, and a variable scope. The variable name is the name of the variable, as used from a JSP. The variable name in Listing 16.28 is `scriptVar`. The classname indicates the type of the variable, such as `java.lang.String`. If the declaration flag is `true`, then the tag automatically declares the variable. Otherwise, a JSP must declare the variable explicitly before using the tag. For example, in Listing 16.28, the `scriptVar` declaration flag is `true`, so a JSP can automatically use a variable named `scriptVar` after using the tag that declares the variable. The scope indicates when the variable is visible. The `AT_END` scope indicates that the variable is only visible after the end tag. The `AT_START` scope indicates that the variable is visible just after the start tag, so it can be used within the body of the tag. The `NESTED` scope indicates that you can only use the variable between the start and end tags and not outside the tag.

The tag itself doesn't need to know about the extra info class, but it does need to put the scripting variables into the page context so the Java Server Page can extract the value of each variable and place it in a local Java variable. Listing 16.29 shows a custom tag that puts a value into the page context.

LISTING 16.29 SOURCE CODE FOR ScriptTag.java

```
import javax.servlet.jsp.tagext.*;
import javax.servlet.jsp.*;
import java.io.*;

public class ScriptTag extends TagSupport
{
    public int doStartTag()
        throws JspException
    {
        pageContext.setAttribute("scriptVar", "This is the script variable");

        return SKIP_BODY;
    }

    public int doEndTag()
    {
        return EVAL_PAGE;
    }
}
```

Listing 16.30 shows a Java Server Page that calls the `ScriptTag` custom tag and then accesses `scriptVar` as if it was a local variable.

LISTING 16.30 SOURCE CODE FOR TestScriptTag.jsp

```
<%@ taglib uri="/scripttag" prefix="xx" %>
<html>
<body>
<xx:setVar/>
<h1><%= scriptVar %></h1>
</body>
</html>
```

Note

> You might be wondering how a value gets from the page context into a Java variable automatically. It isn't as automatic as you might think. According to the JSP specification, the JSP engine is responsible for getting the value from the page context and copying it to the local variable. If you examine the servlet generated from a JSP using a tag-generated scripting variable, you'll see a line that copies the value out of the page context.

To match a `TagExtraInfo` class to its associated tag, you must include a `<teiclass>` tag in the Tag Library Descriptor for the custom tag. Listing 16.31 shows the TLD for the `ScriptTag` class.

LISTING 16.31 SOURCE CODE FOR scripttag.tld

```
<?xml version="1.0"?>
<!DOCTYPE taglib
    PUBLIC "-//Sun Microsystems, Inc.//DTD JSP Tag Library 1.1//EN"
    "http://java.sun.com/j2ee/dtds/web-jsptaglibrary_1_1.dtd">

<taglib>
    <tlibversion>1.0</tlibversion>
    <jspversion>1.1</jspversion>
    <shortname>scripttag</shortname>
    <uri></uri>
    <info>
        An example scripting variable tag
    </info>

    <tag>
        <name>setVar</name>
        <tagclass>ScriptTag</tagclass>
        <teiclass>ScriptExtraInfo</teiclass>
    </tag>
</taglib>
```

If you are having trouble defining scripting variables, see "Scripting Variables" in the "Troubleshooting" section at the end of this chapter.

The TagExtraInfo class actually serves two purposes. In addition to defining scripting variables, it has an isValid method that allows you to validate attribute values at JSP compile time. The isValid method takes an argument of type TagData and returns true if the combination of attributes in TagData is valid, or false if there is an error in the attributes. The idea here is that you can't define what constitutes a good attribute value or a good set of values without evaluating the values. By evaluating them when the JSP is compiled, you avoid any unnecessary runtime overhead.

The TagData class contains the following methods for examining the attributes for a tag:

```
Object getAttribute(String attrName)
Enumeration getAttributes()
String getAttributeString(String attrName)
String getId()
void setAttribute(String attrName, Object value)
```

Most of these methods are self-explanatory. The getId method is a shortcut for getAttributeString("id").

Because some attribute values must be evaluated at request time instead of compile time, the getAttribute method returns a special object named TagData.REQUEST_TIME_VALUE for any value that must be evaluated at request time. A request time attribute value is a value that can be described using the <%= %> tag pair.

TROUBLESHOOTING

COMPILE TIME INCLUDES

Why won't my included file show up?

If you entered the correct filename and the JSP engine didn't report an error while including the file, chances are that the place you included the file causes it to not show up. For example, if you include some tags within the `<head>` tag, they probably won't show up. Likewise, if you include the file within an HTML comment it won't show up. Choose View Source in your browser and see what's being sent from your JSP.

Why doesn't my JSP recompile when I change the contents of the included file?

The JSP specification doesn't require JSP engines to check included files to see if they have changed. Yours probably doesn't.

RUNTIME INCLUDES

My Java Server Pages have been running fine in other JSP engines; why does ServletExec report an error with my `<jsp:include>` tags?

ServletExec enforces the requirement that you put `flush="true"` in the `<jsp:include>` tag. Many others JSP engines do not. Consider it a shortcoming of the other products that they did not report the error.

Why do I get an HTTP Error 500 when I try to access a JSP with an included file?

Most likely, the included file has some error that prevents it from being compiled. Check the log files of your JSP engine to see what the error is, or just try to access the included file directly. By accessing it directly, you should see any errors on your screen.

SCOPE PROBLEMS

Why does it create a new object whenever I call `<jsp:useBean>`?

You probably forgot to specify a `scope` for the bean. Remember, the default `scope` for a bean is `page`, and all beans with `page scope` disappear when the page finishes executing.

I changed some bean properties in one page, so why don't they show up on my other page?

You might have a `scope` problem on one of the pages. For example, if you set the properties on a bean with `session scope` and then you try to access the bean on another page but you give the bean `request scope` on the other page, you have two different beans. The second page looks in its `request` for the bean and, not finding one there, creates a new instance of the bean ignoring the one in the session.

I checked to see that the scope is correct; why do I still not see the changes?

You should probably check the bean `ids`, too. Make sure they are absolutely identical, character-for-character. A bean `id` of `Fred` is different from a bean `id` of `fred`.

BEAN PROPERTY PROBLEMS

Why don't some of my parameters get copied into properties?

Chances are, you have a spelling difference between the parameter and the bean property name. Remember, unless you have a `BeanInfo` class that says otherwise, your bean property names are going to start with a lowercase letter (except when the first few letters of the property are capitalized). The property name looks capitalized in methods, such as `getFirstName` and `setFirstName`, but the property name is still `firstName`. Make sure your parameter name matches the case of the property name.

INSTALL PROBLEMS

Why do I see my custom tag in the HTML output?

You most likely forgot to put the `taglib` directive at the top of the page. You also might not have remembered to use the prefix you defined in the `taglib` directive, or you mistyped the prefix or the tag name.

Why do I get a compile error when I use a custom tag?

Well, the first thing to check is that it's really the tag that's causing the problem. Try removing the tag and see if that clears up the problem. Next, make sure that you have installed the tag library on the Web server. The class files should be under the `WEB-INF/classes` directory (`WEB-INF` must be capitalized, don't count on web-inf working the same way). Also make sure you have a TLD file and that the `web.xml` file in the `WEB-INF` directory has the correct pathname for the TLD. Because custom tags are a recent addition, not all JSP engines implement them the same way (some might not even implement them correctly). You might need to consult the documentation for your JSP engine to see if there are any additional notes for installing custom tag libraries.

ATTRIBUTE VALUES

Why do I get a runtime error when I try to set an attribute value?

There is probably some mismatch between the attribute type in the custom tag and the attribute value you are trying to set. For instance, trying to store the string `"Fred"` into an integer value isn't going to work.

I created get and set methods, so why doesn't the JSP engine recognize my attributes?

Don't forget that you must also define the names of the attributes in the TLD file.

BODY TAGS

When I use a body tag, why does the JSP engine stop responding?

You are probably stuck in an infinite loop caused by your `doAfterBody` method returning `EVAL_BODY_TAG` over and over instead of returning `SKIP_BODY`.

I tried to write out some code in `<% %>` *and re-evaluated the body text; why do the* `<% %>` *tags show up in the output?*

Remember, the JSP engine only parses the body text one time. It might evaluate custom tags in the body text multiple times, but after the text is parsed, that's it.

I rewrote the body text and returned `EVAL_BODY_TAG`, *so why do I still see the original body text?*

Again, the JSP engine only parses the body text once. You will always receive the original body text in `doAfterBody`.

SCRIPTING VARIABLES

I put a value in the page context; why doesn't the JSP have a variable to hold the value?

You might have forgotten to create the `TagExtraInfo` object, or you forgot to link the `TagExtraInfo` object to the tag class by adding a `<teiclass>` item in the TLD file.

PART III

Additional J2EE Technologies

CHAPTER 17

CORBA

In this chapter

What Is CORBA?

The Common Object Request Broker Architecture (CORBA) is a framework for creating distributed object applications that are language and platform independent. You can create a CORBA object in Java running on Linux that talks to a C++ CORBA object running on Windows. If you look at the overall features of CORBA, you'll find that it competes with J2EE in many ways. At their very core, CORBA and J2EE are fairly similar. As you start looking at features beyond the core, however, you see that CORBA and J2EE go in different directions. You find areas that J2EE address where CORBA has no equivalent and areas that CORBA addresses where J2EE hasn't gone.

Note

> The Object Management Group (OMG), which is the standards organization that publishes CORBA, approved the CORBA 3.0 specification in late 1999. The 3.0 specification includes the CORBA Component Model (CCM), which is basically Enterprise JavaBeans. In fact, the CORBA Component Model was designed specifically to be compatible with EJB. Oddly enough, this is a case of CORBA growing toward EJB.

The Object Request Broker (ORB) is the basic building block of CORBA. Other than some differences in how you define the interfaces, you'll find that the ORB is similar to Java RMI. Figure 17.1 illustrates the basic ORB and its relation to the client and server. As you can see, CORBA uses the stub and skeleton pattern just like RMI.

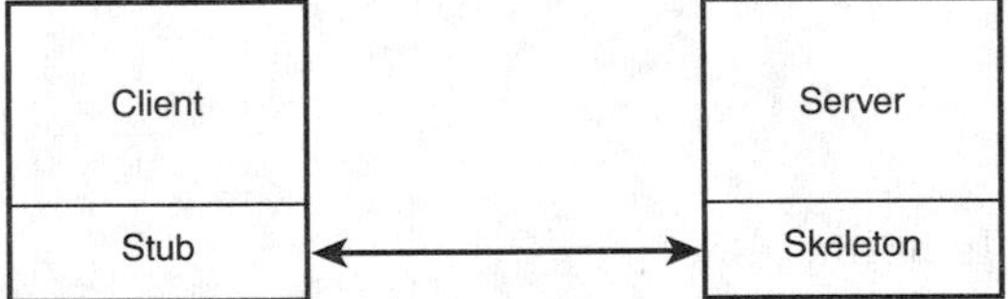

Figure 17.1
CORBA uses stubs and skeletons, just like RMI.

Although the basic features of the ORB still change occasionally, most of the CORBA work in recent years has been in the area of CORBA services. If you stand back and look at the overall plan of CORBA, the idea is to expand an object-oriented program and spread it out over a network. Where you normally create objects and invoke methods locally in a program, CORBA lets you perform the same operations over a network. CORBA adds a naming service, an event service, and even object persistence. The services really distinguish CORBA from other similar technologies.

Although CORBA and J2EE share many similar goals (Java's CORBA support is actually part of J2EE), they also diverge on some key points, causing some overlap in features. Consequently, although Sun states that CORBA support is a part of J2EE, it looks fairly obvious that J2EE supports CORBA ORBs and a few crucial services, but prefers its Java-only alternatives to some of the other services. That doesn't mean there is anything wrong with CORBA; it's just that Sun is pushing a platform that revolves around Java. J2EE doesn't try to support many different languages, and can afford to take some shortcuts.

Although you will certainly find many companies that use many of the CORBA services, you'll find that most companies use the basic ORB services and the naming service and very little else. Most people use CORBA to link distributed programs together in a language-independent way, but they don't design their whole architecture around CORBA. This is not necessarily a reflection on the quality of CORBA's services, but rather that most companies find they don't need the additional services. Even if you don't buy into the whole CORBA architecture, however, it's good to have CORBA at your disposal. You never know when your Java program might need to access objects written in another language, such as Delphi or C++.

THE INTERFACE DEFINITION LANGUAGE (IDL)

With basic RMI (and of course with the RMI-based Enterprise JavaBeans), you start by defining the interface between the client and the server. CORBA is no different in that respect. RMI, however, has the advantage in that you can define the interface with a Java interface object. CORBA must support several different programming languages, many of which don't have the equivalent of a Java interface. Instead, CORBA has its own separate language for defining interfaces. This language is appropriately called the Interface Definition Language (IDL).

An IDL file consists of one or more module definitions. In Java terms, a module is like a package—it's a namespace that can contain various interface definitions. Within a module, you define interfaces, exceptions, and data types. Listing 17.1 shows a sample IDL file for a Message-of-the-Day server.

LISTING 17.1 SOURCE CODE FOR `MOTD.idl`

```
module usingj2ee
{
    module motd
    {
        interface MOTD
        {
            string getMOTD();
        };
    };
};
```

Notice that the `MOTD.idl` file contains nested modules. The end result of this nesting is that the MOTD interface is contained within a Java package called `usingj2ee.motd`. The MOTD interface contains a single method called `getMOTD`, which returns a string. Notice that the IDL keyword string is all lowercase, unlike the Java String class. Also, very importantly, notice that the } brackets always have a ; after them. Unlike Java, you *must* include the ; after a }.

An IDL interface can contain two types of definitions: methods and attributes. A method definition is just what you'd expect—it adds a method to the interface. An attribute definition is a little different, however. It's more akin to a JavaBean property. When you compile the IDL file to Java, you end up with a method to get the attribute and a method to set the attribute value. Although the methods don't have the familiar `get` and `set` names, they still perform the same kind of function. You might define a string attribute this way:

```
attribute string myAttribute;
```

Table 17.1 shows the basic CORBA types and their Java equivalents. You can use any of these types as CORBA attributes, method parameters, and structure variables.

TABLE 17.1 CORBA TYPES AND THEIR JAVA EQUIVALENTS

CORBA Type	Java Type
`boolean`	`boolean`
`char`	`char`
`wchar`	`char`
`octet`	`byte`
`short`	`short`
`unsigned short`	`short`
`long`	`int`
`unsigned long`	`int`
`long long`	`long`
`unsigned long long`	`long`
`float`	`float`
`double`	`double`
`fixed`	`BigDecimal`
`string`	`String`
`wstring`	`String`

The `wstring` and `wchar` types indicate wide characters. In languages such as C and C++, the `char` type is an 8-bit value, so 16-bit Unicode characters must be stored in separate wide types, such as `wchar`. Java, of course, uses 16 bits for all characters, so there's no need to distinguish between `char` and `wchar`.

Note

One of the most annoying features of CORBA is that it doesn't allow `null` strings. You *must* initialize all string variables before using them in a method invocation.

Also, notice that CORBA doesn't have an `int` type. If you're like most people, you'll probably try to use `int` in your IDL files a few times before you train yourself to use `long` instead.

You declare CORBA methods in much the same way that you declare Java methods, except that you must specify whether each method parameter is an `in`, `out`, or `inout` parameter. In

Java, you always pass parameters by value, which means that when you change the value of the parameter within the method, the caller never sees the new value. CORBA, however, allows you to declare methods where you receive changed parameter values back from the method call. An `out` parameter means that you don't actually pass in a value for the parameter, you just expect to get one back. An `inout` parameter means you pass in a parameter value and expect to get the value back (possibly changed).

Note

You might sometimes hear people say that Java passes parameters by value except in the case of an object. That's not true. When you pass an object to another method, you are really passing an object reference, and you pass that reference *by value*. In other words, Java *always* passes parameters by value. That object reference value can't change, although you *can* change the contents of the object. For example, if you declare a string variable `name` and pass it to a method that reassigns the value of `name`, your original `name` variable is unchanged because the object reference is passed by value.

Because `out` and `inout` parameters actually return values, you can create methods with multiple return values—something you can't do in a Java program (without cramming all the values into an array or an object). For example, you can declare a method that retrieves a person's name as a series of `out` parameters:

```
void getName(out string firstName, out string middleName, out string lastName)
```

As you can see, the basic pattern for a CORBA method is the same as for a Java method, except for the additional `in`, `out`, or `inout` specifier before the parameter type.

Now that you've seen the basic structure of an IDL file and have some idea of the data types, you need to see a CORBA program in action to get the feel for how a program works. There's a lot more to IDL yet to go, but seeing a CORBA program in action first should help you see how everything fits together.

CREATING A CORBA SERVER

When you create a CORBA server, you create an implementation for a CORBA object and create a `main` method that creates one or more instances of the CORBA object. After you create a CORBA object, you register it with the CORBA naming service to allow clients to access it.

Before you create the object implementation, of course, you need an IDL file. Because the IDL file in Listing 17.1, shown earlier, is a very simple IDL, it makes a good starting point for CORBA development. After you create the IDL file, you must compile it. Each ORB implementation has a different IDL compiler with different options. JDK 1.3 comes with an IDL compiler called `idlj` that is easy to use. For some strange reason, `idlj` doesn't generate server classes by default—only client classes. You must use the `-fall` or at least `-fserver` to generate the server classes (`-fall` generates both client and server classes).

Why would you need to compile only client classes or only server classes? Remember that CORBA is language independent. You might be developing a server in C++ or Ada, using Java only for the client (perhaps as a servlet or Java Server Page). You don't need the server classes in this case, only the client classes. Likewise, you might be developing a Java server that you will access with a Delphi front end, in which case you just need the server-side classes. Of course, there's no harm in creating both the client and server classes every time.

To compile the IDL file in Listing 17.1, use the following command:

```
idlj -fall MOTD.idl
```

The IDL-to-Java compiler generates a number of classes, but the one you're most interested in for server development is the implementation base class. The classname of the implementation base takes the form `_xxxxImplBase`, where *xxxx* is the name of the interface. For example, the implementation base class for the `MOTD` is called `_MOTDImplBase`.

Listing 17.2 shows a simple implementation for the `MOTD` interface.

LISTING 17.2 SOURCE CODE FOR `MOTDImpl.java`

```
package usingj2ee.motd;

import org.omg.CosNaming.*;
import org.omg.CosNaming.NamingContextPackage.*;
import org.omg.CORBA.*;

import java.io.*;

public class MOTDImpl extends _MOTDImplBase
{
/** The name of the file containing the message */
    protected String motdFileName;

/** Creates a new instance of the MOTD server assigned to a
 *  specific filename.
 */
    public MOTDImpl(String aMotdFileName)
    {
        motdFileName = aMotdFileName;
    }

    public String getMOTD()
    {
        try
        {
// Open the message file
            BufferedReader reader = new BufferedReader(
                new FileReader(motdFileName));

// Create a buffer to hold the resulting message
            StringBuffer buffer = new StringBuffer();

            String line;
```

```
// Read all the lines in the file
            while ((line = reader.readLine()) != null)
            {
// Put each line into the buffer separated by newlines
                buffer.append(line);
                buffer.append("\n");
            }

            reader.close();

// Return the message
            return buffer.toString();
        }
        catch (IOException exc)
        {
// If there's an error, just return an empty message
            return "";
        }
    }

    public static void main(String[] args)
    {
        String motdFile = System.getProperty("file", "motd.txt");
        String motdService = System.getProperty("service",
            "MessageOfTheDay");
        try
        {
// Create a reference to the CORBA orb
            ORB orb = ORB.init(args, null);

// Create an instance of the MOTD implementation
            MOTDImpl impl = new MOTDImpl(motdFile);

// Register the MOTD implementation with the ORB
            orb.connect(impl);

// Locate the CORBA naming service
            org.omg.CORBA.Object objRef =
                orb.resolve_initial_references("NameService");

// Cast the CORBA Object to NamingContext using the narrow method
            NamingContext ncRef = NamingContextHelper.narrow(objRef);

// Create a NameComponent representing the path for the MOTD service
            NameComponent nc = new NameComponent(motdService, "");
            NameComponent[] path = new NameComponent[] { nc };

// Register the MOTD implementation with the naming service
            ncRef.rebind(path, impl);

// Go into an infinite loop while the ORB services requests
            java.lang.Object sync = new java.lang.Object();
            synchronized (sync)
            {
                sync.wait();
            }
        }
        catch (Exception exc)
```

LISTING 17.2 CONTINUED

```
            {
                exc.printStackTrace();
            }
        }
    }
```

Aside from the main method, the MOTDImpl class looks like a typical Java object. The getMOTD method reads a message from a file and returns it.

The main method in the MOTDImpl class first creates an instance of the ORB by calling ORB.init. One thing to keep in mind is that you always call ORB.init no matter what ORB you are using. The ORB object you get back is an implementation-specific ORB object. In other words, if you use the Visibroker ORB, the ORB.init method returns an instance of Visibroker's ORB object.

You are probably wondering how the CORBA API figures out what implementation you want to use. After all, JDK 1.3 has a built-in ORB, how does it know that you want to use Orbix or Visibroker instead? The answer lies in two system properties called org.omg.CORBA.ORBClass and org.omg.CORBA.ORBSingletonClass. The ORBClass property specifies the classname of the ORB implementation. The ORBSingletonClass property specifies the name of the class returned by the ORB.init method.

When you use Visibroker, the properties settings are

```
org.omg.CORBA.ORBClass=com.inprise.vbroker.orb.ORB
org.omg.CORBA.ORBSingletonClass=com.inprise.vbroker.orb.ORB
```

For Orbix, the properties are

```
org.omg.CORBA.ORBClass=com.iona.corba.art.artimpl.ORBImpl
org.omg.CORBA.ORBSingletonClass= com.iona.corba.art.artimpl.ORBSingleton
```

If you start seeing strange behavior in your CORBA application and you're using a third-party ORB, make sure you have set both of these properties.

After the MOTDImpl class has initialized the ORB, it creates an instance of MOTDImpl and calls orb.connect to activate the object within the ORB. After you connect an object to the ORB, it is available to any clients. Before a client can locate the object, however, you must register the object with the CORBA naming service.

> **Note**
>
> In case you're wondering if you ever connect an object to the ORB without registering it with the naming service, the answer is yes. You will soon see a common CORBA pattern called a *factory* that creates objects without registering them with the naming service.

You locate the naming service using the orb.resolve_initial_references method. When you first locate the naming service, you get a CORBA Object instance. You can't use the Java cast operator to convert the Object to a NamingContext object. In other words, you can't do this:

```
NamingContext ncRef = (NamingContext) objRef;
```

Instead, you must use the narrow method:

```
NamingContext ncRef = NamingContextHelper.narrow(objRef);
```

In fact, you must always use narrow to convert from a CORBA Object to a specific type. The IDL-to-Java compiler generates helper classes that implement the narrow method for each CORBA object you define in IDL. In the case of the NamingContext interface, the helper class has already been generated for you.

To associate an object with a name, you call the rebind method in the NamingContext object, passing it an array containing various parts of the name. Many applications just use a single name (that is, an array containing a single name), but others arrange the names in a directory structure to make it easier to organize the names. The rebind method overwrites any existing object bound to the same name. If you just call bind instead of rebind, you must make sure you unbind the old name using the unbind method.

Finally, the MOTDImpl main method creates a dummy object and synchronizes on it. This is just a simple way to wait forever. If you don't do this, your program will exit. In other words, unlike other libraries that can spawn additional threads that continue to run, the ORB spawns daemon threads that don't cause the program to keep running when the main method terminates.

CREATING A CORBA CLIENT

Creating a CORBA client program is much easier than creating a server. You use the same procedure to initialize the ORB in the client as you do in the server. Once again, you must set system properties to specify different ORB implementation classes if you use an ORB other than the one built into the JDK. You also locate the naming service the same way in the client as you do in the server.

After you locate the naming service, use the resolve method to locate the CORBA object. Resolve takes an array of NameComponent objects just like you use in the rebind method. After you locate the object, use the narrow method to cast the Object reference to the type you want.

Listing 17.3 shows the MOTDClient program that interacts with the MOTDImpl class.

LISTING 17.3 SOURCE CODE FOR MOTDClient.java

```
package usingj2ee.motd;

import org.omg.CORBA.*;
import org.omg.CosNaming.*;

public class MOTDClient
{
    public static void main(String[] args)
    {
```

LISTING 17.3 CONTINUED

```
        try
        {
            ORB orb = ORB.init(args, null);

// Locate the CORBA naming service
            org.omg.CORBA.Object objRef =
                orb.resolve_initial_references("NameService");

// Instead of using the Java cast operator, the correct way to convert
// a CORBA Object into a specific type is to use that type's helper
            NamingContext ncRef = NamingContextHelper.narrow(objRef);

// Create a name component path for locating the MOTD service
            NameComponent nc = new NameComponent("MessageOfTheDay", "");
            NameComponent path[] = new NameComponent[] { nc };

// Locate the MOTD service
            org.omg.CORBA.Object motdObj = ncRef.resolve(path);

// Narrow (that is, cast) the reference to an object of type MOTD
            MOTD motdRef = MOTDHelper.narrow(motdObj);

// Display the message of the day
            System.out.println(motdRef.getMOTD());
        }
        catch (Exception exc)
        {
            exc.printStackTrace();
        }
    }
}
```

To run this example, you should first compile both the client and server code—make sure you've already run the `idlj` program or the code won't compile at all. Next, start the CORBA name service. If you're using the JDK, the name service is called `tnameserv` and you simply enter this command:

```
tnameserv
```

The `tnameserv` program allows the client to locate the server. After `tnameserv` is running, start the server program and then start the client. You may need to wait a few seconds for the server to start up before starting the client. Otherwise, the client might look for the server object before it has been created.

ATTRIBUTES

When you define an attribute in IDL, you are really just defining two methods: a getter and a setter. Unlike the JavaBeans API, you don't use `get`*XXX* and `set`*XXX* as method names for CORBA attributes. Instead, the method names are the same as the attribute name. The getter is a method with the same name as the attribute that takes no parameters and returns a value. The setter is a `void` method that takes a parameter that is the new attribute value. For example, suppose you define an attribute like this:

```
attribute string description;
```

The IDL-to-Java compiler adds the following two methods to your interface:

```
public String description();
public void description(String newDescription);
```

As with the method declarations, you must implement these methods yourself.

More About IDL

So far, you've seen how to declare methods and attributes in IDL. You can also declare exceptions, structures, and alternate data types.

Exceptions

You declare an IDL exception using the following form:

```
exception exceptionName
{
    member declarations
}
```

As you can see, an exception can have member variables. When you declare member variables for an exception, the IDL-to-Java compiler generates two constructors for the exception, one that takes no parameters and one that takes values for each member variable in the same order that you declared them in the IDL file.

Listing 17.4 shows an example exception declaration.

Listing 17.4 Example Exception Declaration

```
exception InvalidDataException
{
    string reason;
    long errorCode;
};
```

Although Java uses the `throws` keyword to indicate that a method can throw an exception, CORBA uses the `raises` keyword to indicate that a method throws an exception. Also, unlike the `throws` keyword, the `raises` keyword required you to enclose the exception list in parentheses. In other words, while a Java exception declaration looks like this:

```
throws InvalidDataException, ClassRollFullException
```

The CORBA equivalent looks like this:

```
raises (InvalidDataException, ClassRollFullException)
```

STRUCTURES

You can declare a structure using the `struct` keyword, like this:

```
struct structureName
{
    member declarations
};
```

Listing 17.5 shows an example structure declaration.

LISTING 17.5 EXAMPLE STRUCTURE DECLARATION

```
struct Person
{
    string firstName;
    string middleName;
    string lastName;
    short age;
};
```

The IDL-to-Java compiler creates a Java object with the same name as the structure, containing public data fields for each member of the structure. It also creates a default constructor and a constructor that accepts values for every member in the same order as they are defined in the IDL file.

One thing to keep in mind when it comes to CORBA is that structures are only data holders—you can't define any methods for a structure. Version 3.0 of the CORBA specification includes a new form of structure called a `valuetype` that does include method declarations.

typedef

Sometimes, you might want to make an alias for a type name. For instance, you might want to make a `Name` type that is really of type `string`. Use the `typedef` keyword to create an alternate type name:

```
typedef originaltype newname
```

For example, to make a new `string` type called `Name`, use the following declaration:

```
typedef string Name;
```

Now, you can use `Name` as if it were a built-in CORBA type, for example

```
struct Person
{
    Name firstName;
    Name middleName;
    Name lastName;
};
```

ARRAYS AND SEQUENCES

You sometimes need to declare array types in IDL files. CORBA supports two different kinds of arrays: fixed-size arrays and variable-sized arrays called sequences. To define an array type, add square brackets and an array size to the type, for example

```
typedef long ages[10];
```

To define a variable-length array, or sequence, use the sequence keyword with the type name in angle brackets, for example

```
typedef sequence<string> nameSeq;
```

You can also provide an optional maximum sequence length, like this:

```
typedef sequence<string, 10> nameSeq;
```

Both fixed-length and variable-length arrays translate into Java arrays.

Note

Be careful when passing array indices as CORBA parameters. Because CORBA is language-independent, it might deal with arrays differently depending on the language. If the language starts numbering array elements at 1 instead of 0, the array index you pass from a Java program might refer to the wrong element.

ENUMERATED TYPES

You can define enumerated types in CORBA using the `enum` keyword:

```
enum Colors { red, orange, yellow, green, blue, indigo, violet};
```

Because Java doesn't support enumerated types, the IDL-to-Java compiler generates a Java class for the enumeration with static member variables representing each enumerated value. For example, it generates a `Color` class with member variables named `red`, `orange`, `yellow`, and so on.

`out` AND `inout` PARAMETERS

So far, you know that CORBA allows parameters to be declared as `in`, `out`, or `inout`. Java normally only supports `in` parameters as far as the structure of the language goes. The IDL-to-Java compiler must pull a few tricks to make `out` and `inout` parameters work. For every basic data type in CORBA (`long`, `short`, `float`, and so on) there are corresponding `Holder` classes (`LongHolder`, `ShortHolder`, `FloatHolder`, and so on). In addition, for any data type you define (structures, `typedefs`) the IDL-to-Java compiler generates `Holder` classes. A `Holder` class is a simple wrapper class with a single `value` field that holds a particular value. The `value` field in the `LongHolder` class is of type `long`, while the `value` field in the `StringHolder` class is of type `String`.

Whenever a parameter is an `out` or an `inout` parameter, the Java version of the method uses a `Holder` class for the parameter value. To return a value to the caller, store the new value in the holder's `value` field. When you call a method that has an `out` or an `inout` parameter, you must supply a holder object. When the method returns, you can pull the returned value from the holder's `value` field.

ANY TYPES

It seems like every language has its own form of generic object reference. In C and C++, you have the `void` pointer (`void *`). In Java, it's a reference to `Object` just as it is in Smalltalk. In CORBA, it's called the `any` type. In your IDL file, you can declare a parameter or a structure member as `any`, meaning it can hold any type of value (a number, a string, an object reference, a structure, and so on), for example

```
void doSomething(in any theParam);
```

The `Any` class represents an `any` value and has methods for storing and retrieving various types of values. To store a primitive value in an `Any` object, use a method of the form `insert_xxx` where *xxx* is the type you are storing (short, long, string, float, double, and so on). For structures and other user-defined types, the helper class generated by the IDL-to-Java compiler contains a static `insert` method to insert a value into an `Any`. For example, if you define a struct called `Person`, the `PersonHelper` class contains an `insert` method declared, like this:

```
public static void insert(org.omg.CORBA.Any theAny, Person thePerson)
```

To retrieve a primitive value from an `Any` object, use the `extract_xxx` method where *xxx* is the type you are retrieving. Once again, for user-defined types, the helper class contains a utility class to retrieve a value from an `Any`. The `extract` method in the `PersonHelper` class looks like this:

```
public static void Person extract(org.omg.CORBA.Any theAny)
```

VALUE TYPES

Value types are a huge addition to CORBA. CORBA structures are nice for grouping data together, but the biggest frustration they present is that you can't add methods to them. Many times you want to add validation methods to let the client know when a structure contains invalid data. Before value types came along, you had to create additional utility classes for your validation code. Now, you can declare the methods together with the data as part of a value type. The important thing to remember about the value type is that it is an object that you pass by value. When a method returns a value type object, the client actually receives a copy of the object. When a client invokes methods on the object, the method invocations occur locally on the client—they don't go back to the server.

When you declare a value type, there are three things you can declare: member variables, methods, and constructors. The basic form of the value type declaration is

```
valuetype typeName
{
    declarations
};
```

When you declare a member variable, you must specify whether it is `public` or `private` (there is no `protected` specifier in IDL). To declare a private string variable called `firstName`, use the following declaration:

```
private string firstName;
```

Constructors are a little odd in IDL. You declare a `factory init` method. All the parameters to the constructor must be `in` parameters.

Listing 17.6 shows an IDL file with a value type declaration.

Listing 17.6 Source Code for `Values.idl`

```
module usingj2ee
{
    module value
    {
        valuetype Person
        {
            private string firstName;
            private string middleName;
            private string lastName;

            factory init(in string aFirstName, in string aMiddleName,
                in string aLastName);

            string getFirstName();
            void setFirstName(in string aFirstName);

            string getMiddleName();
            void setMiddleName(in string aMiddleName);


            string getLastName();
            void setLastName(in string aLastName);
        };

        interface Values
        {
            void getPerson(out Person aPerson);
        };
    };
};
```

When you compile an IDL file with a `valuetype` declaration, the IDL-to-Java compiler creates a helper and holder (as it does for structs), some special factory classes, and an abstract base class containing the member variables. The abstract base class has the same name as the value type object. For instance, for the IDL file in Listing 17.6 shown previously, the IDL-to-Java compiler generates a class named `Person`. You must create a concrete implementation class named `xxxxImpl` where *xxxx* is the name of the value type. Listing 17.7 shows an implementation for the `Person` value type.

LISTING 17.7 SOURCE CODE FOR PersonImpl.java

```
package usingj2ee.value;

public class PersonImpl extends Person
{
    public PersonImpl()
    {
    }

    public PersonImpl(String aFirstName, String aMiddleName,
        String aLastName)
    {
        firstName = aFirstName;
        middleName = aMiddleName;
        lastName = aLastName;
    }

    public String getFirstName() { return firstName; }
    public void setFirstName(String aFirstName)
    {
        firstName = aFirstName;
    }

    public String getMiddleName() { return middleName; }
    public void setMiddleName(String aMiddleName)
    {
        middleName = aMiddleName;
    }

    public String getLastName() { return lastName; }
    public void setLastName(String aLastName)
    {
        lastName = aLastName;
    }
}
```

Listing 17.8 shows an example server that creates a new instance of a value type object and returns it to the client.

LISTING 17.8 SOURCE CODE FOR ValuesImpl.java

```
package usingj2ee.value;

import org.omg.CosNaming.*;
import org.omg.CosNaming.NamingContextPackage.*;
import org.omg.CORBA.*;

import java.io.*;

public class ValuesImpl extends _ValuesImplBase
{
    public ValuesImpl()
    {
    }
```

```
    public void getPerson(PersonHolder holder)
    {
        Person newPerson = new PersonImpl("Val", "U.", "Tipe");

        holder.value = newPerson;
    }

    public static void main(String[] args)
    {
        try
        {
// Create a reference to the CORBA orb
            ORB orb = ORB.init(args, null);

// Create an instance of the Values implementation
            ValuesImpl impl = new ValuesImpl();

// Register the Values implementation with the ORB
            orb.connect(impl);

// Locate the CORBA naming service
            org.omg.CORBA.Object objRef =
                orb.resolve_initial_references("NameService");

// Cast the CORBA Object to NamingContext using the narrow method
            NamingContext ncRef = NamingContextHelper.narrow(objRef);

// Create a NameComponent representing the path for the Values service
            NameComponent nc = new NameComponent("Values", "");
            NameComponent[] path = new NameComponent[] { nc };

// Register the Values implementation with the naming service
            ncRef.rebind(path, impl);

// Go into an infinite loop while the ORB services requests
            java.lang.Object sync = new java.lang.Object();
            synchronized (sync)
            {
                sync.wait();
            }
        }
        catch (Exception exc)
        {
            exc.printStackTrace();
        }
    }
}
```

Finally, Listing 17.9 shows a client that receives a value type object and invokes some of its methods.

LISTING 17.9 SOURCE CODE FOR ValuesClient.java

```
package usingj2ee.value;

import org.omg.CORBA.*;
```

LISTING 17.9 CONTINUED

```
import org.omg.CosNaming.*;

public class ValuesClient
{
    public static void main(String[] args)
    {
        try
        {
            ORB orb = ORB.init(args, null);

// Locate the CORBA naming service
            org.omg.CORBA.Object objRef =
                orb.resolve_initial_references("NameService");

// Instead of using the Java cast operator, the correct way to convert
// a CORBA Object into a specific type is to use that type's helper
            NamingContext ncRef = NamingContextHelper.narrow(objRef);

// Create a name component path for locating the Values service
            NameComponent nc = new NameComponent("Values", "");
            NameComponent path[] = new NameComponent[] { nc };

// Locate the Values service
            org.omg.CORBA.Object valuesObj = ncRef.resolve(path);

// Narrow (that is, cast) the reference to an object of type Values
            Values valuesRef = ValuesHelper.narrow(valuesObj);

// Get the person object
            PersonHolder holder = new PersonHolder();

            valuesRef.getPerson(holder);

            Person person = holder.value;

// Print out the person attributes
            System.out.println(person.getFirstName()+" "+
                person.getMiddleName()+" "+person.getLastName());
        }
        catch (Exception exc)
        {
            exc.printStackTrace();
        }
    }
}
```

FACTORIES

One of the things that is conspicuously absent from IDL is a constructor declaration (other than the `factory init` method for value types). With CORBA, you usually create a special object called a *factory* that creates object instances. You register the factory with the naming service, and clients only need to perform a naming lookup on the factory. After a client has located a factory, it can invoke methods to create the actual objects.

Figure 17.2 shows the relationship between a factory, a client, and the object the factory creates.

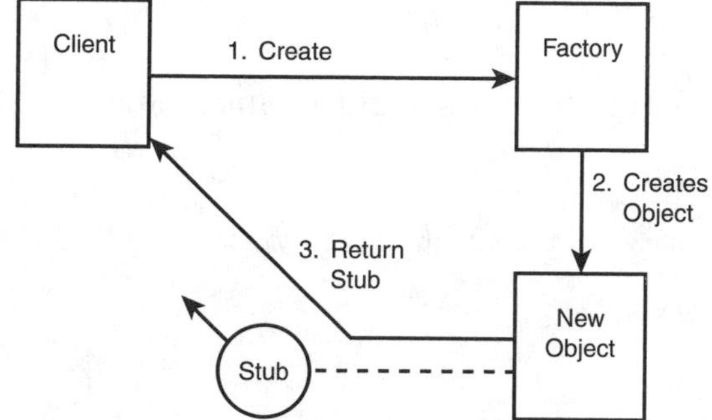

Figure 17.2 The client uses the factory to create specific objects.

Listing 17.10 shows an IDL file for a CORBA interface and a corresponding factory interface.

LISTING 17.10 SOURCE CODE FOR factory.idl

```
module usingj2ee
{
    module factories
    {
        interface Flight
        {
            attribute string flightNumber;
            attribute string origin;
            attribute string destination;
            attribute string departureTime;
            attribute string arrivalTime;

            void save();
            void remove();
        };

        interface FlightFactory
        {
            Flight createFlight(in string flightNumber);
        };
    };
};
```

Listing 17.11 shows a sample factory implementation. The factory just creates new objects and returns them; it's really simple to write.

LISTING 17.11 SOURCE CODE FOR FlightFactoryImpl.java

```
package usingj2ee.factories;

import org.omg.CosNaming.*;
import org.omg.CosNaming.NamingContextPackage.*;
import org.omg.CORBA.*;

import java.io.*;

public class FlightFactoryImpl extends _FlightFactoryImplBase
{
    protected static ORB orb;

/** Creates a new instance of the Flight Factory server
 */
    public FlightFactoryImpl()
    {
    }

    public Flight createFlight(String flightNumber)
    {

// Create a new flight (if you have a flight database, you would perform
// a lookup here to see if the flight already exists

        Flight theFlight = new FlightImpl(flightNumber, "", "", "", "");

// Connect the new flight to the orb
        orb.connect(theFlight);

        return theFlight;
    }

    public static void main(String[] args)
    {
        try
        {
// Create a reference to the CORBA orb
            orb = ORB.init(args, null);

// Create an instance of the FlightFactory implementation
            FlightFactoryImpl impl = new FlightFactoryImpl();

// Register the FlightFactory implementation with the ORB
            orb.connect(impl);

// Locate the CORBA naming service
            org.omg.CORBA.Object objRef =
                orb.resolve_initial_references("NameService");

// Cast the CORBA Object to NamingContext using the narrow method
            NamingContext ncRef = NamingContextHelper.narrow(objRef);

// Create a NameComponent representing the path for the FlightFactory service
            NameComponent nc = new NameComponent("FlightFactory", "");
            NameComponent[] path = new NameComponent[] { nc };
```

```
// Register the FlightFactory implementation with the naming service
            ncRef.rebind(path, impl);

// Go into an infinite loop while the ORB services requests
            java.lang.Object sync = new java.lang.Object();
            synchronized (sync)
            {
                sync.wait();
            }
        }
        catch (Exception exc)
        {
            exc.printStackTrace();
        }
    }
}
```


Listing 17.12 shows a client that uses a factory. Basically, it looks up the factory in the naming service and then invokes the factory method to create the real object.

LISTING 17.12 SOURCE CODE FOR FlightFactoryClient.java

```
package usingj2ee.factories;

import org.omg.CORBA.*;
import org.omg.CosNaming.*;

public class FlightFactoryClient
{
    public static void main(String[] args)
    {
        try
        {
            ORB orb = ORB.init(args, null);

// Locate the CORBA naming service
            org.omg.CORBA.Object objRef =
                orb.resolve_initial_references("NameService");

// Instead of using the Java cast operator, the correct way to convert
// a CORBA Object into a specific type is to use that type's helper
            NamingContext ncRef = NamingContextHelper.narrow(objRef);

// Create a name component path for locating the FlightFactory service
            NameComponent nc = new NameComponent("FlightFactory", "");
            NameComponent path[] = new NameComponent[] { nc };

// Locate the FlightFactory service
            org.omg.CORBA.Object flightFactoryObj = ncRef.resolve(path);

// Narrow (that is, cast) the reference to an object of type FlightFactory
            FlightFactory flightFactoryRef =
                FlightFactoryHelper.narrow(flightFactoryObj);

// Create a new Flight instance
            Flight flight = flightFactoryRef.createFlight("795");
```

LISTING 17.12 CONTINUED

```
// Update some of the flight attributes
            flight.origin("SAN");
            flight.destination("OGG");
            flight.departureTime("1300");
            flight.arrivalTime("1545");

// Save the flight
            flight.save();
        }
        catch (Exception exc)
        {
            exc.printStackTrace();
        }
    }
}
```

CALLBACKS

Sometimes, a CORBA server needs to invoke methods on a client. For example, when you publish stock quotes or aircraft positions, you don't want the clients polling the server over and over to get the new positions. You want the server to notify the clients when it receives data. One way to accomplish this is to use callback interfaces.

The idea is simple, a client program creates a CORBA object and registers the object with the local ORB. The client then invokes a method on the server, passing the CORBA object to the server. CORBA doesn't pass the whole object, of course; it just passes a remote reference to the object. The server then uses the remote reference to invoke methods on the client.

Figure 17.3 illustrates a typical use of a callback.

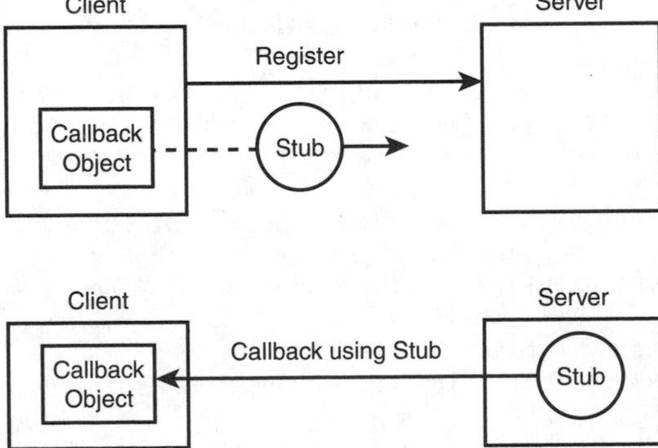

Figure 17.3
A client registers a callback object with the server.

Listing 17.13 shows an IDL file for a simple message callback that continuously publishes a string message to any listeners.

LISTING 17.13 SOURCE CODE FOR Callbacks.idl

```
module usingj2ee
{
    module callbacks
    {
        interface CallbackReceiver
        {
            void handleCallback(in string message);
        };

        interface Callback
        {
            void registerCallback(in CallbackReceiver receiver);
            void unregisterCallback(in CallbackReceiver receiver);
        };
    };
};
```


Listing 17.14 shows the client application. The client application creates a CORBA object, registers it with the server, and then waits for incoming calls from the server.

LISTING 17.14 SOURCE CODE FOR CallbackClient.java

```
package usingj2ee.callbacks;

import org.omg.CORBA.*;
import org.omg.CosNaming.*;

public class CallbackClient extends _CallbackReceiverImplBase
{
    public CallbackClient()
    {
    }

    public void handleCallback(String message)
    {
        System.out.println(message);
    }

    public static void main(String[] args)
    {
        try
        {
            ORB orb = ORB.init(args, null);

// Locate the CORBA naming service
            org.omg.CORBA.Object objRef =
                orb.resolve_initial_references("NameService");

// Instead of using the Java cast operator, the correct way to convert
// a CORBA Object into a specific type is to use that type's helper
            NamingContext ncRef = NamingContextHelper.narrow(objRef);
```

LISTING 17.14 CONTINUED

```
// Create a name component path for locating the Callbacks service
            NameComponent nc = new NameComponent("Callbacks", "");
            NameComponent path[] = new NameComponent[] { nc };

// Locate the Callbacks service
            org.omg.CORBA.Object callbackObj = ncRef.resolve(path);

// Narrow (that is, cast) the reference to an object of type Callback
            Callback callbackRef =
                CallbackHelper.narrow(callbackObj);

// Create a callback receiver
            CallbackClient receiver = new CallbackClient();

// Register the receiver with the ORB
            orb.connect(receiver);

// Register the receiver with the callback server
            callbackRef.registerCallback(receiver);

// Go into an infinite loop while the ORB listens for callbacks
            java.lang.Object sync = new java.lang.Object();
            synchronized (sync)
            {
                sync.wait();
            }
        }
        catch (Exception exc)
        {
            exc.printStackTrace();
        }
    }
}
```

Listing 17.15 shows the callback server. It spawns a thread that publishes a message every five seconds. One of the things you'll notice about the server is that it automatically removes clients if an exception occurs while writing to the client. When it decides to remove the client, it places the client in a separate vector. After it has published to all the clients, it removes any clients that it had saved in the separate vector. Under JDK 1.1, you don't have the fancy new container classes; the `Vector` and its `Enumeration` class are all you have to work with. Unfortunately, the `Enumeration` class gets lost and skips elements when you remove elements as you enumerate through the vector. The `Iterator` class doesn't suffer from the same problem, as long as you don't try to remove the elements using a method other than the `remove` method in the `Iterator` class. Listing 17.15 shows you the old JDK 1.1 way to handle the problem in case you still need to support JDK 1.1.

LISTING 17.15 SOURCE CODE FOR `CallbackImpl.java`

```
package usingj2ee.callbacks;

import org.omg.CosNaming.*;
```

```
import org.omg.CosNaming.NamingContextPackage.*;
import org.omg.CORBA.*;

import java.io.*;
import java.util.*;

public class CallbackImpl extends _CallbackImplBase
{
    protected Vector callbacks;
    protected String callbackMessage;

/** Creates a new instance of the Flight Factory server
 */
    public CallbackImpl(String aCallbackMessage)
    {
        callbacks = new Vector();
        callbackMessage = aCallbackMessage;

// Create the thread for publishing messages
        CallbackSender sender = new CallbackSender();
        Thread callbackThread = new Thread(sender);
        callbackThread.start();
    }

    public void registerCallback(CallbackReceiver receiver)
    {
// Only add the callback to the callback vector if it isn't already there
        Enumeration e = callbacks.elements();

        while (e.hasMoreElements())
        {
            CallbackReceiver r = (CallbackReceiver) e.nextElement();

// Use the CORBA _is_equivalent instead of relying on the Java equals method
            if (r._is_equivalent(receiver)) return;
        }

        System.out.println("Added new listener");
        callbacks.addElement(receiver);
    }

    public void unregisterCallback(CallbackReceiver receiver)
    {
        Enumeration e = callbacks.elements();

        while (e.hasMoreElements())
        {
            CallbackReceiver r = (CallbackReceiver) e.nextElement();

// Don't rely on equals(), use the CORBA version
            if (r._is_equivalent(receiver))
            {
                callbacks.removeElement(r);
                return;
            }
        }
    }
```

LISTING 17.15 CONTINUED

```
    class CallbackSender implements Runnable
    {
        public void run()
        {
            for (;;)
            {
                Enumeration e = callbacks.elements();

                Vector itemsToRemove = null;

                while (e.hasMoreElements())
                {
                    CallbackReceiver r = (CallbackReceiver) e.nextElement();

// Try to send a message to a client
                    try
                    {
                        r.handleCallback(callbackMessage);
                    }
                    catch (Exception exc)
                    {
// If there is an exception while sending, add this client to the list
// of clients that must be removed from the callbacks vector
// You can't remove them directly from the vector because it messes
// up the enumeration.
// You don't need to bother with this if you use an Iterator (Iterators
// don't lose their place when you remove an element). If you must
// use JDK 1.1, however, you need to use the itemsToRemove vector
                        if (itemsToRemove == null)
                        {
                            itemsToRemove = new Vector();
                        }
                        itemsToRemove.addElement(r);
                    }
                }

// If the callbacks vector isn't empty, remove the defunct clients
                if (itemsToRemove != null)
                {
                    e = itemsToRemove.elements();

                    while (e.hasMoreElements())
                    {
                        callbacks.removeElement(e.nextElement());
                        System.out.println("Removed a listener");
                    }
                }

                try
                {
                    Thread.sleep(5000);
                }
                catch (Exception ignore) {}
            }
        }
    }
```

```
    public static void main(String[] args)
    {
        try
        {
// Create a reference to the CORBA orb
            ORB orb = ORB.init(args, null);

// Create an instance of the Callbacks implementation
            CallbackImpl impl = new CallbackImpl("Hello Listeners!");

// Register the FlightFactory implementation with the ORB
            orb.connect(impl);

// Locate the CORBA naming service
            org.omg.CORBA.Object objRef =
                orb.resolve_initial_references("NameService");

// Cast the CORBA Object to NamingContext using the narrow method
            NamingContext ncRef = NamingContextHelper.narrow(objRef);

// Create a NameComponent representing the path for the FlightFactory service
            NameComponent nc = new NameComponent("Callbacks", "");
            NameComponent[] path = new NameComponent[] { nc };

// Register the Callbacks implementation with the naming service
            ncRef.rebind(path, impl);

// Go into an infinite loop while the ORB services requests
            java.lang.Object sync = new java.lang.Object();
            synchronized (sync)
            {
                sync.wait();
            }
        }
        catch (Exception exc)
        {
            exc.printStackTrace();
        }
    }
}
```


Object References

You have already seen that RMI has remote object identifiers and Enterprise JavaBeans have handles. The items represent addresses of remote objects—they tell the various libraries where to find a remote object. CORBA's remote object reference is called an *IOR* (*Inter-ORB Reference*). You use IORs mainly to pass addresses from one ORB to another.

You know, already, that you use a CORBA naming service to locate CORBA objects. Different ORBs have their own custom naming services, however. What happens if a client using the Visibroker ORB wants to access a server running Orbix? Well, because CORBA uses a standard protocol between the client and the server, the only trick is letting the client know where to find the server.

You have two options when trying to run multiple ORBs: You can share the naming service or manage the IORs yourself. The easiest way to mix ORBs together is to use a single naming service. When you start the naming service, you write the IOR of the naming service to a file.

You might have noticed that when you start `tnameserv` (the naming service built into JDK 1.3), it prints out an IOR. Listing 17.16 shows a program that reads the IOR for the naming service from a file and uses it to locate an object.

LISTING 17.16 SOURCE CODE FOR `MOTDClient2.java`

```
package usingj2ee.motd;

import org.omg.CORBA.*;
import org.omg.CosNaming.*;

import java.io.*;

public class MOTDClient2
{
    public static void main(String[] args)
    {
        try
        {
            ORB orb = ORB.init(args, null);

// Read the IOR from a file
            BufferedReader in = new BufferedReader(
                new FileReader("naming.ior"));

            String namingIOR = in.readLine();

            in.close();

// Locate the CORBA naming service by the IOR
            org.omg.CORBA.Object objRef =
                orb.string_to_object(namingIOR);

// Instead of using the Java cast operator, the correct way to convert
// a CORBA Object into a specific type is to use that type's helper
            NamingContext ncRef = NamingContextHelper.narrow(objRef);

// Create a name component path for locating the MOTD service
            NameComponent nc = new NameComponent("MessageOfTheDay", "");
            NameComponent path[] = new NameComponent[] { nc };

// Locate the MOTD service
            org.omg.CORBA.Object motdObj = ncRef.resolve(path);

// Narrow (that is, cast) the reference to an object of type MOTD
            MOTD motdRef = MOTDHelper.narrow(motdObj);

// Display the message of the day
            System.out.println(motdRef.getMOTD());
        }
```

```
        catch (Exception exc)
        {
            exc.printStackTrace();
        }
    }
}
```

Note

When you start `tnameserv`, it writes out a line starting with `IOR:`. Copy this line to a file called `naming.ior` before you try to run the `MOTDClient2` program in Listing 17.16.

If you want to bypass the naming service altogether, you can write the IOR for a particular object to a file (or pass it via a socket). Just use the `orb.object_to_string` method to write out the object reference.

Listing 17.17 shows a simplified CORBA server that writes its IOR to a file instead of using the naming service.

LISTING 17.17 SOURCE CODE FOR `MOTDImplIOR.java`

```
package usingj2ee.motd;

import org.omg.CosNaming.*;
import org.omg.CosNaming.NamingContextPackage.*;
import org.omg.CORBA.*;

import java.io.*;

public class MOTDImplIOR extends _MOTDImplBase
{
/** The name of the file containing the message */
    protected String motdFileName;

/** Creates a new instance of the MOTD server assigned to a
 *  specific filename.
 */
    public MOTDImplIOR(String aMotdFileName)
    {
        motdFileName = aMotdFileName;
    }

    public String getMOTD()
    {
        try
        {
// Open the message file
            BufferedReader reader = new BufferedReader(
                new FileReader(motdFileName));

// Create a buffer to hold the resulting message
            StringBuffer buffer = new StringBuffer();

            String line;
```

LISTING 17.17 CONTINUED

```
// Read all the lines in the file
            while ((line = reader.readLine()) != null)
            {
// Put each line into the buffer separated by newlines
                buffer.append(line);
                buffer.append("\n");
            }

            reader.close();

// Return the message
            return buffer.toString();
        }
        catch (IOException exc)
        {
// If there's an error, just return an empty message
            return "";
        }
    }

    public static void main(String[] args)
    {
        String motdFile = System.getProperty("file", "motd.txt");
        String motdService = System.getProperty("service",
            "MessageOfTheDay");
        try
        {
// Create a reference to the CORBA orb
            ORB orb = ORB.init(args, null);

// Create an instance of the MOTD implementation
            MOTDImplIOR impl = new MOTDImplIOR(motdFile);

// Register the MOTD implementation with the ORB
            orb.connect(impl);

// Open a file for writing out the IOR
            PrintWriter iorOut = new PrintWriter(
                new FileWriter("motd.ior"));

// Write out the IOR to the file
            iorOut.println(orb.object_to_string(impl));

            iorOut.close();

// Go into an infinite loop while the ORB services requests
            java.lang.Object sync = new java.lang.Object();
            synchronized (sync)
            {
                sync.wait();
            }
        }
        catch (Exception exc)
        {
            exc.printStackTrace();
```

```
        }
    }
}
```

Listing 17.18 shows a CORBA client that reads the server's IOR from a file instead of using the naming service.

LISTING 17.18 SOURCE CODE FOR `MOTDClientIOR.java`

```
package usingj2ee.motd;

import org.omg.CORBA.*;
import org.omg.CosNaming.*;

import java.io.*;

public class MOTDClientIOR
{
    public static void main(String[] args)
    {
        try
        {
            ORB orb = ORB.init(args, null);

// Read the IOR from a file
            BufferedReader in = new BufferedReader(
                new FileReader("motd.ior"));

            String motdIOR = in.readLine();

            in.close();

// Locate the MOTD service by the IOR
            org.omg.CORBA.Object motdObj =
                orb.string_to_object(motdIOR);

// Narrow (that is, cast) the reference to an object of type MOTD
            MOTD motdRef = MOTDHelper.narrow(motdObj);

// Display the message of the day
            System.out.println(motdRef.getMOTD());
        }
        catch (Exception exc)
        {
            exc.printStackTrace();
        }
    }
}
```


DYNAMIC INVOCATION

Most of the time, when you use CORBA from a Java program, you're doing static method invocation. That is, you know about the methods that you want to call when you first compile your program. CORBA also supports a mechanism called dynamic method invocation, where you don't need to know what methods an object supports until runtime. The official name for the dynamic method invocation is the Dynamic Invocation Interface, or DII.

Obviously, if you don't know about the methods until runtime, you can hardly expect to have a stub object for invoking methods. Instead, you create a `Request` object based on a method name.

The `Request` object represents a particular method in a distributed object. To create a `Request` object, call the `_request` method on the object whose method you want to invoke. In other words, if you have an instance of the MOTD object and you want to invoke the `getMOTD` method, use the following call:

```
Request req = myMotdRef._request("getMOTD");
```

The way you store parameters in a request is a little quirky, but it's not so bad after you get used to it. You have two ways to add parameters: either add them in the order they are defined in the IDL file, or use the argument names. The quirky thing is that when you add a parameter, you don't add the value, you just tell the request you want to add a parameter and it returns an `Any` object. You then store the parameter value in the `Any`. For instance, suppose you define a method this way:

```
void setName(in string first, in string last)
```

To set the parameters in order, do something like this:

```
Any firstParam = req.add_in_arg();
firstParam.insert_string("Samantha");
Any lastParam = req.add_in_arg();
lastParam.insert_string("Tippin");
```

You can also set the parameters by name, like this:

```
Any lastParam = req.add_named_in_arg("last");
lastParam.insert_string("Tippin");
Any firstParam = req.add_named_in_arg("first");
firstParam.insert_string("Kaitlynn");
```

When a method has a return value (that is, it isn't a `void` method) you must also set the type of the return value you expect. To set the return type, call `set_return_type`, passing in a `TypeCode` object representing the return type you expect. There are two basic ways to get a type code: Call the `get_primitive_tc` object (which takes a `TCKind`) of the `ORB` class, or for a user-defined type, use the helper's `type()` method.

If you call `get_primitive_tc`, use one of the static variables in the `TCKind` class. The values take the form `tc_`*`type`* where *type* is the type of value. For example, to get a type code for a string, use the following call:

```
TypeCode stringTC = orb.get_primitive_tc(TCKind.tk_string);
```

After you have everything set up, use the `invoke` method to invoke the method:

```
request.invoke();
```

Finally, to access any return value, call the `return_value` method, which returns an `Any` object. As usual, you can use the various `extract_`*`xxx`* methods to fetch the value from the `Any`.

Listing 17.19 shows the Dynamic Invocation Interface version of the MOTD client shown earlier in Listing 17.3.

LISTING 17.19 SOURCE CODE FOR DIIMOTDClient.java

```
package usingj2ee.motd;

import org.omg.CORBA.*;
import org.omg.CosNaming.*;

public class DIIMOTDClient
{
    public static void main(String[] args)
    {
        try
        {
            ORB orb = ORB.init(args, null);

// Locate the CORBA naming service
            org.omg.CORBA.Object objRef =
                orb.resolve_initial_references("NameService");

// Instead of using the Java cast operator, the correct way to convert
// a CORBA Object into a specific type is to use that type's helper
            NamingContext ncRef = NamingContextHelper.narrow(objRef);

// Create a name component path for locating the MOTD service
            NameComponent nc = new NameComponent("MessageOfTheDay", "");
            NameComponent path[] = new NameComponent[] { nc };

// Locate the MOTD service
            org.omg.CORBA.Object motdObj = ncRef.resolve(path);

// Locate the getMOTD method and create a request for it
            Request req = motdObj._request("getMOTD");

// The return type should be a string
            req.set_return_type(orb.get_primitive_tc(TCKind.tk_string));

// Invoke the method
            req.invoke();

// Get the return value
            Any retval = req.return_value();

// Display the message of the day
            System.out.println(retval.extract_string());
        }
        catch (Exception exc)
        {
            exc.printStackTrace();
        }
    }
}
```

Like many of the CORBA API calls, DII is a bit more cumbersome to use when compared to typical Java API calls. Remember that CORBA is language-independent and strives to make its API as similar as possible across different programming languages. That's why CORBA doesn't always seem to conform to the Java way of doing things (such as using `return_value` instead of `getReturnValue`).

USING CORBA AND RMI TOGETHER

Although CORBA and RMI are generally considered competing technologies, in the Java realm, they actually work together nicely, thanks to a special blend of CORBA and RMI called *RMI-IIOP*.

One of the biggest knocks against CORBA version 1.0 is that it didn't define a standard protocol for object communication. Every ORB implementation was different, so you couldn't create a client with one ORB and access a server with another ORB. CORBA 2.0 introduced a standard protocol (actually a set of them) to allow different ORBs to communicate with each other. The basic protocol is called the *General Inter-ORB Protocol* (*GIOP*). GIOP defines the data items that an ORB must send for various requests, but doesn't address actual networking protocols. CORBA 2.0 also defines a TCP/IP-based protocol (that is, an Internet protocol) called the *Internet Inter-ORB Protocol* or *IIOP*. Every ORB must implement IIOP regardless of whether it supports any other protocol.

One of the deficiencies of Java RMI is that it is Java-specific. You can't use RMI to invoke methods on a C++ program. Technically, you *can* use RMI to access a C++ program, but to do so, you must implement JRMP (the Java Remote Method Protocol) in C++, which is not a task anyone should take lightly. Take a look again at the basic structure of an RMI client and server, as shown in Figure 17.4.

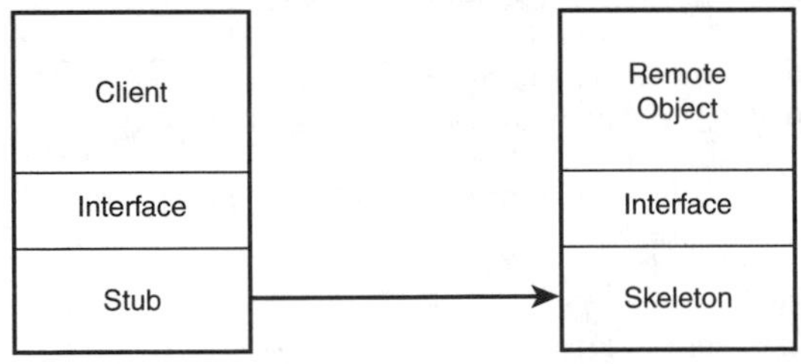

Figure 17.4
An RMI client calls methods on a stub, which talks to a skeleton that invokes server methods.

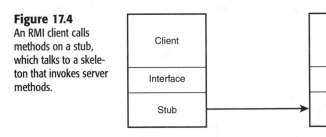

Now, compare the diagram to the one you saw earlier in Figure 17.1. They look almost identical, at least functionally. RMI doesn't really have the concept of an ORB, but both CORBA and RMI use the stub-and-skeleton concept.

The interesting thing here is that the RMI stub and skeleton understand JRMP, but the client and server don't need to know anything about it. In other words, the stub and skeleton hide the underlying protocol from the client and server. If the protocol is hidden, what's to stop you from changing the underlying protocol from JRMP to IIOP? The answer is, nothing. With JDK 1.3, the `rmic` compiler you use to generate your RMI stubs and skeletons can now generate IIOP-aware stubs and skeletons.

Even better, `rmic` can generate IDL files, so you can create CORBA clients in other languages to access RMI server objects. Keep in mind that you typically use RMI-IIOP to create RMI server objects. If you need to access a CORBA server object, you usually just stick with CORBA.

Why is RMI-IIOP so important? Like it or not, some people still want to develop applications in languages other than Java. Many Windows developers despise writing GUI applications in Java because Swing is still somewhat slow compared to a native Windows application. They prefer to stick with traditional Windows GUI programming languages, such as Visual Basic and Delphi. RMI-IIOP allows you to create Enterprise JavaBeans that you can access using CORBA.

Note

For Windows development, you don't need CORBA to access an EJB server from a non-Java application. Sun has a series of libraries called the J2EE Client Access Services (CAS), one of which is called CAS COM. It allows you to use COM (Microsoft's competitor to CORBA) to access Enterprise JavaBeans. The beauty of CAS COM is that you don't need an ORB—just the CAS COM libraries (COM is built directly into Windows).

If you want to make your RMI server available via IIOP, you must do a few things differently. First, you must use the Java Naming API to register your object with the naming service (instead of using RMI's naming classes). Next, you must use a CORBA naming service (such as `tnameserv`) instead of `rmiregistry`. Instead of extending `UnicastRemoteObject` in your server, extend `javax.rmi.PortableRemoteObject`. Finally, when you run `rmic`, you must specify `-iiop` to generate IIOP-aware stubs and skeletons.

Listing 17.20 shows an RMI-IIOP version of the MOTD implementation class.

LISTING 17.20 SOURCE CODE FOR `RMIMOTDImpl.java`

```
package usingj2ee.rmimotd;

import java.io.*;
import java.rmi.*;
import javax.rmi.PortableRemoteObject;
import javax.naming.*;

/** An implementation of the Message-Of-The-Day remote interface. */

public class RMIMOTDImpl extends PortableRemoteObject
    implements RMIMOTD
{
/** The name of the file containing the message */
    protected String motdFileName;

/** Creates a new instance of the MOTD server assigned to a
 *  specific filename.
 */
```

LISTING 17.20 CONTINUED

```
    public RMIMOTDImpl(String aMotdFileName)
        throws RemoteException
    {
        motdFileName = aMotdFileName;
    }

/** Returns the Message-Of-The-Day */
    public String getMOTD()
    {
        try
        {
// Open the message file
            BufferedReader reader = new BufferedReader(
                new FileReader(motdFileName));

// Create a buffer to hold the resulting message
            StringBuffer buffer = new StringBuffer();

            String line;

// Read all the lines in the file
            while ((line = reader.readLine()) != null)
            {
// Put each line into the buffer separated by newlines
                buffer.append(line);
                buffer.append("\n");
            }

            reader.close();

// Return the message
            return buffer.toString();
        }
        catch (IOException exc)
        {
// If there's an error, just return an empty message
            return "";
        }
    }

/** Activates the MOTD service */
    public static void main(String[] args)
    {
        String motdFile = System.getProperty("file", "motd.txt");
        String motdService = System.getProperty("service",
            "MessageOfTheDay");

// Must assign an RMI security manager
        if (System.getSecurityManager() == null)
        {
            System.setSecurityManager(new RMISecurityManager());
        }

        try
        {
// Create an instance of the MOTD service
```

```
            RMIMOTDImpl impl = new RMIMOTDImpl(motdFile);

            Context ctx = new InitialContext();

// Register the service with the RMI registry
            ctx.rebind("//localhost/"+motdService, impl);

        }
        catch (Exception exc)
        {
            exc.printStackTrace();
        }
    }
}
```

Note

The RMIMOTDImpl example requires at least JDK 1.3 because it relies on the RMI-IIOP extensions that weren't added to the JDK until version 1.3.

CORBA APPLICATION ARCHITECTURE

When you create a CORBA application, you must decide how the clients will interact with your objects. You can have one object (or a small group of objects) with many clients, or you can have a separate object for every client. Figure 17.5 illustrates these possibilities.

Figure 17.5
You must decide how many clients a CORBA object can have.

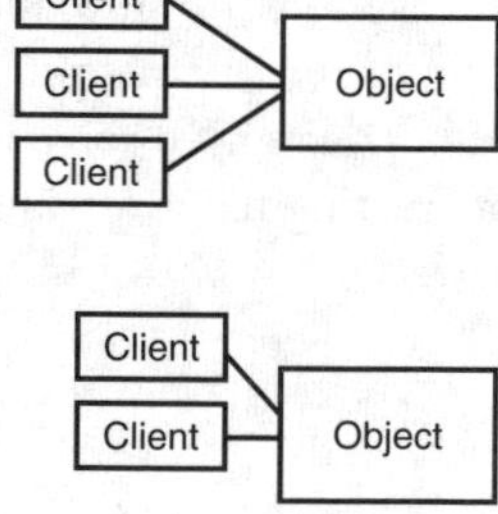

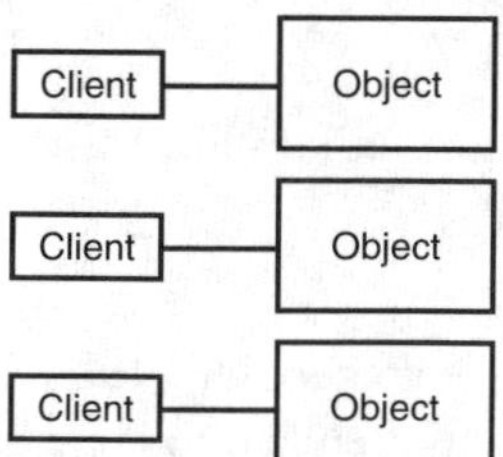

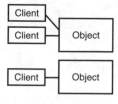

In some applications, the CORBA object represents a business object, like an aircraft or a warehouse. In others, the object represents a set of business operations that you want to perform. When the CORBA objects represent business objects, your application tends to look a lot like an EJB application. You must often define transactions across different objects and you start to perform many of the same persistence operations as you do with EJB. If you see your application heading in this direction, why not make the switch to EJB? Many of the painful parts are already taken care of (persistence, transactions, object lifecycle, caching, and so on).

When you have one CORBA object with many clients, and the CORBA object is just a set of business methods with no real state data (that is, it works like a stateless session bean), you're really doing remote procedure calls—not distributed objects. There's nothing wrong with remote procedure calls. Many times it's easier to maintain your application, and for smaller applications, that might be all you need. You tend to see these remote procedure calls designed for catalog lookups, schedule information, and other fairly static data. You can also use this technique to create an order-entry system, but you must pass all the order information in a single method call because the object doesn't have any state data.

The single-object-per-client design is much like an EJB session bean. Each client has its own object to work with, and the object can store state data related to the client. You usually don't need to worry about transactions—at least not as much—because the objects typically don't participate in joint operations. You might implement a shopping cart object this way, where the CORBA object contains the customer's order.

One of the biggest complaints you see about CORBA is that it is slow. CORBA itself isn't really slow, of course; it's just that CORBA makes it easy to write slow applications. If you use CORBA attributes a lot, you end up making a ton of remote method calls just to get the data you need (entity beans have the same problem, of course). To solve this little problem, you create a view structure. For example, instead of creating name attributes for a person, like this

```
attribute string firstName;
attribute string middleName;
attribute string lastName;
```

You create a `Person` struct, like this:

```
struct Person
{
    string firstName;
    string middleName;
    string lastName;
};
```

Then to store and retrieve the person, you can make methods like this:

```
Person getPerson();
void setPerson(Person aPerson);
```

In the past, this technique was pretty painful because you couldn't extend the structs—you couldn't add local methods to them or anything. You often had to copy data from the structs to your own Java objects. With the addition of value types, however, creating these view objects has become much more palatable. You have more control over the methods you put in the class.

ADDITIONAL CORBA SERVICES

The OMG has defined a number of services for CORBA. There is a small group called the Common Object Services (COS) that consists of the naming service, the Event service and the Lifecycle service. Although only the naming service is included with the JDK, many ORBs provide an event service and lifecycle service.

The lifecycle service defines how you make copies of objects and remove them. The one area the lifecycle doesn't address is object creation—you must create factories on your own to create objects.

The event service allows clients and servers to exchange data in an asynchronous fashion. EJB has a message service that provides essentially the same kinds of features as the CORBA event service. The event service has two basic models: the push model and the pull model. In a *push model*, the supplier (the object generating the events) sends messages to its consumers. In a *pull model*, the consumers ask the supplier if it has any messages for them (pull sounds a lot like poll, which is what the consumers are really doing).

CORBA also defines a persistence service, which has never really taken off. EJB has gotten much further along in the area of persistence. CORBA's Object Transaction Service (OTS) allows you to define transactions that span multiple method invocations. In fact, OTS served as the model for the Java Transaction Service (JTS).

CORBA has many other useful services if you decide to go for a pure CORBA application. Keep in mind, however, that the CORBA APIs tend to be a little more cumbersome than pure Java APIs because of their cross-language nature. If you have no pressing need to use CORBA (that is, if you know you only need to support Java), you should stick with the pure Java APIs.

TROUBLESHOOTING

COMPILING IDL FILES

Why do I get syntax errors when I try to declare a variable that's a sequence of another type?

You usually need to use `typedef` to create an alternate type name for sequences, and then use the `typedef` name to declare your variable.

Why do I get errors when I declare an `int`*?*

You must declare integers as either `short` or `long`. There is no `int` type in IDL.

Why can't I declare an overloaded method?

CORBA doesn't support overloaded method names. Each method name in an interface must be unique.

EXECUTION PROBLEMS

Why do I get strange CORBA errors when I use the `Any` class?

If you are using a third-party ORB, such as Visibroker or Orbix, you must tell the JDK the class name for the ORB using the `-Dorg.omg.CORBA.ORBClass` and `-Dorg.omg.CORBA.ORBSingletonClass` options.

Why do I get error messages about `null` strings?

You can't have a `null` string in CORBA. Every string value must be initialiazed, even if it's just with an empty string. This is probably one of the most annoying features of CORBA.

Why do I get `NoSuchMethod` errors from CORBA?

The most common reason for this error is that the client stub is out of sync with the server skeleton. You usually see this error after you have changed the IDL and recompiled the server, but you haven't copied the new stubs to the client.

CHAPTER 18

JNDI—Java Naming and Directory Interface

In this chapter

A Centralized Directory

Enterprise-level applications use a lot of different directory services—lookup services that locate resources associated with a particular name. When you use RMI, for example, you locate objects with a directory service called the RMI Registry. When you use CORBA, you use the COS Naming facility (CORBA's naming service) to locate objects. When you convert a hostname to an IP address, you usually use a directory service called DNS (Domain Name Service). There are also general directory services that use protocols, such as X.500 (the CCITT directory standard) and LDAP (Lightweight Directory Access Protocol). These directory services can hold many kinds of data.

Although most people tend to use the terms "naming service" and "directory service" interchangeably, there is a difference. A *naming service* associates a single name with a specific resource. A *directory service* associates a name with a set of attributes and resources. When you search a naming service, you can only search for a specific name. When you search a directory, you can search for items matching a specific set of attributes.

One of the interesting things about all these types of naming and directory services is that they generally perform the same task—mapping a name to some set of attributes or objects. Of course, not all directory services are created equally. Some of them have a flat namespace, whereas others offer a tree structure for the names. Some of them allow you to store specific types of objects, whereas others allow you to store almost any kind of object.

The *Java Naming and Directory Interface (JNDI)* draws a distinction between naming services and directory services. A naming service maps a name to an object. The RMI Registry and the CORBA Naming Service are both examples of naming services. You can only store an RMI object in the RMI Registry and you can only store a CORBA object in the CORBA Naming Service. A directory service also stores objects, but these objects can have associated attributes that the directory service recognizes. You can search a directory using the item attributes. For example, you can search an LDAP directory for everyone in a specific department or everyone named Smith.

JNDI provides a uniform way to access naming and directory services. It supports flat namespaces as well as tree namespaces, and it allows you to store many different types of objects. The beauty of JNDI lies it its simplicity and uniformity. After you know the basic JNDI API calls, you can read data out of any kind of directory as long as there is a JNDI service provider for that directory.

You have already encountered JNDI in several earlier chapters. You use JNDI to locate Enterprise JavaBeans and JDBC connection pools from within your EJB container. You might have implemented simple lookup schemes before in your applications; that is, you create a class with static lookup methods or store a `Hashtable` in a static field somewhere. You might choose to use JNDI to replace these kinds of local storage mechanisms, although you might need to write your own service provider.

JNDI is also extremely useful in the area of configuration. If many applications use common configuration data, you might consider storing the data in a directory service, such as LDAP, instead of in a file or database. LDAP is especially good if the configuration information is hierarchical—that is, if it is more like a tree structure than a flat list of values.

One of the hidden benefits of directory services is the fact that there are a lot of directory service browsers and editors—especially for LDAP. You can view the contents of the directory and edit them using an off-the-shelf tool. That saves you from having to write a custom configuration editor.

JNDI BASICS

The `Context` class is the core of the JNDI API. You use it to perform any lookup and to add any new name-value associations. When you use JNDI, you typically create an `InitialContext` object first:

```
Context ctx = new InitialContext();
```

The `InitialContext` constructor looks for a system property called `java.naming.factory.initial` that contains the name of the class that creates the `InitialContext`. Sometimes, you must supply this value yourself. Some EJB containers, like the one that comes with Sun's J2EE SDK, already have this property set.

JDK 1.3 comes with three built-in service providers: RMI, CORBA, and LDAP. The classnames for the different initial context factories are

```
com.sun.jndi.rmi.registry.RegistryContextFactory
com.sun.jndi.cosnaming.CNCtxFactory
com.sun.jndi.ldap.LdapCtxFactory
```


Note Don't worry about setting defining the class for the initial context factory unless you get an error telling you there's no initial context factory.

When you run your program, you can specify the initial context factory on the command-line using the `-D` option:

```
java -Djava.naming.factory.initial=com.sun.jndi.ldap.LdapCtxFactory
➥ usingj2ee.naming.JNDIDemo
```

You can also specify the initial context factory in a `Hashtable` that you can pass to the `InitialContext` constructor:

```
Hashtable props = new Hashtable ();
props.put(Context.INITIAL_CONTEXT_FACTORY,
    "com.sun.jndi.ldap.LdapCtxFactory");
Context ctx = new InitialContext(props);
```

Bear in mind that if you specify the initial context factory using a `Hashtable` object, you might be limiting the portability of your classes. For example, most WebLogic examples tell you to create the `InitialContext` this way:

```
Hashtable props = new Hashtable();
props.put(Context.INITIAL_CONTEXT_FACTORY,
```

```
        "weblogic.jndi.WLInitialContextFactory");
    props.put(Context.PROVIDER_URL,
        "t3://localhost:7001");
    Context = new InitialContext(props);
```

The problem here is that if you want to run your code with another application server, you'll have to recompile your code with a new set of properties. It's better to set these items on the command line:

```
java -Djava.naming.factory.initial=weblogic.jndi.WLInitialContextFactory
➥ -Djava.naming.provider.url=t3://localhost:7001 MyTestClient
```

Tip

Rather than specifying the initial factory on the command line, you can put these associations in a file called `jndi.properties`, which can be located somewhere in your classpath.

When you develop Enterprise Java Beans, you can usually count on the environment being set up properly ahead of time, so you normally don't need to initialize any properties or set any system properties. When you run your client programs to test the EJBs, however, you usually need to specify an initial context factory.

Although most people use the `InitialContext` object as their first entry point into JNDI, there is an alternative. You can use the `javax.naming.spi.NamingManager` class to create a service-specific context for you based on a URL prefix. A fully qualified JNDI name is of the form *`service://itemname`*, where *`service`* is a name such as `iiop`, `rmi`, `ldap`, and so on, and *`itemname`* is the name of the item in that service. The `NamingManager` class lets you create a `Context` object based on the service name. For example, to create an LDAP `Context` object, you can call:

```
Context ctx = NamingManager.getURLContext("ldap", null);
```

One thing to keep in mind when you use this technique is that the `Context` you get back usually doesn't understand names for other services. For example, if you create an initial context that is a CORBA naming service, you can still do an LDAP lookup like this:

```
Object ob = context.lookup("ldap://localhost/dc=wutka,dc=com");
```

The `InitialContext` object knows how to resolve references that use other kinds of services. If you try this with a context returned by `getURLContext`, however, you'll get an error telling you that the name isn't valid for the context you are using.

Okay, now that you have a `Context` object, you can use the `lookup` method to locate an object. For example, when you locate an EJB, you usually make a call like this:

```
Object personHomeRef = context.lookup(
    "java:comp/env/ejb/Person");
```

Tip

Don't forget, if you need to cast the result from `context.lookup` to a specific `Remote` or `Home` interface type, you must use `PortableRemoteObject.narrow`.

The `java` service is available only within an EJB container, and it acts as a local directory service for other objects within the same EJB environment.

To create a new name-value association, use the `bind` method:

```
ctx.bind("rmi://localhost/MyRemoteObject", remoteObject);
```

If the object already exists in the directory, `bind` throws a `NameAlreadyBoundException`. The `rebind` method does the same thing as `bind` except that it doesn't care whether the object already exists:

```
ctx.rebind("rmi://localhost/MyRemoteObject", remoteObject);
```

`rebind` doesn't throw an exception if the object doesn't exist; that is, you can use `rebind` to create a new association as well as to overwrite an old one.

To remove an association, call `unbind`:

```
ctx.unbind("rmi://localhost/MyRemoteObject");
```

To rename an association, call `rename`:

```
ctx.rename("rmi://localhost/MyRemoteObject",
    "rmi://localhost/MyNewRemoteObject");
```

You can close the `InitialContext` by calling the `close` method:

```
ctx.close();
```

Because the context uses resources in the naming or directory service, you should close the context when you are done with it.

Note

Make sure each EJB client creates its own `InitialContext`, especially if you are using EJB security credentials. The credentials are tied to the `InitialContext`, and if you aren't careful, one client may be using another client's credentials. Normally this isn't a problem if the clients are running as separate processes. If you're writing a Web application, however, on a server that acts as multiple clients, you must be careful to keep the contexts separated.

DIRECTORY OPERATIONS

JNDI has directory-specific extensions for performing directory operations as opposed to the simple name-value operations in most naming services. The `DirContext` interface and `InitialDirContext` classes provide additional methods for dealing with directories. The directory-specific classes are all contained within the `javax.naming.directory` package.

If you need to perform directory operations, create an `InitialDirContext` instead of an `InitialContext`. For example

```
DirContext dirCtx = new InitialDirContext();
```

All the same rules apply to `InitialDirContext` as far as the property names for choosing an initial context factory.

The `Attribute` interface and the `BasicAttribute` class represent an attribute of an object stored in a directory. An attribute might have more than one value, but it only has a single name. For example, a directory entry representing a person might have an attribute called `children` that could contain any number of names. A person might also have an `age` attribute containing a single number.

Most of the methods in the `Attribute` interface are for dealing with multi-valued attributes. There are `add` methods and `remove` methods, as well as `get` and `set` methods:

```
public void add(int index, Object value)
public boolean add(Object value)
public Object remove(int index)
public boolean remove(Object value)
public Object get()
public Object get(int index)
public Object set(index, Object value)
```

The `Attributes` interface and the `BasicAttributes` class encapsulate all the attributes. It's easier to manage single-valued attributes from the `Attributes` class than it is to first get an `Attribute` and then perform the manipulation. The main methods you use are `get`, `put`, and `remove`:

```
public Attribute get(String attrName)
public Attribute put(Attribute attr)
public Attribute put(String attrName, Object attrValue)
public Attribute remove(String attrName)
```

The `Attribute` returned by `put` is the attribute being replaced by the new attribute—that is, the attribute previously stored under the same name as the new attribute. If there was no attribute with that name, `put` returns `null`. The `remove` method returns the `Attribute` that is being removed, or `null` if no such attribute exists.

The `bind` and `rebind` methods in the `DirContext` interface let you bind an object with a specific set of attributes:

```
public void bind(String name, Object ob, Attributes attrs)
public void bind(Name name, Object ob, Attributes attrs)
public void rebind(String name, Object ob, Attributes attrs)
public void rebind(Name name, Object ob, Attributes attrs)
```

The `DirContext` interface also provides several variations of a `search` method. One of the things that distinguishes a directory service from a naming service is that you can search for items based on a set of attributes and not a specific name. For instance, find all people with age greater than 18. The various search methods are

```
public NamingEnumeration search(Name name, Attributes[] matchAttributes)
public NamingEnumeration search(Name name, Attributes[] matchAttributes,
    String[] attributesToReturn)
public NamingEnumeration search(Name name, String searchFilter,
    SearchControls controls)
public NamingEnumeration search(Name name, String searchFilter,
    Object[] filterArgs, SearchControls controls)
public NamingEnumeration search(String name, Attributes[] matchAttributes)
public NamingEnumeration search(String name, Attributes[] matchAttributes,
```

```
    String[] attributesToReturn)
public NamingEnumeration search(String name, String searchFilter,
    SearchControls controls)
public NamingEnumeration search(String name, String searchFilter,
    Object[] filterArgs, SearchControls controls)
```

USING LDAP WITH JNDI

Of the directory services supported by JDK 1.3, LDAP is by far the most flexible. You can store a wide variety of items in an LDAP directory and you can get LDAP servers for a wide variety of operating systems. A good place to get a free LDAP server for Linux and Unix is `www.openldap.org`. They are also working on a version for Windows NT.

LDAP stores data in a hierarchical (tree) structure. You refer to an entry in the tree by listing the names of the nodes in the tree, starting at the one you want, working backward to the top of the tree. LDAP paths look confusing at first, but after you understand the notation, it's not so bad. Figure 18.1 shows an example LDAP tree.

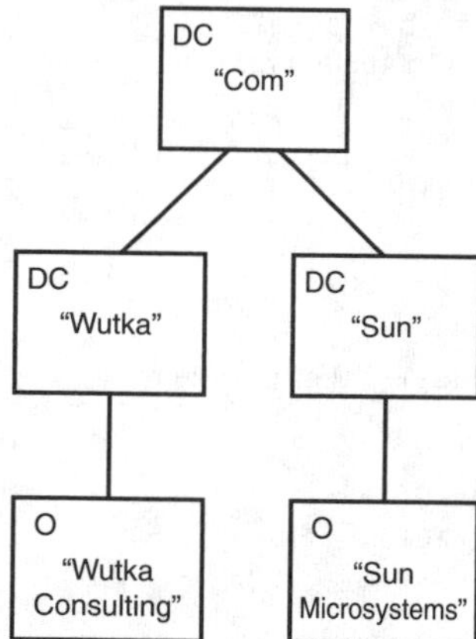

Figure 18.1
LDAP stores its entries in a tree structure.

PART III CH 18

Each node in the tree has a unique name of the form `nodetype=value`. That is, the name includes the type of the node, at least to some extent. For example, the top part of the tree in Figure 18.1 has nodes that represent the LDAP server's domain. These topmost nodes are domain components. For a domain of `wutka.com`, you have two domain components: `wutka` and `com`. Node type for a domain component is `dc`, so the topmost nodes are named `dc=wutka` and `dc=com`. Underneath the `wutka` domain component is an organization called `Wutka Consulting`. An organization has a node type of `o`, so the `Wutka Consulting` node has a name of `o=Wutka Consulting`.

Now, if you're using JNDI to access the `wutkaconsulting` node, you must list the node names starting from the one you want and working backward to the top. In other words, the name you want is `o=Wutka Consulting,dc=wutka,dc=com`.

Listing 18.1 shows a program that reads the `Wutka Consulting` object and prints out its attributes.

LISTING 18.1 SOURCE CODE FOR `ShowWC.java`

```
package usingj2ee.naming;

import javax.naming.*;
import javax.naming.directory.*;

public class ShowWC
{
    public static void main(String[] args)
    {
        try
        {
// Get the initial context
            InitialDirContext ctx = new InitialDirContext();

// Locate the Wutka Consulting object on the server running
// at ldap.wutka.com
            Attributes attrs = ctx.getAttributes(
                "ldap://ldap.wutka.com/o=Wutka Consulting, dc=wutka, dc=com");

// Get the attributes for the object
            NamingEnumeration e = attrs.getAll();

            while (e.hasMoreElements())
            {
// Get the next attribute
                Attribute attr = (Attribute) e.nextElement();

// Print out the attribute's value(s)
                System.out.print(attr.getID()+" = ");
                for (int i=0; i < attr.size(); i++)
                {
                    if (i > 0) System.out.print(", ");
                    System.out.print(attr.get(i));
                }
                System.out.println();
            }
        }
        catch (Exception exc)
        {
            exc.printStackTrace();
        }
    }
}
```

Figure 18.2 shows the output from the `ShowWC` program.

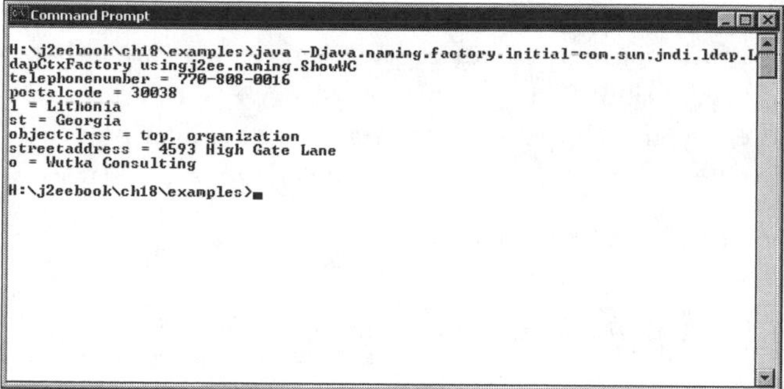

Figure 18.2
It's easy to print the attributes in an LDAP object.

Note

Due to possible network changes, you may not be able to access `ldap.wutka.com` in the future. You might need to set up your own LDAP server to run the example.

LDAP CLASSES AND ATTRIBUTES

Although LDAP entries are really just a collection of attributes, LDAP has the concept of classes. Every LDAP entry has an attribute called `objectClass` that lists the class hierarchy for an object. Not only does `objectClass` contain the object's class, it must contain the entire list of superclasses all the way back to the `top` class. Fortunately, the classes aren't nested too deeply, so the `objectClass` list is usually fairly small.

One other thing to keep in mind: The class hierarchy doesn't dictate the structure of the directory tree. A node in the directory tree can contain one of its superclasses as a child.

Table 18.1 lists some of the common LDAP classes. The complete set of classes is defined in the standard RFC2256, which you can view at `http://www.ietf.org/rfc/rfc2256.txt`.

TABLE 18.1 SOME COMMON LDAP CLASSES

Classname	Parent Class	Required Attribute(s)
`top`	None	`ObjectClass`
`country`	top	`c`
`locality`	top	none
`organization`	top	`o`
`organizationalUnit`	top	`ou`
`person`	top	`sn, cn`
`organizationalPerson`	top	none

The LDAP specification also lists some common attribute names. These attribute names tend to look confusing at first glance because many of them are only one or two characters long. You see these attributes in other places too, such as in X.509 certificates (for digital signatures and encryption). One of the reasons for the similarity is that LDAP uses many of the items defined in the X.500 series of recommendations (standards), which includes X.509.

Table 18.2 lists some of the common attributes and their meanings.

TABLE 18.2 SOME COMMON LDAP ATTRIBUTES

Attribute Name	Meaning
`objectClass`	The classname of the object and its superclasses
`dc`	A domain context—a part of a domain name
`cn`	Common name, usually the name of the object
`sn`	Surname—a person's family name (the last name in most Western cultures)
`c`	The standard two-letter country code
`l`	Locality (city, county, or other region)
`st`	State or province
`o`	Organization
`ou`	Organizational unit
`title`	A person's job title
`personalTitle`	A person's personal (not job-related) title
`description`	A description of the object
`mail`	A person's email address

One other concept you should be aware of is that a context is really a set of names. You can create a context that is a subset of names by calling `createSubcontext` in the `DirContext` object. Essentially, a subcontext is just the set of names starting at a particular node in the directory tree.

The interesting thing is, you create a new node in the tree by creating a new subcontext. Listing 18.2 shows a program that adds two entries to the LDAP directory. Notice that the program must supply a username in the form of a `SECURITY_PRINCIPAL` and a password in the form of `SECURITY_CREDENTIALS` to make changes to the LDAP directory. Most servers let you read the directory anonymously but require a username and password to make changes.

LISTING 18.2 SOURCE CODE FOR `AddPerson.java`

```
package usingj2ee.naming;

import java.util.*;
import javax.naming.*;
```

```
import javax.naming.directory.*;

public class AddPerson
{
    public static void main(String[] args)
    {
        try
        {
// Pass the security information to the directory context
// The LDAP server requires a username (SECURITY_PRINCIPAL)
// and password (SECURITY_CREDENTIALS) to add/remove
// items.
            Hashtable props = new Hashtable();
            props.put(Context.SECURITY_PRINCIPAL,
                "cn=Manager,dc=wutka,dc=com");
            props.put(Context.SECURITY_CREDENTIALS,
                "secret");

// Get the initial context
            InitialDirContext ctx = new InitialDirContext(props);

// Create a new set of attributes
            BasicAttributes attrs = new BasicAttributes();

// The item is an organizationalPerson, which is a subclass of person.
// Person is a subclass of top. Store the class hierarchy in the
// objectClass attribute
            Attribute classes = new BasicAttribute("objectclass");
            classes.add("top");
            classes.add("person");
            classes.add("organizationalPerson");

// Add the objectClass attribute to the attribute set
            attrs.put(classes);

// Store the other attributes in the attribute set
            attrs.put("sn", "Tippin");
            attrs.put("title", "Computer Expert");
            attrs.put("mail", "samantha@wutka.com");

// Add the new entry to the directory server
            ctx.createSubcontext("ldap://ldap.wutka.com/cn=Samantha Tippin,"+
                "o=Wutka Consulting,dc=wutka,dc=com", attrs);

// Create another set of attributes
            attrs = new BasicAttributes();

// Use the same objectClass attribute as before
            attrs.put(classes);

// Set the other attributes
            attrs.put("sn", "Tippin");
            attrs.put("title", "Computer Expert");
            attrs.put("mail", "kaitlynn@wutka.com");

// Add another entry to the directory server
            ctx.createSubcontext("ldap://ldap.wutka.com/cn=Kaitlynn Tippin,"+
                "o=Wutka Consulting,dc=wutka,dc=com", attrs);
```

LISTING 18.2 CONTINUED

```
        }
        catch (Exception exc)
        {
            exc.printStackTrace();
        }
    }
}
```

It's fairly easy to search through an LDAP directory using JNDI. You just call the `search` method in the `DirContext`. There are two main ways to search: by specifying either a set of attributes to match or an LDAP filter string.

Attribute matching is very straightforward, as you can see in Listing 18.3.

LISTING 18.3 SOURCE CODE FOR `NameSearch.java`

```
package usingj2ee.naming;

import javax.naming.*;
import javax.naming.directory.*;

public class NameSearch
{
    public static void main(String[] args)
    {
        try
        {
// Get the initial context
            InitialDirContext ctx = new InitialDirContext();

// Create the search attributes - look for a surname of Tippin
            BasicAttributes searchAttrs = new BasicAttributes();

            searchAttrs.put("sn", "Tippin");

// Search for items with the specified attribute starting
// at the top of the search tree
            NamingEnumeration objs = ctx.search(
                "ldap://ldap.wutka.com/o=Wutka Consulting, dc=wutka, dc=com",
                searchAttrs);

// Loop through the objects returned in the search
            while (objs.hasMoreElements())
            {
// Each item is a SearchResult object
                SearchResult match = (SearchResult) objs.nextElement();

// Print out the node name
                System.out.println("Found "+match.getName()+":");

// Get the node's attributes
                Attributes attrs = match.getAttributes();
```

```
                NamingEnumeration e = attrs.getAll();

// Loop through the attributes
                while (e.hasMoreElements())
                {
// Get the next attribute
                    Attribute attr = (Attribute) e.nextElement();

// Print out the attribute's value(s)
                    System.out.print(attr.getID()+" = ");
                    for (int i=0; i < attr.size(); i++)
                    {
                        if (i > 0) System.out.print(", ");
                        System.out.print(attr.get(i));
                    }
                    System.out.println();
                }
                System.out.println("---------------------------------------");
            }
        }
        catch (Exception exc)
        {
            exc.printStackTrace();
        }
    }
}
```


Searching by filter is a little more complicated. Any LDAP filter string must be surrounded by parentheses. To match all objects in the directory, you can use a filter string, such as `(objectClass=*)`.

You can do comparisons using =, >=, <=, and ~= (approximately), like `(age>=18)`.

The syntax for `and`, `or`, and `not` is a little strange. If you want to test `age>=18` and `sn=Smith`, the expression is `(&(age>=18)(sn=Smith))`. Use `&` for `and`, `|` for `or`, and `!` for `not`. For `and` and `or`, you can list as many expressions as you want to after the `&` or `|` characters. For `not`, you can only have a single expression.

For example, because you can only do a greater-than-or-equal-to comparison (>=), you do a greater-than by doing not-less-than-or-equal-to. For example, if age must be strictly greater than 18, use `(!(age<=18))`. If you need to combine the `and` and `or` operators, you must use parentheses to separate the expressions.

For example, you might want to search for age>=18 or (age >=13 and parentalPermission=true). The expression would be `(|(age>=18)(&(age>=13)(parentalPermission=true)))`. The two expressions being `or`ed together are `(age>=18)` and `(&(age>=13)(parentalPermission=true))`.

You can find a full definition of the LDAP search filter syntax in RFC1558 (`http://www.ietf.org/rfc/rfc1558.txt`).

Listing 18.4 shows a program that performs a simple filter search to dump out the entire contents of the directory.

LISTING 18.4 SOURCE CODE FOR AllSearch.java

```
package usingj2ee.naming;

import javax.naming.*;
import javax.naming.directory.*;

public class AllSearch
{
    public static void main(String[] args)
    {
        try
        {
// Get the initial context
            InitialDirContext ctx = new InitialDirContext();

            SearchControls searchControls = new SearchControls();
            searchControls.setSearchScope(SearchControls.SUBTREE_SCOPE);

// Search for items with the specified attribute starting
// at the top of the search tree
            NamingEnumeration objs = ctx.search(
                "ldap://ldap.wutka.com/o=Wutka Consulting, dc=wutka, dc=com",
                "(objectClass=*)", searchControls);

// Loop through the objects returned in the search
            while (objs.hasMoreElements())
            {
// Each item is a SearchResult object
                SearchResult match = (SearchResult) objs.nextElement();

// Print out the node name
                System.out.println("Found "+match.getName()+":");

// Get the node's attributes
                Attributes attrs = match.getAttributes();

                NamingEnumeration e = attrs.getAll();

// Loop through the attributes
                while (e.hasMoreElements())
                {
// Get the next attribute
                    Attribute attr = (Attribute) e.nextElement();

// Print out the attribute's value(s)
                    System.out.print(attr.getID()+" = ");
                    for (int i=0; i < attr.size(); i++)
                    {
                        if (i > 0) System.out.print(", ");
                        System.out.print(attr.get(i));
                    }
                    System.out.println();
                }
                System.out.println("---------------------------------------");
            }
        }
```

```
        catch (Exception exc)
        {
            exc.printStackTrace();
        }
    }
}
```

TROUBLESHOOTING

INITIAL CONTEXT

Why do I get an error when I create the initial context?

You might need to specify an initial context factory property. You may also need to specify a `PROVIDER_URL` or other properties. Consult the documentation for your JNDI implementation to see what properties it requires.

GENERAL ERRORS

Why can't I store my object in the naming service?

Some services only allow certain types of objects. The RMI Registry only accepts RMI object and the CORBA Naming service only accepts CORBA objects. Other services might require that your object is serializable.

CHAPTER 19

JMS—The Java Message Service

In this chapter

THE IMPORTANCE OF MESSAGING

When you think of two software components communicating, you usually think in terms of one object invoking a method on another object. You can, however, think of a method invocation as one object sending a message to another. For instance, when you call `getName` on a `Person` object, you are sending a message to the `Person` saying "Hey! Tell me who you are!" In general, system designers like to think in terms of messages between objects—method calls are just one way to implement messages.

Method invocations work well on a small scale, and they are useful even for a distributed system. As you deal with larger systems, method calls (both local and remote) start to cause problems. Many times you need to connect two components that have totally different concepts of time. One system might be an interactive GUI application that requires immediate responses, whereas the other might be a large, batch-oriented system that processes huge groups of records at scheduled times.

When your GUI application sends data to the batch system, you don't want to sit there waiting for a response—especially if it might be an hour before you get one. You want to send your data to the batch system and go about your business. You really just need to send a message to the batch system telling it to process your data when it gets a chance.

Messaging is such a popular way to connect system components that an entire industry is devoted to Message-Oriented Middleware (MOM). One of the big attractions of messaging is that the coupling between the client and the server is much looser. As Figure 19.1 shows, components that interact with method calls have a tighter coupling and are more time-sensitive.

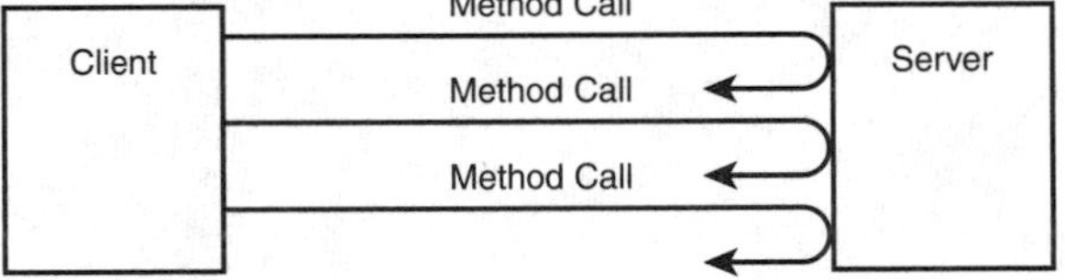

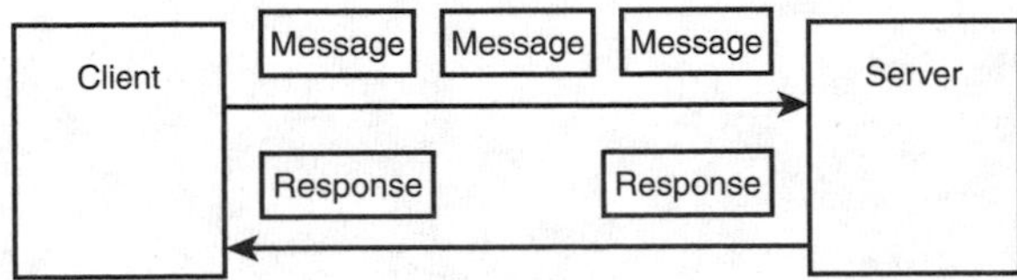

Figure 19.1
Messaging creates a loose coupling between components.

Messaging has a lot of things going for it. First, it is reasonably language- and operating system independent. A Java program on a PC can send a message to a COBOL program running on a mainframe. Although you get some of these cross-platform and cross-language benefits from CORBA, it's easier to write an interface to a messaging system than it is to make a CORBA language binding.

Don't get the impression that messages are the ideal way to do everything. Some of the advantages of messages are also disadvantages. It doesn't make sense to use messages between local Java classes when method calls satisfy your requirements. Messages are typically unidirectional; that is, they are like one-way message calls. To emulate the functionality of a method call, you must also send a reply message back to the original sender. When you start dealing with request and response messages, you encounter sequencing issues. What happens if you send `getFirstName` and `getLastName` messages to a `Person` and get `Curtis` and `Anthony` back? Is the person's name Curtis Anthony or Anthony Curtis? Unless you assign some sort of identifier to match the response to the request, you have no way of knowing. If you invoke `getFirstName` and `getLastName` as methods, however, you know which name goes with which method call.

Consider, too, that methods allow you to throw exceptions and also synchronize against simultaneous access. These are things that are possible with messaging, but require extra work.

So, when do you use messaging and when do you use method calls? Sometimes it's a tough decision. For communications between Java classes that always run inside the same program—that is, for non-network communications, method calls are almost always your best bet.

If one component does its processing on a different time scale than another (for example, one requires immediate response, whereas the other takes a long time to perform processing) then messaging is probably a better solution. A message queue reduces the time-dependency between processes because one process can put data in the queue and go on about its business. When the other process is ready, it can pull data from the queue and begin processing.

If you must send data to a legacy system (an older, established system that is still in use) see if there is messaging software available for the legacy system. IBM, for example, makes a messaging product called MQSeries that makes it easy to exchange data with a mainframe. IBM even has a Java library for sending and receiving MQSeries messages.

TYPES OF MESSAGING

There are two main ways to send messages: point-to-point and publish-subscribe. A point-to-point messaging application has a single producer (usually) and a single consumer. The producer produces messages while the consumer consumes them. Figure 19.2 illustrates a point-to-point messaging model.

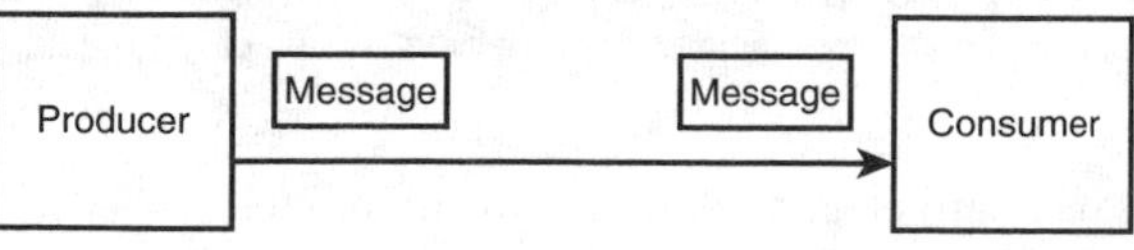

Figure 19.2
A point-to-point messaging system involves a single producer and a single consumer.

A point-to-point system can actually have multiple producers,but usually only a single consumer. Think of a print server, for instance. Any machine on the network can send a print job to a particular print server. Of course, you can have multiple print servers, but that really just means you have multiple point-to-point message queues. Figure 19.3 illustrates a typical multi-producer point-to-point queue.

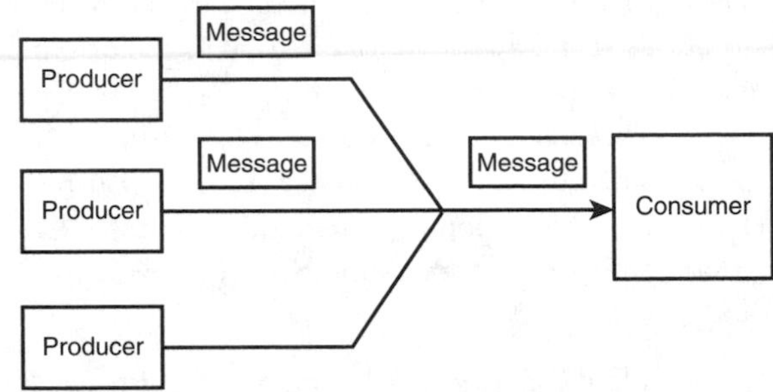

Figure 19.3
A point-to-point system can have multiple producers.

The publish-subscribe messaging model (*pub-sub*) is more of a broadcast-oriented model. Publish-subscribe is based on the idea of topics and typically has many consumers—and potentially many producers as well. An Internet mailing list is similar to a typical publish-subscribe messaging system. The topic is the subject of the mailing list. For example, you might subscribe to Sun's JSP-INTEREST mailing list. In this case, JSP-INTEREST is the topic. Everyone who subscribes to the list receives messages. Anyone who sends a message to the list is a publisher. Of course, with a mailing list, the set of potential publishers is also the set of subscribers, but in a more general publish-subscribe system, the producers usually don't subscribe to the topics they publish on. Figure 19.4 illustrates a typical publish-subscribe setup.

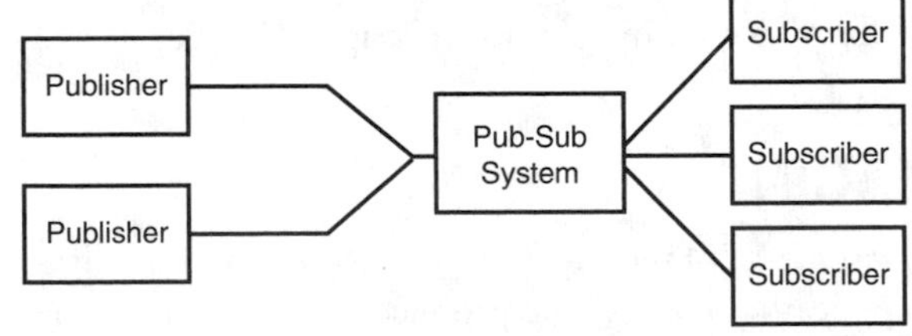

Figure 19.4
A typical publish-subscribe architecture is shown here.

Note

A point-to-point messaging system delivers only a single copy of the message to one consumer. A pub-sub messaging system delivers a copy of the message to *every* consumer.

There is something neat and elegant about a pub-sub model. It's far less coupled than even a message queue system. A component broadcasts the information, never caring about who listens to the data. You can add new components to process the data without the publisher even knowing about the components. Pub-sub is popular in applications that handle data on a real-time basis (or close to real-time, at least). For example, at an airline, you might publish flight information. At a bank, you might publish currency exchange information or stock quotes. At a sports network, you might publish updated scores. Although a producer using point-to-point messaging might never know about the consumer, there is only one consumer in a point-to-point messaging system. The advantage of pub-sub is that you can add new consumers without affecting existing consumers.

After you see how simple and powerful pub-sub can be, you might be tempted to use it for all your component-based communication. Keep in mind, however, there is a big potential drawback to using pub-sub everywhere. With most pub-sub systems, message ordering isn't guaranteed. The message ordering really comes into play when you have a system in which one pub-sub event triggers another. Figure 19.5 illustrates the message-ordering problem. Producer A sends a message that producer B receives. Producer B then publishes another message related to the one from producer A. Now consumer C happens to see the message from producer B and doesn't understand what's going on because the message from producer A hasn't arrived yet.

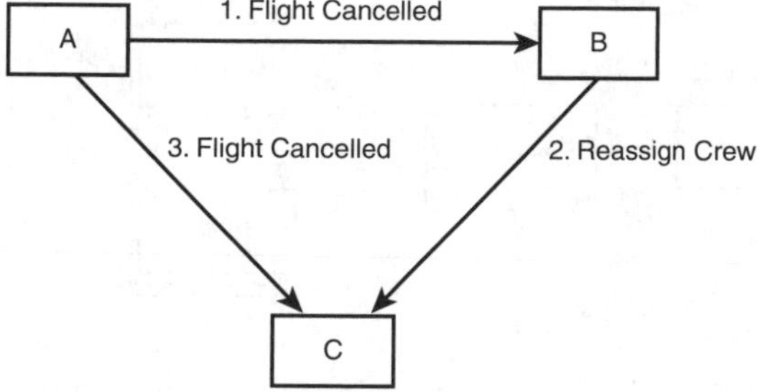

Figure 19.5 When pub-sub messages can trigger other pub-sub messages, message order can be a problem.

It might be difficult to find a messaging system that can preserve message order—it's a fairly complex task. Remember, it's one thing to preserve the order on a single topic, but an entirely different (and harder) task to preserve the order across multiple different topics. Your best bet, unfortunately, is to avoid situations in which message order matters. This limits the number of places you can apply pub-sub, but you're still left with a rich set of possibilities.

THE JAVA MESSAGE SERVICE (JMS)

An enterprise-level platform such as J2EE wouldn't be complete without a messaging API. Thanks to the Java Message Service (JMS), J2EE has good support for messaging. JMS is similar to JDBC in that it is a standard API for existing message systems, just as JDBC is a standard API for accessing databases. Like JDBC, JMS can't stand on its own two feet. It only defines the interfaces and major classes that are used to communicate with a messaging system, and does not actually implement any messaging.

Most of the top J2EE application servers support messaging, so you shouldn't have too hard a time finding an implementation of the messaging service. Sun provides a list of JMS vendors at `http://java.sun.com/products/jms/vendors.html`.

JMS supports both point-to-point messaging and publish-subscribe. You send point-to-point messages using queues and you publish messages to subscribers via topics.

Note

Although JMS supports point-to-point and pub-sub messaging, the specification doesn't require a vendor to implement both types of messaging. A particular implementation might contain only point-to-point or pub-sub.

JMS seems a little complicated when you first start using it because it you must create a lot of classes just to send a message. After you understand the structure of the classes, however, it is easy to use. The `QueueConnection` and `TopicConnection` classes manage all your interactions with the message server, but to interact with the message server, you must create either a `QueueSession` or a `TopicSession`. Figure 19.6 shows the relationship between connections, sessions, queues, and topics.

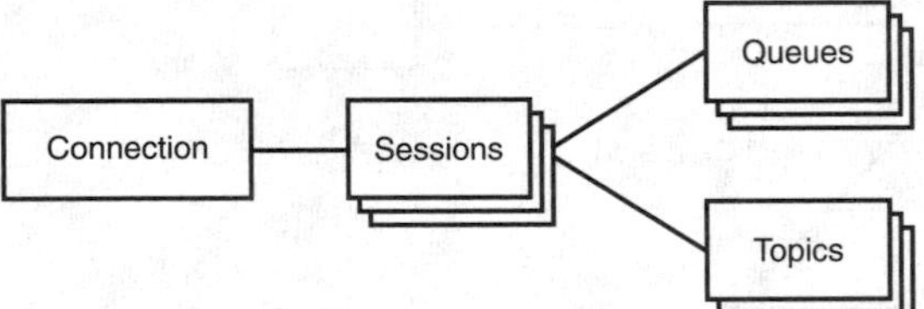

Figure 19.6
Although the connection is your link to the message server, you do your work using other objects.

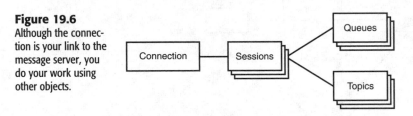

In many ways, JMS connections are like JDBC connections. They represent your connection to a server and you use them to create other objects, but you don't normally do your work by using them directly. The `QueueSession` and `TopicSession` classes are also similar to JDBC connections in that you use them to create objects, but again, you don't interact with them directly to send and receive messages.

The session objects let you create the senders, receivers, queues, and topics you need to actually send and receive messages.

One of the big benefits of JMS is that you can perform message operations as part of a transaction. When you create a `QueueSession` or a `TopicSession`, you can specify that the session is transactional. The reason transactions are so important for messaging is that you get into situations in which you read a message off a message queue and then try to insert the message in a database. If the database operation fails, you can't just stick the message back on the queue. If the operation is transactional, however, when the database operation fails, your message stays in the queue. Transactions can also ensure that the messaging system delivers the messages in the order you send them.

SENDING QUEUE MESSAGES

Before you can perform any kind of queue operations in JMS, you must first create a `QueueConnection`. You use JNDI to locate a `QueueConnectionFactory` and then create the connection. Next, you use the `QueueConnection` to create a `QueueSession`. Next, you create the `Queue` (although you usually look for the queue in the naming service first, in case someone has already created it). When you create the queue, you must give it a name. Every queue must have a unique name.

After you have a `Queue`, you're almost ready. All you need is a `QueueSender` to send messages on the queue and one or more `Message` objects. You use the `QueueSession` to create both the `QueueSender` and the messages.

Listing 19.1 shows a message queue version of the ever-popular "Hello World" program. In this case, the program sends "Hello" messages over a message queue.

LISTING 19.1 SOURCE CODE FOR `HelloQueueSender.java`

```
package usingj2ee.messages;

import javax.jms.*;
import javax.naming.*;

public class HelloQueueSender
{
    public static void main(String[] args)
    {
        try
        {
// Locate the JNDI naming service
            Context ctx = new InitialContext();

// Locate the Queue Connection Factory via JNDI
            QueueConnectionFactory factory =
                (QueueConnectionFactory) ctx.lookup(
                    "javax.jms.QueueConnectionFactory");

// Create a new Queue Connection
            QueueConnection conn = factory.createQueueConnection();

// Create a Queue Session, ask JMS to acknowledge the messages
// The session is non-transactional; you don't send messages
// as part of a transaction.
            QueueSession session = conn.createQueueSession(false,
                Session.AUTO_ACKNOWLEDGE);

            Queue queue = null;

            try
            {
// See if someone has already created the queue
                queue = (Queue) ctx.lookup("HelloQueue");
            }
            catch (NameNotFoundException exc)
            {
```

LISTING 19.1 CONTINUED

```
// If not, create a new Queue and store it in the JNDI directory
                queue = session.createQueue("HelloQueue");
                ctx.bind("HelloQueue", queue);
            }

// Create a simple text message
            TextMessage message = session.createTextMessage("Hello Client!");

// Create a QueueSender (so you can send messages)
            QueueSender sender = session.createSender(queue);

// Tell the Queue Connection you are ready to interact with the message service
            conn.start();

            for (;;)
            {
// Send a message
                sender.send(message);

// Wait 5 seconds (5,000 milliseconds) before sending another message
                try { Thread.sleep(5000); } catch (Exception ignore) {}
            }
        }
        catch (Exception exc)
        {
            exc.printStackTrace();
        }
    }
}
```

RECEIVING QUEUE MESSAGES

Most of the setup you do for sending messages is the same as for receiving them. Of course, instead of creating a `QueueSender`, you create a `QueueReceiver`. There are two different ways to receive messages. You can call the `receive` method, which waits for messages, or you can create a listener object that receives messages when they become available.

Listing 19.2 shows a simple message receiver that uses the `receive` method to retrieve the queue messages. Notice that most of the setup is the same as in Listing 19.1.

LISTING 19.2 SOURCE CODE FOR `HelloQueueReceiver.java`

```
package usingj2ee.messages;

import javax.jms.*;
import javax.naming.*;

public class HelloQueueReceiver
{
    public static void main(String[] args)
    {
        try
        {
```

```
// Locate the JNDI naming service
            Context ctx = new InitialContext();

// Locate the Queue Connection Factory via JNDI
            QueueConnectionFactory factory =
                (QueueConnectionFactory) ctx.lookup(
                    "javax.jms.QueueConnectionFactory");

// Create a new Queue Connection
            QueueConnection conn = factory.createQueueConnection();

// Create a Queue Session, ask JMS to acknowledge the messages
// This program receives messages, so it doesn't really care.
// The session is non-transactional

            QueueSession session = conn.createQueueSession(false,
                Session.AUTO_ACKNOWLEDGE);

            Queue queue = null;
            try
            {
// See if someone has already created the queue
                queue = (Queue) ctx.lookup("HelloQueue");
            }
            catch (NameNotFoundException exc)
            {
// If not, create a new Queue and store it in the JNDI directory
                queue = session.createQueue("HelloQueue");
                ctx.bind("HelloQueue", queue);
            }

// Create a QueueReceiver to receive messages
            QueueReceiver receiver = session.createReceiver(queue);

// Tell the Queue Connection you are ready to interact with the message service
            conn.start();

            for (;;)
            {
// Receive the next message
                TextMessage message = (TextMessage) receiver.receive();

// Print the message contents
                System.out.println(message.getText());
            }
        }
        catch (Exception exc)
        {
            exc.printStackTrace();
        }
    }
}
```

PART III CH 19

If you don't want to wait for messages, but instead prefer to have the `QueueReceiver` notify you when a message comes in, you can implement the `MessageListener` interface. You tell the `QueueReceiver` about your message listener and it will automatically let you know when a message comes in. Listing 19.3 shows the listener version of the message receiver in Listing 19.2.

LISTING 19.3 SOURCE CODE FOR `HelloQueueListener.java`

```
package usingj2ee.messages;

import javax.jms.*;
import javax.naming.*;

public class HelloQueueListener implements MessageListener
{
    HelloQueueListener()
    {
    }

/** Called by the QueueReceiver to handle the next message in the queue */
    public void onMessage(Message message)
    {
        try
        {
// Assume the message is a text message
            TextMessage textMsg = (TextMessage) message;

// Print the message text
            System.out.println(textMsg.getText());
        }
        catch (JMSException exc)
        {
            exc.printStackTrace();
        }
    }

    public static void main(String[] args)
    {
        try
        {
// Locate the JNDI naming service
            Context ctx = new InitialContext();

// Locate the Queue Connection Factory via JNDI
            QueueConnectionFactory factory =
                (QueueConnectionFactory) ctx.lookup(
                    "javax.jms.QueueConnectionFactory");

// Create a new Queue Connection
            QueueConnection conn = factory.createQueueConnection();

// Create a non-transactional Queue Session
            QueueSession session = conn.createQueueSession(false,
                Session.AUTO_ACKNOWLEDGE);

            Queue queue = null;
            try
            {
// See if someone has already created the queue
                queue = (Queue) ctx.lookup("HelloQueue");
```

```
            }
            catch (NameNotFoundException exc)
            {
// If not, create a new Queue and store it in the JNDI directory
                queue = session.createQueue("HelloQueue");
                ctx.bind("HelloQueue", queue);
            }

// Create a QueueReceiver to receive messages
            QueueReceiver receiver = session.createReceiver(queue);

// Tell the Queue Connection you are ready to interact with the message service
            conn.start();


// Tell the receiver to call your listener object when a new message arrives
            receiver.setMessageListener(new HelloQueueListener());

// Normally you would do other processing here...
            Thread.sleep(999999999);
        }
        catch (Exception exc)
        {
            exc.printStackTrace();
        }
    }
}
```

You typically have one queue receiver and one or more queue senders. Although JMS allows you to have multiple receivers on a queue, it is up to the individual implementations to decide how to handle multiple receivers. Some might distribute the messages evenly across all receivers, and others might just send all the messages to the first receiver you create.

Note Because sessions are single-threaded, you can only process one message at a time. If you need to process multiple messages concurrently, you must create multiple sessions.

PUBLISHING MESSAGES

Although the overall concept of publish-subscribe is a bit different from point-to-point messages, the JMS calls for creating a topic and publishing messages are remarkably similar to the calls for sending queue messages. In fact, if you go through the program in Listing 19.1 earlier in this chapter and change all the occurrences of `Queue` to `Topic`, you'll *almost* have a working topic publisher. You must also change the `createSender` call to `createPublisher`.

As with queues, each topic must have a unique name. Unlike queues, in which you only have one receiver, you normally have many subscribers to a topic. You can also have multiple publishers.

Listing 19.4 shows the publish-subscribe version of the ubiquitous "Hello World," at least the publishing half.

LISTING 19.4 SOURCE CODE FOR HelloTopicPublisher.java

```
package usingj2ee.messages;

import javax.jms.*;
import javax.naming.*;

public class HelloTopicPublisher
{
    public static void main(String[] args)
    {
        try
        {
// Locate the JNDI naming service
            Context ctx = new InitialContext();

// Locate the Topic Connection Factory via JNDI
            TopicConnectionFactory factory =
                (TopicConnectionFactory) ctx.lookup(
                    "javax.jms.TopicConnectionFactory");

// Create a new Topic Connection
            TopicConnection conn = factory.createTopicConnection();

// Create a non-transactional TopicSession
            TopicSession session = conn.createTopicSession(false,
                Session.AUTO_ACKNOWLEDGE);

            Topic topic = null;

            try
            {
// See if someone has already created the topic
                topic = (Topic) ctx.lookup("HelloTopic");
            }
            catch (NameNotFoundException exc)
            {
// If not, create a new topic and store it in the JNDI directory
                topic = session.createTopic("HelloTopic");
                ctx.bind("HelloTopic", topic);
            }

// Create a new text message
            TextMessage message = session.createTextMessage("Hello Client!");

// Create a publisher to publish messages
            TopicPublisher sender = session.createPublisher(topic);

// Tell the Topic Connection you are ready to interact with the message service
            conn.start();

            for (;;)
            {
// Publish the message
                sender.publish(message);

// Wait 5 seconds before sending another message
                try { Thread.sleep(5000); } catch (Exception ignore) {}
```

```
            }
        }
        catch (Exception exc)
        {
            exc.printStackTrace();
        }
    }
}
```

You can run multiple copies of this program with no problems. Your clients will just see more messages than they do if only one copy is running.

SUBSCRIBING TO TOPICS

Subscribing to a topic is just as easy as listening on a queue. Again, you can just about convert the program in Listing 19.2 earlier in the chapter to work with topics just by changing all the occurrences of `Queue` to `Topic`. Listing 19.5 shows the subscriber for the "Hello World" pub-sub example.

LISTING 19.5 SOURCE CODE FOR `HelloTopicReceiver.java`

```
package usingj2ee.messages;

import javax.jms.*;
import javax.naming.*;

public class HelloTopicReceiver
{
    public static void main(String[] args)
    {
        try
        {
// Locate the JNDI naming service
            Context ctx = new InitialContext();

// Locate the Topic Connection Factory via JNDI
            TopicConnectionFactory factory =
                (TopicConnectionFactory) ctx.lookup(
                    "javax.jms.TopicConnectionFactory");

// Create a new Topic Connection
            TopicConnection conn = factory.createTopicConnection();

// Create a non-transactional Topic Session
            TopicSession session = conn.createTopicSession(false,
                Session.AUTO_ACKNOWLEDGE);

            Topic topic = null;
            try
            {
// See if someone has already created the topic
                topic = (Topic) ctx.lookup("HelloTopic");
            }
            catch (NameNotFoundException exc)
            {
```

LISTING 19.5 CONTINUED

```
// If not, create a new topic and store it in the JNDI directory
                topic = session.createTopic("HelloTopic");
                ctx.bind("HelloTopic", topic);
            }

// Create a subscriber to receive messages
            TopicSubscriber subscriber = session.createSubscriber(topic);

// Tell the Topic Connection you are ready to interact with the message service
            conn.start();

            for (;;)
            {
// Get the next published message
                TextMessage message = (TextMessage) subscriber.receive();

// Print the message text
                System.out.println(message.getText());
            }
        }
        catch (Exception exc)
        {
            exc.printStackTrace();
        }
    }
}
```

As with the `QueueReceiver` class, you can choose to receive message notifications asynchronously by using the `MessageListener` interface. The actual listener implementation for topics is identical to the one for queues.

DURABLE SUBSCRIPTIONS

Most pub-sub systems you see today deal with frequently published data and tend to provide real-time monitoring and status updates. Pub-sub is good for these kinds of operations. Many pub-sub implementations have a peculiar limitation that makes them *only* suitable for applications with frequently published data—more specifically, applications in which it doesn't matter if you miss a message because there will be another one in a few minutes.

The reason pub-sub usually only works in these types of applications is that pub-sub doesn't usually have the concept of a persistent, or durable subscription. For example, suppose you are publishing flight cancellations for LaGuardia Airport. Although it's true that they do seem to occur often enough that there will be another one in a few minutes, you really don't want to miss one. Now, suppose you have a program that makes a list of passengers who need to be rebooked for the next available flight (tomorrow, next week, sometime next year, and so on). If the program shuts down for a few minutes, it might miss three or four cancellations! You want the message server to hold on to your messages while your program is down.

JMS supports durable subscription. After you create a durable subscription, the JMS server keeps any messages you miss while your program isn't running. To create a durable subscription, use the `createDurableSubscriber` method in the `TopicSession` class:

```
public TopicSubscriber createDurableSubscriber(Topic topic,
    String subscriptionName)
```

You must always use the same subscription name when reconnecting your program to its durable subscription. That is, if you call the subscription `RebookFlightCx` (that's the subscription name, not the topic name), you must always ask for `RebookFlightCx` when resuming that subscription. Keep in mind that durable connections are expensive for the server to maintain, so only use them when absolutely necessary.

Messages can have an expiration time, so when a message expires, the server can safely remove it from the durable subscription. This helps keep the database size down when you don't resume a durable subscription for a long time.

More About Messages

So far, you've seen a lot about queues and topics, but not much about messages. Messages are the most important part of JMS, and there are many different types of messages and many interesting features common to all messages.

A JMS message has three parts, as shown in Figure 19.7.

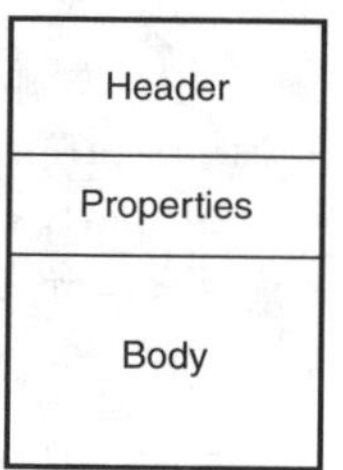

Figure 19.7
A JMS message has a header, properties, and a body.

The message header is a set of values that is present on every message. The properties are similar to header values in that they are separate from the actual message content and can appear on any type of message. You can think of the properties as header values that you define yourself. The message body can be any number of different types. JMS defines five different types of message.

Message Headers

The message headers are a set of common values assigned to every message. They include the message priority, message type, and several other items. You can't add your own header types, but the properties section of the message functions like custom headers. Table 19.1 lists the standard JMS message header values.

TABLE 19.1 JMS MESSAGE HEADER VALUES

Header Value	Description
`JMSCorrelationID`	A string or byte-array value relating one message to another.
`JMSDeliveryMode`	The message delivery mode (persistent or non-persistent).
`JMSDestination`	Where the message was sent (this will be a topic or a queue).
`JMSExpiration`	The time when this message expires.
`JMSMessageID`	A unique message ID assigned by the message server.
`JMSPriority`	The message priority (0–9) in which 9 is the highest (most important). 0–4 is normal, and 5–9 is high priority.
`JMSRedelivered`	If true, this message might have been delivered before but the receiver didn't acknowledge it.
`JMSReplyTo`	A destination where a reply can be sent.
`JMSTimestamp`	The time the message was first sent to the message server.
`JMSType`	A provider-specific message type.

The `Message` class has `get/set` methods for examining and modifying the header attributes. The message server sets the value of some of these attributes when you send the message. For example, it stores the destination in the message automatically. You don't need to set the value yourself.

MESSAGE PROPERTIES

Message properties are essentially custom header fields. You store properties in a message with an associated name and retrieve them using the name. A property can be one of the following types: `boolean`, `byte`, `double`, `float`, `int`, `long`, `Object`, `short`, or `String`. The `MessageClass` has `get/set` methods for setting properties of each type. For example, to set a `long` property, call `setLongProperty`:

```
myMessage.setLongProperty("TimeNoSee", 1234);
```

To retrieve the value, call `getLongProperty`:

```
long timeNoSee = myMessage.getLongProperty("TimeNoSee");
```

Caution

Don't use any property names starting with JMS. That prefix is reserved for the JMS API.

MESSAGE TYPES

There are five different types of JMS messages:

- `BytesMessage`
- `MapMessage`
- `ObjectMessage`

- StreamMessage
- TextMessage

The BytesMessage and StreamMessage message types work much like Java IO streams in that you can read and write different data values. For instance, both messages have writeInt, writeDouble, readBytes, and readUTF just like the DataInputStream and DataOutputStream classes. The difference between BytesMessage and StreamMessage is that StreamMessage also writes out data types, so it can determine whether you try to read the wrong kind of value. It can also perform any necessary type conversions. The BytesMessage class just reads and writes raw bytes. It is most useful for matching existing message formats.

The ObjectMessage class lets you store a single serializable Java object in a message using setObject. You can retrieve the object with getObject.

The MapMessage class lets you create a group of name-value pairs for a message. You can store the same data types as you can in the message properties, plus you can store an array of bytes. To store a long value, call setLong:

```
myMsg.setLong("TimeNoSee", 1234);
```

To retrieve a long value, call getLong:

```
long timeNoSee = myMsg.getLong("TimeNoSee");
```

The other data types follow a similar pattern (getShort, setShort, getString, setString, and so on).

Finally, the TextMessage class lets you store a single string in a message using setText and retrieve the string with getText.

MESSAGE SELECTORS

Many message servers let you filter messages at the server, saving the receivers and subscribers a lot of trouble. If you publish a data item that only 1 in 100 subscribers is interested in, should all 100 have to see the message? If you use message selectors, they don't have to. A message selector lets you define a string similar to a database query that filters a message based on header and property values.

The format of the query is basically the same as an SQL WHERE clause. For example, to filter all messages where the StockSymbol property equals SUNW, use the filter StockSymbol='SUNW'.

The filters come into play when you first create your QueueReceiver or TopicSubscriber. You can supply an additional parameter to the createReceiver and createSubscriber methods specifying a message selector (filter).

For example, commercial aircraft use a system called *ACARS* (*Aircraft Communication and Reporting System*) to transmit position data and other information to sites on the ground. A typical ACARS feed sends data for all aircraft, not just for a specific airline. You might set up a program to listen for ACARS messages and then publish them, setting various message properties to help identify the message. For example, you would likely include the airline and the flight number in the header file.

A program monitoring all United flights might set up a subscriber like this:

```
TopicSubscriber sub = topicSession.createSubscriber(
    "ACARS", "Airline='UA'");
```

A program tracking a specific Delta flight might create a subscriber this way:

```
TopicSubscriber sub = topicSession.createSubscriber(
    "ACARS", "Airline='DL' AND FlightNumber=1579");
```

MESSAGE-DRIVEN BEANS

Version 2.0 of the EJB specification introduced a new kind of EJB: the message-driven bean. Unlike entity or session beans, message-driven beans don't have a public interface. The only way you can communicate with message-driven beans is via messages.

Message-driven beans are much easier to write than either session beans or entity beans. You must still write `ejbCreate` and `ejbRemove` to initialize the bean and clean up when you're done. You must also implement `ejbActivate` and `ejbPassivate` just because they're required by the EJB specification, but they are not a part of the message-driven bean lifecycle. Because message-driven beans have no public interface, they have no `Home` or `Remote` interfaces.

You must implement the `setMessageDrivenContext` method so the container can give you your entity bean context and, finally, you must implement the `onMessage` method from the `MessageListener` interface to receive messages.

One of the advantages of message-driven beans as compared to non-EJB message listeners is that the EJB container might create multiple beans to handle incoming messages. The EJB container dispatches queue messages to as many message-driven beans as it sees fit (the EJB container might only use a single bean if it desires).

One of the disadvantages of message-driven beans is that they can only listen to a single queue or topic. A single message-driven bean can't listen to messages from two different queues.

When you create a `QueueSession`, you must specify an acknowledgement mode. The three possible modes are `Session.AUTO_ACKNOWLEDGE`, `Session.CLIENT_ACKNOWLEDGE`, and `Session.DUPS_OK_ACKNOWLEDGE`. The `AUTO_ACKNOWLEDGE` mode causes the session to acknowledge messages automatically. The `CLIENT_ACKNOWLEDGE` mode requires the consumer to acknowledge each message manually by calling the message's `acknowledge` method. The `DUPS_OK_ACKNOWLEDGE` mode causes the session to acknowledge the messages lazily—that is, it acknowledges the messages when it sees it. In `DUPS_OK_ACKNOWLEDGE` mode, it's possible for a consumer to receive a message twice if the message service has a problem. Although the mode can allow messages to flow through the system faster, you should only use it if you can tolerate the presence of duplicate messages.

Listing 19.7 shows a simple message-driven bean that echoes messages back to the sender. It uses the JMSReplyTo property to figure out where to send the reply. Also, notice that it creates a QueueSender with a null Queue. This creates an anonymous producer that can send to any queue.

LISTING 19.7 SOURCE CODE FOR EchoMessageBean.java

```
package usingj2ee.messages;

import javax.ejb.*;
import javax.jms.*;
import javax.naming.*;

public class EchoMessageBean implements MessageDrivenBean
{
    private MessageDrivenContext mdContext;

// The following Queue objects are only needed because this bean
// sends a reply message back to the sender. For a message-driven bean,
// the EJB container handles the Queue and Topic objects for the incoming
// messages.

    protected QueueConnection qConn;
    protected QueueSession qSession;
    protected QueueSender qSender;

    public EchoMessageBean()
    {
    }

    public void ejbCreate()
        throws CreateException
    {
        try
        {
// Locate the JNDI naming instance
            InitialContext context = new InitialContext();

// Locate the Queue Connection Factory
            QueueConnectionFactory qcFact = (QueueConnectionFactory)
                context.lookup("javax.jms.QueueConnectionFactory");

// Create a Queue Connection
            qConn = qcFact.createQueueConnection();

// Create a non-transactional Queue Sender
            qSession = qConn.createQueueSession(false,
                Session.AUTO_ACKNOWLEDGE);

// Create an unidentified producer (a producer that isn't associated
// with a particular queue)
            qSender = qSession.createSender(null);
        }
        catch (Exception exc)
        {
            exc.printStackTrace();
```

LISTING 19.7 CONTINUED

```
                throw new CreateException(
                    "Error initializing EchoMessageBean: "+
                        exc.toString());
            }
        }

        public void setMessageDrivenContext(MessageDrivenContext ctx)
        {
            mdContext = ctx;
        }

        public void ejbActivate()
        {
        }

        public void ejbPassivate()
        {
        }

        public void ejbRemove()
        {
            try
            {
// Close the Queue connection
                qConn.close();
            }
            catch (Exception exc)
            {
                exc.printStackTrace();
            }
        }

        public void onMessage(Message message)
        {
            try
            {
// Set a property that lets the client know for sure that the
// message bean saw the message
                message.setStringProperty("MessageBeanACK",
                    "The message bean saw this message");

// Figure out where to send the reply
                Destination replyTo = message.getJMSReplyTo();

                if ((replyTo != null) && (replyTo instanceof Queue))
                {
// Send the reply
                    qSender.send((Queue) replyTo, message);
                }
            }
            catch (Exception exc)
            {
                exc.printStackTrace();
            }
        }
}
```

TROUBLESHOOTING

GENERAL ERRORS

Why do I get an error when I create the `InitialContext`?

You might need to tell JNDI the name of the `InitalContextFactory` class by setting the `java.naming.factory.initial` property. There might be other reasons for this error. You should consult the documentation for your EJB server to find other possible causes. For example, the Inprise Application Server might require you to run the OSAgent naming service, although WebLogic required you to supply the provider URL.

Why do I get an error when I try to bind my `Queue` or `Topic`?

In the examples in this chapter, there is a slight chance that if the producer and consumer start at the same time, they might both try to create the queue or topic. One will bind successfully, whereas the other will get an error. You might want to add code to try locating the queue or topic again if the bind fails.

MESSAGE-DRIVEN BEANS

Why doesn't my EJB server support message-driven beans?

EJB 2.0 is still a fairly new specification. It might take some time for all the EJB servers to support the new specification.

CHAPTER 20

Connecting to Existing Systems

In this chapter

TYPES OF EXTERNAL SYSTEM CONNECTIONS

Unless you're at a brand new startup company, you'll probably need to integrate your application with existing systems. If you need to interface with a CORBA-based system or with a Java application, you should already have a pretty good idea how to proceed. Many times, however, the situation is a little cloudier. You might need to interface with a mainframe application or some other kind of system that might not be very talkative when it comes to inter-application communication.

Note

Older systems and applications are usually referred to as "legacy" systems. Many times, a company is willing to spend extra money to develop code to access the legacy system without adding code to the legacy system. The idea is that if the legacy system works now, don't mess with it. You're more likely to break it. This is especially true when it's hard to find people to maintain the legacy system.

Although you might have a variety of ways to connect to an existing system, the four most common (ignoring CORBA and RMI) are

- A socket connection using either a custom protocol or a terminal-emulation protocol
- A message queue service, such as MQSeries
- A custom access library
- The J2EE Connector interface, although this is so new, it won't be "common" for quite a while

SOCKET CONNECTIONS TO EXISTING SYSTEMS

Although mainframes are notoriously unfriendly toward Unix and Windows applications, they have become a little more accessible in the last few years. Most mainframe operating systems support socket connections (TCP/IP network connections). One of the problems you still face, however, is that most mainframe applications aren't very cooperative.

If you're lucky, someone else has already faced the connectivity problem and written a communication library for you. The rest of the time, however, you must develop a communication protocol yourself. If you're new to socket programming, you can find out more about it in Chapter 27, "Network Programming." Basically, you'll need to write some sort of server on the existing system. As you'll see in Chapter 27, you can create a simple protocol for passing messages back and forth. From there, you can determine what kind of information you need to send back and forth.

If you don't have the luxury of being able to write code for the mainframe, you have another option, although not a pretty one. You can write a program that emulates a mainframe terminal. The idea, of course, is that your program logs on to the mainframe application just like any other user. It sends whatever input codes are necessary to behave just like a terminal. The program then reads through the response from the mainframe, pulling out the data it's looking for. This technique is called *screen scraping*.

Screen scraping is the least-intrusive way to get data from the mainframe. The mainframe application can't tell the difference between a regular terminal and a screen-scraping program. Unfortunately, this technique is also tedious, slow, and error-prone. If you make changes to the mainframe, you might break the existing screen-scraping programs. Believe it or not, you'll still find screen-scraping programs in banks and airlines, as well as other industries. They aren't pretty, but they get the job done.

If you create a socket-based interface into an existing system, you should encapsulate it with a Java class. In other words, create a single point of access for your code to talk to the mainframe. That way, if you change the way you access the mainframe, you only change a single Java class instead of many.

You can use sockets in an EJB—you can at least connect to other systems, although you can't listen for incoming connections. Unfortunately, your socket interface can't participate in a transaction. If you save some data to the database and then to the mainframe, but you then decide to roll the transaction back, you can't undo the changes you make to the mainframe. Although this might be sufficient for some applications, it can become a headache if you must keep the database tightly coordinated with mainframe operations.

SENDING MESSAGES TO EXISTING SYSTEMS

Messaging systems can help you solve some of the woes you experience when you use s ockets. For example, using JMS to send messages, you can send a message as part of a transaction. If you roll the transaction back, you don't send the message.

Many mainframe systems support various types of messaging systems. One of the most popular messaging systems is one called MQSeries, available on IBM systems. IBM even makes a JMS interface for MQSeries so you can use it from an EJB.

Although your message might be part of a transaction, you might still have some problem completing a transaction. For example, suppose you create an application to book a seat on an airline. You create a session bean that stores the reservation using some entity beans and also sends a message to the reservations mainframe. When you commit the transaction, you save your data and send your message. Unfortunately, the mainframe can decide that the flight is full. At this point, however, your transaction has already completed and you have already informed the customer that the seat has been booked. Messages are good for queuing information, but not necessarily for completing transactions. In other words, you might want to send a message indicating that the flight has been booked—just an informational message for any application that needs to know—but you don't necessarily want the message to be part of the actual booking process.

Using Custom Access Libraries

Custom access libraries can be a good alternative to a socket-based or message-based solution. Basically, you don't need to write any custom code on the mainframe (or you write only a small bit) and you use a special access library to send your requests. IBM, for example, makes a CICS gateway that lets you invoke transactions on a CICS system.

Because many of these libraries use native libraries, you can't use them from an EJB. You can, however, create an RMI or CORBA server that your EJBs can talk to. The server then uses the native library to talk to the mainframe.

As with socket-based solutions, custom libraries can't participate in EJB transactions, so you might have trouble synchronizing your data.

Using the J2EE Connector API

The J2EE Connector API is a framework for connecting to other systems. The connector architecture doesn't actually deal with connectivity, however. It is more concerned with resource and transaction management. Although the Java Messaging API gives you some support for transactions when dealing with existing systems, you can't make the entire operation part of the transaction—only the act of sending the message is part of the transaction. The Connector API lets you perform an operation on an existing system as part of a transaction.

The Connector API is similar to JDBC, both in its design and its various parts. Like JDBC, the API itself is an abstract framework with no concrete implementation. To connect to a specific machine or application, you need a custom Connector implementation. You can expect some of the more popular mainframe applications and operating systems to have Connectors over the next year or so.

The most important part of the Connector API, from an EJB development standpoint, is the Common Client Interface (CCI). The CCI gives you a standard way to create a connection and send and receive data—just like JDBC gives you a standard way to make a connection, create statements, and retrieve results.

The Major Components of CCI

Although CCI and JDBC are different APIs, they share a similar structure. Many of the major classes in CCI have similar counterparts in JDBC, although the names are slightly different.

Figure 20.1 shows the major parts of CCI and their relationships with each other.

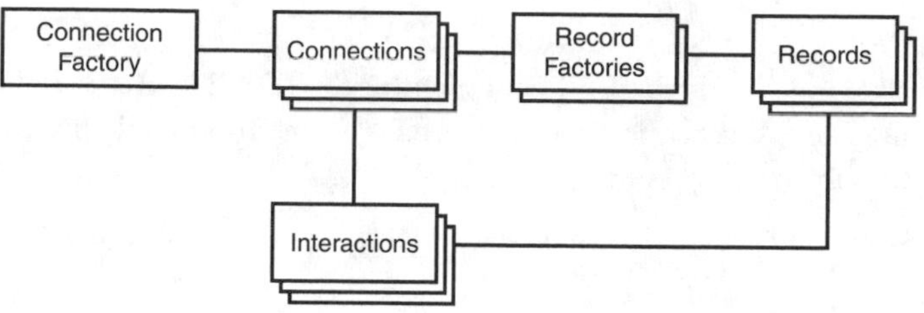

Figure 20.1
The CCI object model is similar in structure to JDBC.

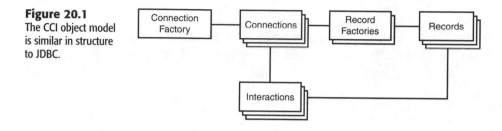

`ConnectionFactory`

The `ConnectionFactory` class is the CCI equivalent of the JDBC `Driver` class or the `DataSource` class. You use it to create `Connections` for accessing other systems. Typically, you access a `ConnectionFactory` using JNDI, just like you do with a `DataSource`. As usual, each EJB vendor might have different ways of configuring connectors.

To create a CCI connection, after you have located a connection factory, call the `getConnection` method. You can either call `getConnection` with no parameters, or you can pass a `ConnectionSpec` object containing various connector-specific parameters.

You can also use the connection factory to access the `RecordFactory` for a particular system. You use the record factory to create new `Record` objects, which you use when making requests.

Like JDBC, CCI provides you with a logging object for writing connector-related information. `ConnectionFactory` has a `getLogWriter` method that returns the `PrintWriter` used for logging messages. You can call `setLogWriter` to change the destination of the log messages. Most of the time, you'll probably use `setLogWriter` more often than `getLogWriter`, because you're usually more interested in specifying where the connector's log message goes than adding your own messages to the log.

`Connection`

The `Connection` object represents a single connection to an external system, much like a JDBC connection represents a single connection to a database. Most of the time, you just use the connection to create `Interaction` objects for executing requests. The `createInteraction` method takes no parameters and returns a new `Interaction` object that is tied to the connection.

One of the aspects that the `Connection` object shares with its JDBC counterpart is the notion of auto-commit for transactions. You can tell the connection to decide when to commit a transaction, or you can control the transaction directly. As with JDBC, the methods to control auto-commit are `setAutoCommit` and `getAutoCommit`. One big difference between CCI and JDBC auto-commit is that in CCI, auto-commit defaults to *off*, whereas in JDBC, it defaults to *on*.

Unlike JDBC, the CCI `Connection` class doesn't contain methods to begin, commit, and rollback a transaction. Instead, you call `getLocalTransaction` to get a `LocalTransaction` interface. The `LocalTransaction` interface contains the `begin`, `commit`, and `rollback` methods. If you have auto-commit turned on, you can't access the local transaction.

Interaction

The `Interaction` class is the CCI equivalent of the JDBC `Statement` object. You use an interaction to invoke a request on an external system. You mainly use the `execute` method, which comes in two flavors:

```
public boolean execute(InteractionSpec spec,
    Record input, Record output)
public Record execute(InteractionSpec spec,
    Record input)
```

The `InteractionSpec` object contains information for invoking the remote request. Most importantly, it contains a string called `FunctionName`, which is the name of the remote function you want to call. You use the input and output `Record` objects to pass data to the remote function and receive data back.

Record

A `Record` represents data that you want to send to another system or data returned by another system. Although databases can have a reasonably common format for exchanging data, applications and operating systems as a whole don't have a common data exchange model. The `Record` interface attempts to encapsulate many different types of data formats.

The Connector API specification defines three basic `Record` types: `MappedRecord`, `IndexedRecord`, and `ResultSet`. A `MappedRecord` implements the `java.util.Map` interface and represents a set of name-value pairs, similar to a `HashMap` or a `Properties` object. The `IndexedRecord` interface represents a container of objects. Both the `MappedRecord` and `IndexedRecord` objects can contain other `Record` objects.

The `ResultSet` interface is an extension of the JDBC `ResultSet` interface. One of the interesting aspects of the Connector API is that you can use it to access existing database systems.

You can also create a Java Bean that represents data for an external system.

The Connector API is still fairly new and it might be some time before you begin to see many connectors available. They certainly hold a lot of promise, however, because you might soon be able to define transactions across several systems.

CASE STUDY

Airlines have traditionally been the poster children for external system connections. Many of the larger airlines use a fairly old operating system called TPF (Transaction Processing Facility) for their reservations systems. Although TPF is fast, it hasn't been very friendly to other operating systems until fairly recently. Airlines have had to resort to custom solutions when connecting to their existing TPF systems.

One airline developed a screen-scraping application that used a combination of TCP sockets, X.25, and a custom network to communicate with TPF. Over its lifetime, the application suffered occasional outages when the mainframe developers changed the format of the various screens. The advantage, however, is that the application developers didn't require any special code on the mainframe, so they were able to develop their applications quickly (TPF development tends to take longer than with other operating systems).

Later, this same airline came up with a more efficient solution. By adding a small bit of code to the TPF mainframe, they were able to communicate directly with TPF applications, bypassing the need for screen scraping. Consequently, applications accessing mainframe data were able to run much faster and didn't suffer outages when the screen formats changed.

CHAPTER 21

PACKAGING AND INSTALLING A J2EE APPLICATION

In this chapter

USING AN AUTOMATED EJB PACKAGING TOOL

In the previous chapters, you have seen examples of graphical deployment tools for deploying an Enterprise Java Bean (EJB). These graphical tools are extremely useful, especially when you are new to EJB. There is no standard as to what these tools should support, but most of them enable you to specify the classes to include, set special deployment options, and even run a verifier to make sure your bean complies with the EJB specification.

The typical packaging sequence for an automated tool is that you specify the name of a JAR file that will contain the EJB(s) you are packaging; you should be able to add to an existing JAR file if you need to.

Next, you select the classes that make up the EJB, although you might first need to tell the tool that you want to define an EJB. After you select the classes, you specify which classes implement the Home and Remote interfaces and which class contains the bean implementation. Some tools can guess whether a bean is a session bean or an entity bean, and others require you to specify.

If you use container-managed persistence (CMP), you might need to specify how the bean is mapped to the database. You might also need to run an additional program to complete the mapping because CMP is vendor-specific.

You also can specify what other resources your bean uses, whether they are additional EJBs or database connections. You specify the transaction type for your session bean methods and also set up any necessary security restrictions.

Finally, you usually have the option to deploy the bean into the server, which might result in the generation of a client JAR file—a file that client programs might use to connect to your newly deployed EJB. Not all servers generate a client JAR and the JAR files are rarely (if ever) compatible between different EJB vendors.

HOW ENTERPRISE JAVABEANS ARE PACKAGED

One of the disadvantages of a graphical deployment tool is that it is often cumbersome when you just need to make a quick change. Some companies also make a policy of doing a software build every night, and those builds must be automated. It is much easier to automate EJB builds and deployments when you don't need to go through a graphical tool.

You can build an EJB JAR file manually, just by creating one or two XML deployment descriptors that describe the bean or beans you want to deploy. According to the EJB specification, the only deployment descriptor you are required to provide is a standard one called `ejb-jar.xml`. Some EJB vendors such as WebLogic, however, require an additional file that fills in some of the gaps that the EJB specification doesn't cover. For instance, the WebLogic-specific XML file contains the JNDI name of the bean's Home interface.

A Deployment Descriptor for a Session Bean

The best way to get a feel for the format of the deployment descriptor file is to examine a simple one. Listing 21.1 shows the deployment descriptor for the HelloWorldSession bean from Chapter 6, "Creating a Session Bean."

Listing 21.1 Deployment Descriptor for the HelloWorldSession Bean

```
<?xml version="1.0"?>

<!DOCTYPE ejb-jar PUBLIC '-//Sun Microsystems, Inc.//DTD Enterprise
JavaBeans 1.1//EN' 'http://java.sun.com/j2ee/dtds/ejb-
jar_1_1.dtd'>

<ejb-jar>
    <display-name>HelloWorld</display-name>
    <enterprise-beans>
      <session>
    <ejb-name>HelloWorldSessionImpl</ejb-name>
    <home>usingj2ee.hello.HelloWorldSessionHome</home>
    <remote>usingj2ee.hello.HelloWorldSession</remote>
    <ejb-class>usingj2ee.hello.HelloWorldSessionImpl</ejb-class>
    <session-type>Stateful</session-type>
    <transaction-type>Container</transaction-type>
      </session>
    </enterprise-beans>
    <assembly-descriptor></assembly-descriptor>
    <ejb-client-jar>helloworldclient.jar</ejb-client-jar>
  </ejb-jar>
```

The first three tags—<?xml?>, <!DOCTYPE>, and <ejb-jar>—are required in every deployment descriptor. The <display-name> tag defines a name for the JAR file that is just used for display purposes in automated deployment tools and similar programs. It has nothing to do with the actual definition of the bean.

The <enterprise-beans> tag surrounds the definitions of all enterprise beans in the file. You can specify multiple EJBs in a single deployment descriptor, but they must all occur inside the <enterprise-beans> tag. A <session> tag identifies a session bean, whereas an <entity> tag identifies an entity bean.

The <ejb-name> tag defines a unique name for the bean within the deployment descriptor file; that is, each <ejb-name> in a single deployment descriptor must be unique. The name defined by the <ejb-name> tag isn't used by any EJB code or the container. It serves to uniquely identify the bean in the file because various other tags in the file must refer to a particular bean by name.

The next three tags—<home>, <remote>, and <ejb-class>—define the Home, Remote, and implementation classnames. Notice that the classnames must be fully qualified. That is, they must include the package name as well as the class or interface name.

For a session bean, you must also indicate whether the bean is stateless or stateful by specifying either `Stateless` or `Stateful` in the `<session-type>` tag. Also, you must specify whether the bean uses container-managed or bean-managed transactions by putting either `Bean` or `Container` in the `<transaction-type>` tag.

Listing 21.2 shows the additional `weblogic-ejb-jar.xml` file required by the WebLogic server.

LISTING 21.2 A WEBLOGIC-SPECIFIC DEPLOYMENT DESCRIPTOR

```
<?xml version="1.0"?>

<!DOCTYPE weblogic-ejb-jar PUBLIC '-//BEA Systems, Inc.//DTD WebLogic 5.1.0 EJB//EN'
'http://www.bea.com/servers/wls510/dtd/weblogic-ejb-jar.dtd'>

<weblogic-ejb-jar>
    <weblogic-enterprise-bean>
      <ejb-name>HelloWorldSessionImpl</ejb-name>
      <jndi-name>HelloWorld</jndi-name>
    </weblogic-enterprise-bean>
  </weblogic-ejb-jar>
```

The `<ejb-name>` tag in the WebLogic descriptor file must match an `<ejb-name>` in the `ejb-jar.xml` file. Again, the name is only used to uniquely identify a bean in the file. The `<jndi-name>` tag specifies the JNDI name for the bean's Home interface.

A DEPLOYMENT DESCRIPTOR FOR AN ENTITY BEAN

An entity bean's deployment descriptor is similar to the deployment descriptor for a session bean, at least for a simple bean. Listing 21.3 shows the deployment descriptor for the `Person` entity bean from Chapter 7, "Creating an Entity Bean."

LISTING 21.3 DEPLOYMENT DESCRIPTOR FOR THE `Person` ENTITY BEAN

```
<?xml version="1.0"?>

<!DOCTYPE ejb-jar PUBLIC '-//Sun Microsystems, Inc.//
DTD Enterprise JavaBeans 1.1//EN'
'http://java.sun.com/j2ee/dtds/ejb-jar_1_1.dtd'>

<ejb-jar>
    <enterprise-beans>
      <entity>
    <ejb-name>PersonImpl</ejb-name>
    <home>usingj2ee.addressbook.PersonHome</home>
    <remote>usingj2ee.addressbook.Person</remote>
    <ejb-class>usingj2ee.addressbook.PersonImpl</ejb-class>
    <persistence-type>Bean</persistence-type>
    <prim-key-class>usingj2ee.addressbook.PersonPK</prim-key-class>
    <reentrant>True</reentrant>
      </entity>
    </enterprise-beans>
    <assembly-descriptor></assembly-descriptor>
```

```
  <ejb-client-jar>/home/mark/j2eebook/ch07/examples/wlpersonClient.jar
  </ejb-client-jar>
</ejb-jar>
```

As you can see, the descriptor looks much like the one for the session bean. Instead of specifying a transaction type, you must specify a persistence type of `Bean` if you're using BMP or `Container` if you're using CMP. You must also specify the classname of the primary key using the `<prim-key-class>` tag. Again, the classname must be fully qualified. Also, you must specify whether the bean is *reentrant*—that is, whether it can handle multiple method invocations at the same time.

EJB Deployment Descriptor Options

Although the EJB deployment descriptors you have seen so far are short, the descriptor can contain quite a few tags. Many of these tags relate to container-managed persistence, and others relate to transaction control and security.

General Options

The general options for a bean let you specify various aspects of the bean that are common across all types of EJBs. Most of the general options involve various names, descriptions, and icons associated with the bean.

`description`

The `<description>` tag is a general text item used to describe a particular element. It can be used with many tags in the deployment descriptor. The general rule of thumb for description use is that if the tag normally contains other tags, you can also add a description. There are a few such tags, such as `<assembly-descriptor>` and `<enterprise-beans>`, that don't allow a description, however.

`display-name`

The `<display-name>` tag enables you to specify a name that various deployment tools can use when referring to the JAR file or items in the JAR. The display name doesn't have an effect on the actual deployment of the bean.

`large-icon` AND `small-icon`

You can supply image filenames that deployment tools can use when displaying the JAR file or various items in the JAR with the `<large-icon>` and `<small-icon>` tags. As with the `<display-name>` and `<description>` tags, these tags don't affect the deployment.

Bean Options

When you describe the beans contained in the JAR, you create a series of bean descriptions, all contained within the `<enterprise-beans>` tag.

`session`, `entity`, AND `message-driven`

The `<session>`, `<entity>`, and `<message-driven>` tags enable you to describe the deployment information for various types of beans. Although the different types of beans have different behaviors, the tags you use to configure these beans are remarkably similar. There are only a few minor differences between the three types of beans.

`ejb-name`

The `<ejb-name>` tag gives the bean a unique name that is used to reference the bean within the JAR file. There are other tags in the JAR file that are not contained within the bean's main tag (`session`, `entity`, or `message-driven`), and these tags must have a way to refer to a specific bean. The `ejb-name` tag doesn't affect the deployment of the bean and has nothing to do with the JNDI name for the bean's home interface.

`home`, `remote`, AND `ejb-class`

The `<home>`, `<remote>`, and `<ejb-class>` tags enable you to specify the classnames for the Home, Remote, and implementation classes. Don't forget that the classnames must include the package name as well.

`prim-key-class`

The `<prim-key-class>` tag specifies the classname for an entity bean's primary key. Once again, you must use the fully qualified pathname, including the package name.

`session-type`

The `<session-type>` tag controls whether the session bean is stateless or stateful. The legal values for the session type are `Stateless` and `Stateful`.

`transaction-type` AND `persistence-type`

The `<transaction-type>` tag indicates whether a session bean or message driven bean has control over its own transactions or whether the container controls the transactions. For an entity bean, the `<persistence-type>` tag indicates whether the bean uses BMP or CMP. The legal values for the both tags are `Bean` and `Container`.

`reentrant`

The `<reentrant>` tag tells whether an entity bean is reentrant (whether it can handle multiple threads at the same time). The legal values for this tag are `True` and `False`. A value of `True` means that the bean can handle multiple simultaneous threads.

`cmp-version`

Because CMP is so different between version 1.1 and version 2.0 of the EJB specification, you must specify which version of CMP a particular entity bean uses. The legal values for the `<cmp-version>` tag are `1.x` and `2.x`.

cmp-field

The <cmp-field> tag indicates that a particular field is stored using CMP. You must provide a <field-name> tag within this tag specifying the name of the field, and optionally add a <description> tag to describe the field.

PACKAGING JAVA SERVER PAGES AND SERVLETS

Servlets and Java Server Pages have their own special type of JAR file for deployment. This JAR file is called a WAR file (short for Web Archive).

When you create a WAR file, you must include a web.xml file that describes the application. Usually, you will at least need descriptions of the various servlets in your application. Listing 21.4 shows a crude servlet that calls a Java Server Page.

LISTING 21.4 SOURCE CODE FOR ExampleWARServlet.java

```
package usingjsp.warexample;

import javax.servlet.*;
import javax.servlet.http.*;

import java.io.*;

public class ExampleWARServlet extends HttpServlet
{
    public void service(HttpServletRequest request,
        HttpServletResponse response)
        throws ServletException, IOException
    {
// Just call the JSP
        RequestDispatcher dispatcher =
            getServletContext().getRequestDispatcher(
                "/ExampleWARJSP.jsp");

        dispatcher.forward(request, response);
    }
}
```

Without a WAR file, you would need to put the ExampleWARJSP.jsp file in your Web server's root directory. Listing 21.5 shows ExampleWARJSP.jsp.

LISTING 21.5 SOURCE CODE FOR ExampleWARJSP.jsp

```
<html>
<body>

<h1>Hello From the WAR!</h1>

<p>
This page was invoked by ExampleWARServlet!
</body>
</html>
```

The web.xml file for the example application assigns a name to the example servlet and sets up a URL mapping. The mapping is relative to the base path of the installed application. In other words, if the mapping says that the servlet's name is /ExampleWARServlet and the base path is /example, the full path for the example servlet would be /example/ExampleWARServlet.

Listing 21.6 shows the web.xml file.

LISTING 21.6 SOURCE CODE FOR web.xml

```
<!DOCTYPE web-app PUBLIC
    "-//Sun Microsystems, Inc.//DTD Web Application2.2//EN"
    "http://java.sun.com/j2ee/dtds/web-app_2_2.dtd">
<web-app>
    <display-name>WARExample</display-name>
    <description>
        A skeletal application to demonstrate WAR files
    </description>
    <servlet>
        <servlet-name>ExampleWARServlet</servlet-name>
        <servlet-class>usingjsp.warexample.ExampleWARServlet</servlet-class>
    </servlet>
    <servlet-mapping>
        <servlet-name>ExampleWARServlet</servlet-name>
        <url-pattern>/ExampleWARServlet</url-pattern>
    </servlet-mapping>
</web-app>
```

You will soon learn what each of the elements in the web.xml file mean. Most of them are probably obvious because their names are descriptive.

When you create the WAR file, the web.xml file must be in a directory named WEB-INF, and any Java classes you need, such as the servlet, must be in a classes directory under WEB-INF. If you have ExampleWARJSP.jsp, ExampleWARServlet.java, and web.xml in the same directory, you can use the following Windows commands to create example.war:

```
mkdir WEB-INF
copy web.xml WEB-INF
mkdir WEB-INF\classes
javac -d WEB-INF\classes ExampleWARServlet.java
jar cvf example.war *.jsp WEB-INF
```

If you are running Unix or Linux, the procedure is almost identical:

```
mkdir WEB-INF
cp web.xml WEB-INF
mkdir WEB-INF/classes
javac -d WEB-INF/classes ExampleWARServlet.java
jar cvf example.war *.jsp WEB-INF
```

WAR CONFIGURATION OPTIONS

A number of different elements might appear in the `web.xml` file. Although most of them are discussed here, some are discussed in Chapter 16, "Extending JSP with New Tags," and others in Chapter 37, "J2EE Security."

GENERAL APPLICATION OPTIONS

The general application options deal with the parts of the application that are above a servlet. For example, the description of the application, the initial startup file, and the various error pages to use are general application options.

display-name

The `display-name` option is a short description of the application. It is intended to be the kind of name you would expect to see in a GUI tool and is similar to the `Application Name` option in the JRun WAR deployment screen.

Example:

```
<display-name>ExampleWAR</display-name>
```

description

The `description` option is the long description of the application. When this option is a direct child of `<web-app>`, it describes the application; otherwise, it describes the item it is a child of. That is, other things can have a description, so when you see a `<description>` tag, don't assume that it's a description of the application.

Example:

```
<description>
This application demonstrates how you use a WAR file to deploy an
    application in different Web servers.
</description
```

distributable

The `distributable` option indicates that this application might be distributed across multiple containers (servlet engines). One of the things you must ensure when you create a distributable application is that all the items you place in a session can be serialized. The container might need to copy objects from one session object to another if a browser session accesses a different server.

Example:

```
<distributable/>
```

`context-param`

The `context-param` option lets you set initialization parameters that are accessible through the `ServletContext` class. Use the `<param-name>` and `<param-value>` tags to set the parts of the context parameter. You can also include an optional description tag.

Example:

```
<context-param>
    <param-name>initParam1</param-name>
    <param-value>Foo!</param-value>
    <description>A simple init parameter</description>
</context-param>
```

`mime-mapping`

You might find it odd that you can set mime mappings for files in a WAR file, because most of the time you set content types in a servlet or a JSP. If you forward to a non-servlet, non-JSP resource, however, the content type for the response will be the mime type of the resource you are returning. The `mime-mapping` option allows you to control those content types.

Example:

```
<mime-mapping>
    <extension>wml</extension>
    <mime-type>text/vnd.wap.wml>
</mime-mapping>
```

`welcome-file-list`

When you access a Web site, you rarely enter a filename. For instance, you might enter `http://www.slashdot.org` without entering a filename such as `index.html` or `default.html`. The `welcome-file-list` option enables you to specify the possible names for the default application file. In other words, if the application is named `example` and you go to `http://localhost/example`, the welcome file list indicates the possible files that you might run. If the list includes `index.html`, `index.htm`, and `default.jsp` and the only file in the application is `default.jsp`, that's what you'll see.

Example:

```
<welcome-file-list>
    <welcome-file>index.html</welcome-file>
    <welcome-file>index.htm</welcome-file>
    <welcome-file>default.jsp</welcome-file>
</welcome-file-list>
```

`error-page`

The `error-page` option allows you to specify the pages that handle various errors that might occur. You can map HTTP errors to specific error pages and also map Java exceptions to specific error pages. To map an HTTP error, use the `<error-code>` tag and specify the error number, such as 404. To map a Java exception, make sure you use the fully qualified class-name of the exception, such as `java.lang.NullPointerException`.

Example:

```
<error-page>
    <error-code>404</error-code>
    <location>Handle404Error.jsp</location>
</error-page>
<error-page>
    <exception-type>java.lang.NullPointerException
        </exception-type>
    <location>HandleNullPointerServlet</location>
</error-page>
```

session-config

The `session-config` option enables you to change various settings related to sessions created by the application. Under the current servlet specification, the only option you can change is the session timeout, which is specified in minutes.

SERVLET OPTIONS

Servlet options allow you to change the options at the servlet level. Although there are several servlet options, they are all specified within one of two tags, either `<servlet>` or `<servlet-mapping>`.

servlet

The `servlet` option is the main option for changing the attributes of a servlet. You can specify a servlet's name, class, description, initialization parameters, and startup information.

The `<servlet-name>` tag lets you specify the name of the servlet. This name can be used in the `<servlet-mapping>` tag to create a URL mapping for the servlet. The servlet name alone is not enough to specify the name you use to access the servlet.

The `<servlet-class>` tag specifies the fully qualified pathname for the servlet. Instead of a servlet class, you might specify the name of a JSP file for this servlet by using the `<jsp-file>` tag.

Only the `<servlet-name>` and either `<servlet-class>` or `<jsp-file>` tags are required for the `<servlet>` tag, all others are optional.

The `<display-name>` tag specifies the short name of the servlet and might be used in a GUI tool. Likewise, the `<description>` tag specifies the long description of the servlet.

The `<init-param>` tag allows you to specify any number of initialization parameters for the servlet, which are passed in to the servlet via the `ServletConfig` class. The `<init-param>` tag must contain a single `<param-name>` and a single `<param-value>` tag and might optionally contain a `<description>` tag.

The `<load-on-startup>` tag indicates that you want the servlet to be loaded when the Web server first starts up. The data value associated with the tag is a priority number that allows you to specify an order for servlet startup. The lowest numbers are started first.

Example:

```
<servlet>
    <servlet-name>MyServlet</servlet-name>
    <servlet-class>com.wutka.MyServlet</servlet-class>
    <display-name>MyVeryOwnServlet</display-name>
    <description>It's mine, all mine!</description>
    <init-param>
        <param-name>owner</param-name>
        <param-value>me</param-value>
    </init-param>
    <init-param>
        <param-name>belongsTo</param-name>
        <param-value>me</param-value>
    </init-param>
    <load-on-startup>1</load-on-startup>
</servlet>
```

servlet-mapping

The `servlet-mapping` option enables you to map URLs to servlets. At a minimum, you can use the servlet's name as the URL pattern, like this:

```
<servlet-mapping>
    <servlet-name>MyServlet</servlet-name>
    <url-pattern>MyServlet</url-pattern>
</servlet-mapping>
```

You can also map a servlet so it handles any path that starts with a certain pattern. For example, when a path starts with `/servlet`, the Web server runs a special invoker servlet that extracts the servlet name from the rest of the path and executes it. The `<servlet-mapping>` definition for the invoker looks like this:

```
<servlet-mapping>
    <url-pattern>/servlet/*</url-pattern>
    <servlet-name>invoker</servlet-name>
</servlet-mapping>
```

You can also use servlet mapping to handle various file extensions. For example, the Resin server has a special servlet that handles requests for Java Server Pages. The server maps any URL ending with `.jsp` to this servlet using the following servlet mapping:

```
<servlet-mapping>
    <url-pattern>*.jsp</url-pattern>
    <servlet-name>com.caucho.jsp.JspServlet</servlet-name>
</servlet-mapping>
```

APPLICATION DEPLOYMENT

You can package Enterprise Java Beans, Java Server Pages, and servlets into a single application file called an Enterprise Archive, or EAR file. The EAR file is, of course, a JAR file with an additional descriptor file describing the JAR files included in the EAR file. The descriptor file must be in the `META-INF` directory and must be named `application.xml`.

EAR DESCRIPTOR OPTIONS

There isn't much to the deployment descriptor for an EAR file; you can give it a display name and description using the `<display-name>` and `<description>` tags. You then list the various JARs by using the `<module>` type. Within each module tag, you have one of three tags: `<ejb>`, `<java>`, or `<web>`. For the `ejb` and `java` tags, you specify the URI of the JAR file. For the `web` tag, you use the `<web-uri>` tag to specify the URI for the JAR file and `<context-root>` to specify the root for the Web application.

TROUBLESHOOTING

WEB INSTALLATION PROBLEMS

Why doesn't the Resin Servlet Engine use my WAR file?

Resin doesn't unpack WAR files automatically. You must unpack the file in Resin's doc directory. When you restart the server, it will see the application.

Why isn't Tomcat unpacking my WAR file?

If you have already installed a WAR file, Tomcat might not unpack it again, even if you have changed the WAR file. When you install a new WAR file, make sure you delete the directory where Tomcat unpacked the previous version. Then you can be sure Tomcat will unpack the WAR file when it restarts.

I reinstalled my WAR file in JRun; why hasn't anything changed?

You still need to restart the server. All the old class files (servlets and JSPs) are still present in the Java Virtual Machine.

EJB INSTALLATION PROBLEMS

Why does the EJB container complain about missing classes when I install my EAR file or JAR file?

Many EJB servers require you to perform an extra compilation step before installing a packaged application. If you're using WebLogic, you might need to use the `weblogic.ejbc` program to compile the application into a WebLogic-specific JAR file. Some EJB containers perform the compilation step after you install the file. Consult the documentation for your EJB container to see if it requires an extra step.

PART IV

Using XML with J2EE

CHAPTER 22

XML—The Extensible Markup Language

In this chapter

WHAT XML IS AND ISN'T

The Extensible Markup Language (XML) represents an important step in data representation. In the past, programs used many different formats for storing data. There have been text files with comma-delimited or pipe-delimited fields, binary files in any number of formats, and even plain ASCII text. Unfortunately, most programs use slightly different ways to store data, even if the overall format is similar. Unfortunately, you don't usually have an easy way to describe the format of the data. XML not only gives you a common way to store data, it also gives you a common way to describe the data.

Another problem you encounter when storing data is that most representations tend to be tabular in nature. That is, when you write data into a file, you typically put all the information for a particular data element on a single line in the file. What happens when you want to write structured data that doesn't fit neatly on a single line? It's often difficult to store structured data on a single line with a prescribed set of fields.

XML solves this problem by defining a standard way to represent data, a standard way to tag the data with its type, and a way to describe the overall data structure. XML is simple, easy to read, and easy to understand. There are a few things XML is not:

- **Although related, XML is not a replacement for HTML**—XML and HTML belong to the same family, derived from SGML. Although there is an XML-compliant version of HTML called XHTML, XML does not define how to represent data on a Web browser.
- **XML is not a cure-all for the data-format ills**—Various software vendors and the business sector must still agree on a common representation for data. For example, the travel industry needs a standard format to represent reservation information. The banking industry needs a standard format to represent account information.
- **XML is not a programming language**—XML lets you describe data, but it doesn't let you describe how to process the data.

WHY XML IS IMPORTANT IN J2EE

The popularity of XML emphasizes one important point: People (and applications) need to exchange data. If not, why would anyone care about a standard way to represent data? You might not need XML to exchange recipes with your next-door neighbor, but if you're a doctor and you need to exchange patient records with a hospital, XML sure comes in handy.

Imagine, for instance, that you work for a large company that does a lot of long-distance calling. You arrange with your long-distance company to receive detailed call summaries every month. You certainly wouldn't want the company to make a huge number of remote method invocations to send you the information—it might take them a whole month just to send you a month's worth of data. Instead, you're better off getting a huge file of XML data. You might still use EJB or at least JDBC when storing the data in a database, but the long-distance company doesn't have to sit and wait while you process the data. XML gives you a good, portable way to transfer large data records from one system to another. This is especially useful when one system is a legacy system that doesn't run Java.

The other area where XML lends J2EE a hand is in configuration. In Chapter 21, "Packaging and Installing a J2EE Application," you might have noticed that the configuration files for Enterprise JavaBeans, servlets, and Java Server Pages are all XML files. Because XML is human-readable, it's easy for you to edit. Because XML can represent structured data, it simplifies configuration file formats. Because XML is portable, you can use the same configuration files on different application servers.

Before XML became popular, most Java applications used properties files for configuration (plenty of them still do!) Properties files are somewhat one-dimensional, however. You end up doing things like this:

```
connection.conn1.url="http://localhost/foo"
connection.conn1.description="My local connection"
connection.conn1.bufferSize=500
```

In XML, however, you can group the items together nicely:

```
<connection name="conn1">
    <url>http://localhost/foo</url>
    <description>My local connection</description>
    <bufferSize>500</bufferSize>
</connection>
```

BASIC XML SYNTAX

An XML page consists of two sections: a prolog and the root element. You can't have more than one root element—all the data in the XML document must be enclosed by a single root element. The XML prolog begins with an XML processing instruction identifying the document as an XML document. XML processing instructions begin with <?. Usually, the tag looks like this:

```
<?xml version="1.0"?>
```

Next, when you create an XML page, you have the option of specifying a Document Type Definition (DTD) that defines what tags are permitted in the XML page. DTDs let you create standard definitions of XML pages. You can then use an XML validator to check an XML page to make sure it conforms to its DTD. Use the `<!DOCTYPE` declaration to specify the DTD for your page. The `<!DOCTYPE` declaration is part of the XML prolog. Listing 22.1 shows an example DTD.

LISTING 22.1 SOURCE CODE FOR `Simple.dtd`

```
<!ELEMENT phone-book (entry*)>
<!ELEMENT entry (person? | number*)+>
<!ELEMENT person (first-name? | middle-name? | last-name?)+>
<!ELEMENT first-name (#PCDATA)>
<!ELEMENT middle-name (#PCDATA)>
<!ELEMENT last-name (#PCDATA)>
<!ELEMENT number (#PCDATA)>
```

You'll learn how to create a DTD a little later in this chapter. Listing 22.2 shows the source code for `Simple.xml`.

LISTING 22.2 SOURCE CODE FOR Simple.xml

```
<?xml version="1.0"?>
<!DOCTYPE person SYSTEM "http://localhost/Simple.dtd">
<person>
    <first-name>Samantha</first-name>
    <middle-name>Lauren</middle-name>
    <last-name>Tippin</last-name>
</person>
```

A DTD is optional, of course. You can create an XML page with any set of tags you want. For each start tag you must have an end tag.

The exception to this rule is that you can end a tag with `/>` to indicate that it doesn't need an end tag. This kind of tag is called an *empty-element tag*.

Remember, the `<jsp:include/>` and `<jsp:forward/>` tags end with `/>` and thus take no closing tag. You can't interleave tags, either. In other words, if tag B starts within tag A, then tag B must be closed before tag A closes. The following combination of tags is illegal in XML:

```
<foo>
   <bar>
</foo>
    </bar>
```

Because the `<bar>` tag starts inside the `<foo>` tag, it must also close within the `<foo>` tag. An XML element is an item represented by either start and end tags or an empty-element tag. An XML element can contain other elements.

You can also specify attributes within a tag. Although HTML is lenient about quotes in attributes, XML requires that the value of every attribute is enclosed in quotes. In other words, where you might have an HTML tag like this:

```
<img src="katy.jpg" width=140 height=150>
```

A valid XML version of the `<IMG>` tag would look like this:

```
<img src="katy.jpg" width="140" height="150"/>
```

Notice that the XML version of `<IMG>` ends with `/>` because it doesn't need a closing tag.

Sometimes you need to include data in an XML file that might contain XML-like tags and other data that you don't want XML to interpret. XML has a special section called CDATA that you can use to enclose text data. A CDATA section starts with `<![CDATA[` and ends with `]]>`. You might, for example, want to include an HTML page as the data portion of an XML tag. You don't want the XML parser to interpret the HTML tags; you just want them to be part of a tag's data. Listing 22.3 shows an example XML page that contains HTML as text data.

LISTING 22.3 SOURCE CODE FOR HTMLData.xml

```
<?xml version="1.0"?>
<info>
    <description>The Hello World! Page</description>
    <html-text>
        <![CDATA[
            <html>
            <body>
            <h1>Hello World!</h1>
            </body>
            </html>
        ]]>
    </html-text>
</info>
```

As far as XML is concerned, the `<html-text>` tag, which is just a made-up name, contains text data and has no XML tags contained beneath it.

You can insert comments in an XML file by surrounding them with `<!--` and `-->`, like this:

```
<!-- This is a comment -->
```

CREATING A DOCUMENT TYPE DEFINITION (DTD)

XML is remarkably flexible. If you don't use a DTD, you can create a document using almost any kind of structure you want. You might choose to represent a person's name through attributes:

```
<person first-name="Samantha" last-name="Tippin">
```

Or, you might create separate tags for the various data items associated with a person:

```
<person>
    <first-name>Samantha</first-name>
    <last-name>Tippin</last-name>
</person>
```

Flexibility, of course, is a two-edged sword. Because you are able to format your data however you like, it's unlikely you'll use the same format as someone else. A Document Type Definition enables you to define a specific format for an XML document. You can specify which tags might appear in a document, which attributes a tag might have, and what kind of content each tag has.

The core of a DTD file is the `<!ELEMENT>` (Element Type) declaration. It defines a tag that is valid for your XML file. The general format for the `<!ELEMENT>` (Element Type) declaration is

```
<!ELEMENT tagname content-type>
```

The tag name is the name of the XML tag, such as `person` or `first-name`. The content specification can be `EMPTY`, `ANY`, or a list or sequence of elements, including a special `#PCDATA type` that indicates text data.

Most of the time, the content specification is a list of elements, like this:

```
<!ELEMENT person (first-name|middle-name|last-name)>
```

If the items in the content specification are separated by pipe characters (|), the content specification is referred to as a *choice*. You can have one of the elements specified, but only one. In other words, in the previous declaration, if you specify a first name inside a `<person>` tag, you can't specify a middle name or a last name.

If the items in the content type are separated by commas, each of the elements in the list must appear in the document in the order it is declared. This kind of list is called a *sequence*. For example, the following declaration requires a person to have a first name, middle name, and last name in that order:

```
<!ELEMENT person (first-name,middle-name,last-name)>
```

You are probably wondering how you can declare that the middle name is optional, or that the first and last names don't have to be in a specific order. The `?`, `+`, and `*` characters after an element or even a whole list enable you to control the number of times an element can appear.

The `?` character indicates that an element or a list might occur exactly zero or one times. Because a middle name is often optional, you might still require the first and last names in order but allow the middle name to be optional, like this:

```
<!ELEMENT person (first-name,middle-name?,last-name)>
```

If you don't care about the order, you can use a choice instead of a sequence, and make the choice occur one or more times, with each element occurring zero or one times. In other words, this way:

```
<!ELEMENT person (first-name? | middle-name? | last-name?)+>
```

This declaration lets you declare the first, middle, and last names in any order, but it does not keep you from entering multiple names. The reason is, the `?` that indicates that an item might occur zero or one times is only valid within a single choice. Each time the choice occurs (the `+` indicates it might occur 1 or more times), you can have a first name, middle name, or last name. You can even have nothing at all, because each item is optional.

The `*` character indicates that an item might occur zero or more times. Whereas the `+` sign requires there be at least one instance, the `*` character allows for the possibility that the tag doesn't occur at all.

You can also nest choices and sequences within other choices. For example, the following declaration allows you to enter at most one of each kind of name but in any order:

```
<!ELEMENT person ((first-name?,middle-name?,last-name?) |
                  (first-name?,last-name?,middle-name?) |
                  (middle-name?,first-name?,last-name?) |
                  (middle-name?,last-name?,first-name?) |
                  (last-name?,first-name?,middle-name?) |
                  (last-name?,middle-name?,last-name?))>
```

When an element can contain text data, you can specify a choice in which #PCDATA is the first item in the choice. If the element can contain *only* text data, make #PCDATA the only item in the choice. Most <description> tags are defined this way:

```
<!ELEMENT description (#PCDATA)>
```

Tip

You can't use the #PCDATA type without the surrounding parentheses, and it must always be the first item in the list if there are multiple items.

If a tag might include text as well as other tags, you can include the tags after the #PCDATA type, like this:

```
<!ELEMENT sentence (#PCDATA|comma|period)*>
```

Although you can specify the types this way, you can't specify their order or the number of times they occur.

The second most important tag in a DTD is the <!ATTLIST> (Attribute List) declaration, which defines the attributes that a tag might have. Odd as it might seem, you don't define an element's attributes in the <!ELEMENT> (Element Type) declaration. Here is an example <!ATTLIST> (Attribute List) declaration that defines the first, middle, and last names of a person as attributes:

```
<!ATTLIST person first-name CDATA #IMPLIED
                 middle-name CDATA #IMPLIED
                 last-name CDATA #IMPLIED>
```

The general format for the <!ATTLIST> (Attribute List) declaration is that it contains the element name first (person in the previous example) followed by any number of declarations of the form: *name type default-declaration*. The name, of course, is the name of the attribute. The type is usually either CDATA to indicate a text string or a list of possible values like this: (value1|value2|value3). As you can see, the list of possible attribute values is similar to a choice list in the <!ELEMENT> (Element Type) declaration.

The default declaration can be one of four possibilities: #REQUIRED, #IMPLIED, a string value, or #FIXED followed by a string value. If an attribute is required, it must always be present. If an attribute is implied, there is no default value if there is no such attribute in the document. The third option, the string value, is the opposite of an implied value. If the attribute isn't in the document, then you (or an XML parser) should consider the attribute as being there with the specified default value. The last option, #FIXED, is like a default constant. If the attribute is there, its value must be the value specified just after #FIXED. Here is an attribute definition that shows you the various ways to define attributes:

```
<!ATTLIST person sex (male|female) #REQUIRED
          age CDATA #IMPLIED
          breathes CDATA #FIXED "air"
          smile CDATA ":-)">
```

You can include comments in a DTD using the <!-- --> tags just as you can in an XML document.

OTHER XML SPECIFICATIONS

One of the overwhelming things you discover when you start delving into the world of XML is that there are so many different specifications related to XML. So far, everything you have seen is from the original XML specification. There are a number of extensions to XML that deal with various ways to manipulate and describe XML documents.

Although the core of XML is fairly stable, there have been new standards arising to address some of the holes that the original XML specification doesn't cover. The W3C (the XML/HTML standards body) has been slow to approve some of the recent standards. Some of the standards listed here might not be fully approved as you read this.

You can read the standards yourself at `http://www.w3c.org`.

XML NAMESPACES

Namespaces are similar to Java packages. As you might have seen before in Java, some packages have classes with the same name—`java.lang.Object` and `org.omg.CORBA.Object`, for example. You have the same problem in XML, where you might have `<rank>Admiral</rank>` for a naval Web site, and `<rank>7</rank>` to describe the position of a chess piece. XML namespaces enable you to assign a prefix to a tag to specify what the tag refers to. The `<rank>` tag with a namespace prefix might look like `<naval:rank>` or `<chess:rank>`. When you use a namespace, you associate it with a specific URI. The URI doesn't need to exist; it's used as a unique way to identify the namespace. When you first use an element from a specific namespace, you use the `xmlns` attribute to declare the namespace. For example

```
<naval:rank xmlns:naval="http://www.navy.mil/schema">
```

When you include a namespace in an element, you can use that namespace in other elements within that element.

XSL

XSL (Extensible Stylesheet Language) is complex enough and powerful enough to deserve an entire chapter in this book—Chapter 23, "Using XSL to Translate XML Documents," to be exact. Briefly, XSL allows you to define a translation from one form of XML document to another. Most people think of XSL as a transformation from XML data to XHTML, but it's a lot more general than that. XSL also includes a style sheet similar to HTML's cascading style sheets.

XPATH

The XPath standard provides a standard for referring to portions of an XML document. Because it is used so heavily in XSL, you'll learn more about XPath in Chapter 23. To try to relate XPath to some Java equivalent, if you have an array of `Person` objects in Java and you want to access the last name of the fifth person, you use a statement such as `people[4].lastName`. In XPath, if you have a `<people>` tag that contains `<person>` tags, which can contain `<lastName>` tags, you can reference the last name of the fifth person with `/people/person[5]/lastName`.

XLINKS

The XLinks specification defines how XML documents refer to other documents, somewhat like HTML documents use hyperlinks to refer to other HTML documents. Because XML isn't specifically a display-oriented language, the links aren't necessarily things that you click. Instead, XLinks describe much more complex relationships.

XPOINTERS

When you make a hyperlink in HTML, you sometimes want to jump to a specific section of a page. When you do, you create an anchor tag and append the anchor name to the URL, like this: `http://localhost/mydoc.html#jumphere`. The XPointers standard uses the XPath standard to enable you to refer to specific sections of an XML document. XPointers are more useful from within XLinks. That is, XPointers exist so that XLinks can refer to a specific element in a specific XML document.

If you take a really optimistic view of XLinks and XPointers, you can imagine that all over the world there are servers with a lot of XML documents containing any kind of data you can imagine. You can create new documents and reference this data using XLinks and XPointers. For example, suppose the U.S. National Archives put the U.S. Census data into XML format (this is a *really* optimistic view). When you work on your family tree and you want to reference data from a census, you can just include an XLink to the census data rather than copying the data.

The census isn't the best example of the power of XLinks, however, because the data doesn't change. Suppose Major League Baseball sets up XML documents containing the current statistics for all baseball players. If you want to display an XHTML page containing the statistics for the Atlanta Braves, you can create an XML document that uses XLinks to refer to various statistics in `atlantabraves.xml`. You then use XSL to transform your XML document into XHTML. If everything goes well, you're displaying statistics that come right from Major League Baseball without having to copy them yourself or write a script to go out and fetch them periodically.

XML SCHEMA

XML is a subset of a language called SGML, which was originally developed for creating text documents. XML documents, although containing readable text, usually contain data. To be more specific, text is something like `<soliloquy>To be or not to be... </soliloquy>`, whereas data is more like `<birthdate>05/11/1965</birthdate>`. If you look back at the DTD specification, you'll see that XML doesn't have any concept of data types (other than CDATA, which is XML-speak for "text").

The XML Schema standard is intended as a replacement for DTDs and allows you to assign data types to XML tags. Not only does it define data types, it also defines a standard for understanding those data types as printable text. If you've ever had to read and write dates, you know what a boon this is. One of the biggest obstacles to standard data exchange formats is the fact that different companies represent data values different ways. With XML Schema, a lot of these differences disappear.

JAVA MEETS XML

Although they are different from a technology standpoint, XML and Java share a strange similarity. Many people originally thought XML would mainly be used for displaying data, or at least represent data in a way that would make it easy to display, but now XML is used heavily in server-side applications for data storage and data exchange. Java, of course, got its start as a language for a small handheld device and is now wildly popular for server-side programming.

XML is platform independent and has the potential to be application independent if various application providers can agree on a standard document format. Java is reasonably platform independent, being available on most major computing platforms. Another portable aspect of both XML and Java is that they both use Unicode to represent characters, allowing them to represent data from a large number of written languages (such as English, German, French, and so on).

These similarities make Java and XML an excellent combination.

Of course, to combine the two technologies, you need to be able to read XML documents into a Java program and create XML documents from a Java program.

CREATING XML DOCUMENTS WITH JAVA

Because an XML document is simply a text file (or a stream of text), you can create one just by using a `PrintWriter` or even `System.out.println`. Listing 22.4 shows a simple Java program that prints out an XML document.

LISTING 22.4 SOURCE CODE FOR PrintXML.java

```
package usingj2ee.xml;

public class PrintXML
{
    public static void main(String[] args)
    {
        System.out.println("<?xml version=\"1.0\"?>");
        System.out.println("<greeting>");
        System.out.println("   Hello XML World!");
        System.out.println("</greeting>");
    }
}
```

Obviously, there's nothing to printing out an XML file. Now, from a Java Server Page, you have one extra challenge. The content type for an XML page is different from the content type for an HTML page. By default, a JSP has a content type of `text/html`, but for XML, you want a content type of `text/xml`. You change the content type by specifying it in the `<%@ page %>` directive. Listing 22.5 shows the JSP equivalent of the program in Listing 22.4.

Listing 22.5 Source Code for XMLHelloWorld.jsp

```
<%@ page contentType="text/xml" %>

<?xml version="1.0"?>
<greeting>
    Hello XML World!
</greeting>
```

As you can see, Java Server Pages are a natural fit for XML because you can enter the XML content exactly as you want it to appear.

You can also generate XML from a servlet, again by using `println` statements, as Listing 22.6 shows.

Listing 22.6 Source Code for XMLHelloWorldServlet.java

```
package usingj2ee.xml;

import javax.servlet.*;
import javax.servlet.http.*;
import java.io.*;

public class XMLHelloWorldServlet extends HttpServlet
{
    public void service(HttpServletRequest request,
        HttpServletResponse response)
        throws ServletException, IOException
    {
        response.setContentType("text/xml");

        PrintWriter out = response.getWriter();

        out.println("<?xml version=\"1.0\"?>");
        out.println("<greeting>");
        out.println("    Hello XML World!");
        out.println("</greeting>");
    }
}
```

Parsing an XML Document with Java

As you can see, generating an XML document is fairly trivial. Reading an XML document is a little trickier, and that's where a parser comes in. There are two main flavors of XML parsers: SAX and DOM. SAX stands for Simple API for XML and is an event-based parser. When a SAX parser reads through an XML file, it sends an event to a handler class that you write. SAX parsers tend to be fast, but they can be cumbersome to use for complex documents.

Document Object Model (DOM) parsers read the whole document and create a Java representation of the object. The advantage of DOM is that it is usually easier to navigate through the document because you have everything you need. When you use SAX, you must keep track of where the parser is, and you can't search through the rest of the document until the parser has finished with it. With DOM, you have access to the entire document at once. The biggest disadvantage with DOM is that it tends to be very slow for large documents. The general rule of thumb is that for large, simple documents, SAX is better. For smaller, more complex documents, use DOM. For large, complex documents, you've got a tough job whichever way you go.

Note

A DTD is not a valid XML document itself, so you can't use an XML parser to parse a DTD. As people move away from DTDs and to XML Schemas, this should be less of an issue because XML Schemas are valid XML. In the meantime, if you need to parse a DTD, there is a free DTD Parser available at `http://www.wutka.com/dtdparser.html`.

USING A DOM PARSER

When you use a DOM parser, the hardest part is actually navigating the document. Parsing it is a snap. You create a document parser and tell it to parse your document. One of the important things about the Java API for XML Parsing (JAXP) is that it supports multiple implementations. You can use the one supplied by Sun, or go with Apache's Xerces parser. Either way, your Java code works the same way. You locate a `DocumentBuilderFactory` and then create a `DocumentBuilder`. Under DOM, a document builder is really just a parser.

Listing 22.7 shows a program that parses a document using DOM, but doesn't do anything with the content. You can use the program to check for errors in your XML, however, because the parser reports any errors it encounters.

LISTING 22.7 SOURCE CODE FOR `DOMValidate.java`

```
package usingj2ee.xml;

import java.io.*;
import javax.xml.parsers.*;
import org.xml.sax.*;
import org.w3c.dom.*;

public class DOMValidate
{
    public static void main(String[] args)
    {
        try
        {

// Locate the document builder factory
            DocumentBuilderFactory factory =
                DocumentBuilderFactory.newInstance();

// Tell the document builder to create a validating
// parser (one that checks to make sure the
// document is valid)
            factory.setValidating(true);

// Ask the factory to create a document builder
            DocumentBuilder builder = factory.newDocumentBuilder();
```

```
// By default, try to parse the file "Simple.xml"
            String filename = "Simple.xml";

// If the user specifies a filename on the command line, use it instead
            if (args.length > 0)
            {
                filename = args[0];
            }

// Ask the document builder to parse the file
            Document doc = builder.parse(new File(filename));

// This is where you would normally do something with the document content
        }
        catch (Exception exc)
        {
            exc.printStackTrace();
        }
    }
}
```

If your XML file contains no errors, the program in Listing 22.7 doesn't appear to do anything. It only fails if there is an error in the XML file. You can try inserting errors into the XML file to see kinds of errors you get when you parse a file containing errors.

When you use DOM, parsing the document is the easy part. It's navigating through the `Document` object and all its children that's tough.

THE DOCUMENT OBJECT MODEL (DOM)

One of the first things you'll notice about the Document Object Model is that it just doesn't work the way most Java object models do. DOM doesn't use the standard Java collections—no vectors, enumerations, or hash tables. After you get used to these differences, DOM isn't so bad to use.

`Node`, `NodeList`, AND `NamedNodeMap`

The `Node` class is the real workhorse of DOM, because almost every major class in the object model is a subclass of `Node`. A node has a name, a type, and possibly a value. It can also have attributes, children, siblings, and a single parent.

If a node is an element, the node name is the XML tag for the element. If the node is an attribute, the node name is the attribute name. Otherwise, for most of the common node types, you can ignore the node's name. The declaration for `getNodeName` is as follows:

```
public String getNodeName()
```

If a node is a text node (there are several types of text nodes) the node's value is the actual text from the document. If the node is an attribute, the node's value is the attribute value. The following is the declaration for `getNodeValue`:

```
public String getNodeValue() throws DOMException
```

You can test the node's type two ways, either with the `instanceof` keyword checking for a specific class type, or with the `getNodeType` method. The `getNodeType` method returns a short integer, which has a value equal to one of the type constants defined in the `Node` class. Some of the common constant names are `DOCUMENT_NODE`, `ELEMENT_NODE`, `ATTRIBUTE_NODE`, `CDATA_SECTION_NODE`, and `TEXT_NODE`. There are, of course, several other types, but in day-to-day parsing, these are the most common.

The following are the common methods for getting and setting related nodes (attributes, parents, children, and siblings):

```
public Node appendChild(Node newChild) throws DOMException
public NamedNodeMap getAttributes()
public NodeList getChildNodes()
public Node getFirstChild()
public Node getLastChild()
public Node getNextSibling()
public Node getParentNode()
public Node getPreviousSibling()
public boolean hasChildNodes()
public Node insertBefore(Node nodeToInsert, Node whereToInsert)
    throws DOMException
public Node removeChild(Node childToRemove) throws DOMException
public Node replaceChild(Node newChild, Node oldChild)
    throws DOMException
```

The `NodeList` class returned by `getChildNodes` is similar to an enumeration or an iterator. It has only two methods: `getLength` and `item`. The `getLength` method returns the number of items in the list, whereas `item` returns the item at a specific position in the list. These methods are declared as follows:

```
public int getLength()
public Node item(int whichItem)
```

The `NamedNodeMap` class is the DOM equivalent of a hash table, although it can also be accessed sequentially. The three name-oriented methods in the `NamedNodeMap` are listed here:

```
public Node getNamedItem(String itemName)
public Node setNamedItem(Node newItem) throws DOMException
public Node removeNamedItem(Node oldItem) throws DOMException
```

Because nodes have built-in names, the `set` and `remove` methods don't require you to provide the name, they just ask the node itself for its name.

The `NamedNodeMap` also includes the same `getLength` and `item` methods found in `NodeList` so you can access the items sequentially.

Document

The `Document` class represents an XML document, and is a subclass of `Node`. Most of the methods in the `Document` class create new items to put in the document. A DOM document isn't necessarily a static thing that you just read from a file and process. You can create new documents dynamically with DOM. You use the `Document` class to create new items (in other words, when you create an element, you don't use the `Element` constructor, you call `document.createElement`).

When you're just reading a document, the two most important methods for you are `getDocumentElement`, which returns the root element in the document, and `getElementsByTagName`, which returns all the elements in the document with a specific tag name (regardless of how deep into the structure they are). These methods are declared as

```
public Element getDocumentElement()
public NodeList getElementsByTagName(String tagName)
```

To create new items to add to a document, you can use the following methods:

```
public Attr createAttribute(String attrName) throws DOMException
public CDATASection createCDATASection(String data) throws DOMException
public Comment createComment(String comment) throws DOMException
public Element createElement(String tagName) throws DOMException
public Text createTextNode(String data) throws DOMException
```

There are, of course, some other kinds of items that you can create, but they are fairly rare.

Incidentally, to create a `Document` object, you use the `newDocument` method in the `DocumentBuilder` class. Don't try to create one yourself—`Document` is really an interface, not a class! The same goes for the other items, such as `Element` and `Attr`.

`Element`

Most of the methods in the `Element` class deal with getting, setting, and removing attributes. When you deal with attributes in an `Element` object, you can either work with `Attr` objects, or just work with names and values. The attribute-related methods in the `Element` class are

```
public String getAttribute(String attributeName)
public Attr getAttributeNode(String attributeName)

public void removeAttribute(String attributeName) throws DOMException
public void removeAttributeNode(Attr oldAttribute) throws DOMException
public void setAttribute(String attrName, String attrValue)
    throws DOMException
public void setAttributeNode(Attr newAttr) throws DOMException
```

You can also use the `getElementsByTagName` method just like the one in the `Document` class.

`CharacterData`

The `CharacterData` class is the parent class for the three types of text classes in a document: `CDATASection`, `Comment`, and `Text`. A `CharacterData` object represents a sequence of characters and behaves somewhat like a `StringBuffer` object because you can modify the contents of the object, unlike the `String` class. The following are the methods in the `CharacterData` class:

```
public void appendData(String moreData) throws DOMException
public void deleteData(int startingOffset, int characterCount)
    throws DOMException
public String getData() throws DOMException
public int getLength()
public void insertData(int insertAtOffset, String dataToInsert)
    throws DOMException
public void replaceData(int replaceAtOffset, int numCharsToReplace,
```

```
   String newData) throws DOMException
public void setData(String newData) throws DOMException
public String substringData(int startingOffset, int characterCount)
    throws DOMException
```

The `Text` class, which is a subclass of `CharacterData` and also the parent class of `CDATASection`, includes one extra method that lets you split a text node into two separate nodes:

```
public Text splitText(int splitAtOffset) throws DOMException
```

Attr

The `Attr` class represents an attribute (a name and a value). Remember that in the DTD, you had default values for attributes? The `Attr` class can tell you if the value of the attribute came from a default value or if it was explicitly specified (if `getSpecified` returns `true`, the value was explicitly specified). If an attribute is declared as `#IMPLIED` and it isn't present in the document, there won't be a corresponding `Attr` object for it at all.

The following are the methods in the `Attr` class:

```
public String getName()
public boolean getSpecified()
public String getValue()
public void setValue(String newValue)
```

A DOM Example Program

Listing 22.8 shows a DTD for a simple list of people.

Listing 22.8 Source Code for `people.dtd`

```
<!ELEMENT people (person*)>
<!ELEMENT person (first-name? | middle-name? | last-name?)+>
!ELEMENT first-name (#PCDATA)>
<!ELEMENT middle-name (#PCDATA)>
<!ELEMENT last-name (#PCDATA)>
```

Listing 22.9 shows a sample XML input file using the DTD defined in Listing 22.8.

Listing 22.9 Source Code for `people.xml`

```
<?xml version="1.0"?>
<!DOCTYPE people SYSTEM "people.dtd">

<people>
    <person>
        <first-name>Samantha</first-name>
        <middle-name>Lauren</middle-name>
        <last-name>Tippin</last-name>
    </person>
    <person>
        <first-name>Kaitlynn</first-name>
        <middle-name>Dawn</middle-name>
        <last-name>Tippin</last-name>
```

```
    </person>
    <person>
        <first-name>Edward</first-name>
        <middle-name>Alexander</middle-name>
        <last-name>Wutka</last-name>
    </person>
    <person>
        <first-name>Norton</first-name>
        <middle-name>Alexander</middle-name>
        <last-name>Wutka</last-name>
    </person>
</people>
```

Listing 22.10 shows you a program that uses DOM to navigate through a document containing people using the DTD defined in Listing 22.8.

LISTING 22.10 SOURCE CODE FOR `ListPeopleDOM.java`

```
package usingj2ee.xml;

import java.io.*;
import javax.xml.parsers.*;
import org.xml.sax.*;
import org.w3c.dom.*;

public class ListPeopleDOM
{
    public static void main(String[] args)
    {
        try
        {

// Locate the document builder factory
            DocumentBuilderFactory factory =
                DocumentBuilderFactory.newInstance();

// Tell the document builder to create a validating
// parser (one that checks to make sure
// the document is valid)
            factory.setValidating(true);

// Ask the factory to create a document builder
            DocumentBuilder builder = factory.newDocumentBuilder();

// By default, try to parse the file "people.xml"
            String filename = "people.xml";

// If the user specifies a filename on the command line, use it instead
            if (args.length > 0)
            {
                filename = args[0];
            }

// Ask the document builder to parse the file
            Document doc = builder.parse(new File(filename));

// Get the root element
```

LISTING 22.10 CONTINUED

```
            Element peopleElement = doc.getDocumentElement();

// Get the people from the element
            NodeList peopleList = peopleElement.getChildNodes();

            for (int i=0; i < peopleList.getLength(); i++)
            {
                Node item = peopleList.item(i);

// Skip the items that aren't elements
                if (item.getNodeType() != Node.ELEMENT_NODE) continue;

                Element person = (Element) item;

// Get a list of all the first names, but only print the first one
                NodeList firstNames = person.getElementsByTagName(
                    "first-name");

                if (firstNames.getLength() > 0)
                {
                    System.out.print(getElementText(
                        (Element) firstNames.item(0)));
                    System.out.print(' ');
                }

// Get a list of all the middle names, but only print the first one
                NodeList middleNames = person.getElementsByTagName(
                    "middle-name");

                if (middleNames.getLength() > 0)
                {
                    System.out.print(getElementText(
                        (Element) middleNames.item(0)));
                    System.out.print(' ');
                }

// Get a list of all the last names, but only print the first one
                NodeList lastNames = person.getElementsByTagName(
                    "last-name");

                if (lastNames.getLength() > 0)
                {
                    System.out.print(getElementText(
                        (Element) lastNames.item(0)));
                    System.out.print(' ');
                }
                System.out.println();
            }
        }
        catch (Exception exc)
        {
            exc.printStackTrace();
        }
    }
```

```
/** Retrieves all the text items below an element as a single string */
    public static String getElementText(Element elem)
    {
        StringBuffer buff = new StringBuffer();

// Get the element's children
        NodeList list = elem.getChildNodes();

        for (int i=0; i < list.getLength(); i++)
        {
            Node item = list.item(i);

// If the child is a text item, add its data to the buffer
            if (item instanceof Text)
            {
                Text charItem = (Text) item;

                buff.append(charItem.getData());
            }
        }
        return buff.toString();
    }
}
```

Note

Notice that the program in Listing 22.10 intentionally ignores extra names. Because a DTD can't always specify an exact number of allowable elements, you often must make these corrections in your program.

USING A SAX PARSER

The Simple API for XML (SAX) is, as its name implies, simple. To be more specific, SAX is lightweight and fast. The API itself is simple in that it doesn't have as many classes as DOM. Where SAX is not so simple is in its day-to-day usage. When you try to parse even a simple data structure with SAX, you begin to realize the complexity of parsing a nested data structure with an event-driven parser.

To parse a document with SAX, you must create an event handler that listens to the parsing events that the SAX parser fires. Some example parsing events are `startElement`, `endElement`, and `characters`. The parser generates quite a few different events, but you don't have to handle them all. When you create your event handler, just subclass the `DefaultHandler` class. It has default implementations for all the SAX events.

You must also create an instance of `SAXParser` in much the same way that you create a `DocumentBuilder` when you use DOM.

Listing 22.11 shows an example SAX program that reads through the same kind of XML document as the DOM program in Listing 22.10.

LISTING 22.11 SOURCE CODE FOR ListPeopleSAX.java

```
package usingj2ee.xml;

import java.io.*;
import javax.xml.parsers.*;
import org.xml.sax.*;
import org.xml.sax.helpers.*;
import org.w3c.dom.*;

public class ListPeopleSAX extends DefaultHandler
{
    protected static boolean parsingFirstName;
    protected static StringBuffer currFirstName;

    protected static boolean parsingMiddleName;
    protected static StringBuffer currMiddleName;

    protected static boolean parsingLastName;
    protected static StringBuffer currLastName;

    public static void main(String[] args)
    {
        try
        {
// Locate the parser factory
            SAXParserFactory factory = SAXParserFactory.newInstance();

// Tell the parser factory to create a validating parser (one that checks
// to make sure the document is valid)
            factory.setValidating(true);

// Ask the factory to create a SAX parser
            SAXParser builder = factory.newSAXParser();

// By default, try to parse the file "people.xml"
            String filename = "people.xml";

// If the user specifies a filename on the command line, use it instead
            if (args.length > 0)
            {
                filename = args[0];
            }

            DefaultHandler eventHandler = new ListPeopleSAX();

// Ask the parser to parse the file
            builder.parse(new File(filename), eventHandler);
        }
        catch (Exception exc)
        {
            exc.printStackTrace();
        }
    }

    public void startElement(String namespaceURI, String localName,
        String qualifiedName, Attributes attributes)
```

```
    {
// If this is the start of a person element, clear out all the name
// buffers
        if (localName.equals("person"))
        {
            currFirstName = null;
            currMiddleName = null;
            currLastName = null;
        }

// If this is the start of a first name, create a new name buffer
        else if (localName.equals("first-name"))
        {
            parsingFirstName = true;
            currFirstName = new StringBuffer();
        }

// If this is the start of a middle name, create a new name buffer
        else if (localName.equals("middle-name"))
        {
            parsingMiddleName = true;
            currMiddleName = new StringBuffer();
        }

// If this is the start of a last name, create a new name buffer
        else
        if (localName.equals("last-name"))
        {
            parsingLastName = true;
            currLastName = new StringBuffer();
        }
    }

    public void characters(char[] chars, int start, int length)
    {
// See if the characters should be appended to one of the name buffers
        if (parsingFirstName)
        {
            currFirstName.append(chars, start, length);
        }
        else if (parsingMiddleName)
        {
            currMiddleName.append(chars, start, length);
        }
        else if (parsingLastName)
        {
            currLastName.append(chars, start, length);
        }
    }

    public void endElement(String namespaceURI, String localName,
        String qualifiedName)
    {
// If this is the end of the person element, print out the names
        if (localName.equals("person"))
        {
            if (currFirstName != null)
```

LISTING 22.11 CONTINUED

```
                {
                    System.out.print(currFirstName.toString());
                    System.out.print(" ");
                }
                if (currMiddleName != null)
                {
                    System.out.print(currMiddleName.toString());
                    System.out.print(" ");
                }
                if (currLastName != null)
                {
                    System.out.print(currLastName.toString());
                }
                System.out.println();
            }
// Otherwise, if this is the end of one of the names, indicate that
// the program is no longer parsing a name
            else if (localName.equals("first-name"))
            {
                parsingFirstName = false;
            }
            else if (localName.equals("middle-name"))
            {
                parsingMiddleName = false;
            }
            else if (localName.equals("last-name"))
            {
                parsingLastName = false;
            }
        }
}
```

As you can see, SAX is easy to use. You just handle the tags as they come along. Although SAX may seem simple, it is still incredibly powerful. In fact, many other XML APIs use SAX as their basic XML parser.

When you process a reasonably shallow XML document like the one in Listing 22.9, SAX is a good choice. In fact, SAX is probably as easy to use as DOM in these situations. For more complex documents, however, you must do more work to keep track of where you are in the document. If you need to build your own model of the data, SAX is probably a better choice than DOM. After all, why build a DOM version of the data if you still need to create your own model? If, on the other hand, you're happy with DOM's representation of the data, you might want to skip SAX and use DOM.

The biggest knock against DOM is that it can be slow for large documents, whereas SAX handles large documents easily.

TROUBLESHOOTING

USING SUN'S XML LIBRARIES

Why can't the Java compiler find the XML libraries?

Make sure that `jaxp.jar` is in your classpath.

My program compiles okay; why does it tell me it can't find the parser library?

The parser library is in `jaxp.jar`, but the parser implementation is in a separate `JAR` file. Depending on the release of the parser, the file may be called `parser.jar` or `crimson.jar`. You can also use the Xerces parser from Apache with Sun's libraries.

DOM PROBLEMS

Why do I keep getting `ClassCastException` when I loop through the children of an element?

The `NodeList` class is a list of node objects, and even though you might expect all the nodes to be one particular type (like `Element`), it's possible that there are other nodes. Specifically, `Comment` objects might pop up or even the occasional `Text` object. Make sure you check the type of the node before trying to cast it to another type.

CHAPTER 23

Using XSL to Translate XML Documents

In this chapter

What Is XSL?

Although XML has been gathering heaps of praise as the next "big thing," the Extensible Style Language (XSL) has been lurking quietly, waiting to be noticed. XSL is a language for translating XML from one format into another. For example, you might have a set of XML elements that describe a person (`<firstName>`, `<lastName>`, and so on) and you want to represent those elements with HTML. You can create a style sheet to tell the XSL processor how to translate the person XML into HTML.

There are actually two distinctly different kinds of XSL. The XSL Transformation Language is the kind of XSL discussed in this chapter. You will often see the XSL Transformation Language referred to as XSLT. There is also an XSL formatting language called XSLFO (XSL Formatting Objects) that is more of a layout language, such as HTML with cascading style sheets (CSS). This chapter does not address the XSL formatting language at all. The idea is that presenting an XML document involves two steps: You transform the document into a structure that the user can understand and then format the elements into a form that's more user-friendly.

You can read the specification for both XSLT and XSLFO in the XSL Specification at `http://www.w3.org/TR/xsl/`.

In some ways, XSL looks like a competitor to Java Server Pages. XSL can process data in XML form and render a Web page. Many people tout XSL as the solution for creating Web applications and wireless Web applications using the same set of data. You just write two style sheets, one to generate HTML and one to generate WML. Where you normally write a Java Server Page to fetch data and render it, you could write an XSL style sheet to take XML data and render it. Of course, XSL can't fetch the data like JSP can; it's not that powerful.

As you will see, however, XSL isn't really a competitor to JSP. Instead, it complements JSP and servlets nicely by giving you a template language for formatting XML. As you will soon see, XSL isn't the prettiest language in the world. It isn't easy to read and is frequently difficult to write. There are cases where you would be better off using Java Server Pages to format your data. Still, adding XSL to your toolchest is a wise decision.

A Simple XSL Style Sheet

The best way to get a feel for how XSL style sheets work is to see one in action. Listing 23.1 shows an XML file describing two people. Notice the `<?xml-stylesheet?>` processing instruction that specifies the name of the XSL style sheet that accompanies this XML file.

Listing 23.1 Source Code for `Person.xml`

```
<?xml version="1.0"?>
<?xml-stylesheet type="text/xsl" href="PersonToHTML.xsl"?>
<people>
    <person>
```

```
        <firstName>Samantha</firstName>
        <middleName>Lauren</middleName>
        <lastName>Tippin</lastName>
        <age>7</age>
    </person>
    <person>
        <firstName>Kaitlynn</firstName>
        <middleName>Dawn</middleName>
        <lastName>Tippin</lastName>
        <age>4</age>
    </person>
</people>
```


Listing 23.2 shows the `PersonToHTML.xsl` style sheet that translates the XML definitions into HTML.

LISTING 23.2 SOURCE CODE FOR PersonToHTML.xsl

```
<?xml version="1.0"?>
<xsl:stylesheet
    xmlns:xsl="http://www.w3.org/1999/XSL/Transform"
    version="1.0">

    <xsl:template match="people">
        <html>
        <body bgcolor="#ffffff">
        <table border="4">
            <tr><th>First Name</th><th>Middle Name</th><th>Last Name</th>
            <th>Age</th></tr>

        <xsl:apply-templates/>

        </table>
        </body>
        </html>
    </xsl:template>

    <xsl:template match="person">
        <tr>
            <td>
                <xsl:value-of select="firstName"/>
            </td>
            <td>
                <xsl:value-of select="middleName"/>
            </td>
            <td>
                <xsl:value-of select="lastName"/>
            </td>
            <td>
                <xsl:value-of select="age"/>
            </td>
        </tr>
    </xsl:template>
</xsl:stylesheet>
```

XSL might look a little odd at first, but it's really not so bad after you get used to it. Because an XSL style sheet is a value XML document, it must start with the `<?xml?>` XML declaration. The root element for an XSL style sheet is `xsl:stylesheet`, which includes a reference to the XSL namespace (the `xmlns:xsl=...`).

Probably the most common XSL element you'll see is `xsl:template`.

In an XSL style sheet, you set up template rules that match various XML elements. For instance, `<xsl:template match="people"/>` defines the actions the XSL processor should take when it encounters a `<people>` element. A template rule consists of two parts: the pattern and the template. When the XSLT processor finds a rule that matches a particular element, it spits out the template. The template can contain other rules that apply to the current element's content, and also elements that aren't XSL elements at all. The XSLT processor simply adds the non-XSL elements to the output stream without modifying them.

In Listing 23.2, the action for the `<people>` element type is to set up the beginning of the HTML document by outputting the `<html>` and `<body>` tags and then outputting HTML tags that begin a table.

The `xsl:apply-templates` element tells the XSL processor to look for templates that apply to elements within the body of the `people` element. In other words, look at all the child elements of `people` and see whether there is an `xsl:template` element defined for any of them. If so, apply the template and insert the output right here. After the `xsl:apply-templates` element, you see that the template closes off the table, the body, and the HTML page. The remaining template rule defines the actions for `person` elements.

> **Note**
>
> **Keep in mind that although a template can match multiple items in the XML file, the XSL processor executes the template once for each match. You don't need to worry about what happens if there are multiple matches.**

The second template rule in the style sheet makes use of another handy element: `xsl:value-of`.

The template rule for the `person` element starts a row in the HTML table, and then creates `<td>` tags for each of the four child elements defined by *`person.xml`* (first name, middle name, last name, and age). The `xsl:value-of` element lets you insert the text from a child element into the current output.

Listing 23.3 shows the HTML output from the combination of the `Person.xml` data file and the `PersonToHTML.xsl` style sheet.

LISTING 23.3 HTML OUTPUT FROM `PersonToHTML` STYLE SHEET

```
!DOCTYPE html PUBLIC '-//W3C/DTD HTML 4.0 Frameset//EN'
    'http://www.w3c.org/TR/REC-html40/frameset.dtd'>
<html>
  <body bgcolor="#ffffff">
    <table border="4">
```

```
        <tr>
          <th>First Name</th>
          <th>Middle Name</th>
          <th>Last Name</th>
          <th>Age</th>
        </tr>
      <tr>
          <td>Samantha</td>
          <td>Lauren</td>
          <td>Tippin</td>
          <td>7</td>
        </tr>
      <tr>
          <td>Kaitlynn</td>
          <td>Dawn</td>
          <td>Tippin</td>
          <td>4</td>
        </tr>
  </table>
    </body>
  </html>
```


Figure 23.1 shows the page as displayed by the browser.

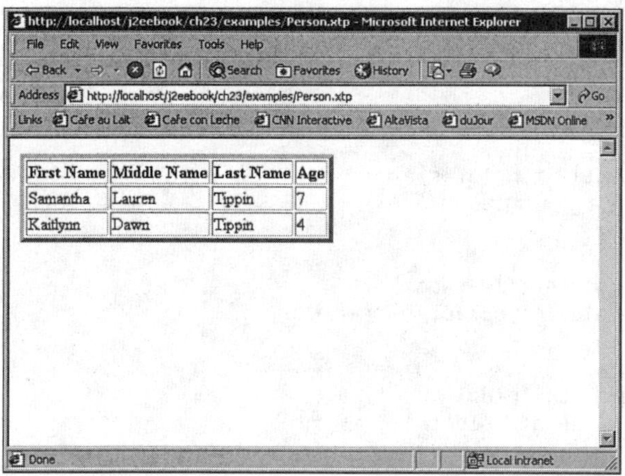

Figure 23.1 You can generate HTML from an XSL style sheet.

Note The Resin Web Server from `http://www.caucho.com` has a built-in XSL style sheet processor that makes it easy to add XSL to your existing JSP/Servlet applications. To run the XSL processor, just rename your `.xml` files to `.xtp`. For example, to view the `Person.xml` file, just rename it `Person.xtp`.

Rather than using `<xsl:value-of>` to extract values from child elements, you can set up additional `<xsl:template>` elements. When you want to insert the value of the current element into the output, use `<xsl:value-of select="."/>`. The "." value in the `select` attribute means "the value of the current node." It's similar to the way "." means the current directory when you're working with a file system.

Listing 23.4 shows an alternate version of `PersonToHTML.xsl` that displays the output in exactly the same format, but matches the children of `<person>` with separate template rules. When you specify multiple template rules this way, the XSLT processor must check each template rule against the current element to see if there's a match. The more template rules you create, the more work the XSLT processor must do—making it run slower.

LISTING 23.4 SOURCE CODE FOR `PersonToHTML2.xsl`

```
<?xml version="1.0"?>
<xsl:stylesheet
    xmlns:xsl="http://www.w3.org/1999/XSL/Transform"
    version="1.0">

    <xsl:template match="people">
        <html>
        <body bgcolor="#ffffff">
        <table border="4">
            <tr><th>First Name</th><th>Middle Name</th><th>Last Name</th>
            <th>Age</th></tr>

        <xsl:apply-templates/>

        </table>
        </body>
        </html>
    </xsl:template>

    <xsl:template match="person">
        <tr>
            <xsl:apply-templates/>
        </tr>
    </xsl:template>

    <xsl:template match="firstName">
        <td><xsl:value-of select="."/></td>
    </xsl:template>

    <xsl:template match="middleName">
        <td><xsl:value-of select="."/></td>
    </xsl:template>

    <xsl:template match="lastName">
        <td><xsl:value-of select="."/></td>
    </xsl:template>

    <xsl:template match="age">
        <td><xsl:value-of select="."/></td>
    </xsl:template>

</xsl:stylesheet>
```

Using a Standalone XSL Processor

Using a standalone XSL processor is as easy as running a Java compiler. You just need to download an XSL processor. The Saxon XSL processor is fast and easy to use. It also has a special Windows-only executable version so you can get going quickly. You can get Saxon at `http://users.iclway.co.uk/mhkay/saxon`. If you're running windows, try instant-saxon. Unpack a `ZIP` file to get to the `saxon.exe` file, and then just type the following:

```
saxon yourXMLfile.xml yourstylesheet.xsl
```


You can also use the Apache Xalan XSL processor (available at `http://xml.apache.org`) as a standalone processor. After you unpack Xalan, make sure the Xalan `JAR` file is in your classpath and then type this:

```
java org.apache.xalan.xslt.Process -IN yourXMLfile.XML -XSL
➥yourXSLfile.XSL
➥-OUT theoutputfile
```

Note

> You might also want to look at the XSL Debugger at `http://www.xsldebugger.com`. The XSLT Test tool at `http://www.netcrucible.com/xslt/xslt-tool.htm` is also useful.

Applying XSL Templates on the Browser

Internet Explorer 5 has a built-in XSL processor that can apply templates on the client side. This gives you a lot of flexibility because you can generate XML from a Java Server Page and have the browser apply the style sheet to the XML. You must modify the XML file to explicitly embed the style sheet, however. That is, the XML file must use the `xsl-stylesheet` processing directive to tell the browser which style sheet to use.

The advantage of processing the style sheet on the browser is that you have much more flexibility on your server, and the server isn't bogged down processing style sheets for every user. The main disadvantage is that Internet Explorer 5 is the only browser as of December, 2000 that supports XSL. If your application must support general Web users, you'll still need to apply the style sheet on the server.

Applying XSL Templates from a Servlet

XSL becomes a powerful tool when you combine it with the power of servlets and Java Server Pages. You can create XML documents within your server-side Java code and use a style sheet to format the XML into something the client understands.

To apply an XSL style sheet to an XML document from a servlet or JSP, you must have an XSL processor installed in your servlet engine's classpath. The Apache Group's Xalan XSL processor (`http://xml.apache.org`) is an excellent XSL processor and works well in a servlet environment. IBM's LotusXSL processor, available from `http://www.alphaworks.ibm.com`, is also good.

Listing 23.5 shows a servlet that takes an XML document or a filename from the `request` object along with a style sheet filename and applies a style sheet to the document. As an added bonus, it checks to see if the request came from a wireless application and, if so, it applies a different style sheet. The servlet assumes that the HTML style sheets are in a subdirectory named `html` and the wireless WML style sheets are in a subdirectory named `wml`.

→ For more information on Wireless Web applications, **see** Chapter 53, "Creating a Wireless Web Application."

LISTING 23.5 SOURCE CODE FOR `XSLServlet.java`

```
package usingj2ee.xsl;

import java.io.*;

import javax.servlet.*;
import javax.servlet.http.*;

import org.apache.xalan.xslt.*;
import org.w3c.dom.*;
import org.xml.sax.*;

public class XSLServlet extends HttpServlet
{
    public void service(HttpServletRequest request,
        HttpServletResponse response)
        throws IOException, ServletException
    {

// Get the XML source passed in the request
        Object source = request.getAttribute("source");

        XSLTInputSource xmlSource = null;

// See if the source is an XML document
        if (source instanceof Document)
        {
            xmlSource = new XSLTInputSource((Document) source);
        }
// Otherwise see if it is a file or a filename
        else if ((source instanceof File) || (source instanceof String))
        {
            if (source instanceof File)
            {
                xmlSource = new XSLTInputSource(
                    new FileReader((File) source));
            }
            else
            {
                xmlSource = new XSLTInputSource(
                    new FileReader((String) source));
            }
        }

// Get the URL for the style sheet (assume for now that it's local)
        String stylesheet = (String) request.getAttribute("stylesheet");
```

```
        String stylesheetPath = null;

// If the request came from a wireless application, pull the style sheet
// from the wml directory, otherwise use the html directory
        if (isWML(request))
        {
            stylesheetPath = "wml"+File.separator+stylesheet;
            response.setContentType("text/vnd.wap.wml");
        }
        else
        {
            stylesheetPath = "html"+File.separator+stylesheet;
            response.setContentType("text/html");
        }

// Create an input source for reading the style sheet (use the servlet
// context to get an input stream for the style sheet)

        XSLTInputSource stylesheetSource = new XSLTInputSource(
            getServletContext().getResourceAsStream(stylesheetPath));


// Create a result target that writes to the servlet's output stream
        XSLTResultTarget target = new
➥       XSLTResultTarget(response.getWriter());

// Create an XSL processor and process the XML source and the style sheet
        try
        {
            XSLTProcessor processor = XSLTProcessorFactory.getProcessor();

            processor.process(xmlSource, stylesheetSource, target);
        }
        catch (SAXException exc)
        {
            throw new ServletException(exc);
        }
    }

    public static boolean isWML(HttpServletRequest request)
    {
// Checks to see if the request came from a wireless app
        String accept = request.getHeader("Accept");
        if (accept == null) return false;

        if (accept.indexOf("text/vnd.wap.wml") >= 0)
        {
            return true;
        }

        return false;
    }
}
```

Listing 23.6 shows a Java server page that creates an XML document on-the-fly and then passes it to the XSL servlet using the `<jsp:forward>` tag.

LISTING 23.6 SOURCE CODE FOR TestXSL.jsp

```
<%@ page import="org.w3c.dom.*,org.apache.xerces.dom.*" %>
<%

/* The following statement creating a Document object is not
 * part of the standard DOM API. To pass a Document
 * object to the Xalan style sheet processor, the Document must
 * be from the Xerces (Apache's XML parser) implementation.
 * If you have the Sun XMl parser installed, which you need for
 * Tomcat, you won't be able to create a Document object that
 * Xalan understands.
 */
    Document doc = new DocumentImpl();

// Create the root element
    Element root = doc.createElement("mainpage");

    doc.appendChild(root);

// Create the greeting
    Element greeting = doc.createElement("greeting");

    greeting.appendChild(doc.createTextNode("Welcome to the Demo!"));

    root.appendChild(greeting);

// Create the main menu
    Element menu = doc.createElement("menu");

    Element menuItem1 = doc.createElement("item");
    menuItem1.setAttribute("name", "Products");
    menuItem1.setAttribute("link", "products.jsp");
    menu.appendChild(menuItem1);

    Element menuItem2 = doc.createElement("item");
    menuItem2.setAttribute("name", "Services");
    menuItem2.setAttribute("link", "service.jsp");
    menu.appendChild(menuItem2);

    Element menuItem3 = doc.createElement("item");
    menuItem3.setAttribute("name", "Support");
    menuItem3.setAttribute("link", "support.jsp");
    menu.appendChild(menuItem3);

    root.appendChild(menu);

    request.setAttribute("source", doc);
    request.setAttribute("stylesheet", "mainpage.xsl");
%><jsp:forward page="XSLServlet"/>
```

The JSP in Listing 23.8 creates an XML document that would look like this if written to a file:

```
<mainpage>
    <greeting>Welcome to the Demo!</greeting>
```

```
    <menu>
        <item name="Products" link="products.jsp"/>
        <item name="Services" link="services.jsp"/>
        <item name="Support" link="support.jsp"/>
    </menu>
</mainpage>
```

By using style sheets, you can display this XML any number of ways. Listing 23.7 shows a style sheet that converts the XML document into an HTML document.

Listing 23.7 Source Code for an HTML Version of `mainpage.xsl`

```
<?xml version="1.0"?>
<xsl:stylesheet
    xmlns:xsl="http://www.w3.org/1999/XSL/Transform"
    version="1.0">

    <xsl:template match="/">
        <xsl:apply-templates/>
    </xsl:template>

    <xsl:template match="mainpage">
        <html>
        <body bgcolor="#ffffff">
            <xsl:apply-templates/>
        </body>
        </html>
    </xsl:template>

    <xsl:template match="greeting">
        <h1><xsl:value-of select="."/></h1>
        <p></p>
    </xsl:template>

    <xsl:template match="menu">
        <p>Please choose from the following menu options:</p>
        <bl>
            <xsl:apply-templates/>
        </bl>
    </xsl:template>

    <xsl:template match="item">
        <li><a>
            <xsl:attribute name="href">
                <xsl:value-of select="@link"/>
            </xsl:attribute>
            <xsl:value-of select="@name"/>
            </a></li>
    </xsl:template>
</xsl:stylesheet>
```

Figure 23.2 shows the output of XSLServlet when it applies the style sheet to the XML document for HTML output.

Figure 23.2
You can use an XSL style sheet from a servlet to generate HTML.

Listing 23.8 shows a style sheet that formats the same XML document as the style sheet in Listing 23.7, only the target format is WML—the markup language for wireless Web applications.

Listing 23.8 Source Code for a WML Version of mainpage.xsl

```
<?xml version="1.0"?>
<xsl:stylesheet
    xmlns:xsl="http://www.w3.org/1999/XSL/Transform"
    version="1.0">

    <xsl:output doctype-public="-//WAPFORUM//DTD WML 1.1//EN"
        doctype-system="http://www.wapforum.org/DTD/wml_1.1.xml"/>

    <xsl:template match="/">
        <xsl:apply-templates/>
    </xsl:template>

    <xsl:template match="mainpage">
        <wml>
        <card id="mainpage">
            <xsl:apply-templates/>
        </card>
        </wml>
    </xsl:template>

    <xsl:template match="greeting">
        <p><xsl:value-of select="."/></p>
    </xsl:template>

    <xsl:template match="menu">
            <p>
            <xsl:apply-templates/>
            </p>
    </xsl:template>

    <xsl:template match="item">
        <a>
            <xsl:attribute name="href">
```

```
                <xsl:value-of select="@link"/>
            </xsl:attribute>
            <xsl:attribute name="title">
                <xsl:value-of select="@name"/>
            </xsl:attribute>
            <xsl:value-of select="@name"/>
            </a>
    </xsl:template>
</xsl:stylesheet>
```


NAVIGATING AN XML DOCUMENT WITH XPATH

The XPath standard defines how you refer to an element in an XML document. XPath is basically a query mechanism that lets you identify nodes based on a certain pattern. The pattern can be the node's value, its children, its attributes, and even its relationship to other nodes. For example, you've already seen XSL template rules that use `/` to match the root element and `.` to match the current element. These are both XPath expressions.

For example, if you want to refer to the `firstName` element that is a child of the `person` element, you can use the XPath expression `person/firstName`. In some ways, it is similar to the convention you use for naming files. XPath is more than just a naming standard, however; it is used for pattern matching. You use XPath expressions in the `match` attribute of the `xsl:template` element. So far, all you have seen are element names for the match target, but you can look for far more interesting items.

Suppose you have several elements in your document that have a child node of `name`. If you want to handle the `name` element differently depending on its parent element, you must use an XPath expression to match the name. For example, to create a template that matches only `name` elements that are children of `company` elements, you would use the following `xsl:template` element:

```
<xsl:template match="company/name"/>
```

You can also use `*` to match all children. For example, in listing 23.4, there are templates to match each child node of `<person>`, but the templates are doing the same thing. You can reduce the four separate templates to a single template by specifying `match="person/*"`, as shown in listing 23.9.

LISTING 23.9 SOURCE CODE FOR PersonToHTML3.xsl

```
<?xml version="1.0"?>
<xsl:stylesheet
    xmlns:xsl="http://www.w3.org/1999/XSL/Transform"
    version="1.0">

    <xsl:template match="people">
        <html>
        <body bgcolor="#ffffff">
        <table border="4">
            <tr><th>First Name</th><th>Middle Name</th><th>Last Name</th>
            <th>Age</th></tr>
```

LISTING 23.9 CONTINUED

```
        <xsl:apply-templates/>

        </table>
        </body>
        </html>
    </xsl:template>

    <xsl:template match="person">
        <tr>
            <xsl:apply-templates/>
        </tr>
    </xsl:template>

    <xsl:template match="person/*">
        <td><xsl:value-of select="."/></td>
    </xsl:template>
</xsl:stylesheet>
```

XPath has two types of syntax representation: abbreviated and unabbreviated. The syntax you have seen so far is abbreviated.

In the unabbreviated form, an XPath expression contains an axis expression, a node test, and a predicate. An axis points to the part of the tree you want. To understand the axis, you should also understand that XPath has the notion of a context node—the current node that you're processing. An *axis* is a collection of elements that may have some relationship to the context node. For example, the `child` axis contains all immediate children of the context node, whereas the `descendant` axis contains *all* children of the context node regardless of their depth (that is, all children, grandchildren, greatgrandchildren, and so on). Given an axis, you can then specify a *node test*—a matching pattern for a node within an axis. For example, `child::firstName` selects all elements that are children of the context node.

The predicate portion of the path lets you specify additional matching parameters for the node. For example, a predicate of `[5]` selects the fifth node in the axis. `Child::firstName[5]` selects the fifth `firstName` element that is a child of the current node. You can create combinations of axes and nodes using `::` to separate the axes.

The unabbreviated syntax for matching an element named `person` is `match="person"`. The syntax for matching all children of the `<person>` node is `match="person/child::*"`.

Listing 23.10 shows the unabbreviated version of `PersonToHTML.xsl`.

LISTING 23.10 SOURCE CODE FOR `PersonToHTML4.xsl`

```
<?xml version="1.0"?>
<xsl:stylesheet
    xmlns:xsl="http://www.w3.org/1999/XSL/Transform"
    version="1.0">

    <xsl:template match="people">
```

```
        <html>
        <body bgcolor="#ffffff">
        <table border="4">
            <tr><th>First Name</th><th>Middle Name</th><th>Last Name</th>
            <th>Age</th></tr>

        <xsl:apply-templates/>

        </table>
        </body>
        </html>
    </xsl:template>

    <xsl:template match="person">
        <tr>
            <xsl:apply-templates/>
        </tr>
    </xsl:template>

    <xsl:template match="person/child::*">
        <td><xsl:value-of select="self"/></td>
    </xsl:template>

</xsl:stylesheet>
```


Table 23.1 shows the abbreviated and unabbreviated XPath syntax for various common patterns that you might want to use.

TABLE 23.1 ABBREVIATED AND UNABBREVIATED SYNTAX EXAMPLES FOR XPATH

Abbreviated	Unabbreviated	Description
`elem`	`child::elem`	Selects all children of current node named `elem`
`*`	`child::*`	Selects all children of current node
`text()`	`child::text()`	Selects all text nodes that are children of the current node
`@attr`	`attribute::attr`	Selects attribute named `attr` from current node
`@*`	`attribute::*`	Selects all attributes from the current node
`elem[1]`	`child::elem[position()=1]`	Selects first child of current node named `elem`
`*/elem`	`child::*/child::elem`	Selects all grandchildren of the current node named `elem`
`elem[@attr="foo"]`	`child::elem[attribute::attr="foo"]`	Selects all children of the current node whose `attr` attribute has the value of `"foo"`

TABLE 23.1 CONTINUED

Abbreviated	Unabbreviated	Description
`elem[something]`	`child::elem[child::something]`	Selects all children named `elem` that have children named `something`
`elem[foo or bar]`	`child::elem[child::foo or child::bar]`	Selects all children named `elem` that have children named either `foo` or `bar`

JSP or Style Sheets?

There is some overlap between the features of Java Server Pages and XSL style sheets. You might be wondering how to decide which one to use.

XSL works best when you already have XML files, or when you generate an XML document as part of your normal processing. There are now applications that can query a database and return an XML document representing the data. XSL is ideal for formatting these documents.

JSP is better when you are working with pure Java objects, which is probably what you'll be using most of the time. Even if you read in XML data, if you do any processing on it, you'll likely be converting the XML into a Java object and then invoking methods on the Java object. If you have Java objects and want to use XSL style sheets, you must first take the extra step of representing your Java objects as XML documents, which is not a pleasant task.

Troubleshooting

Translator Problems

Why won't Resin apply my XSL style sheet to my XML file?

Resin doesn't realize it needs to run the XSL processor unless you change the extension to `.xtp`.

Why doesn't the XSL processor process elements contained within one of the elements I defined in my style sheet?

You probably forgot the `xsl:apply-templates` element.

Why doesn't the XSL processor do anything with my XML file?

Some XSL processors, notably IE, require you to specify a rule for `/` to match the document itself.

CHAPTER 24

Using Java-XML Tools

In this chapter

THE NEED FOR ADDITIONAL TOOLS

So far, you can read and write XML files and use XSL to translate an XML file from one form to another. You can go a long way with just these capabilities, but there are many more tools out there that solve common problems as well. Tools that automatically copy data from Java objects to XML and from XML to Java are extremely useful. DOM might give you a representation of the data in the XML file, but as a developer, you're better off working with objects that represent the data. In other words, it's better to work with a `Person` object than it is to work with a DOM `Element` whose tag name is `Person`.

There are two basic philosophies when it comes to automatically translating between XML and Java, and the difference is in the style of the XML. One approach uses XML tags that describe a Java object (`<class>`, `<field>`, `<bean>`, and so on). The other approach uses any kind of XML document and uses various techniques to map the XML to one or more Java classes.

There are advantages and disadvantages with each approach. If you use Java-specific XML tags, you can write out just about any Java object you can think of. Even better, you don't need to define a specific mapping, as you do when your XML isn't Java-specific. This approach essentially gives you Java object serialization, but to a human-readable file instead of the binary format Java uses. It also reduces the impact of changes that normally plague applications that rely on object serialization.

The Koala Bean Markup Language (KBML) uses Java-specific tags when reading and writing data. You can read and write just about any Java object you can think of. KBML makes a great alternative to Java's built-in serialization and is easy to use. The obvious disadvantage to the Java-specific XML tags is that you can't just accept anyone else's XML file. It is unlikely that you'll find someone else willing to use the Java-specific tags, especially if they aren't using Java.

When you try to map any kind of XML document to one or more Java classes, you encounter an interesting problem: For a given XML element, what Java class or field should contain the value in that element? For example, if you have a `person` element, how does your program know to use the `Person` object? There are several approaches to this problem. The JOX (Java Objects in XML) library uses a combination of relaxed name matching and bean properties to make reasonable guesses. The Quick library uses a special markup language that explicitly maps attributes and elements to Java classes and fields. Each of these approaches has advantages and disadvantages.

For JOX, the advantage is simplicity. You don't need to create any additional definition files, although you can supply a DTD when JOX writes out an object to tell it what element names are valid. The big disadvantages with JOX are that it only works with beans (specifically bean properties), and the names of the bean properties must at least loosely match the XML element names.

Quick, on the other hand, requires that you create a separate schema file that describes how each XML element maps to Java and vice-versa. Although it is still easy to use, it takes a little more time to set up than JOX. Of course, Quick works with any Java field and can handle many types of data structures that JOX can't.

The important thing to remember is that you don't have to stick with one solution. If KBML (Koala Bean Markup Language) fits your needs for one project, but Quick works for another, use them both.

Note

The combination of XML and Java has been a hot topic and there are plenty of other projects that combine Java and XML for easy data storage. Sun has two projects in the works. Project Adelard specifies a Java-XML data binding providing the same capabilities as JOX and Quick. The Long Term JavaBeans Persistence project is defining an XML version of Java Object serialization. The Castor project at `http://www.exolab.org` also provides a nice Java-XML data binding library.

THE EXAMPLE XML AND JAVA BEAN FILES

Assume you have an XML file that looks like the one shown in Listing 24.1.

LISTING 24.1 SOURCE CODE FOR `people.dtd`

```
<!ELEMENT people (person*)>

<!ELEMENT person (first-name|middle-name|last-name)+>

<!ELEMENT first-name (#PCDATA)>
<!ELEMENT middle-name (#PCDATA)>
<!ELEMENT last-name (#PCDATA)>
```

Furthermore, you have two Java bean classes, `People` and `Person`, shown in Listings 24.2 and 24.3.

LISTING 24.2 SOURCE CODE FOR `People.java`

```
package usingj2ee.xml;

import java.util.Vector;

public class People implements java.io.Serializable
{

    protected Vector personVec;

    public People()
    {
        personVec = new Vector();
    }

    public Person[] getPerson()
    {
        Person[] retval = new Person[personVec.size()];
```

LISTING 24.2 CONTINUED

```
        personVec.copyInto(retval);
        return retval;
    }

    public void setPerson(Person[] values)
    {
        personVec = new Vector(values.length);
        for (int i=0; i < values.length; i++)
        {
            personVec.addElement(values[i]);
        }
    }

    public Person getPerson(int i)
    {
        return (Person) personVec.elementAt(i);
    }

    public void setPerson(int i, Person value)
    {
        personVec.setElementAt(value, i);
    }

    public static People createDefault()
    {
        People people = new People();

        Person[] persons = new Person[4];

        persons[0] = new Person("Samantha", "Lauren", "Tippen");
        persons[1] = new Person("Kaitlynn", "Dawn", "Tippen");
        persons[2] = new Person("Edward", "Alexander", "Wutka");
        persons[3] = new Person("Norton", "Alexander", "Wutka");

        people.setPerson(persons);

        return people;
    }

    public String toString()
    {
        StringBuffer buff = new StringBuffer();

        buff.append("People [\n");

        for (int i=0; i < personVec.size(); i++)
        {
            buff.append("         ");
            buff.append(personVec.elementAt(i).toString());
            buff.append("\n");
        }
        buff.append("]\n");

        return buff.toString();
    }
}
```

LISTING 24.3 SOURCE CODE FOR `Person.java`

```
package usingj2ee.xml;

import java.util.Vector;

public class Person implements java.io.Serializable
{
    public String firstName;
    public String middleName;
    public String lastName;


    public Person()
    {
    }

    public Person(String aFirstName, String aMiddleName,
        String aLastName)
    {
        firstName = aFirstName;
        middleName = aMiddleName;
        lastName = aLastName;
    }

    public String getFirstName()
    {
        return firstName;
    }

    public void setFirstName(String theFirstName)
       {
        firstName = theFirstName;
    }

    public String getMiddleName()
    {
        return middleName;
    }

    public void setMiddleName(String theMiddleName)
    {
        middleName = theMiddleName;
    }

    public String getLastName()
    {
        return lastName;
    }

    public void setLastName(String theLastName)
    {
        lastName = theLastName;
    }

    public String toString()
    {
```

LISTING 24.3 CONTINUED

```
        StringBuffer buff = new StringBuffer();

        if (firstName != null)
        {
            buff.append(firstName);
            buff.append(' ');
        }

        if (middleName != null)
        {
            buff.append(middleName);
            buff.append(' ');
        }

        if (lastName != null)
        {
            buff.append(lastName);
        }

        return buff.toString();
    }
}
```

In this chapter, you will see how to read data into and out of these Java beans using three different libraries: KBML, JOX, and Quick.

USING KBML TO SERIALIZE AND DESERIALIZE JAVA BEANS

The Koala Bean Markup Language (KBML) writes beans to XML using a Java-specific format. Specifically, it writes out beans using a `<bean>` tag and writes bean properties using a `<property>` tag. Because KBML uses its own specific XML format, it isn't suitable for most XML data exchange. It makes an excellent serialization tool, however.

You can get the latest version of KBML from `http://www-sop.inria.fr/koala/kbml/`.

Listing 24.4 shows a program that writes a `Person` object out to an XML file using KBML.

LISTING 24.4 SOURCE CODE FOR `KoalaWrite.java`

```
package usingj2ee.xml;

import java.io.*;
import fr.dyade.koala.xml.kbml.*;

public class KoalaWrite
{
    public static void main(String[] args)
    {
        try
        {
```

```
            People people = People.createDefault();

            FileOutputStream out = new FileOutputStream("koala.xml");

            KBMLSerializer beanWriter = new KBMLSerializer(out);

            beanWriter.writeXMLDeclaration();
            beanWriter.writeDocumentTypeDefinition();
            beanWriter.writeKBMLStartTag();
            beanWriter.writeBean(people);
            beanWriter.writeKBMLEndTag();
            beanWriter.flush();
            beanWriter.close();
        }
        catch (Exception exc)
        {
            exc.printStackTrace();
        }
    }
}
```


As you can see in Listing 24.4, KBML has a `KBMLSerializer` class for writing XML files. You first create an output stream and then create the serializer from the output stream. Then you use the various methods in the serializer to write the XML file.

The `writeXMLDeclaration` method writes out the XML Declaration, and then the `writeDocumentTypeDefinition` method writes out the `DOCTYPE` declaration.

Next, the `writeKBMLStartTag` writes the `<kbml>` document root tag. The `writeBean` method serializes a bean to XML, of course, and then the `writeKBMLEndTag` writes the closing `</kbml>` tag. When you use KBML, don't forget to flush the serializer output stream and close it.

Listing 24.5 shows the XML generated by KBML. The output has been formatted for easy reading, however.

Listing 24.5 Java Bean Serialized by KBML

```
<?xml version="1.0" encoding="UTF-8" ?>
<!DOCTYPE kbml (View Source for full doctype...)>

<kbml version="2.3" copyright="(c) Dyade 2000">
    <bean class="usingj2ee.xml.People" id="KBML_0">
        <property name="person">
            <valueArray id="KBML_1">
                <bean class="usingj2ee.xml.Person" id="KBML_2">
                    <property name="middleName">
                        <value id="KBML_3">Lauren</value>
                    </property>
                    <property name="lastName">
                        <value id="KBML_4">Tippen</value>
                    </property>
                    <property name="firstName">
                        <value id="KBML_5">Samantha</value>
                    </property>
```

LISTING 24.5 CONTINUED

```
                    </bean>
                    <bean class="usingj2ee.xml.Person" id="KBML_6">
                        <property name="middleName">
                            <value id="KBML_7">Dawn</value>
                        </property>
                        <property name="lastName">
                            <value source="KBML_4" />
                        </property>
                        <property name="firstName">
                            <value id="KBML_8">Kaitlynn</value>
                        </property>
                    </bean>
                    <bean class="usingj2ee.xml.Person" id="KBML_9">
                        <property name="middleName">
                            <value id="KBML_10">Alexander</value>
                        </property>
                        <property name="lastName">
                            <value id="KBML_11">Wutka</value>
                        </property>
                        <property name="firstName">
                            <value id="KBML_12">Edward</value>
                        </property>
                    </bean>
                    <bean class="usingj2ee.xml.Person" id="KBML_13">
                        <property name="middleName">
                            <value source="KBML_10" />
                        </property>
                        <property name="lastName">
                            <value source="KBML_11" />
                        </property>
                        <property name="firstName">
                            <value id="KBML_14">Norton</value>
                        </property>
                    </bean>
                </valueArray>
            </property>
        </bean>
</kbml>
```

Reading a bean with KBML is even easier than writing one. You just create an input stream, wrap a `KBMLDeserializer` around the input stream, and read the bean. Listing 24.6 shows a program that reads a bean using KBML.

LISTING 24.6 SOURCE CODE FOR `KoalaRead.java`

```
package usingj2ee.xml;

import java.io.*;
import fr.dyade.koala.xml.kbml.*;
```

```
public class KoalaRead
{
    public static void main(String[] args)
    {
        People people = null;

        try
        {
            FileInputStream in = new FileInputStream("koala.xml");

            KBMLDeserializer beanReader = new KBMLDeserializer(in);

            people = (People) beanReader.readBean();

            beanReader.close();

            System.out.println(people);
        }
        catch (Exception exc)
        {
            exc.printStackTrace();
        }
    }
}
```


Note

KBML automatically recognized several different SAX parsers, but unfortunately the Xerces parser from Apache isn't one of them. If you use Xerces, make sure you include a system property setting of `Dorg.xml.sax.parser=org.apache.xerces.parsers.SAXParser`.

If you don't care what the XML looks like, KBML is excellent for serializing and deserializing Java beans. It makes an excellent testing tool because you can dump the contents of a bean out to a file, edit the file, and then read the contents back in. It also helps for automated testing when you want to set the various properties of a bean to certain values before running a test.

USING JOX TO READ AND WRITE OBJECTS IN XML

Java Objects in XML (JOX) is a library that reads XML data into a Java bean and writes Java beans out to XML without using any additional configuration files. The idea is simple: When reading an XML file, you give JOX either a Java bean, or a Java class that can be instantiated as a bean, and JOX tries to map the XML elements underneath the root element to properties in the bean. You can get JOX from `http://www.wutka.com/jox.html`.

JOX applies a loose matching strategy by removing all dashes, dots and underscores from the XML element name and ignoring any capitalization in both the XML element and the property name. For example, JOX thinks of `first-name` and `firstName` as being the same (it thinks they're both `firstname`).

JOX understands all the Java primitive types (`char`, `int`, `double`, and so on), the object wrappers for the primitive types (`Character`, `Integer`, `Double`, and so on), and also strings and dates. If JOX sees a property that is one of these types, it automatically tries to convert the XML text to the particular data type.

If a property is not one of the core types, but is actually a Java bean, JOX will try to read data into the bean. For example, if inside a `Person` object you have a bean property called `Address`, perhaps defined this way:

```
public Address getAddress()

public class Address {
    private String street;
    private String city;
    private String state;
    private String zip;
    public String getAddress() {...)
    public String setAddress() {...)
    . . .
}
```

JOX can handle a situation like this:

```
<person>
   <address>
      <street>123 Fourth St.</street>
```

When it sees the `address` element, it notices that `Person` has a matching `address` property, so it creates a new `Address` object (it knows the type from the bean property type) and begins to read `street` and other address elements into the `Address` object.

JOX can also handle indexed properties (the bean equivalent of an array-like structure). In case you aren't familiar with indexed properties, you define two `get` and `set` methods for an indexed property. One version takes an array of property values, like the following:

```
public void setGrades(int[] gradeValues);
public int[] getGrades()
```

The other version lets you set individual values:

```
public void setGrades(int position, int gradeValue)
public int getGrades(int position)
```

The `People` object back in Listing 24.2 has an indexed property called `person`.

Tip

When you create an indexed property, your natural urge is to give the property a pluralized name (grades, people, and so on). When using JOX, however, this would require the XML element for an individual item to have a pluralized name `<grades>100</grades>` when you really want it to be singular. If you're using JOX, consider making the indexed property names singular.

Listing 24.7 shows a program that uses JOX to read a `Person` object from an XML file.

LISTING 24.7 SOURCE CODE FOR `JOXRead.html`

```
package usingj2ee.xml;

import java.io.*;
import com.wutka.jox.*;

public class JOXRead
{
    public static void main(String[] args)
    {
        try
        {
            JOXBeanReader beanReader = new JOXBeanReader(
                new FileReader("people.xml"));

            People people = (People) beanReader.readObject(People.class);

            System.out.println(people);
        }
        catch (Exception exc)
        {
            exc.printStackTrace();
        }
    }
}
```

Listing 24.8 shows the XML file that the program in Listing 24.7 reads.

LISTING 24.8 SOURCE CODE FOR `people.xml`

```
<?xml version="1.0"?>

<people>
    <person>
        <first-name>Samantha</first-name>
        <middle-name>Lauren</middle-name>
        <last-name>Tippin</last-name>
```

LISTING 24.8 CONTINUED

```
    </person>
    <person>
        <first-name>Kaitlynn</first-name>
        <middle-name>Dawn</middle-name>
        <last-name>Tippin</last-name>
    </person>
    <person>
        <first-name>Edward</first-name>
        <middle-name>Alexander</middle-name>
        <last-name>Wutka</last-name>
    </person>
    <person>
        <first-name>Norton</first-name>
        <middle-name>Alexander</middle-name>
        <last-name>Wutka</last-name>
    </person>
</people>
```

JOX has a little bit of a handicap when it comes to writing out a document. It's not always likely that the bean property name will match the XML element name you want. When JOX reads a file, it knows the XML element names and the bean property names, so it is able to match them up. When it writes an XML document, JOX has only the bean to work with, so it can't magically come up with the correct element name. Fortunately, there is a solution to this problem. You can give JOX a DTD that tells it what element names to use. The added bonus is that JOX won't try to write out properties that have no equivalent in the DTD, so you won't accidentally create a document that can't be read by another program using the same DTD.

The one thing that JOX can't figure out, even with a DTD, is what the name of the root element should be. When you write out a bean, you must supply the root element name.

Listing 24.9 shows a program that uses JOX to write out a bean to an XML file.

LISTING 24.9 SOURCE CODE FOR `JOXWrite.java`

```
package usingj2ee.xml;

import com.wutka.jox.*;
import java.io.*;

public class JOXWrite
{
    public static void main(String[] args)
    {
        try
        {
            FileWriter out = new FileWriter("joxperson.xml");

            JOXBeanWriter beanWriter = new JOXBeanWriter(
                "file:///h:/j2eebook/ch24/examples/people.dtd", out);

            People people = People.createDefault();
```

```
// Write out the people object using <people> as the root element
            beanWriter.writeObject("people", people);

            out.close();
        }
        catch (Exception exc)
        {
            exc.printStackTrace();
        }
    }
}
```

Note Don't forget to change the location of the DTD in Listing 24.9 before you try to run it.

USING QUICK TO READ AND WRITE OBJECTS IN XML

The Quick library, from `http://www.jxml.com` is not as simple as JOX, but it's also not as simplistic. Quick lets you map XML data to Java classes and fields, but doesn't require the Java classes to be beans. Although JOX handles a somewhat limited set of Java classes (only beans), Quick handles any kind of Java class, and includes some data structures that JOX can't handle, such as maps (hash tables).

To achieve this tremendous flexibility, Quick requires you to create a file that describes the structure of your XML document and how it maps to Java. The file format is called QJML and is very simple to understand. Listing 24.10 shows a QJML file that maps the `Person` class to the format described in the `person.dtd` file. Because Quick can return an array of objects, the QJML file skips over the `People` class and just stores `Person` objects in an array.

LISTING 24.10 SOURCE CODE FOR `people.qjml`

```
<?xml version="1.0" encoding="ISO-8859-1"?>
<qjml root="people">
    <element name="people">
        <targetClass>java.util.ArrayList</targetClass>
        <child element="person"
                repeating="True"
                optional="True"
                class="com.jxml.quick.access.QListAccess"/>
    </element>
    <element name="person">
        <targetClass>usingj2ee.xml.Person</targetClass>
        <child element="first-name" field="firstName" optional="True"/>
        <child element="middle-name" field="middleName" optional="True"/>
        <child element="last-name" field="lastName" optional="True"/>
    </element>
    <element content="string" name="first-name" />
    <element content="string" name="middle-name" />
    <element content="string" name="last-name" />
</qjml>
```

As you can see, QJML looks like an XML version of a DTD; it defines elements and indicates what elements can be children of other elements. Defining the QJML is definitely the hardest part of using Quick. After you have it defined, reading and writing objects is a snap.

Listing 24.11 shows a program that reads the `person.xml` file from Listing 24.8.

LISTING 24.11 SOURCE CODE FOR `QuickRead.java`

```
package usingj2ee.xml;

import java.util.*;
import java.io.*;
import com.jxml.quick.*;
import org.xml.sax.*;
import org.xml.sax.helpers.*;

public class QuickRead
{
    public static void main(String[] args)
    {
        try
        {
            QDoc peopleSchema = Quick.parseQJML("people.qjml");

            QDoc peopleDoc = Quick.parse(peopleSchema, "people.xml");

            ArrayList people = (ArrayList) Quick.getRoot(peopleDoc);

            Iterator i = people.iterator();

            while (i.hasNext())
            {
                Person p = (Person) i.next();
                System.out.println(p);
            }
        }
        catch (Exception exc)
        {
            exc.printStackTrace();
        }
    }
}
```

To write an XML file using Quick, you create a `Qdoc` object and then ask Quick to turn it into a string. Listing 24.12 shows a program that writes a set of `Person` objects out to an XML file.

LISTING 24.12 SOURCE CODE FOR `QuickWrite.java`

```
package usingj2ee.xml;

import java.util.*;
import java.io.*;
import com.jxml.quick.*;
```

```
import org.xml.sax.*;
import org.xml.sax.helpers.*;

public class QuickWrite
{
    public static void main(String[] args)
    {
        try
        {
            People people = People.createDefault();

            Person[] persons = people.getPerson();

            ArrayList list = new ArrayList(persons.length);

            for (int i=0; i < persons.length; i++)
            {
                list.add(persons[i]);
            }

            QDoc peopleSchema = Quick.parseQJML("people.qjml");

            QDoc peopleDoc = Quick.createDoc(list, peopleSchema);

            PrintWriter out = new PrintWriter(new
➥          FileWriter("quickout.xml"));

            out.println(Quick.express(peopleDoc));

            out.close();
        }
        catch (Exception exc)
        {
            exc.printStackTrace();
        }
    }
}
```

Quick is a robust library that has been in use for several years. Don't let the QJML file scare you; after you get the hang of it, you'll find that Quick is one of the most powerful tools you can have in your Java arsenal.

JOX, Quick, and KBML are only three out of a variety of Java-XML tools available to you. Using these tools, you can accomplish any number of interesting things. For example, one project used JOX for testing EJBs. They used JOX to serialize a copy of the bean's data, then edited the file, and used JOX to copy the data back into the bean. They were able to see which `get` and `set` methods in the bean were working and which ones weren't.

TROUBLESHOOTING

KOALA PROBLEMS

I get a `ClassNotFound` *exception when I read a bean but not when I write it.*

If you put the KBML JAR file in the `jre\lib\ext` directory for your JDK, the class loader might not see the classes you want to load. Take the KBML JAR file out of the `jre\lib\ext` directory and just put it in your classpath.

QUICK PROBLEMS

I get a `ClassNotFound` *exception when I read a bean but not when I write it.*

As with KBML, if you put the Quick JAR file in the `jre\lib\ext` directory for your JDK, the class loader might not see the classes you want to load. Take the Quick JAR file out of the `jre\lib\ext` directory and just put it in your classpath.

CHAPTER 25

Remote Method Calls with XML-SOAP

In this chapter

WHAT IS SOAP?

XML allows you to describe structured data in a platform-independent and language-independent manner, but it has no mechanism for transporting this data. If two systems want to pass XML data back and forth, they must still decide on a transport protocol. In many ways, CORBA addresses some of the same aspects as XML, but it includes a way to transport data and to package the data into individual requests. Unfortunately, CORBA doesn't use XML for data representation. The *Simple Object Access Protocol* (*SOAP*) is a remote procedure call mechanism that uses XML to encode the request and the result. XML is not a transport protocol; it's just a data representation protocol. SOAP can use any number of transport protocols, the most common of which is HTTP (you can also send SOAP requests via email using the SMTP and POP3 protocols!). Although SOAP still doesn't solve the problem of picking a transport protocol, it provides a standard way to package requests; that is, it adds the concept of business methods to complement XML's data representation. Figure 25.1 illustrates the typical path of a SOAP request.

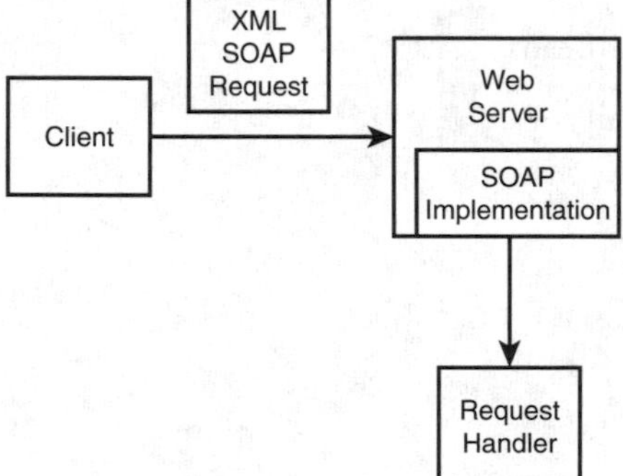

Figure 25.1
You can receive and process SOAP requests in a Web server.

SOAP was originally proposed to the IETF (the organization that publishes Internet standards such as TCP, FTP, HTTP, and so on) and then the World Wide Web Consortium (W3C). A quick glance at the SOAP standard (available at `http://www.w3.org/TR/SOAP/`) shows that the SOAP specification was written by several people from Microsoft, a couple of people from IBM/Lotus, Don Box (a noted COM guru), and Dave Winer (the creator of a SOAP-like protocol called XML-RPC). It might seem odd to see Microsoft pushing a standard such as SOAP, but Microsoft has really embraced XML and some of its related technologies. SOAP can be a nice bridge between the Java world and the Microsoft world.

With other options, such as CORBA and RMI, you might wonder why you need yet another remote procedure call mechanism. SOAP might not be the fastest protocol, and it might not integrate as naturally with Java as RMI, but because it works so naturally over HTTP, you can deploy SOAP applications in many places where RMI and CORBA don't work well. Many companies block off their Internet connections to only allow Web traffic and email in and out of the company network. Because SOAP can use the same protocol as a Web server, you can use it wherever you can use a Web server.

Note

Many Web sites can't handle large XML documents, often because they use parsers that create an in-memory representation of the entire document rather than parsing it bit-by-bit. Because of these problems, some Web sites have started to limit the size of incoming messages. If you design a SOAP-based application that requires large messages, you should check with your Web site administrator to make sure your server will accept large messages.

Because all SOAP messages are XML documents, it's easy to read the SOAP protocol and easy to make different languages work with SOAP. RMI, of course, is a Java-only solution. Before you can use another programming language with CORBA, you need a way to translate IDL into your programming language, and then you need an IIOP library for your language so you can send and receive CORBA requests. For SOAP, on the other hand, you just need an XML parser, which is often readily available, and a library for sending HTTP requests, also readily available for a number of languages.

Listing 25.1 shows an example SOAP request. You won't necessarily need to generate SOAP XML yourself when you use SOAP because libraries do it for you. Still, it helps to understand how SOAP works.

LISTING 25.1 EXAMPLE SOAP REQUEST

```
<SOAP-ENV:Envelope xmlns:SOAP-ENV="http://schemas.xmlsoap.org/soap/envelope/"
    xmlns:xsi="http://www.w3.org/1999/XMLSchema-instance"
    xmlns:xsd="http://www.w3.org/1999/XMLSchema">
    <SOAP-ENV:Body>
        <ns1:getAddressFromName xmlns:ns1="urn:AddressFetcher"
            SOAP-ENV:encodingStyle="http://schemas.xmlsoap.org/soap/encoding/">
            <nameToLookup xsi:type="xsd:string">John B. Good</nameToLookup>
        </ns1:getAddressFromName>
    </SOAP-ENV:Body>
</SOAP-ENV:Envelope>
```

The main document element in a SOAP request is the `<Envelope>` tag. In Listing 25.1, the tag also contains the namespace for the tag (that is, `<SOAP-ENV:Envelope>`). Listing 25.1 looks formidable because of all the namespace information. If you boil it down, however, you see that it's not that complex. Listing 25.2 shows the same request with the namespace information removed.

LISTING 25.2 SIMPLIFIED SOAP REQUEST

```
<Envelope>
    <Body>
        <getAddressFromName>
            <nameToLookup type="string">John B. Good</nameToLookup>
        </getAddressFromName>
    </Body>
</Envelope>
```

The example SOAP request in Listing 25.2 calls a remote method called `getAddressFromName` and passes a single string parameter named `nameToLookup`, which has a value of `"John B. Good"`.

Listing 25.3 shows an example SOAP response.

Listing 25.3 Example SOAP Response

```
<SOAP-ENV:Envelope xmlns:SOAP-ENV="http://schemas.xmlsoap.org/soap/envelope/"
➥xmlns:xsi="http://www.w3.org/1999/XMLSchema-instance"
    xmlns:xsd="http://www.w3.org/1999/XMLSchema">
    <SOAP-ENV:Body>
        <ns1:getAddressFromNameResponse xmlns:ns1="urn:AddressFetcher"
            SOAP-ENV:encodingStyle="http://schemas.xmlsoap.org/soap/encoding/">
            <return xmlns:ns2="urn:xml-soap-address-demo"
                xsi:type="ns2:address">
                <phoneNumber xsi:type="ns2:phone">
                    <exchange xsi:type="xsd:string">456</exchange>
                    <areaCode xsi:type="xsd:int">123</areaCode>
                    <number xsi:type="xsd:string">7890</number>
                </phoneNumber>
                <zip xsi:type="xsd:int">12345</zip>
                <streetNum xsi:type="xsd:int">123</streetNum>
                <streetName xsi:type="xsd:string">Main Street</streetName>
                <state xsi:type="xsd:string">NY</state>
                <city xsi:type="xsd:string">Anytown</city>
            </return>
        </ns1:getAddressFromNameResponse>
    </SOAP-ENV:Body>
</SOAP-ENV:Envelope>
```

Again, the response looks formidable with all the namespace information in there, but when you strip it away, you see how simple SOAP really is. Listing 25.4 shows the response from Listing 25.3 with the namespace information stripped out.

Listing 25.4 Simplified SOAP Response

```
<Envelope>
    <Body>
        <getAddressFromNameResponse>
            <return type="address">
                <phoneNumber type="phone">
                    <exchange type="string">456</exchange>
                    <areaCode type="int">123</areaCode>
                    <number type="string">7890</number>
                </phoneNumber>
                <zip type="int">12345</zip>
                <streetNum type="int">123</streetNum>
                <streetName type="string">Main Street</streetName>
                <state type="string">NY</state>
                <city type="string">Anytown</city>
            </return>
        </getAddressFromNameResponse>
    </Body>
</Envelope>
```

As with the request, the main tag for the response is the `<Envelope>` tag. Notice that the return type is a structured address value containing a structured phone number and some additional information.

As you can see, SOAP itself is simple after you wade through all those annoying namespaces. From a Java standpoint, SOAP is even simpler, because the Apache group has created a nice SOAP implementation with a Java client library to create the SOAP request and interpret the response. You don't have to generate the SOAP XML yourself!

USING SOAP WITH JAVA

The Apache group has created a nice SOAP implementation for Java that makes it simple to create SOAP clients and to make objects accessible via SOAP. You can get the package from `http://xml.apache.org/soap`. The Apache version of SOAP is based on a previous implementation from IBM.

The Apache SOAP implementation is just a set of client libraries, a set of server libraries, and a servlet to process the incoming requests. You use the client libraries to create a request and send it to the server. The server decodes the request, invokes the method, and packages the result. The client libraries then decode the result and return it to you.

Figure 25.2 shows the sequence of a SOAP request using the Apache SOAP implementation.

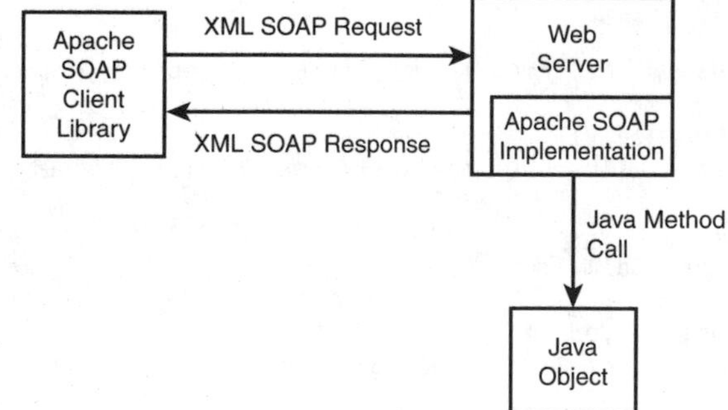

Figure 25.2
The Apache SOAP implementation creates the XML for SOAP requests and responses.

Listing 25.5 shows a simple Java class that you can use on the server side for testing SOAP requests.

LISTING 25.5 SOURCE CODE FOR `SoapHello.java`

```
package usingj2ee.soap;public class SoapHello{    protected String helloString;

    public SoapHello()
    {
        helloString = "Hello!";
    }
```

LISTING 25.5 CONTINUED

```
    public String getHello(String extra1, int extra2)
    {
        return helloString+" "+extra1+" "+extra2;
    }

    public void setHello(String newHello)
    {
        helloString = newHello;
    }
}
```

Notice that the server-side class doesn't need to know anything at all about SOAP. It's just a normal Java class. The client, on the other hand, must use SOAP routines to construct the remote request.

Listing 25.6 shows the client routine that creates and executes the SOAP request.

LISTING 25.6 SOURCE CODE FOR GetHello.java

```
import java.io.*;import java.net.*;import java.util.*;import org.w3c.dom.*;
import org.apache.soap.*;import org.apache.soap.encoding.*;
import org.apache.soap.encoding.soapenc.*;
import org.apache.soap.rpc.*;
import org.apache.soap.util.xml.*;

public class GetHello
{
    public static void main(String[] args) throws Exception
    {
// The URL for the SOAP servlet
        URL url = new URL("http://localhost/soap/servlet/rpcrouter");

// Create a new call
        Call call = new Call();

// Tell SOAP which object you want
        call.setTargetObjectURI("urn:HelloApp");

// Tell SOAP which method to invoke
        call.setMethodName("getHello");

// Tell SOAP to use the regular SOAP encoding style
        call.setEncodingStyleURI(Constants.NS_URI_SOAP_ENC);

// Create a vector to hold the method parameters
        Vector params = new Vector();

// Add a string parameter called extra1 with a value of "Hello info"
// Specify null for the encoding style
        params.addElement(new Parameter("extra1", String.class,
            "Hello info", null));

// Add an int parameter called extra2 with a value of 123
// Specify null for the encoding style
```

```
        params.addElement(new Parameter("extra2", Integer.class,
            new Integer(123), null));

// Store the parameters in the request
        call.setParams(params);

        Response resp = null;

// Invoke the call method
        try
        {
            resp = call.invoke(url, "");
        }
        catch (SOAPException e)
        {
            e.printStackTrace();
            System.exit(0);
        }

// See if the response contains an error
        if (!resp.generatedFault())
        {
// If not, get the return value
            Parameter ret = resp.getReturnValue();

// Expect it to be a string
            String value = (String) ret.getValue();

            System.out.println(value);
        }
        else
        {
            Fault fault = resp.getFault();

            System.err.println("Generated fault: ");
            System.out.println ("  Fault Code   = " + fault.getFaultCode());
            System.out.println ("  Fault String = " + fault.getFaultString());
        }
    }
}
```

To create a SOAP request, you create a new `Call` object. You tell the `Call` object the name of the object you want to call (you set up the name-to-class mapping when you install the SOAP service). You must also tell SOAP the name of the method you want to invoke and the encoding style to use (it's best to stick with the default for now).

You then create a vector of `Parameter` objects containing the parameters you want to send. After you invoke the remote method, you can extract the `Parameter` object containing the return value from the `Response` object returned by the method invocation.

Apache has a Web-based configuration utility for SOAP, but it also has a simple XML-based utility that makes it easy to install and uninstall services from the command line. Listing 25.7 shows the deployment descriptor for the `SoapHello` class.

LISTING 25.7 `DeploymentDescriptor.xml` **FOR** `SoapHello`

```
<isd:service xmlns:isd="http://xml.apache.org/xml-soap/deployment"
    id="urn:HelloApp">
    <isd:provider type="java" scope="Application"
        methods="getHello setHello">
        <isd:java class="usingj2ee.soap.SoapHello" static="false"/>
    </isd:provider>
</isd:service>
```

To install the deployment descriptor, you can run Apache's command-line utility (make sure `soap.jar` is in your classpath):

```
java org.apache.soap.server.ServiceManagerClient
➥http://localhost/soap/servlet/rpcrouter
➥deploy DeploymentDescriptor.xml
```

Assuming that you have SOAP installed and that your Web server's classpath can see the `SoapHello` class, you should be able to run the `GetHello` program and see the results of the remote call to `SoapHello`.

USING SOAP WITH ENTERPRISE JAVABEANS

Because your server-side object doesn't rely on anything specific to SOAP, and because it can be just about any kind of Java class, there's no reason your server-side object can't use an EJB. In other words, you can use SOAP as a way to access an EJB remotely without using RMI-IIOP. Of course, you must write a layer to go between SOAP and EJB.

Listing 25.8 shows an example server-side object that accesses the `Person` bean from Chapter 12, "EJB Design."

LISTING 25.8 SOURCE CODE FOR `SoapPerson.java`

```
package usingj2ee.addressbook;

import java.util.*;
import javax.naming.*;
import javax.rmi.PortableRemoteObject;

public class SoapPerson
{
    public SoapPerson()
    {
    }

    public FullPersonViewer locatePerson(String firstName, String lastName)
    {
        try
        {
// Set up properties for WebLogic so you don't have to do
// this on the command line
            Properties props = new Properties();
            props.put(Context.INITIAL_CONTEXT_FACTORY,
```

```
                "weblogic.jndi.WLInitialContextFactory");

/** Creates a JNDI naming context for location objects */
            Context context = new InitialContext(props);

/** Asks the context to locate an object named "Person" and expects the
    object to implement the PersonHome interface */

            PersonHome home = (PersonHome)
                PortableRemoteObject.narrow(context.lookup("PersonHome"),
                    PersonHome.class);

// Locate the person
            Collection people = home.findByFirstAndLastName(
                firstName, lastName);

            Iterator iter = people.iterator();

            if (!iter.hasNext())
            {
                return null;
            }

            Person person = (Person) iter.next();

// Get a view of the person's data
            FullPersonViewer view = (FullPersonViewer) person.getAsView(
                FullPersonViewer.class.getName());

            return view;
        }
        catch (Exception exc)
        {
            exc.printStackTrace();

            return null;
        }
    }
}
```


Because the `SoapPerson` class returns an object instead of a simple type, you must do a little extra work on your client to send and receive an object. You must create a type-mapping object that tells how to translate a particular object to a local Java class. The Apache SOAP implementation lets you create various serializers to translate objects to and from XML. It also comes with a built-in `BeanSerializer` class for passing Java beans.

Listing 25.9 shows an example client program that sets up the type mapping for reading the `SoapPersonViewer` object from the server.

LISTING 25.9 SOURCE CODE FOR `GetAddress.java`

```
import java.io.*;import java.net.*;
import java.util.*;

import org.w3c.dom.*;
```

LISTING 25.9 CONTINUED

```
import org.apache.soap.*;
import org.apache.soap.encoding.*;
import org.apache.soap.encoding.soapenc.*;
import org.apache.soap.rpc.*;
import org.apache.soap.util.xml.*;

import usingj2ee.addressbook.*;
import usingj2ee.soap.SoapPersonViewer;

public class GetAddress
{
    public static void main(String[] args) throws Exception
    {
// The URL for the SOAP servlet
        URL url = new URL("http://localhost/soap/servlet/rpcrouter");

// Create a new call
        Call call = new Call();

// Tell SOAP which object you want
        call.setTargetObjectURI("urn:AddressApp");

// Tell SOAP which method to invoke
        call.setMethodName("locatePerson");

// Tell SOAP to use the regular SOAP encoding style
        call.setEncodingStyleURI(Constants.NS_URI_SOAP_ENC);

// Create a bean serializer to decode the incoming reply
        BeanSerializer ser = new BeanSerializer();

// Create a mapping Registry to map SOAP data structures to Java objects
        SOAPMappingRegistry reg = new SOAPMappingRegistry();

// Add a mapping for the SoapPersonViewer class
// The urn:soapdemo refers to the type mapping defined in the deployment
// descriptor for the SOAP service.
        reg.mapTypes(Constants.NS_URI_SOAP_ENC,
            new QName("urn:soapdemo", "person"),
                SoapPersonViewer.class, ser, ser);

// Create a vector to hold the method parameters
        Vector params = new Vector();

// Add the parameters
        params.addElement(new Parameter("firstName", String.class,
            args[0], null));
        params.addElement(new Parameter("lastName", String.class,
            args[1], null));

// Store the parameters in the request
        call.setParams(params);

        Response resp = null;
```

```
// Invoke the call method
        try
        {
            resp = call.invoke(url, "");
        }
        catch (SOAPException e)
        {
            e.printStackTrace();
            System.exit(0);
        }

// See if the response contains an error
        if (!resp.generatedFault())
        {
// If not, get the return value
            Parameter ret = resp.getReturnValue();

            SoapPersonViewer person = null;
            person = (SoapPersonViewer) ret.getValue();

            System.out.println(person.getFirstName()+" "+
                person.getMiddleName()+" "+person.getLastName());
            System.out.println(person.getAddress1());
            System.out.println(person.getAddress2());
            System.out.println(person.getCity()+" "+person.getState()+", "+
                person.getZip());
            System.out.println("Home: "+person.getHomePhone());
            System.out.println("Work: "+person.getWorkPhone());
            System.out.println("Mobile: "+person.getMobilePhone());
        }
        else
        {
            Fault fault = resp.getFault();

            System.err.println("Generated fault: ");
            System.out.println ("  Fault Code   = " + fault.getFaultCode());
            System.out.println ("  Fault String = " + fault.getFaultString());
        }
    }
}
```


When you set up the mapping, the `QName` class refers to a name in the deployment descriptor. The first part of the `QName` is the namespace you define (`urn:soapdemo` in this case) and the second part is the object name (`person`).

Listing 25.10 shows the deployment descriptor for the `SoapPerson` service. You can see how the `SoapPersonStructure` is defined in the descriptor, requiring the `BeanSerializer` class to serialize and deserialize the class. In the client, you specify the serializer in the mapping Registry, but on the server, you specify it in the deployment descriptor.

LISTING 25.10 DEPLOYMENT DESCRIPTOR FOR `SoapPerson`

```
<isd:service xmlns:isd="http://xml.apache.org/xml-soap/deployment"
   id="urn:HelloApp">
   <isd:provider type="java" scope="Application"
```

LISTING 25.10 CONTINUED

```
        methods="getHello setHello">
        <isd:java class="usingj2ee.soap.SoapHello" static="false"/>
    </isd:provider>
    <isd:mappings>
        <isd:map encodingStyle="http://schemas.xmlsoap.org/soap/encoding/"
            xmlns:x="urn:soapdemo" qname="x:person"
            javaType="usingj2ee.soap.SoapPersonViewer"
            java2XMLClassName="org.apache.soap.encoding.soapenc.BeanSerializer"
            xml2JavaClassName="org.apache.soap.encoding.soapenc.BeanSerializer"
        />
    </isd:mappings>
</isd:service>
```

SENDING SOAP REQUESTS VIA EMAIL

One of the interesting add-ons for the Apache SOAP implementation is a pair of utilities for receiving SOAP requests and sending a response via email. You set up a small POP3 server that listens for mail to a particular mailbox. Whenever the server sees a message, the server forwards it to the SOAP server. The server then takes the response and emails it back to the sender.

It might sound a little wacky to send requests via email, but email has the capability to penetrate through a corporate firewall better than any other protocol. You can often set up an email SOAP server well inside your corporate network where Web browsers have no hope of reaching. Although this isn't the most efficient way of doing business, for low-volume messages that don't require immediate responses, it's a good alternative.

For example, although this wasn't a SOAP application, I once had a program that could retrieve information from the mainframe at my company—information I often needed while on the road. I set up an email service on my desktop Sun workstation to receive requests via email and send a reply. As long as I was in a place that had dial-up Internet access, I could query the mainframe and get a response. You can use SOAP to do the same kind of thing.

SOAP appears to have a bright future. Microsoft's .NET strategy includes SOAP, and Sun's Open Network Environment (ONE) should at least support SOAP. Although SOAP works well with Java, its future as an integral part of J2EE and ONE is still murky. Sun has recently endorsed another protocol called ebXML that is a competitor to SOAP. Between Microsoft and Apache, however, SOAP has a strong support base to grow on.

TROUBLESHOOTING

INSTALLING SOAP

Why can't my Web server find the SOAP `rpcrouter` *servlet?*

You probably haven't set up a path to it in your Web server configuration. See the SOAP installation guides to see how to configure SOAP for your servlet engine.

Why can't SOAP find my server class?

Your servlet engine's classpath must include the path to your server class. After you add the path to the servlet engine's configuration, you most likely will need to restart the server before it picks up the change.

PART V

NETWORKING

CHAPTER 26

Networks and Network Protocols

In this chapter

THE IMPORTANCE OF UNDERSTANDING THE NETWORK

It's difficult to do enterprise-level development without using a network. If you're deploying an Internet application, it's vital that you have some idea of how your network is configured and how clients access your application. Sooner or later, you're going to have a client who is unable to access your server even though you can access it yourself. When you know the possible things that can go wrong, you have a much better chance of figuring out the problem.

Aside from debugging, it's important to understand the network when you design your application. If someone must access your application through a firewall, you need to know how the firewall affects various network techniques. You might discover that an approach you were planning won't work because of the way your network is designed. As a developer, you don't need to know how to configure a router or a firewall, but you should know what routers and firewalls do.

THE INTERNET PROTOCOL

The Internet Protocol (IP) is the foundation upon which all other Internet protocols are built. The irony of IP is that it predates the Internet itself. When IP was created, it was intended as a protocol to link one network to another—an inter-network protocol. Eventually, as various large networks became permanently connected, everyone began to refer to the overall network as the Internet.

There are plenty of computers that use IP every day that aren't connected to the Internet. Many companies maintain large internal networks that, for security or economic reasons, have no access to the Internet.

Most people think that the Internet is synonymous with the World Wide Web. In some ways this is true, but the truth is, the Internet is a worldwide network of computers that all use the Internet Protocol. The World Wide Web, as you will see in chapter 29, "The HTTP Protocol," uses a protocol called HTTP that is built on top of IP. Although every computer on the Internet can understand IP, not all of them have Web servers or Web browsers running on them, so they aren't part of the World Wide Web.

IP is a packet-oriented protocol; that is, data is always transmitted in small blocks called *packets*. IP networks are called packet-switched networks because they focus on sending packets from point A to point B. Packet-switched networks tend to be flexible and resilient to failures. To understand why this is so, you must first look at the main alternative to packet switching: circuit switching.

Although phone systems are much more complex now than they used to be, and some systems now use packet switching in various places, the traditional phone network is a circuit-switched network. Figure 26.1 shows a phone network with a series of switches that can each handle a number of connections. The switches are connected to each other.

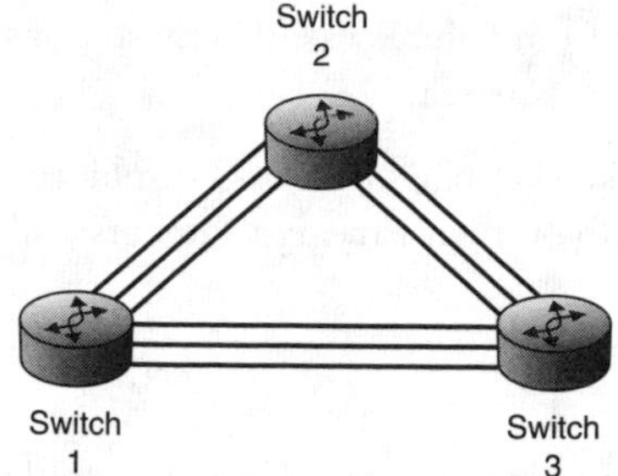

Figure 26.1
A circuit-switched network is a series of connected switches.

Now, to make a connection from point A to point B, the switch at point A makes a connection to another switch, which then connects to another switch. The overall connection is really a series of connections between switches. Figure 26.2 shows how this series of connections results in a connection between point A and point B.

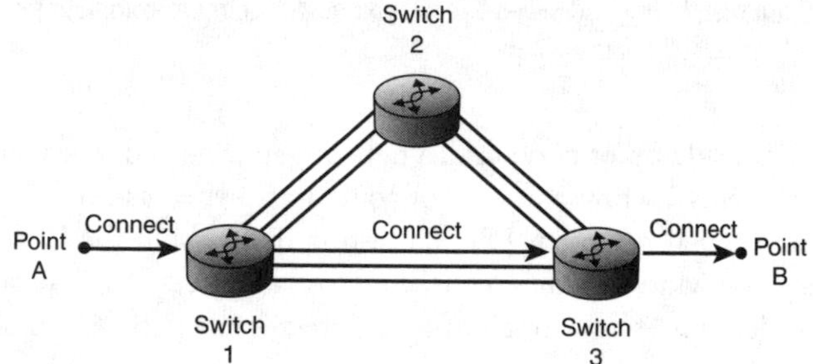

Figure 26.2
The small connections between switches create an overall connection between two points.

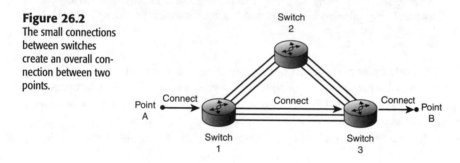

One of the problems with a circuit-switched network is that if a switch goes down for some reason, the connection is terminated (or it is at least difficult to recover from a lost switch).

Now, a packet-switched network still has interconnected switches, but to get data from point A to point B, the switches send packets along any valid path. That is, each packet of data might take a different path from point A to point B. Figure 26.3 shows how a packet-switched network routes data.

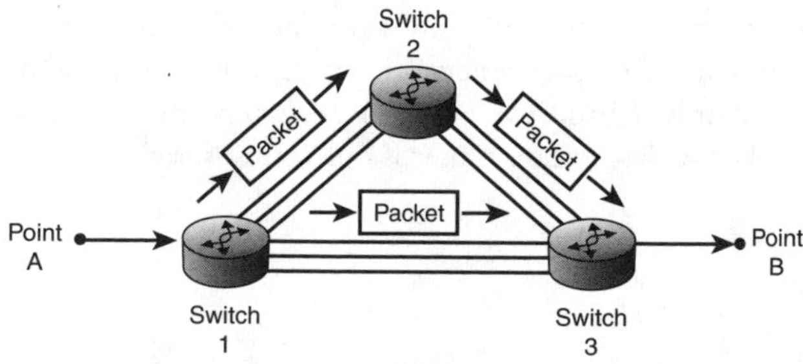

Figure 26.3
A packet-switched network can route packets along any valid path.

A packet-switched network can recover from failures easily because it just sends packets along a different path, skirting the disabled switch.

The underlying technical details of packet-switched networks can be complex, but you don't really need to know much about them if you're just trying to understand IP and the protocols built on it.

IP ADDRESSES

Every computer on an IP network has a unique IP address—that combination of four numbers that you frequently see when you use the Internet. For example, 192.168.1.2 is an IP address. In general, each of the four numbers are 8-bit values, meaning they can range from 0 to 255.

Note

There is a new IP standard called IPv6 that uses larger addresses. It represents the next generation in IP networking and solves some of the problems that have plagued the Internet. In the next several years, you might see more companies switching over to IPv6, but it is still relatively new.

Every IP address is made up of two parts: a network address and a host address. The network address represents a whole network of computers, whereas the host address represents a single computer on that network. The interesting thing about the IP address is that there are different ways to divide it into network and host addresses. You use something called a network mask to determine how much of the address is the network and how much is the host.

A network mask takes the same form as the IP address, but it has a peculiar restriction. If you were to write the values out in binary, the network mask should start with only 1s and at some point switch over to only 0s. For example, the typical network mask for the address 192.168.1.2 is 255.255.0.0. The value 255 in binary is, of course, 11111111, so the network mask in binary is 11111111.11111111.0.0. The reason for this restriction is that you retrieve the network address from the IP address by performing a binary AND between the network mask and the IP address. Thus, for the address 192.168.1.2, when you perform the binary AND, you get a network address of 192.168.0.0.

Figure 26.4 shows a sample IP network configuration with two separate connected networks. You can see that each separate network has its own network address and each host on the network has a separate IP address. Between the two networks is a router, which you will learn more about shortly. Basically, a router is one form of packet switch.

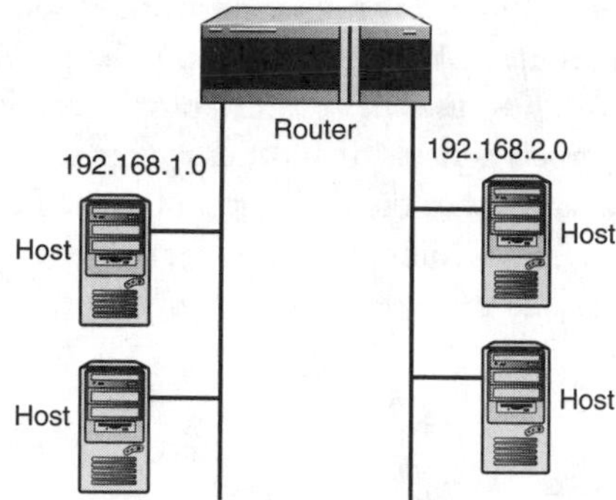

Figure 26.4
An IP network has its own network address and can be connected to other networks by a router.

SUBNETTING

You might have heard of something called a *subnet*. The idea is that a company can have a network address that can have a tremendous number of hosts. For example, if your network address is 192.168.0.0, you can have 65,536 host addresses (256 values for the third number times 256 values for the fourth number). That's a pretty big network. In general, when two networks are connected by a router, each network must have a separate network address. When you need to set up several networks in several buildings, you need multiple network addresses. You typically divide your existing network address into several subnetworks. For instance, you might create three networks with network addresses of 192.168.1.0, 192.168.2.0, and 192.168.3.0. The network masks for these networks would be 255.255.255.0, as opposed to the original 255.255.0.0. This technique is called *subnetting* and is done in almost every large company.

HOW HOSTS COMMUNICATE ON THE NETWORK

Although hosts on an IP network can communicate with each other, hosts on an IP network can only send packets directly to other machines on the same local network (other machines with the same IP network address). A host actually has two different addresses: a physical hardware address and the IP address. Every network card has a globally unique address, so no two cards ever have the same address. When a host sends a packet to another host on the same network, it addresses the packet to the other host's physical address, as shown in Figure 26.5.

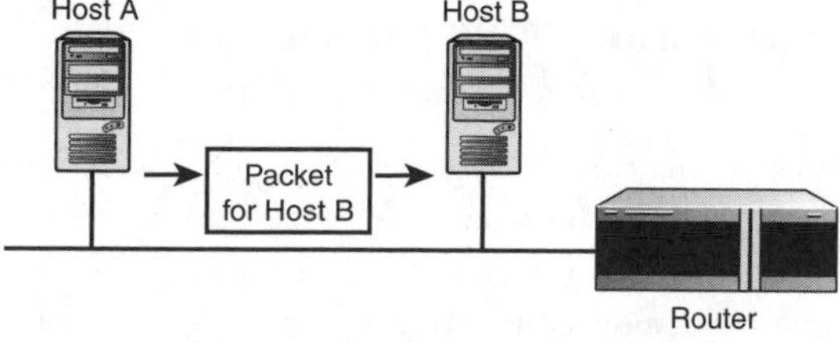

Figure 26.5
Hosts on the same network communicate using physical addresses.

When a host needs to send a packet to a host on another network, it sends the packet to the local router on the network and the router takes care of sending the packet where it needs to go. As you can see in Figure 26.6, a host uses the router's physical address to send the packet. The router then uses the physical address of another router to forward the packet. The second router uses the physical address of the destination host to finally deliver the packet. The various hosts and routers use a combination of protocols to discover the physical addresses for various IP addresses and to discover routers on the network.

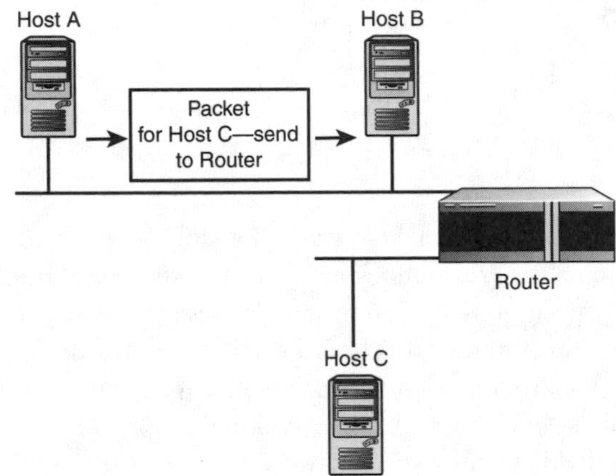

Figure 26.6
A host always uses a physical address when sending a packet.

A host should always have a router that it sends packets to when it needs to send a packet outside the network. This router is called the *default gateway*. You've probably seen the term before; you almost always need to set up a default gateway when setting up a network connection for a PC.

Note

Hosts on the same network learn about each other's physical addresses using the Address Resolution Protocol. A host broadcasts an ARP message saying "I am looking for the host with address 192.168.1.2." The host with that address responds with its physical address.

TRANSMISSION CONTROL PROTOCOL (TCP)

The Transmission Control Protocol (TCP) is the real workhorse of the Internet. Although the Internet Protocol is called IP, you usually see the suite of Internet protocols (IP and the things built on top of it) referred to as TCP/IP. Technically, TCP can work on top of other protocols, but in practice, it's most often used on top of IP.

The Internet Protocol is a simple *packet-oriented protocol*. That is, it defines a way to send a packet of data from point A to point B. There are a lot of things that can happen to a packet along the way, however. It might go to a router that suddenly crashes, losing the packet. One packet might travel along a slow connection while one sent right after it gets a fast connection. In other words, you can receive packets out of order, or not at all.

TCP enables two hosts to communicate without worrying about lost packets or packet order. It keeps track of the packet sequence and can reassemble packets in the correct order even if they arrive out of sequence. If a packet is lost, TCP has a resend protocol so it can request that the sending host resend the lost packet. The design of TCP is fairly complicated, but you don't really need to understand its inner workings to use it.

Although the capability to make a connection from one machine to another is important, you still have a big problem. How can you distinguish between an email connection and a Web connection? TCP solves that problem with the concept of ports. A port isn't a physical device; it's an extended address.

If you think of a TCP connection as a phone call between two hosts, the port number is each party's extension. When a company has a single incoming phone number, it usually gives each phone a separate extension number so you have a way to talk to a specific phone. You know the main number for XYZ Company is 765-4321, and you know Fred's extension is 123, so a phone connection to Fred is identified by the number 764-4321 x123. In the TCP world, a Web server's extension (port number) is usually 80. If XYZ company's Web host has an IP address of 192.168.1.2, a TCP connection to the company's Web host goes to 192.168.1.2 port 80.

Just like a phone call, there is a caller and a receiver (usually called the listener). The listener listens for connections on a specific port number (such as 80 for Web connections or 25 for email). When you make a phone call and there's no one there to answer the phone, you eventually stop calling. When a caller tries to establish a connection to a host and port number where there's no listener, the TCP software refuses to establish the connection. In other words, you can't connect to a port if there's no listener for that port.

Some operating systems don't allow you to listen for connections on port numbers less than 1,024 (unless you are a system administrator) because these ports are commonly used for common services such as Web access and email. If you were allowed to listen for connections on port 80, for instance, you could intercept Web page requests and return phony results.

Tip

Most Windows and Unix systems have a command called `netstat` that allows you to display information about your network access. Specifically, `netstat -a` shows you all the active TCP connections as well as other network resources. You can see what ports are being used for listening, what connections exist, and what ports those connections are using.

A TCP connection always has port numbers on both endpoints, but when you make the connection, you usually don't care about the caller's port number—only the port number of the listening side. The operating system usually picks a random port number (it's not really random, but it might as well be) for the caller's port number. Technically, you can specify the caller's port number, but in practice, you almost always let the operating system pick the port number.

In fact, if you tell the operating system to listen for connections on port number 0, it will also pick a random port number.

Why would you want to listen on a random port number? Because there can only be one listener for a port number, you must be careful not to use a port that another application uses. For instance, if you pick port number 5,000 for your application and someone else picks the same port number, you can't run both applications on the same host. The easy solution for this problem is to make the port number a configurable parameter in your application. That is, allow the user to change the port number on the command line or in a configuration file.

The other solution is to pick a random free port number by listening on port 0. The one guarantee of a random port number is that it isn't being used by another program at the moment. Obviously, you need an alternate means of publishing port number information to potential clients for this method to work.

For instance, you could use the User Datagram Protocol (UDP) (described in the next section) to send out port number information. You might also write the port number to a file or store it in a directory using JNDI. Many CORBA and RMI implementations use this technique.

Tip

Because port numbers below 1,024 are usually reserved for operating system services, you won't get a random free port number below 1,024.

USER DATAGRAM PROTOCOL (UDP)

The User Datagram Protocol (UDP) is a packet-oriented protocol that adds some extra capabilities to IP. If a TCP connection is like a phone call, a UDP datagram is like a pager message. When you send a page, you dial a number and enter a numeric or text message. After that, you don't know whether the page was received. The only way you know is that you eventually hear from the person you paged. A datagram works the same way. You send a datagram to a specific host address and port number, but you have no guarantee that the packet ever gets there.

UDP also allows packets to be broadcast to a particular port number on all the hosts on the network.

If there was such a capability with pagers, you would be able to send the same page to everyone with a pager—or at least some subset of those people. The effectiveness of broadcasts is directly related to the router configuration, however. Most system administrators configure their routers to block broadcast packets to keep network traffic to a minimum. You should usually just count on broadcasts working on your local network and not across different networks or subnetworks.

Note

Many lookup services, such as some CORBA naming services and RMI naming services, use UDP broadcasts to perform lookups. These services might not work well across different networks because the routers usually block broadcast packets. You must either change the router configuration (which is not usually a network administrator's favorite choice) or change the naming service configuration. Most naming services have ways to work around these broadcast limitations.

IP also has the concept of multicast addresses. You can send a UDP packet to a specific group of hosts that belong to a particular IP multicast group. If this capability was available in phone pagers, you could set up a pager number that would send the same page to everyone in your department or family.

NAMED PORT NUMBERS

You can usually assign a name to a particular port number by adding it to a special file called `services`. On Windows 95/98/ME, this file is in the main Windows directory. On Windows NT and Windows 2000 systems, it's under `WINNT\System32\Drivers\etc`. On Unix/Linux systems, it's in the `etc` directory. The `services` file contains a list of names with associated port numbers and services. One thing to keep in mind with port numbers is that they are protocol-specific. Port 80 for TCP connections is not the same as port 80 for UDP datagrams. An entry in the `services` file looks like this:

```
ftp           21/tcp
```

The File Transfer Protocol (FTP) normally uses port 21 for incoming connections, so this entry in the `services` file associates the name `ftp` with port 21. The other bonus in using the services file is that it removes the port from the list of free ports. If you need to reserve TCP port 5,000 for your application, put an entry like this in the `services` file:

```
myapp       5000/tcp
```

This doesn't keep other applications from intentionally listening on port 5,000, but it will prevent the operating system from handing out 5,000 as a port number when an application asks for a free port.

INTERNET CONTROL MESSAGE PROTOCOL (ICMP)

The Internet Control Message Protocol (ICMP) allows routers and hosts to send errors and other control messages. Unlike TCP and UDP, ICMP isn't used by applications. There are different types of ICMP messages, and chances are, you don't need to know anything about them. The one ICMP message that you might have already unknowingly used is ICMP ECHO. An ICMP ECHO message is better known as a *ping*. When you need to see if your machine can talk to another machine, you can send a ping to the other machine and see if it responds. The `ping` command is available on Unix and Windows machines, so there's a good chance you have access to it. Figure 26.7 shows the output when you ping a host successfully.

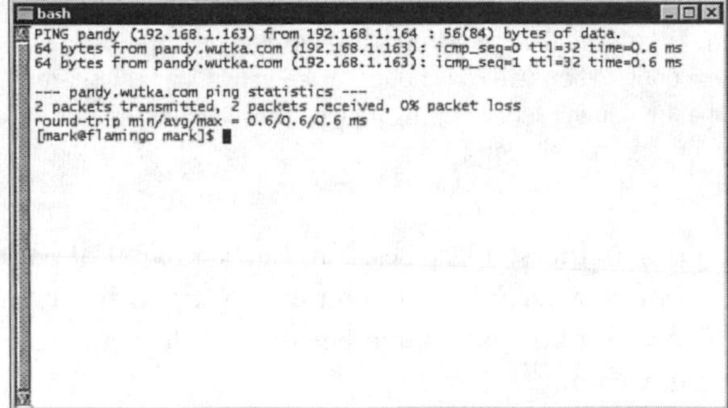

bash
PING pandy (192.168.1.163) from 192.168.1.164 : 56(84) bytes of data.
64 bytes from pandy.wutka.com (192.168.1.163): icmp_seq=0 ttl=32 time=0.6 ms
64 bytes from pandy.wutka.com (192.168.1.163): icmp_seq=1 ttl=32 time=0.6 ms
--- pandy.wutka.com ping statistics ---
2 packets transmitted, 2 packets received, 0% packet loss
round-trip min/avg/max = 0.6/0.6/0.6 ms
[mark@flamingo mark]$

Figure 26.7
When a ping succeeds, it usually tells you how long it took to get a reply.

When a ping fails, ping will either tell you immediately or just sit there doing nothing. It all depends on the particular version of the `ping` command you're using.

An Interesting Use of Ping

The funniest use of ping to date was described in January 1991 by Steve Hayman on the Usenet group *`comp.sys.next`*. He was trying to isolate a faulty cable segment on a TCP/IP Ethernet hooked up to a NeXT machine, and got tired of having to run back to his console after each cabling tweak to see if the ping packets were getting through. So he used the sound-recording feature on the NeXT, then wrote a script that repeatedly invoked `ping(8)`, listened for an echo, and played back the recording on each returned packet. Result? A program that caused the machine to repeat, over and over, "Ping…, ping…, ping…" as long as the network was up. He turned the volume to maximum, ferreted through the building with one ear cocked, and found a faulty tee connector in no time.

From The Jargon File version 4.2.2 at `http://www.tuxedo.org/~esr/jargon`

DOMAIN NAME SERVICE (DNS)

The Domain Name Service (DNS) is the phone book of the Internet. DNS is what gets you from `xyz.com` to 192.168.1.2. If you could only use numbers for Internet addresses, there are two things you could count on: The Internet wouldn't be nearly as popular as it is, and someone would shell out millions of dollars for the address 1.2.3.4.

Fortunately for everyone, the early designers of the Internet realized that it would be much easier to refer to hosts by name instead of address. Not only are they easier for humans to remember, the names also allow you to switch machines without reconfiguring other programs. For example, the popular news site `www.slashdot.org` has gone through several hardware upgrades over the past few years as it has become more and more popular. Whenever they upgraded the machine, the loyal readers didn't have to remember a new IP address. The DNS entry for `www.slashdot.org` referred everyone's Web browsers to the new address.

When you ask a DNS server to locate `www.slashdot.org`, it might end up asking one of the huge top-level DNS servers to look up `slashdot.org`. These top-level servers know every name that comes right before `.org`, `.com`, or any of the other common endings. That is, they know slashdot.org, but not necessarily anything else in the address, like the www. After your DNS server receives the address for slashdot.org, it asks the name server for slashdot.org to find www.slashdot.org. All of this takes place in less than a second. You often don't notice. Plus, because DNS servers cache frequently requested addresses, there's a good chance the server already has the address you want.

You might be wondering why you need to know anything about DNS. Obviously, it's nice to know how things work, but when it comes to debugging a system, there's a more important reason. When you try to connect to a host for one reason or another, if the DNS server is down or you have trouble using DNS, it might look like the server itself is down, even though you're just having a DNS problem. In other words, you might try to connect to www.xyz.com and get an error because the DNS lookup failed. Knowing that there is an extra point of failure possible (the DNS server), you should try using the actual IP address for the server if you know it.

Note

Windows and Unix systems also keep a local file called hosts that associates names with IP addresses. Under Windows 95/98/ME, the file is under the main Windows directory. On a new installation, there's a hosts.sam sample file to show you the format of the hosts file. You can rename (or copy) this file to hosts and then edit it. On Windows NT/2000 systems, the hosts file is in WINNT\System32\Drivers\etc, and on Unix/Linux systems, the file is in /etc.

FIREWALLS

Firewalls are one of the most important components in an enterprise network, yet they are frequently ignored and misunderstood by most developers. The main purpose of the firewall is to keep malicious people out of your network while still allowing your internal users to access the Internet and allowing external users to access various parts of your network. Figure 26.8 shows a typical firewall setup.

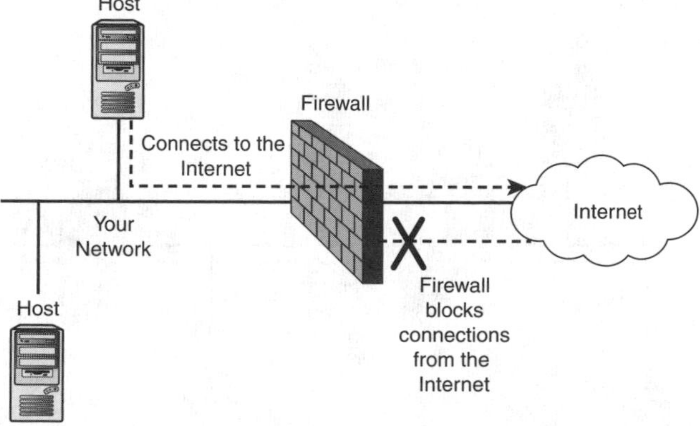

Figure 26.8
A firewall blocks most incoming connections, but usually allows outbound connections.

Firewalls vary tremendously in capabilities, but there are some common capabilities, and also some common network configurations. Many firewalls employ a technique of blocking off certain ports and/or certain network addresses. For example, if you are running a Web server, you want to allow outside users to connect to your server on ports 80 and 443 (80 is for normal Web traffic, 443 is for encrypted Web traffic). Many firewalls allow you to block all incoming connections that aren't on ports 80 or 443. This lessens the possibility that someone will break into your system. Firewalls can also block outgoing connections. Your site might not want you making certain types of outbound connections or might not want you to make outbound connections at all.

Some firewalls understand network protocols and can validate the data being sent for various reasons. For instance, there are firewalls that filter Web traffic to remove Java applets and other executable content from Web pages. This lessens the chance that someone will accidentally download something that compromises network security. This can sometimes cause problems if the firewall thinks a port number is for a different protocol than the one you're using.

For example, Sun's Java Web Server uses port number 7070 for encrypted Web traffic by default. Unfortunately, port 7070 is also used by RealAudio. Some firewalls might suddenly drop Java Web Server connections because they don't look like RealAudio data streams. When this happens, the system administrators need to change the firewall configuration. Most firewalls can perform filtering on a per-host basis, so you can turn off the RealAudio filter just for your Java Web Server host (and turn on the secure Web filter if you want).

In addition to the configuration you saw in Figure 26.8, many sites use a configuration called a *Demilitarized Zone* or *DMZ*. The idea is that you create a subnet for your Web servers and other Internet-accessible machines, and protect that subnet with a firewall. Then you put a much stronger firewall between the DMZ and your internal network where your database and application servers reside. Figure 26.9 shows a typical DMZ configuration.

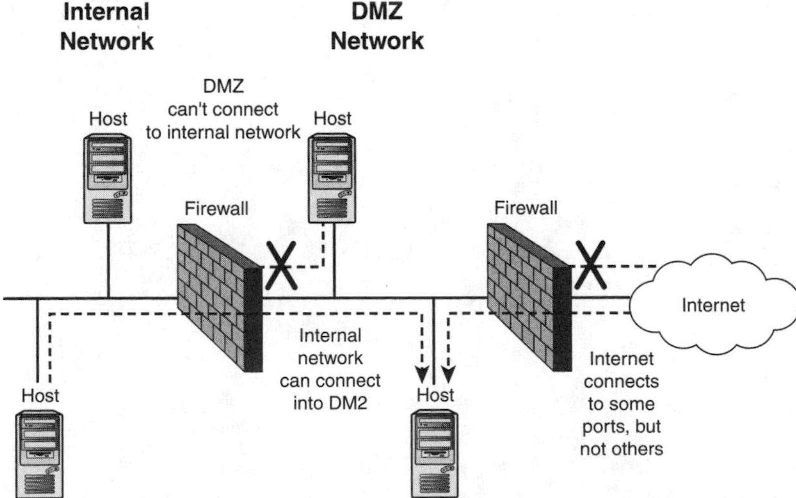

Figure 26.9
A DMZ separates the internal network from the Internet-accessible network.

In many DMZ configurations, hosts on the internal network can freely connect to hosts on the DMZ, but DMZ hosts can't connect to hosts on the internal network. The whole idea is that even if a machine on the DMZ is compromised, your internal network is still safe. You often must open holes in the firewall between the DMZ and the internal network, if Web servers must access data from your application and database servers.

You probably won't be the network administrator's best friend for doing this, but there are ways to get around some firewall restrictions. If the firewall just blocks ports and ignores the actual content, you might be able to change the port number of the service you're accessing. For example, a consultant was working at a site that allowed outbound connections only on ports 80 and 443. The consultant needed to open a Telnet connection to his computer at home, which ran Linux. He changed the configuration on his Linux machine to allow Telnet connections on port 443 as well as the usual port 23. The firewall, thinking he was making a secure Web connection, allowed the connection. Obviously, to use a technique like this you must have control of the machine you are connecting to. Whatever you do, make sure you aren't compromising your network security if you try to skirt firewall restrictions. In general, avoid anything that would allow someone to create an inbound connection.

Remember that applications can choose to listen on a random free port number instead of using a well-known port number. This technique causes all kinds of havoc when there's a firewall between the listener and the caller. Because CORBA and RMI frequently use this technique, it's often difficult to uses these technologies when there's a firewall involved.

Many companies make various kinds of gateway programs that use specific port numbers for relaying CORBA and RMI calls. These gateways allow CORBA and RMI to work over a firewall (in most cases).

In extreme cases, the firewall is so restrictive that it only allows Web traffic. When faced with this proposition, you have two choices: use a Web-based protocol such as XML-SOAP, or use a Web gateway for CORBA or RMI. A Web gateway for CORBA or RMI encapsulates a CORBA or RMI call in a regular Web-page request. This technique tends to be slow, but it does make it easier to use a firewall.

CHAPTER 27

Network Programming

In this chapter

SOCKET PROGRAMMING

The term *socket* might sound a little strange, but sockets are the objects that let you communicate with the network. A socket doesn't represent a physical device, just an endpoint of a network connection. There are three main socket classes in Java—`Socket`, `ServerSocket`, and `DatagramSocket`. Of these, only the `Socket` and `ServerSocket` classes are used for connection-oriented data (that is, they support the TCP protocol). The `DatagramSocket` class does connectionless networking (the UDP protocol).

CREATING A SERVER

Remember from Chapter 26, "Networks and Network Protocols," that to create a TCP connection, you must first have a listener. The `ServerSocket` class lets you listen for incoming connections. You create a `ServerSocket` and specify the port number it should listen on, or 0 to get any free port. Next, you call the `accept` method, which waits for an incoming connection. Keep in mind that the `accept` method will not return until there is an incoming connection. If you need to do other things while waiting for a connection, you need to use multiple threads.

You might set up a `ServerSocket` like this:

```
ServerSocket server = new ServerSocket(1234);
Socket = server.accept();
```

When the `ServerSocket` receives an incoming connection, the `accept` method returns a `Socket` object representing the listener's side of the connection. After you have a connected socket object, you can call `getInputStream` and `getOutputStream` methods to get streams for reading and writing data.

Most servers spawn a thread to handle a connection from a client. That is, after `accept` returns a `Socket` for an incoming connection, the server creates a client-handler thread that talks to the new client, and the server calls `accept` again to wait for a new client.

Listing 27.1 shows a server that echoes back any data sent to it.

LISTING 27.1 SOURCE CODE FOR `EchoServer.java`

```
package usingj2ee.net;

import java.io.*;
import java.net.*;

/** Implements a simple echo server that echoes back any
 *  data it receives. */

public class EchoServer
{
    public static void main(String[] args)
    {
        try
        {
```

```
// Allow the user to override the port number using a system property
// You can set the property with the -D option on the command-line:
// java -Dport=4321 usingj2ee.net.EchoServer

            String portNumStr = System.getProperty("port", "1234");

            int port = 1234;

            try
            {
                port = Integer.parseInt(portNumStr);
            }
            catch (Exception exc)
            {
                System.out.println("Invalid port number: "+portNumStr);
                System.exit(0);
            }

// Create the server socket
            ServerSocket server = new ServerSocket(port);

// Wait for an incoming connection
            for (;;)
            {
                Socket newClient = server.accept();

// Create a client handler to handle the new client
                ClientHandler handler = new ClientHandler(newClient);

// Create a thread for running the client handler
                Thread clientThread = new Thread(handler);
                clientThread.start();
            }
        }
        catch (Exception exc)
        {
            exc.printStackTrace();
        }
    }
}

/** Handles incoming data from a client and echoes it back */
class ClientHandler implements Runnable
{
    protected Socket clientSocket;

    public ClientHandler(Socket aClientSocket)
    {
        clientSocket = aClientSocket;
    }

    public void run()
    {
        try
        {
// First, get an input stream for reading client data and an output stream
// for writing client data
```

LISTING 27.1 CONTINUED

```
            InputStream in = clientSocket.getInputStream();

            OutputStream out = clientSocket.getOutputStream();

// Create a buffer for reading data
            byte[] inputBuffer = new byte[5000];


            for (;;)
            {
// Read data from the input stream into the input buffer
                int numBytesRead = in.read(inputBuffer);

// If there are no more bytes to read (the client disconnected)
// exit the loop
                if (numBytesRead <= 0)
                {
                    break;
                }

// Write the bytes to the output stream -- for writing,
// you must also specify a buffer offset and a number
// of bytes. In this case, the buffer offset is 0,
// meaning the start of the input buffer, and the
// number of bytes is the number of bytes returned
/  by the read method.

                out.write(inputBuffer, 0, numBytesRead);
            }

// The loop only terminates when the client disconnects.
// It's safe to close down the connection. Just ignore
// any errors that happen when closing.
            try
            {
                clientSocket.close();
            }
            catch (Exception ignore) {}
        }
        catch (Exception exc)
        {
            exc.printStackTrace();

// It's possible that the socket is still open at this
// point, so try to close it just in case
            try
            {
                clientSocket.close();
            }
            catch (Exception ignore) {}
        }
    }
}
```

You don't need to write a client program to test the echo server; you can use the `telnet` command to test it. Just start the server with the command `java usingj2ee.net.EchoServer`, and then from another command prompt type `telnet localhost 1234`. If you're running Windows 95/98/ME/NT, a Telnet window will pop up on the screen. If you're running Windows 2000, Unix, or Linux, you should see a screen somewhat similar to the one shown in Figure 27.1. Try typing things in the Telnet window. You should see them echoed back. You might or might not need to hit return to see the echoed text.

Note

To exit from the `telnet` command from Windows, either close the window (using the Close button or by choosing Connect, Disconnect). Under Unix, Linux, and Windows 2000, press Ctrl+] and type `quit`. To stop the server, press Ctrl+C.

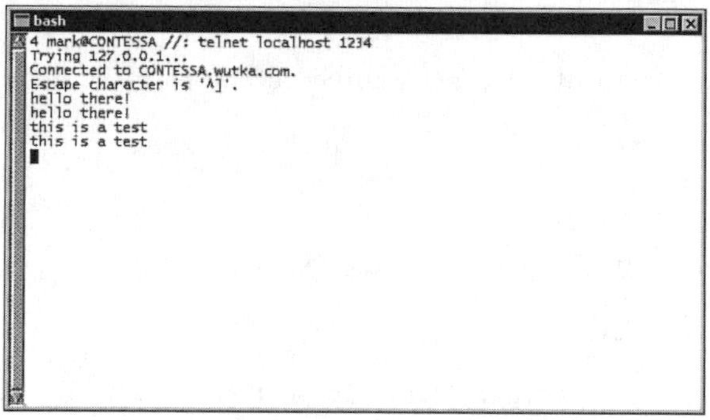

Figure 27.1
You can test the echo server with the `telnet` command.

```
bash
4 mark@CONTESSA //: telnet localhost 1234
Trying 127.0.0.1...
Connected to CONTESSA.wutka.com.
Escape character is '^]'.
hello there!
hello there!
this is a test
this is a test
```

Tip

Because the `telnet` command opens up a TCP connection to another host and port, you can use it to test network connectivity. If you have trouble connecting to the `www.xyz.com` Web site, try telnetting to port 80 on `www.xyz.com` and see if you can get a connection.

CREATING A CLIENT

To create a TCP connection with the `Socket` class, just create a new `Socket` with the host-name and port you want to connect to. For instance, to create a `Socket` that connects to the test program from Listing 27.1, just do the following:

```
Socket clientSock = new Socket("localhost", 1234);
```

The `Socket` class you create when you call `new Socket` is the same kind of `Socket` returned by `ServerSocket.accept`, so you can call `getInputStream` and `getOutputStream` to get streams for reading and writing data.

Listing 27.2 shows a test client that connects to the echo server, passes some test data, and prints the response.

LISTING 27.2 SOURCE CODE FOR EchoClient.java

```
package usingj2ee.net;

import java.io.*;
import java.net.*;

/** Implements a simple client that connects to the echo server */

public class EchoClient
{
    public static void main(String[] args)
    {
        try
        {

// Allow the user to override the port number using a system property
// You can set the property with the -D option on the command-line:
// java -Dport=4321 usingj2ee.net.EchoClient

            String portNumStr = System.getProperty("port", "1234");

            int port = 1234;

            try
            {
                port = Integer.parseInt(portNumStr);
            }
            catch (Exception exc)
            {
                System.out.println("Invalid port number: "+portNumStr);
                System.exit(0);
            }

// Allow the user to override the destination host with -Dhost
            String host = System.getProperty("host", "localhost");

// Create the socket
            Socket clientSock = new Socket(host, port);

// Get the input and output streams

            InputStream in = clientSock.getInputStream();
            OutputStream out = clientSock.getOutputStream();

            PrintStream ps = new PrintStream(out);

            String strToWrite = "Hello, Server!\n";

// Write the string to the output stream (send it to the server)
            ps.println(strToWrite);
            ps.flush();  // make sure all the bytes get written

// Create a buffer for reading data
            byte[] inputBuffer = new byte[5000];


// Count the total bytes read from the server
```

```
            int totalRead = 0;

            for (;;)
            {
// Read data from the input stream into the input buffer
                int numBytesRead = in.read(inputBuffer);

// Echo the bytes to the screen
                System.out.write(inputBuffer, 0, numBytesRead);

// If there are no more bytes to read (the server disconnected)
// exit the loop
                if (numBytesRead <= 0)
                {
                    break;
                }

                totalRead = totalRead + numBytesRead;

// Quit when the server has echoed back all the bytes sent.
// If you don't do this, the client never knows when to
// quit because the server just waits for the client to
// send more data
                if (totalRead >= strToWrite.length()) break;

            }
            clientSock.close();
        }
        catch (Exception exc)
        {
            exc.printStackTrace();
        }
    }
}
```

One of the most important things to remember about a TCP connection is that it is a stream of bytes with no notion of message boundaries. When a client sends 500 bytes to a server, the server might receive the data as 150 bytes followed by 350 more. If you want to break up the data into messages with specific sizes, you must send the size along with each message. You will see how to do that in a moment.

First, there are a few other items you should be aware of. You should almost always use a buffered input stream when reading data from a socket connection, and use a buffered output stream to write the data. This is especially true if you are reading only a few bytes at a time. If you don't use a buffered input stream, every time you call the `read` method, the Java VM makes a call to the operating system to read data. Such calls take a lot of extra time. A buffered stream reads and writes in large chunks, minimizing the number of times the VM must interact with the operating system.

The `DataInputStream` and `DataOutputStream` classes really help when you must send various types of data. You can send an `int` value over a TCP connection by calling the `DataOutputStream`'s `writeInt` method. When you do network programming in a language other than Java, you usually have to worry about byte ordering when it comes to numeric values. A Sun machine represents numbers differently than a Pentium machine does. For example, the hex number 0x12345678 on a Sun is stored as 0x12, 0x34, 0x56, 0x78, in successive memory locations. This storage mechanism is called *big endian* because the high-order bytes—or the big end of the number—is stored first. Other machines, such as the Pentium, store 0x12345678 as 0x78, 0x56, 0x43, 0x12. This method is called *little endian* because the least significant bytes, or little end of the number, is stored first.

Because machines represent numbers differently, it's important to have a standard way to represent these numbers when transmitting data over a network. Otherwise, you must figure out each time whether two machines represent numbers the same way or not. The standard representation for a number is big-endian, which is also referred to as "network byte order."

The Java VM shields you from these byte-ordering concerns. You never see how the CPU represents a number in memory, so you don't really care. The only place you see any kind of byte ordering is when you use methods such as `writeInt`, `writeShort`, `readInt`, and so on. These methods read and write data in network byte order, regardless of the CPU type. After all, if a Java program behaved differently on one type of CPU, that would break the write-once-run-anywhere philosophy.

If the server and the client are both Java, you couldn't care less how the data streams represent numbers. It's when you must interact with non-Java programs that it becomes an issue. As long as you remember that the Java streams use network byte order, you should have no problem working with existing network protocols. Most of them use network byte order anyway.

SENDING AND RECEIVING MESSAGES

Most application-level network protocols have the notion of a message. Some of them terminate messages with special characters, such as newline characters, whereas others use fixed-size message blocks. One of the problems with using special characters is that you must scan through each message character-by-character looking for the message terminator. Fixed-size messages are extremely easy to deal with, because you know how much data you must read. You lose some flexibility, however, because you must always fit your data into the fixed size. For messages with very little content, you also waste network bandwidth sending unused bytes.

Another common messaging solution is to first write out a byte count and then write out the message bytes. This way, you can still work with messages, you don't have to scan for a terminating character, and the messages can be any size you want. You can send a 10-byte message followed by a 10,000-byte message.

Listing 27.3 shows a pair of utility methods for reading and writing variable-sized messages. Notice that the `readMessage` method uses `readFully` to read the byte array. The `read` method might return less than the number of bytes you wanted to read, but `readFully` either reads the full number of bytes or it throws an exception, which usually occurs only if you lose the connection while reading. The `readFully` method is part of the `DataInputStream` class.

LISTING 27.3 SOURCE CODE FOR Messages.java

```
package usingj2ee.net;

import java.io.*;
import java.net.*;

public class Messages
{
    public static byte[] readMessage(DataInputStream in)
        throws IOException
    {
// Get the message length
        int messageLen = in.readInt();

// Create a buffer for reading the message
        byte[] buff = new byte[messageLen];

// Read the full number of bytes
        in.readFully(buff);

        return buff;
    }

    public static void writeMessage(byte[] message, int len,
        DataOutputStream out)
        throws IOException
    {
// Write out the message length
        out.writeInt(len);

// Write out the message
        out.write(message, 0, len);

// Flush the output stream in case it's buffered
        out.flush();
    }
}
```

You can also use `DataInputStream` and `DataOutputStream` to store data into a byte array for messaging and read data back out. You just use the `ByteArrayInputStream` and `ByteArrayOutputStream` classes to work with the byte arrays, and use the `DataInputStream` and `DataOutputStream` classes around the byte-array streams. Keep in mind, however, that creating a new stream every time you read and write a message can waste a lot of CPU time and memory. If your server must handle a large volume of messages, you can't afford to create a lot of objects just to handle a single message. In fact, even the `Messages` class could be pretty inefficient because it creates a new byte array for every message.

Listing 27.4 shows a client handler for a simple chat program. It uses byte-array streams for encoding and decoding messages.

LISTING 27.4 SOURCE CODE FOR ChatClientHandler.java

```
package usingj2ee.net;

import java.io.*;
import java.net.*;
import java.util.Date;

public class ChatClientHandler implements Runnable
{
    protected ChatServer server;
    protected Socket clientSocket;

    protected DataInputStream clientIn;
    protected DataOutputStream clientOut;

    protected String userName;
    protected Date loginTime;
    protected boolean isLoggedIn;

    public ChatClientHandler(ChatServer theServer, Socket theClientSocket)
    {
        clientSocket = theClientSocket;
        userName = null;
        isLoggedIn = false;
        server = theServer;
    }

    public void run()
    {
        try
        {
// Make sure the input stream is buffered
            clientIn = new DataInputStream(
                new BufferedInputStream(clientSocket.getInputStream()));

// Make sure the output stream is buffered
            clientOut = new DataOutputStream(
                new BufferedOutputStream(clientSocket.getOutputStream()));

            for (;;)
            {
// Read the message from the client
                byte[] message = Messages.readMessage(clientIn);

// Create a DatanputStream to decode the message
                DataInputStream msgDecode = new DataInputStream(
                    new ByteArrayInputStream(message));

// Get the message type
                int messageType = msgDecode.readInt();

// Process the message based on the type
                switch (messageType)
                {
                    case ChatProtocol.LOGIN:
// Get the username from the message
```

```
                        userName = msgDecode.readUTF();
                        loginTime = new Date();

// Tell the server that the user has logged in
                        if (server.login(this))
                        {
                            isLoggedIn = true;
                        }
                        break;

                    case ChatProtocol.CHAT:
                        if (!isLoggedIn)
                        {
                            sendError("You're not logged in");
                        }

// Get the chat message
                        String chatMessage = msgDecode.readUTF();

// Relay the chat message to the server
                        server.chat(chatMessage, this);
                        break;

                    case ChatProtocol.ACTION:
                        if (!isLoggedIn)
                        {
                            sendError("You're not logged in");
                        }

// Get the action message
                        String actionMessage = msgDecode.readUTF();

// Relay the action message to the server
                        server.action(actionMessage, this);
                        break;

                    case ChatProtocol.PRIVATE:
                        if (!isLoggedIn)
                        {
                            sendError("You're not logged in");
                        }

// Get the user who should receive the private message
                        String destinationUser = msgDecode.readUTF();

// Get the private message
                        String pvtMessage = msgDecode.readUTF();

// Relay the private message to the server
                        server.privateMessage(destinationUser,
                            pvtMessage, this);
                        break;

                    case ChatProtocol.WHO:
                        if (!isLoggedIn)
                        {
                            sendError("You're not logged in");
```

LISTING 27.4 CONTINUED

```
                    }
                    server.who(this);
                    break;

                default:
                    sendError("Protocol error: Invalid
➥                  message type.");
            }
        }
    }
    catch (Exception exc)
    {
// Tell the server that the user has logged out
        if (isLoggedIn)
        {
            server.logout(this);
        }
        try
        {
            clientSocket.close();
        }
        catch (Exception ignore) {}
    }
}

/** Encodes and sends a chat message back to the client */
public synchronized void sendChat(String fromUser, String message)
{
    try
    {
        ByteArrayOutputStream byteOut = new ByteArrayOutputStream();
        DataOutputStream chatOut = new DataOutputStream(byteOut);

        chatOut.writeInt(ChatProtocol.CHAT);
        chatOut.writeUTF(fromUser);
        chatOut.writeUTF(message);

        sendMessage(byteOut.toByteArray());
    }
    catch (Exception ignore) {}
}

/** Encodes and sends an action message back to the client */
public synchronized void sendAction(String fromUser, String message)
{
    try
    {
        ByteArrayOutputStream byteOut = new ByteArrayOutputStream();
        DataOutputStream chatOut = new DataOutputStream(byteOut);

        chatOut.writeInt(ChatProtocol.ACTION);
        chatOut.writeUTF(fromUser);
        chatOut.writeUTF(message);

        sendMessage(byteOut.toByteArray());
```

```
        }
        catch (Exception ignore) {}
    }

/** Encodes and sends an error message back to the client */
    public synchronized void sendError(String message)
    {
        try
        {
            ByteArrayOutputStream byteOut = new ByteArrayOutputStream();
            DataOutputStream chatOut = new DataOutputStream(byteOut);

            chatOut.writeInt(ChatProtocol.ERROR);
            chatOut.writeUTF(message);

            sendMessage(byteOut.toByteArray());
        }
        catch (Exception ignore) {}
    }

/** Encodes and sends a private message back to the client */
    public synchronized void sendPrivateChat(String fromUser,
➥          String message)
    {
        try
        {
            ByteArrayOutputStream byteOut = new ByteArrayOutputStream();
            DataOutputStream chatOut = new DataOutputStream(byteOut);

            chatOut.writeInt(ChatProtocol.PRIVATE);
            chatOut.writeUTF(fromUser);
            chatOut.writeUTF(message);

            sendMessage(byteOut.toByteArray());
        }
        catch (Exception ignore) {}
    }

/** Encodes and sends a login message back to the client */
    public synchronized void sendLogin(String user, Date loginTime)
    {
        try
        {
            ByteArrayOutputStream byteOut = new ByteArrayOutputStream();
            DataOutputStream chatOut = new DataOutputStream(byteOut);

            chatOut.writeInt(ChatProtocol.LOGIN);
            chatOut.writeUTF(user);
            chatOut.writeLong(loginTime.getTime());

            sendMessage(byteOut.toByteArray());
        }
        catch (Exception ignore) {}
    }

/** Encodes and sends a logout message back to the client */
    public synchronized void sendLogout(String user, Date logoutTime)
```

LISTING 27.4 CONTINUED

```
    {
        try
        {
            ByteArrayOutputStream byteOut = new ByteArrayOutputStream();
            DataOutputStream chatOut = new DataOutputStream(byteOut);

            chatOut.writeInt(ChatProtocol.LOGOUT);
            chatOut.writeUTF(user);
            chatOut.writeLong(logoutTime.getTime());

            sendMessage(byteOut.toByteArray());
        }
        catch (Exception ignore) {}
    }

/** Encodes and sends a privatesent message back to the client */
    public synchronized void sendPrivateSent(String user, String message)
    {
        try
        {
            ByteArrayOutputStream byteOut = new ByteArrayOutputStream();
            DataOutputStream chatOut = new DataOutputStream(byteOut);

            chatOut.writeInt(ChatProtocol.PRIVATE_SENT);
            chatOut.writeUTF(user);
            chatOut.writeUTF(message);

            sendMessage(byteOut.toByteArray());
        }
        catch (Exception ignore) {}
    }


/** Encodes and sends a WHO message back to the client */
    public synchronized void sendWho(String[] users, Date[] loginTimes)
    {
        try
        {
            ByteArrayOutputStream byteOut = new ByteArrayOutputStream();
            DataOutputStream chatOut = new DataOutputStream(byteOut);

            chatOut.writeInt(ChatProtocol.WHO);
            chatOut.writeInt(users.length);
            for (int i=0; i < users.length; i++)
            {
                chatOut.writeUTF(users[i]);
                chatOut.writeLong(loginTimes[i].getTime());
            }

            sendMessage(byteOut.toByteArray());
        }
        catch (Exception ignore) {}
    }

    public void sendMessage(byte[] message)
    {
```

```
        try
        {
            Messages.writeMessage(message, message.length, clientOut);
        }
        catch (Exception ignore) {}
    }

    public String getUserName()
    {
        return userName;
    }

    public Date getLoginTime()
    {
        return loginTime;
    }
}
```

The ChatClientHandler class uses some constants to define message types. These message types are defined in a class called ChatProtocol, which is shown in Listing 27.5.

LISTING 27.5 SOURCE CODE FOR ChatProtocol.java

```
package usingj2ee.net;

/** Defines constant message types used in messages between
 *  the chat client and the chat server. */

public class ChatProtocol
{
    public static final int LOGIN = 1;
    public static final int CHAT = 2;
    public static final int ACTION = 3;
    public static final int PRIVATE = 4;
    public static final int LOGOUT = 5;
    public static final int ERROR = 6;
    public static final int PRIVATE_SENT = 7;
    public static final int WHO = 8;
}
```

The chat server is pretty simple. The ChatClientHandler class does all the interaction with the individual clients. The only thing the server needs to do is listen for new clients and process any requests from the clients. Whenever a client sends a message, the server relays the message to the other clients. Listing 27.6 shows the ChatServer class.

LISTING 27.6 SOURCE CODE FOR ChatServer.java

```
package usingj2ee.net;

import java.io.*;
import java.net.*;
import java.util.*;

public class ChatServer implements Runnable
```

LISTING 27.6 CONTINUED

```
{
    protected Hashtable users;
    protected int portNumber;

    public ChatServer()
    {
        portNumber = 1234;
        users = new Hashtable();
    }

    public ChatServer(int aPortNumber)
    {
        portNumber = aPortNumber;
        users = new Hashtable();
    }

    public void run()
    {
        try
        {
// Create a socket for receiving incoming connections
            ServerSocket serverSock = new ServerSocket(portNumber);

            for (;;)
            {
// Get the next incoming connection
                Socket clientSocket = serverSock.accept();

// Create a ChatClientHandler to interact with the new connection
                ChatClientHandler handler = new ChatClientHandler(
                    this, clientSocket);

// Start the ChatClientHandler in a separate thread
                Thread clientThread = new Thread(handler);
                clientThread.start();
            }
        }
        catch (Exception exc)
        {
            exc.printStackTrace();
        }
    }

    public synchronized boolean login(ChatClientHandler loginClient)
    {
        String userName = loginClient.getUserName();
        Date loginTime = loginClient.getLoginTime();

// If the user already exists, send an error
        if (users.get(userName) != null)
        {
            loginClient.sendError("That user name is already taken.");
            return false;
        }
```

```
// Put the user in the user table
        users.put(userName, loginClient);

// Tell all the users that the new user has logged on
        Enumeration e = users.elements();

        while (e.hasMoreElements())
        {
            ChatClientHandler handler = (ChatClientHandler)
➥           e.nextElement();

            handler.sendLogin(userName, loginTime);
        }

        return true;
    }


    public synchronized void logout(ChatClientHandler client)
    {
        String userName = client.getUserName();

// Remove the user from the table
        users.remove(userName);

// Tell all the users that the user has logged off
        Enumeration e = users.elements();

        Date logoutTime = new Date();

        while (e.hasMoreElements())
        {
            ChatClientHandler handler = (ChatClientHandler)
➥           e.nextElement();

            handler.sendLogout(userName, logoutTime);
        }
    }

    public void chat(String message, ChatClientHandler client)
    {
        String userName = client.getUserName();

        Enumeration e = users.elements();

        while (e.hasMoreElements())
        {
            ChatClientHandler handler = (ChatClientHandler)
➥           e.nextElement();

            handler.sendChat(userName, message);
        }
    }

    public void action(String message, ChatClientHandler client)
    {
        String userName = client.getUserName();
```

LISTING 27.6 CONTINUED

```
        Enumeration e = users.elements();

        while (e.hasMoreElements())
        {
            ChatClientHandler handler = (ChatClientHandler)
➥           e.nextElement();

            handler.sendAction(userName, message);
        }
    }

    public void privateMessage(String destUser, String message,
        ChatClientHandler client)
    {
        String userName = client.getUserName();

        ChatClientHandler destClient =
            (ChatClientHandler) users.get(destUser);

        if (destClient == null)
        {
            client.sendError("Unknown user - "+destUser);
        }
        else
        {
            destClient.sendPrivateChat(userName, message);
            client.sendPrivateSent(destUser, message);
        }
    }

    public synchronized void who(ChatClientHandler client)
    {
        int numUsers = users.size();

        String[] userNames = new String[numUsers];
        Date[] loginTimes = new Date[numUsers];

        int i=0;

        Enumeration e = users.elements();

        while (e.hasMoreElements())
        {
            ChatClientHandler whoClient = (ChatClientHandler)
➥           e.nextElement();

            userNames[i] = whoClient.getUserName();
            loginTimes[i] = whoClient.getLoginTime();
            i++;
        }

        client.sendWho(userNames, loginTimes);
    }
```

```
    public static void main(String[] args)
    {
        int portNumber = 1234;

        String portNumStr = System.getProperty("port", "1234");

        try
        {
            portNumber = Integer.parseInt(portNumStr);
        }
        catch (Exception exc)
        {
            System.out.println("Invalid port number: "+portNumStr);
            System.exit(0);
        }

        try
        {
            ChatServer server = new ChatServer(portNumber);

// The server doesn't need to run in a separate thread,
// just call its run method.
            server.run();
        }
        catch (Exception exc)
        {
            exc.printStackTrace();
        }
    }
}
```

The `ChatClient` class is a text-based client for the chat server. You can create a graphical interface pretty easily, too, but a text-based client is the easiest. As a user of the chat program, you want to watch messages go by without having to type anything. When you want to say something, you type it in and press Enter. When you read from `System.in`, however, your thread blocks while waiting for input, so you must have a second thread that reads the messages from the server. The `ChatClient` spawns a thread for reading messages from the server and uses the main thread for reading console input. Listing 27.7 shows the `ChatClient` program.

LISTING 27.7 SOURCE CODE FOR ChatClient.java

```
package usingj2ee.net;

import java.io.*;
import java.net.*;
import java.text.*;
import java.util.Date;

public class ChatClient implements Runnable
{
    protected DataInputStream clientIn;
    protected DateFormat format;

    public ChatClient(DataInputStream aClientIn)
```

Listing 27.7 Continued

```
    {
        clientIn = aClientIn;

// Create a formatter for printing times and dates
        format = DateFormat.getDateTimeInstance(
            DateFormat.SHORT, DateFormat.SHORT);
    }

    public void run()
    {
        try
        {
            for (;;)
            {
// Read the next message from the server
                byte[] message = Messages.readMessage(clientIn);

// Create a DataInputStream for decoding the message
                ByteArrayInputStream byteIn = new ByteArrayInputStream(
                    message);
                DataInputStream msgDecoder = new DataInputStream(byteIn);

                int messageType = msgDecoder.readInt();

// For each possible message type, extract the data from the message
// and call the appropriate routine to handle the message
                switch (messageType)
                {
                    case ChatProtocol.CHAT:
                        String fromUser = msgDecoder.readUTF();
                        String chat = msgDecoder.readUTF();
                        printChat(fromUser, chat);
                        break;

                    case ChatProtocol.ACTION:
                        fromUser = msgDecoder.readUTF();
                        String action = msgDecoder.readUTF();
                        printAction(fromUser, action);
                        break;

                    case ChatProtocol.ERROR:
                        String error = msgDecoder.readUTF();
                        printError(error);
                        break;

                    case ChatProtocol.PRIVATE:
                        fromUser = msgDecoder.readUTF();
                        String pvtMsg = msgDecoder.readUTF();
                        printPrivate(fromUser, pvtMsg);
                        break;

                    case ChatProtocol.PRIVATE_SENT:
                        String toUser = msgDecoder.readUTF();
                        pvtMsg = msgDecoder.readUTF();
                        printPrivateSent(toUser, pvtMsg);
```

```
                    break;

                case ChatProtocol.LOGIN:
                    String loginUserName = msgDecoder.readUTF();
                    Date loginTime = new Date(msgDecoder.readLong());
                    printLogin(loginUserName, loginTime);
                    break;

                case ChatProtocol.LOGOUT:
                    String user = msgDecoder.readUTF();
                    Date logoutTime = new Date(msgDecoder.readLong());
                    printLogout(user, logoutTime);
                    break;

                case ChatProtocol.WHO:
                    int numUsers = msgDecoder.readInt();
                    String[] users = new String[numUsers];
                    Date[] loginTimes = new Date[numUsers];

                    for (int i=0; i < numUsers; i++)
                    {
                        users[i] = msgDecoder.readUTF();
                        loginTimes[i] = new
➥                       Date(msgDecoder.readLong());
                    }
                    printWho(users, loginTimes);
                    break;
            }

        }
    }
    catch (Exception exc)
    {
        exc.printStackTrace();
        System.exit(0);
    }
}

public void printChat(String userName, String message)
{
    System.out.println("<"+userName+">: "+message);
}

public void printAction(String userName, String message)
{
    System.out.println(userName+" "+message);
}

public void printError(String message)
{
    System.out.println("!ERROR! "+message);
}

public void printPrivate(String fromUser, String message)
{
    System.out.println("*Private from "+fromUser+"* "+message);
}
```

LISTING 27.7 CONTINUED

```
    public void printPrivateSent(String toUser, String message)
    {
        System.out.println("Sent private message to "+toUser);
    }

    public void printLogin(String user, Date loginTime)
    {
        System.out.println("User "+user+" logged in at "+
            format.format(loginTime));
    }

    public void printLogout(String user, Date logoutTime)
    {
        System.out.println("User "+user+" logged off at "+
            format.format(logoutTime));
    }

    public void printWho(String[] users, Date loginTimes[])
    {
        for (int i=0; i < users.length; i++)
        {
            System.out.println(users[i]+" on since "+
                format.format(loginTimes[i]));
        }
    }

    public static void main(String[] args)
    {
        int portNumber = 1234;

        String portNumStr = System.getProperty("port", "1234");

        try
        {
            portNumber = Integer.parseInt(portNumStr);
        }
        catch (Exception exc)
        {
            System.out.println("Invalid port number: "+portNumStr);
            System.exit(0);
        }

        String host = System.getProperty("host", "localhost");

        if (args.length == 0)
        {
            System.out.println(
                "Please provide a user name on the command line");
            System.exit(0);
        }

        try
        {
// Connect to the server
```

```
            Socket sock = new Socket(host, portNumber);

// Create the streams for reading from and writing to the server

            DataInputStream clientIn = new DataInputStream(
                new BufferedInputStream(sock.getInputStream()));

            DataOutputStream clientOut = new DataOutputStream(
                new BufferedOutputStream(sock.getOutputStream()));

// Create a ChatClient to handle incoming server messages
            ChatClient theClient = new ChatClient(clientIn);


// Start the ChatClient in a separate thread
            Thread clientInThread = new Thread(theClient);
            clientInThread.start();

// Log the user in
            sendLogin(args[0], clientOut);

            DataInputStream userInput = new DataInputStream(System.in);

            String line;

// Read input from the System.in and handle the input appropriately
            while ((line = userInput.readLine()) != null)
            {
                if (!line.startsWith("/"))
                {
                    sendChat(line, clientOut);
                }
                else if (line.startsWith("/me "))
                {
                    sendAction(line.substring(4).trim(), clientOut);
                }
                else if (line.startsWith("/quit"))
                {
                    System.exit(0);
                }
                else if (line.startsWith("/msg "))
                {
                    String pvtStr = line.substring(5).trim();
                    int spacePos = pvtStr.indexOf(' ');
                    if (spacePos < 0)
                    {
                        System.out.println("Format: /msg username
➥                       message");
                        continue;
                    }

                    String destUser = pvtStr.substring(0, spacePos);
                    String message = pvtStr.substring(spacePos).trim();

                    sendPrivate(destUser, message, clientOut);
                }
                else if (line.startsWith("/who"))
```

LISTING 27.7 CONTINUED

```
                {
                    sendWho(clientOut);
                }
                else
                {
                    System.out.println("Invalid command");
                }
            }
        }
        catch (Exception exc)
        {
            exc.printStackTrace();
        }
    }

    public static void sendChat(String message, DataOutputStream
➥          clientOut)
    {
        try
        {
            ByteArrayOutputStream byteOut = new ByteArrayOutputStream();
            DataOutputStream chatOut = new DataOutputStream(byteOut);

            chatOut.writeInt(ChatProtocol.CHAT);
            chatOut.writeUTF(message);

            sendMessage(byteOut.toByteArray(), clientOut);
        }
        catch (Exception exc)
        {
            exc.printStackTrace();
        }
    }

    public static void sendAction(String message, DataOutputStream
➥          clientOut)
    {
        try
        {
            ByteArrayOutputStream byteOut = new ByteArrayOutputStream();
            DataOutputStream chatOut = new DataOutputStream(byteOut);

            chatOut.writeInt(ChatProtocol.ACTION);
            chatOut.writeUTF(message);

            sendMessage(byteOut.toByteArray(), clientOut);
        }
        catch (Exception exc)
        {
            exc.printStackTrace();
        }
    }

    public static void sendPrivate(String destUser, String message,
        DataOutputStream clientOut)
```

```
    {
        try
        {
            ByteArrayOutputStream byteOut = new ByteArrayOutputStream();
            DataOutputStream chatOut = new DataOutputStream(byteOut);

            chatOut.writeInt(ChatProtocol.PRIVATE);
            chatOut.writeUTF(destUser);
            chatOut.writeUTF(message);

            sendMessage(byteOut.toByteArray(), clientOut);
        }
        catch (Exception exc)
        {
            exc.printStackTrace();
        }
    }

    public static void sendLogin(String userName, DataOutputStream
➥          clientOut)
    {
        try
        {
            ByteArrayOutputStream byteOut = new ByteArrayOutputStream();
            DataOutputStream chatOut = new DataOutputStream(byteOut);

            chatOut.writeInt(ChatProtocol.LOGIN);
            chatOut.writeUTF(userName);

            sendMessage(byteOut.toByteArray(), clientOut);
        }
        catch (Exception exc)
        {
            exc.printStackTrace();
        }
    }

    public static void sendWho(DataOutputStream clientOut)
    {
        try
        {
            ByteArrayOutputStream byteOut = new ByteArrayOutputStream();
            DataOutputStream chatOut = new DataOutputStream(byteOut);

            chatOut.writeInt(ChatProtocol.WHO);

            sendMessage(byteOut.toByteArray(), clientOut);
        }
        catch (Exception exc)
        {
            exc.printStackTrace();
        }
    }

    public static void sendMessage(byte[] message, DataOutputStream out)
    {
        try
```

LISTING 27.7 CONTINUED

```
        {
            Messages.writeMessage(message, message.length, out);
        }
        catch (Exception exc)
        {
            exc.printStackTrace();
        }
    }
}
```

The chat server and client represent a fairly typical client/server application in Java. Although you might not package messages the same way, you usually create a main server and separate client handlers, each with its own thread.

USING DATAGRAM SOCKETS

UDP datagram sockets are easy to use, after you understand how they work. A datagram socket has a specific port number assigned to it. You can specify the port number when you create the socket, or use port number 0 to allocate a random free port number. When you send a datagram packet, you can send it as a broadcast, meaning it goes to every host on the network, or you can send it to a specific host. The important thing to keep in mind is that you *always* send it to a port number, and not necessarily the same port number as your datagram socket.

Tip

When you send a datagram packet, you must always specify a host address. To broadcast a packet, set the host portion of the IP address to all 1s. For instance, if your network mask is 255.255.0.0, the broadcast host address is 0.0.255.255. If your host's IP address is 192.168.1.2, you take the network address—192.168.0.0—and combine it with the broadcast address—0.0.255.255—to get the final broadcast address of 192.168.255.255. Although your local router should stop it, please resist sending a broadcast with an address of 255.255.255.255. It's considered rude because the rest of the world doesn't want your broadcast packets clogging up the network.

For example, you can create a datagram socket and assign it a port of 1234. Other datagram sockets, regardless of their port numbers, can send datagrams to port 1234, either by broadcasting them or by sending them to a specific host.

If there is no datagram socket listening on a particular port number, the datagram packet is ignored. Remember, it's like sending someone a pager message. You send it out, but you never know that the person got the page unless they happen to call you back.

Note

UDP datagrams are connectionless in that there is no permanent session between the client and the server. If you look at the `DatagramSocket` API documentation, you will notice a `connect` and a `disconnect` method. Don't let these terms fool you into thinking there is an actual connection. The connection merely forces all the packets to go to a specific hostname and port number. If you disconnect a datagram socket from one address and connect it to another, neither the old receiver nor the new receiver receives any notification.

UDP datagram sockets are used primarily for two things: alerts and lookups. You can set up an alert datagram for your applications so that whenever there is an error, your application can send out a packet indicating the problem. Although you probably already write errors out to a log file, sending an alert means you don't have to write a program that scans through the log file for something interesting.

Note

Because datagrams are connectionless, a sender never knows when the receiving program terminates. Likewise, the receiver never knows when the sender terminates.

Many naming services use UDP for lookups because the broadcast capabilities of UDP allow you to perform a lookup without knowing even the address of the naming service.

Listing 27.8 shows a class that sends alerts to datagram port 1234. You can use a class like this for application-level alerting.

Listing 27.8 Source Code for `AlertSender.java`

```
package usingj2ee.net;

import java.net.*;
import java.io.*;

public class AlertSender
{
    protected static DatagramSocket socket = null;
    protected static String broadcastAddress = "192.168.255.255";

// Create the datagram socket
    static
    {
        try
        {
            socket = new DatagramSocket();
        }
        catch (SocketException exc)
        {
            exc.printStackTrace();
        }
    }


    public static void sendAlert(String alertString)
        throws IOException
    {
// Convert the string to an array of bytes
        byte[] alertBytes = alertString.getBytes();
```

LISTING 27.8 CONTINUED

```
// Create a datagram packet containing the bytes from the string
        DatagramPacket packet = new DatagramPacket(
            alertBytes, alertBytes.length);

// Create an InetAddress containing the broadcast address
        InetAddress broadcastAddr =
➥       InetAddress.getByName(broadcastAddress);

// Tell the packet its destination
        packet.setAddress(broadcastAddr);

// Send alerts to port 1234
        packet.setPort(1234);

// Send the packet
        socket.send(packet);
    }

    public static void main(String[] args)
    {
        try
        {
// Allow the broadcast address to be overridden with -Dbroadcast
            broadcastAddress = System.getProperty("broadcast",
                broadcastAddress);

            int i=0;

            for (;;)
            {
// Send an alert of the form <n> where n is a number
                i=i+1;
                sendAlert("<"+i+">");

// Wait 1 second (1000 milliseconds) before sending another alert
                Thread.sleep(1000);
            }
        }
        catch (Exception exc)
        {
            exc.printStackTrace();
        }
    }
}
```

Note

You might need to change the broadcast address in the `AlertSender` class to match your network configuration.

Listing 27.9 shows a simple alert receiver that listens for alerts on port 1234. You can only run one instance of the receiver on a particular host, but you can run multiple copies of the sender. Only one program can open a socket on a specific port, and the receiver specifies a port number—the sender just uses any free port.

LISTING 27.9 SOURCE CODE FOR AlertReceiver.java

```
package usingj2ee.net;

import java.net.*;
import java.io.*;

public class AlertReceiver
{
    public static void main(String[] args)
    {
        try
        {

// Create the datagram socket for receiving the packets
            DatagramSocket receiveSocket = new DatagramSocket(1234);

// Create a buffer to hold the incoming data
            byte[] buffer = new byte[1024];

// Create a packet for the incoming data
            DatagramPacket packet = new DatagramPacket(buffer,
➥           buffer.length);

            for (;;)
            {
// Reset the packet size to the original size of the buffer (it gets set
// to the received data size after a packet has been received)
                packet.setLength(buffer.length);

// Receive the incoming packet
                receiveSocket.receive(packet);

// Get the data from the packet and print it out as a string
                String alert = new String(packet.getData(), 0,
                    packet.getLength());
                System.out.println(alert);
            }
        }
        catch (Exception exc)
        {
            exc.printStackTrace();
        }
    }
}
```

To run the `AlertSender` and `AlertReceiver` programs, just start them in different windows. If you have several machines on your network, run `AlertReceiver` on several machines at once to see that each program receives the datagram.

Choosing Between TCP and UDP

Most of the time, it should be pretty easy to decide between UDP datagrams and TCP connections. If you must be sure that a message has been received or that it hasn't, you should use TCP. Also, if you need to know when a client or server terminates, use TCP. Because UDP datagram packets have a size limitation of roughly 1,100 bytes, you should use TCP connections if you need to send more than about 1,000 bytes of data.

If you need to send data to anyone that might be listening, especially to multiple receivers, a UDP datagram is probably a better idea—especially if it doesn't matter if the message is never received. UDP datagrams are also good for sending data quickly because there's less setup overhead. If you need to send a lot of small pieces of data quickly and the destination might change frequently, UDP is probably a better choice.

Of course, there's no reason you can't use both of these technologies in your application. Use the one that best fits your requirements.

Troubleshooting

Startup Problems

Why does it say the port is in use?

There is probably another program running that uses that socket number. Type `netstat -a` (if you're running Windows or Unix/Linux) and look for the port number you are trying to use. If you find the port and see the word `LISTENING` off to the right, that socket is in use.

Using `netstat`

What does `TIME_WAIT` mean in `netstat -a`, and why do I get a `port in use` error when the port has a `TIME_WAIT` status?

Sometimes when you stop a server, it takes some time to shut down all the socket connections. You usually see `TIME_WAIT` occur when you stop a server that has active connections without first stopping all the clients. Give it a minute or two and it should stop waiting.

UDP Problems

Why don't I see any of the datagrams I am sending?

First, make sure that you have the address and port correct. Next, if you are sending between different hosts and the message is a broadcast message, the router might be eating the broadcast. Try changing the destination address to the specific host address of the receiver and see whether it gets through. If so, you might need to talk to your network administrator about allowing broadcasts, or don't use broadcasts.

CHAPTER 28

Overview of Internet Protocols

In this chapter

WHO DEFINES INTERNET PROTOCOLS

The Internet Engineering Task Force (IETF) is the standards body that publishes Internet standards. As a standards body, the IETF has done an excellent job defining reasonable standards in a timely manner. One of the reasons that IETF has been so successful is that it relies on working implementations for standards. That is, although some standards bodies hand down cumbersome standards before they have been implemented, the IETF takes a practical approach and often works with existing standards and software. The result is that the software is often available by the time the standard becomes finalized.

One of the interesting aspects of the IETF is that it is not a membership organization. You don't have to pay a large fee to join. To quote the IETF Web page, "no cards, no dues, no secret handshakes :-)." Anyone who is interested in working on Internet standards may join a working group (the people who do the actual work) by joining the working group's mailing list.

When you consider the number of standards that the IETF has created and how many of them are in constant use throughout the world, you can't help but be amazed at the success of the organization.

WHERE TO FIND INTERNET STANDARDS

When the IETF publishes a standard, it creates a document called an RFC (Request For Comments). There are actually several types of RFCs, only one of which defines a standard. The other types are Best Current Practices, Experimental, Historical, and Informational. In other words, in addition to defining Internet standards, the IETF publishes information on how best to use the standards and also provides other interesting information.

An RFC passes through three stages: proposed standard, draft standard, and standard. For an RFC to be a proposed standard, it must be complete—no holes remaining to be fleshed out. You must also be able to demonstrate the usefulness of the proposed technology. For an RFC to become a draft standard, there must be multiple implementations of the standard and they must all interoperate. After the draft standard has been given a thorough operational testing, it becomes a standard.

The IETF sets certain time limits on how long an RFC can stay at a particular stage before being reevaluated. An RFC must remain at the proposed-standard level for at least six months. An RFC must remain at the draft-standard level for at least 4 months and until there has been an IETF meeting. If an RFC doesn't make it all the way to standard within two years, the IETF reviews the status of the RFC to see whether it should still proceed.

The RFCs are available on the IETF Web site at `http://www.ietf.org`. Even the RFC standards process is defined in an RFC—specifically, RFC 2026—Internet Standards Process. RFC 2026 is, incidentally, a Best Current Practice RFC, not an Internet standard.

Basic Features of Internet Protocols

Obviously, because there are Internet standards for everything from the format of individual data packets to real-time video and audio conferencing, it's tough to find common features in protocols. If you look at some of the most common protocols, however, you see many similarities.

First of all, most of the upper-level protocols use either TCP or UDP as a transport mechanism. Of the upper-level protocols, the most commonly used are HTTP (Hypertext Transfer Protocol), FTP (File Transfer Protocol), and SMTP (Simple Mail Transfer Protocol). These protocols all use TCP and are all text-based. That is, the commands and responses used in these protocols are all human-readable text. Some of the other protocols are binary protocols that require a program to decode.

You'll notice many common features in the text-based protocols. First of all, many of them use the same convention for responses. The response begins with a number whose first digit indicates the kind of response:

- 1xx indicates that the action has started and that you should expect further responses indicating whether the request completed successfully.
- 2xx indicates that the request completed successfully.
- 3xx indicates that although the request has been accepted, the server needs further information from you before it can continue. For instance, when you send a username under the FTP protocol, you get a 331 response indicating that you must also supply a password.
- 4xx indicates that the request can't be completed for some temporary or correctable reason. For instance, in the HTTP (Web) protocol, a 404 error means that the server can't find the page you requested.
- 5xx indicates that the request can't be completed due to a permanent failure. A 500 error in HTTP means that the server encountered an internal server error while processing your request.

Other protocols such as POP3 (mailbox) use `+` or `-` at the beginning of a response to indicate success or failure. For instance, you might get `+OK` after you send a valid `USER` request, but get `-ERR` if you send an unrecognized command.

Some Common Internet Protocols

You have already encountered a few of the interesting protocols. Here is a list of some of the most common ones:

- **RFC 791 The Internet Protocol**—This is the granddaddy of them all. It is the low-level Internet protocol (IP).
- **RFC 792 Internet Control Message Protocol (ICMP)**—Defines the informational messages that hosts and routers use to exchange control information as opposed to data.

- **RFC 793 Transmission Control Protocol (TCP)**—Defines the standard, connection-oriented, guaranteed-delivery protocol that so much of the Internet is based on.
- **RFC 768 User Datagram Protocol (UDP)**—Defines the standard datagram protocol used by many standard Internet protocols.
- **RFC 826 Ethernet Address Resolution Protocol (ARP)**—Defines how a host can convert an IP address into a physical network address.
- **RFC 903 Reverse Address Resolution Protocol (RARP)**—Defines how a host can convert a physical network address into an IP address.
- **RFC 959 File Transfer Protocol (FTP)**—The standard file transfer protocol used by FTP and by Web browsers (when given an `ftp://` URL).
- **RFC 2616 Hypertext Transfer Protocol 1.1 (HTTP)**—The newest version of the standard Web protocol. As of December 2000, this is still just a draft standard even though most Web servers support it.
- **RFC 854 Telnet Protocol**—A protocol for logging in to remote hosts.
- **RFC 821 Simple Mail Transfer Protocol (SMTP)**—The protocol for sending email.
- **RFC 1939 Post Office Protocol version 3 (POP3)**—A common protocol for retrieving email.
- **RFC 2060 Internet Message Access Protocol 4 (IMAP4)**—An alternative to POP3 for reading mail, although not as commonly used.
- **RFC 1035 Domain names: implementation and specification**—Defines the protocol for resolving names into IP addresses.
- **RFC 1157 Simple Network Management Protocol (SNMP)**—Defines a protocol for network devices to send and receive management information (configuration, errors, statistics, and so on).
- **RFC 1777 Lightweight Directory Access Protocol (LDAP)**—Defines a protocol for quick directory lookups. This is one of the naming protocols supported by JNDI.

Note

If you read these protocols, you will notice that a large number of them were written by J. Postel, who died in October of 1998. Jon Postel was one of the true pioneers of the Internet, and through his work, he made a huge impact on our world. You can learn more about him at `www.postel.org`.

AN IN-DEPTH LOOK AT THE FILE TRANSFER PROTOCOL

The File Transfer Protocol is one of the workhorses of the Internet, although it has been surpassed by HTTP over the past several years. FTP is interesting in that it uses two separate connections: a command connection and a data connection.

Like HTTP and SMTP, FTP is text based and uses numeric response codes. One of the neat features of the text-based protocols is that you can use them with the Telnet program. If you want to try out the FTP protocol, for example, you can Telnet to port 21 on a machine that is running an FTP server.

To log on to an FTP server, you must specify a username and password. You specify the username with the `USER` command:

```
USER myusername
```

You specify the password with the `PASS` command:

```
PASS mypassword
```

Figure 28.1 shows a Telnet session with an FTP server.

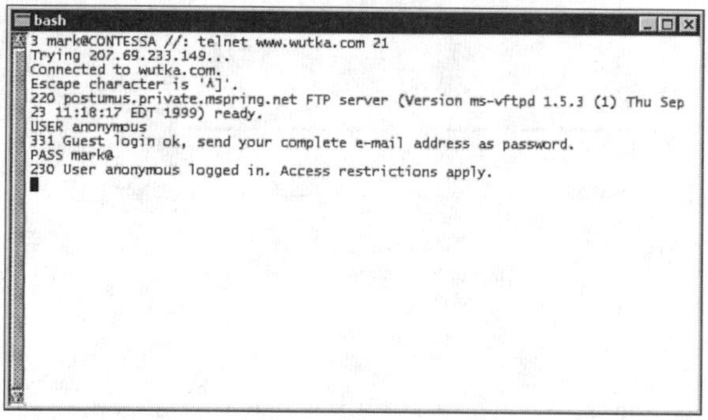

Figure 28.1 You can use Telnet to communicate with an FTP server.

bash
3 mark@CONTESSA //: telnet www.wutka.com 21
Trying 207.69.233.149...
Connected to wutka.com.
Escape character is '^]'.
220 postumus.private.mspring.net FTP server (Version ms-vftpd 1.5.3 (1) Thu Sep 23 11:18:17 EDT 1999) ready.
USER anonymous
331 Guest login ok, send your complete e-mail address as password.
PASS mark@
230 User anonymous logged in. Access restrictions apply.

Notice that the response numbers in FTP use the 1xx, 2xx, 3xx, 4xx, 5xx numbering scheme discussed in the previous section.

Whenever you transfer a file or get a directory listing in FTP, you use a data connection to get or send the information. If you've ever used the `ftp` command (as opposed to a graphical FTP client), you might have noticed the message `PORT command accepted` after certain commands. The `PORT` command tells the FTP server the address of the data connection.

Normally, the FTP server creates the data connection by connecting back to the client. That might sound strange, but it's true. The client initiates the command connection, and then the server connects back to the client for data transfer. Figure 28.2 shows the connection sequence between an FTP client and server.

The big problem with the reverse data connection is that it doesn't work with firewalls and proxies. In these situations, the server either doesn't know the true IP address of the client, or its inbound connections are blocked by the firewall. The FTP protocol supports another transfer method called *passive transfer mode*. Basically, a passive transfer just means that the client instead of the server creates the data connection.

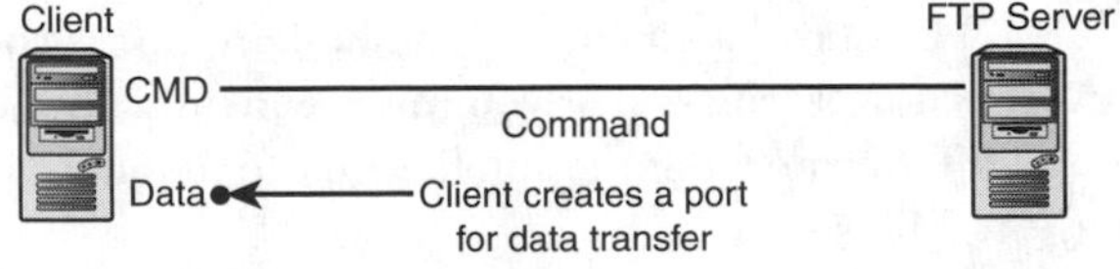

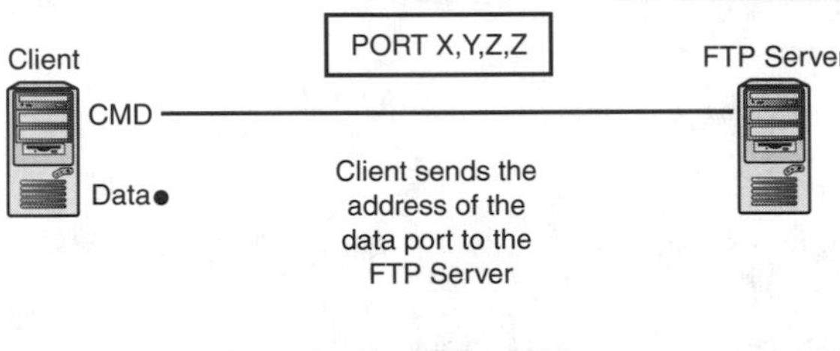

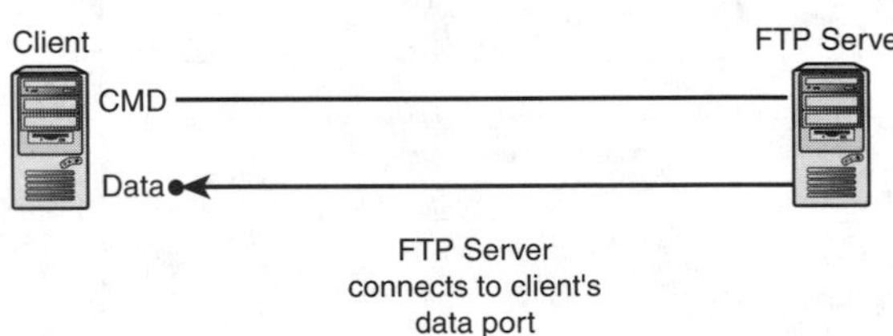

Figure 28.2
The client creates the command connection and the server creates the data connection.

Figure 28.3 shows a Telnet session with the FTP server that uses passive transfers. The PASV command tells the server to listen for an incoming data connection. The response from PASV is a list of six numbers. The first four numbers make up the IP address of the server, whereas the last two are the port number. To convert the last two numbers to a single port number, multiply the first number by 256 and add the second number. In the example in Figure 28.3, the resulting port number is 39,130 (152×256 + 218).

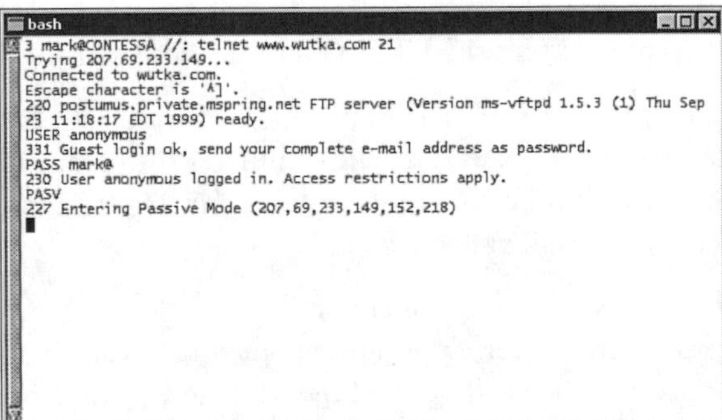

Figure 28.3
The PASV command initiates passive transfer mode.

After you compute the port number, you can create a second Telnet connection, this time to the newly created port. Then, from the original command connection, enter the LIST command to list the files in the current directory. The file list appears in the second window, as shown in Figure 28.4.

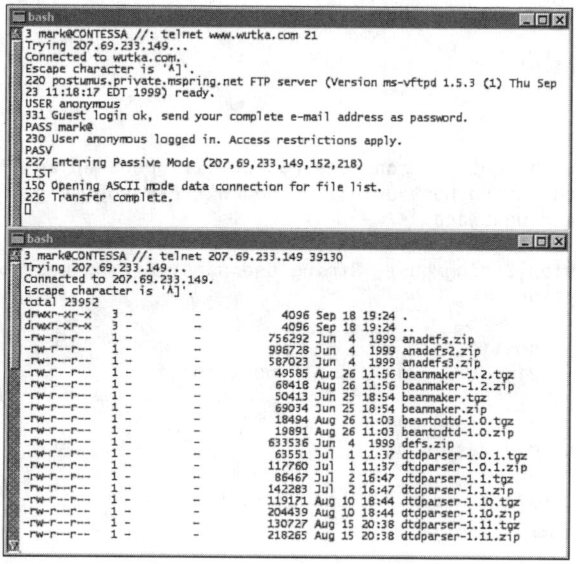

```
3 mark@CONTESSA //: telnet www.wutka.com 21
Trying 207.69.233.149...
Connected to wutka.com.
Escape character is '^]'.
220 postumus.private.mspring.net FTP server (Version ms-vftpd 1.5.3 (1) Thu Sep
23 11:18:17 EDT 1999) ready.
USER anonymous
331 Guest login ok, send your complete e-mail address as password.
PASS mark@
230 User anonymous logged in. Access restrictions apply.
PASV
227 Entering Passive Mode (207,69,233,149,152,218)
LIST
150 Opening ASCII mode data connection for file list.
226 Transfer complete.
```

```
3 mark@CONTESSA //: telnet 207.69.233.149 39130
Trying 207.69.233.149...
Connected to 207.69.233.149.
Escape character is '^]'.
total 23952
drwxr-xr-x   3 -        -            4096 Sep 18 19:24 .
drwxr-xr-x   3 -        -            4096 Sep 18 19:24 ..
-rw-r--r--   1 -        -          756292 Jun  4  1999 anadefs.zip
-rw-r--r--   1 -        -          996728 Jun  4  1999 anadefs2.zip
-rw-r--r--   1 -        -          587023 Jun  4  1999 anadefs3.zip
-rw-r--r--   1 -        -           49585 Aug 26 11:56 beanmaker-1.2.tgz
-rw-r--r--   1 -        -           68418 Aug 26 11:56 beanmaker-1.2.zip
-rw-r--r--   1 -        -           50413 Jun 25 18:54 beanmaker.tgz
-rw-r--r--   1 -        -           69034 Jun 25 18:54 beanmaker.zip
-rw-r--r--   1 -        -           18494 Aug 26 11:03 beantodtd-1.0.tgz
-rw-r--r--   1 -        -           19891 Aug 26 11:03 beantodtd-1.0.zip
-rw-r--r--   1 -        -          633536 Jun  4  1999 defs.zip
-rw-r--r--   1 -        -           63551 Jul  1 11:37 dtdparser-1.0.1.tgz
-rw-r--r--   1 -        -          117760 Jul  1 11:37 dtdparser-1.0.1.zip
-rw-r--r--   1 -        -           86467 Jul  2 16:47 dtdparser-1.1.tgz
-rw-r--r--   1 -        -          142283 Jul  2 16:47 dtdparser-1.1.zip
-rw-r--r--   1 -        -          119171 Aug 10 18:44 dtdparser-1.10.tgz
-rw-r--r--   1 -        -          204439 Aug 10 18:44 dtdparser-1.10.zip
-rw-r--r--   1 -        -          130727 Aug 15 20:38 dtdparser-1.11.tgz
-rw-r--r--   1 -        -          218265 Aug 15 20:38 dtdparser-1.11.zip
```

Figure 28.4
You can even receive data from an FTP server using Telnet.

Listing 28.1 shows a class that uses the FTP protocol to get a file, send a file, or get a list of files.

LISTING 28.1 SOURCE CODE FOR FTPSession.java

```
package usingj2ee.net;

import java.io.*;
import java.net.*;
import java.util.*;

/** This class implements file storage and retrieval using the
 *  FTP protocol. Your server must support the PASV command
 *  for this to work.
 */

public class FTPSession extends Object
{
    public String host;        // Host name to connect to
    public int port;           // port number to connect to, default=21
    public String username;    // Username to log in with
    public String password;    // Password to log in with
    public String acct;        // optional acct for logging in
    public boolean doPassive; // Indicates whether to use passive transfers

    protected Socket sessionSock;      // The control socket
    protected ServerSocket server;    // The data connection server socket
```

LISTING 28.1 CONTINUED

```
    protected DataInputStream inStream;
    protected DataOutputStream outStream;

    public FTPSession()
    {
    }

/** This should be the most common constructor, it opens up an FTP
    session with the named host using the default FTP port and logs on using
    the username and password. */

    public FTPSession(String host, String username, String password)
    throws IOException
    {
        this.host = host;
        this.port = 21;     // default FTP port is 21

        this.username = username;
        this.password = password;

        logon();    // go ahead and log on to the server
    }

/** Opens up an FTP session with the named host using the default FTP
    port and logs on using the username and password, and account.
    The account field is pretty rare on FTP servers. */

    public FTPSession(String host, String username, String password,
         String acct)
    throws IOException
    {
        this.host = host;
        this.port = 21;     // default FTP port is 21

        this.username = username;
        this.password = password;
        this.acct = acct;

        logon();    // go ahead and log on to the server
    }

/** Opens up an FTP session with the named host using an alternate
    port number and if logOn is true, logs on using the username and
    password. */

    public FTPSession(String host, int port, String username,
        String password, boolean logOn)
    throws IOException
    {
        this.host = host;
        this.port = port;
        if (this.port <= 0) this.port = 21;

        this.username = username;
```

```
        this.password = password;

        if (logOn)
        {
            logon();
        }
    }

/** Opens up an FTP session with the named host using an alternate
    port number and if logOn is true, logs on using the username,
    password, and account. */

    public FTPSession(String host, int port, String username,
        String password, String acct, boolean logOn)
    throws IOException
    {
        this.host = host;
        this.port = port;
        if (this.port <= 0) this.port = 21;

        this.username = username;
        this.password = password;
        this.acct = acct;

        if (logOn)
        {
            logon();
        }
    }

/** Close down the session */

    public void close()
    throws IOException
    {
        sessionSock.close();
        sessionSock = null;
        if (server != null)
        {
            server.close();
        }
    }

/** Connect to the server */

    public void connect()
    throws IOException
    {
        sessionSock = new Socket(host, port);
        inStream = new DataInputStream(
            new BufferedInputStream(
                sessionSock.getInputStream()));
        outStream = new DataOutputStream(
            new BufferedOutputStream(
                sessionSock.getOutputStream()));

    }
```

LISTING 28.1 CONTINUED

```
/** Send a command and wait for a response */

    public String doCommand(String commandString)
    throws IOException
    {
        outStream.writeBytes(commandString+"\n");
        outStream.flush();
        String response = getResponse();
        return response;
    }

/** Get a response back from the server. Handles multi-line responses
    and returns them as part of the string. */

    public String getResponse()
    throws IOException
    {
        String response = "";

        for (;;)
        {
            String line = inStream.readLine();

            if (line == null)
            {
                throw new IOException(
                    "Bad response from server.");
            }

// FTP response lines should at least have a 3-digit number

            if (line.length() < 3)
            {
                throw new IOException(
                    "Bad response from server.");
            }
            response += line + "\n";

// If there isn't a '-' immediately after the number, you have
// received the complete response. ('-' is the continuation character
// for FTP responses)

            if ((line.length() == 3) ||
                (line.charAt(3) != '-')) return response;
        }
    }


/** Logs on to the FTP server */

    public void logon()
    throws IOException
    {
        connect();
```

```
// After connecting, the FTP server will send a response string. Make
// sure it starts with a '2' (responses in the 200s are positive
// responses.

        String response = getResponse();
        if (response.charAt(0) != '2')
        {
            throw new IOException(response);
        }

// Send a logon command
        response = doCommand("USER "+username);

// If you get a response in the 300s, send a password

        if (response.charAt(0) == '3')
        {
            response = doCommand("PASS "+password);

// If you get a response in the 300s on the password command,
// send the account
            if (response.charAt(0) == '3')
            {
                response = doCommand("ACCT "+acct);
            }
        }

// If the last response you received wasn't in the 200s, there
// was an error during the logon.

        if (response.charAt(0) != '2')
        {
            throw new IOException(response);
        }
    }

/** For normal transfers, calls doPort to create the server socket,
 for passive transfers, gets a connection to the server */

    protected Socket getPort()
        throws IOException
    {
        if (doPassive)
        {
            return doPasvPort();
        }
        else
        {
            doPort();
            return null;
        }
    }

/** Creates a server socket if necessary and sends a port command
    to the server */
    protected void doPort()
```

LISTING 28.1 CONTINUED

```
        throws IOException
    {
        try
        {
// Only create the server socket if one doesn't exist
            if (server == null)
            {
                server = new ServerSocket(0);
            }

// Get the local host address
            InetAddress socketAddr = InetAddress.getLocalHost();

// Convert the address into an array of bytes
            byte[] addrBytes = socketAddr.getAddress();

// Get the port number for the server socket
            int portNumber = server.getLocalPort();

// Create a PORT command
            StringBuffer portCommand = new StringBuffer("PORT ");

            for (int i=0; i < 4; i++)
            {
// By AND-ing the byte with 255, you get a value between 0 and 255
instead
// of the normal -128 to 127 range
                portCommand.append(addrBytes[i] & 255);
                portCommand.append(',');
            }
            portCommand.append(portNumber / 256);
            portCommand.append(',');
            portCommand.append(portNumber % 256);

// Send the PORT command
            String response = doCommand(portCommand.toString());

            if (response.charAt(0) != '2')
            {
                throw new IOException(response);
            }
        }
        catch (Exception exc)
        {
            throw new IOException(exc.toString());
        }
    }

/** Creates a data connection to the server by using the PASV
    command.
    Normally the data connection is set up by the client sending the
    server an address and port number using the PORT command.
    Unfortunately, because an applet cannot listen for incoming
    connections, you can't work that way. The PASV command asks the
    server to accept a connection.
```

```
    The response for the PASV command contains a host address and port
    number in the form h,h,h,h,p,p where h is a byte in the host address
    and p is a byte in the port. */

    protected synchronized Socket doPasvPort()
    throws IOException
    {

// Send the PASV command
        String response = doCommand("PASV");

// If it wasn't in the 200s, there was an error

        if (response.charAt(0) != '2')
        {
            throw new IOException(response);
        }

// The pasv response looks like:
// 227 Entering Passive Mode (127,0,0,1,4,160)
// Look for the ()'s at the end first

        int parenStart = response.lastIndexOf('(');
        int parenEnd = response.lastIndexOf(')');

// Make sure they're both there and that the ) comes after the (
        if ((parenStart < 0) || (parenEnd < 0) ||
            (parenStart >= parenEnd))
        {
            throw new IOException("PASV response format error");
        }

// Extract the address bytes
        String pasvAddr = response.substring(parenStart+1, parenEnd);

// Create a tokenizer to parse the bytes
        StringTokenizer tokenizer = new StringTokenizer(pasvAddr,
",");

// Create the array to store the bytes
        int[] addrValues = new int[6];

// Parse each byte
        for (int i=0; (i < 6) && tokenizer.hasMoreTokens(); i++)
        {
            try
            {
                addrValues[i] = Integer.valueOf(
                    tokenizer.nextToken()).intValue();
            }
            catch (Exception e)
            {
                throw new IOException(
                    "PASV response format error");
            }
        }
```

LISTING 28.1 CONTINUED

```
// This class ignores the host addresses, assuming that the host
// address is
// the same as the host address you used to connect the first time.

        Socket newSock = new Socket(host, (addrValues[4] << 8) +
            addrValues[5]);

        return newSock;
    }

/** Fetches a file in binary mode if doBinary is true, or ascii mode
    if it's false, and returns it as an array of bytes. */

    public synchronized void get(String remoteFile, OutputStream
toStream,
        boolean doBinary)
        throws IOException
    {

// If transferring in binary mode, send a type command for type I
(IMAGE)
        if (doBinary)
        {
            String response = doCommand("TYPE I");
            if (response.charAt(0) != '2')
            {
                throw new IOException(response);
            }
// If transferring in ascii mode, send a type command for type A
(ASCII)
        }
        else
        {
            String response = doCommand("TYPE A");
            if (response.charAt(0) != '2')
            {
                throw new IOException(response);
            }
        }

// Set up the data connection

        Socket getSock = getPort();

// Tell the server to send the file over
        String response = doCommand("RETR "+remoteFile);

// If the request is successful, the server should send a response
// in the 100s and then start sending the file. After the file
// is sent, it should send a response in the 200s.

// Check for an initial response in the 100s

        if (response.charAt(0) != '1')
```

```
        {
            if (getSock != null)
            {
                getSock.close();
            }
            throw new IOException(response);
        }

        if (getSock == null)
        {
            getSock = server.accept();
        }

// For binary transfers, read one byte at a time and store it in
// the array.
        if (doBinary)
        {
            InputStream in = new BufferedInputStream(
                getSock.getInputStream());

            int ch;

            while ((ch = in.read()) >= 0)
            {
                toStream.write(ch);
            }

// For ascii transfers, read a line at a time and strip off whatever
// newline you received.
        }
        else
        {
            DataInputStream in = new DataInputStream(
                new BufferedInputStream(
                    getSock.getInputStream()));
            PrintStream dataOut = new PrintStream(toStream);

            String line;

            while ((line = in.readLine()) != null)
            {
                dataOut.println(line);
            }
        }

// Close the data connection
        getSock.close();

// Make sure you got a response in the 200s saying the transfer was
// successful.
        response = getResponse();
        if (response.charAt(0) != '2')
        {
            throw new IOException(response);
        }
    }
```

LISTING 28.1 CONTINUED

```
// Stores an array of bytes in the named file, using binary mode if
// doBinary is true, ascii mode otherwise.

    public synchronized void put(String remoteFile, InputStream
fromStream,
        boolean doBinary)
    throws IOException
    {

// If transferring in binary mode, send a type command for type I(IMAGE)
        if (doBinary)
        {
            String response = doCommand("TYPE I");
            if (response.charAt(0) != '2')
            {
                throw new IOException(response);
            }

// If transferring in ascii mode, send a type command for type A(ASCII)
        }
        else
        {
            String response = doCommand("TYPE A");
            if (response.charAt(0) != '2')
            {
                throw new IOException(response);
            }
        }

// Open up a data connection
        Socket putSock = getPort();

// Tell the server where you want it to store the data you are sending

        String response = doCommand("STOR "+remoteFile);

// If the request is successful, the server should send a response
// in the 100s and then start receiving the bytes. After the
// data connection is closed, it should send a response in the 200s.

        if (response.charAt(0) != '1')
        {
            if (putSock != null)
            {
                putSock.close();
            }
            throw new IOException(response);
        }

        if (putSock == null)
        {
            putSock = server.accept();
        }
```

```
// If binary mode, just write all the bytes
        if (doBinary)
        {
            BufferedOutputStream out = new BufferedOutputStream(
                putSock.getOutputStream());

            byte[] buffer = new byte[4096];
            int len;

            while ((len = fromStream.read(buffer)) > 0)
            {
                out.write(buffer, 0, len);
            }

            out.flush();

// If ascii mode, write the data a line at a time

        }
        else
        {
            DataInputStream in = new DataInputStream(fromStream);

            DataOutputStream out = new DataOutputStream(
                new BufferedOutputStream(
                    putSock.getOutputStream()));

            String line;

            while ((line = in.readLine()) != null)
            {
                out.writeBytes(line+"\r");
            }
            out.flush();
        }

        putSock.close();

        response = getResponse();

// Make sure you got a 200 response

        if (response.charAt(0) != '2')
        {
            throw new IOException(response);
        }
    }

    public synchronized String[] list()
        throws IOException
    {
// Set up the data connection

        Socket getSock = getPort();

// Tell the server to send a list of files
```

LISTING 28.1 CONTINUED

```
        String response = doCommand("LIST");

// If the request is successful, the server should send a response
// in the 100s and then start sending the file. After the file is
// sent, it should send a response in the 200s.

// Check for an initial response in the 100s

        if (response.charAt(0) != '1')
        {
            if (getSock != null)
            {
                getSock.close();
            }
            throw new IOException(response);
        }

        if (getSock == null)
        {
            getSock = server.accept();
        }

        DataInputStream in = new DataInputStream(
            new BufferedInputStream(
                getSock.getInputStream()));

        Vector v = new Vector();

        String line;

        while ((line = in.readLine()) != null)
        {
            v.addElement(line);
        }

// Close the data connection
        getSock.close();

// Make sure you got a response in the 200s saying the transfer was
// successful.
        response = getResponse();
        if (response.charAt(0) != '2')
        {
            throw new IOException(response);
        }

        String[] list = new String[v.size()];
        v.copyInto(list);

        return list;
    }
}
```

Listing 28.2 shows a simple test program that demonstrates how to use the `FTPSession` class.

LISTING 28.2 SOURCE CODE FOR `TestFTPSession.java`

```
package usingj2ee.net;

public class TestFTPSession
{
    public static void main(String[] args)
    {
        try
        {
            FTPSession sess = new FTPSession("flamingo", "testuser",
                "testpass");

            String[] fileList = sess.list();

            for (int i=0; (i < fileList.length) && (i < 10); i++)
            {
                System.out.println(fileList[i]);
            }
        }
        catch (Exception exc)
        {
            exc.printStackTrace();
        }
    }
}
```

You can use the `FTPSession` class to send and receive files via FTP. In a Java applet, for example, when you can't access local files, you can use FTP to access files on the Web server that aren't normally available via HTTP. You can also use the `FTPSession` class to perform automated file transfers.

CASE STUDY

A software integrator ran a sales-reporting system for a large telecommunications company. The reporting system used a combination of Java and Visual Basic to create an application for entering sales data. The telecom company also had a separate sales-reporting system containing additional sales that needed to be entered.

The telecom company created a batch job that extracted new sales data periodically and placed the data on an FTP server. The software integrator used the `FTPSession` class to periodically check for new files and download them. Using the `doCommand` method, the software integrator was able to delete files using the `DELE` command to avoid downloading the same file twice.

CHAPTER 29

THE HTTP PROTOCOL

In this chapter

The HTTP protocol is one of the most important of all the Internet protocols because it runs the World Wide Web. Most of the time, a Web browser communicates with the Web server using the HTTP protocol. In some cases, the browser uses FTP and communicates with an FTP server, but overall, HTTP carries the bulk of Web traffic.

Although the `URL` and `URLConnection` classes let you access Web servers via HTTP, and Java Server Pages and servlets let you handle incoming HTTP requests, it's still useful to see how the HTTP protocol works.

THE HTTP PROTOCOL

An HTTP connection is a simple network socket connection. The Web server usually listens for incoming connections on port 80. After the connection is established, the browser sends a few lines of text indicating which Web page it wants to see, some request headers telling the Web server which kind of browser is making the request, and a few other interesting items.

The only part of the request that is required is the first line, which tells the server what file the browser wants. The rest is optional. Each line in the request is a human-readable text line, separated by a newline character. The request header ends with a blank line. The protocol is so simple, you can even interact manually with a Web server using the `telnet` command.

For example, you can view the HelloWorld Java Server Page from Chapter 15, "Common JSP Tasks," by telnetting to port 80 on your Web server, entering `GET <the path of the JSP> HTTP/1.0`, and pressing Enter twice. The path in an HTTP request is the portion of the URL that comes after the host name and includes the leading `/`. Thus, if you access `HelloWorld.jsp` with `http://localhost/j2eebook/ch15/examples/HelloWorld.jsp`, you would enter `/j2eebook/ch15/examples/HelloWorld.jsp` as the path.

Figure 29.1 shows a Telnet session requesting and receiving the Hello World JSP.

```
bash
6 mark@CONTESSA //: telnet localhost 80
Trying 127.0.0.1...
Connected to CONTESSA.wutka.com.
Escape character is '^]'.
GET /j2eebook/ch15/examples/HelloWorld.jsp HTTP/1.0

HTTP/1.0 200 OK
Server: Resin/1.1
Cache-Control: no-cache="set-cookie,set-cookie2"
Expires: Thu, 01 Dec 1994 16:00:00 GMT
Set-Cookie: JSESSIONID=wBzSq5swr7KOBzOoHO;Path=/;Version=1
Content-Type: text/html
Content-Length: 59
Date: Fri, 29 Sep 2000 22:36:15 GMT

<HTML>
<BODY>
<H1>Hello World!</H1>

</BODY>
</HTML>
Connection closed by foreign host.
7 mark@CONTESSA //:
```

Figure 29.1
You can interact with a Web server directly using the `telnet` command.

Note

You might need to turn on local echo in your Telnet window to see what you are typing. Also, if you make any typing errors, don't be surprised if the Web server doesn't understand the Backspace key and complains that you sent it a garbled command.

Notice that the request to the server indicated it was using version 1.0 of the HTTP protocol (the `HTTP/1.0` at the end of the `GET` request), whereas the server responded with version 1.1 of HTTP. HTTP version 1.1 adds a number of options that can optimize Web access and allow the browser to retrieve multiple pages over a single connection.

Under HTTP 1.1, there is an additional line that must be present in each request. You must specify the name of the host you are accessing. This is important in multi-home hosts in which a single Web server supports many host names.

Figure 29.2 shows a Telnet session that again fetches the `HelloWorld.jsp` file, this time using HTTP 1.1.

```
bash
3 mark@CONTESSA //: telnet localhost 80
Trying 127.0.0.1...
Connected to CONTESSA.wutka.com.
Escape character is '^]'.
GET /j2eebook/ch15/examples/HelloWorld.jsp HTTP/1.1
Host: localhost

HTTP/1.1 200 OK
Server: Resin/1.1
Cache-Control: no-cache="set-cookie,set-cookie2"
Expires: Thu, 01 Dec 1994 16:00:00 GMT
Set-Cookie: JSESSIONID=jgKyhJE8v_WP8AvMv3;Path=/;Version=1
Content-Type: text/html
Content-Length: 59
Date: Fri, 29 Sep 2000 22:35:10 GMT

<HTML>
<BODY>
<H1>Hello World!</H1>

</BODY>
</HTML>
```

Figure 29.2
HTTP 1.1 requires you to specify a host name in the request.

Notice, too, that the Web server did not automatically close down the connection as it did when you used HTTP/1.0. One of the optimizations of HTTP 1.1 is that a browser can make multiple requests using the same connection. Setting up a connection is a time-consuming process. You can force the server to close the connection by specifying `Connection: close` in the request. Figure 29.3 shows a Telnet session that asks the server to close the connection.

```
bash
8 mark@CONTESSA //: telnet localhost 80
Trying 127.0.0.1...
Connected to CONTESSA.wutka.com.
Escape character is '^]'.
GET /j2eebook/ch15/examples/HelloWorld.jsp HTTP/1.1
Host: localhost
Connection: close

HTTP/1.1 200 OK
Server: Resin/1.1
Cache-Control: no-cache="set-cookie,set-cookie2"
Expires: Thu, 01 Dec 1994 16:00:00 GMT
Set-Cookie: JSESSIONID=ucgcaLWaEHetMe3vD-;Path=/;Version=1
Content-Type: text/html
Content-Length: 59
Date: Fri, 29 Sep 2000 22:36:48 GMT

<HTML>
<BODY>
<H1>Hello World!</H1>

</BODY>
</HTML>
Connection closed by foreign host.
9 mark@CONTESSA //:
```

Figure 29.3
If you want the server to automatically close the connection in HTTP 1.1, you must explicitly say so.

VIEWING THE REQUEST HEADERS MADE BY A BROWSER

A browser sends quite a bit more information than the minimum. The request object has methods that allow you to retrieve all the header values sent by the browser. Listing 29.1 shows you a JSP file that displays all the headers sent to it.

LISTING 29.1 SOURCE CODE FOR `DumpHeaders.jsp`

```
<html>
<body>
<pre>
<%
    java.util.Enumeration e = request.getHeaderNames();

    while (e.hasMoreElements())
    {
        String headerName = (String) e.nextElement();
        out.print(headerName+": ");

        java.util.Enumeration h = request.getHeaders(headerName);

        while (h.hasMoreElements())
        {
            String header = (String) h.nextElement();
            out.print(header);
            if (h.hasMoreElements()) out.print(", ");
        }
        out.println();
    }
%>
</pre>
</body>
</html>
```

Figure 29.4 shows the headers sent to `DumpHeaders.jsp`.

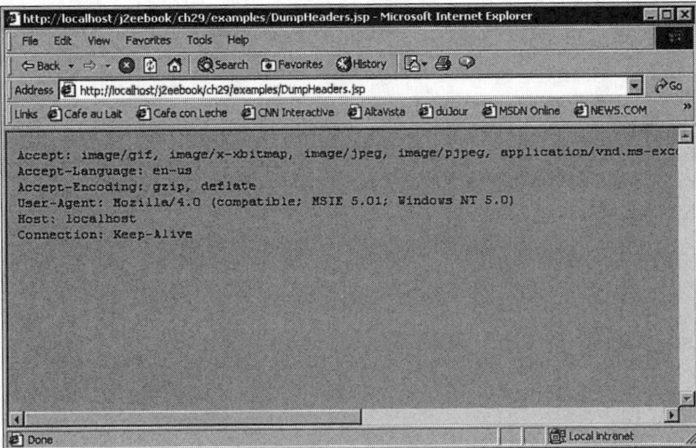

Figure 29.4
A JSP or servlet can examine all the request headers.

How can you be sure that you are really seeing all the header values? Because HTTP works over a simple socket connection, you can create a program that accepts an incoming connection and dumps out anything sent to it.

Listing 29.2 shows the `Dumper.java` program you can use to verify that you are seeing all the header values.

LISTING 29.2 SOURCE CODE FOR `Dumper.java`

```
import java.net.*;
import java.io.*;

public class Dumper
{
    public static void main(String[] args)
    {
        try {
            int portNumber = 1234;
            try {
                portNumber = Integer.parseInt(System.getProperty("port"));
            } catch (Exception e) {
            }
            ServerSocket serv = new ServerSocket(portNumber);

            for (;;) {
                Socket sock = serv.accept();
                InputStream inStream = sock.getInputStream();
                int ch;
                while ((ch = inStream.read()) >= 0) {
                    System.out.print((char) ch);
                }
                sock.close();
            }
        } catch (Exception e) {
            e.printStackTrace();
        }
    }
}
```

Figure 29.5 shows the output from the Dumper program. When you run Dumper on your local machine, point the browser to the URL `http://localhost:1234`. Because the Dumper doesn't understand HTTP and doesn't know to shut down the connection, you'll need to either click the stop button on your browser or terminate the Dumper program.

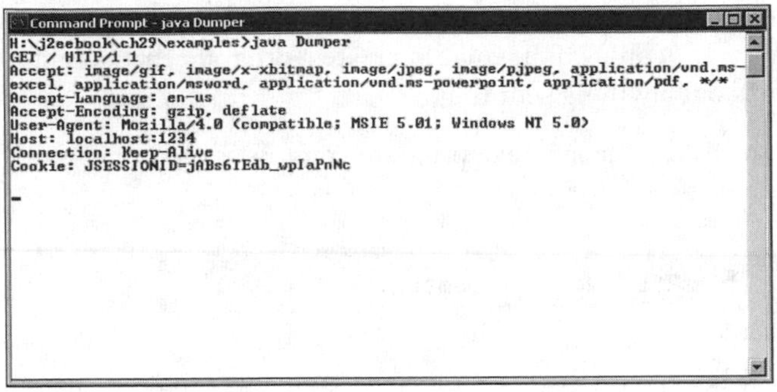

Figure 29.5
You can view the headers sent by a browser using a simple socket program.

```
Command Prompt - java Dumper
H:\j2eebook\ch29\examples>java Dumper
GET / HTTP/1.1
Accept: image/gif, image/x-xbitmap, image/jpeg, image/pjpeg, application/vnd.ms-
excel, application/msword, application/vnd.ms-powerpoint, application/pdf, */*
Accept-Language: en-us
Accept-Encoding: gzip, deflate
User-Agent: Mozilla/4.0 (compatible; MSIE 5.01; Windows NT 5.0)
Host: localhost:1234
Connection: Keep-Alive
Cookie: JSESSIONID=jABs6TEdb_wpIaPnNc
```

COMMON REQUEST HEADERS

The headers you saw in Figures 29.4 and 29.5 represent the most common set of request headers you'll receive. Netscape browsers might also send an `Accept-Charset` request header.

THE `Accept` HEADER

The `Accept` header indicates the kind of content the browser is able to accept. The order of the items is typically the order the browser prefers. In other words, when the browser lists `application/msword` before `application/pdf`, it indicates that it prefers MS Word documents to Adobe Acrobat documents (obviously this is a Microsoft browser!). Usually, you'll see `*/*` at the end of the list, indicating that the browser will accept anything, but it prefers those it has already listed.

If you look at the `Accept` header sent by a wireless phone (which you'll learn more about in Chapter 53, "Creating a Wireless Web Application"), you'll see that it lists HTML text and bitmap images after the `*/*`, indicating that it prefers just about anything to HTML or bitmaps! Here is the `Accept` header sent from a wireless phone:

```
Accept: application/x-hdmlc, application/x-up-alert, application/x-up-cacheop,
   application/x-up-device, application/x-up-digestentry, text/x-hdml;version=3.1,
   text/x-hdml;version=3.0, text/x-hdml;version=2.0, text/x-wap.wml,
   text/vnd.wap.wml, */*, image/bmp, text/html
```

THE `Accept-Language` HEADER

The `Accept-Language` header gives you a hint as to what language the browser prefers (really the browser's user, because the browser doesn't speak human languages itself). For English, you might see just `en` or you might see `en-us` or `en-uk`, specifying English for a particular locale like the United States or the United Kingdom. You can use this header to provide language-specific content automatically. You will learn more about this idea in Chapter 52, "Internationalization."

THE Accept-Charset HEADER

If present, the `Accept-Charset` header indicates the preferred character set(s) that the browser will accept. For Netscape running in an English-speaking locale, you'll most likely see this kind of header:

```
Accept-Charset: iso-8859-1,*,utf-8
```

THE User-Agent HEADER

Of all the headers sent by the browser, `User-Agent` is probably the most useful because it indicates what kind of browser is making the request. Oddly, both Netscape and Internet Explorer identify themselves as Mozilla, which was the nickname for the Netscape browser.

Note

In case you're wondering where the name Mozilla came from, Netscape was founded by the folks who wrote the old Mosaic Web browser. Netscape Navigator was intended to be a monstrous version of Mosaic–the Godzilla Mosaic, or Mozilla.

When Internet Explorer first came out, it lagged behind Netscape in usage, and gradually added in features to become a reasonable alternative by the time IE version 3 came along. By identifying itself as being Mozilla compatible, IE is telling the Web server that it can handle anything Mozilla can.

If you want to figure out whether the browser is Netscape or Internet Explorer, only IE sends the `MSIE` string as part of its `User-Agent` header. Thus, you can do the following test in your JSP or servlet:

```
if (request.getHeader("USER-AGENT").
    indexOf("MSIE") >= 0)
{
    // do Internet-Explorer specific stuff here
}
else
{
    // do Netscape-specific stuff here
}
```

You can perform similar tests to detect other browsers, such as Opera.

COMMON RESPONSE HEADERS

If you look all the way back to Figure 29.1, you'll see a typical response sent by a Web server. There are quite a few variations of response headers, but you only need to worry about a few when you write Java Web applications.

THE Content-Type HEADER

The `Content-Type` header is the most important response header. It tells the browser how to interpret the data it receives. A JSP has a default content type of `text/html`, although you can use the `<%@page` directive to change the content type. If you are returning XML data, for instance, you use a content type of `text/xml`.

THE `Content-Length` HEADER

The `Content-Length` header is important for many types of content that contain binary data. It tells the browser exactly how many bytes are in the body of the response. That way the browser can read the full response without worrying whether it has gotten everything.

THE `Cache-Control` HEADER

The `Cache-Control` header allows you to control how long the browser will keep a particular page cached. As you saw in Figure 29.1, a JSP normally isn't cached at all. You can request that a page be cached for 5 minutes (300 seconds) using the following response header:

```
Cache-Control: maxage=300
```

THE HTTP POST COMMAND

So far, the only HTTP command you have seen in this chapter is the `GET` command. As you know, the `POST` command is also frequently used to send form information to the Web server. Technically, the `POST` command can be used for more things than just form data, but form data is by far the most common kind of data sent via `POST`.

When a browser sends a `POST` command, the first line of the request looks just like the `GET` request, except that instead of `GET`, the command is `POST`. The difference comes about just after the request header. In a `GET` request, there is no data after the request header. After the server sees the blank line indicating the end of the header, it processes the request. In a `POST` request, the browser sends the form data after the header.

Listing 29.3 shows a bare bones form that posts its data to the Dumper program so you can see what a `POST` request looks like.

LISTING 29.3 SOURCE CODE FOR `PostForm.html`

```
<html>
<body>
<form action="http://localhost:1234" method="post">
<input type="text" name="foo" value="Foo!"><br>
<input type="text" name="bar" value="Bar?"><br>
<input type="text" name="baz" value="<<BAZ>>"><br>
<input type="submit">
</form>
</body>
</html>
```

Figure 29.6 shows the output from the Dumper program after it receives a `POST` request.

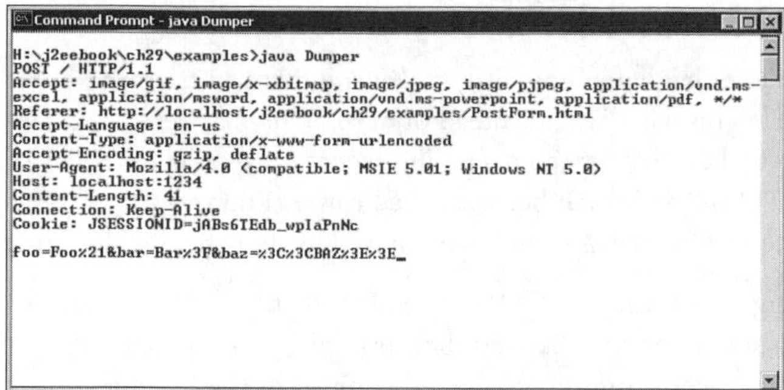

Command Prompt - java Dumper
H:\j2eebook\ch29\examples>java Dumper
POST / HTTP/1.1
Accept: image/gif, image/x-xbitmap, image/jpeg, image/pjpeg, application/vnd.ms-excel, application/msword, application/vnd.ms-powerpoint, application/pdf, */*
Referer: http://localhost/j2eebook/ch29/examples/PostForm.html
Accept-Language: en-us
Content-Type: application/x-www-form-urlencoded
Accept-Encoding: gzip, deflate
User-Agent: Mozilla/4.0 (compatible; MSIE 5.01; Windows NT 5.0)
Host: localhost:1234
Content-Length: 41
Connection: Keep-Alive
Cookie: JSESSIONID=jABs6TEdb_wpIaPnNc
foo=Foo%21&bar=Bar%3F&baz=%3C%3CBAZ%3E%3E_

Figure 29.6
A POST request sends form data in the body of the request.

Notice that there is a content type and content length in the request. No matter which direction the data is going, if you are sending content, you need to specify a content type and usually a content length.

GET VERSUS POST

You might wonder why someone would choose to do a `GET` instead of a `POST` or vice-versa. Why is there even a choice? When you send form data using the `GET` request, you're really taking advantage of a performance hack. By appending the form variables to the end of the pathname, you simplify the work that the server needs to do, because it takes a little more work to read posted data. For example, the corresponding `GET` request for the form data posted from the `PostForm` page looks like this:

```
GET /?foo=Foo%21&bar=Bar%3F&baz=%3C%3CBAZ%3E%3E HTTP/1.1
```

There is a limit to the length of the pathname for a `GET` request, however, so if the total length of your form variables is pretty long—more than 4,000 bytes—you can't use a `GET` request at all. Some servers won't even accept 2,000 bytes in a pathname. If you think the total length of your form data could be anywhere near the limit, you should use a `POST` instead of a `GET`.

Besides the size limitations, there are other reasons to choose `POST` over `GET` or vice-versa. If you submit a form using the `GET` request and then bookmark the resulting page, the bookmark contains the form variables because they are part of the URL. You might consider this a good thing, because it saves the user from having to type in the data. It might also be a bad thing if one of the form items is a password. Not only is the password now saved as a bookmark, defeating the purpose of requiring a password, but also the password is visible in the browser's address window.

> **Tip**
>
> If your form contains sensitive data, such as a password, use `POST` instead of `GET`.

HTTPS—SECURE HTTP

You might notice that when you visit a Web site that wants you to enter a credit card, the URL usually begins with `https` instead of `http`. The browser recognizes `https` as a request to use secure sockets to pass the data. The secure sockets layer (SSL) allows you to send encrypted data back and forth between the browser and the server. (Technically, it just provides encrypted traffic between any two endpoints, not specifically browsers and servers.)

The nice thing about using HTTP over SSL is that the HTTP protocol is still the same; just the Transport layer has changed. For example, if you had an SSL library that you could use with the Dumper program, you could connect to the Dumper with `https` and still see the HTTP headers exactly as you see them with an unencrypted connection. Figure 29.7 shows the relationship between the HTTP protocol and the SSL protocol as compared to an unencrypted HTTP connection.

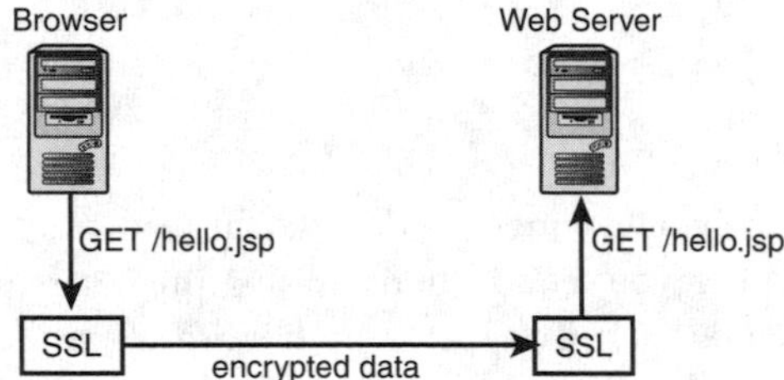

Figure 29.7 The Secure Socket Layer takes the place of a regular TCP/IP socket connection when sending encrypted HTTP traffic.

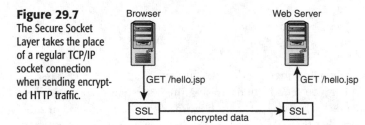

CASE STUDY

Knowing the HTTP protocol is frequently helpful in debugging Web applications. For example, suppose you try to redirect the browser to a different site and for some reason, you get a `404 - Page not found` error. Using the Telnet program, you access the Web site and look at the redirect request to see what it's sending the browser.

A developer was working on a Java Web application that wasn't tracking sessions correctly. The application sent a redirect to the browser, and although the browser displayed the new page correctly, the session information was gone. Using the Telnet program, the developer captured the redirect request on the screen and realized that the browser was being redirected to a different URL. The session information stored in the browser's cookie was not valid for the new URL (which contained a different hostname).

CHAPTER 30

SMTP, POP3, AND IMAP4—THE E-MAIL PROTOCOLS

In this chapter

THE SIMPLE MAIL TRANSPORT PROTOCOL

The Simple Mail Transport Protocol (SMTP) has been around in one form or another for 20 years. The original mail transfer protocol was defined in September of 1980 (RFC 772), although the current version of the protocol wasn't published until RFC 821 came out in August of 1982. Since then, the protocol has remained the same. Some servers might not support some functions, but SMTP is still the email workhorse for the Internet.

Like many of the common Internet protocols, SMTP is text based and uses TCP, so you can use the `telnet` command to create an SMTP session. The SMTP server usually runs on port 25. Keep in mind, of course, that if you're running Windows, you probably don't have an SMTP server on your local machine. You typically use your Internet service provider's SMTP server (or your company's server).

There are a minimum of four commands required to send email via SMTP: `HELO`, `MAIL FROM`, `RCPT TO`, and `DATA`. The `HELO` command tells the mail server your identity (you, in this case, are an email program, not a person). The `MAIL FROM` command identifies the person who is sending the mail. The `RCPT TO` command specifies the recipient of the mail, and the `DATA` command specifies the body of the message.

Notice that the message subject is not part of the protocol. The subject and other header information is part of the message body.

Figure 30.1 shows a Telnet-based SMTP session that creates and sends an email from a fictitious address.

```
bash
[mark@flamingo mark]$ telnet localhost 25
Trying 127.0.0.1...
Connected to localhost.
Escape character is '^]'.
220 flamingo.wutka.com ESMTP Sendmail 8.9.3/8.9.3; Wed, 27 Sep 2000 21:14:39 -04
00
HELO usingj2ee.com
250 flamingo.wutka.com Hello IDENT:mark@localhost [127.0.0.1], pleased to meet y
ou
MAIL FROM: senorcoffeebean@usingj2ee.com
250 senorcoffeebean@usingj2ee.com... Sender ok
RCPT TO: mark
250 mark... Recipient ok
DATA
354 Enter mail, end with "." on a line by itself
Subject: Ola!

Hello!  It is I, Senor Coffee Bean!  I bring you greetings
from the wonderful world of telnet!
   S.C.B. Esp.
.
250 VAA09936 Message accepted for delivery
```

Figure 30.1
You can send an email with the `telnet` command.

Notice in Figure 30.1 that there is a blank line between the subject and the message body. Some SMTP servers, such as the Lotus Notes server, consider all the lines up to the first blank line to be header information. You must include a blank line before the message body or the message will be blank.

SMTP servers are not as helpful as they once were, mainly because of the rising popularity of spam emails (mass bulk-mailing). In the past, you could contact any SMTP server, send mail from any sender, and send it to anyone. The SMTP server would then forward the message on to where it needed to go. These days, however, most SMTP servers require that either the sender or the recipient is in the same domain as the SMTP server, or at least that the host you are sending the mail from is in the same domain as the server. Although these restrictions don't prevent spam, they keep innocent organizations from bearing the brunt of the anger caused by spam.

For example, one organization I worked for started getting many angry emails accusing them of sending spam emails. After some investigation, it turned out that one of their SMTP servers didn't have any restrictions on forwarding, so the spammers were sending email through their server making it appear that the innocent company had sent the mail.

Note

The term "*spam*" comes from a Monty Python's Flying Circus skit, in which a restaurant menu has such entries as "spam, spam, spam, spam, spam, baked beans, spam, spam, spam, spam, and spam." Originally, spamming meant to send a message repeatedly to cause a failure or to just be annoying. The term is now used more often to refer to bulk email (when it isn't referring to the canned, spiced ham from Hormel).

Listing 30.1 shows a Java class that can send an email via SMTP.

LISTING 30.1 SOURCE CODE FOR `SMTPSession.java`

```
package usingj2ee.net;

import java.io.*;
import java.net.*;
import java.util.*;

/** Sends an e-mail message via SMTP */
public class
SMTPSession extends Object
{
    public String host; // Hostname to connect to
    public int port;    // port number to connect to, default=25

    public String recipient;
    public String sender;
    public String senderDomain;
    public String[] message;

    protected Socket sessionSock;

    protected DataInputStream inStream;
    protected DataOutputStream outStream;

    public SMTPSession()
    {
    }

    public SMTPSession(String host, String recipient,
        String sender, String[] message)
    throws IOException
    {
        this.host = host;
        this.port = 25;    // default SMTP port is 25
```

LISTING 30.1 CONTINUED

```
        this.recipient = recipient;
        this.message = message;
        this.sender = sender;
    }

    public SMTPSession(String host, int port, String recipient,
        String sender, String[] message)
    throws IOException
    {
        this.host = host;
        this.port = port;
        if (this.port <= 0) this.port = 25;

        this.recipient = recipient;
        this.message = message;
        this.sender = sender;
    }

// Close down the session

    public void close()
    throws IOException
    {
        sessionSock.close();
        sessionSock = null;
    }

// Connect to the server

    protected void connect()
    throws IOException
    {
        sessionSock = new Socket(host, port);

        inStream = new DataInputStream(
            new BufferedInputStream(
                sessionSock.getInputStream()));

        outStream = new DataOutputStream(
            new BufferedOutputStream(
                sessionSock.getOutputStream()));

    }

// Send a command and wait for a response

    protected String doCommand(String commandString)
    throws IOException
    {
        outStream.writeBytes(commandString+"\n");
        outStream.flush();
        String response = getResponse();
        return response;
    }

// Get a response back from the server. Handles multi-line responses
// and returns them as part of the string.
```

```
    protected String getResponse()
    throws IOException
    {
        String response = "";

        for (;;)
        {
            String line = inStream.readLine();

            if (line == null)
            {
                throw new IOException(
                    "Bad response from server.");
            }

// FTP response lines should at least have a 3-digit number

            if (line.length() < 3)
            {
                throw new IOException(
                    "Bad response from server.");
            }
            response += line + "\n";

// If there isn't a '-' immediately after the number, you have
// received the complete response.
// ('-' is the continuation character for FTP
// responses)

            if ((line.length() == 3) ||
                (line.charAt(3) != '-')) return response;
        }
    }


/** Sends a message using the SMTP protocol */

    public void sendMessage()
    throws IOException
    {
        connect();

// After connecting, the SMTP server will send a response string.
// Make sure it starts with a '2' (responses in the 200s are
// positive responses.

        String response = getResponse();
        if (response.charAt(0) != '2')
        {
            throw new IOException(response);
        }

// If the user hasn't specified a domain for the sender, try
// extracting it from the sender's email address

        if (senderDomain == null)
        {
            int atPos = sender.indexOf('@');
            if (atPos >= 0)
            {
```

LISTING 30.1 CONTINUED

```
                senderDomain = sender.substring(atPos+1);
            }
        }

// The session introduces itself to the SMTP server with a polite
// "HELO"
        response = doCommand("HELO "+senderDomain);

        if (response.charAt(0) != '2')
        {
            throw new IOException(response);
        }

// Tell the server who this message is from

        response = doCommand("MAIL FROM: " + sender);

        if (response.charAt(0) != '2')
        {
            throw new IOException(response);
        }


// Now tell the server who you want to send a message to

        response = doCommand("RCPT TO: " + recipient);

        if (response.charAt(0) != '2')
        {
            throw new IOException(response);
        }

// Okay, now send the mail message

        response = doCommand("DATA");

// Expect a response beginning with '3' indicating that the server
// is ready for data.

        if (response.charAt(0) != '3')
        {
            throw new IOException(response);
        }

// Send each line of the message

        for (int i=0; i < message.length; i++)
        {

// Check for a blank line
            if (message[i].length() == 0)
            {
                outStream.writeBytes("\n");
                continue;
            }

// If the line begins with a ".", put an extra "." in front of it.
```

```
            if (message[i].charAt(0) == '.')
            {
                outStream.writeBytes("."+message[i]+"\n");
            }
            else
            {
                outStream.writeBytes(message[i]+"\n");
            }
        }

        outStream.flush();

// A "." on a line by itself ends a message.

        response = doCommand(".");

        if (response.charAt(0) != '2')
        {
            throw new IOException(response);
        }

        close();
    }
}
```

Listing 30.2 shows a program that uses the `SMTPSession` class to send an email message.

LISTING 30.2 SOURCE CODE FOR SendSMTP.java

```
package usingj2ee.net;
import java.io.*;
public class SendSMTP extends Object
{
  public static void main(String[] args)
  {
    String[] message = {
      "Subject: Message from JAVA!",
      "",
            "Mark-",
            "This is a message you sent yourself from Java.",
            "   Senor Coffee Bean, Esp."
        };

        try
        {
            SMTPSession sess = new SMTPSession("flamingo.wutka.com",
                "mark@flamingo.wutka.com",
"senorcoffeebean@usingj2ee.com",
                message);

            sess.sendMessage();
        } catch (Exception e) {
            e.printStackTrace();
        }
    }
}
```

Note

Although it's instructive to see how SMTP works within Java code, if you're developing a commercial application, you should use the Java Mail API to send messages.

THE POST OFFICE PROTOCOL, VERSION 3

The Post Office Protocol version 3 (POP3) allows you to read your email over the network. In the early days, you had an SMTP server on your machine that would store your email in a local mailbox file. As the Internet grew, more people with small machines needed to read their email. It was impractical to expect each of these machines to run an SMTP server for receiving mail. Instead, Internet service providers set up POP3 servers that allowed users to read their email over the network, either keeping it on the ISP's server, or downloading it to a local mailbox.

As with many other Internet protocols, POP3 is a text-based protocol. Once again, you can interact with a POP3 server using the `telnet` command. Listing 30.3 shows an example POP3 session that logs on and reads a message.

LISTING 30.3 EXAMPLE POP3 SESSION

```
Trying 207.69.200.157...
Connected to mail.mindspring.com.
Escape character is '^]'.
+OK ngpopper@mindspring.com ready.
USER markwutka
+OK
PASS pass1234
+OK wutka has 1 messages (1418 octets).
TOP 1 5
+OK 1418 octets
Return-Path: <mark@wutka.com>
Received: from blount.mail.mindspring.net ([207.69.200.226])
    by runyon.mail.mindspring.net (Mindspring Mail Service) with
ESMTP id ssssrn.tg8.37kbi7f
    for <wutka@mindspring.com>; Sun, 24 Sep 2000 17:34:47 -0400
(EDT)
Received: from severus.mspring.net (severus-z.mspring.net
[207.69.231.74])
    by blount.mail.mindspring.net (8.9.3/8.8.5) with SMTP id
RAA18219
    for <wutka@mindspring.com>; Sun, 24 Sep 2000 17:34:47 -0400
(EDT)
X-MindSpring-Loop: mark@wutka.com
Received: from darius.concentric.net ([207.155.198.79])
    by severus.mspring.net (Mindspring Mail Service) with ESMTP id
sssss6.e9.37kbpqa
    for <mark@wutka.com>; Sun, 24 Sep 2000 17:35:02 -0400 (EDT)
Received: from newman.concentric.net (newman.concentric.net
[207.155.198.71])
    by darius.concentric.net (8.9.1a/(98/12/15 5.12))
    id RAA01365; Sun, 24 Sep 2000 17:34:46 -0400 (EDT)
```

```
        [1-800-745-2747 The Concentric Network]
Errors-To: <mark@wutka.com>
Received: from flamingo.wutka.com (w164.z208176122.atl-ga.dsl.cnc.net
[208.176.122.164])
        by newman.concentric.net (8.9.1a)
        id RAA15255; Sun, 24 Sep 2000 17:34:45 -0400 (EDT)
Date: Sun, 24 Sep 2000 17:33:43 -0400 (EDT)
From: Mark Wutka <mark@wutka.com>
To: mark@wutka.com
Subject: Hello there!
Message-ID: <Pine.LNX.4.21.0009241733300.26068-
100000@flamingo.wutka.com>
MIME-Version: 1.0
Content-Type: TEXT/PLAIN; charset=US-ASCII

I see you are reading your mail. Very good!


.
QUIT
+OK
```


As you can see, the USER command tells the POP3 server your username and the PASS command tells it your password. The LIST command shows you what messages are available and the RETR command retrieves an entire message. You can also use the TOP command to look at the first few lines of a message. For instance, the following command shows the first 10 lines of message number 2:

```
top 2 10
```

You can delete a message using the DELE command. Also the RSET command resets any changes you made during the session. Finally, the STAT command shows you how many messages there are. You can find out more details about POP3 in RFC 1939.

Listing 30.4 shows a Java class that implements the POP3 protocol.

LISTING 30.4 SOURCE CODE FOR POP3Session.java

```
package usingj2ee.net;

import java.io.*;
import java.net.*;
import java.util.*;

/** This class implements a POP3 (Post Office Protocol 3) session
    with a mail server. It allows you to create remote mail readers.
    You create a POP3 session by providing a hostname and a
    username/password combination for the user whose mailbox you are reading.
    After creating an instance of this class, you must call the
    connect method to actually connect to the server. You must always close
    the connection manually with the close method.
*/

public class POP3Session extends Object
```

LISTING 30.4 CONTINUED

```
{
    protected Socket pop3Sock;
    protected DataInputStream inStream;
    protected DataOutputStream outStream;

// The hostname and port to connect to. Default POP3 port is 110
    public String host;
    public int port;

// The username and password of the mailbox you want
    public String userName;
    public String password;

    public POP3Session()
    {
    }

    public POP3Session(String host, String userName, String password)
    {
        this.host = host;
        this.port = 110;
        this.userName = userName;
        this.password = password;
    }

    public POP3Session(String host, int port, String userName,
        String password)
    {
        this.host = host;
        this.port = port;
        this.userName = userName;
        this.password = password;
    }

/** POP3 positive responses start with a '+', negative responses
    start with '-' isErrorResponse returns true if a response does not start with
    a '+'
 */

    protected boolean isErrorResponse(String str)
    {
        return str.charAt(0) != '+';
    }

/** fetches the current number of messages using the POP3 STAT
    command */

    public int getMessageCount()
    throws IOException
    {

// Send the command
        String response = doCommand("STAT");
```

```
// Check for error
        if (isErrorResponse(response))
        {
            throw new IOException(response);
        }

// The format of the response is +OK # other text, you are interested
// in the number after the OK, but you need to stop parsing before
// the other text.
// You take the substring from offset 4 (the start of the number) and
// go up to the first space, then convert that string to a number.

        try
        {
            int count = Integer.valueOf(response.substring(4,
                response.indexOf(' ', 4))).
                intValue();
            return count;
        }
        catch (Exception e)
        {
            throw new IOException("Invalid response - "+response);
        }
    }

/** Get headers returns a list of message numbers along with some
    sizing information, and possibly other information depending on the
    server.
*/

    public String[] getHeaders()
    throws IOException
    {
        String response = doCommand("LIST");

        if (isErrorResponse(response))
        {
            throw new IOException(response);
        }

        return getData();
    }

/** Get header returns the message number and message size for
    a particular message number. It can also contain other
    information
*/

    public String getHeader(int messageNumber)
    throws IOException
    {
        String response = doCommand("LIST "+messageNumber);

        if (isErrorResponse(response))
        {
            throw new IOException(response);
        }
```

LISTING 30.4 CONTINUED

```
        return response;
    }

/** Retrieves the entire text of a message using the POP3 RETR
    command */

    public String[] getMessage(int messageNumber)
    throws IOException
    {
        String response = doCommand("RETR "+messageNumber);

        if (isErrorResponse(response))
        {
            throw new IOException(response);
        }

        return getData();
    }

/** Retrieves the first <linecount> lines of a message using the POP3
    TOP command. Note: this command might not be available on all
    servers. If it isn't available, you'll get an exception.
*/

    public String[] getMessageHead(int messageNumber, int lineCount)
    throws IOException
    {
        String response = doCommand("TOP "+messageNumber+" "+
            lineCount);

        if (isErrorResponse(response))
        {
            throw new IOException(response);
        }

        return getData();
    }

/** deletes a particular message */

    public void deleteMessage(int messageNumber)
    throws IOException
    {
        String response = doCommand("DELE "+messageNumber);

        if (isErrorResponse(response))
        {
            throw new IOException(response);
        }
    }

/** Undoes any pending deletions */

    public void reset()
```

```
    throws IOException
    {
        String response = doCommand("RSET");

        if (isErrorResponse(response))
        {
            throw new IOException(response);
        }
    }

/** Initiates a graceful exit */

    public void quit()
    throws IOException
    {
        String response = doCommand("QUIT");

        if (isErrorResponse(response))
        {
            throw new IOException(response);
        }
    }

/** Connects to the POP3 server and logs on with the USER and PASS commands */

    public void connect()
    throws IOException
    {

// Make the connection
        pop3Sock = new Socket(host, port);
        inStream = new DataInputStream(
            new BufferedInputStream(pop3Sock.getInputStream()));
        outStream = new DataOutputStream(
            new BufferedOutputStream(pop3Sock.getOutputStream()));

// The POP3 server should start out with a status message
        String response = inStream.readLine();
        if (isErrorResponse(response))
        {
            throw new IOException(response);
        }

// Send a logon (USER) command
        response = doCommand("USER "+userName);
        if (isErrorResponse(response))
        {
            throw new IOException(response);
        }

// Send a PASS command
        response = doCommand("PASS "+password);
        if (isErrorResponse(response))
        {
            throw new IOException(response);
        }
    }
```

Listing 30.4 Continued

```
/** Shuts down the connection immediately. You should call this if you
    get an exception. */

    public void close()
    throws IOException
    {
        pop3Sock.close();
        pop3Sock = null;
    }

/** Sends a POP3 command and retrieves the response */
    protected String doCommand(String command)
    throws IOException
    {
        outStream.writeBytes(command+"\n");
        outStream.flush();
        String response = inStream.readLine();
        return response;
    }

/** Retrieves a multi-line POP3 response. If a line contains "." by
    itself, it is the end of the response. If a line starts with a ".",
    it should really start with two of them. You strip off the leading "."
*/

    protected String[] getData()
    throws IOException
    {

// Don't know how many lines you're getting, so put them in a vector first
        Vector lines = new Vector();

        String line;

// Read lines from the server
        while ((line = inStream.readLine()) != null)
        {

// If you get a "." on a line by itself, that's the end of the multi-
// line response. Create a string array and copy the lines of the
// response into it.
            if (line.equals("."))
            {

// Create the array to return
                String response[] = new String[
                    lines.size()];

// Copy the strings from the vector into the array
                lines.copyInto(response);
                return response;
            }
```

```
// If a line starts with a ".", strip it off.

            if ((line.length() > 0) && (line.charAt(0) == '.'))
            {
                line = line.substring(1);
            }
            lines.addElement(line);
        }
        throw new IOException("Connection closed.");
    }
}
```


Listing 30.5 shows a program that uses the `POP3Session` class to examine a mailbox.

LISTING 30.5 SOURCE CODE FOR `TestPOP3.java`

```
package usingj2ee.net;

public class TestPOP3 extends Object
{
    public static void main(String[] args)
    {
        try
        {
            POP3Session pop3 = new POP3Session("YourPOP3Host",
                "YourUserName", "YourPassword");
// Connect to the server
            pop3.connect();

// Get a message count
            System.out.println("There are "+pop3.getMessageCount()+
            " messages.");

// Get a list of messages (the results look pretty boring)
            String[] headers = pop3.getHeaders();

            System.out.println("Message headers:");

            for (int i=0; i < headers.length; i++)
            {
                System.out.println(headers[i]);
            }

// Try fetching message #1, hopefully there will be one

            String[] message = pop3.getMessage(1);
            System.out.println("Message #1");

            for (int i=0; i < message.length; i++)
            {
                System.out.println(message[i]);
            }

// Try fetching message #99. Unless your mailbox is really full,
// there won't be one. For this test, the assumption is that there
// isn't one.
```

LISTING 30.5 SOURCE CODE FOR `TestPOP3.java`

```
            try
            {
                String header = pop3.getHeader(99);
            }
            catch (Exception e)
            {
                System.out.println("Got error getting message #99, good!");
            }

// Tell the server you're through
            pop3.quit();

// Close down the socket
            pop3.close();
        }
        catch (Exception e)
        {

// If you get any error at all, just print a stack trace

            e.printStackTrace();
        }
    }
}
```

THE INTERNET MESSAGE ACCESS PROTOCOL 4

The Internet Message Access Protocol version 4 (IMAP4) is similar to POP3 in that it lets you read email messages, but IMAP4 is a much more advanced protocol. Although POP3 lets you access only one mailbox, IMAP4 lets you access multiple mailboxes. Not only that, IMAP4 lets you execute multiple commands simultaneously over a single connection.

To support multiple commands, IMAP4 requires you to preface every command with a tag—an alphanumeric identifier that is used to indicate responses for various commands. The idea is that you could execute one command with a tag of `A001` and then start a second command with a tag of `A002`. When the server sends a response for one of the commands, it shows the tag name of the command it is responding to. The tags are what allows IMAP4 to support multiple commands.

Listing 30.6 shows a sample IMAP4 session. Notice that you send the username and password on a single line. The `SELECT` command chooses which inbox you want to work with. The `SEARCH` command lets you search for messages in various ways, and the `FETCH` command lets you display the contents of a message.

LISTING 30.6 EXAMPLE IMAP4 SESSION

```
Trying 127.0.0.1...
Connected to localhost.
Escape character is '^]'.
```

```
* OK localhost IMAP4rev1 2000.281 at Sun, 24 Sep 2000 17:36:34 -0400 (EDT)
A1 LOGIN mark mypass123
A1 OK LOGIN completed
a1 SELECT INBOX
* 57 EXISTS
* 0 RECENT
* OK [UIDVALIDITY 958516989] UID validity status
* OK [UIDNEXT 3951] Predicted next UID
* FLAGS (\Answered \Flagged \Deleted \Draft \Seen)
* OK [PERMANENTFLAGS (\* \Answered \Flagged \Deleted \Draft \Seen)] Permanent
flags
a1 OK [READ-WRITE] SELECT completed
a1 FETCH 57 body[TEXT]
* 57 FETCH (BODY[TEXT] {49}

I see you are reading your mail. Very good!

)
a1 OK FETCH completed
a1 LOGOUT
* BYE imapserver.wutka.com IMAP4rev1 server terminating connection
a1 OK LOGOUT completed
```


The IMAP4 protocol is defined in RFC 2060. Because the IMAP4 protocol is so much more complex than SMTP and POP3, it's much more difficult to write a Java class that understands IMAP4. You are better off using Sun's Java Mail API, which supports IMAP4.

THE JAVA MAIL API

Although it is nice to be able to write your own Java routines to speak the various email protocols, it can get pretty tedious, too. The `SMTPSession` and `POP3Session` classes you saw earlier in this chapter don't handle attachments. Although you could probably add attachments with some work, you don't have to because you have the Java Mail API is at your disposal.

The Java Mail API is a generic mail framework that supports the sending and retrieving of mail messages. The best part is, it supports multiple mail protocols through the same set of objects.

SENDING EMAIL WITH THE JAVA MAIL API

The `Transport` object represents a mail-delivery protocol like SMTP. You can use a `Transport` object to send `Message` objects. When you create the `Transport` object, you specify what protocol you want to use. Most of the time, you'll probably use `"smtp"` as the protocol.

After you create a `Transport`, you just create a `Message` and ask the `Transport` to send it. For normal email messages, you create a `MimeMessage` object. You can set the recipient, the sender, the subject, and the content of the message. If you want to support multiple message parts (that is, attachments) you can set the content of the message to be a `MimeMultipart` object. You can then add the different message parts to the `MimeMultipart` object.

After you have created the message, you must call the `saveChanges` method in the `Message` before sending it.

Listing 30.7 shows a program that sends an SMTP mail message using the Java Mail API.

LISTING 30.7 SOURCE CODE FOR SendJavaMail.java

```
package usingj2ee.net;

import java.util.*;
import javax.mail.*;
import javax.mail.internet.*;

/** Uses the Java Mail API to send a message via SMTP. */

public class SendJavaMail
{
    public static void main(String[] args)
    {
        try
        {
// Create a properties file containing the host address of
// your SMTP server
            Properties mailProps = new Properties();
            mailProps.put("mail.smtp.host", "smtp.myispserver.net");

// Create a session with the Java Mail API
            Session mailSession =
Session.getDefaultInstance(mailProps);

// Create a transport object for sending mail
            Transport transport = mailSession.getTransport("smtp");

// Create a new mail message
            MimeMessage message = new MimeMessage(mailSession);

// Set the From and the Recipient
            message.setFrom(new InternetAddress(
                "senorcoffeebean@wutka.com"));

            message.setRecipient(Message.RecipientType.TO,
                new InternetAddress("mark@wutka.com"));

// Set the subject
            message.setSubject("Hello from Java Mail!");

// Set the message text
            message.setText("Hello!\n"+
                "It is I, Senor Coffee Bean!  I bring you greetings \n"+
                "from the Java Mail API!. \n"+
                "    Senor Coffee Bean, Esp.\n");

// Save all the changes you have made to the message
            message.saveChanges();

// Send the message
            transport.send(message);
        }
        catch (Exception exc)
```

```
        {
            exc.printStackTrace();
        }
    }
}
```

ADDING ATTACHMENTS TO MAIL MESSAGES

The only difference between a regular email message and a message with attachments is that when there are attachments, the message content is a `MimeMultipart` object. To make a message with attachments, create a new `MimeMultipart` object, and then for each part of the message, create a new `MimeBodyPart` object. Add the body parts to the `MimeMultipart` object, and then call `setContent` on the main `Message` class, passing the `MimeMultipart` object as the content.

Listing 30.8 shows a Java program that sends its own source code as an attachment to an email message.

LISTING 30.8 SOURCE CODE FOR `SendAttachment.java`

```
package usingj2ee.net;

import java.io.*;
import java.util.*;
import javax.mail.*;
import javax.mail.internet.*;

/** Uses the Java Mail API to send a message via SMTP. */

public class SendAttachment
{
    public static void main(String[] args)
    {
        try
        {
// Create a properties file containing the host address of
// your SMTP server
            Properties mailProps = new Properties();
            mailProps.put("mail.smtp.host", "smtp.myispserver.net");

// Create a session with the Java Mail API
            Session mailSession =
Session.getDefaultInstance(mailProps);

// Create a transport object for sending mail
            Transport transport = mailSession.getTransport("smtp");

// Create a new mail message
            MimeMessage message = new MimeMessage(mailSession);

// Set the From and the Recipient
            message.setFrom(new InternetAddress(
                "senorcoffeebean@wutka.com"));

            message.setRecipient(Message.RecipientType.TO,
```

LISTING 30.8 CONTINUED

```
                new InternetAddress("mark@wutka.com"));

// Set the subject
             message.setSubject("Hello from Java Mail!");

// Create the multipart object for doing attachments
             MimeMultipart multi = new MimeMultipart();

// Create the message part for the main message text

             BodyPart textBodyPart = new MimeBodyPart();
// Set the message text
             textBodyPart.setText("Hello!\n"+
                 "It is I, Senor Coffee Bean!  I bring you an
➥               attachment \n"+
                 "from the Java Mail API!. \n"+
                 "    Senor Coffee Bean, Esp.\n");

// Add the body part to the multipart object
             multi.addBodyPart(textBodyPart);

// Create an input stream to read the attachment data
             FileInputStream in = new
➥            FileInputStream("SendAttachment.java");

// Create the body part for the attachment
             BodyPart fileBodyPart = new MimeBodyPart(in);

// Give the attachment a filename (the name that appears when someone
// reads the message--it doesn't have to be the same as the file
// you're reading).
             fileBodyPart.setFileName("SendAttachment.java");

// Add the attachment to the multipart object
             multi.addBodyPart(fileBodyPart);

// The multipart object is the content for the email message
             message.setContent(multi);

// Save all the changes you have made to the message
             message.saveChanges();

// Send the message
             transport.send(message);
         }
         catch (Exception exc)
         {
             exc.printStackTrace();
         }
     }
}
```

READING EMAIL WITH THE JAVA MAIL API

A Store object represents a place where email messages are stored—a mailbox. A mailbox consists of one or more folders, which might contain messages. The mailbox itself doesn't contain messages, just folders. For protocols such as POP3, which only support one mailbox, the Store still uses the folder concept, and there's just a single folder. For POP3, the folder is named INBOX.

A Folder object represents a mailbox folder and can contain any number of Message objects. A Message object, of course, represents an email message.

Listing 30.9 shows a program that reads a message from a POP3 mailbox using the Java Mail API.

LISTING 30.9 SOURCE CODE FOR JavaMailPOP3.java

```
package usingj2ee.net;

import java.util.*;
import javax.mail.*;
import javax.mail.internet.*;

/** Reads a message in a POP3 mailbox */

public class JavaMailPOP3
{
    public static void main(String[] args)
    {
        try
        {
// Create an empty properties object
            Properties mailProps = new Properties();

// Create a session with the Java Mail API
            Session mailSession = Session.getDefaultInstance(mailProps);

// Create a Store that references your POP3 mailbox
            Store store = mailSession.getStore(new URLName(
                    "pop3://myaccount:mypassword@pop3.myispserver.com"));

// Connect to the POP3 server
            store.connect();

// Locate the INBOX (POP3 has only one folder and its name is INBOX)
            Folder inbox = store.getFolder("INBOX");

// Open the folder
            inbox.open(Folder.READ_ONLY);

// Find out how many messages are in the folder
            System.out.println("There are "+inbox.getMessageCount()+
                " messages in your inbox.");

// Get the first message (if there isn't one, this will throw an exception)
            Message msg = inbox.getMessage(1);
```

Listing 30.9 Continued

```
// Print out the first sender and the subject
            Address senders[] = msg.getFrom();
            System.out.println("Message from: "+senders[0]);
            System.out.println("Subject: "+msg.getSubject());

// If the message is a MimeMessage (most are), print out the content.
// The content is returned as an Object, but if it's just plain text,
// it will print out as a string.
            if (msg instanceof MimeMessage)
            {
                System.out.println("Message text:");
                System.out.println(((MimeMessage)msg).getContent());
            }
        }
        catch (Exception exc)
        {
            exc.printStackTrace();
        }
    }
}
```

Notice that in Listing 30.9, the program creates a URL for the POP3 mailbox address. Instead of specifying a URL, you can also just specify a protocol and then specify the username, password and hostname in the `connect` method call. Listing 30.10 shows a program that reads an IMAP4 inbox using the Java Mail API. Notice that it provides the username, password, and hostname in the `connect` method.

Listing 30.10 Source Code for `JavaMailIMAP4.java`

```
package usingj2ee.net;

import java.util.*;
import javax.mail.*;
import javax.mail.internet.*;

/** Reads a mail message from an IMAP4 server */
public class JavaMailIMAP4
{
    public static void main(String[] args)
    {
        try
        {
// Create an empty properties object
            Properties mailProps = new Properties();

// Create a session with the Java Mail API
            Session mailSession =
Session.getDefaultInstance(mailProps);

// Create a Store object for working with an IMAP4 server
            Store store = mailSession.getStore("imap");

// Connect to the IMAP4 server
```

```
            store.connect("myimap4server", "mark", "myimappassword"
);

// Get the INBOX folder
            Folder inbox = store.getFolder("INBOX");

// Open the INBOX folder
            inbox.open(Folder.READ_ONLY);

// Find out how many messages are in the folder
            System.out.println("There are "+inbox.getMessageCount()+
                " messages in your inbox.");

// Get the first message, hopefully there is one
            Message msg = inbox.getMessage(1);

// Print out the sender and the subject
            Address senders[] = msg.getFrom();
            System.out.println("Message from: "+senders[0]);
            System.out.println("Subject: "+msg.getSubject());

// Print out the message content
            if (msg instanceof MimeMessage)
            {
                System.out.println("Message text:");
                System.out.println(((MimeMessage)msg).getContent());
            }
        }
        catch (Exception exc)
        {
            exc.printStackTrace();
        }
    }
}
```

Notice how similar the programs in Listings 30.9 and 30.10 look. The beauty of the Java Mail API is that it hides the specifics of the underlying protocol. You don't need to worry that IMAP4 is more complex than POP3 or that it requires you to tag each command with an identifier. The Java Mail API frees you from having to worry about the protocol so you can concentrate on getting the job done.

TROUBLESHOOTING

SMTP PROBLEMS

My SMTP server tells me that it won't forward a message.

Either the sender or the recipient of the message must belong to the same domain as the SMTP server, or at least the computer you're running your program on must be in the same domain. Forwarding usually invites spammers to forward spam through your server.

If I try to send mail with a sender that doesn't exist, why won't Java Mail let it through?

Java Mail checks the sender to make sure it is a valid email address. If you really need to send such mail, use the `SMTPSession` class.

JAVA MAIL PROBLEMS

Why do I get a `ClassNotFoundException` *for* `javax.activation.DataSource` *when I try to use the Java Mail API?*

The Java Mail API also needs the Java Beans Activation Framework—specifically, the `activation.jar` file or the `j2ee.jar` file.

CHAPTER 31

Proxies and Relays

In this chapter

CONNECTIONS ARE EVERYWHERE

When you stop and look at all the software packages that work over a network, you realize that your computer makes a lot of network connections. You make a connection to read mail and a connection to send mail. Your browser makes connections to Web servers. If you use a database server, such as Informix, Oracle, DB2, or SQL Server, you make a network connection to those databases.

The fact that these packages all use a standard protocol such as TCP or UDP gives you tremendous flexibility. Think of a TCP connection as an electrical cord. One end goes into a lamp or a stereo, the other end plugs into a socket (how appropriate!). Suppose you want to move the lamp to the other side of the room. You just plug it into an extension cord and then plug the extension cord into the socket where the lamp was originally plugged in. You can do similar things with TCP connections, and there are some good reasons why you might want to.

Suppose your company is creating a database application for a Saudi Arabian oil company. You develop the application and test it thoroughly, but when you deliver it to your customer, you encounter problems because the customer's database is configured to use a different language. You need to troubleshoot the application from a machine at your company. You have a network connection to your customer's site, but it has severe network limitations. Basically, you have a server that has a connection to one machine at the customer's site. Your server can't connect to any other machines at the customer's site, and none of the other machines on your network can connect to any machines on the customer's site. Figure 31.1 illustrates the network connectivity you have.

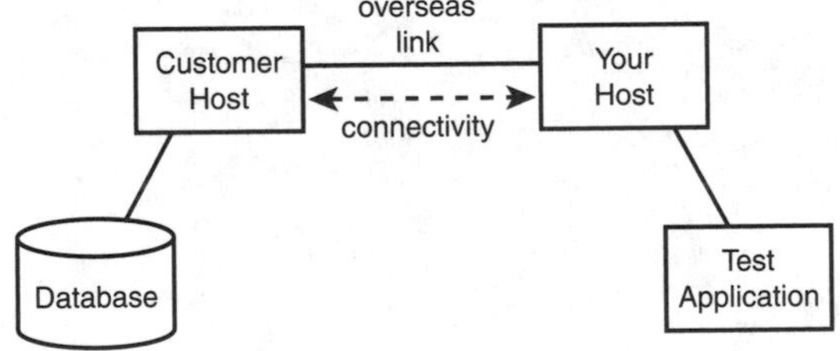

Figure 31.1
You have a single machine that can talk to a single machine at the customer's site.

Now, you want to test your application against the customer's database, but for technical reasons, you can't run the application on the one server that can connect to the customer's site. Even if you could, the database isn't running on the one machine you can connect to. Through an interesting configuration of relay programs, you can still make the connection you need!

Imagine you have a relay program that listens for connections on one port and makes a connection to another port either on the same machine or on another machine. Figure 31.2 shows how a relay might make a connection to another machine.

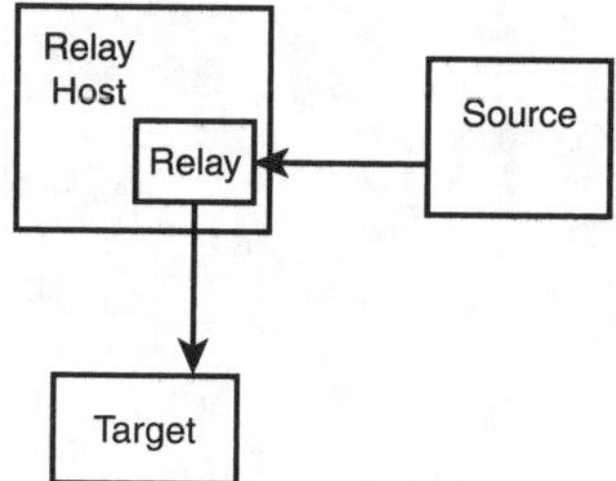

Figure 31.2
A relay works like an extension cord, relaying a connection from one machine to another.

Remember there is nothing special about a TCP connection; it's just a stream of bytes. As long as you relay every byte from one connection to another, neither the client nor the server knows there is even a relay between them.

To solve any kind of connectivity problem, just look at what you have to work with and see whether you can trace a path of connectivity. You want to connect point A to point D, but you can't. You *can* connect point A to point B, however, and you *can* connect point B to point C and point C to point D. Sure, it won't be fast, but it's better than nothing.

Your solution, then, for connecting to the customer's database, is to set up a relay program on your server, and connect it to the one machine on the customer's site that you can access. Then, run a relay on the customer's machine and connect it to the database. Finally, change your application program to make it think the database is running on your server on the port number where you have the relay running.

Figure 31.3 illustrates the working result.

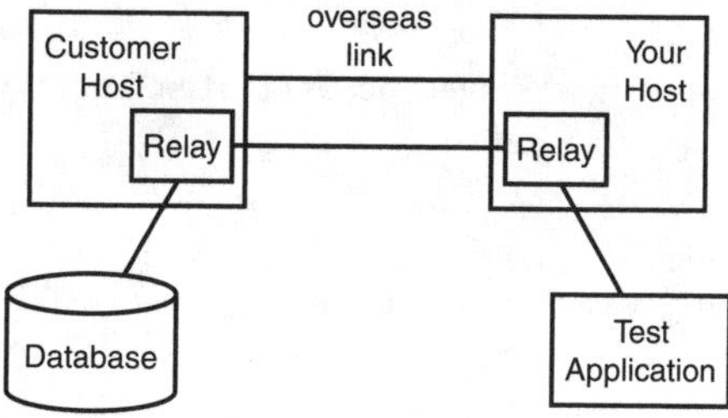

Figure 31.3
A pair of connected relays lets you make the connection you need.

Listing 31.1 shows the multi-threaded relay program that you can use for creating these relay connections.

Listing 31.1 Source Code for `Relay.java`

```
package usingj2ee.net;

import java.net.*;
import java.io.*;
```

LISTING 31.1 CONTINUED

```
/** Relays a connection from a local port to another port, possibly
 *  on another host.
 */

public class Relay implements Runnable
{

/** The local port number for accepting connections */
    public int listenPort;

/** The remote host where the relay connections will be made */
    public String relayHost;

/** The remote port where the relay connections will be made */
    public int relayPort;

    public Relay()
    {
    }

    public Relay(int aListenPort, String aRelayHost, int aRelayPort)
    {
        listenPort = aListenPort;
        relayHost = aRelayHost;
        relayPort = aRelayPort;
    }

    public void run()
    {
        try
        {
// Listen for incoming connections
            ServerSocket server = new ServerSocket(listenPort);

            for (;;)
            {
// Accept the next incoming connection
                Socket sock = server.accept();

                try
                {
// Create the connection to the remote host
                    Socket relaySocket = new Socket(relayHost, relayPort);

// Start a thread to read from the incoming connection and write
// to the remote connection
                    startRelay(sock.getInputStream(),
                        relaySocket.getOutputStream());

// Start a thread to read from the remote connection and write
// to the incoming connection
                    startRelay(relaySocket.getInputStream(),
                        sock.getOutputStream());
                }
                catch (Exception exc)
                {
                    exc.printStackTrace();
```

```
                    sock.close();
                }
            }
        }
        catch (Exception exc)
        {
            exc.printStackTrace();
        }
    }

/** Starts a thread that relays data from an input stream to an
    output stream */

    public void startRelay(InputStream in, OutputStream out)
        throws IOException
    {
        DataRelay relayer = new DataRelay(in, out);
        Thread relayerThread = new Thread(relayer);
        relayerThread.start();
    }

/** A runnable class that continuously relays data from an input stream
 *  to an output stream.
 */
    class DataRelay implements Runnable
    {
        protected InputStream in;
        protected OutputStream out;

        public DataRelay(InputStream relayIn, OutputStream relayOut)
        {
            in = relayIn;
            out = relayOut;
        }

        public void run()
        {
// Create a buffer for reading data
            byte[] buffer = new byte[4096];

            try
            {
                for (;;)
                {
// Read a block of data
                    int len = in.read(buffer);

// If End-of-stream, quit
                    if (len == 0) break;

// Relay the block of data to the output stream
                    out.write(buffer, 0, len);
                }
// When done, close both streams
                try { in.close(); } catch (Exception ignore) {}
                try { out.close(); } catch (Exception ignore) {}
            }
```

LISTING 31.1 CONTINUED

```
            catch (Exception exc)
            {
// If there's an error, close both streams
                try { in.close(); } catch (Exception ignore) {}
                try { out.close(); } catch (Exception ignore) {}
            }
        }
    }

    public static void main(String[] args)
    {
        if (args.length < 3)
        {
            System.out.println("Please supply a local port, a remote host "+
                " and a remote port.");
            System.exit(0);
        }

        int localPort = 0;

        try
        {
            localPort = Integer.parseInt(args[0]);
        }
        catch (Exception exc)
        {
            System.out.println("Invalid local port: "+args[0]);
            System.exit(0);
        }

        int remotePort = 0;

        try
        {
            remotePort = Integer.parseInt(args[2]);
        }
        catch (Exception exc)
        {
            System.out.println("Invalid remote port: "+args[2]);
            System.exit(0);
        }

        Relay theRelay = new Relay(localPort, args[1], remotePort);

        theRelay.run();
    }
}
```

There are other practical applications for the `Relay` class. An application server on a company's internal network needs to open a secure Web connection (HTTPS) to another company's Web server. The company uses a DMZ-style firewall configuration and doesn't allow machines on the internal network to connect to the Internet. Figure 31.4 illustrates the configuration.

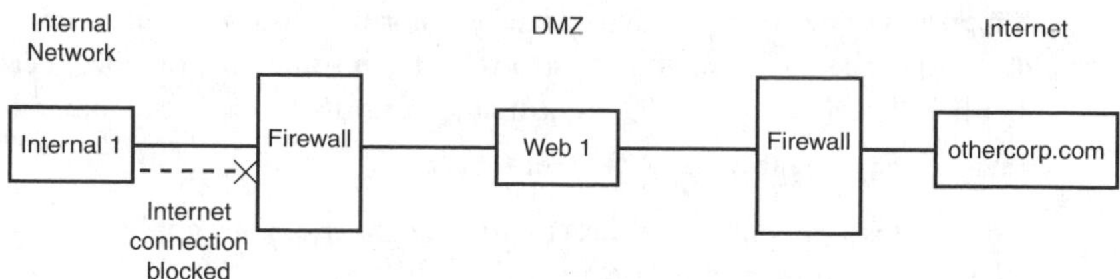

Figure 31.4 A host on the internal network wants to make an Internet connection.

Normally, the application on the Internal 1 host would use the URL `https://othercorp.com/postdata.cgi` to send information. When you break down the HTTPS URL, you see that it indicates that you should open a connection to port 443 (the secure HTTP port) on `othercorp.com` and then request the document `/postdata.cgi`.

Because you're setting up a relay, you want to change the host part of the URL, but not the document. The reason the document doesn't change is that you request the document after the connection has been established. The document path is one of the first things sent over the connection.

To set up the relay, you run the `Relay` program on the Web1 host, picking a specific port to listen for connections on. Suppose you choose to listen on port 4444. You start the relay on Web 1 with the following command:

```
java usingj2ee.net.Relay 4444 othercorp.com 443
```

Now, you change the URL you are requesting from Internal1 to `https://web1:4444/postdata.cgi`. Figure 31.5 shows the end result of this relay. The Internal1 host connects to the relay program on Web 1, which then relays the connection to `othercorp.com`.

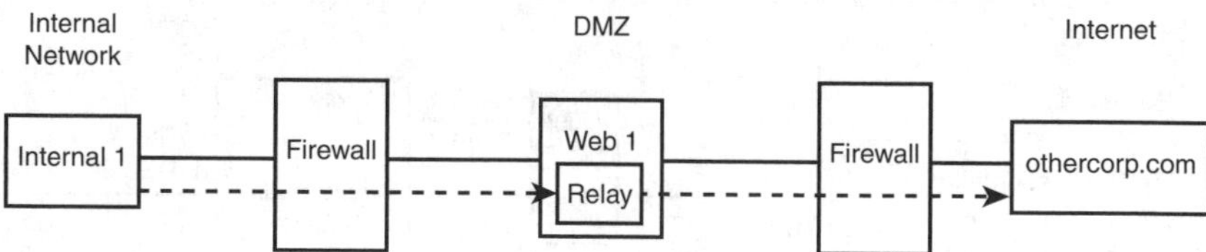

Figure 31.5 The `Relay` class lets you navigate around firewall restrictions.

> **Note**
>
> If you want to get a better feel for using the `Relay` class, try relaying various connections you often use. If you telnet to `xyz.com`, set up a relay from some local port to port 23 on `xyz.com` and then telnet to the relay port. You'll see that you end up connected to `xyz.com`. Likewise, set up a relay from port 1234 to port 80 at `www.slashdot.org` and then point your browser to `http://localhost:1234` and you'll see that you end up reading `www.slashdot.org`.

You can also use the `Relay` class to see how your application reacts to network outages. For example, suppose you want to see what happens to your application when the database goes down. You don't want to actually take the database down, you just want to simulate it.

Suppose, furthermore, that your database normally accepts connections on the hostname `db1` on port 5400. Now, you set up a relay from some port on your local machine, maybe 1234, and relay to port 5400 on host `db1` using the following command:

```
java usingj2ee.net.Relay 1234 db1 5400
```

Now, instead of connecting directly to the database, your application is going through a relay, as shown in Figure 31.6.

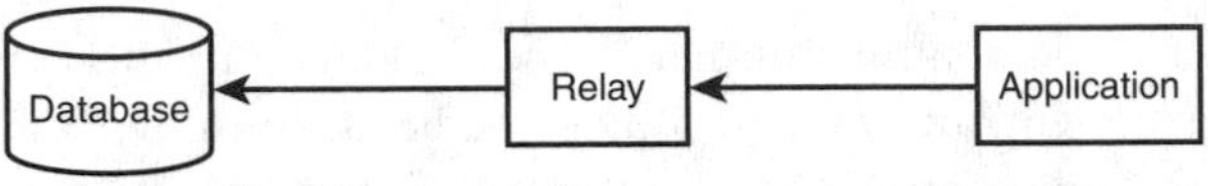

Figure 31.6
The relay sits between your application and the database.

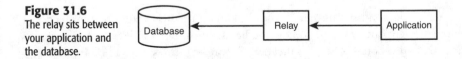

Now, to simulate a database crash, just kill the relay program. Your application loses its connection to the database so you can see how it reacts, but the database is still running!

One of the patterns you often see in a network is the use of network address translation (NAT). NAT is often used when there are a limited number of IP addresses available for Internet use and there are more machines than there are IP addresses. For example, you might have a home network with several machines, but a single dialup or DSL connection to the Internet with only one IP address. You can use a feature of Linux called *IP masquerading* to allow the other machines on your network to access the Internet. The Linux machine connects to the Internet, and other machines use the Linux machine as their default gateway. When one of the other machines tries to make a connection, the Linux machine forwards the connection to the Internet, changing the source address of the connection to match the lone IP address you have.

Figure 31.7 illustrates a network using IP masquerading.

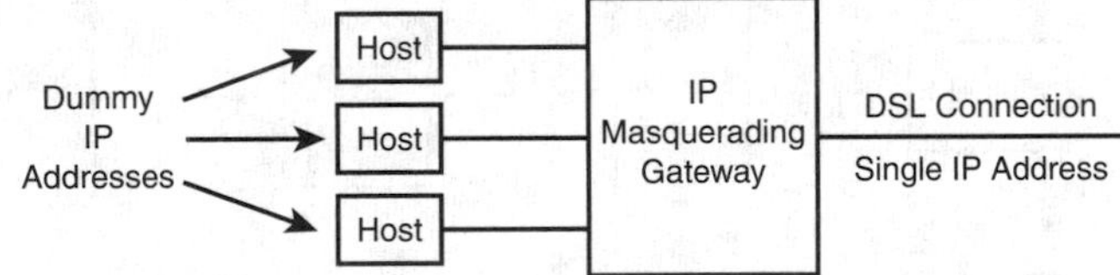

Figure 31.7
An IP masquerading gateway allows multiple hosts to share a single Internet address.

There are other forms of Internet connection sharing and network address translation. Some routers allow you to configure a pool of valid IP addresses. When a machine accesses the Internet, the router pulls an address from the pool and changes the source address of the connection.

What does network address translation have to do with relays? Suppose a machine out on the network wants to connect to one of the machines on your local network. Because you're using IP masquerading, the local machine doesn't have a valid IP address. You set up a relay on the Linux machine (your IP masquerading gateway) and relay the connection to the local machine.

Suppose, for example, that you and your mom like to play Scrabble over the Internet. Your machine is sitting behind an IP masquerading gateway, whereas your mom just has a dialup to the Internet. The Scrabble program listens for connections on port 3000, so you set up a relay on the Linux machine to relay connections on port 3000 to your computer. You give your mom the IP address of your Linux box, and when she connects to port 3000, the relay sends the connection over to your machine. Figure 31.8 illustrates the configuration.

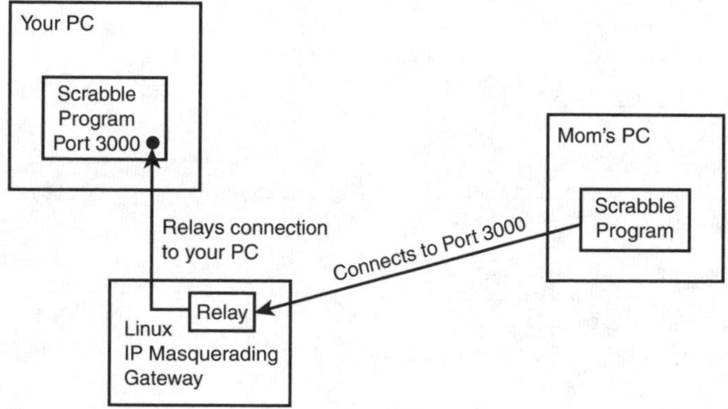

Figure 31.8
A relay enables hosts on the Internet to connect to hosts behind an IP masquerading gateway.

Using a Relay to Trace Data

If you want to see the data sent back and forth between a client and a server and you don't have a network sniffer, you can modify the `Relay` class so it writes data out to trace files. Listing 31.2 shows the `Trace` class, which works just like the `Relay` class with an additional parameter indicating the prefix for the trace filenames. The `Trace` class appends a connection count to the filename prefix and appends `.send` to the trace file for the data sent to the remote host and `.recv` to the trace file for data received from the remote host.

Listing 31.2 Source Code for `Trace.java`

```
package usingj2ee.net;

import java.net.*;
import java.io.*;

/** Relays a connection from a local port to another port, possibly
 *  on another host.
 */

public class Trace implements Runnable
{

/** The local port number for accepting connections */
    public int listenPort;

/** The remote host where the relay connections will be made */
    public String relayHost;
```

LISTING 31.2 CONTINUED

```
/** The remote port where the relay connections will be made */
    public int relayPort;

/** The prefix for trace filenames */
    public String tracePrefix;

/** The current count for trace filenames */
    public int traceCount;

    public Trace()
    {
        traceCount = 0;
    }

    public Trace(int aListenPort, String aRelayHost, int aRelayPort,
        String theTracePrefix)
    {
        listenPort = aListenPort;
        relayHost = aRelayHost;
        relayPort = aRelayPort;
        tracePrefix = theTracePrefix;
    }

    public void run()
    {
        try
        {
// Listen for incoming connections
            ServerSocket server = new ServerSocket(listenPort);

            for (;;)
            {
// Accept the next incoming connection
                    Socket sock = server.accept();

                    try
                    {
// Create the connection to the remote host
                        Socket relaySocket = new Socket(relayHost, relayPort);

// Bump up the trace count so the filename changes
                        traceCount++;

// Start a thread to read from the incoming connection and write
// to the remote connection
                        startRelay(sock.getInputStream(),
                            relaySocket.getOutputStream(),
                            tracePrefix+traceCount+".send");

// Start a thread to read from the remote connection and write
// to the incoming connection
                        startRelay(relaySocket.getInputStream(),
                            sock.getOutputStream(),
                            tracePrefix+traceCount+".recv");
                    }
                    catch (Exception exc)
```

```
                    {
                        exc.printStackTrace();

                        sock.close();
                    }
                }
            }
            catch (Exception exc)
            {
                exc.printStackTrace();
            }
        }

    /** Starts a thread that relays data from an input stream to an
        output stream */

        public void startRelay(InputStream in, OutputStream out,
            String relayFilename)
            throws IOException
        {
            DataRelay relayer = new DataRelay(in, out, relayFilename);
            Thread relayerThread = new Thread(relayer);
            relayerThread.start();
        }

    /** A runnable class that continuously relays data from an input stream
     *  to an output stream.
     */
        class DataRelay implements Runnable
        {
            protected InputStream in;
            protected OutputStream out;
            protected OutputStream trace;

            public DataRelay(InputStream relayIn, OutputStream relayOut,
                String traceFilename)
            {
                in = relayIn;
                out = relayOut;
                try
                {
                    trace = new FileOutputStream(traceFilename);
                }
                catch (Exception exc)
                {
                    exc.printStackTrace();
                }
            }

            public void run()
            {
// Create a buffer for reading data
                byte[] buffer = new byte[4096];

                try
                {
                    for (;;)
                    {
```

LISTING 31.2 CONTINUED

```
// Read a block of data
                    int len = in.read(buffer);

// If End-of-stream, quit
                    if (len == 0) break;

// Relay the block of data to the output stream
                    out.write(buffer, 0, len);

// If the trace file is open, write out trace data
                    if (trace != null)
                    {
                        trace.write(buffer, 0, len);
                    }
                }
// When done, close both streams
                try { in.close(); } catch (Exception ignore) {}
                try { out.close(); } catch (Exception ignore) {}
                try { trace.close(); } catch (Exception ignore) {}
            }
            catch (Exception exc)
            {
// If there's an error, close both streams
                try { in.close(); } catch (Exception ignore) {}
                try { out.close(); } catch (Exception ignore) {}
                try { trace.close(); } catch (Exception ignore) {}
            }
        }
    }

    public static void main(String[] args)
    {
        if (args.length < 4)
        {
            System.out.println("Please supply a local port, a remote host, "+
                " a remote port, and a prefix for the trace filename.");
            System.exit(0);
        }

        int localPort = 0;

        try
        {
            localPort = Integer.parseInt(args[0]);
        }
        catch (Exception exc)
        {
            System.out.println("Invalid local port: "+args[0]);
            System.exit(0);
        }

        int remotePort = 0;

        try
        {
            remotePort = Integer.parseInt(args[2]);
```

```
        }
        catch (Exception exc)
        {
            System.out.println("Invalid remote port: "+args[2]);
            System.exit(0);
        }

        Trace theRelay = new Trace(localPort, args[1], remotePort,
            args[3]);

        theRelay.run();
    }
}
```

RELAYING DATAGRAMS

Following the idea of the TCP relay, a UDP datagram relay receives datagrams on a particular port number and resends them to another address and port.

Listing 31.3 shows a simple datagram relay.

LISTING 31.3 SOURCE CODE FOR DatagramRelay.java

```
package usingj2ee.net;

import java.net.*;
import java.io.*;

public class DatagramRelay
{
    public static void main(String[] args)
    {
        if (args.length < 3)
        {
            System.out.println("Please supply a local port, a remote host "+
                " and a remote port.");
            System.exit(0);
        }

        int localPort = 0;

        try
        {
            localPort = Integer.parseInt(args[0]);
        }
        catch (Exception exc)
        {
            System.out.println("Invalid local port: "+args[0]);
            System.exit(0);
        }

        int remotePort = 0;

        try
        {
```

LISTING 31.3 CONTINUED

```
            remotePort = Integer.parseInt(args[2]);
        }
        catch (Exception exc)
        {
            System.out.println("Invalid remote port: "+args[2]);
            System.exit(0);
        }

        try
        {
            InetAddress destAddr = InetAddress.getByName(args[1]);

// Create the datagram socket for receiving the packets
            DatagramSocket receiveSocket = new DatagramSocket(1234);

// Create a buffer to hold the incoming data
            byte[] buffer = new byte[1024];

// Create a packet for the incoming data
            DatagramPacket packet = new DatagramPacket(buffer, buffer.length);

            for (;;)
            {
// Reset the packet size to the original size of the buffer (it gets set
// to the received data size after a packet has been received)
                packet.setLength(buffer.length);

// Receive the incoming packet
                receiveSocket.receive(packet);

// Change the destination address and port for the packet
                packet.setAddress(destAddr);
                packet.setPort(remotePort);

// Relay the packet to the remote host and port
                receiveSocket.send(packet);
            }
        }
        catch (Exception exc)
        {
            exc.printStackTrace();
        }
    }
}
```

The `DatagramRelay` class is only a simplistic datagram relay. For an effective relay, you need to create separate datagram sockets for every host and port number you receive a datagram from. The reason is that when you relay the connection to the destination host and port, the receiving application might want to send a reply back to the original sender. If you have only a single datagram socket, you can't tell where the response should go. By creating separate datagram sockets, however, when the reply comes back it will go to only one datagram socket, and if you keep track of which host and port the datagram socket belongs to, you know where to relay the response back to.

Now, the tricky part is that you don't know whether you need to create new datagram sockets or not. You also don't know how long to keep them around. Because datagrams are connectionless, you don't know whether the sending application is even around anymore. You also don't know whether the relay host will send multiple responses back to the original sender.

If you need to relay datagrams, examine how the datagrams are used so you can create a relay program that responds appropriately.

CREATING A CUSTOM SOCKET

When you use certain technologies such as RMI (Remote Method Invocation), it's tougher to deal with firewalls. RMI normally listens for connections on any free port, so you end up having to open up all ports on the firewall over 1024. If you want to open just one port on the firewall, you can create a relay program that accepts a hostname and port number and then connects to the named host and port.

Caution

It's *extremely* dangerous to make a relay that allows users outside the firewall to make connections to any address inside the firewall. You have essentially turned off the firewall and opened up your network to the world. You must limit the hosts and ports that you allow the user to connect to.

Although the relay server can help you work around firewall restrictions, you really end up duplicating the features of the firewall because you must still restrict the addresses that clients can connect to.

The relay server is helpful when you write Java applets, which can only connect back to the Web server from where they were loaded. The relay server lets you write an applet that connects to other servers.

Listing 31.4 shows a relay server that accepts a host address and port number as the destination for the relay, as opposed to the previous `Relay` class in which the host and port are specified on the command line.

LISTING 31.4 SOURCE CODE FOR `RelayServer.java`

```
package usingj2ee.net;

import java.net.*;
import java.io.*;

/** Relays a connection from a local port to another port, possibly
 *  on another host.
 */

public class RelayServer implements Runnable
{
```

LISTING 31.4 CONTINUED

```
/** The local port number for accepting connections */
    public int listenPort;

    public RelayServer()
    {
    }

    public RelayServer(int aListenPort)
    {
        listenPort = aListenPort;
    }

    public void run()
    {
        try
        {
// Listen for incoming connections
            ServerSocket server = new ServerSocket(listenPort);

            for (;;)
            {
// Accept the next incoming connection
                Socket sock = server.accept();

                try
                {
                    InputStream in = sock.getInputStream();

                    DataInputStream dataIn = new DataInputStream(in);

                    String relayHost = dataIn.readUTF();
                    int relayPort = dataIn.readInt();

                    if (!isValidRelayAddress(relayHost, relayPort))
                    {
                        sock.close();
                        continue;
                    }

// Create the connection to the remote host
                    Socket relaySocket = new Socket(relayHost, relayPort);

// Start a thread to read from the incoming connection and write
// to the remote connection
                    startRelay(in, relaySocket.getOutputStream());

// Start a thread to read from the remote connection and write
// to the incoming connection
                    startRelay(relaySocket.getInputStream(),
                        sock.getOutputStream());
                }
                catch (Exception exc)
                {
                    exc.printStackTrace();
```

```
                    sock.close();
                }
            }
        }
        catch (Exception exc)
        {
            exc.printStackTrace();
        }
    }

/** Starts a thread that relays data from an input stream to an
    output stream */

    public void startRelay(InputStream in, OutputStream out)
        throws IOException
    {
        DataRelay relayer = new DataRelay(in, out);
        Thread relayerThread = new Thread(relayer);
        relayerThread.start();
    }

/** A runnable class that continuously relays data from an input stream
 *  to an output stream.
 */
    class DataRelay implements Runnable
    {
        protected InputStream in;
        protected OutputStream out;

        public DataRelay(InputStream relayIn, OutputStream relayOut)
        {
            in = relayIn;
            out = relayOut;
        }

        public void run()
        {
// Create a buffer for reading data
            byte[] buffer = new byte[4096];

            try
            {
                for (;;)
                {
// Read a block of data
                    int len = in.read(buffer);

// If End-of-stream, quit
                    if (len == 0) break;

// Relay the block of data to the output stream
                    out.write(buffer, 0, len);
                }
// When done, close both streams
                try { in.close(); } catch (Exception ignore) {}
                try { out.close(); } catch (Exception ignore) {}
            }
            catch (Exception exc)
```

LISTING 31.4 CONTINUED

```
            {
// If there's an error, close both streams
                try { in.close(); } catch (Exception ignore) {}
                try { out.close(); } catch (Exception ignore) {}
            }
        }
    }

/** Returns true if you want to allow clients to connect to this
 *  host address (should be a numeric address) and port.
 *  For safety reasons, this method returns false by default, meaning
 *  the relay won't work until you add valid addresses.
 */
    public boolean isValidRelayAddress(String host, int port)
    {
        return false;
    }

    public static void main(String[] args)
    {
        if (args.length < 1)
        {
            System.out.println("Please supply a local port");
            System.exit(0);
        }

        int localPort = 0;

        try
        {
            localPort = Integer.parseInt(args[0]);
        }
        catch (Exception exc)
        {
            System.out.println("Invalid local port: "+args[0]);
            System.exit(0);
        }

        RelayServer theRelay = new RelayServer(localPort);

        theRelay.run();
    }
}
```

You can create a custom socket to connect to the relay server. By creating a custom socket, you make it easier to use the relay with packages such as RMI, which allow you to substitute alternate socket implementations to provide special capabilities.

Listing 31.5 shows the `RelaySocket` class that uses system properties of `relayHost` and `relayPort` to determine where the relay server is running. The class takes the original hostname and port number and passes them to the relay server. The end result is that it looks like you're connected to the place you wanted, and you don't realize you're going through a relay server.

Listing 31.5 Source Code for RelaySocket.java

```
package usingj2ee.net;

import java.net.*;
import java.io.*;

/** A socket that connects to a relay server in order to make a connection.
 *  This socket can be used to make connections through a firewall, although
 *  you must be extremely careful when setting up the relay server.
 *  If your relay server allows you to make a connection to any host and
 *  port, you have essentially deactivated your firewall and opened up
 *  your network to hackers.
 */

public class RelaySocket extends Socket
{
    protected static boolean checkedRelayConfig = false;
    protected static String relayHost;
    protected static int relayPort;

    protected OutputStream out;

/** Creates a RelaySocket that uses a relay to connect to the specified
 *  address and port.
 */
    public RelaySocket(InetAddress address, int port)
        throws IOException
    {
        super(getRelayHost(address.getHostAddress()), getRelayPort(port));

        doRelay(address, port);
    }

/** Creates a RelaySocket that uses a relay to connect to the specified
 *  address and port. The localAddr and localPort indicate the local
 *  address and port number for the socket.
 */
    public RelaySocket(InetAddress address, int port, InetAddress localAddr,
        int localPort)
        throws IOException
    {
        super(getRelayHost(address.getHostAddress()), getRelayPort(port),
            localAddr, localPort);

        doRelay(address, port);
    }

/** Creates a RelaySocket that uses a relay to connect to the specified
 *  host and port.
 */
    public RelaySocket(String host, int port)
        throws IOException
    {
        super(getRelayHost(host), getRelayPort(port));

        doRelay(InetAddress.getByName(host), port);
    }
```

Listing 31.5 Continued

```
/** Creates a RelaySocket that uses a relay to connect to the specified
 *  address and port. The localAddr and localPort indicate the local
 *  address and port number for the socket.
 */
    public RelaySocket(String host, int port, InetAddress localAddr,
        int localPort)
        throws IOException
    {
        super(getRelayHost(host), getRelayPort(port), localAddr, localPort);

        doRelay(InetAddress.getByName(host), port);
    }

/** Creates a relay connection through the relay server */
    protected void doRelay(InetAddress destAddr, int destPort)
        throws IOException
    {
        if ((relayHost == null) && (relayPort == 0)) return;

        out = super.getOutputStream();

        DataOutputStream dataOut = new DataOutputStream(
            new BufferedOutputStream(out));

// Tell the relay server the hostname and port to connect to
        dataOut.writeUTF(destAddr.getHostAddress());
        dataOut.writeInt(destPort);
        dataOut.flush();
    }

    public OutputStream getOutputStream()
        throws IOException
    {
        if (out != null) return out;
        return super.getOutputStream();
    }

    protected static String getRelayHost(String origHost)
        throws IOException
    {
        if (relayHost != null) return relayHost;
        if (checkedRelayConfig) return origHost;

        checkRelayConfig();

        if (relayHost == null) return origHost;
        return relayHost;
    }

    protected static int getRelayPort(int origPort)
        throws IOException
    {
        if (relayPort != 0) return relayPort;
        if (checkedRelayConfig) return origPort;
```

```
        checkRelayConfig();

        if (relayPort != 0) return relayPort;
        return origPort;
    }

/** Looks at the system properties for the hostname and port number
 *  of the relay server.
 */
    protected static void checkRelayConfig()
        throws IOException
    {
        relayHost = System.getProperty("relayHost");
        String relayPortStr = System.getProperty("relayPort");
        try
        {
            relayPort = Integer.parseInt(relayPortStr);
        }
        catch (Exception exc)
        {
            throw new IOException("Invalid relay port: "+relayPortStr);
        }
        checkedRelayConfig = true;
    }
}
```


Don't forget that you must add the allowable host addresses and port numbers to the `isValidRelayAddress` method in the `RelayServer` class or the relay won't work. Once again, the relay server has the potential to render your firewall useless by allowing the connections that the firewall would otherwise block. Handle it with care.

Listing 31.6 shows the `TestRelaySocket` class that demonstrates how to make use of a relay. It creates a connection to `www.cnn.com` and retrieves the HTML data from the CNN Web site. It assumes that the relay is running on the local host on port 4321, but allows you to change the relay settings with system properties.

LISTING 31.6 SOURCE CODE FOR `TestRelaySocket.java`

```
package usingj2ee.net;

import java.io.*;
import java.net.*;

public class TestRelaySocket
{
    public static void main(String[] args)
    {
        try
        {
            System.setProperty("relayHost", "localhost");
            System.setProperty("relayPort", "4321");

            RelaySocket relay = new RelaySocket("www.cnn.com", 80);
```

LISTING 31.6 CONTINUED

```
                PrintStream ps = new PrintStream(
                    relay.getOutputStream());
                InputStream in = relay.getInputStream();

                ps.println("GET / HTTP/1.0");
                ps.println();

                byte[] buff = new byte[4096];
                int len;

                while ((len = in.read(buff)) > 0)
                {
                    System.out.write(buff, 0, len);
                }
            }
            catch (Exception exc)
            {
                exc.printStackTrace();
            }
        }
    }
```

Using proxies and relays requires that you understand your network architecture and also the possible security risks involved in circumventing network restrictions. You should coordinate with your network administrator before running any programs that may compromise your network.

CASE STUDY

A check-printing company implemented an online ordering system using Java Server Pages and CORBA. The company needed to send copies of any new orders to the customer's bank. The system sent the orders using a secure HTTP connection. The system was originally deployed into a DMZ configuration, with both the JSP and the CORBA services running on a single machine. The DMZ firewall allowed the application server to make outgoing connections using port 443 (the secure HTTP port).

The company eventually split the application so that the CORBA services ran inside the company network and only the Java Server Pages ran in the DMZ area—thus making the application a little more secure. Unfortunately, the CORBA services were no longer able to send data to the banks because the internal network couldn't get through the firewall. The company set up a relay inside the DMZ that relayed connections from the CORBA services on the internal network to the various banks.

PART VI

SECURITY

CHAPTER 32

Introduction to Encryption Techniques

In this chapter

WHAT IS ENCRYPTION?

Encryption is the process of hiding information by encoding it. You've probably seen numerous examples of encryption, such as the cryptogram quiz in your local newspaper or the ROT13 encoding of material on the Usenet. If you aren't familiar with ROT13, it replaces a letter with the letter that is 13 places over in the alphabet. A becomes N, B becomes O, M becomes Z, N becomes A, and so on. The interesting thing about ROT13 is that you use the same process to decode ROT13 that you use to encode it. Because A becomes N and N becomes A, if you encode something with ROT13 and then encode the result again with ROT13, you'll end up with the original text you started with.

The ROT13 encoding for the phrase "the password is xyzzy" is "gur cnffjbeq vf klmml".

Note

An encryption/decryption algorithm or technique is usually referred to as a *cipher*.

Cryptograms and ROT13 are examples of an encryption technique called *substitution*. To put it simply, you substitute one letter for another. *Transposition* is another form of encryption, where you rearrange the letters of a message according to some fixed pattern. For example, writing the message backward is a simple form of transposition cipher. You can also make a transposition cipher by writing the phrase in a grid pattern, writing horizontally, and then reading off the letters vertically. For example, you can write the phrase "the password is xyzzy" in a grid like this:

```
T H E P A S
S W O R D I
S X Y Z Z Y
```

Now, you read off the letters vertically, getting the encrypted phrase "TSSHWXEOYPRZA DZSIY". As long as the person decoding the message knows the original size of the grid, they can decode the message easily. There are many interesting variations on transposition and substitution ciphers and their combinations.

Although these forms of encryption can be fun and challenging for puzzle enthusiasts, they take on a whole new dimension when computers enter into the encryption process.

Although many encryption algorithms can involve complex combinations of transpositions and substitutions, they are often so complicated that it is almost impossible to decode the data without a computer, even if you know what to do. Computer-based encryption algorithms don't work with characters, they work with bits. They shift the bits around and change the values according to certain patterns.

One of the most interesting aspects of encryption is that it is even difficult to know how good an encryption algorithm is. Some of them have various weaknesses where you might predict the value of certain bits or given a certain pattern of bits, you might be able to gain some information about the algorithm. Most encryption algorithms must be studied in depth by many experts before they are believed to be safe. Computer encryption algorithms tend to be math-oriented, and many of the top encryption experts have doctoral degrees in mathematics.

Note

Don't be deceived by the idea that an algorithm must be secret to be secure. The chances are pretty good that if a vendor tells you its encryption algorithm is a secret, you probably can't trust it. Most of the commonly used algorithms are published openly. The security comes from the use of secret encryption keys and not some secret technique. If you use different encryption keys for each message and someone figures out a key, only one message is exposed. If someone figured out your algorithm, however, everything is exposed. It's safest to stay away from vendors who won't reveal their encryption algorithms.

ENCRYPTION TERMINOLOGY

When you deal with encryption software, you'll probably encounter a few terms you might not have heard before. First of all, as you have already seen, a *cipher* is an encryption algorithm. The encrypted data is called *ciphertext*, whereas the unencrypted data is called *plaintext*. A *key* is a piece of information used to encrypt or decrypt the data but is not part of the data.

A *stream cipher* is a simple single-character-in, single-character-out cipher. That is, it performs the encryption one character at a time. Each time a stream cipher reads a character, it uses the key and accumulated data from the other characters it has processed to figure out how to scramble the next byte of data. Unlike some of the simple ciphers you might be familiar with, a good stream cipher does not simply map one character to another. If you feed two A's in a row to a stream cipher, chances are you will not get two identical characters in a row in the encrypted text. Figure 32.1 illustrates a stream cipher in action.

Figure 32.1
A stream cipher encodes a single character at a time.

A block cipher, on the other hand, encrypts whole blocks of data at a time. Unlike a stream cipher, the block cipher can scramble all the bits within a block, so that the bits for the first byte of the block can be scrambled and placed in strange places. Of course, the key and the actual values of the bits determine what the encoded block looks like. The first bit in a block can end up in one position using a certain key, and a different position using a different key. Figure 32.2 illustrates a block cipher in action.

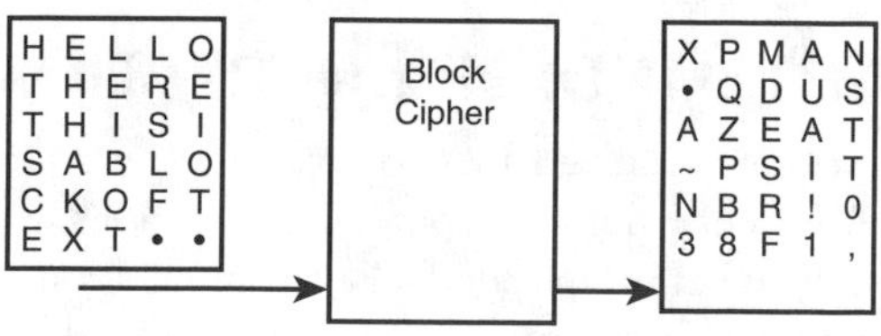

Figure 32.2
A block cipher scrambles whole blocks of data at one time.

Another way to classify encryption algorithms is based on the kind of key used. Some algorithms use a private key, also referred to as a *symmetric key*, whereas others use a public/private key pair, known as an *asymmetric pair*.

Private key encryption is probably the one you are most familiar with. Two parties agree on a secret key. The sender encrypts the data with the secret key, and the receiver decrypts the data with the same key. If anyone else finds out the secret key, they can spy on the data being exchanged. Figure 32.3 illustrates a data exchange using a private key.

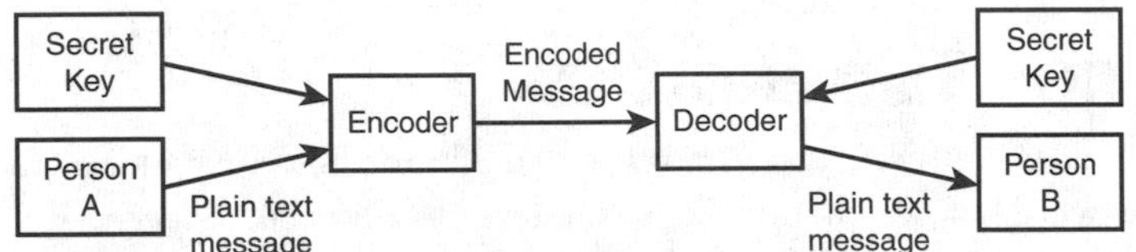

Figure 32.3 Both parties agree on a private key and use that key for encryption and decryption.

One of the problems with private keys is that you have to find some way of agreeing on the key ahead of time. How do two people exchange encrypted communications if they have had no way to exchange keys to begin with? Public key encryption provides a neat solution to this problem.

With public key encryption, every person who wants to receive encrypted data creates a private decryption key and a public encryption key. This is called an *asymmetric key cipher* because the encryption key and the decryption key are different. The important part of this scheme is that although you can determine the public key based on the private key, you cannot figure out the private key from the public key.

Anyone wanting to send you encrypted data would look up your public key, which can be published in a number of ways, and use it to encrypt a message to you. You would receive this message and decrypt it with your private key (see Figure 32.4).

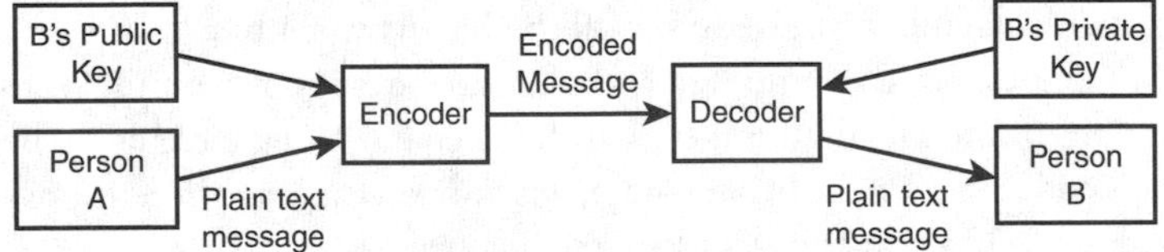

Figure 32.4 The data is encrypted with the public key and decrypted with the private key.

Choosing the Right Kind of Encryption

Given the fact that a stream cipher handles 1 byte, or even 1 bit at a time, you might think that a stream cipher is better for encrypting computer login sessions, which are more byte-oriented. As it turns out, block ciphers aren't too bad for login sessions, because the blocks are often only 64 bits (8 bytes) in size. Essentially, your choice of cipher shouldn't depend on whether it is a block or stream cipher.

The following are some of the factors that will influence your choice of encryption:

- **The amount of security required**—Some encryption algorithms can bc broken in a matter of hours, and some would take many years. Others would take several times the anticipated lifetime of the universe to break, given machines many times more powerful than the ones in use today. Of course, the price you pay for more security is the encryption time, among other things. If the data will be useless in an hour, you don't need an algorithm that will protect it for your lifetime.
- **The speed of the algorithm**—Some algorithms are prohibitively slow for common use. If you need a Cray mainframe to encrypt and decrypt the data in a reasonable time, it probably is not a good choice for an applet.
- **Licensing fees**—The number of patents for encryption algorithms is amazing compared to the rest of the computing field. Many algorithms, although publicly available, are still patented and subject to licensing fees for commercial use. The patent on the popular RSA public-key encryption algorithm expired on September 21, 2000, allowing developers to use the algorithm in the United States without paying a royalty fee to RSA Data Security (`www.rsa.com`). Interestingly, RSA actually released the algorithm into the public domain about two weeks before the patent was due to expire.
- **Availability for Java**—At the outset, Java and encryption algorithms didn't get along too well because Java was a byte-code interpreted language, and encryption algorithms require a lot of computations. As JIT compilers have emerged, Java has improved at meeting the high demands of these algorithms.
- **Native versus 100% Java implementations**—Several vendors have taken a shortcut in implementing encryption for Java by implementing some of the more compute-intensive parts of the algorithms as native methods. When you start relying on native methods, you lose the cross-platform advantages of Java.
- **Export restrictions**—The United States has stringent restrictions on the export of encryption software, although the restrictions have been relaxed in recent years. If your application uses a restricted algorithm, you could be violating U.S. law if someone outside the United States is running your application. Of course, if you are already outside the United States, you don't have this problem. Sometimes an entire algorithm is not restricted, only the use of keys above a certain size.

GUARDING AGAINST MALICIOUS ATTACKS

Your choice of private keys versus private/public key pairs depends on the kind of communications you are doing and the possible ways someone might attack your communications.

Presumably, the reason you are encrypting your data is to hide something in the data from prying eyes. This hidden information might be a credit card number, it might be the password to another system somewhere, or it might just be personal information.

When you create secure applications, you need to have some idea of the ways someone can attack your application. In general, there are two types of attack:

- **Simple eavesdropping**—An eavesdropping attack is a passive attack that can be conducted by monitoring network traffic. You should assume that anyone who might want to listen in on a conversation will have access to such a monitor. Because so many computers can act as network monitors with only a minor amount of programming, this is a safe assumption.
- **Impersonation**—An impersonation attack is an insidious attack, in which someone has the capability of impersonating another person or computer. The person sending confidential information sends the information to the imposter rather than the real recipient. This is typically the hardest attack to defend against, and is also the most difficult attack to implement.

You can see how encryption solves various attacks by starting first with a conversation that doesn't involve encryption. Then, as encryption is added to solve various problems, you can see how the attackers respond. After you are able to see how devious an attacker can be, you can design your applications appropriately. In other words, you start with an unsecure application, analyze the possible attacks, fix the security holes, and then look for new ways to break the security. It helps to look at ways that other people have attacked applications in the past, but keep in mind that people are always devising new ways to defeat security.

Figure 32.5 shows a simple conversation between two people with an eavesdropper watching the conversation.

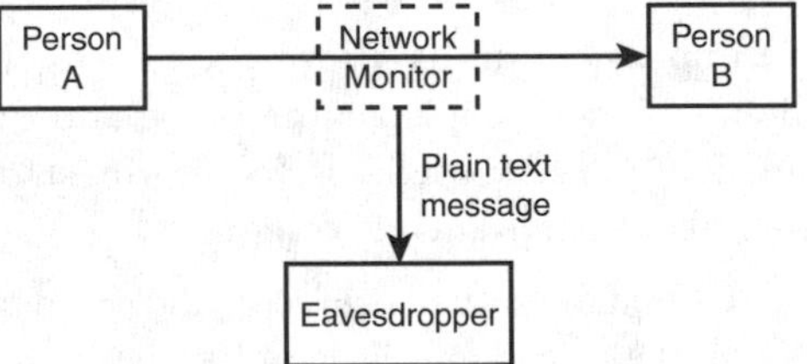

Figure 32.5
Unencrypted conversations are easy prey for an eavesdropper.

To solve the simple eavesdropping problem, the participants in the conversation agree on a secret key and encrypt their conversation. Now, the eavesdropper doesn't know what they're saying. In certain cases, the eavesdropper might not need to know what they're saying to perform an attack. Suppose, for instance, that the participants in the conversation are an automatic teller machine and a bank. As shown in Figure 32.6, the eavesdropper records the conversation between the teller machine and the bank as someone at the automatic teller makes a withdrawal.

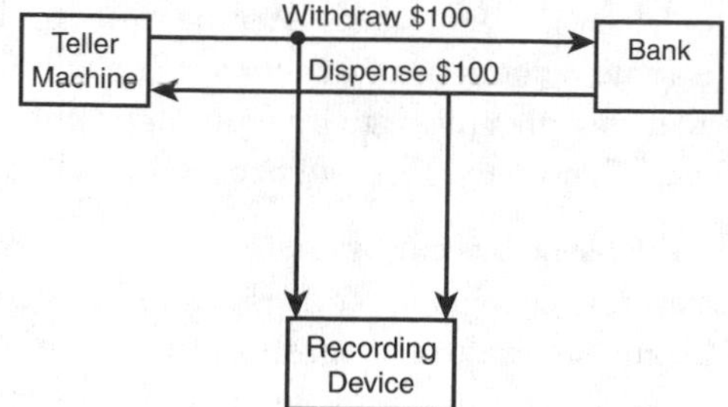

Figure 32.6
The eavesdropper records an encrypted conversation.

Some time later, the eavesdropper taps back into the connection between the bank and the teller machine and replays the encrypted conversation, which results in the bank performing another cash withdrawal from the customer's account, and the teller machine spitting out the cash (see Figure 32.7).

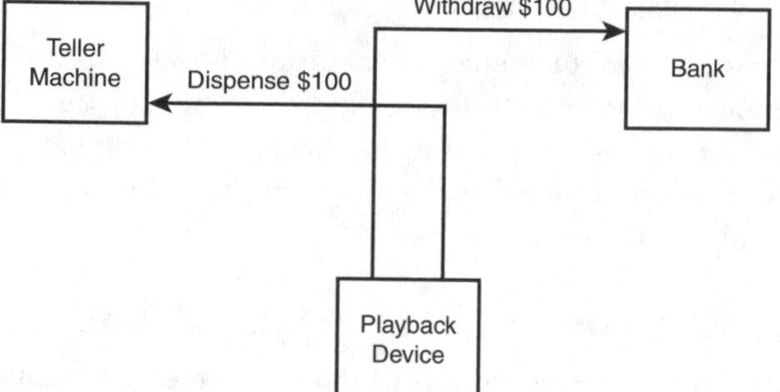

Figure 32.7
The eavesdropper can duplicate a transaction by playing it back at a later time.

RESISTING A PLAYBACK ATTACK

This sort of attack is often useful when encryption is used to set up a login connection or similar session, but the rest of the session is unencrypted. An eavesdropper could play back the login sequence and establish a login connection some time after the original login without ever knowing the secret key. You can solve the playback attack in the case of a login like this, but you should encrypt the entire login session anyway. If someone wanted to infiltrate your system, he could interfere with your unencrypted session and send bogus commands, intercepting the responses so you never knew they were there.

A simple trick for thwarting the playback attack is to insure that the messages change slightly from one session to the next. Not just that they change, but that they are required to change.

A simple solution for this problem is as follows:

1. The receiver generates a random number and sends it to the sender.
2. The sender must use the randomly generated number inside the message it sends to the receiver.
3. The receiver ignores any messages with an invalid number.

Now, the eavesdropper cannot play back the messages later, because it is highly unlikely that the receiver would generate the same random number the next time. In the worst case, the eavesdropper could get the sender to send a message by replaying a previous number sent by the receiver, but the receiver would ignore the message because it had the wrong number.

The eavesdropper could still wreak havoc by replaying previous messages during the current session. In other words, the eavesdropper waits for the session to be established and begins recording the conversation. At some point, the eavesdropper interferes and plays back an earlier part of the conversation, possibly causing some kind of security breach.

If each message has a sequence number associated with it, however, even that playback attack will not work. Each time a message is sent, it is given a sequence number that is one greater than the previous sequence number. Any out-of-sequence message is ignored. If the eavesdropper plays back a message from earlier in the session, it will have a sequence number that is out of order and the message is ignored.

Don't Store Keys in Your Software

Java makes simple symmetric communication almost impossible for applets. The problem here is that someone could get your software, find the secret key, and decrypt a conversation or actually impersonate either or both of the participants. You probably still want to use symmetric keys for communication, but the sender needs a way to generate a random session key and send it to the receiver.

Using Public Key Encryption to Exchange Session Keys

One of the reasons you don't see public keys used for encrypted communication channels is that the asymmetric encryption algorithms tend to take a lot longer than symmetric key encryption. Public keys are useful, however, for passing a random session key to a potential receiver.

The sequence for this is simple:

1. The sender generates a random session key and encrypts it with the receiver's public key.
2. The receiver decrypts the session key using the private key, and the two are ready to talk.

To make sure you are using the correct public key, you should use a digitally signed certificate that authenticates the key.

Digital Signatures

Many times, you want to verify that a document hasn't been tampered with, but you don't necessarily need to encrypt the document. A digital signature is essentially a way to verify that a document hasn't been changed and that the document comes from the party you think it does.

There are two basic components to a digital signature: a secure hash function and public key encryption. A secure hash algorithm takes a block of data and boils it down into a smaller block of bits. The algorithm should produce the same hash value for a particular pattern of bit every time it runs. That is, when you compute the hash value before you send the document, you want the receiver to compute the same hash value. A good hash algorithm also changes the value significantly for even a small change in the document. The idea is that you don't want someone tampering with the document in such a way that the hash value still comes out the same.

For example, suppose you created a hash algorithm that computed a value based solely on the individual characters in a document, ignoring the order of the characters. That is, ABC has the same hash value as CBA. Suppose you used this hash value in digitally signing a transaction with an amount of $123.00. Because your hash algorithm doesn't care about the order of the characters, someone could change the transaction to have a value of $321.00 without changing the hash, and thus keeping the signature valid.

Secure hash algorithms such as MD5 and SHA do take the order of the bytes into account, making it almost impossible to make small changes to a document and still have the same hash value.

Now, the second part of a digital signature is a kind of reverse public key algorithm. Normally when you use a public key encryption algorithm, you encrypt the data with the public key and use the private key to decrypt the data. With a digital signature, you do the opposite. You use the private key to encrypt the hash value for your block of text. Anyone wanting to verify the validity of your signature can use your public key to verify that a hash value has been encrypted with your private key.

Figure 32.8 shows the sequence for signing a document and verifying the signature.

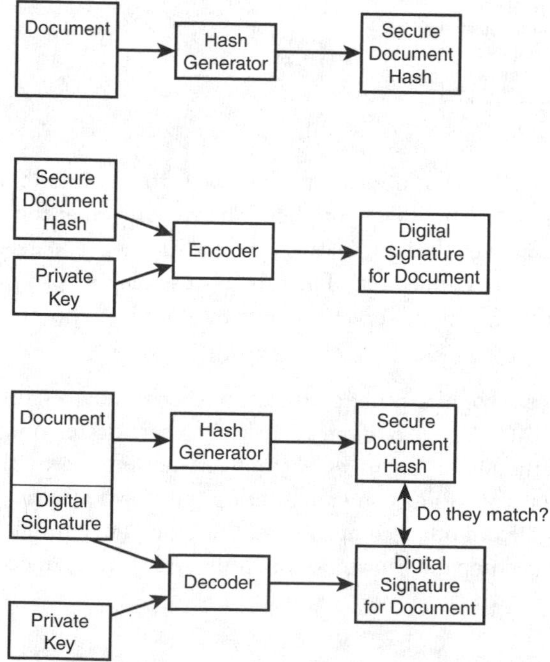

Figure 32.8
To sign a document, you create a secure hash of the document and encrypt the hash value with a private key.

DIGITAL CERTIFICATES

If you've ever set up a Web server that supports encrypted HTTP connections, you've probably had to obtain a digital certificate from a company such as Verisign. Digital certificates solve an important key-exchange problem: How can you be sure that someone's public key is what they say it is? To thwart possible man-in-the-middle attacks, you should have some piece of information at hand that you don't get from the network. In other words, if the only thing you know is what the network tells you, how do you know that the network is telling you the right things?

A digital certificate is just a digitally signed public key. A Web browser comes with some built-in knowledge about various certificate authorities, one of which is Verisign. A certificate authority (CA) is an organization whose signature the browser trusts. The browser also trusts any certificates signed by the CA.

Now, when you install your Web server, the Web server generates a private key and a public key that it uses to initiate secure Web connections. After you generate these keys, you send the public key off to Verisign in a file called a Certificate Signing Request (CSR). After Verisign verifies your identity, they digitally sign your public key and send it back in the form of a digital certificate. Figure 32.9 shows the general contents of a digital certificate.

Figure 32.9
A digital certificate contains your public key and identification and a digital signature of your key and information.

Your Identity
Your Public Key
Digital signature of identity and public key signed by a certificate authority

One of the things that seems to confuse a lot of people is that you can't just move digital certificates around from one machine to another. The reason is that the certificate doesn't contain the server's private key. It can't, because the certificate gets passed to any client wanting to establish a secure connection. The server must keep its private key secret. If you want to move a certificate from one server to another, you must also find a way to move the private key.

You can make a browser recognize other certificate authorities by installing a certificate called a CA root certificate. A *root certificate* is basically a certificate containing a CA's public key. The browser uses the public key in a CA's root certificate to verify the signature in a certificate signed by that CA. Some companies set up their own internal CA, so they don't need to order certificate from other companies all the time. They install their internal CA root certificates on their company browsers, which then recognize any certificates signed by the internal CA.

Verisign issues test certificates that usually have a period of 14 days. You can download the Test CA root certificate—the certificate for verifying test certificates. You can then install this Test CA root certificate on a browser when you want to try out your test certificate. Make sure, however, that you remove the Test CA root certificate when you're done with it. Otherwise, you might accidentally trust someone else's server that is using a test certificate.

CASE STUDY

A bank needed to exchange account data with another bank. In addition to keeping the data hidden, the banks needed to identify each other to make sure they weren't getting phony data. Because each bank's server was accessible over the Internet, it was possible that someone would try to send fake data.

The banks used HTTPS over secure sockets to transmit the data in encrypted form. By using a standard protocol such as HTTPS, the banks didn't need to change their firewall configurations to exchange data. To verify each other's identities, the banks opted to digitally sign every message they exchanged, which included the date and time of the transaction. This allowed the banks to verify the authenticity of the messages. By including the date and time in the message, the banks reduced the possibility of a playback attack where someone resends an earlier message.

CHAPTER 33

ENCRYPTING DATA

In this chapter

THE JAVA CRYPTOGRAPHY EXTENSION

The standard Java Development Kit comes with a security framework called the *Java Cryptography Architecture* (JCA). The interesting thing about the JCA is that it doesn't provide you a way to do cryptography. Instead, it provides some useful utilities and cryptography-related items, such as digital signatures. If you want to encrypt or decrypt data, you must use the *Java Cryptography Extension* (JCE) or a third-party encryption library.

Technically, the JCE is a framework for encryption providing various software vendors with a standard way to make their encryption libraries available to Java developers. The JCE does come with a reference implementation that includes several common encryption algorithms, so you won't necessarily need to buy any additional software.

Note

Starting with version 1.2.1, JCE recognizes only "trusted" security providers. This means that a security provider must go through an approval process with Sun to supply a pluggable cryptography implementation for JCE. The reason for this restriction is that it allows the JCE to be exportable from the United States and makes it easier to create exportable encryption software because the JCE is responsible for enforcing any restrictions. The bad part of this restriction is that there is always a nagging suspicion that software vendors will be forced to include back doors into their software for various law enforcement agencies.

The main classes that the JCE introduces are the `Cipher` class, which represents an encryption algorithm; the `CipherInputStream` and `CipherOutputStream` classes, which allow you to read and write encrypted data; and the `SealedObject` class, which acts as a holder for an encrypted Java object.

In addition, the JCE includes a mechanism for exchanging encryption keys securely. Whenever you use symmetric private key encryption, you need a way for both parties to agree on a particular key. Typically, one part generates the key and sends it to the other via some secure mechanism. As you will see, JCE provides that secure mechanism in the form of a `KeyAgreement` object.

JCE comes with three different ciphers: DES, Triple-DES (also called DESede), and Blowfish. DES is the Data Encryption Standard (the official U.S. Government standard encryption cipher) and is a block cipher, which means that it operates on a block of data at a time instead of one byte or bit at a time.

Note

On October 2, 2000, the U.S. National Institute of Standards and Technologies announced that it had chosen an algorithm for the proposed new Advanced Encryption Standard (AES)—the successor to DES. The new algorithm is called Rijndael (pronounced "Rhine Doll") and is named after its two Dutch inventors: Rijmen and Daemen. By sometime in 2001, you should expect this algorithm to become the new U.S. government encryption standard.

Triple-DES, or DESede, is a variation of DES in which the data is encrypted three times with two different keys. Normal DES has a key size of only 56 bits, which was once large enough to be considered safe. Computers have become powerful enough, however, that they can, given enough time and CPU power, break a 56-bit key. Triple-DES expands the key to 112 bits by first encrypting the data with one key, then decrypting it with a second key, and finally encrypting again with the first key. This encrypt-decrypt-encrypt sequence is why Triple-DES is also called DESede (DES encrypt-decrypt-encrypt).

Note

In 1998, Electronic Frontier Foundation (EFF) built a supercomputer for around $250,000 for the sole purpose of breaking a 56-bit DES encryption key. The EFF's purpose was to show that the U.S. government's restrictions on the export of cryptography software were useless. It took the EFF only 56 hours to break a 56-bit DES key!

The other cipher included in the JCE is Bruce Schneier's Blowfish cipher. Blowfish, like DES and Triple-DES, is a block cipher and supports key lengths of up to 448 bits.

Note

For more information on Blowfish and other algorithms, read Bruce Schneier's *Applied Cryptography* (John Wiley & Sons, Inc. ISBN: 0-471-11709-9). It is one of the most in-depth, informative introductions to cryptography you can find.

Installing the Java Cryptography Extension

You can download the JCE from Sun at `http://java.sun.com/products/jce/index.html`. The JCE comes in the form of a `ZIP` file that you must first unpack. The `ZIP` file contains several `JAR` files and instructions on installing the JCE. The easiest way to install JCE is to make it an installed extension. Copy the `JAR` files in JCE's `lib` directory to the `jre/lib/ext` directory of your JDK.

Next, edit the `java.security` file in your `jre/lib` directory. After a series of comment lines, you see several lines of the form: `security.provider.`*`n=some Java Package name`*. Add a new line that looks something like this:

```
security.provider.3=com.sun.crypto.provider.SunJCE
```

The provider number (3 in the previous example line) should be one higher than the current highest number. In other words, if your provider list has a single line that starts with `security.provider.1=`, the next provider you add should start with `security.provider.2=`.

Once you have installed the `JAR` files and edited the `java.security` file, you can use JCE. Because you install the `JAR` files as a JDK extension, you don't need to edit your classpath. The compiler and the JVM both recognize extension `JAR`s automatically.

Generating an Encryption Key

The JCE represents keys two different ways. First, there is a class called `SecretKey` that is an opaque version of the key. That is, although the `SecretKey` class represents a key, you don't have access to the individual bits in the key. The other representation is called a *key specification*. A key specification, or key spec, is represented by the `SecretKeySpec` class and by algorithm-specific subclasses such as `DESKeySpec` or `PBEKeySpec`.

The easiest way to generate a random key is just to use a `KeyGenerator` class. Use the `getInstance` method to get a key generator for the particular algorithm you want to use. For example, to generate a random key for DESede, you first call

```
KeyGenerator keyGen = KeyGenerator.getInstance("DESede");
```

Next, you call `generateKey` to create a `SecretKey` object:

```
SecretKey theKey = keyGen.generateKey();
```

You can also generate a random key by first creating a random sequence of bytes, storing them in a key spec object, and then using the `SecretKeyFactory` class to create a secret key from the key spec, as you can see in Listing 33.1.

LISTING 33.1 EXCERPT FROM `GenerateRandomKey.java`

```
// Create an array to hold the random key
            byte[] randomKey = new byte[24];

// Create the SecureRandom object for generating the key
            SecureRandom random = new SecureRandom();

// Generate random bytes and store them in randomKey
            random.nextBytes(randomKey);

// Create a DESede key spec from the random key
            DESedeKeySpec spec = new DESedeKeySpec(randomKey);

// Get the secret key factor for generating DESede keys
            SecretKeyFactory keyFactory =
SecretKeyFactory.getInstance(
                "DESede");

// Generate a DESede SecretKey object
            SecretKey theKey = keyFactory.generateSecret(spec);
```

The `SecretKeyFactory` class can also convert a `SecretKey` object into a key spec object. When you encrypt and decrypt data, you use a `SecretKey` object. Most of the time, you won't need to convert the key to a key spec. If you need to access the actual bytes in the key, that's when you perform the conversion.

The following code converts a `SecretKey` object to a `DESedeKeySpec`:

```
// Get the DESede secret key factory
SecretKeyFactory keyFactory = SecretKeyFactory.getInstance(
    "DESede");

// Convert the key into an instance of DESedeKeySpec
DESedeKeySpec keySpec = (DESedeKeySpec)
    keyFactory.getKeySpec(theKey, DESedeKeySpec.class);
```

ENCRYPTING DATA

If you're using JCE's built-in cryptography provider, the only ciphers available to you are symmetric key block ciphers. Recall from Chapter 32, "Introduction to Encryption Techniques," that a symmetric key algorithm uses the same key for encryption and decryption and that a block cipher works on a block of data rather than one byte at a time.

When you deal with block ciphers, there are two additional aspects of the encryption that you must specify in addition to the actual cipher. First, there is the block mode, which can be Electronic Code Book (ECB), Cipher Block Chaining (CBC), Cipher Feedback (CFB), Output Feedback (OFB), and Propagating Cipher Block Chaining (PCBC).

ECB mode means that you encrypt each block separately. The problem with ECB is that you might be able to determine certain aspects of the message content based on how the encrypted data repeats. Cipher Block Chaining (CBC) addresses the problems with ECB by combining the results of the previous encryption with the data being encrypted.

CBC uses the exclusive-OR (`XOR`) operation to combine the previous results with the next block. `XOR` is common in encryption routines because it is easy to undo the results of an `XOR`. That is, if `A XOR B = C`, then `C XOR B = A` and `X XOR A = B`. Now, if you encrypt something using CBC, you encrypt the first block just like you would with ECB—you just apply the encryption algorithm to the block. Now, for the next block, you first `XOR` the block with the encrypted version of the last block. You perform a similar operation on successive blocks. When you decrypt the data, you decrypt the first block normally, then decrypt the second one and `XOR` the encrypted version of the first block.

Of course, you don't need to do this yourself when you use JCE: it does it automatically if you just specify a mode of CBC instead of ECB.

Cipher Feedback (CFB) and Output Feedback (OFB) modes are somewhat similar to CBC in that they involve the combination of other parts of the encrypted and unencrypted text to generate the next block. The important thing about CFB and OFB is that they make a block cipher behave like a stream cipher. Because the JCE doesn't come with a stream cipher, you can use CFB or OFB to simulate a stream cipher. These modes are especially handy when you want to use the built-in encrypted streams for sending data. When you specify a mode, you can append the number of bytes you want to send at one time. To treat the block cipher like a byte-oriented stream cipher, choose a mode of CFB8 or OFB8.

PCBC allows you to detect transmission errors because it `XOR`s the original plaintext into the message in such a way that if there are errors, you can detect them programmatically.

The other thing you must worry about is padding. The JCE understands three padding types: `NoPadding`, `PKCS5Padding`, and `SSL3Padding`. The SunJCE provider that comes with JCE doesn't support SSL3 padding, however. The reason for padding is that your data doesn't always fit neatly into blocks. When you decrypt the data, how do you know how many bytes you are supposed to end up with? Obviously you could send a byte length along with the data, but that's not always the most convenient thing.

PKCS5 padding involves padding the end of the message with 1 to 8 bytes of data. The value of each padding byte is the number of padding bytes that have been appended. If you must append 2 padding bytes, the last 2 bytes in the block will be `02 02`. If you must pad with 4 bytes, the last 4 bytes will be `04 04 04 04`. If you use PKCS5 padding and the number of bytes fits evenly within a block, you end up with an extra block of padding. That is, you end up with a block containing `08 08 08 08 08 08 08 08`. By using this padding mechanism, you don't need to send the number of bytes along with the message because the count can be determined from the padding.

SSL3 padding works roughly the same way as PCKS5 padding, except that the padding length is always present and is separate from the actual padding bytes.

To encrypt a block of data, you can either use a `Cipher` class or use a `CipherOutputStream`. If you use a `CipherOutputStream`, you must still start with a `Cipher` object, however.

To obtain a `Cipher`, you must use the `getInstance` method in the `Cipher` class, passing it either the encryption algorithm by itself or a combination of the algorithm, the mode, and the padding in the form *`algorithm/mode/padding`*. For example, you can create a DES cipher this way:

```
Cipher c = Cipher.getInstance("DES");
```

To create a DES cipher using CBC mode and PKCS5 padding, use the following statement:

```
Cipher c = Cipher.getInstance("DES/CBC/PKCS5Padding");
```

After you create the cipher, you must initialize it with the type of operation you want to perform (decrypt, encrypt) and the encryption key. The `init` method has several different versions because some algorithms can accept various parameters. Also, if you are performing public-key encryption and you want to use the public key from a digital certificate, you can use the certificate as the key. The various versions of `init` are

```
void init(int mode, Certificate cert)
void init(int mode, Certificate cert, SecureRandom random)
void init(int mode, Key key)
void init(int mode, Key key, SecureRandom random)
void init(int mode, Key key, AlgorithmParameters params)
void init(int mode, Key key, AlgorithmParameterSpec paramSpec)
void init(int mode, Key key, AlgorithmParameters params, SecureRandom
random)
void init(int mode, Key key, AlgorithmParameterSpec paramSpec,
    SecureRandom random)
```

The mode for the `init` method is typically either `Cipher.ENCRYPT_MODE` or `Cipher.DECRYPT_MODE`.

Some algorithms require additional parameters. If you use either of the DES algorithms or Blowfish and you choose a mode other than ECB (that is, you use CBC, CFB, OFB, or PCBC), you must create an initialization vector that contains the initial block values that are merged into the plaintext before encryption. For instance, remember that CBC (Cipher Block Chaining) combines the previous encrypted block with the current plaintext block before encrypting. Because there is no previous block when you encrypt the first block, the initialization vector supplies a dummy block to combine with the plaintext.

If your algorithm requires an initialization vector, you can create a new `IvParameterSpec` object, like this:

```
IvParameterSpec ivBlock = new IvParameterSpec(
    new byte[] { 12, 34, 56, 78, 12, 34, 56, 78 } );
```

Because DES works in 8-byte blocks, the initialization vector must be 8 bytes.

You can encrypt blocks in partial increments by calling the `update` method for all the blocks except the last one. There are several forms of `update`:

```
byte[] update(byte[] plaintext)
byte[] update(byte[] plaintext, int offset, int len)
int update(byte[] plaintext, int offset, int len,
    byte[] encrypted)
int update(byte[] plaintext, int offset, int len,
    byte[] encrypted, int encryptedOffset)
```

If you're using a block cipher and you use one of the versions of `update` that returns a byte array, you'll get a `null` if there aren't enough bytes to make a full block. If you use the version that writes to a byte buffer and the buffer is too small, you'll get a `ShortBufferException`. You can use the `getOutputSize` method to determine the minimum buffer size to hold the remaining encrypted bytes.

To encrypt a whole block at once, or encrypt the final block in a series (when you used `update` for the rest), use the `doFinal` method. Again, there are several versions of `doFinal`:

```
byte[] doFinal()
byte[] doFinal(byte[] encrypted)
byte[] doFinal(byte[] encrypted, int offset, int len)
int doFinal(byte[] encrypted, byte[] plaintext)
int doFinal(byte[] encrypted, int offset, int len, byte[] plaintext)
int doFinal(byte[] encrypted, int offset, int len,
    byte[] plaintext, int plaintextOffset)
```


Listing 33.2 shows a program that encrypts a block of data using a simple text string as the key.

LISTING 33.2 SOURCE CODE FOR `EncryptData.java`

```
package usingj2ee.security;

import java.io.*;
import javax.crypto.*;
import javax.crypto.spec.*;

public class EncryptData
{
    public static void main(String[] args)
    {
        try
        {
// Create an array to hold the key
            byte[] encryptKey = "This is a test DESede
key".getBytes();

// Create a DESede key spec from the key
```

LISTING 33.2 CONTINUED

```
            DESedeKeySpec spec = new DESedeKeySpec(encryptKey);

// Get the secret key factor for generating DESede keys
            SecretKeyFactory keyFactory =
SecretKeyFactory.getInstance(
                "DESede");

// Generate a DESede SecretKey object
            SecretKey theKey = keyFactory.generateSecret(spec);

// Create a DESede Cipher
            Cipher cipher =
Cipher.getInstance("DESede/CBC/PKCS5Padding");

// Create an initialization vector (necessary for CBC mode)

            IvParameterSpec IvParameters = new IvParameterSpec(
                new byte[] { 12, 34, 56, 78, 90, 87, 65, 43 });

// Initialize the cipher and put it into encrypt mode
            cipher.init(Cipher.ENCRYPT_MODE, theKey, IvParameters);

            byte[] plaintext =
                "This is a sentence that has been
encrypted".getBytes();

// Encrypt the data
            byte[] encrypted = cipher.doFinal(plaintext);

// Write the data out to a file
            FileOutputStream out = new FileOutputStream("encrypted.dat");
            out.write(encrypted);
            out.close();
        }
        catch (Exception exc)
        {
            exc.printStackTrace();
        }
    }
}
```

If you are having trouble running the `EncryptData` *program and you have already installed the JCE,* *see "Locating Algorithms" in the "Troubleshooting" section at the end of this chapter.*

If you need to write encrypted data to a stream, don't bother using the `update` or `doFinal` methods. The `CipherOutputStream` class lets you write data to an output stream, encrypting the data as you write it. To create a `CipherOutputStream`, you need to supply the base output stream (where the data will be written) and the cipher to use for encrypting the data.

Listing 33.3 shows a variation of the program from Listing 33.2 using a `CipherOutputStream` to perform the encryption and write the data.

LISTING 33.3 SOURCE CODE FOR EncryptStream.java

```
package usingj2ee.security;

import java.io.*;
import javax.crypto.*;
import javax.crypto.spec.*;

public class EncryptStream
{
    public static void main(String[] args)
    {
        try
        {
// Create an array to hold the key
            byte[] encryptKey = "This is a test DESede key".getBytes();

// Create a DESede key spec from the key
            DESedeKeySpec spec = new DESedeKeySpec(encryptKey);

// Get the secret key factor for generating DESede keys
            SecretKeyFactory keyFactory = SecretKeyFactory.getInstance(
                "DESede");

// Generate a DESede SecretKey object
            SecretKey theKey = keyFactory.generateSecret(spec);

// Create a DESede Cipher
            Cipher cipher = Cipher.getInstance("DESede/ECB/PKCS5Padding");

            cipher.init(Cipher.ENCRYPT_MODE, theKey);

// Create a CipherOutputStream for writing to an encrypted stream
            CipherOutputStream ciphOut =
                new CipherOutputStream(
                    new FileOutputStream("encrypted2.dat"),
                    cipher);

// Wrap a print stream around the cipher stream
            PrintStream ps = new PrintStream(ciphOut);

// Print some data that will be encrypted
            ps.println("This is a sentence that has been encrypted");

            ciphOut.close();
        }
        catch (Exception exc)
        {
            exc.printStackTrace();
        }
    }
}
```

DECRYPTING DATA

Decrypting the data is just as easy (or hard) as encrypting it. You've already seen the steps you must take, because you still create a key and initialize a `Cipher` object. The major difference is that the cipher mode must be `Cipher.DECRYPT_MODE` instead of `Cipher.ENCRYPT_MODE`. Other than that, you still use `update` and `doFinal` to process the data, or use `CipherInputStream` to read encrypted data from a stream and decrypt it.

Listing 33.4 shows a program that decrypts the data encrypted by the program in Listing 33.2.

LISTING 33.4 SOURCE CODE FOR `DecryptData.java`

```
package usingj2ee.security;

import java.io.*;
import javax.crypto.*;
import javax.crypto.spec.*;
import java.security.*;

public class DecryptData
{
    public static void main(String[] args)
    {
        try
        {
// Create an array to hold the key
            byte[] encryptKey = "This is a test DESede key".getBytes();

// Create a DESede key spec from the key
            DESedeKeySpec spec = new DESedeKeySpec(encryptKey);

// Get the secret key factor for generating DESede keys
            SecretKeyFactory keyFactory = SecretKeyFactory.getInstance(
                "DESede");

// Generate a DESede SecretKey object
            SecretKey theKey = keyFactory.generateSecret(spec);

// Create a DESede Cipher
            Cipher cipher = Cipher.getInstance("DESede/CBC/PKCS5Padding");

// Create the initialization vector required for CBC mode
            IvParameterSpec ivParameters = new IvParameterSpec(
                new byte[] { 12, 34, 56, 78, 90, 87, 65, 43 } );

// Initialize the cipher and put it in decrypt mode
            cipher.init(Cipher.DECRYPT_MODE, theKey, ivParameters);

            File encryptedFile = new File("encrypted.dat");

// Create a byte block to hold the entire encrypted file
            byte[] encryptedText = new byte[(int) encryptedFile.length()];

            FileInputStream fileIn = new FileInputStream(encryptedFile);
```

```
// Read the entire encrypted file
            fileIn.read(encryptedText);

            fileIn.close();

// Decrypt the data
            byte[] plaintext = cipher.doFinal(encryptedText);

            String plaintextStr = new String(plaintext);

            System.out.println("The plaintext is:");
            System.out.println(plaintextStr);
        }
        catch (Exception exc)
        {
            exc.printStackTrace();
        }
    }
}
```

Listing 33.5 shows a program that uses a `CipherInputStream` to read the file written by the program in Listing 33.3.

LISTING 33.5 SOURCE CODE FOR `DecryptStream.java`

```
package usingj2ee.security;

import java.io.*;
import javax.crypto.*;
import javax.crypto.spec.*;

public class DecryptStream
{
    public static void main(String[] args)
    {
        try
        {
// Create an array to hold the key
            byte[] encryptKey = "This is a test DESede key".getBytes();

// Create a DESede key spec from the key
            DESedeKeySpec spec = new DESedeKeySpec(encryptKey);

// Get the secret key factor for generating DESede keys
            SecretKeyFactory keyFactory = SecretKeyFactory.getInstance(
                "DESede");

// Generate a DESede SecretKey object
            SecretKey theKey = keyFactory.generateSecret(spec);

// Create a DESede Cipher
            Cipher cipher = Cipher.getInstance("DESede/ECB/PKCS5Padding");

            cipher.init(Cipher.DECRYPT_MODE, theKey);

// Create a CipherInputStream for reading from an encrypted stream
```

LISTING 33.5 CONTINUED

```
            CipherInputStream ciphIn =
                new CipherInputStream(
                    new FileInputStream("encrypted2.dat"),
                    cipher);

            byte[] buff = new byte[4096];

            int len;

// Read the stream and write out the contents
            while ((len = ciphIn.read(buff)) > 0)
            {
                System.out.write(buff, 0, len);
            }
            System.out.println();
        }
        catch (Exception exc)
        {
            exc.printStackTrace();
        }
    }
}
```

ENCRYPTING OBJECTS

Sometimes, you might want to encrypt a Java object and write it to a file or send it over a network. Although you could combine the `ObjectOutputStream` class with `CipherOutputStream` to write the object and use `CipherInputStream` and `ObjectInputStream` to read it, there is a better way.

The `SealedObject` class is a special container that encrypts serialized objects and lets you retrieve them again.

To store an object in a `SealedObject` container, you must first create a `Cipher`, just as you do for other encryption/decryption processes. Then, just pass the object you want to encrypt and the `Cipher` to the `SealedObject` constructor:

```
SealedObject sealed = new SealedObject(myObject, myCipher);
```

Because the `SealedObject` class is serializable, you can write it out to a file or send it over the network. It also contains all the information needed to decrypt the object—except for the key. That is, it contains the algorithm and possibly the initialization vector or other algorithm parameters.

To decrypt a sealed object, just call `getObject`, passing it either a `Cipher` that matches the cipher used to encrypt the object, or just pass the encryption key:

```
Object myObject = sealed.getObject("thekeyisthekey");
```

or

```
Object myObject = sealed.getObject(myCipher);
```

You can also determine the algorithm used to encrypt the object by calling `getAlgorithm`.

A QUICK AND DIRTY PUBLIC KEY IMPLEMENTATION

The JCE is frustrating in that it omits two very useful types of encryption: stream ciphers and public key ciphers. Although the JDK includes some support for public key encryption, it is only enough to support digital signatures and not full public key encryption. What is interesting about the JDK is that it has just enough support for public keys that you can create your own public key encryption and decryption routines with very little effort.

The RSA encryption algorithm, named for its inventors—Rivest, Shamir, and Adleman—is one of the oldest and best-known forms of public key encryption. Although the mathematics behind the algorithm might be a little complex, the algorithm itself is not. An RSA key, public or private, consists of two parts: an exponent and a modulus. Both the public and private keys share the same modulus, but they each have different exponents.

To encrypt a block of bytes using RSA, you treat the bytes as one big number, raise that number to the power of the public key exponent, and then perform the `mod` function on the resulting number and the modulus value. The beauty of this operation is that the JDK `BigInteger` class makes it really easy to perform these operations.

First, you can take a block of bytes and convert it to a `BigInteger`:

```
byte[] byteblock = "This is a test".getBytes();
BigInteger bytenum = new BigInteger(byteblock);
```

Now, assuming for a moment that the public key exponent and modulus values are also `BigInteger` values, you can perform the RSA public key encryption in one step:

```
BigInteger result = bytenum.modPow(publicExp, modulus);
```

The `toByteArray` method lets you convert the `BigInteger` back to an array of bytes:

```
byte[] encrypted = result.toByteArray();
```

To decrypt the block, you use the same procedure, except that you use the private key exponent instead of the public key exponent.

Now, here's the real kicker. The JDK comes with a key generator that lets you generate RSA key pairs. You don't need to worry about the mathematical gyrations necessary to compute the exponent and modulus!

Listing 33.6 shows a simple round-trip encryption example that first generates a public-private key pair, then encrypts with the public key, and decrypts with the private key.

LISTING 33.6 SOURCE CODE FOR RSADemo.java

```
package usingj2ee.security;

import java.security.*;
import java.security.interfaces.*;
import java.math.*;

public class RSADemo
{
    public static void main(String[] args)
    {
        try
        {
// Get a key generator to create RSA key pairs
            KeyPairGenerator gen = KeyPairGenerator.getInstance("RSA");

// Generate the key pair
            KeyPair pair = gen.genKeyPair();

            RSAPrivateKey pvtKey = (RSAPrivateKey) pair.getPrivate();

            RSAPublicKey pubKey = (RSAPublicKey) pair.getPublic();

            byte[] plainText =
                "This is a test of a simple RSA public key encryption".
                getBytes();

// Convert the bytes into a BigInteger
            BigInteger plainTextInt = new BigInteger(plainText);

// Perform the RSA encryption algorithm
            BigInteger encryptedText = plainTextInt.modPow(
                pubKey.getPublicExponent(), pubKey.getModulus());

            System.out.println("The encrypted text is: "+
                encryptedText.toString(16));

// Perform the RSA decryption algorithm
            BigInteger decryptedText = encryptedText.modPow(
                pvtKey.getPrivateExponent(), pvtKey.getModulus());

            System.out.println("The decoded text is: "+
                new String(decryptedText.toByteArray()));
        }
        catch (Exception exc)
        {
            exc.printStackTrace();
        }
    }
}
```

Due to U.S. export restrictions, the source code for RSADemo.java can't be included on the CD-Rom accompanying this book.

The RSA encryption algorithm is like a block cipher in that it can encrypt a limited number of characters (usually 1,024 bits or 128 bytes). Because the bytes represent a single number, if there are fewer bytes than a full block, there's no need for padding. You'll only get out as many bytes as you put in.

The other thing you need to know about RSA is that it is not very fast. You might only be able to do 5 or 10 of these per second. The nice thing is, you don't need any additional software libraries; you only need the JDK.

Accessing the Keystore

The JDK comes with a program called `keytool` that lets you manage a database of keys and certificates. With `keytool`, you can create new keys, request a digital certificate, and manage a database of keys and certificates. The keystore would be useless, however, if you couldn't access it from a Java program.

You can create an RSA key with the following `keytool` command:

```
keytool -genkey -alias j2eetest -keyalg "RSA"
```

Note

When you create a key, you have the option of supplying a separate password for the key itself. The examples in this chapter use a password of "kspass" for the keystore and "thekeypass" for the key password.

To access the keystore, you create a `KeyStore` object and then load the keys from the keystore file on the disk. By default, `keytool` stores the keys in a file called `.keystore` in the user's home directory.

After you load the keystore, you can access keys and certificates by the alias you specified when you created the key or imported the certificate. If you load a key, you must specify the key's password.

Listing 33.7 shows a program that loads an RSA key from the keystore and prints out the exponent and modulus. It then accesses the certificate associated with the key and prints out the public exponent (remember, the modulus is the same for public and private RSA keys).

Listing 33.7 Source Code for `GetKey.java`

```
package usingj2ee.security;

import java.security.*;
import java.security.interfaces.*;
import java.io.*;

public class GetKey
{
    public static void main(String[] args)
    {
        try
        {
```

LISTING 33.7 CONTINUED

```
            String keystorePassword = "kspass";
            String testAlias = "j2eetest";
            String testKeyPassword = "thekeypass";

// Create a keystore
            KeyStore keystore = KeyStore.getInstance("JKS");

// Figure out where the user's keystore is located
            String keystoreFilename = System.getProperty("user.home")+
                File.separator+".keystore";

// Load the keystore from the keystore file
            keystore.load(new FileInputStream(keystoreFilename),
                keystorePassword.toCharArray());

// Locate the key with the specified alias and password
            Key testkey = keystore.getKey(testAlias,
                testKeyPassword.toCharArray());

// Assume that the key is an RSA key
            RSAPrivateKey pvtKey = (RSAPrivateKey) testkey;

            System.out.println("Private key modulus = "+
                pvtKey.getModulus().toString(16));

            System.out.println("Private key exponent = "+
                pvtKey.getPrivateExponent().toString(16));

// Get the certificate associated with the alias
            java.security.cert.Certificate cert =
                keystore.getCertificate(testAlias);

// Assume it contains an RSA key
            RSAPublicKey pubKey = (RSAPublicKey) cert.getPublicKey();

            System.out.println("Cert public key exponent = "+
                pubKey.getPublicExponent().toString(16));
        }
        catch (Exception exc)
        {
            exc.printStackTrace();
        }
    }
}
```

EXCHANGING KEYS

In the grand scheme of things, how you manage your encryption keys and certificates is just as important as your encryption algorithm. What good is it to have a really powerful encryption algorithm if you don't protect your keys?

When you want to perform encrypted communications between two programs on a network, key management becomes crucial. It's not easy to distribute new keys to potential clients, and no two clients should know each other's keys, so each client must have a separate key. Public keys make key distribution easier because you don't have to hide the public key, but public key encryption is far slower than symmetric private key encryption. It would be nice to have the key management of public key encryption combined with the speed of symmetric private key encryption.

Fortunately, there's a solution to this problem. You use both forms of encryption. Figure 33.1 illustrates a sequence in which you generate a secret symmetric key, encrypt it with a public key, and send it to the other party who decrypts it with the private key. After both parties have the symmetric key, they can use a normal symmetric encryption algorithm to communicate.

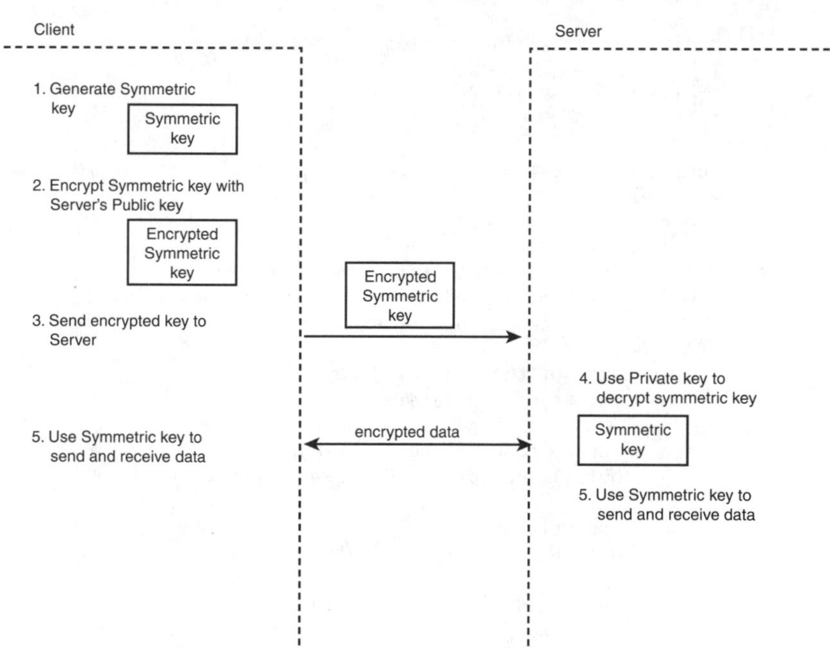

Figure 33.1 Use public key encryption to agree on a key, and then use symmetric private key encryption.

Listing 33.8 shows a server program that receives an encrypted key and then uses the Blowfish algorithm for communications. It uses a CFB8 as its mode, so it doesn't care about how many bytes it sends at one time. That way, it can use `CipherInputStream` and `CipherOutputStream` to send data. The server echoes back any data sent to it.

LISTING 33.8 SOURCE CODE FOR `KeyExchangeServer.java`

```
package usingj2ee.security;

import java.io.*;
import java.net.*;
```

LISTING 33.8 CONTINUED

```
import java.math.*;
import java.security.*;
import java.security.interfaces.*;
import javax.crypto.*;
import javax.crypto.spec.*;

/** A simple echo server that first receives a key encrypted using RSA
 *  and then uses that key for symmetric encryption.
 */

public class KeyExchangeServer implements Runnable
{
    protected Socket sock;
    protected static BigInteger privateKeyExponent;
    protected static BigInteger modulus;

    public KeyExchangeServer(Socket theSock)
    {
        sock = theSock;
    }

    public void run()
    {
        try
        {
// Create a DataInputStream for reading the key
            DataInputStream dataIn = new DataInputStream(
                sock.getInputStream());

// Read the size of the encrypted key
            int keySize = dataIn.readShort();

// Create an array to hold the incoming key
            byte[] encryptedKeyBytes = new byte[keySize];

// Read the encrypted key
            dataIn.readFully(encryptedKeyBytes);

// Turn the encrypted key into a BigInteger
            BigInteger encryptedKey = new BigInteger(encryptedKeyBytes);

// Use the RSA algorithm to decrypt the key
            BigInteger theKey = encryptedKey.modPow(
                privateKeyExponent, modulus);

            byte[] keyBytes = theKey.toByteArray();

// Create a SecretKeySpec from the key bytes
            SecretKeySpec keySpec = new SecretKeySpec(keyBytes, "Blowfish");

// Set up the Initialization Vector
            IvParameterSpec IvParameters = new IvParameterSpec(
                new byte[] { 12, 34, 56, 78, 90, 87, 65, 43 });
```

```
// Use the Blowfish cipher, but use CFB8 mode to make it act like
// a stream cipher
            Cipher encryptCipher = Cipher.getInstance(
                "Blowfish/CFB8/NoPadding");

            encryptCipher.init(Cipher.ENCRYPT_MODE, keySpec, IvParameters);

// Create an output stream for encrypting bytes
            CipherOutputStream cipherOut = new CipherOutputStream(
                sock.getOutputStream(), encryptCipher);

// Repeat the procedure to create a cipher for reading data
            Cipher decryptCipher = Cipher.getInstance(
                "Blowfish/CFB8/NoPadding");

            decryptCipher.init(Cipher.DECRYPT_MODE, keySpec, IvParameters);

            CipherInputStream cipherIn = new CipherInputStream(
                sock.getInputStream(), decryptCipher);

// Create a buffer for reading the data
            byte[] buff = new byte[4096];
            int len;

            while ((len = cipherIn.read(buff)) > 0)
            {

// Echo the bytes back out to the client
                cipherOut.write(buff, 0, len);
            }

            try
            {
                sock.close();
            }
            catch (Exception ignore) {}
        }
        catch (Exception exc)
        {
            exc.printStackTrace();

            try
            {
                sock.close();
            }
            catch (Exception ignore) {}
        }
    }

    public static void main(String[] args)
    {
        try
        {
            String keystorePassword = "kspass";
            String testAlias = "j2eetest";
            String testKeyPassword = "thekeypass";
```

LISTING 33.8 CONTINUED

```
// Create a keystore
            KeyStore keystore = KeyStore.getInstance("JKS");

// Figure out where the user's keystore is located
            String keystoreFilename = System.getProperty("user.home")+
                File.separator+".keystore";

// Load the keystore from the keystore file
            keystore.load(new FileInputStream(keystoreFilename),
                keystorePassword.toCharArray());

// Get the private key that will be used for decrypting the symmetric key
            Key testKey = keystore.getKey(testAlias,
                testKeyPassword.toCharArray());

            RSAPrivateKey pvtKey = (RSAPrivateKey) testKey;

// Store the key parts in static variables so each thread can access them
            privateKeyExponent = pvtKey.getPrivateExponent();
            modulus = pvtKey.getModulus();

// Create the ServerSocket to listen for incoming connections
            ServerSocket server = new ServerSocket(4567);

            for (;;)
            {
                Socket newClient = server.accept();

// Create the handler for handling each client
                KeyExchangeServer clientHandler =
                    new KeyExchangeServer(newClient);

// Start the handler
                Thread clientHandlerThread = new Thread(clientHandler);
                clientHandlerThread.start();
            }
        }
        catch (Exception exc)
        {
            exc.printStackTrace();
        }
    }
}
```

Due to U.S. export restrictions, the source code for RSADemo.java can't be included on the CD-Rom accompanying this book.

The `KeyExchangeServer` class listens for new client connections. When a client connects, the server reads an encrypted symmetric key value from the client. Using the RSA decryption algorithm along with a private RSA key from the keystore, the server decrypts the encrypted symmetric key. The server then uses the symmetric key to decrypt messages from the client and also to encrypt a response message, which is simply the original message from the client.

In other words, the KeyExchangeServer class just echoes messages back to the client, but it uses encryption to send and receive the messages. You start the server with this command:

```
java usingj2ee.security.KeyExchangeServer
```

You won't see any output from the server program. Make sure you have used the keytool program to create a key named "j2eetest" with a password of "thekeypass". The keystore password should be "kspass". If your keystore has different values, make sure you change the keystorePassword, testAlias, and testKeyPassword variables in the KeyExchangeServer program.

Listing 33.9 shows the client side of the encrypted socket connection.

LISTING 33.9 SOURCE CODE FOR KeyExchangeClient.java

```
package usingj2ee.security;

import java.io.*;
import java.net.*;
import java.math.*;
import java.security.*;
import java.security.interfaces.*;
import javax.crypto.*;
import javax.crypto.spec.*;

public class KeyExchangeClient
{
    public static void main(String[] args)
    {
        try
        {
            String keystorePassword = "kspass";
            String testAlias = "j2eetest";
            String testKeyPassword = "thekeypass";

// Create a keystore
            KeyStore keystore = KeyStore.getInstance("JKS");

// Figure out where the user's keystore is located
            String keystoreFilename = System.getProperty("user.home")+
                File.separator+".keystore";

// Load the keystore from the keystore file
            keystore.load(new FileInputStream(keystoreFilename),
                keystorePassword.toCharArray());

// Get the certificate associated with the alias
            java.security.cert.Certificate cert =
                keystore.getCertificate(testAlias);

// Assume it contains an RSA key
            RSAPublicKey pubKey = (RSAPublicKey) cert.getPublicKey();

// Create a generator for creating Blowfish keys
            KeyGenerator keyGen = KeyGenerator.getInstance("Blowfish");
```

LISTING 33.9 CONTINUED

```
// Generate a random key for blowfish
            SecretKey theKey = keyGen.generateKey();

// Get the raw bytes for the symmetric key
            byte[] keyBytes = theKey.getEncoded();

// Turn the bytes into a BigInteger
            BigInteger keyBignum = new BigInteger(keyBytes);

// Use the RSA encryption algorithm to encrypt the symmetric key
// using the public key from the Certificate
            BigInteger encodedKey = keyBignum.modPow(
                pubKey.getPublicExponent(), pubKey.getModulus());

// Connect to the server
            Socket sock = new Socket("localhost", 4567);

            DataOutputStream dataOut = new DataOutputStream(
                sock.getOutputStream());

            byte[] encryptedKeyBytes = encodedKey.toByteArray();

// Send the number of encrypted key bytes to the server
            dataOut.writeShort(encryptedKeyBytes.length);

// Send the encrypted key bytes to the server
            dataOut.write(encryptedKeyBytes, 0, encryptedKeyBytes.length);

            SecretKeySpec keySpec = new SecretKeySpec(keyBytes, "Blowfish");

// Create the Initialization Vector
            IvParameterSpec IvParameters = new IvParameterSpec(
                new byte[] { 12, 34, 56, 78, 90, 87, 65, 43 });

// Create a Blowfish cipher using CFB8 mode to simulate a stream cipher
            Cipher encryptCipher = Cipher.getInstance(
                "Blowfish/CFB8/NoPadding");

            encryptCipher.init(Cipher.ENCRYPT_MODE, keySpec, IvParameters);

// Create an output stream for writing encrypted data
            CipherOutputStream cipherOut = new CipherOutputStream(
                sock.getOutputStream(), encryptCipher);

// Repeat the procedure to create a cipher for reading data
            Cipher decryptCipher = Cipher.getInstance(
                "Blowfish/CFB8/NoPadding");

            decryptCipher.init(Cipher.DECRYPT_MODE, keySpec, IvParameters);

            CipherInputStream cipherIn = new CipherInputStream(
                sock.getInputStream(), decryptCipher);

// Create a thread to read data from the server and print it out
            Thread echoThread = new Thread(new EchoPrinter(cipherIn));
            echoThread.start();
```

```
            BufferedReader in = new BufferedReader(
                new InputStreamReader(System.in));

            String line;

            System.out.println("Enter text to send to server:");

// Read a line from the console
            while ((line = in.readLine()) != null)
            {
// Send the line to the server followed by a newline
                cipherOut.write(line.getBytes());
                cipherOut.write('\n');
            }
        }
        catch (Exception exc)
        {
            exc.printStackTrace();
        }
    }
}

/** Reads data from a stream and prints it to the console */
class EchoPrinter implements Runnable
{
    protected InputStream in;

    public EchoPrinter(InputStream theInputStream)
    {
        in = theInputStream;
    }

    public void run()
    {
        try
        {
            byte[] buff = new byte[4096];
            int len;

            while ((len = in.read(buff)) > 0)
            {
                System.out.write(buff, 0, len);
            }
        }
        catch (Exception exc)
        {
        }
    }
}
```

Due to U.S. export restrictions, the source code for KeyExchangeClient.java can't be included on the CD-Rom accompanying this book.

The `KeyExchangeClient` program creates a random symmetric key for the Blowfish encryption algorithm. It then uses a public RSA key to encrypt the symmetric key. After it has encrypted the symmetric key, the client program connects to the server and transmits the encrypted symmetric key. After the connection is made, the client program prompts you for input. Every time you type a line of text, the client uses the symmetric key to encrypt the line and then sends it to the server. The client also decrypts the response returned by the server, so you should see your original text echo back on the screen.

To run the client program, make sure the server is already running, and then type

```
java usingj2ee.security.KeyExchangeClient
```

Like the `KeyExchangeServer` class, the `KeyExchangeClient` class assumes you have created a key named "j2eetest" with a password of "thekeypass". The keystore password should be "kspass". If your keystore has different values, make sure you change the `keystorePassword`, `testAlias`, and `testKeyPassword` variables in the `KeyExchangeClient` program.

TROUBLESHOOTING

LOCATING ALGORITHMS

Why can't I create a Cipher that uses DES?

You probably don't have the JCE installed correctly. If you took the easy way and installed the JCE JAR files to your `jre\lib\ext` directory, you must still add the new security provider to the `jre\lib\security\java.security` file. The line you add usually looks something like this:

```
security.provider.3=com.sun.crypto.provider.SunJCE
```

I know the JCE is installed properly; why can't I find DES?

Make sure you spell it properly: DES, all capital letters. If that doesn't work, try specifying "SunJCE" as the second parameter, which is the security provider.

ENCRYPTION AND DECRYPTION

I can encrypt with DES, DESede, or Blowfish; why do I get an error about missing parameters when I try to decrypt?

If you're using a mode other then ECB, you must specify the initialization vector for the algorithm. Make sure you use the same vector for encryption and decryption.

Why is my decrypted data still scrambled?

Make sure you used the right key value; also make sure you initialized your `Cipher` object with a mode of `Cipher.DECRYPT_MODE`.

CHAPTER 34

Digitally Signing Data

In this chapter

HOW DIGITAL SIGNATURES WORK

Digital signatures are a special form of encryption used for verifying the authenticity of some piece of data. Although a digital signature is a form of encryption, it doesn't mean that data itself is encrypted. In other words, digitally signed data is not encrypted—or rather, it doesn't need to be encrypted. There is nothing to stop you from encrypting the data as an additional step.

When you use digital signatures, you deal with three items: the original data, the digital signature, and the public key of the signer. Of course, if you need the public key of the signer, you can bet that the signer's private key enters into the mixture, too. Figure 34.1 shows the basic sequence in signing a document and verifying the signature. The signer creates a signature from a piece of data and a private key. The receiver uses the public key to verify that the data hasn't been tampered with and that the signer is indeed the person who has signed the data.

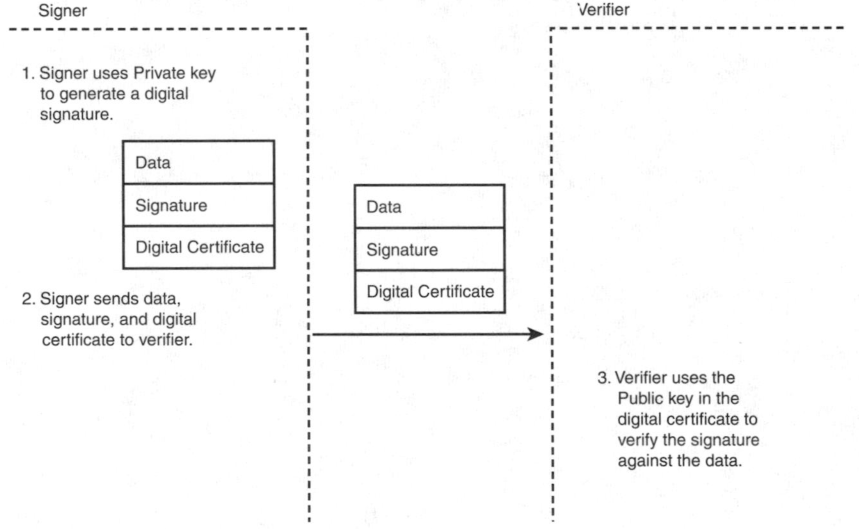

Figure 34.1
A signer signs a document with a private key, and the receiver verifies the signature with a public key.

The thing that makes digital signatures tick is the message-digest algorithm. When you digitally sign your data, you use an algorithm, such as the Message Digest algorithm or the Secure Hash Algorithm, which computes a reasonably small value that represents the content of the document. A message digest is similar to a checksum—it's just a number based on the byte values contained in the data. If you change the data, the digest changes. Although it's possible for two documents to have the same digest value, it's extremely unlikely. There are two important things to remember about the message digest. First, you can't determine anything about the content of the data based on the digest. That is, you can't figure out what is in the data just by looking at the message digest. Second, you can't make minor changes to the data and expect the digest to be the same.

For instance, if you used a simple checksum value as a message digest, a dollar amount of $123.00 could have the same checksum value as $321.00 because the checksum doesn't care about the order of the data values. Someone could tamper with the data and still come up with the same checksum. A message digest is complex enough that you can't make minor changes to the data and get the same digest back out. Obviously, because the message digest is a small version of the data, there are different sets of data that can have the same digest. It is virtually impossible, however, to intentionally create a sequence of bytes that generates a specific message digest.

Remember, a digital signature tells you two things: whether the data has been tampered with and who sent the data. The message digest part of the signature lets you determine whether the data has been tampered with and the public key encryption part lets you determine who signed the data.

To digitally sign a piece of data, you compute the message digest for the data and then encrypt the digest using your private key. You don't need to encrypt the data, just the digest. One of the interesting things about public key encryption is that you can encrypt with the private key and decrypt with the public key. It might seem strange to encrypt with the private key because anyone in the world can decrypt the data—it's not very useful for passing secret data. In the case of digital signatures, it's very useful. Because only your public key decrypts the encrypted message digest correctly, anyone can verify that you signed the data.

Figure 34.2 illustrates the sequence you go through to digitally sign your data.

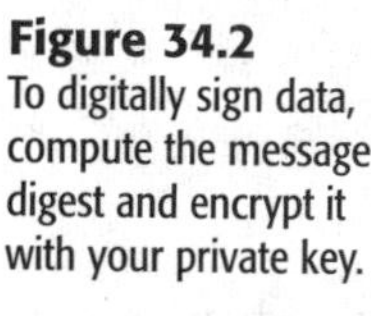

Figure 34.2
To digitally sign data, compute the message digest and encrypt it with your private key.

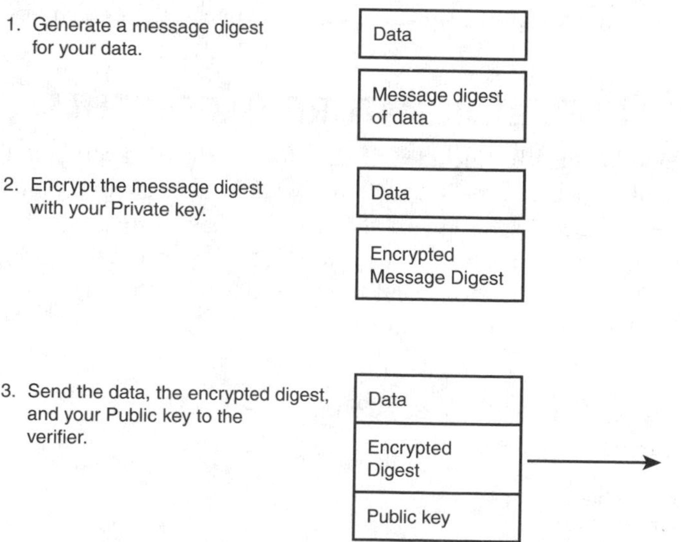
1. Generate a message digest for your data.
Data
Message digest of data
2. Encrypt the message digest with your Private key.
Data
Encrypted Message Digest
3. Send the data, the encrypted digest, and your Public key to the verifier.
Data
Encrypted Digest
Public key

When someone wants to verify your signature, she computes the message digest for the data, decrypts your signature, and compares it with the computed message digest, as shown in Figure 34.3.

Figure 34.3
To verify a signature, compute the message digest, decrypt the signature, and compare it with the message digest.

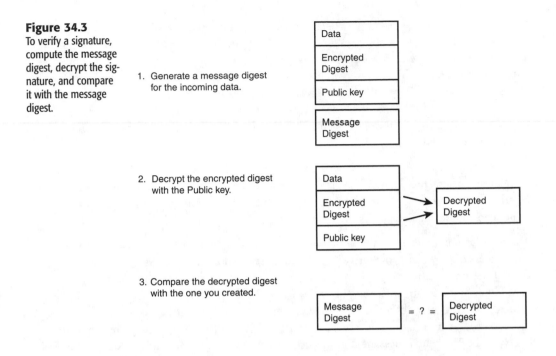

1. Generate a message digest for the incoming data.

Data
Encrypted Digest
Public key
Message Digest

2. Decrypt the encrypted digest with the Public key.

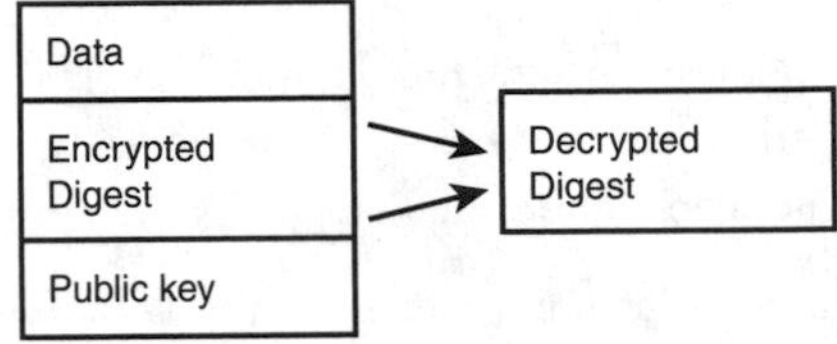

3. Compare the decrypted digest with the one you created.

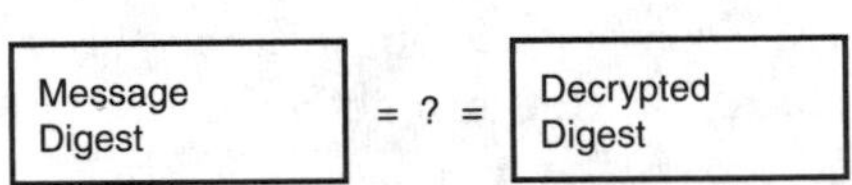

If the decrypted message digest doesn't match the digest you compute, then one of two things has happened. Either the data has changed, which makes the digest come out wrong, or the key used to encrypt the signature isn't the same as the one you used to decrypt it.

A SIMPLE DIGITAL SIGNATURE ALGORITHM

The Java Development Kit includes routines for creating and verifying digital signatures, but you might get a better feel for how they work by seeing a program that creates a signature and then verifies it. Listing 34.1 shows a digital signature demo that uses the RSA encryption algorithm introduced in Chapter 33, "Encrypting Data," to encrypt a message digest. It then decrypts the digest and compares the decrypted digest with the original, which is the signature-verification process.

LISTING 34.1 SOURCE CODE FOR `SignatureDemo.java`

```
package usingj2ee.security;

import java.security.*;
import java.security.interfaces.*;
import java.math.*;

public class SignatureDemo
{
    public static void main(String[] args)
    {
        String messageText =
```

```
            "To Whom It May Concern,"+
            "  I, Argle Bargle, being a sound-minding body, "+
            "do hereby object to the loud music played by that "+
            "jerk downstairs!"+
            "    Argle Bargle";

        try
        {
// Get a Message Digest implementation (use either SHA or MD5)
            MessageDigest theDigest = MessageDigest.getInstance("SHA");

// Add the message text to the digest
            theDigest.update(messageText.getBytes());

// Compute the message digest for the text you added to the digest
            byte[] digestBytes = theDigest.digest();

// For demo purposes, create a public and private key
            KeyPairGenerator gen = KeyPairGenerator.getInstance("RSA");

            KeyPair pair = gen.generateKeyPair();

// Get the public and private keys
            RSAPrivateKey pvtKey = (RSAPrivateKey) pair.getPrivate();
            RSAPublicKey pubKey = (RSAPublicKey) pair.getPublic();

// Now perform the RSA private key encryption algorithm, encrypting
// the message digest with the private key

// Convert the digest bytes into a BigInteger
            BigInteger digestNum = new BigInteger(digestBytes);

// Do the RSA algorithm
            BigInteger signature = digestNum.modPow(
                pvtKey.getPrivateExponent(), pvtKey.getModulus());

            byte[] signatureBytes = signature.toByteArray();

// At this point, signatureBytes contains the digital signature for
// the message text. Someone wanting to verify the signature needs
// the original message text, the signature bytes, and the
// public key.

// The following code verifies the signature (you would normally
// do this in a different program)

// You need to compute the message digest for the message, but because
// it was already done above, just use the digestBytes that you
// already computed.

// Take the signature bytes and decrypt them with the RSA algorithm

            BigInteger sigVerify = new BigInteger(signatureBytes);

// Use the RSA algorithm with the public key to decrypt the signature
            BigInteger checkDigest = sigVerify.modPow(
                pubKey.getPublicExponent(), pubKey.getModulus());
```

LISTING 34.1 CONTINUED

```
            byte[] checkDigestBytes = checkDigest.toByteArray();

// At this point, if the signature worked correctly, digestBytes and
// checkDigestBytes should have the same data

            boolean matched = true;

// If the signature lengths are different, they definitely don't match
            if (digestBytes.length != checkDigestBytes.length)
            {
                matched = false;
            }
            else
            {
// Compare each individual byte in the signature
                for (int i=0; i < digestBytes.length; i++)
                {
                    if (digestBytes[i] != checkDigestBytes[i])
                    {
                        matched = false;
                        break;
                    }
                }
            }

            if (matched)
            {
                System.out.println("The signatures match!");
            }
            else
            {
                System.out.println("The signatures don't match!");
            }
        }
        catch (Exception exc)
        {
            exc.printStackTrace();
        }
    }
}
```

Due to U.S. export restrictions, the source code for KeyExchangeClient.java can't be included on the CD-ROM for this book.

DIGITALLY SIGNING DATA

Now that you know how to digitally sign data, you'll be happy to know that the `Signature` class in the `java.security` package takes care of most of the work for you. You don't have to go through the trouble of computing the message digest or encrypting it. You just create a

Signature object, feed it a public or private key along with the data, and ask it either to sign the data or verify a signature.

There are a few combinations of message digests and encryption algorithms you can use. First, there are two types of public key encryption you can use: DSA (Digital Signature Algorithm) or good old RSA. There are three message digest algorithms available with the JDK: MD2 (Message Digest version 2), MD5 (Message Digest version 5), and SHA1 (Secure Hash Algorithm version 1). If you use DSA for encryption, you must use SHA1 for the message digest. The general format for describing the signature combination is *DDDwithCCC* where *DDD* is the name of the digest algorithm and *CCC* is the name of the encryption algorithm. Thus, for the SHA1 digest with DSA encryption, you create a Signature object with the following statement:

```
Signature sig = Signature.getInstance("SHA1withDSA");
```

The other available options are SHA1withRSA, MD2withRSA, and MD5withRSA.

To create a signature, you must first create and initialize a Signature object. Next, you add the data you want to sign by invoking the update method as many times as you need to. Finally, invoke the sign method to create the digital signature. Listing 34.2 shows a program that uses a private key stored in the keystore to digitally sign a file and write out a signature file, along with a certificate for verifying the signature.

LISTING 34.2 SOURCE CODE FOR SignData.java

```
package usingj2ee.security;

import java.security.*;
import java.security.interfaces.*;
import java.io.*;

/** Computes a digital signature for a file */

public class SignData
{
    public static void main(String[] args)
    {
        try
        {
            String keystorePassword = "kspass";
            String testAlias = "j2eetest";
            String testKeyPassword = "thekeypass";

// Create a keystore
            KeyStore keystore = KeyStore.getInstance("JKS");

// Figure out where the user's keystore is located
            String keystoreFilename = System.getProperty("user.home")+
                File.separator+".keystore";

// Load the keystore from the keystore file
            keystore.load(new FileInputStream(keystoreFilename),
                keystorePassword.toCharArray());
```

LISTING 34.2 CONTINUED

```
// Locate the key with the specified alias and password
            Key testkey = keystore.getKey(testAlias,
                testKeyPassword.toCharArray());

// Assume that the key is an RSA key
            RSAPrivateKey pvtKey = (RSAPrivateKey) testkey;

// Get the certificate for the key (not for computing the signature,
// just for writing out to a separate file for later signature verification)
            java.security.cert.Certificate cert =
                keystore.getCertificate(testAlias);

// Create and initialize a signer to use SHA1 and RSA
            Signature signer = Signature.getInstance("SHA1withRSA");
            signer.initSign(pvtKey);

// Open the data file
            FileInputStream in = new FileInputStream(args[0]);

// Create a block of bytes for reading the file
            byte[] buffer = new byte[4096];
            int len;

// Read a block of the file and add it to the signature object
            while ((len = in.read(buffer)) > 0)
            {
                signer.update(buffer, 0, len);
            }
            in.close();

// Compute the digital signature
            byte signatureBytes[] = signer.sign();

// Write the signature out to a file
            FileOutputStream out = new FileOutputStream(args[0]+".sig");
            out.write(signatureBytes);
            out.close();

// Write the certificate out to the file in encoded format
            out = new FileOutputStream(args[0]+".cer");
            out.write(cert.getEncoded());
            out.close();
        }
        catch (Exception exc)
        {
            exc.printStackTrace();
        }
    }
}
```

Before you run the `SignData` program, you must create a key store and a private key. To create a private key, use the `keytool` command that comes with the JDK. Because you want to use RSA encryption, you must specify RSA as the key algorithm. The program assumes that the key store password is `kspass` and the key password is `thekeypass`. The key alias is `j2eetest`. Use the following command to add the key to the key store and create the key store if it doesn't exist:

```
keytool -genkey -alias j2eetest -keyalg RSA -keypass thekeypass
```

When you run `keytool`, it will ask you for the key store password. If you have never created a key store, the password you enter will be the password for the new key store.

If you are having trouble running the `SignData` *program, see "Signature Algorithms" in the "Troubleshooting" section at the end of this chapter.*

Listing 34.3 shows a program that verifies a digital signature by taking a file, a signature, and a certificate and checking the signature. The program also prints out the contents of the certificate so you can verify that it came from the person you think it came from.

LISTING 34.3 SOURCE CODE FOR `VerifyData.java`

```
package usingj2ee.security;

import java.io.*;
import java.security.*;
import java.security.cert.*;
import java.security.interfaces.*;

/** Verifies a digital signature against a file using the public
 *  key from a certificate (that is, it uses the original data file and
 *  the two files generated by the SignData program)
 */
public class VerifyData
{
    public static void main(String[] args)
    {
        try
        {
            if (args.length < 3)
            {
                System.out.println(
                    "Please supply the data file, the sig file "+
                    "and the cert file.");
                System.exit(1);
            }

            FileInputStream certFile = new FileInputStream(args[2]);

// Create a certificate factory to read an X.509 certificate
            CertificateFactory certFact = CertificateFactory.
                getInstance("X.509");

// Load the certificate from the certificate file
            java.security.cert.Certificate cert =
                certFact.generateCertificate(certFile);

            certFile.close();

// Extract the public key from the certificate (assume it's an RSA key)
            RSAPublicKey pubKey = (RSAPublicKey) cert.getPublicKey();
```

LISTING 34.3 CONTINUED

```
// Create and initialize a Signature object for SHA1 and RSA
            Signature sigVerifier = Signature.getInstance("SHA1withRSA");
            sigVerifier.initVerify(pubKey);

// Open the data file
            FileInputStream dataFile = new FileInputStream(args[0]);

// Create a buffer for reading the file
            byte[] buffer = new byte[4096];

            int len;

// Read block of bytes from the file and add them to the signature
            while ((len = dataFile.read(buffer)) > 0)
            {
                sigVerifier.update(buffer, 0, len);
            }

            dataFile.close();

// Create a byte buffer for the original signature
            File sigFile = new File(args[1]);
            byte sigBytes[] = new byte[(int) sigFile.length()];

// Read the signature from a file
            FileInputStream sigIn = new FileInputStream(sigFile);
            sigIn.read(sigBytes);
            sigIn.close();

// Compare the signature from the file with the data file
// and the public key from the certificate
            if (sigVerifier.verify(sigBytes))
            {
                System.out.println("The signature matches.");
            }
            else
            {
                System.out.println(
                    "The signature doesn't match.");
            }
        }
        catch (Exception exc)
        {
            exc.printStackTrace();
        }
    }
}
```

TROUBLESHOOTING

SIGNATURE ALGORITHMS

Why can't the JDK find the signature algorithm I asked for?

Make sure you are using a security provider that supports it. If you're using one of the ones mentioned in this chapter, the JDK should have built-in support already. Also make sure that you have the capitalization correct and that you put the digest algorithm first and not the encryption (`SHA1withDSA`, not `DSAwithSHA1`).

Why do I get an exception telling me that it can't find my key?

You might have forgotten to run `keytool` to create the key, or you might have entered the key alias incorrectly. Type `keytool -list` to see the keys in your key store.

COMPARING SIGNATURES

Why don't the signatures match up?

Either the file you're checking has been changed, you're using the wrong public key to verify the signature, or you're using the wrong algorithm.

CHAPTER 35

Using the Secure Socket Layer (SSL)

In this chapter

HOW THE SECURE SOCKET LAYER WORKS

The *Secure Socket Layer* (SSL) is a special form of the standard socket API that does encrypted communications. The advantage of using SSL as opposed to the cryptography routines in Java Cryptography Extension (JCE) is that SSL is almost seamless. You can take an existing socket-based network program, change just a few lines, and you have a secure network program. You have probably used SSL frequently without even knowing it. Whenever you see a URL that starts with https, it's using SSL.

There are several third-party SSL libraries for Java, and Sun has recently released its own SSL library called JSSE—the Java Secure Sockets Extension. The two core classes in JSSE are `SSLSocket` and `SSLServerSocket`. These classes are subclasses of `Socket` and `ServerSocket`, so they can plug into existing applications in a snap. The only difference is that you must use a special factory class to create the `SSLSocket` and `SSLServerSocket` instances rather than just creating them with the `new` keyword.

SSL is a robust protocol supporting many kinds of encryption. The client and server actually negotiate to figure out which protocols they each support and what would be the strongest protocol they have in common. Although you don't need to know much about SSL to use it, you need to understand it to debug connectivity problems.

Figure 35.1 shows the sequence of messages exchanged between an SSL client and server. The messages marked with dotted lines are optional.

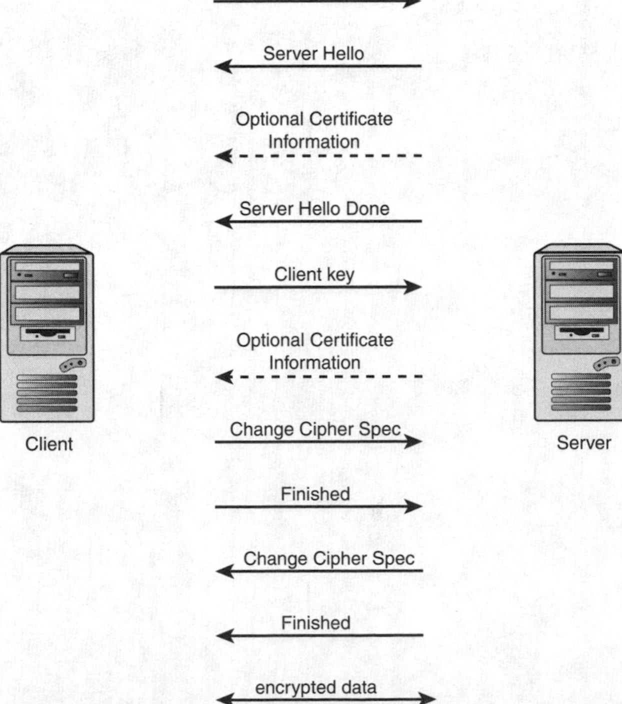

Figure 35.1
The client and server exchange several messages before exchanging data.

After the client connects to the server, it sends a hello message. The server then sends a hello back to the client. Next, the client and server exchange certificate information. Typically, the server just sends its certificates to the client. Using public key encryption, the client and server negotiate a private encryption key for data communications. Finally, the client and server switch over to encrypted communications and begin exchanging data.

If you have ever set up a secure Web server, you know that the server needs a digital certificate to do SSL communication. Typically, the digital certificate must be issued by a common signing agency, such as Verisign (`www.verisign.com`). A signing agency is usually referred to as a Certificate Authority, or CA. To understand the necessity for a CA, you must understand the nature of establishing trust.

When two parties communicate over a network, they need a way to verify each other's identities. The problem is, how can you be sure that you are getting the correct information? What if someone is impersonating the other person and intercepting your information? Anything that the real person can send you, the impersonator can, too. The root of the problem is that you must have a piece of information that you aren't getting from the network. If your only source of information is the network, you can never be sure that you aren't talking to an impersonator.

Figure 35.2 illustrates how an impersonator might operate to intercept your data.

Figure 35.2
An impersonator can intercept data and send false information.

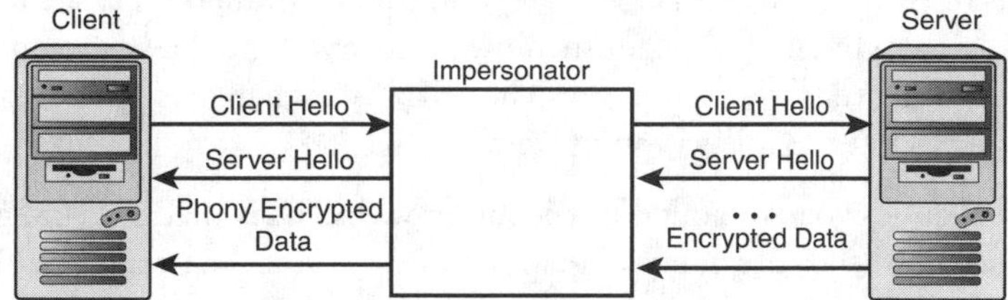

The piece of information that you have, in this case, is the public key of the certificate authority. Web browsers and servers, as well as other SSL-enabled software, come equipped with a list of trusted CAs. When a client connects to a server using SSL, the server sends its digital certificate. Remember, a digital certificate is the server's public key, digitally signed by a known CA. The client examines the certificate and verifies the signature. Because the client has a built-in list of trusted CAs, the client can verify the certificate using a piece of information that didn't come from the network. An impersonator can't just insert a phony certificate because the impersonator's certificate won't match any of the entries in the list of trusted CAs. Of course, the impersonator might have a valid certificate, but it would be issued to the impersonator and not the person you really wanted to talk to.

Figure 35.3 shows the sequence the client and server go through to establish a trusted connection.

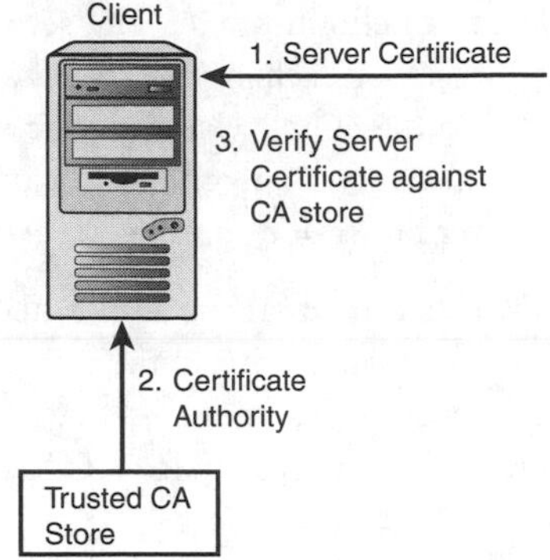

Figure 35.3
The client uses its list of trusted Certificate Authorities to verify the server's certificate.

Most of the time, the client is more concerned about the authenticity of the server than the server is about the client. That's because the server is usually just sending files back to the client. There are times, however, when the server wants to verify the authenticity of the client. In these cases, you use a special option of SSL called *client authentication*. For client authentication, the client must present the server with a certificate.

The certificate isn't just for verifying authenticity, of course. The certificate also contains the server's public key (or the client's public key in the case of client authentication). When the client receives the server's certificate, it generates a random private key for symmetric private key encryption. The client then uses the server's public key to encrypt the symmetric private key and sends it to the server. The SSL key exchange is similar to the key exchange you saw in Chapter 33, "Encrypting Data."

One of the issues you are bound to encounter with SSL is that the U.S. government places restrictions on the export of cryptography software. You can't export certain types of strong encryption without certain built-in safeguards. The general rule in the past was that you could only export 40-bit encryption products (that was later lengthened). Recently, however, some of those restrictions have been relaxed, allowing vendors to export strong encryption software to other countries. For example, you can get international versions of Netscape Navigator and Internet Explorer that support full 128-bit encryption. The 128-bit encryption had only been available within the United States for several years. Now, to support the international versions of the 128-bit Web browsers, you need a special digital certificate. The interesting thing here is that the digital certificate by itself is normally unrelated to the size of the symmetric private key you are using. Remember, you use the certificate to perform public key encryption on a randomly generated private key. The certificate typically contains a 1,024-bit public key, which can encrypt up to 1,024 bits of data—easily large enough to hold a 128-bit key. If you visit one of the CA Web sites, you'll see that a global 128-bit certificate costs a good deal more than a domestic certificate. You might be inclined to think that it's just a scam—a way to grab extra money from businesses that don't care about a couple hundred bucks. Believe it or not, the global certificates (or "super" certificates) aren't scams—there *is* a difference.

The global certificates contain a flag that indicates that the server supports SGC—Server Gated Cryptography. When you export an SSL-based product with strong encryption, you must support the SGC protocol. Now, rather than restricting the export of the software, the U.S. government restricts the export of the global certificates, but generally the number of restricted countries is very small (somewhere around 10). A regular digital certificate will allow you to do 128-bit encryption within the United States using a non-exportable version of a browser. The exportable versions can do 128-bit encryption only if you have a global certificate and will revert back to 40-bit encryption if the server presents them with a regular domestic certificate.

Note

From a programmer's perspective, you don't need to worry about the certificates when you write your code. It's when you try to run it that the certificates matter.

MANAGING KEYS AND CERTIFICATES

JSSE uses two kinds of repositories for data exchange: a key store and a trust store. The server uses the key store to locate its private keys and its certificates, whereas the client uses the trust store to locate trusted CAs, as illustrated in Figure 35.4.

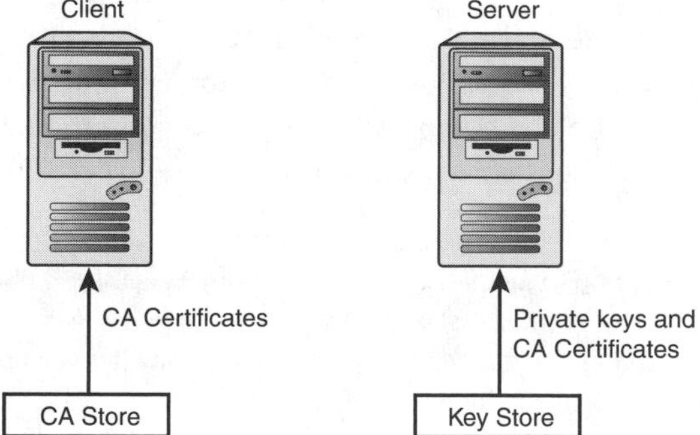

Figure 35.4
The server uses a key store, and the client uses a trusted CA store.

The difference between a key store and a trust store is really more of a difference in terminology. A trust store is just a key store without any keys—only certificates. You can use the JDK's `keytool` program to manage key stores and trust stores. JDK 1.3 ships with a default trust store called `cacerts` that is located in the `jre/lib/security` directory underneath the main JDK installation directory. To see the contents of the `cacerts` directory, go to the `jre/lib/security` directory and type

```
keytool -list -keystore cacerts
```

Note

When you list the contents of the keystore, the `keytool` program prompts you for the keystore password. The examples in this book use "kspass" as the keystore password. If you have an existing keystore, however, you may need to change the example programs to use your own keystore password.

CREATING A KEY

Use the `keytool` program to create a public-private key pair for your SSL server program. If you intend to write a server program that interacts with a Web browser, you should use a key algorithm of RSA. When you create a key, you can specify a key store file with the `-keystore` option. If you don't specify a file, `keytool` stores the keys in your home directory in a file called `.keystore`. If you use the default key store location, you can always get the location in Java code with the following statement:

```
String keystoreLoc = System.getProperty("user.home")+
    File.separator+".keystore";
```

Now, to create a new key, run `keytool` like this:

```
keytool -genkey -alias j2eebook -keyalg RSA -sigalg MD5withRSA
```

The key `alias` is simply a name for the key; you can use whatever you like for the alias.

When you create a key, `keytool` prompts you for various pieces of information that will be needed if you want to obtain a digital certificate from a Certificate Authority (CA), such as Verisign. The `keytool` program asks you for an "organizational unit," which is usually equivalent to a department or division at a company. After the "organizational unit," `keytool` asks you for an organization, which is usually your company name.

Caution

When `keytool` asks you for a key password, just hit Enter to let the key password default to the key store password. Otherwise, SSL won't recognize the key. When you create a key, `keytool` first asks you for the keystore password, then after you enter the various data items, `keytool` asks you for the key password.

When you use the `-genkey` option, `keytool` creates a public-private key pair and a self-signed digital certificate. A self-signed certificate means the certificate is its own CA.

Now, if you just want to test your programs locally and aren't putting your software into production, you can use the self-signed certificate. You just need to copy the certificate into your `cacerts` file so your clients will recognize your new key as a valid CA. To do that, you must first export the self-signed certificate:

```
keytool -export -alias j2eebook -file j2eebook.cert
```

After you export the certificate, you'll see a file called `j2eebook.cert` in your current directory. You can use `keytool` to print out the contents of this certificate:

```
keytool -printcert -file j2eebook.cert
```

Tip

The `keytool -printcert` command is one of the most useful commands when you must deal with a lot of certificates. Certificate files are not human-readable.

Now, to insert this new certificate into your `cacerts` file, go to the `jre/lib/security` directory and type

```
keytool -import -keystore cacerts -alias j2eebook -file somedir/j2eebook.cert
```

Tip

The initial password for the `cacerts` file is "changeit".

Obviously, *`somedir`* refers to the directory where the `j2eebook.cert` file is located. Also, you might need to adjust the permissions on the `cacerts` file to give yourself write access.

Caution

The `cacerts` file is a list of CAs that you trust. Only add your own keys to the file if you are working on a development machine or you have a good, secure, key management policy in place at your company. You shouldn't put your own keys into a production version of `cacerts` unless you know what you are doing. If you aren't careful about protecting your key store, someone could get your private key and sign documents that will then be trusted by your server.

Note

If you have a file called `jssecacerts` in your `jre/lib/security` directory, JSSE uses this file instead of `cacerts`. Make sure you import your certificate into the alternate file instead. The initial password is also "changeit".

When you decide to put your application into production, you need to get a digital certificate from one of the commercial CAs, such as Verisign or CyberTrust. Once again, you use the `keytool` command to create a certificate request:

```
keytool -certreq -alias j2eebook -sigalg MD5withRSA -file j2eecert.crq
```

The certificate request is stored in a file called `j2eecert.crq` (unless you used a different filename for the `-file` argument). The contents of the file are in a special format called MIME64. Listing 35.1 shows an example certificate request file.

Listing 35.1 Example Certificate Request


```
-----BEGIN NEW CERTIFICATE REQUEST-----
MIIBuDCCASECAQAweDELMAkGA1UEBhMCVVMxEDAOBgNVBAgTB0dlb3JnaWExETAPBgNVBAcTCExp
dGhvbmlhMRkwFwYDVQQKExBXdXRrYSBDb25zdWx0aW5nMRQwEgYDVQQLEwtEZXZlbG9wbWVudDET
MBEGA1UEAxMKTWFyayBXdXRrYTCBnzANBgkqhkiG9w0BAQEFAAOBjQAwgYkCgYEAyiJq6fGDaSCw
ATpq1RGSTpQ5Hd6MPZpGffwCr85ph5RsfjHPsYOaFSJtaJNRpDaaykw7gcMYHFCC0DqPAcvWIRt3
liQ0aoaz3+aTUf0spoX3ZoRW/+DORYTS3BeOFjZAA7TGIyGw/ufMd+AGohSYb78j4YIG0EE/7Nd6
etC+wUkCAwEAAaAAMA0GCSqGSIb3DQEBBAUAA4GBAAhHQtPutLA0ySdVzGBwDCQ6Hs1HhBpanAT2
av5C61MV73O6lTtEqPy1waArQaY/dL1mxuUBzxF47hyfC+TbWfOLzmFjAM63o3Jrvu6pNxWQjq0j
TogKYH2zeLhCZ8mZ6IlqWhzWNtcv8ikJrNnJ6biHDNsC3w/Ht42fUCyek+Dj
-----END NEW CERTIFICATE REQUEST-----
```


After you choose a Certificate Authority, follow the CA's instructions for requesting a certificate. At some point, the CA will ask you to send it a certificate request. Send the file you generated from the `keytool -certreq` command.

At some point, the CA will send you back a digitally signed certificate. You can import this certificate into your key store with this command:

```
keytool -import -alias j2eebook -file mysignedcert.cert
```

You want the certificate in your key store, not your trust store. The server uses the key store, and the server needs to present the certificate to the client.

Creating an SSL Server Program

The key management aspect of SSL is by far the toughest part. If you've made it this far, it's all downhill from here. Using the `javax.net.ssl.SSLServerSocket` class is just like using the `ServerSocket` class except that you must create the socket a different way. Also, you must tell Java your key store password one way or another.

To create an `SSLServerSocket` object, you must create an `SSLServerSocketFactory` and then ask the factory to create the `SSLServerSocket`, as shown in Listing 35.2.

Listing 35.2 `SSLServerSocket` Creation

```
// Create a socket for receiving incoming connections
SSLServerSocketFactory sslServerFactory =
    (SSLServerSocketFactory)
    SSLServerSocketFactory.getDefault();

SSLServerSocket serverSock = (SSLServerSocket) sslServerFactory.
    createServerSocket(portNumber);
```

You can specify the key store password and location using system properties, which you can either set on the command-line or in your Java code. To set the properties in your code, you can make a call like this:

```
// Use the default keystore
System.setProperty("javax.net.ssl.keyStore",
```

```
    System.getProperty("user.home")+File.separator+".keystore");
System.setProperty("javax.net.ssl.keyStorePassword",
"kspass");
```

To illustrate how easy it is to convert a program from regular sockets to SSL, Listing 35.3 shows an excerpt from the `ChatServer` class from Chapter 27, "Network Programming." In this excerpt, the chat server creates a `ServerSocket` to listen for incoming connections.

LISTING 35.3 EXCERPT FROM `ChatServer.java`

```
    public void run()
    {
        try
        {
// Create a socket for receiving incoming connections
            ServerSocket serverSock = new ServerSocket(portNumber);

            for (;;)
            {
// Get the next incoming connection
                Socket clientSocket = serverSock.accept();
```

Listing 35.4 shows the same section of code modified to use `SSLServerSocket`.

LISTING 35.4 EXCEPTION FROM SSL VERSION OF `ChatServer.java`

```
    public void run()
    {
// Use the default keystore
        System.setProperty("javax.net.ssl.keyStore",
            System.getProperty("user.home")+File.separator+".keystore");
        System.setProperty("javax.net.ssl.keyStorePassword", "kspass");

        try
        {
// Create a socket for receiving incoming connections
            SSLServerSocketFactory sslServerFactory =
                (SSLServerSocketFactory)
                    SSLServerSocketFactory.getDefault();

            SSLServerSocket serverSock = (SSLServerSocket) sslServerFactory.
                createServerSocket(portNumber);

            for (;;)
            {
// Get the next incoming connection
                Socket clientSocket = serverSock.accept();
```

The only other change required to make this conversion is that the SSL version must have the following import statement at the top of the file:

```
import javax.net.ssl.*;
```

The rest of the ChatServer class stays exactly the same. Even though the SSLServerSocket.accept method returns an SSLSocket instead of a plain Socket, you don't have to change anything because SSLSocket is a subclass of Socket.

If you are having trouble running the ChatServer program or any other examples from this chapter, see the "Troubleshooting" section at the end of this chapter.

CREATING AN SSL CLIENT PROGRAM

It's even easier to convert a client program to SSL because you don't need to worry about the key store. You just create an SSLSocketFactory and ask the factory to create an SSLSocket object.

Listing 35.5 shows an excerpt from the ChatClient class from Chapter 27.

LISTING 35.5 EXCERPT FROM ChatClient.java

```
        try
        {
// Connect to the server
            Socket sock = new Socket(host, portNumber);
```

Listing 35.6 shows the SSL version of the same section of code.

LISTING 35.6 EXCEPTION FROM SSL VERSION OF ChatClient.java

```
        try
        {
// Connect to the server
            SSLSocketFactory sslFactory =
                (SSLSocketFactory) SSLSocketFactory.getDefault();

            SSLSocket sock = (SSLSocket) sslFactory.
                createSocket(host, portNumber);
```

Once again, the only other change you need to make is the additional import statement at the top of the file.

COMMUNICATING WITH A WEB BROWSER

By now, it should be obvious that if you know how to do normal socket programming, using SSL is a no-brainer. One interesting application of SSL is that you can make your own HTTPS server that can accept simple requests.

Listing 35.7 shows a simple Hello World HTTPS server that sends some HTML back to a browser.

LISTING 35.7 SOURCE CODE FOR `HTTPSHelloServer.java`

```
package usingj2ee.ssl;import javax.net.ssl.*;import java.io.*;import
java.net.*;public class HTTPSHelloServer implements Runnable
{
    protected Socket sock;

    public HTTPSHelloServer(Socket aSocket)
    {
        sock = aSocket;
    }

    public void run()
    {
        try
        {
// Create the streams to read the request and send the response
            BufferedReader in = new BufferedReader(
                new InputStreamReader(sock.getInputStream()));
            PrintWriter out = new PrintWriter(
                new OutputStreamWriter(sock.getOutputStream()));

            String line;

// Read the request, quit at end-of-file or a blank line
            for (;;)
            {
                line = in.readLine();
                if (line == null) break;
                if (line.trim().length() == 0) break;
            }

// If you didn't hit EOF (that is, you got a blank line), send a response
            if (line != null)
            {
// Send the response code
                out.println("HTTP/1.0 200 OK");
// Send the content type
                out.println("Content-type: text/html");
// Blank line means end of header
                out.println();
// Send the HTML
                out.println("<html><body>");
                out.println("<h1>Hello World</h1>");
                out.println("</body></html>");
                out.println();
                out.flush();
            }
        }
        catch (Exception exc)
        {
        }
        finally
        {
// Make sure you close the socket whether or not there was an error
            try { sock.close(); } catch (Exception ignore) {}
        }
    }
```

LISTING 35.7 CONTINUED

```
    public static void main(String[] args)
    {
// Tell SSL where the keystore is and what the keystore password is
        System.setProperty("javax.net.ssl.keyStore",
            System.getProperty("user.home")+File.separator+".keystore");
        System.setProperty("javax.net.ssl.keyStorePassword", "kspass");

        try
        {
// Create the SSLServerSocketFactory
            SSLServerSocketFactory sslServerFactory =
                (SSLServerSocketFactory) SSLServerSocketFactory.getDefault();

// Create an SSLServerSocket on port 443 (the standard HTTPS port)
            ServerSocket server = sslServerFactory.createServerSocket(443);

            for (;;)
            {
// Accept a new client connection (even though sock is declared as Socket,
// it's really an SSLSocket, you just don't care at this point)
                Socket sock = server.accept();

// Create an HTTPSHelloServer instance to service the client
                HTTPSHelloServer clientHandler = new HTTPSHelloServer(sock);

// Start a thread to service the client
                (new Thread(clientHandler)).start();
            }
        }
        catch (Exception exc)
        {
            exc.printStackTrace();
        }
    }
}
```

AN SSL RELAY PROGRAM

Remember the `Relay` program from Chapter 31, "Proxies and Relays"? With a few quick changes, you can use it to relay an SSL connection to a non-SSL connection. For example, if you have a Web server that doesn't support secure connections, you can set up the relay to forward SSL connections to your Web browser. By now, you already know the drill. You just change the way you create the `ServerSocket` and you're done.

ACCESSING WEB SERVERS WITH SSL

One of the most popular uses of JSSE is in the area of HTTPS requests. That is, you want to write a Java program that accesses a Web server via HTTPS—either to retrieve data or to send data. Although you could write a socket program to mimic the HTTP protocol over SSL (that's all HTTPS really is—HTTP over an SSL socket connection), there's a better way.

JSSE comes with an HTTPS protocol handler that plugs into the Java URL framework to recognize requests for `https` URLs.

Listing 35.8 shows a program that performs an HTTPS `GET` request using the `URL` class.

LISTING 35.8 SOURCE CODE FOR `GetHTTPS.java`

```
package usingj2ee.ssl;import java.io.*;import
java.net.*;public class GetHTTPS{    public static void main(String[] args)
    {         try
        {
// Add the protocol handler to the built-in defaults. If you have additional
// protocol handlers, list them here
            System.setProperty("java.protocol.handler.pkgs",
                "com.sun.net.ssl.internal.www.protocol");

// Create a URL to access Verisign
            URL verisign = new URL("https://www.verisign.com");

// Open a connection to Verisign
            URLConnection urlConn = verisign.openConnection();

            InputStream in = urlConn.getInputStream();

            byte[] buffer = new byte[4096];

            int len;

// Read the response from Verisign and dump it out to the console
            while ((len = in.read(buffer)) > 0)
            {
                System.out.write(buffer, 0, len);
            }
        }
        catch (Exception exc)
        {
            exc.printStackTrace();
        }
    }
}
```

USING SSL WITH RMI

RMI makes it easy to integrate SSL. RMI has two special interfaces—`RMIClientSocketFactory` and `RMIServerSocketFactory`—that allow you to substitute your own socket implementations for the sockets and RMI usually uses. All you need to do is create your own implementation of these interfaces to return SSL sockets and you have encrypted RMI.

Listing 35.9 shows an implementation of both of the RMI socket factory interfaces.

Listing 35.9 Source Code for `RMISSLSocketFactory.java`

```
package usingj2ee.ssl;import javax.net.ssl.*;import
java.rmi.server.*;import java.io.*;import java.net.*;public class
RMISSLSocketFactory
    implements RMIServerSocketFactory, RMIClientSocketFactory,
Serializable
{
    public ServerSocket createServerSocket(int port)
        throws IOException
    {
        SSLServerSocketFactory fact =
            (SSLServerSocketFactory)
SSLServerSocketFactory.getDefault();

        return fact.createServerSocket(port);
    }

    public Socket createSocket(String host, int port)
        throws IOException
    {
        SSLSocketFactory fact =
            (SSLSocketFactory) SSLSocketFactory.getDefault();
        return fact.createSocket(host, port);
    }
}
```

Now, interestingly enough, you only need to change your RMI server to use the new factories. The client stub automatically picks up the client factory when it locates the server. To change your RMI server to use SSL, change the constructor for your implementation class to pass the socket factory to its parent class (which is `UnicastRemoteObject`). Your constructor might look something like this:

```
public StockQuoteImpl()
    throws RemoteException
{
    super(0, new RMISSLSocketFactory(),
        new RMISSLSocketFactory());
// do other initialization here
}
```

After you make this simple change, your RMI is encrypted!

Troubleshooting

Compile Problems

Why can't I find `javax.net.ssl.*`?

You might not have installed JSSE or the JSSE JAR files are not in your classpath. The default install method for JSSE puts the JAR files in your `jre/lib/ext` directory, which doesn't require classpath changes, so there's a good chance you just haven't installed JSSE.

Why do I get illegal assignment errors when I create a factory or an SSL socket?

The SSL factories use new standard extensions called `SocketFactory` and `ServerSocketFactory`. The `getDefault` methods in the factories return `SocketFactory` and `ServerSocketFactory` references instead of the SSL-specific factories. The underlying objects are the SSL-specific types; you just need to cast them to their SSL-equivalents. The same goes for the sockets you create.

RUNTIME PROBLEMS

Why do I keep getting an error saying there's no SSL socket or no SSL implementation available?

You probably don't have the key store set up properly. SSL must be able to find your key store, and it must have the correct password. Also, make sure the password for at least one of your keys is the same as the key store password (that is, don't assign passwords for individual keys).

JSSE doesn't like to see keys in the keystore whose passwords don't match the keystore password. If you still have the `j2eetest` key from previous chapters, delete it from the keystore with `keytool -delete -alias j2eetest`.

What does "untrusted cert chain" mean?

The client received a certificate from a server, but the signer of the certificate isn't in the client's trust store. If you're doing your own testing with a self-signed certificate, export the certificate from your key store and import it into the client's trust store. If you are using Verisign's test certificate, the client needs Verisign's Test CA root certificate in its trust store. Verisign signs test certificates with a different key than it uses for regular certificates. Browsers and other products don't have the Test CA root certificate in their list of trusted CAs, so they don't trust the test certificates.

When I try to access my SSL service from a browser, why am I getting a message that there's no cipher suites in common?

Most browsers, including IE and Netscape, use RSA for public key encryption. When you use `keytool` to generate a key, it uses DSA by default. When you create a key, make sure you specify `-keyalg RSA` and either `-sigalg MD5withRSA` or `-sigalg SHA1withRSA`.

CHAPTER 36

Java Security Features

In this chapter

THE ADVANTAGES OF BUILT-IN SECURITY

As the Internet has become more popular, security has become a much more important issue than it was back in the days when computers weren't constantly connected to each other. When Java first hit the scene, it was mainly used for downloaded applets that had restricted sandbox environments—preventing people from writing malicious applets that could spy on other users or damage computers.

The applet sandbox originally relied on a simple security manager that determined whether a class could perform a specific operation. Although the security manager framework wasn't applet-specific, few developers ever created their own security managers for their applications.

Java's original applet security model was helpful in making Java popular because people generally felt safe about running Java applets. As Java became more popular, applet developers needed a way to create more powerful applets. They wanted to read and write files and make network connections to different sites—things that the applet sandbox didn't allow. The various browser vendors came up with digital signature mechanisms that allowed you to digitally sign code and mark it as being safe. Of course, you had to trust the person signing the code, but at least you could feel sure that someone else didn't replace the signed code with a malicious program.

The code-signing support for Internet Explorer is an all-or-nothing approach. If the code is signed, it has all the capabilities of a regular Java application. In fact, this is the same approach the Microsoft uses for ActiveX controls—an alternative to Java applets. Netscape takes a more conservative approach, allowing you to grant certain permissions to an applet without giving it free reign over your system.

The Security Framework introduced with JDK 1.2 supports digitally signed code and enables you to grant privileges based on the signer. You can set up security policies that allow a signed applet to access only a certain area of your file system or connect to certain network addresses.

Digitally signed code will become more important in the future as smaller devices become Internet-aware. Already Sun is developing special Java virtual machines to run in cars and mobile phones. These devices can't hold a large number of applications at one time, so downloadable code will become more important. You can already see it happening with mobile phones—the Wireless Markup Language (WML) is becoming more robust because people need it to do more than just show simple text forms.

There's no reason you can't use the Java security framework for other types of security as well. Suppose, for example, that you want to set up a Web host to provide JSP and servlet access to various subscribers. Each subscriber has its own directory on your server and you want to allow the subscriber to access only its own directories from its servlets and Java Server Pages. You can use the Java Security Framework to set up a security policy to implement these restrictions.

THE JAVA SECURITY FRAMEWORK

The Java Security Framework is built around the `java.security.Permission` class. Although there are a lot of support classes, the final determination of whether you can perform an operation comes down to the comparison of two `Permission` objects.

A permission has two basic components: a name and a list of actions. For example, a `FilePermission` object has a name that is either a filename or a directory name and a list of actions that can include `read`, `write`, `execute`, and `delete`. The list of actions is a string of comma-separated action names.

The `Permission` class also includes an `implies` method that returns true if one permission implies another. The `implies` method is used to determine whether the permission is ultimately granted or refused. When you try to read a file, the Java I/O libraries create a `FilePermission` object with the name of the file you want to read and an action of `read`. The security framework then checks the permission against all the things you are allowed to do (using the `implies` method), and if there is an existing permission that implies the permission you are asking for, the security framework lets the operation proceed.

You can actually create permission objects and compare them with the `implies` method to see if a particular name and set of actions would be permitted. Listing 36.1 shows a program that compares file permissions.

LISTING 36.1 SOURCE CODE FOR FilePermTest.java

```
package usingj2ee.security;

import java.security.*;
import java.io.*;

public class FilePermTest
{
    public static void main(String[] args)
    {

// Create a permission allowing read/write access to all files
// in the h:\j2eebook\ch36\examples directory
        FilePermission dirPerm =
            new FilePermission("h:\\j2eebook\\ch36\\examples\\*",
                "read,write");

// Create a permission for read access to the FilePermTest.java file
// in the h:\j2eebook\ch36\examples directory
        FilePermission goodFilePerm =
            new FilePermission(
                "h:\\j2eebook\\ch36\\examples\\FilePermTest.java",
                "read");

// Create a permission for write access to the c:\windows\hosts file
        FilePermission badFilePerm =
            new FilePermission(
                "c:\\windows\\hosts", "write");
```

LISTING 36.1 CONTINUED

```
// See if the permission in dirPerm allows the permission in goodFilePerm
        if (dirPerm.implies(goodFilePerm))
        {
            System.out.println("You are allowed "+goodFilePerm.getActions()+
                " on "+goodFilePerm.getName());
        }
        else
        {
            System.out.println("You are NOT allowed "+
                goodFilePerm.getActions()+
                " on "+goodFilePerm.getName());
        }

// See if the permission in dirPerm allows the permission in badFilePerm
        if (dirPerm.implies(badFilePerm))
        {
            System.out.println("You are allowed "+badFilePerm.getActions()+
                " on "+badFilePerm.getName());
        }
        else
        {
            System.out.println("You are NOT allowed "+
                badFilePerm.getActions()+
                " on "+badFilePerm.getName());
        }
    }
}
```

When you run the `FilePermTest` program, it tells you whether you can access two different files based on the permissions granted for a specific directory.

You don't normally check permissions this way, of course. If you must check permissions at all, you use the `AccessController` class. Basically, you still create a `Permission` object for the permission you want to check, but instead of using the `implies` method of another permission, you call the `checkPermission` method in `AccessController`.

For example, given a `FilePermission` object, you can check the permission with the following:

```
AccessController.checkPermission(myFilePerm);
```

It's important to understand how the `AccessController` checks a permission. It can be confusing to diagnose a permission problem if you don't know what to look for.

When you call `checkPermission`, the `AccessController` searches back through the call stack, checking to make sure that *each* object making a method call in the call stack has permission to perform the operation. Suppose, for example, that you have a class called `FileParser` that reads a data file. You set up a security policy that allows the `FileParser` class to read any file on the system (you'll learn how to set up security policies later in this chapter). Now, suppose an applet tries to use the `FileParser` class to read a file. Figure 36.1 illustrates how the call stack for this operation might look.

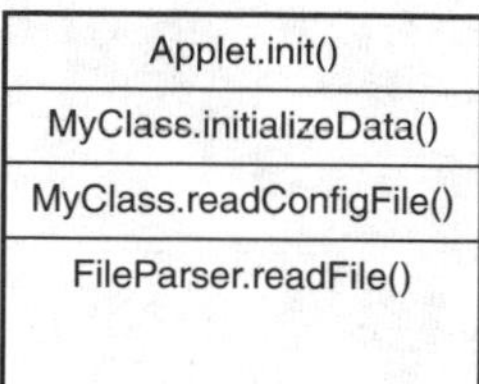

Figure 36.1 The `AccessController` examines the entire call stack.

The `AccessController` class sees that `FileInputStream` is allowed to read the file, and so is `FileParser`, but because the applet is not allowed to read the file, the `AccessController` throws an `AccessControlException`.

There are times when a class needs to access a resource regardless of the permissions of the calling class. For example, the `Signature` class accesses the key store file to digitally sign data and verify signatures. You might not have access to the file, but you should still be able to at least verify signatures, if not sign, data. The `Signature` class must tell the security service that it needs to perform the permitted operations regardless of the permissions of the caller. It does so by telling the `AccessController` to start a privileged operation.

The `doPrivileged` method in `AccessController` takes an object implementing the `PrivilegedAction` interface and invokes the object's `run` method. When the `AccessController` finds an object in the call stack that implements `PrivilegedAction`, it doesn't look any higher in the call stack when verifying permissions. Suppose the `FileParser` object from Figure 36.1 performs a privileged operation. As Figure 36.2 illustrates, the `AccessController` doesn't look at the applet's permissions because the `FileParser` is performing a privileged operation.

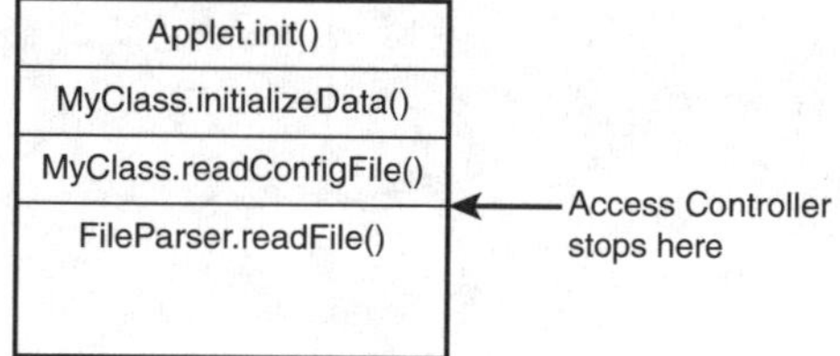

Figure 36.2 A privileged operation tells the `AccessController` not to look any further up in the call stack.

Listing 36.2 shows a program that executes a privileged action to verify some file permissions. The program checks the permissions manually rather than allowing one of the `java.io` classes to do it.

Listing 36.2 Source Code for `AccessControlTest.java`

```
package usingj2ee.security;

import java.security.*;
import java.io.*;
```

LISTING 36.2 CONTINUED

```
public class AccessControlTest
{
    public static void main(String[] args)
    {
        try
        {
// Start a privileged operation using a quirky-looking
// anonymous class
            AccessController.doPrivileged(new PrivilegedAction() {
                public Object run()
                {
// Create a permission for read access to the FilePermTest.java file
// in the h:\j2eebook\ch36\examples directory
                    FilePermission goodFilePerm =
                        new FilePermission(
                            "h:\\j2eebook\\ch36\\examples\\FilePermTest.java",
                            "read");

// Check for permission to access the file
                    AccessController.checkPermission(goodFilePerm);


// Create a permission for write access to the c:\windows\hosts file
                    FilePermission badFilePerm =
                        new FilePermission(
                            "c:\\windows\\hosts", "write");

// Check for permission to access the file
                    AccessController.checkPermission(badFilePerm);

                    return null;
                }
            });
        }
        catch (Exception exc)
        {
            exc.printStackTrace();
        }
    }
}
```

The `AccessControlTest` program throws an exception when you run it.

Caution

Be *very* careful about performing privileged operations. You must make sure that you aren't opening any security holes that would allow an untrusted class to access sensitive data. Try to keep the privileged part of the operation as short as possible. Don't do anything inside a privileged operation that doesn't need to be privileged.

Obviously, if there is a way to make a permission fail, there must be a way to grant the permission. You grant permissions through policy files. As far as Java is concerned, a *policy* is a collection of permissions describing all the things you are permitted to do. A *permission* describes a single operation (although that single operation may imply many associated operations).

Java recognizes two policy files by default:

- **A system policy**—The system policy is defined in a file called `java.policy` located in the `jre/lib/security` directory wherever you have installed the JDK/JRE.
- **A user policy**—The user policy file is stored in a file called `.java.policy` and is stored in a user's home directory (the directory specified by the `user.home` system property).

Java loads a system policy first, and then loads the user policy file to augment the system policy. You can also specify an additional policy on the command-line by setting the `java.security.policy` system property (Java still uses the system and user policies in this case). For example, to specify an additional policy for the `AccessControlTest` class, you can use the following command:

```
java -Djava.security.policy=mytest.policy usingj2ee.security.AccessControlTest
```

If you want the policy file to take the place of the system and user policy files instead of augmenting them, define the policy with two equal signs (==), like the following:

```
-Djava.security.policy==mytest.policy
```

You can also add additional default policy files by editing the `jre\lib\security\java.security` file. There are lines of the form:

```
policy.url.n=...
```

These lines specify the locations of the default policy files. The JDK usually comes with two policies, defined as the following:

```
policy.url.1=file:${java.home}/lib/security/java.policy
policy.url.2=file:${user.home}/.java.policy
```

A policy file consists of a number of permissions of the form:

```
grant SignedBy signer, CodeBase codebase
{
    permission;
    permission;
    permission;
};
```

Both the `SignedBy` and the `CodeBase` specifiers are optional. If you only specify one of the two, you don't need the comma, either. The *`signer`* parameter indicates that you are granting permission for code signed by a specific person or organization. The *`codebase`* parameter indicates the location of the code you are granting permissions for. It might be a JAR file (signed or unsigned) or a URL. If the URL represents a directory and not a single file, make sure it ends with a slash. Also, the order of `SignedBy` and `CodeBase` doesn't matter.

The following is the format of a permission:

```
permission permissionClass "name","action(s)",SignedBy "signers"
```

The *permissionClass* parameter is the name of the Java class that represents the permission (for example, `java.io.FilePermission`).

When you define permissions, you typically grant permissions for a block of resources. For example, you don't grant permission for every file in a directory individually, you just grant the permission on the directory itself.

The *name* parameter is the name of the resource you are specifying the permission for. It might be a filename, a directory, even an IP address. Each permission has a single *name* parameter, you can't specify multiple names separated by commas as you can with the actions and signers. In any of the names, you can substitute system properties with the expression `${propertyname}`. For example, to insert your home directory (defined by `user.home`), use `${user.home}`. Also, because Unix and Windows use different path separators, you can use `${/}` to represent the path separator for the operating system you're using.

The *action* parameter is a list of actions that you are allowed to perform on the resource. For files, the actions are `read`, `write`, `execute`, and `delete`. For a socket, the possible actions are `connect`, `accept`, `listen`, and `resolve`. The *action* parameter is optional; some permissions don't need actions (`java.awt.AWTPermission`, for example, which allows access to several AWT functions).

The *signers* parameter is an optional list of potential code signers. The permission is only granted if the code has been signed by *all* of the people in the *signers* list. This list is similar to the list of signers for the `grant` command itself, except that it is specific to a permission.

Note

If the signers parameter includes more than one signer, the code must be signed by all the signers because it's not a list of possible signers; it's a list of required signers.

Jumping back to the example in Listing 36.2, if you try to run the program you should get an exception on at least one of the two calls to `checkPermission`. To eliminate the exception, you must explicitly grant permission to access the directories in question. Listing 36.3 shows a policy file that grants access to these directories.

LISTING 36.3 SOURCE CODE FOR `unrestrict.policy`

```
grant codeBase "file:/h:/j2eebook/ch36/examples/" {
  permission java.io.FilePermission "h:/-", "read, write";
  permission java.io.FilePermission "c:/windows/hosts", "read, write";
};
```

Note

On some Windows systems, such as Windows 98, you may need to specify `h:\\-` or `h:${/}-` instead of `h:/-`.

The policy file in listing 36.3 grants permission to read and write the entire H: drive and to the `c:\windows\hosts` file.

java.io.FilePermission

As you have already seen, the `java.io.FilePermission` class grants permission to access files and directories. You can specify either a specific filename or you can use wildcards. When you grant permission on a directory, if you don't end the directory name with `*` or `-`, you are granting permissions *only* on the directory and not on the files within it. For example, the following permission allows you to get a list of the files in a directory, but does not give you any permission to access the files:

```
permission java.io.FilePermission "/usr/local/src/","read"
```

If a directory name ends with `*`, the permission applies to all files within the directory, but does not include files in any subdirectories. For example, the following permission allows you to read all the files in `/usr/local/src`, but not in `/usr/local/src/java`:

```
permission java.io.FilePermission "/usr/local/src/*","read"
```

If you want a directory permission to cover subdirectories, use `-` instead of `*`. The following permission declaration allows you to read all files in `/usr/local/src` and any subdirectories below it:

```
permission java.io.FilePermission "/usr/local/src/-","read"
```

The `FilePermission` class also recognizes a special filename that applies to all files in the file system. The special name is `<<ALL FILES>>`. For example, the following permission lets you read all files on the computer:

```
permission java.io.FilePermission "<<ALL FILES>>","read"
```

Keep in mind, of course, that these permissions can't override the operating system's permissions. If Java thinks you can read a file but the operating system says you can't, you can't.

java.net.SocketPermission

The `java.net.SocketPermission` class lets you grant permission for socket operations. The *name* parameter for a socket permission is a combination of a host address (either by name or by IP address) and possibly a port number or a range of port numbers. You can use wildcards in the host name, but only on the leftmost part of the name. In other words, you can do `*.wutka.com`, but you can't do `wutka.*`.

The port number can be a single number; a range of numbers (2000–2999); a dash followed by a number indicating port numbers up to and including the specified number (–4000); or a port number followed by a dash, indicating all port numbers greater than or equal to the specified number (1024–).

The possible socket actions are `connect`, `accept`, `listen`, and `resolve`. Because `connect`, `accept`, and `listen` all imply `resolve`, you don't need to specify `resolve` unless you want to allow a class to perform a name lookup on a particular address without performing any socket operations on that address.

The `connect` action grants the code permission to connect to a particular address.

The `listen` action grants the code permission to listen for connections to a particular port, but does *not* grant permission to actually receive the connections. You must also grant `accept` permission for any external addresses that you want to accept connections from.

java.net.NetPermission

The `NetPermission` class lets you grant a few permissions for some of the `URL` class operations. The three possible names are `requestPasswordAuthentication`, `setDefaultAuthenticator`, and `specifyStreamHandler`. You don't need to specify an action for any of these names—you either have the permission or you don't.

java.lang.RuntimePermission

The `RuntimePermission` class grants permission to perform various operations associated with the Java runtime. None of the runtime permissions require an action, but a few of them allow you to specify particular class, file, and package names or use `*` as a wildcard. The permissions that can include specific names are as follows:

- `loadLibrary.`*`libraryName`*
- `accessClassInPackage.`*`packageName`*
- `defineClassInPackage.`*`packageName`*
- `accessDeclaredMembers.`*`className`*

The other possible names are `createClassLoader`, `getClassLoader`, `setContextClassLoader`, `setSecurityManager`, `createSecurityManager`, `exitVM`, `setFactory`, `setIO`, `modifyThread`, `stopThread`, `modifyThreadGroup`, `getProtectionDomain`, `shutdownHooks`, `readFileDescriptor`, `writeFileDescriptor`, and `queuePrintJob`.

java.util.PropertyPermission

The `PropertyPermission` class lets you grant permission to read and/or write system properties. The name in the permission is the property name, and can end with `*`. The possible actions are `read` and `write`.

java.security.SecurityPermission

The `SecurityPermission` class allows access to various parts of the security API. There are a few permissions whose names can include a specific key name or provider name. None of the security permissions require an action.

The following are the properties that take an additional key name or provider name:

- `getProperty.`*`key`*
- `setProperty.`*`key`*
- `insertProvider.`*`providerName`*
- `removeProvider.`*`providerName`*
- `clearProviderProperties.`*`providerName`*
- `putProviderProperty.`*`providerName`*
- `removeProviderProperty.`*`providerName`*

The other possible security permission names are `getPolicy`, `setPolicy`, `setSystemScope`, `setIdentityPublicKey`, `setIdentityInfo`, `printIdentity`, `addIdentityCertificate`, `removeIdentityCertificate`, `getDomainController`, `createAccessControlContext`, `getSignerPrivateKey`, and `setSignerKeyPair`.

java.io.SerializablePermission

The `SerializablePermission` class lets you control a few potential security holes in the Java Serialization API. The possible names are `enableSubclassImplementation` and `enableSubstitution`. There are no actions.

java.lang.reflect.ReflectPermission

The `ReflectPermission` class lets you grant permission for classes to use the Java Reflection API to access protected and private members of a class (certain utility libraries such as database tools might need to do this). The only name for this permission is `suppressAccessChecks`, and there are no actions.

java.awt.AWTPermission

The `AWTPermission` class lets you grant permission for performing certain AWT procedures that could potentially create security holes. The possible names are `accessClipboard`, `accessEventQueue`, `listenToAllAWTEvents`, `readDisplayPixels`, `createRobot`, and `showWindowWithoutWarningBanner`. There are no actions for these names.

java.security.AllPermission

The `AllPermission` class grants permission for anything that can possibly have a permission. If a class has `AllPermission`, it doesn't need any of the other permissions. Obviously, this is a dangerous permission to grant, but it does keep you from having to list every possible permission if you totally trust a particular library or signer. This permission doesn't require any names or actions.

SIGNING A JAR FILE

To make use of permissions granted to a particular signer, you need to know how to sign code. This is done by signing JAR files. If you already know how to manipulate the key store, which you have seen over the past few chapters, signing a JAR file is a piece of cake. You just type the following:

```
jarsigner jarfile alias
```

The *jarfile* parameter is, of course, the name of the JAR file you want to sign and *alias* is the alias for a key in the key store that you will use to sign the JAR file. In case you don't remember how to create a key, just type the following:

```
keytool -genkey -alias somekeyalias
```

This generates a new key for signing code and gives it the specified alias. Now, if you want to distribute the code to other users, you probably want to request a certificate from Verisign or another trusted Certificate Authority. To do that, you must create a certificate request with this:

```
keytool -certreq -alias somekeyalias -file outputreqfile
```

You can then send the certificate request off to the CA to get it digitally signed. When you get the signed certificate back from the CA, you can import it back into your key store with the following:

```
keytool -import -alias somekeyalias -file certfile
```

When you distribute the signed JAR file to someone else, he must recognize your certificate (it must be in his key store). Before you can send someone your certificate, you must extract it from your key store, which you can do with the `-export` option:

```
keytool -export -alias somekeyalias -file outputcertfile
```

Now, you send the certificate to the other person, who then uses the `-import` option to import the certificate into his key store with a specific alias (his alias doesn't need to be the same as yours).

Remember that the `SignedBy` keyword takes a list of signers. You might have wondered where the name for the signer comes from. As it turns out, the signer name must be the name of an alias in your key store.

To see the entire process in action, store the `AccessControlTest` classes in a JAR file with the following:

```
jar cvf actsigned.jar usingj2ee\security\AccessControlTest*.class
```

Now, create a key for signing the JAR:

```
keytool -genkey -alias j2eebooksign
```

Use the new key to sign the JAR file (don't bother with the expense of getting a full certificate from Verisign, the self-signed certificate that `keytool` creates is good enough for this demonstration):

```
jarsigner actsigned.jar j2eebooksign
```

Now, update the policy file to include your key store location and restrict the permissions to code signed by `j2eebooksign`. The new policy should look like the file in Listing 36.4.

LISTING 36.4 `permitsigned.policy` **SECURITY POLICY FILE**

```
keystore "file:/c:/Documents and Settings/mark/.keystore", "jks";

grant signedBy "j2eebooksign" {
  permission java.io.FilePermission "h:\\-", "read, write";
  permission java.io.FilePermission "c:\\windows\\hosts", "read, write";
};
```

Note

You might need to change the keystore path and the file permission paths to match your particular system. For a Unix system, you should use a single forward slash (`/`) instead of `\\`. It's best to use `${/}` as a platform-independent slash.

Now, just run the program with the following command:

```
java -cp actsigned.jar -Djava.security.policy=permitsigned.policy
➥usingj2ee.security.AccessControlTest
```

If everything went right, the program should terminate with no errors and no output.

Tip

If you have trouble getting permissions to work correctly, try defining the property `-Djava.security.debug=all`. You'll get a ton of diagnostic output, some of which might be useful.

TROUBLESHOOTING

SETTING PERMISSIONS

Why can't I grant myself permission to access a file?

You probably typed the filename incorrectly. If you're using backslashes in the filename, make sure you use two of them. The backslash character (\) is usually used as an escape character, indicating that the next character shouldn't be interpreted as a special character but rather as just a plain character. Two backslashes (\\) turn into a single backslash because the first one says "take the next character as just a plain character."

I granted my code permission to listen for incoming socket connections; why can't I receive any?

You must also grant permission to accept incoming connections from any hosts that might want to connect, or use `*` for all hosts.

CODE SIGNING

Why aren't my permissions working for my signed code?

There are a number of possibilities. First, the permissions themselves could be wrong. Try specifying the JAR file as the codebase while leaving the `SignedBy` keyword out and see whether the permissions work. If not, it's probably an error in the permissions and not in the signing. If the permissions work when you just specify a code base, the next possibility is that you didn't specify the key store correctly or that the signer name isn't an alias in your key store. The fastest way to find the problem is to turn on debugging with `-Djava.security.debug=all` and look through the volumes of debug messages.

Why do I see an `X.509 not found` error message in the debug output when it reads my key store?

If you have either JCE or JSSE loaded, there might be a conflict. Try disabling JCE and/or JSSE in your `jre\lib\security\java.security` file and see whether the problem goes away.

CHAPTER 37

J2EE Security

In this chapter

ROLE-BASED SECURITY

One of the challenges you often face in developing a distributed, multi-user application is how to handle security.

The authentication mechanism in the J2EE specification uses a technique called *role-based security*. The idea is that rather than restricting resources at the user level, you create groups of users called roles and restrict the resources by role. A single user can have more than one role. For example, a company might have employees and contractors, so you might have an application that permits different operations depending on whether you are an employee or a contractor. You might also have a manager role. If a contractor happens to be a manager, he would have two roles—contractor and manager.

There are no predefined roles. You can come up with role names as you see fit. As far as creating users and roles, each J2EE server has its own method for defining them.

Because authentication is becoming increasingly important for all applications, not just J2EE applications, Sun has created a new standard package called the Java Authentication and Authorization Service (JAAS). JAAS augments the original Java Security framework by adding subjects, principals, and credentials. For example, under Java 1.3, you can grant security permissions with a security setting like this:

```
grant Codebase "http://wutka.com", Signedby "mark"
{
    permission java.io.FilePermission "c:\windows", "read";
}
```

With JAAS, you can further restrict the permission by adding a principal, like this:

```
grant Codebase "http://wutka.com", Signedby "mark",
    Principal com.wutka.Principal "mark"
{
    permission java.io.FilePermission "c:\windows", "read";
}
```

Although earlier Java security frameworks used a principal as the basic unit of authentication, JAAS uses a subject, which can contain one or more principals. The idea is that a single user can use different names for different systems. A subject might have a principal (an I.D.) containing an e-mail address, and another principal containing a Social Security number. If you log in as a particular subject, any system that authenticates by e-mail address can access the e-mail principal, whereas systems that authenticate by Social Security number can access the Social Security number principal. JAAS authenticates subjects using credentials, which can take many forms. A simple login password is one form of credential, whereas a digital certificate is another form. A *credential* is basically a piece of information that the subject supplies to the security system to verify the subject's identity.

Although JAAS will be part of the JDK in a future release, most likely JDK 1.4, J2EE will also use JAAS for authentication. Sun is developing a standard for integrating J2EE with JAAS, which might or might not be present in the final J2EE 1.3 specification.

BASIC AUTHENTICATION

Both the EJB and Servlet specifications support authentication and if you use servlets and EJBs in the same server, you might be able to create users one time and use the same users for both the servlets and the EJBs. In other cases, however, your servlet container is separate from the EJB container, so you must configure the authentication separately.

Eventually, the J2EE-JAAS integration will solve this problem, allowing you to authenticate a user from the Web container and pass the authorization context along to the EJB container. Some J2EE servers already pass authorization information between different containers. Most of the time, you must be running the containers within the same server, although some servers might even pass authentication information from one machine to another.

EJB AUTHENTICATION

As with several other aspects of EJB, authentication has a basic framework but the actual implementation of authentication is left to the container provider. Unfortunately, too much has been left up to the container providers, so you might have difficulty even using authentication from your standalone client applications or from your Web clients.

For standalone applications, EJB provides an application client. An *application client* is essentially a client program that is packaged along with a set of Enterprise JavaBeans. When you deploy the application, the deployment tool generates a client JAR file. You run the JAR file with a special application client program that first asks the user for authentication. That way, your client program doesn't need to know anything about authentication.

For example, in the J2EE Reference Implementation, you can configure an application client from the `deploytool` program. You include any classes for the client application in the deployment JAR file and specify the main class for the client. Figure 37.1 shows the section of the `deploytool` program where you set up a client.

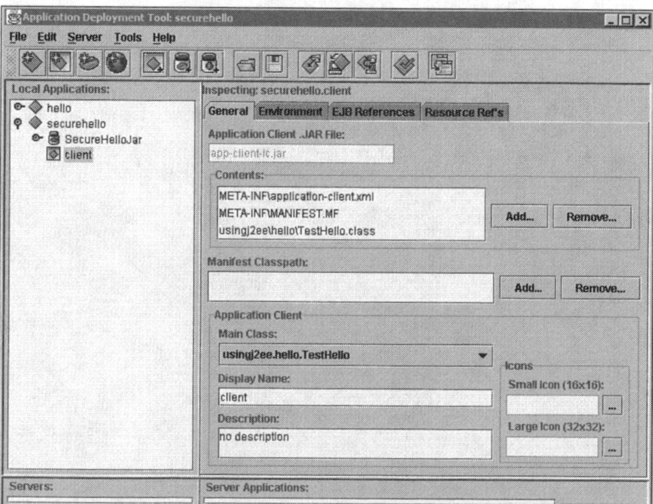

Figure 37.1
The `deploytool` program lets you configure client programs.

To do authentication, of course, you need to add users and user groups. J2EE organizes users by groups and realms. Basically, a group is simply a logical grouping of users. You might create a group called J2EE that organizes users by groups and realms. Basically, a group is simply a logical grouping of users. You might create a group called managers whose members are all managers and a group called `contractors` whose members are all contractors. A user can belong to more than one group, so a manager who is also a contractor can belong to both the `managers` and `contractors` groups. Groups belong to a specific security realm. For example, your Web container can have its own realm and your EJB container can have a separate realm. They can also share the same realm; it really depends on the implementation.

The J2EE Reference Implementation includes a program called `realmtool` for adding users. You can expect other J2EE containers to use a different method to add users.

Now, you can create user groups with `realmtool` by specifying the `-addGroup` option, like this:

```
realmtool -addGroup managers
```

You delete groups with the `-removeGroup` option:

```
realmtool -removeGroup managers
```

You can create a user and specify a password and group (or a comma-separated list of groups) for the user with the `-add` option:

```
realmtool -add mike mikespass managers
```

After you have created users and groups, you can add restrictions for the various methods in your Enterprise JavaBeans. Basically, you create security roles in your EJB deployment. A role can contain any number of users and groups. You then restrict EJB methods by role, specifying which roles can access which groups.

To add security constraints to a bean, you must first add one or more security roles. In the `deploytool` program, you add the roles by selecting an EJB JAR file and then clicking the Roles tab. You see a form like the one shown in Figure 37.2.

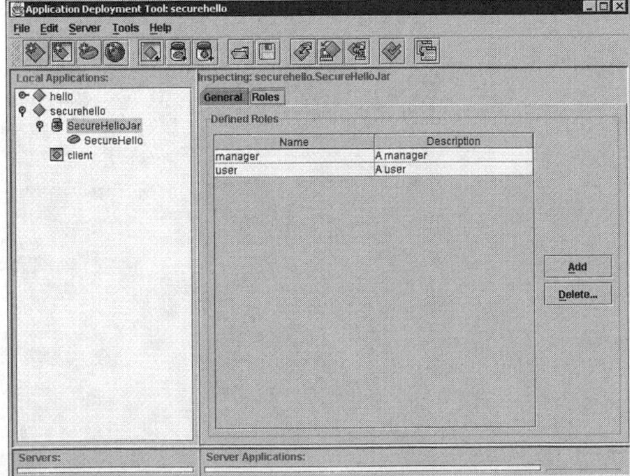

Figure 37.2
You must create roles before you add security constraints.

After you create the roles, you can restrict various methods to specific roles. For example, as Figure 37.3 shows, you can restrict the `setGreeting` method in the `HelloWorldSession` bean to only be accessible to managers.

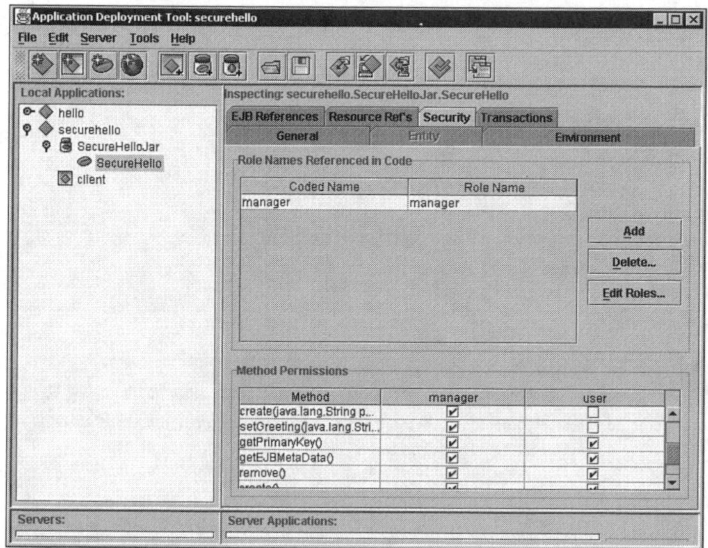

Figure 37.3
You can restrict EJB methods by role name.

Finally, when you deploy the application, you can specify which users and groups belong to which roles. This extra level of separation lets you configure the roles for an EJB just once, while you change the user-role membership whenever you deploy to a new server. The purpose for this logical separation is that when you create an EJB, you don't know what security roles might be used in the deployment container. You use the logical roles in your bean, and then the deployer maps the logical roles to actual roles in the container, allowing you to reuse the bean across many containers with different role sets.

After you generate the client JAR file, you run it with the `runclient` command, like this:

```
runclient -client helloClient.jar -name client
```

The `name` option for the `runclient` command is the display name you set up for the client when you configured it.

Although the user and group configuration changes from server to server, the way you define roles and assign methods to roles remains the same. Listing 37.1 shows an excerpt from an `ejb-jar` file that creates some roles and assigns them to various bean methods.

Listing 37.1 Excerpt from `ejb-jar.xml` for `HelloWorldSession` Bean

```
<assembly-descriptor>
    <security-role>
      <description>A manager</description>
      <role-name>manager</role-name>
```

LISTING 37.1 CONTINUED

```
    </security-role>
    <security-role>
      <description>A user</description>
      <role-name>user</role-name>
    </security-role>
    <method-permission>
      <role-name>user</role-name>
      <method>
    <ejb-name>SecureHello</ejb-name>
    <method-intf>Home</method-intf>
    <method-name>remove</method-name>
    <method-params>
      <method-param>java.lang.Object</method-param>
    </method-params>
      </method>
```

> **Note**
>
> You can also use the `<run-as-specified-identity>` tag to specify a particular identity that the bean should run as. This is important for message-driven beans that can't rely on a client's identity because the client never interacts with the bean.

In the `<assembly-descriptor>` tag, you create a list of roles. Then, you create a `<method-permission>` tag containing a role name and a list of EJB methods that the role can invoke. To grant permission for all methods, you can specify * for the method name.

SERVLET AUTHENTICATION

The servlet specification provides several ways to authenticate users. Although servlet engines are not required to implement the authentication features, you should expect most of the top servlet engines to support them.

The HTTP protocol has a built-in authentication protocol. When you log into a page that requires authentication, the Web server first sends back a message telling the browser to send authentication information. The browser then prompts you for a username and password to send to the server. After the browser sends the username and password, assuming they are correct, the Web server displays the requested page. The browser holds on to the authentication information in case the Web server asks for it again.

To set up basic authentication for a Web application, you must add several new tags to your `web.xml` file. Listing 37.2 shows a basic `web.xml` file that uses authentication.

LISTING 37.2 SOURCE CODE FOR `web.xml` FOR THE `authtest` APPLICATION

```
<!DOCTYPE web-app PUBLIC "-//Sun Microsystems, Inc.//
DTD Web Application 2.2//EN" "http://java.sun.com/j2ee/dtds/web-app_2_2.dtd">
<web-app>
    <display-name>authtest</display-name>
    <description>A test of authentication</description>
    <security-constraint>
```

```
        <web-resource-collection>
            <web-resource-name>Test</web-resource-name>
            <url-pattern>/*</url-pattern>
            <http-method>GET</http-method>
            <http-method>POST</http-method>
        </web-resource-collection>
        <user-data-constraint>
            <transport-guarantee>NONE</transport-guarantee>
        </user-data-constraint>
        <auth-constraint>
            <role-name>manager</role-name>
        </auth-constraint>
    </security-constraint>
    <login-config>
        <auth-method>BASIC</auth-method>
    </login-config>
</web-app>
```


The two main tags that have been added to the basic deployment descriptor are `<security-constraint>` and `<login-config>`.

THE <security-constraint> TAG

The `<security-constraint>` tag tells the servlet engine what security requirements your application has. You can have more than one security constraint if necessary. Within the security constraint, you must specify a Web resource collection with the `<web-resource-collection>` tag.

A Web resource collection is a collection of URL patterns that the security constraint applies to. For instance, you might want to restrict only a single directory in your application. The `<url-pattern>` tag in your resource collection would then contain a pattern matching the directory you want to restrict. The pattern `/*` in Listing 37.2 means that the security constraint applies to all URLs in the application's directory. The `<web-resource-name>` tag specifies the name for the Web resource collection. There is no connection between the name and any of the URLs within it. The name serves little purpose, but might be useful for various development and configuration tools.

The other tag you find in the Web resource collection is the `<http-method>` tag. This specifies which HTTP methods require authentication. If you do not specify an HTTP method, the security applies to all HTTP methods. You might, for example, want to perform authentication for an HTTP POST, but not for a GET. You might also want to perform different kinds of authentication for GET and POST. In the latter case, you specify two separate security constraints, one with an HTTP method of GET and the other with an HTTP method of POST.

The `<user-data-constraint>` tag tells the servlet engine what kind of data security your application needs. You might include a `<description>` tag to describe the constraint, but it's optional. The `<transport-guarantee>` tag indicates the kind of transport-level data security your application needs. The value for the `<transport-guarantee>` tag can be one of three values:

- NONE indicates that the application doesn't require any special data security
- INTEGRAL indicates that the client and server should insure that the data can't be changed by anyone. Although you would typically use an encrypted protocol such as SSL for this level of security, INTEGRAL does not require that the data can't be observed by a third party. You could send digitally signed unencrypted messages back and forth and still meet the requirements for INTEGRAL.
- CONFIDENTIAL requires that a third party can't tamper with the data or read it. You will almost always use SSL for this level unless you have another encryption transport protocol available.

The <auth-constraint> tag lets you specify the various roles that this security constraint applies to. The <role-name> tag lets you specify a specific role. You can include multiple <role-name> tags within a single <auth-constraint> tag.

THE <login-config> TAG

The <login-config> tag lets you control the type of authentication you want the servlet engine and browser to perform. You specify the type of authentication through the <auth-method> tag. The four kinds of authentication methods supported by the servlet specification are the following:

- BASIC causes the browser to prompt the user for a username and password and then sends them to the server without encrypting them first. If you use BASIC authentication over an SSL (encrypted) connection, the username and password are encrypted by the SSL protocol itself. The password is encoded using base64 encoding, which isn't really a form of encryption.
- DIGEST causes the browser to encrypt the password before sending it. Although this method might prevent someone from reading the password as it travels over the network, it's not as secure as using a fully encrypted session.
- FORM is just like the BASIC authentication method except that the server sends back a login form rather than using the browser's built-in form. The username and password are transmitted as form variables.
- CLIENT-CERT requires the user to provide a public key certificate for authentication. This method is frequently too cumbersome for general users because they rarely have their own digital certificates, but does offer a reasonably high level of security, even over an unencrypted connection.

For basic authentication, you can specify a realm name using the <realm-name> tag. The realms help organize various sections of a Web site that might need authentication. By grouping applications into separate realms, you can require the user to log in to each application. The realm name isn't configured anywhere other than in the <realm-name> tag, so you don't need to worry about setting up different realms. The realm is little more than a name passed back and forth between the browser and the server.

Listing 37.2, shown earlier, uses basic authentication. Figure 37.4 shows the login prompt for a page in the `authtest` application running under Internet Explorer.

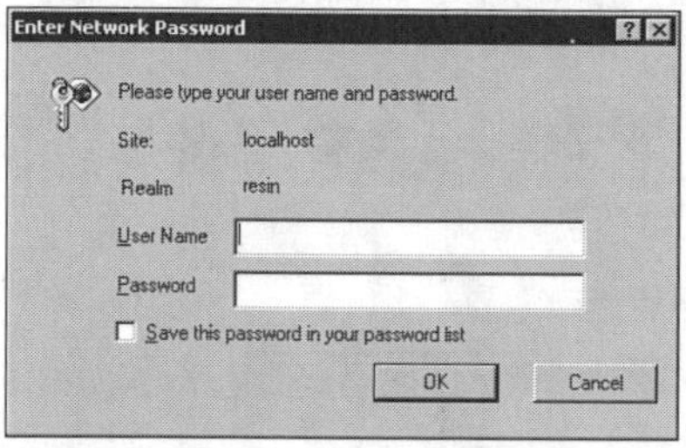

Figure 37.4
The browser prompts for a username and password for basic authentication.

CREATING A CUSTOM LOGIN FORM

When you use the `FORM` authentication method, you must supply a login form to prompt the user for a username and password. The login form must contain form elements named `j_username` and `j_password`. The action in the `<form>` tag must be `j_security_check`. Listing 37.3 shows the HTML source for an example login form.

LISTING 37.3 SOURCE CODE FOR `LoginForm.html`

```
<html>
<body bgcolor="#ffffff">
<center><img src="banner.jpg"></center>
<form action="j_security_check">
<center>
<table border="0">
<tr>
<td><img src="login.jpg"></td>
<td><input type="text" name="j_username"></td>
</tr>
<tr>
<td><img src="password.jpg"></td>
<td><input type="password" name="j_password"></td>
</tr>
</table>
<input type="submit" value="Login!">
</center>
</form>
</body>
</html>
```

Figure 37.5 shows the example login form after the user has tried to access a page that requires authentication.

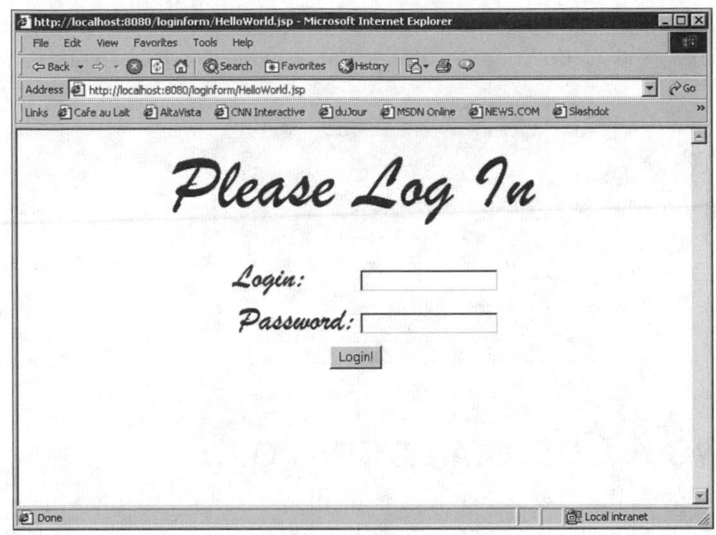

Figure 37.5
You can supply your own custom login form.

You can also create an error page that displays when there is an error in performing the authentication. Listing 37.4 shows a simple error page.

LISTING 37.4 SOURCE CODE FOR `LoginErr.html`

```
<html>
<body bgcolor="#ffffff">
<h1>Sorry</h1>
An error occurred during authorization.
<p>
</body>
</html>
```

Figure 37.6 shows the simple error page in action.

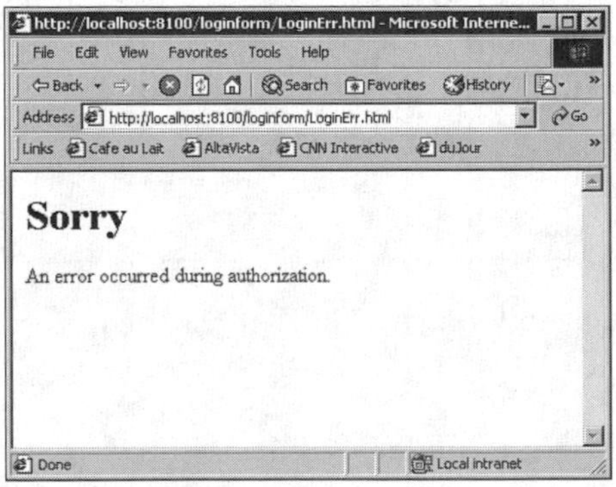

Figure 37.6
You can supply your own custom error page for handling authentication errors.

When you supply your own custom login form, you must supply the name of the login form and the name of the error form inside the <login-config> tag. The <form-login-page> tag specifies the location of the login page, and the <form-error-page> tag specifies the location of the error page. The <form-login-page> and <form-error-page> tags are contained within the <form-login-config> tag.

Listing 37.5 shows the web.xml file for an application with a custom login form.

LISTING 37.5 web.xml FOR THE loginform APPLICATION

```
<!DOCTYPE web-app PUBLIC "-//Sun Microsystems, Inc.//DTD
Web Application 2.2//EN" "http://java.sun.com/j2ee/dtds/web-app_2_2.dtd">
<web-app>
    <display-name>loginform</display-name>
    <description>A test of custom login forms</description>
    <security-constraint>
        <web-resource-collection>
            <web-resource-name>Test</web-resource-name>
            <url-pattern>/*.jsp</url-pattern>
            <http-method>GET</http-method>
            <http-method>POST</http-method>
        </web-resource-collection>
        <user-data-constraint>
            <transport-guarantee>NONE</transport-guarantee>
        </user-data-constraint>
        <auth-constraint>
            <role-name>manager</role-name>
        </auth-constraint>
    </security-constraint>
    <login-config>
        <auth-method>FORM</auth-method>
        <form-login-config>
            <form-login-page>/LoginForm.html</form-login-page>
            <form-error-page>/LoginErr.html</form-error-page>
        </form-login-config>
    </login-config>
</web-app>
```

CHECKING SECURITY ROLES PROGRAMMATICALLY

Role-based authentication is nice when you can partition pages based on a role, but you can rarely make this kind of authentication seamless. Suppose, you want to set up pages that can only be run by someone in a manager role. Obviously you can group the pages into a separate Web resource collection and specify a role name of manager in the <auth-config> tag for the collection. The problem is determining where to put the links to the manager-only pages.

If you put them on a page that everyone can access, the nonmanager users might click the link and see an error page. Although this mechanism does secure your application, it doesn't make it pretty.

Tip A user should never see an error page as part of the normal operation of the site.

Rather than presenting the user with an ugly error page, you can check the user's role programmatically by calling the `isUserInRole` method in the `request` object. For example, in a Java Server Page that links to pages for managers, you might have the following code:

```
<% if (request.isUserInRole("manager")) { %>
<a href="managers/mgrreport.jsp">Manager Report</a>
<a href="managers/personnel.jsp">Personnel Records</a>
<% } %>
```

By checking the user's role in a JSP or servlet, you can customize the Web page to only show the user the items he can access.

If you need the name of the user as it was entered in the authentication form, you can call `getUserPrincipal` in the `request` object.

Listing 37.6 shows the source for a custom tag that lets you specify a required role for all the text contained in the tag body. The beauty of the custom tag is that it is more compact and more readable than using Java code embedded inside `<% %>` tags.

LISTING 37.6 SOURCE CODE FOR RequireRoleTag.java

```
import javax.servlet.jsp.tagext.*;
import javax.servlet.jsp.*;
import javax.servlet.http.*;
import java.util.*;

public class RequireRoleTag extends TagSupport
{
    protected String role = null;

    public int doStartTag()
        throws JspException
    {
        HttpServletRequest request =
            (HttpServletRequest) pageContext.getRequest();

        if ((role != null) && request.isUserInRole(role))
        {
            return EVAL_BODY_INCLUDE;
        }
        else
        {
            return SKIP_BODY;
        }
    }

    public int doEndTag()
    {
        return EVAL_PAGE;
    }
```

```
    public String getRole() { return role; }
    public void setRole(String aRole) { role = aRole; }
}
```

Listing 37.7 shows a Java Server Page that tests the custom tag in Listing 37.6.

Listing 37.7 Source Code for CheckRole.jsp

```
<%@ taglib uri="/rolecheck" prefix="rc" %>
<html>
<body>

<h1>Welcome</h1>

Here are the things you can do:<br>
<a href="complain.jsp">Complain</a><br>
<a href="checkstocks.jsp">Check Your Stocks</a><br>
<a href="clock.jsp">Look At The Clock</a><br>
<rc:require-role role="manager">
    <a href="fire.jsp">Fire Someone At Random</a><br>
    <a href="meeting.jsp">Call A 10-Hour Meeting</a><br>
</rc:require-role>
</body>
</html>
```

Listing 37.8 shows the `rolecheck.tld` file used to define the custom tag library.

Listing 37.8 Source Code for rolecheck.tld

```
<?xml version="1.0"?>
<!DOCTYPE taglib
    PUBLIC "-//Sun Microsystems, Inc.//DTD JSP Tag Library 1.1//EN"
    "http://java.sun.com/j2ee/dtds/web-jsptaglibrary_1_1.dtd">

<taglib>
    <tlibversion>1.0</tlibversion>
    <jspversion>1.1</jspversion>
    <shortname>rolecheck</shortname>
    <uri></uri>
    <info>
        A tag to require a specific authentication role for its body
    </info>

    <tag>
        <name>require-role</name>
        <tagclass>RequireRoleTag</tagclass>
    </tag>
</taglib>
```

Listing 37.9 shows the `web.xml` file that describes the application.

LISTING 37.9 `web.xml` FILE FOR THE `rolecheck` APPLICATION

```
<!DOCTYPE web-app PUBLIC "-//Sun Microsystems, Inc.//DTD Web
Application 2.2//EN" "http://java.sun.com/j2ee/dtds/web-app_2_2.dtd">
<web-app>
    <display-name>authtest</display-name>
    <description>A test of authentication</description>
    <taglib>
        <taglib-uri>/rolecheck</taglib-uri>
        <taglib-location>/WEB-INF/tld/rolecheck.tld</taglib-location>
    </taglib>
    <security-constraint>
        <web-resource-collection>
            <web-resource-name>Test</web-resource-name>
            <url-pattern>/*</url-pattern>
            <http-method>GET</http-method>
            <http-method>POST</http-method>
        </web-resource-collection>
        <user-data-constraint>
            <transport-guarantee>NONE</transport-guarantee>
        </user-data-constraint>
        <auth-constraint>
            <role-name>manager</role-name>
        </auth-constraint>
    </security-constraint>
    <login-config>
        <auth-method>BASIC</auth-method>
    </login-config>
</web-app>
```

CHECKING ROLES FROM AN EJB

An EJB might also check to see whether a user is in a particular role using the `isCallerInRole` method. The `isCallerInRole` method is available in the `EJBContext` class (and thus in `EntityContext` and `SessionContext`). Listing 37.10 shows the `getGreeting` method in the `HelloWorldSession` bean that has been modified to look for managers and enhance the greeting slightly.

LISTING 37.10 `getGreeting` METHOD IN `HelloWorldSessionImpl.java`

```
public String getGreeting()
{
    if (context.isCallerInRole("manager"))
    {
        return "<<< "+greeting+" >>>";
    }
    else
    {
        return greeting;
    }
}
```

Tip

Never hard-code a role name directly into your code (as was done in Listing 37.10). Instead, create a public static final string to hold the value. If you use the string in multiple classes, put the constant in a separate class so you only need to define it once. It's much easier to find errors if the string is in only one place.

The role name you specify in your EJB is *not* the same role name that you configure in your `<assembly-descriptor>` tag (or in your deployment tool). Instead, EJB adds an extra mapping layer that lets you map the coded string to a role that you have configured for deployment. That way, if you deploy the bean in a container where you have assigned different roles, you remap the coded role name to whatever real role name you want. You don't need to rewrite the bean.

Note

You must include a `<security-role-ref>` tag in your `ejb-jar.xml` file to use `isCallerInRole` from within a particular bean. The `<security-role-ref>` tag establishes a logical role name that a deployer must then map to an actual role name in the EJB container.

If you want to find the name of the principal, you can call the `getCallerPrincipal` method in the `EJBContext` class.

USING CLIENT CERTIFICATES FOR AUTHENTICATION

There are at least two ways to use client certificates for authentication, but only one is likely to be supported by most servlet engines. The safest way to do certification authentication is to set the authentication method in the `<auth-method>` tag to `CLIENT-CERT`.

After the client has been authenticated, you can access the `java.security.Principal` object that represents the user by calling `getUserPrincipal`.

Note

Because certificate authentication is rarely used in typical applications, you might have difficulty finding a servlet engine that supports certificate authentication.

Your second option is to not use the normal authentication mechanism and go back to checking authentication manually, like you did in Chapter 5, "Overview of Enterprise JavaBeans." If you use an SSL-enabled servlet engine, you might be able to access the client's certificate by accessing the `javax.servlet.request.X509Certificate` attribute in the `request` object.

The idea is that you keep a database of valid certificate numbers and when a user accesses your site, you check the certificate number against the list of valid numbers. If the numbers match, you allow the user in. Because the certificates are digitally signed by a trusted certificate authority, it is almost impossible to forge a certificate.

Listing 37.11 shows a segment of code that accesses the client's certificate.

LISTING 37.11 CODE TO ACCESS A CLIENT CERTIFICATE

```
    X509Certificate cert = (X509Certificate) request.
        GetAttribute("javax.servlet.request.X509Certificate");

    if (cert != null)
    {
        String serialNumber = cert.getSerialNumber().toString();
        String issuer = cert.getIssuerDN().getName();

// validate the serialNumber/issuer against a valid list here…
    }
```

The serial number alone is not necessarily unique. The serial number is only required to be unique for a single certificate authority. For extra safety, you should check both the serial number and the name of the certificate issuer to make sure that you have the correct certificate.

TROUBLESHOOTING

SERVLET AUTHENTICATION

Why doesn't the servlet engine prompt me for authentication information?

Most likely it's because the servlet engine doesn't support the kind of authentication you want. If the servlet engine doesn't support authentication, you might still be able to user the Web server's authentication if the servlet engine is just acting as a plug-in for a Web server, such as Apache or Netscape. Another possibility is that even though you changed the servlet configuration to require authentication, you might have forgotten to restart the servlet engine to pick up the changes.

CERTIFICATE PROBLEMS

Why doesn't the servlet engine pass me the certificate information when I use SSL?

Very few servlet engines support the certificate attribute. The Java Web Server from Sun does, but as of March 2000, neither JRun, ServletExec, Tomcat, or Resin supported it. When the servlet engine acts as a plug-in to a Web server, you are less likely to get the certificate information because the Web server probably isn't passing the information to the servlet engine in the first place.

EJB PROBLEMS

I defined roles in my `ejb-jar.xml` *file; why doesn't my container recognize them?*

Each container can choose to implement the roles differently, and might require you to perform additional configuration steps to create a role. Consult the documentation for your EJB server to see whether you must perform additional steps.

Why do I get an error when I call `isCallerInRole`?

Most likely, you forgot to use the `<security-role-ref>` tag to define the role in your `ejb-jar.xml` file. You must use this tag whenever you do programmatic role checking in an EJB.

PART VII

DYNAMIC JAVA

CHAPTER 38

Serialization

In this chapter

THE MANY USES OF SERIALIZATION

By now, you should be reasonably familiar with serialization. You know that you mark an object as serializable by implementing `java.io.Serializable`, and that you mark fields as transient when you don't want them to be serialized. Serialization has a lot of features, however, that can help you improve your code and make your system more robust. There are also many interesting ways to use serialization.

STORING OBJECTS IN FILES

There are plenty of times when you need to store data in a file so it's available the next time you run your program. For instance, you might need to save the user's preferences or store the application's state data so the application can start right back where it left off.

You have many options when it comes to writing application data to a file. You can write a simple text file, you can store XML data, you can write out `Properties` objects, and you can serialize the objects. One of the major drawbacks of serialization is that it uses a binary storage format, so you can't edit the serialized data (unless you have a hex editor, a copy of the serialization specification, and a lot of time on your hands). Data items, such as server configuration options and user preferences, are poor choices for serialization because you often want to edit them while the application isn't running.

If you spend a great deal of time computing tables of values every time the program starts, it might be faster to compute them once and serialize them. For example, suppose you need a large table of prime numbers. You can compute the table once, serialize it, and then read it in every time you run the program.

To store an object in a file, you create a `FileOutputStream` and then wrap an `ObjectOutputStream` around it. The `writeObject` method lets you write an object to the stream. Incidentally, the `ObjectOutputStream` class also implements the `DataOutput` interface, so you can write integers, strings, and other data types along with objects.

To read an object from a file, you create a `FileInputStream` and wrap an `ObjectInputStream` around it. The `readObject` method then reads an object from the stream and returns it to you. The `ObjectInputStream` class also implements the methods from `DataInputStream`, so you can read data types other than objects.

Listing 38.1 shows a program that computes all prime numbers under a specific maximum value and serializes them as a `BitSet` object, in which a value of 1 for a bit indicates a prime and a value of 0 indicates a non-prime.

LISTING 38.1 SOURCE CODE FOR `ComputePrimes.java`

```
package usingj2ee.ser;

import java.io.*;
import java.util.*;

public class ComputePrimes
```

```
{
    public static void main(String[] args)
    {
        int maxValue = 0;

        if (args.length < 2)
        {
            System.out.println(
                "Please supply a maximum value and an output filename");
            System.exit(0);
        }

// Allow the user to specify the maximum value on the command line
        try
        {
            maxValue = Integer.parseInt(args[0]);
        }
        catch (Exception exc)
        {
            System.out.println("Invalid maximum value: "+args[0]);
            System.exit(0);
        }

        String outputFilename = args[1];

// Create a BitSet with one bit for every number up to the maximum
        BitSet primes = new BitSet(maxValue);

// Initialize all the bits to 1 (assume everything's a prime to start with)
        for (int i=0; i < maxValue; i++)
        {
            primes.set(i);
        }

// Use the Sieve of Eratosthenes to eliminate non-primes (start at 2,
// mark off all multiples of 2, then proceed to the next number that
// isn't marked off, mark off all its multiples. When you're done, the
// numbers that haven't been marked off are prime).

        for (int i=2; i < maxValue; i++)
        {
// Skip the non-primes
            if (!primes.get(i)) continue;

// Figure out how many multiples there can be
            int max = maxValue / i;

// Clear off the multiples of i
            for (int j=2; j <= max; j++)
            {
                primes.clear(i * j);
            }
        }

// At this point, the bitset contains bit indicating all the primes
// up to the specified maximum. Serialize the bitset to a file.
```

LISTING 38.1 CONTINUED

```
        try
        {
// Create the output stream for serialization
            ObjectOutputStream out = new ObjectOutputStream(
                new FileOutputStream(outputFilename));

// Serialize the object
            out.writeObject(primes);

            out.close();
        }
        catch (Exception exc)
        {
            exc.printStackTrace();
        }
    }
}
```

Now that the `BitSet` of primes is serialized to a file, you can quickly read the table back again without having to recompute the prime table. A table of the primes up to 50,000,000 can take 30 seconds or more to compute on a reasonably fast machine, but you can read in the table in just a few seconds.

Listing 38.2 shows a class that uses the serialized prime `BitSet` to tell you whether a number is prime or not.

LISTING 38.2 SOURCE CODE FOR `Primes.java`

```
package usingj2ee.ser;

import java.io.*;
import java.util.*;

public class Primes
{
    protected BitSet primes;

/** Creates a Primes object from a specific serialized BitSet file */
    public Primes(String primesFile)
        throws IOException
    {
        try
        {
// Open the file containing the BitSet
            ObjectInputStream in = new ObjectInputStream(
                new FileInputStream(primesFile));

// Read the BitSet
            primes = (BitSet) in.readObject();

            in.close();
        }
        catch (ClassNotFoundException exc)
```

```
        {
            throw new IOException("Got exception reading primes file: "+
                exc.toString());
        }
    }

/** Returns the maximum value stored in the table (might or might not be prime) */
    public int getMaxValue()
    {
        return primes.size() - 1;
    }

/** Returns true if i is a prime. If i is larger than the maximum value in
 *  the table, this method throws an exception.
 */
    public boolean isPrime(int i)
    {
        if (i > getMaxValue())
        {
            throw new RuntimeException(
                "Number exceeds maximum prime in table");
        }
        return primes.get(i);
    }
}
```


Listing 38.3 shows an amusing application of prime numbers. Every whole number is either a prime number or a composite number. Remember that a prime number is a number that has no factors other than 1 and itself (you can't divide it by any other numbers but 1 and itself). For example, 2 and 3 are prime, but 4 is composite because $2 \times 2 = 4$. If a number is a composite, then it has a unique set of prime factors that multiply together to create the composite.

In Chapter 33, "Encrypting Data," you saw an encryption example that converted a string to a very large number to encrypt it. The program in Listing 38.3 takes a string, converts it to a large number, and then computes the prime factorization of the string. Now you can impress people at parties by reciting the prime factorization of your name.

LISTING 38.3 SOURCE CODE FOR PrimeFact.java

```
package usingj2ee.ser;

import java.math.*;
import java.util.*;

public class PrimeFact
{
    protected Primes primes;

    public PrimeFact(Primes thePrimes)
    {
        primes = thePrimes;
    }
```

LISTING 38.3 CONTINUED

```
/** Returns a vector of integers containing the prime factorization of N */
    public Vector getFactorization(BigInteger n)
    {
        Vector results = new Vector();

// Start with 2 - the lowest prime
        int factor = 2;

// Get a BigInteger version of 2, as well
        BigInteger bigFactor = BigInteger.valueOf((long) factor);

// Keep dividing N until it reaches 1
        while (!n.equals(BigInteger.ONE))
        {
// Divide N by the current factor and get both the dividend and the remainder
            BigInteger[] divRem = n.divideAndRemainder(bigFactor);

// If the remainder is 0, factor is a prime factor of N
            if (divRem[1].equals(BigInteger.ZERO))
            {
// Add the factor to the list of factors
                results.addElement(new Integer(factor));

// N is now N / factor
                n = divRem[0];
                continue;
            }
            else
            {
// If the remainder isn't 0, factor isn't a prime factor of N, so go
// find the next prime number > factor
                factor = findNextPrime(factor);

// If factor < 0, there are no more factors
                if (factor < 0)
                {
                    throw new RuntimeException(
                        "Can't factor "+n);
                }
// Get a BigInteger version of the factor
                bigFactor = BigInteger.valueOf((long) factor);
            }
        }

        return results;
    }

/** Returns the next prime number > startPrime, or -1 if there are no
 *  more primes in the prime table > startPrime.
 */
    public int findNextPrime(int startPrime)
    {
        startPrime = startPrime + 1;

// Loop through the prime table looking for the next prime
```

```
        while ((startPrime <= primes.getMaxValue()) &&
            !primes.isPrime(startPrime))
        {
            startPrime = startPrime + 1;
        }

// If there are no more primes in the table, return -1
        if (startPrime > primes.getMaxValue())
        {
            return -1;
        }
        else
        {
            return startPrime;
        }
    }

    public static void main(String[] args)
    {
        if (args.length < 2)
        {
            System.out.println(
                "Please supply a primes file and a string to factor.");
            System.exit(0);
        }

        try
        {
// Load the primes table from disk
            Primes primes = new Primes(args[0]);

            String factorMe = args[1];

// Convert the string into a BigInteger
            BigInteger stringVal = new BigInteger(factorMe.getBytes());

// Create a PrimeFact object with the given primes table
            PrimeFact fact = new PrimeFact(primes);

// Get the prime factorization of the string (as a number)
            Vector v = fact.getFactorization(stringVal);

// Print out the string and its associated BigInteger value
            System.out.println("The prime factors of "+factorMe+"("+
                stringVal+") are:");

            Enumeration e = v.elements();

// Create a check value to make sure the factorization is correct
            BigInteger checkValue = BigInteger.ONE;

// Loop through the factors
            while (e.hasMoreElements())
            {
                Integer factor = (Integer) e.nextElement();

// Print out the factor
                System.out.println(factor);
```

LISTING 38.3 CONTINUED

```
// Multiply the check value by the factor
                checkValue = checkValue.multiply(
                    BigInteger.valueOf(factor.longValue()));
            }

// At this point, checkValue contains all the factors multiplied
// together. If everything worked out correctly, when you convert
// checkValue to an array of bytes and then convert the array to
// a string, you should get the original value back.
            String checkString = new String(checkValue.toByteArray());

// Make sure you got the original value back
            if (factorMe.equals(checkString))
            {
                System.out.println("The factors passed the validity check!");
            }
            else
            {
                System.out.println("The factors failed the validity check.");
            }
        }
        catch (Exception exc)
        {
            exc.printStackTrace();
        }
    }
}
```

As Figure 38.1 shows, my wife Cecilia and I have nothing in common—mathematically, at least.

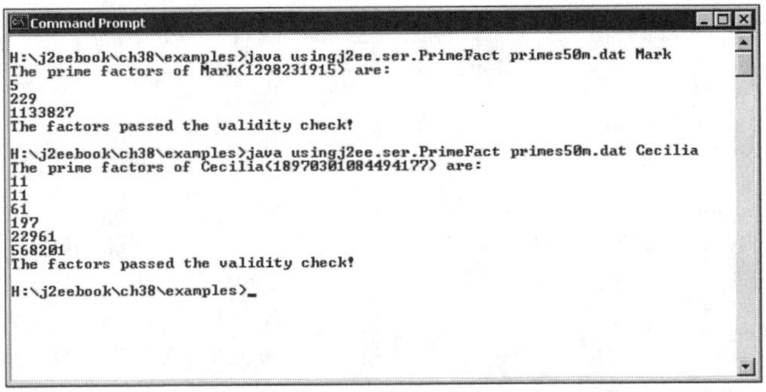

```
Command Prompt

H:\j2eebook\ch38\examples>java usingj2ee.ser.PrimeFact primes50m.dat Mark
The prime factors of Mark(1298231915) are:
5
229
1133827
The factors passed the validity check!

H:\j2eebook\ch38\examples>java usingj2ee.ser.PrimeFact primes50m.dat Cecilia
The prime factors of Cecilia(18970301084494177) are:
11
11
61
197
22961
568201
The factors passed the validity check!

H:\j2eebook\ch38\examples>_
```

Figure 38.1
Thanks to the serialized table of primes, you can perform quick prime factorizations.

SENDING OBJECTS OVER A NETWORK

The `ObjectInputStream` and `ObjectOutputStream` classes are particularly useful for sending objects over a socket connection. RMI, for example, uses object serialization to pass objects from the client to the server and back again.

One thing you should understand about serialization is that it isn't the most efficient way to send data. For example, if you have an object containing two strings and an integer, and you want to send it over a network connection, it's much more efficient to use a `DataOutputStream` and call `writeUTF` to write the strings and `writeInt` to write the integer. The object-serialization routines write out a lot of extra information on top of the actual data in the objects.

There are always trade-offs between runtime efficiency and development time. It might be faster to use `DataOutputStream` at runtime, but it's much easier to develop using `ObjectOutputStream`. It's usually best to go with the solution that's easiest for development unless there is an overriding efficiency requirement.

When you use `ObjectInputStream` and `ObjectOutputStream` for network operations, you must take a few things into consideration. First, `ObjectOutputStream` keeps track of the objects it writes to the stream to make sure it doesn't write an object more than once. Because you'll probably be sending multiple "messages" that might contain the same object, you want to make sure that `ObjectOutputStream` sends the object again. The `reset` method in `ObjectOutputStream` resets the table of sent objects. You should reset the stream before you begin a new set of objects.

Next, the `ObjectOutputStream` class sends the stream header when you first create it. When you create an `ObjectInputStream`, it immediately reads the header. When you set up your client and server, you must flush the `ObjectOutputStream` by invoking the `flush` method. Otherwise, your client and server might never be able to initiate communications. The problem is that the stream header might be buffered, so it doesn't necessarily get sent over the socket connection immediately. As Figure 38.2 shows, you might end up in a deadlock situation, in which the client and server each wait for each other's stream headers.

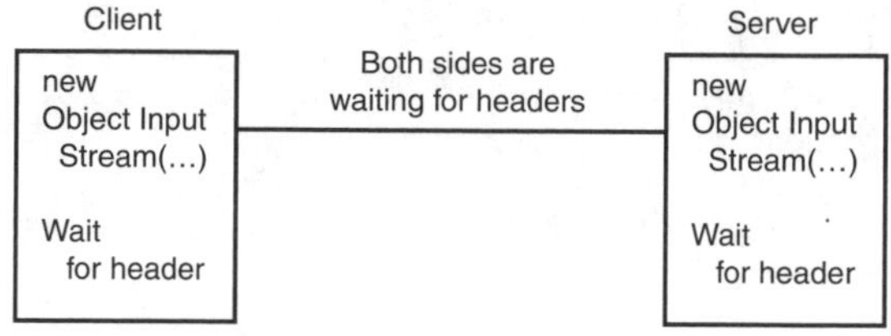

Figure 38.2
If you don't flush the `ObjectOutputStream` after you create it, you could cause a deadlock.

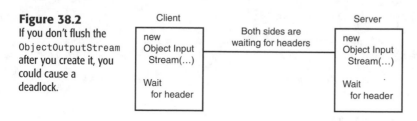

You should also use a `BufferedInputStream` between the `ObjectInputStream` and the input stream returned by the socket's `getInputStream` method. The buffering cuts down on the number of native method calls you make when sending the object. Likewise, you should use a `BufferedOutputStream` between the `ObjectOutputStream` and the socket's output stream. Regardless of whether you use the buffered streams or not, you should invoke the `flush` method whenever you want to make sure the data goes over to the server.

For example, suppose you write a server that accepts three objects, performs some calculations with the objects, and then sends a response. On the client side, you call `writeObject` once for each object and then invoke the `flush` method to make sure the `ObjectOutputStream` sends the three objects over to the server.

You can design a server in many ways: One interesting way is to create a RemoteFunction interface, in which you send objects that implement this interface to the server and the server simply invokes the interface methods on them. The difference between remote-function invocation and remote-method invocation is that you are sending the entire remote function object to the server, whereas remote-method invocation invokes a method on an object that lives on the server.

Listing 38.4 shows a simple RemoteFunction interface.

LISTING 38.4 SOURCE CODE FOR RemoteFunction.java

```
package usingj2ee.ser;

public interface RemoteFunction
{
    public Object invoke();
}
```

Listing 38.5 shows a server that reads RemoteFunction objects from an ObjectInputStream, invokes the remote function, and writes the results back to the client using an ObjectOutputStream.

LISTING 38.5 SOURCE CODE FOR RemoteServer.java

```
package usingj2ee.ser;

import java.io.*;
import java.net.*;

public class RemoteServer implements Runnable
{
// The socket of a client connection
    protected Socket clientSock;

/** Creates a new RemoteServer instance to handle a specific client socket */
    public RemoteServer(Socket aClientSock)
    {
        clientSock = aClientSock;
    }

/** Reads requests from the client socket and executes them */
    public void run()
    {
        try
        {
// Wrap a buffered object output stream around the socket output stream
            ObjectOutputStream objOut = new ObjectOutputStream(
                new BufferedOutputStream(clientSock.getOutputStream()));

// Always flush the ObjectOutputStream after you create it—at least
// if you're doing socket operations.
            objOut.flush();
```

```
// Wrap a buffered object input stream around the socket input stream
            ObjectInputStream objIn = new ObjectInputStream(
                new BufferedInputStream(clientSock.getInputStream()));

            for (;;)
            {
// Read an object, expecting it to implement the RemoteFunction interface
                RemoteFunction func = (RemoteFunction) objIn.readObject();

// Reset the output stream before you send the response to ensure
// that the object will be written to the stream
                objOut.reset();

// Invoke the function object and write its result to the stream
                objOut.writeObject(func.invoke());

// Make sure the stream sends the result back immediately
                objOut.flush();
            }
        }
        catch (EOFException ignoreEof)
        {
        }
        catch (Exception exc)
        {
            exc.printStackTrace();
        }
        finally
        {
// It's easiest to close the socket from a finally clause to make sure
// it gets closed no matter what exception gets thrown
            try
            {
                clientSock.close();
            }
            catch (Exception ignore) {}
        }
    }

    public static void main(String[] args)
    {
        try
        {
// Get the port number to listen on, use 4321 as a default
            String portNumStr = System.getProperty("port", "4321");

            int portNumber = Integer.parseInt(portNumStr);

// Create the server socket to listen on the port
            ServerSocket sock = new ServerSocket(portNumber);

            for (;;)
            {

// Accept an incoming client connection
                Socket clientSock = sock.accept();
```

LISTING 38.5 CONTINUED

```
// Create a handler to talk to the client
                RemoteServer clientHandler = new RemoteServer(clientSock);

// Create a thread to execute the handler and start it
                (new Thread(clientHandler)).start();
            }
        }
        catch (Exception exc)
        {
            exc.printStackTrace();
        }
    }
}
```

The interesting thing about the RemoteServer class is that it has no idea what the remote functions do; it just invokes the functions and returns the results. You can expand the server's capabilities just by adding new types of function classes. Listing 38.6 shows a simple Hello function that prints "Hello" to the server's console.

LISTING 38.6 SOURCE CODE FOR RemoteHello.java

```
package usingj2ee.ser;

public class RemoteHello implements java.io.Serializable, RemoteFunction
{
    public RemoteHello()
    {
    }

    public Object invoke()
    {
        System.out.println("Hello!");

        return null;
    }
}
```

Listing 38.7 shows a slightly more complicated remote function that prints a message to the server's console and then returns the server's host name.

LISTING 38.7 SOURCE CODE FOR RemotePrint.java

```
package usingj2ee.ser;

public class RemotePrint implements java.io.Serializable,
RemoteFunction
{
    protected String message;

    public RemotePrint()
    {
    }
```

```
    public RemotePrint(String aMessage)
    {
        message = aMessage;
    }

    public Object invoke()
    {
        System.out.println(message);

// Return the name of the host where the message was printed, or "Unknown"
// if you can't determine the host name
        try
        {
            return java.net.InetAddress.getLocalHost().getHostName();
        }
        catch (java.net.UnknownHostException exc)
        {
            return "Unknown";
        }
    }
}
```


Finally, Listing 38.8 shows a client program that sends some remote functions to the server and then prints the results returned from the functions.

LISTING 38.8 SOURCE CODE FOR RemoteClient.java

```
package usingj2ee.ser;

import java.io.*;
import java.net.*;

public class RemoteClient
{
    public static void main(String[] args)
    {
        try
        {
// Get the port number of the server, use 4321 as a default
            String portNumStr = System.getProperty("port", "4321");

            int portNumber = Integer.parseInt(portNumStr);

// Get the host name of the server, use "localhost" as a default
            String host = System.getProperty("host", "localhost");

// Create a socket connection to the server
            Socket sock = new Socket(host, portNumber);

// Wrap a buffered object output stream around the socket's output stream
            ObjectOutputStream objOut = new ObjectOutputStream(
                new BufferedOutputStream(sock.getOutputStream()));

// Make sure you flush the new ObjectOutputStream if you're doing
// socket communications
```

LISTING 38.8 CONTINUED

```
            objOut.flush();

// Wrap a buffered object input stream around the socket's input stream
            ObjectInputStream objIn = new ObjectInputStream(
                new BufferedInputStream(sock.getInputStream()));

// Create a new RemoteHello function object and send it to the server
            objOut.writeObject(new RemoteHello());

// Flush the stream to make sure the server gets the object now
            objOut.flush();

// Read the result back from the server (if you don't flush the stream
// before this point, your program could hang here because the RemoteHello
// object could still be sitting in the buffer waiting to go to the server,
// and the server would never see it and would never send a response for you
// to read right here.)
            Object result = objIn.readObject();

// Reset the output stream to make the stream forget about the objects
// it has already written
            objOut.reset();

// Create a new RemoteFunction object and write it
            objOut.writeObject(
                new RemotePrint("This is a message from the client"));

// Always flush at the end of a request
            objOut.flush();

// Read the response from the server
            result = objIn.readObject();

// Print out the response
            System.out.println("Sent a message to "+result);

            sock.close();
        }
        catch (Exception exc)
        {
            exc.printStackTrace();
        }
    }
}
```

Although the remote function invocation technique might be useful in some situations, it has some drawbacks. The biggest drawback is that the function objects have server-specific code. If the server has special libraries that the remote function needs to call, those libraries must be present on the client even if they aren't used there, because the client must be able to create an instance of the function object.

STORING OBJECTS IN A DATABASE

One of the difficulties in marrying object-oriented languages with relational databases is that relational databases tend to be rather flat. If you want to show that one object can contain several instances of another object, the relational database requires you to set up multiple tables and create relationships between the tables.

Instead of a relational database, you might opt for an object database that understands the nature of object relationships and can store objects efficiently while still providing query capabilities. Although object databases have gained some popularity, they haven't reached the same acceptability level as relational databases, such as Oracle, Informix, DB2, and SQL Server. Some relational databases even provide some object database features, although not to the level that most object databases do.

You can store Java objects as serialized BLOBs in a relational database as long as the database supports BLOBs (Binary Large Objects). You can't perform queries against the data in the BLOB, but at least you have a centralized place to store the data.

Why would you want to store a Java object in a BLOB rather than using the relational structure? When you have complex objects, the relational structure can be cumbersome. For large volumes of data spread across many tables, it might not be feasible to reconstruct an object using queries every time the user wants an object. For example, suppose you are writing a program to plan conventions. A particular convention has a list of attendees, room vacancies, and various events. You have a call center of people who handle convention bookings, and these people can't afford to wait five minutes for you to gather all the database information for a specific meeting.

You decide to store some of the meeting information in a BLOB, although you still keep the data in the relational tables, too. The idea is that the BLOB acts like a data cache. Every night (or at least at some scheduled period of time), a program takes the data from the BLOB and stores it back to database tables for reporting purposes.

There might be items in the BLOB that you still want to query for. You can create additional database columns in the database row where you store the BLOB. For instance, you might want the convention date, the convention name, and the client name (the company holding the convention) stored in columns that you can query against.

Of course, for a large convention, a single BLOB is unwieldy. You don't want to retrieve and save 50MB of data every time someone signs up for a convention. You must consider what data you want to cache in a BLOB and what data you can still keep in relational tables (or in separate BLOBs).

Listing 38.9 shows the SQL command used to create the simplified convention database.

LISTING 38.9 SOURCE CODE FOR `create_conventions.sql`

```
create table conventions
(
    name varchar(40) not null primary key,
```

LISTING 38.9 CONTINUED

```
    client varchar(40),
    start_date DATE,
    end_date DATE,
    convention BLOB
);
```

Listing 38.10 shows a program that reads and writes a BLOB using serialization. Notice how it uses a `ByteArrayOutputStream` to create a byte array representing the object.

LISTING 38.10 SOURCE CODE FOR `UpdateAttendees.java`

```
package usingj2ee.ser;
import java.sql.*;
import java.util.*;
import java.io.*;

public class UpdateAttendees
{
    public static void main(String[] args)
    {
        try
        {
// Make sure the DriverManager knows about the driver
            Class.forName("oracle.jdbc.driver.OracleDriver").newInstance();

// Create a connection to the database
            Connection conn = DriverManager.getConnection(
                "jdbc:oracle:thin:@flamingo:1521:j2eebook",
                    "j2eeuser", "j2eepass");

// Turn off auto-commit so you can execute multiple statements
// in a single transaction
            conn.setAutoCommit(false);

// Grab the convention from the database
            PreparedStatement stmt = conn.prepareStatement(
                "SELECT convention from conventions where name=?");
            stmt.setString(1, "Java-oni");

            ResultSet results = stmt.executeQuery();

            if (!results.next())
            {
                System.out.println("Can't find the convention.");
                System.exit(0);
            }

// Get the blob containing the convention data
            Blob blob = results.getBlob("convention");

// Create an ObjectInputStream to read the blob
            ObjectInputStream objIn = new ObjectInputStream(
                blob.getBinaryStream());
```

```
// Read the blob
            Convention conv = (Convention) objIn.readObject();

            stmt.close();

// Add an attendee to the convention list
            conv.attendees.addElement("Mark Wutka");

// Create a statement to update the convention
            stmt = conn.prepareStatement(
                "update conventions set convention=? where name=?");

// Store the object into a byte array by first writing to
// a ByteArrayOutputStream
            ByteArrayOutputStream byteOut = new ByteArrayOutputStream();
            ObjectOutputStream objOut = new ObjectOutputStream(
                byteOut);
            objOut.writeObject(conv);

// Store the blob as an array of bytes
            stmt.setBytes(1, byteOut.toByteArray());
            stmt.setString(2, conv.name);

            if (stmt.executeUpdate() == 1)
            {
                System.out.println("Updated convention attendee list");
            }
            else
            {
                System.out.println("Update failed.");
            }

// Commit the database transaction
            conn.commit();

            conn.close();

// List out the attendees for the convention
            Enumeration e = conv.attendees.elements();

            System.out.println("The attendees are:");

            while (e.hasMoreElements())
            {
                System.out.println(e.nextElement());
            }
        }
        catch (Exception exc)
        {
            exc.printStackTrace();
        }
    }
}
```

CUSTOMIZING SERIALIZATION

Most of the time, you will probably be happy with the default serialization mechanism. Sometimes, however, you might need to change the way an object writes itself to a stream and reads itself from a stream.

To create a custom serialization routine for your object, create your own implementations of `writeObject` and `readObject`. The `writeObject` method is declared as the following:

```
private void writeObject(ObjectOutputStream out)
    throws IOException
```

Note

The `writeObject` and `readObject` methods are somewhat peculiar because the method signature must be exact. You can't change the access modifier–it must be `private`. The serialization API only recognizes these methods if they exactly match the documented specification.

You can choose to write out whatever data you want. You have a choice when you implement `writeObject` of whether you want to write out all the fields yourself or just add extra data on top of what would normally be written if you didn't implement `writeObject`.

Call `defaultWriteObject` to perform the normal serialization before you write any additional data. For example, the following `writeObject` method adds an additional string to the regular serialization contents:

```
public void writeObject(ObjectOutputStream out)
    throws IOException
{
    out.defaultWriteObject();
    out.writeUTF("This is an extra string");
}
```

Obviously, if you change the way you write objects, you must also change the way you read objects. The `readObject` method is declared as the following:

```
private void readObject(ObjectInputStream in)
    throws IOException, ClassNotFoundException
```

If you want to read the normal serialization data, you can call `defaultReadObject`. Otherwise, you must handle all the deserialization yourself. Make sure that you read data in the same order you wrote it in the `writeObject` method.

The following routine deserializes an object that has an extra string after the normal serialized data:

```
public void readObject(ObjectInputStream in)
    throws IOException, ClassNotFoundException
{
    in.defaultReadObject();
    String extra = in.readUTF();
}
```

You can also replace an object with another object when you serialize or deserialize it. If you want to substitute a different object when you serialize an object, implement the `writeReplace` method:

```
private Object writeReplace()
    throws ObjectStreamException
```

You can declare `writeReplace` with any access modifier (`private`, `protected`, `public`).

Note

The serialization routines look for `writeReplace` before calling `writeObject`, so you don't need to worry about accidentally writing out two objects.

To replace a deserialized object with another object, declare the `readResolve` method:

```
private Object readResolve()
    throws ObjectStreamException
```

As with `writeReplace`, you can use any access modifier.

Note

The serialization routines call `readResolve` after `readObject`, so you can be sure that the object has been deserialized when `readResolve` is called.

The object you return from `writeReplace` and `readResolve` must be compatible with the original object type.

One of the places you use both the custom `readObject`/`writeObject` methods as well as the `readResolve` method is in Java enumerated type classes. Unlike Pascal, C, and C++, Java doesn't support *enumerated types* (a type that can only have a few certain values). One of the common design patters for enumerated types in Java has been to create a class with a private constructor and then create public static final instances of the class that represent each enumeration value.

Because there can only be a single object instance for any particular enumerated value, you can use two equal signs (==) to compare values.

Listing 38.11 shows a sample enumerated type.

LISTING 38.11 SOURCE CODE FOR `SimpleEnum.java`

```
package usingj2ee.ser;

public class SimpleEnum
{
    public static final SimpleEnum MOE = new SimpleEnum(1);
    public static final SimpleEnum LARRY = new SimpleEnum(2);
    public static final SimpleEnum CURLY = new SimpleEnum(3);

    private int typeCode;
```

LISTING 38.11 CONTINUED

```
    private SimpleEnum(int aTypeCode)
    {
        typeCode = aTypeCode;
    }

    public int getTypeCode()
    {
        return typeCode;
    }

    public boolean equals(Object ob)
    {
        if (ob == this) return true;
        if ((ob == null) || !(ob instanceof SimpleEnum)) return false;
        SimpleEnum other = (SimpleEnum) ob;
        if (typeCode == other.typeCode) return true;
        return false;
    }
}
```

The `SimpleEnum` class works well in a normal application. You can make declarations like this:

```
SimpleEnum foo = SimpleEnum.MOE;
```

You can also make comparisons such as the following:

```
if (foo == SimpleEnum.MOE)
```

Normally, you don't compare objects with `==`, but in the case of the enumerated types, because you manage the object instances, you can use `==` safely.

Unfortunately, object serialization throws a wrench into the enumerated types, because when you deserialize an enumerated type, it's a different object from any of the static values. In other words, when you deserialize an object with the same typecode as `SimpleEnum.MOE`, it becomes a different object from the original `MOE`, and the `==` comparison fails.

All you need to do, however, is implement the `readResolve` method to convert a deserialized object back into one of the static values.

The `SimpleEnum` enumerated type doesn't implement an additional type description, but many other enumerated type implementations do. Although it's nice to use numeric type codes, you sometimes need to print out a string version of the type as well. The additional text field doesn't do any harm, but if you use the type codes a lot, you should use `readObject` and `writeObject` to make the storage a little more efficient by only reading and writing the type code. Because you are resolving the object back into one of the static values anyway, the description value you read in would go to waste anyway.

Listing 38.12 shows an example enumerated type from a Java DTD parser program. It uses `readObject` and `writeObject` to eliminate the description from the serialized object, and `readResolve` to make sure the enumerated types work correctly when you deserialize an object.

LISTING 38.12 SOURCE CODE FOR DTDCardinal.java

```
package com.wutka.dtd;

import java.io.*;

/** Represents the various cardinality values for a DTD item.
 * <bl>
 * <li>NONE indicates no cardinality</li>
 * <li>OPTIONAL indicates an optional value (specified by ?)</li>
 * <li>ZEROMANY indicates zero-to-many values (specified by *)</li>
 * <li>ONEMANY indicates an one-to-many values (specified by +)</li>
 * </bl>
 *
 * @author Mark Wutka
 */
public class DTDCardinal implements Serializable
{
/** Indicates no cardinality (implies a single object) */
    public static final DTDCardinal NONE = new DTDCardinal(0, "NONE");

/** Indicates that an item is optional (zero-to-one) */
    public static final DTDCardinal OPTIONAL = new DTDCardinal(1, "OPTIONAL");

/** Indicates that there can be zero-to-many occurrences of an item */
    public static final DTDCardinal ZEROMANY = new DTDCardinal(2, "ZEROMANY");

/** Indicates that there can be one-to-many occurrences of an item */
    public static final DTDCardinal ONEMANY = new DTDCardinal(3, "ONEMANY");

    public int type;
    public String name;

    public DTDCardinal(int aType, String aName)
    {
            type = aType;
            name = aName;
    }

    public boolean equals(Object ob)
    {
        if (ob == this) return true;
        if (!(ob instanceof DTDCardinal)) return false;

        DTDCardinal other = (DTDCardinal) ob;
        if (other.type == type) return true;
        return false;
    }

/** Writes the notation for this cardinality value */
    public void write(PrintWriter out)
        throws IOException
    {
        if (this == NONE) return;
        if (this == OPTIONAL)
        {
            out.print("?");
```

Listing 38.12 Continued

```
            }
            else if (this == ZEROMANY)
            {
                out.print("*");
            }
            else if (this == ONEMANY)
            {
                out.print("+");
            }
        }

/** Custom serialization to only write out the type code */
        private void writeObject(ObjectOutputStream out)
            throws IOException
        {
            out.writeInt(type);
        }

/** Custom serialization to only read the type code */
        private void readObject(ObjectInputStream in)
            throws IOException
        {
            type = in.readInt();
        }

/** Custom serialization to replace an incoming object with one of the
  * static object values. */
        private DTDCardinal readResolve()
            throws ObjectStreamException
        {
            if (type == NONE.type)
            {
                return NONE;
            }
            else if (type == OPTIONAL.type)
            {
                return OPTIONAL;
            }
            else if (type == ZEROMANY.type)
            {
                return ZEROMANY;
            }
            else if (type == ONEMANY.type)
            {
                return ONEMANY;
            }
            else
            {
                throw new StreamCorruptedException(
                    "Invalid DTDCardinal type found in input stream");
            }
        }
}
```

If you want even more control over object serialization, you can use the `Externalizable` interface instead of `Serializable`. The `Externalizable` interface extends `Serializable`, but adds methods that allow you to completely control an object's external format:

```
public interface Externalizable extends Serializable
{
    public void writeExternal(ObjectOutput out)
        throws IOException;
    public void readExternal(ObjectInput in)
        throws IOException, java.lang.ClassNotFoundException;
}
```

When an object implements the `Externalizable` interface, its `writeExternal` and `readExternal` methods must perform all the serialization tasks for the object; you can't rely on a default implementation as you can when you use `writeObject` and `readObject`.

DEALING WITH MULTIPLE VERSIONS

One of the more frustrating aspects of serialization is in the area of versioning. If you serialize a class, change it, and then try to deserialize the old data into an object with the new class definition, the deserialization will fail. Although there might be many cases in which you want it to fail, there's a pretty good chance that you really wanted to read the old data, ignoring any fields that aren't there, and using default initialization values for the fields that are there.

When the serialization libraries write out a serialized object, they first compute a serialization version number called the serial version UID. The version number is a hash value computed from the various methods and member variables in the class. Because the version number includes the method names and types as part of its calculation, you make your class incompatible with previous versions just by changing the type on a single method. That's pretty annoying considering the fact that you haven't changed the data at all.

The Java serialization specification carefully spells out the procedure the serialization routines use when resolving version differences, even though the slightest change in a class definition creates incompatible version. The trick is, there's a way to tell Java not to treat a new version as incompatible with the old one. You must define a variable called `serialVersionUID` to declare that this version of a class is compatible with a previous version.

For example, suppose you have serialized many instances of a particular class and you now want to update the class. Before you do, run the `serialver` program to get the original `serialVersionUID` for the class:

```
serialver usingj2ee.ser.Convention
```

The `serialver` program prints out a declaration for the `serialVersionUID` program you should add to the class definition. For example

```
static final long serialVersionUID = -3778671264112558151L;
```

If you add this declaration to the `Convention` class and then change the `Convention` class, you can still deserialize the previous version of the class because they will have the same `serialVersionUID`.

If a class contains its own `serialVersionUID`, Java doesn't perform its normal computation for the version number. It just uses the value you supplied. In other words, you can specify the `serialVersionUID` as the following:

```
static final long serialVersionUID = 1234L;
```

When Java tries to read an older version of an object, it ignores any fields that were present in the old version and not present in the new version. If there are fields in the new version of the object that aren't in the old version, the values are initialized to the normal defaults (zero or `null`).

TROUBLESHOOTING

VERSIONING PROBLEMS

All I did was change a method; why can't I deserialize my data anymore?

Any change to a class makes it incompatible with the previous version unless you use the `serialVersionUID` field.

NETWORKING PROBLEMS

Why won't my client and server talk to each other when using object streams?

You must make absolutely sure that you flush the `ObjectOutputStream` after you create it (before you write any data). It writes some header information that the `ObjectInputStream` constructor tries to read.

CHAPTER 39

REFLECTION

In this chapter

WHAT IS REFLECTION?

The Java Reflection API gives you a way to examine objects at runtime as well as dynamically update fields and invoke methods. Although Reflection is useful in a few places in day-to-day application programming, most of the common uses of Reflection are in the area of middleware tools. For example, the TOPLink database-mapping tool uses Reflection to copy database values into Java objects and vice-versa. Reflection isn't hard to use, and it's extremely powerful.

EXAMINING OBJECTS AT RUNTIME

The Reflection classes, for the most part, represent parts of a class. The main classes, found in the `java.lang.reflect` package, are `Field`, `Method`, `Constructor`, `Modifier`, and `Array`. There are also some other support classes that you will learn about shortly. You access the Reflection classes through a `Class` object, which you can get by calling either `Class.forName` or `getClass` on an object.

Listing 39.1 defines a simple `Person` class that can be used to demonstrate Reflection.

LISTING 39.1 SOURCE CODE FOR Person.java

```
package usingj2ee.reflect;

public class Person implements java.io.Serializable
{
    public String firstName;
    public String middleName;
    public String lastName;


    public Person()
    {
    }

    public Person(String aFirstName, String aMiddleName,
        String aLastName)
    {
        firstName = aFirstName;
        middleName = aMiddleName;
        lastName = aLastName;
    }

    public String getFirstName()
    {
        return firstName;
    }

    public void setFirstName(String theFirstName)
       {
        firstName = theFirstName;
    }
```

```
    public String getMiddleName()
    {
        return middleName;
    }

    public void setMiddleName(String theMiddleName)
    {
        middleName = theMiddleName;
    }

    public String getLastName()
    {
        return lastName;
    }

    public void setLastName(String theLastName)
    {
        lastName = theLastName;
    }

    public String toString()
    {
        StringBuffer buff = new StringBuffer();

        if (firstName != null)
        {
            buff.append(firstName);
            buff.append(' ');
        }

        if (middleName != null)
        {
            buff.append(middleName);
            buff.append(' ');
        }

        if (lastName != null)
        {
            buff.append(lastName);
        }

        return buff.toString();
    }
}
```


ACCESSING FIELDS

To access the fields in a `Person` object, you can create a new `Person`, call `getClass`, and then call `getFields` or `getDeclaredFields`.

Note

Reflection distinguishes between methods/fields declared in the actual class versus methods/fields that are inherited from superclasses. If you want only the methods/fields from the current class, call `getDeclaredFields` or `getDeclaredMethods`. To include all inherited fields and methods, use `getFields` and `getMethods`.

The Field class has methods to get and set values for each of the primitive data types (getByte, getChar, setInt, setDouble, and so on) as well as a generic get and set to store and retrieve objects. If you use the plain get and set methods, you can still store primitive data values by using the object version of the primitive type. In other words, calling set and passing an Integer object is the same thing as calling setInt (assuming the field is an int and not an Integer).

When you use the get and set methods in a Field object, you must specify the object you want to access. Remember, you get the list of fields from a Class object, which describes all instances of the class, not a specific object. A Field object doesn't refer to a specific data object. Of course, the good part is that you can use the same Field object to manipulate several different objects.

You can reuse a Field object, but not to manipulate a field in a different class (unless it's a subclass). In other words, just because two classes have a string field called firstName, you cannot use the same Field object to update fields in both classes.

Listing 39.2 shows a program that prints out the field values from a Person object.

LISTING 39.2 SOURCE CODE FOR ShowPersonFields.java

```
package usingj2ee.reflect;

import java.lang.reflect.*;

public class ShowPersonFields
{
    public static void main(String[] args)
    {
        try
        {
// Create an instance of Person with some initial data values
            Person person = new Person("Samantha", "Lauren", "Tippin");

// Get the Person class
            Class personClass = person.getClass();

// Get only the fields declared in the Person class (that is, the ones
// declared in Person.java)
            Field[] personFields = personClass.getDeclaredFields();

// Loop through the fields
            for (int i=0; i < personFields.length; i++)
            {
// Get the name of the field
                String fieldName = personFields[i].getName();

// Get the field value (they're all String in this example)
                String fieldValue = (String) personFields[i].get(person);

// Print out the field name and field value
                System.out.println(fieldName+"="+fieldValue);
            }
```

```
        }
        catch (Exception exc)
        {
            exc.printStackTrace();
        }
    }
}
```

Figure 39.1 shows the output from the `ShowPersonFields` program.

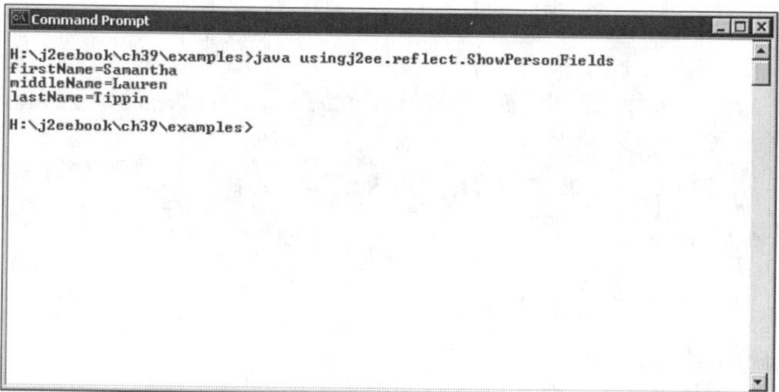

Figure 39.1 You can extract field values using the `Field` class.

The `getType` method in the `Field` class returns the `Class` object that describes the field type. For example, if a field contains a string, the `getType` returns the `Class` object for `java.lang.String`, which is the same class you would get if you called `java.lang.String.class`—which itself is shorthand for `Class.forName("java.lang.String")`.

Obviously, Java needs a way to tell you that a field contains a primitive type, such as `int`. It can't return `Integer.class` because you wouldn't be able to tell the difference between an `int` field and an `Integer` field. Java solves the problem by defining a special `TYPE` field on each of the wrapper classes (`Byte`, `Character`, `Integer`, and so on). This `TYPE` field returns a `Class` object representing the primitive type that the object wraps. In other words, if you need the corresponding `Class` object for `int`, use `Integer. TYPE`.

Tip

You can also use the `.class` notation on native types to retrieve the `Class` object for that type. In other words, `int.class` returns the same object as `Integer.TYPE`.

In addition to using the `getFields` and `getDeclaredFields` methods, you can locate a field by calling `getField` or `getDeclaredField` and passing the name of the field you are looking for. For example, to get the `firstName` `Field` in the `Person` object, call

```
Field fn = Person.class.getDeclaredField("firstName");
```

Accessing Methods

Invoking methods is a little more complicated than accessing fields because you must pass parameters. The `Method` class contains an `invoke` method that takes an `Object` (the object whose method you are invoking) and an array of `Objects` representing the parameters you are passing to the method:

```
public Object invoke(Object target, Object[] params)
```

If you want to pass a native type (such as `int`) as a parameter, use the corresponding object wrapper (such as `Integer`). If the method doesn't take any parameters, pass an empty array for the `params`, *not* `null`!

To invoke a static method, pass `null` as the target.

Listing 39.3 shows a program that invokes the `get` methods in the `Person` object by using Reflection.

LISTING 39.3 SOURCE CODE FOR InvokePersonGets.java

```
package usingj2ee.reflect;

import java.lang.reflect.*;

public class InvokePersonGets
{
    public static void main(String[] args)
    {
        try
        {
// Create an instance of Person with some initial data values
            Person person = new Person("Kaitlynn", "Dawn", "Tippin");

// Get the Person class
            Class personClass = person.getClass();

// Get only the methods declared in the Person class (that is, the ones
// declared in Person.java)
            Method[] personMethods = personClass.getDeclaredMethods();

// Loop through the methods
            for (int i=0; i < personMethods.length; i++)
            {
// Get the name of the method
                String methodName = personMethods[i].getName();

// If it isn't a get method, skip it
                if (!methodName.startsWith("get")) continue;

// Invoke the method with no parameters and get the method result
                String methodValue =
                    (String) personMethods[i].invoke(person,
                        new Object[0]);

// Print out the method name and method value
                System.out.println(methodName+"="+methodValue);
            }
        }
        catch (Exception exc)
```

```
        {
            exc.printStackTrace();
        }
    }
}
```

Figure 39.2 shows the output from the `InvokePersonGets` program.

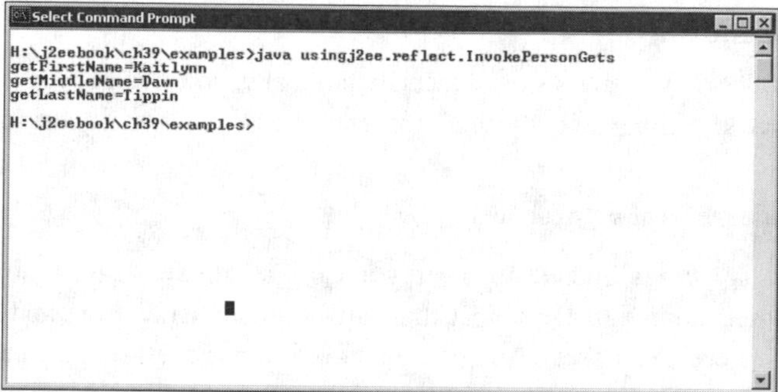

Figure 39.2
You can dynamically invoke methods using Reflection.

You can locate methods by name just like you can with fields, but it's a little tougher because you must also specify the method signature. When you call `getMethod` or `getDeclaredMethod`, you not only pass the method name but also an array of `Class` objects representing the data type of each parameter. For example, to locate the `setLastName` in the `Person` class, you use the following call:

```
Method m = Person.class.getMethod("setLastName",
    new Class[1] { String.class } );
```

If the `new Class[1] { String.class }` syntax looks a little strange to you, it's a way to create and initialize an array without creating a separate variable.

Tip

There's no shorthand way to get the class representing an array. For instance, there's no trick to getting a class for `String[]`. You must use `Class.forName` using a string of the form `[L`*`classname`*`;`. For example, to get the class for an array of strings, use `Class.forName("[Ljava.lang.String;")`. This format is just the way Java represents arrays when it creates `.class` files. This is probably the only situation in which you ever need to use this notation.

Accessing Constructors

A `Constructor` object is like a `Method` object, except you don't invoke it on an object; instead, you just use its `newInstance` method to create a new object. You can use the `getConstructors` and `getDeclaredConstructors` methods to locate all the available constructors, or you can call `getConstructor` or `getDeclaredConstructor` and pass an array of `Class` objects describing the types of the parameters a desired constructor accepts.

For example, the Person object has a constructor that takes three strings. You can locate and use this constructor using the following code:

```
Constructor c = Person.class.getDeclaredConstructor(
    new Class[] { String.class, String.class, String.class });

Person p = (Person) c.newInstance(
    new Object[] { "Samantha", "Lauren", "Tippin" });
```

WORKING WITH ARRAYS

If you need to work with arrays of objects dynamically, you need a way to create an array of objects without knowing the data type until runtime. You normally create an array of objects like this:

```
Integer[] numbers = new Integer[20];
```

If all you have is a Class object, however, you can't create an array of objects—there's no newInstance method in a Class object that can create an array. Fortunately, the Array class makes it easy to create an array. You call the newInstance method and pass the Class of the new array's data type and either an int containing the array size, or an array of int values containing the sizes for each dimension of a multidimensional array.

You can create a Person array this way:

```
Person[] p = (Person[]) Array.newInstance(Person.class, 10);
```

Normally, you work with the array as just an Object, because at compile time you don't know the actual data type—you discover the type at runtime. Working with an array as an Object complicates what you need to do to manipulate its elements. Because the array Object might hold primitives or objects of any type, there are methods in the Array class that let you get and set values of various types. The get and set methods let you get and set object values:

```
public static Object get(Object array, int index)
public static void set(Object array, int index, Object value)
```

The Array class also has methods, such as getInt, setInt, getDouble, setDouble, and so on, for setting native type values.

SUPPRESSING ACCESS RESTRICTIONS

There are times when your Reflection code must access private and protected members of another class. Although that sounds like a violation of good object-oriented principles, it's actually a reasonable thing to do when you're writing a library that does data mapping (such as serialization or object-to-relational mapping).

The reason you normally create access restrictions is to keep other classes from becoming dependent on parts of your class that are implementation specific. For example, if you use a counter to keep track of the number of items in an order, you're better off creating a getItemCount method rather than exposing the counter to any client classes. Otherwise, you'd be obligated to keep the counter, even if you store the order items in a data structure such as a vector that automatically maintains the count.

If you're writing a database-mapping library, however, you aren't building-in any dependencies on specific parts of another class. That is, if someone changes the implementation of a class so it no longer uses a counter variable, the database mapping code doesn't care, although the mapping configuration might need to change. The same goes for serialization. If you remove a field from a class, you don't break the serialization code; it can still read and write your objects. Relaxing the access restrictions for these types of libraries doesn't break the notion of encapsulation.

As a matter of fact, allowing a library to circumvent the access restrictions actually *helps* maintain encapsulation. You as an application developer don't have to create any special access methods to allow the library to access your private data, nor do you have to declare your fields as public when you prefer not to.

For example, suppose you have this simple class:

```
public class MyData
{
    protected String myName;
    protected String myPassword;

    public String getMyName() { return myName; }
    public void setMyName(String aName)
    {
        myName = aName;
    }

    public boolean verifyPassword(String aPassword)
    {
        if (aPassword.equals(myPassword)) return true;
        return false;
    }
}
```


You don't define any accessor methods for the `myPassword` field because you don't want external users to see it. Now, suppose you create a database-mapping library that uses Reflection to copy data between Java objects and a relational database. If you can't relax the access restrictions, you must declare the `myPassword` as public, create accessor methods, or not store the password in the database. In other words, either you break encapsulation or you don't use the mapping library—not very good choices.

To turn off access checking, call `setAccessible(true)` on any `Field`, `Method`, or `Constructor` you want to use. You can also use the static version of `setAccessible` to change the access flag on an array of objects (for instance, the array of `Fields` returned by `getFields`):

```
public void setAccessible(AccessibleObject[] objects,
    boolean relaxAccessRestrictions)
```

The `Field`, `Method`, and `Constructor` classes are all subclasses of `AccessibleObject`, which exists specifically for controlling access restrictions. If your code is subject to security restrictions (for example, if you're running an applet), you'll need permission from the security system before you can change the access restriction.

Also, keep in mind that changing the access restrictions on an instance of `Field` doesn't change the access restrictions for another instance of the same `Field`. In other words, you don't have to worry that relaxing the restrictions on your `Field` object will also affect another `Field` object that refers to the same field. Relaxing the access restrictions on a `Field` (or any other object) doesn't affect the way classes normally access the field. For example, if you called `getField("firstName")` and then called `setAccessible(true)` on the `Field` object, if another object tried to access the `firstName` field directly (assuming that it's private), the other object is *still prohibited* from accessing the field. Again, the accessible flag affects only the `Field` object you're working with.

Listing 39.4 shows a program that relaxes the access restrictions on a class called `PrivatePerson`, which is just like the `Person` class from Listing 39.1 except that all the fields are private.

LISTING 39.4 SOURCE CODE FOR `ShowPrivateFields.java`

```
package usingj2ee.reflect;

import java.lang.reflect.*;

public class ShowPrivateFields
{
    public static void main(String[] args)
    {
        try
        {
// Create an instance of PrivatePerson with some initial data values
            PrivatePerson person =
                new PrivatePerson("Kaitlynn", "Dawn", "Tippin");

// Get the PrivatePerson class
            Class personClass = person.getClass();

// Get only the fields declared in the PrivatePerson class (that is, the ones
// declared in PrivatePerson.java)
            Field[] personFields = personClass.getDeclaredFields();

// Turn off the access checking in all the fields (this is a shortcut
// from the normal procedure of looping through the fields and
// calling setAccessible(true) on each one
            AccessibleObject.setAccessible(personFields, true);

// Loop through the fields
            for (int i=0; i < personFields.length; i++)
            {
// Get the name of the field
                String fieldName = personFields[i].getName();

// Get the field value (they're all String in this example)
                String fieldValue = (String) personFields[i].get(person);
```

```
// Print out the field name and field value
                    System.out.println(fieldName+"="+fieldValue);
                }
            }
            catch (Exception exc)
            {
                exc.printStackTrace();
            }
        }
}
```

CREATING DYNAMIC PROXIES

Of all the features of the Reflection API, dynamic proxies are definitely the most esoteric. Dynamic proxies let you create a proxy class that appears to implement one or more interfaces and can serve as a proxy between an object and its clients. Figure 39.3 illustrates how you can insert a proxy between an object and its users.

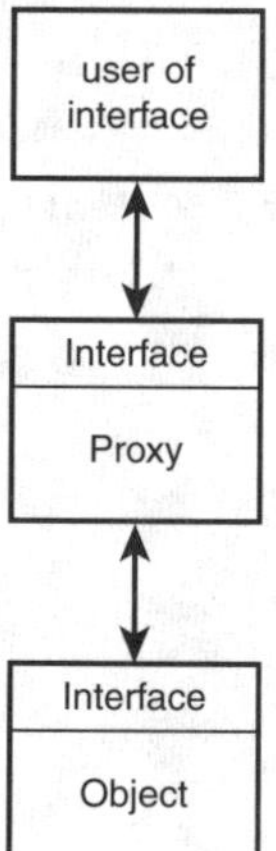

Figure 39.3
A dynamic proxy can sit between an object and its users.

There are a couple of interesting things to note about dynamic proxies. First, the proxy doesn't need to implement the interface that is being proxied; in fact, the whole reason for the dynamic proxy API is to allow you to proxy things on-the-fly. Second, the proxy class isn't required to pass the method invocations on to another object. In other words, instead of sitting between an object and its users, the proxy can impersonate the object and handle all the method calls itself. Third, you can only proxy interfaces. You can't create a proxy that impersonates a whole class—just the interfaces implemented by the class.

Unless you're writing a remote method invocation library or some other kind of library that needs to invoke different methods, you probably won't have much use for dynamic proxies, although they can help with debugging.

The only thing special about a dynamic proxy class is that it must implement the `java.lang.reflect.InvocationHandler` interface. The interface contains only one method, `invoke`:

```
public Object invoke(Object proxy, Method method, Object[] args)
    throws Throwable
```

Listing 39.5 shows a debug proxy program that prints out a message before it calls a method and then prints out the result of the method call.

LISTING 39.5 SOURCE CODE FOR DebugProxy.java

```
package usingj2ee.reflect;

import java.lang.reflect.*;

public class DebugProxy implements InvocationHandler
{
    protected Object targetObj;

    public DebugProxy(Object aTargetObject)
    {
        targetObj = aTargetObject;
    }

    public Object invoke(Object theProxy, Method method, Object[] params)
        throws Throwable
    {
        try
        {
// Print out the name of the method you are invoking
            System.out.print("invoking "+method.getName()+"(");

// Print out the parameters
            for (int i=0; i < params.length; i++)
            {
                if (i > 0) System.out.print(",");
                System.out.print(params[i]);
            }
            System.out.print(") -> ");

// Invoke the real method on the target object
            Object retval = method.invoke(targetObj, params);

// Print out the result
            System.out.println(retval);

            return retval;
        }
        catch (InvocationTargetException exc)
        {
// If the method threw an exception, get the exception
            Throwable error = exc.getTargetException();

// Print out the exception
            System.out.println("threw "+error.toString());
```

```
// Throw it back to the caller
            throw error;
        }
        catch (Exception exc)
        {
// If there's an error just trying to invoke the method, print it out
            System.out.println("Got error: "+exc.toString()+
                " while invoking method");
            throw exc;
        }
    }
}
```

Listing 39.6 shows a simple interface definition for testing the debug proxy program.

LISTING 39.6 SOURCE CODE FOR `TestInterface.java`

```
package usingj2ee.reflect;

public interface TestInterface
{
    public String doTest1(String aStr, int aNumber);
    public void doTest2(String[] strs);
}
```

Listing 39.7 shows a simple implementation of the `TestInterface` interface.

LISTING 39.7 SOURCE CODE FOR `TestTarget.java`

```
package usingj2ee.reflect;

public class TestTarget implements TestInterface
{
    public String doTest1(String aStr, int aNumber)
    {
        return aStr+aNumber;
    }

    public void doTest2(String[] strs)
    {
        throw new RuntimeException("I don't know what to do in doTest2");
    }
}
```

Now, to attach the proxy to a class, you must call the `newProxyInstance` method in the `Proxy` class, passing it the class loader for the proxied interface(s), an array of the proxied interfaces, and the proxy itself (see Listing 39.8). You get back an object that appears to implement whatever interfaces you have specified.

LISTING 39.8 SOURCE CODE FOR RunDebugTest.java

```
package usingj2ee.reflect;

import java.lang.reflect.*;

public class RunDebugTest
{
    public static void main(String[] args)
    {
        try
        {
// Create the real interface implementation
            TestTarget target = new TestTarget();

// Create a proxy to wrap the original implementation
            DebugProxy proxy = new DebugProxy(target);

// Get a reference to the proxy through the TestInterface interface
            TestInterface test = (TestInterface) Proxy.newProxyInstance(
                TestInterface.class.getClassLoader(),
                new Class[] { TestInterface.class }, proxy);

// Invoke some methods on the test interface
            System.out.println(test.doTest1("This is test ", 1));
            test.doTest2(new String[] { "foo", "bar", "baz" });
        }
        catch (Exception exc)
        {
            exc.printStackTrace();
        }
    }
}
```

Figure 39.4 shows the output from RunDebugTest.

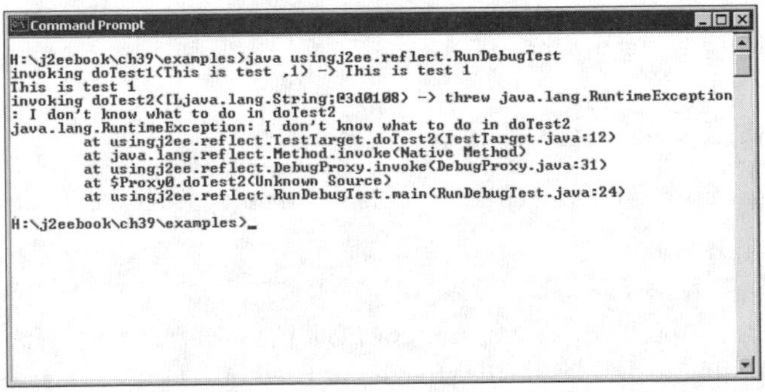

```
Command Prompt
H:\j2eebook\ch39\examples>java usingj2ee.reflect.RunDebugTest
invoking doTest1(This is test ,1) -> This is test 1
This is test 1
invoking doTest2([Ljava.lang.String;@3d0108) -> threw java.lang.RuntimeException
: I don't know what to do in doTest2
java.lang.RuntimeException: I don't know what to do in doTest2
        at usingj2ee.reflect.TestTarget.doTest2(TestTarget.java:12)
        at java.lang.reflect.Method.invoke(Native Method)
        at usingj2ee.reflect.DebugProxy.invoke(DebugProxy.java:31)
        at $Proxy0.doTest2(Unknown Source)
        at usingj2ee.reflect.RunDebugTest.main(RunDebugTest.java:24)

H:\j2eebook\ch39\examples>_
```

Figure 39.4
A dynamic proxy can intercept method invocations.

Notice that DebugProxy is able to intercept the methods of the TestInterface interface even though it doesn't implement the interface. That's the whole purpose behind dynamic proxies.

IMPROVING REFLECTION PERFORMANCE

One of the big knocks against Reflection is that it's quite a bit slower than normal field and method access. When you use Reflection as part of your application, there are a few things you can do to speed things up.

First, if you do a lot of method lookups, consider creating a cache of the methods, possibly by some unique name so you don't have to create a description of the method parameters every time. Any time you can avoid creating a new object you'll save time.

Second, consider creating static arrays for some commonly used, read-only object arrays. For instance, when you invoke a `get` method on an object, you typically pass a zero-length array. You should create a static zero-length object array and use it every time you call a `get` method. Again, try to avoid creating objects.

TROUBLESHOOTING

LOCATING METHODS

Why can't I find the method I'm looking for?

If the method was defined in a superclass of the one you're using, make sure you use `getMethod` instead of `getDeclaredMethod`. Second, double-check the array of method parameters and make sure you are using the correct types. Remember to use `.TYPE` to get native types.

EXCEPTIONS

When a method throws an exception, why do I get an `InvocationTargetException` instead of the real exception?

That's just the way Reflection works. Call `getTargetException` on the `InvocationTargetException` to get the underlying exception.

CHAPTER 40

Dynamic Class Loading

In this chapter

LOADING CLASSES AT RUNTIME

Java's capability to load classes dynamically is one of the biggest boons for developers. Although it's true that other languages have had the capability to load dynamic libraries at runtime, none of them compare to the ease with which you can load a new Java class and create instances of that class.

To load a class dynamically, you only need to do the following:

```
Class someClass = Class.forName("foo.bar.SomeClass");
```

If you only need to use the default constructor for a class, you can use the `newInstance` method in the `Class` object:

```
Object someClassOb = someClass.newInstance();
```

If you need to invoke a static method on the object or call one of the other constructors, you must use Reflection (which you saw in Chapter 39, "Reflection,") to look up the method or constructor you want.

Listing 40.1 shows a handy utility that uses both dynamic class loading and Reflection to run a program while sending `System.out` and `System.err` to different files and using an input file for `System.in`. There are times when you need to run a Java program but you can't use the console for any I/O. Although you could change the program to change the locations of the standard streams, it's much easier to let another program handle it—especially if you don't have the source code for the program you want to run.

LISTING 40.1 SOURCE CODE FOR `OutputRedir.java`

```
package usingj2ee.dynclass;

import java.io.*;
import java.lang.reflect.*;

public class OutputRedir
{
    public static void main(String[] args)
    {
// Allow the user to change the location of stdout with a system property
try
        {
            PrintStream stdout = new PrintStream(
                new FileOutputStream(
                    System.getProperty("stdout", "std.out")));

            System.setOut(stdout);
        }
        catch (Exception ignore)
        {
        }

// Allow the user to change the location of stderr with a system property
        try
        {
```

```
            PrintStream stderr = new PrintStream(
                new FileOutputStream(
                    System.getProperty("stderr", "std.err")));

            System.setErr(stderr);
        }
        catch (Exception ignore)
        {
        }

// Allow the user to change the location of stdin with a system property
        try
        {
            InputStream stdin = new FileInputStream(
                    System.getProperty("stdin", "std.in"));

            System.setIn(stdin);
        }
        catch (Exception ignore)
        {
        }

        try
        {
// Get the arg list: the first one should be the classname, the rest
// should be the args for the class you're about to run
            String[] classArgs = new String[args.length - 1];

// Copy all but the first arg into the new args array
            System.arraycopy(args, 1, classArgs, 0, args.length-1);

// Locate the class you want to run
            Class runClass = Class.forName(args[0]);

// Locate the main method for the class
            Method main = runClass.getMethod("main",
                new Class[] { Class.forName("[Ljava.lang.String;") });

// Invoke the main method
            main.invoke(null, new Object[] { classArgs });
        }
        catch (Exception exc)
        {
            exc.printStackTrace();
        }
    }
}
```

To use the `OutputRedir` class, just type

```
java -Dstdout=outfile -Dstderr=errfile -Dstdin=infile
➥ usingj2ee.dynclass.OutputRedir yourclassname yourclassargs
```

If you don't specify files for `stdout`, `stderr`, and `stdin`, they default to `std.out`, `std.err`, and `std.in`. These filenames are just arbitrary names chosen by the `OutputRedir` program and are not anything specific to Java.

Most of the time when you do dynamic class loading, you don't need to use Reflection. You expect the class you load to implement an interface that you know at compile time. You load a class dynamically, call `newInstance` to create a new instance, and invoke methods on the instance through the known interface.

For example, suppose you expect a class to implement the `Runnable` interface. You can load the class, create an instance using the default constructor, cast the object to `Runnable`, and call the `run` method. Listing 40.2 shows just such a program.

LISTING 40.2 SOURCE CODE FOR `LoadAndRun.java`

```
package usingj2ee.dynclass;

public class LoadAndRun
{
    public static void main(String[] args)
    {
        try
        {
// Dynamically load the class
            Class runClass = Class.forName(args[0]);

// Create a new instance using the default constructor
            Object runOb = runClass.newInstance();

// Make sure the object implements Runnable
            if (runOb instanceof Runnable)
            {
// Cast the object to Runnable and call the run method
                ((Runnable) runOb).run();
            }
            else
            {
                System.err.println("The class doesn't implement Runnable.");
            }
        }
        catch (Exception exc)
        {
            exc.printStackTrace();
        }
    }
}
```

Dynamic class loading lets you create nice server frameworks for running various services based on simple interfaces. Although EJB containers provide a good framework, you might still need your own application server framework. For example, what if you want to listen for incoming socket connections? You can't do that in an EJB.

A typical application framework includes logging, configuration, and other services. You can find one such framework at `http://www.wutka.com/download.shtml`, or on the CD-ROM that comes with this book (in `Wlib.zip`). The framework includes configuration, logging, and a mechanism for dynamically loading services.

To dynamically load services, you need a common interface for all your services. For example, the Wlib framework defines a `Service` interface like the one shown in Listing 40.3.

LISTING 40.3 SOURCE CODE FOR `Service.java` (FROM `Wlib.zip`)

```
package com.wutka.util;

/** Interface implemented by services that can be started automatically
 *  by the ServiceStarter class.
 * <P>
 * Since the name of the service is passed in the startService method,
 * it is a good idea to have your services look for their configuration
 * based on the service name. That way, you can have multiple instances
 * of the same service class with different configuration items.
 * <P>
 * For example, you might have a startService method that fetches
 * configuration like this:
 * <PRE>
 *    String myInfo = Config.getConfigItem(serviceName+".myInfo");
 * </PRE>
 * <P>
 * In your config file, you can list the config items like this:
 * <PRE>
 * instance1.myInfo=Foo
 * instance2.myInfo=Bar
 * </PRE>
 * <P>
 * Then, your service startup file could list the service like this:
 * <PRE>
 * instance1 mypackage.MyServiceClass
 * instance2 mypackage.MyServiceClass
 * </PRE>
 *
 * @author Mark Wutka
 * @version 1.0
 */


public interface Service
{
/** Asks the service to start itself using the specified service name */
    public void startService(String serviceName)
        throws ServiceStartupException;

/** Asks the service to stop itself */
    public void stopService();
}
```

The Wlib framework includes a `ServerMain` class that serves as the main entry point for your server. You always start your application server using the `ServerMain` class—you just use a different configuration file to start a different set of services. Although Wlib gives you a framework for writing application services, it doesn't include any services (other than the built-in logging and configuration services).

DESIGNING SERVERS TO USE DYNAMIC CLASS LOADING

If you spend much time creating socket-based network programs, it won't take long for you to notice a simple pattern. You usually create a main class that listens for incoming socket connections. You then create a separate class (or an inner class) to handle the new connection in a separate thread. Because the only thing that really changes is the way you handle the clients, why not create a generic socket service to make it easier to create socket applications?

You start by creating a common interface for client handlers, like the one shown in Listing 40.4.

LISTING 40.4 SOURCE CODE FOR `ClientHandler.java`

```
package usingj2ee.dynclass;

import java.net.*;

public interface ClientHandler extends Runnable
{
/** Called to give the handler the client's socket */
    public void setClientSocket(Socket sock);

/** Called in a separate thread to execute the client handler */
    public void run();
}
```

Next, you create the code that listens for the socket connections and spawns the client. Listing 40.5 shows the listener class implemented as a Wlib service (so it can use the configuration and logging services).

LISTING 40.5 SOURCE CODE FOR `SocketListenerService.java`

```
package usingj2ee.dynclass;

import java.net.*;
import com.wutka.util.*;

public class SocketListenerService implements Service
{
    protected ServerSocket server;

    public SocketListenerService()
    {
    }

    public void startService(String serviceName)
        throws ServiceStartupException
    {
// Get the port number from the Config class
        String portNumStr = Config.getConfigItem(
            serviceName+".portNumber");
```

```
// Parse the port number
        int portNumber = 0;
        try
        {
            portNumber = Integer.parseInt(portNumStr);
        }
        catch (Exception exc)
        {
            throw new ServiceStartupException(
                "Invalid listen port number: "+portNumber);
        }

// Get the classname of the handler class from the Config class
        String handlerClassName = Config.getConfigItem(
            serviceName+".className");


        Class handlerClass = null;
        try
        {
// Dynamically load the handler class
            handlerClass = Class.forName(handlerClassName);
        }
        catch (Exception exc)
        {
            throw new ServiceStartupException(
                exc.toString());
        }

// Create the server socket
        try
        {
            server = new ServerSocket(portNumber);
        }
        catch (Exception exc)
        {
            throw new ServiceStartupException(
                exc.toString());
        }

        Log.logMessage(LogSeverity.INFORMATION,
            serviceName+" service listening on port "+portNumber);

// If the handler class is invalid, this service logs a message. This
// flag insures that it only logs the message once
        boolean loggedInvalidHandlerClass = false;

        for (;;)
        {
            try
            {
// Accept an incoming connection
                Socket client = server.accept();

// Create a new instance of the handler class
                Object handlerOb = handlerClass.newInstance();
```

LISTING 40.5 CONTINUED

```
// Make sure it implements
                if (handlerOb instanceof ClientHandler)
                {
                    ClientHandler handler = (ClientHandler) handlerOb;

// Give the client's socket to the handler
                    handler.setClientSocket(client);

// Create a new handler thread and start it
                    (new Thread(handler)).start();
                }
                else
                {
// If the handler class is invalid, log an error message—but only once
                    if (!loggedInvalidHandlerClass)
                    {
                        Log.logMessage(LogSeverity.ERROR,
                            serviceName+" handler class "+handlerClassName+
                            " doesn't implement ClientHandler");
                        loggedInvalidHandlerClass = true;
                    }
                    try
                    {
                        client.close();
                    }
                    catch (Exception ignore) {}
                }
            }
            catch (Exception exc)
            {
                Log.logException(LogSeverity.ERROR,
                    serviceName+" received exception: ", exc);
            }
        }
    }

    public void stopService()
    {
// When the service stops, stop listening for connections. This class doesn't
// keep track of the clients so there's no way to stop all the client threads.
        try
        {
            server.close();
        }
        catch (Exception ignore) {}
    }
}
```

Because most client handlers want to wrap either a data or an object stream around the socket streams, why not create an abstract base class that performs some of the housekeeping chores (see Listing 40.6)?

LISTING 40.6 SOURCE CODE FOR ClientHandlerBase.java

```
package usingj2ee.dynclass;

import com.wutka.util.*;
import java.net.*;
import java.io.*;

public abstract class ClientHandlerBase implements ClientHandler
{
    protected Socket clientSocket;

// If the handler doesn't use object streams, use data streams
    protected DataInputStream in;
    protected DataOutputStream out;

// The handler can use object streams if it wants to. You can only
// use object streams if the clients also use them, of course
    protected ObjectInputStream objIn;
    protected ObjectOutputStream objOut;

    public ClientHandlerBase()
    {
    }

    public void setClientSocket(Socket aClientSocket)
    {
        clientSocket = aClientSocket;
        try
        {
// If the client handler wants to use objects streams, create
// buffered object streams. Don't forget to flush the ObjectOutputStream
// after you create it!
            if (useObjectStreams())
            {
                objOut = new ObjectOutputStream(new BufferedOutputStream(
                    clientSocket.getOutputStream()));
                objOut.flush();

                objIn = new ObjectInputStream(new BufferedInputStream(
                    clientSocket.getInputStream()));
            }
            else
            {
// If the client doesn't use object streams, use data streams
                out = new DataOutputStream(new BufferedOutputStream(
                    clientSocket.getOutputStream()));

                in = new DataInputStream(new BufferedInputStream(
                    clientSocket.getInputStream()));
            }

        }
        catch (Exception exc)
        {
            Log.logException(LogSeverity.ERROR,
                "Client handler got exception while creating streams:", exc);
```

LISTING 40.6 CONTINUED

```
        }
    }

    public abstract void run();

    public abstract boolean useObjectStreams();
}
```

Finally, Listing 40.7 shows a simple echo socket service based on the framework.

LISTING 40.7 SOURCE CODE FOR EchoClientHandler.java

```
package usingj2ee.dynclass;

public class EchoClientHandler extends ClientHandlerBase
{
    public void run()
    {
        try
        {
            for (;;)
            {
// Read a line from the client
                String line = in.readLine();

// Echo it back
                out.writeBytes(line);
                out.write('\n');

// Since the stream is buffered, flush it
                out.flush();
            }
        }
        catch (Exception exc)
        {
            try
            {
                clientSocket.close();
            }
            catch (Exception ignore) {}
        }
    }

// This handler doesn't want object streams
    public boolean useObjectStreams() { return false; }
}
```

Note

The `EchoClientHandler` class uses the deprecated `readLine` method in `DataInputStream`. If you will be doing mostly character-based, line-oriented programs, you should change the `ClientHandlerBase` and `EchoClientHandler` to use a `BufferedReader`, which is the proper way to do a `readLine`. Because many networking protocols require you to send and receive different datatypes, the `ClientHandlerBase` class assumes you would be happier with a `DataInputStream` instead of a `BufferedReader`.

Now, to fit the new service into the Wlib framework, you create a services file with the name of the socket listener service. You can start up many listener services with different configuration options. The listener class uses its service name to look for its configuration. For the echo service, your services file (called `echo.services`) only needs one line:

```
echoservice usingj2ee.dynclass.SocketListenerService
```

The service listener also needs two configuration items: the name of the client handler class to dynamically load and the port number to listen on. Your config file (`echo.cfg`) just needs three lines: the name of the services file, the name of the class to load for the echo service, and the listener port number (see Listing 40.8). Notice that the configuration for the echo service starts with the service name. If you look back to the implementation of the service listener, you see that it uses its service name at the beginning of its configuration items.

LISTING 40.8 `echo.cfg` **FILE**

```
services.file=echo.services

echoservice.portNumber=4321
echoservice.className=usingj2ee.dynclass.EchoClientHandler
```

To run the service, use the following command:

```
java -cp .;wlib.zip com.wutka.util.ServerMain echo.cfg
```


Figure 40.1 shows a Telnet session that tests the `EchoClientHandler` class. Because the class uses only character data and not binary data, you can test it with the Telnet program rather than writing a custom client.

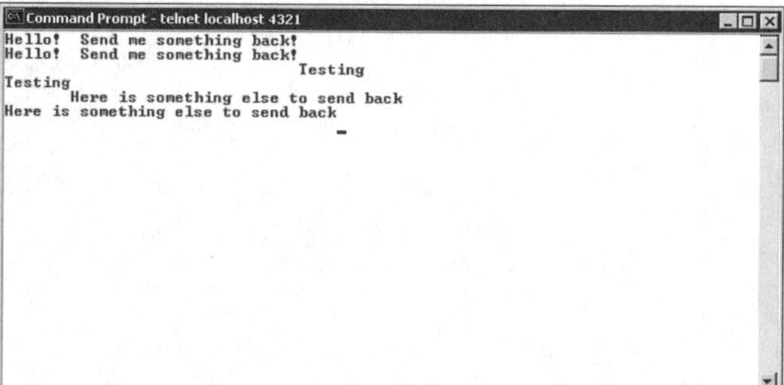

Figure 40.1 You can use the Telnet command to test the `EchoClientHandler` class.

TROUBLESHOOTING

LOADING CLASSES

Why do I get a `ClassNotFoundException` *when I try to load a class?*

The class probably isn't in your classpath or you didn't use the correct name. Remember that it's a classname and not a file, so the name should have periods and no slashes. It shouldn't end in `.class` either. Also, make sure you use the fully qualified classname including the package.

Why can't I instantiate a class with `newInstance`*?*

That usually happens when the default constructor is private or protected. The only thing you can do is use Reflection and try to find a public constructor.

USING WLIB

Why won't any of the Echo service examples compile?

You probably don't have Wlib in your classpath.

CHAPTER 41

Introspection

In this chapter

How Introspection Works

Introspection is a special utility for JavaBeans that uses Reflection to determine the contents of a bean. As you probably know, JavaBeans are just Java classes that use specific naming conventions to support properties, methods, and events.

JavaBeans is Sun's answer to Microsoft's ActiveX controls, which coincidentally support properties, methods, and events. One of the differences between JavaBeans and ActiveX controls is that JavaBeans don't require any additional description files. ActiveX controls often use Interface Definition Language (IDL) files to define interfaces at compile time and have type libraries (essentially compiled IDL files) to define interfaces at runtime. Microsoft's .Net framework is moving away from some of these restrictions, however. Technically, because a bean might use separate `BeanDescriptor` and `BeanInfo` classes, JavaBeans do have their equivalent to type libraries, but you can get along fine without ever writing either a `BeanDescriptor` or a `BeanInfo` class.

The JavaBeans API is able to circumvent the use of description files because of two things: reflection and a standard naming convention for describing properties and events. Methods in JavaBeans, apart from the methods that define properties, are exactly the same as methods in any Java class, so there's no need for a standard method naming convention, other than that the methods must be public.

To create a bean property, you simple create `get` and `set` methods to manipulate the property. Although normal methods have no standard naming convention, methods that define properties have a strict naming convention. For example, to make a property called `firstName`, you create the following methods:

```
public String getFirstName()
public void setFirstName(String aFirstName)
```

If the property has a Boolean value, you usually use `is` instead of `get`:

```
public boolean isReady()
public void setReady(boolean readyFlag)
```

A bean can also have array-like properties that hold multiple values. These properties are called *indexed properties*. You typically create four different methods for an `indexed property`:

```
public Sometype getPropertyName(int index)
public void setPropertyName(int index, Sometype value)
public Sometype[] getPropertyName()
public void setPropertyName(Sometype[] values)
```

Now, the reason for this little refresher course on bean properties and events is that the `java.beans.Introspector` uses these naming conventions to create a `BeanInfo` class that describes the contents of a bean.

Listing 41.1 shows a `Person` bean with a few simple properties and one indexed property.

Listing 41.1 Source Code for Person.java

```
package usingj2ee.introspect;

public class Person implements java.io.Serializable
{
    public String firstName;
    public String middleName;
    public String lastName;
    public String[] pets;


    public Person()
    {
    }

    public Person(String aFirstName, String aMiddleName,
        String aLastName)
    {
        firstName = aFirstName;
        middleName = aMiddleName;
        lastName = aLastName;
    }

    public String getFirstName()
    {
        return firstName;
    }

    public void setFirstName(String theFirstName)
       {
        firstName = theFirstName;
    }

    public String getMiddleName()
    {
        return middleName;
    }

    public void setMiddleName(String theMiddleName)
    {
        middleName = theMiddleName;
    }

    public String getLastName()
    {
        return lastName;
    }

    public void setLastName(String theLastName)
    {
        lastName = theLastName;
    }

    public String[] getPet()
    {
        return pets;
    }
```

LISTING 41.1 CONTINUED

```
    public void setPet(String thePets[])
    {
        pets = thePets;
    }

    public String getPet(int index)
    {
        return pets[index];
    }

    public void setPet(int index, String pet)
    {
        pets[index] = pet;
    }
}
```

To use the introspector on the `Person` class, you can use the following:

```
BeanInfo info = Introspector.getBeanInfo(Person.class)
```

By default, the introspector looks at the entire contents of the bean including any inherited members. Unfortunately, this means that you pick up any part of your superclass that looks like a property. For instance, in the `Object` class you'll find a method called `getClass`. The introspector sees it and thinks you have a property named `class`. Fortunately, you can tell the introspector to stop when it reaches a certain class. You can pass the top-level class (where you want the introspector to stop lookup) as the second parameter to `getBeanInfo`:

```
BeanInfo info = Introspector.getBeanInfo(Person.class, Object.class)
```

Listing 41.2 shows a program that prints out the properties in the `Person` class and then runs the introspector again, telling it to stop when it hits the `Object` class.

LISTING 41.2 SOURCE CODE FOR `IntrospectPerson.java`

```
package usingj2ee.introspect;

import java.beans.*;

public class IntrospectPerson
{
    public static void main(String[] args)
    {
        try
        {
// Introspect the person class
            BeanInfo info = Introspector.getBeanInfo(Person.class);

// Get the list of properties
            PropertyDescriptor[] props = info.getPropertyDescriptors();

            System.out.println("The Person class has "+props.length+
                " properties:");
```

```
// Print out the names of each property
            for (int i=0; i < props.length; i++)
            {
                System.out.println(props[i].getName());
            }

// Look at the Person class again, but this time ignore properties
// defined in the Object class
            info = Introspector.getBeanInfo(Person.class,
                Object.class);

            props = info.getPropertyDescriptors();

            System.out.println("The Person class has "+props.length+
                " properties:");

            for (int i=0; i < props.length; i++)
            {
                System.out.println(props[i].getName());
            }
        }
        catch (Exception exc)
        {
            exc.printStackTrace();
        }
    }
}
```

Figure 41.1 shows the output from the `IntrospectPerson` program.

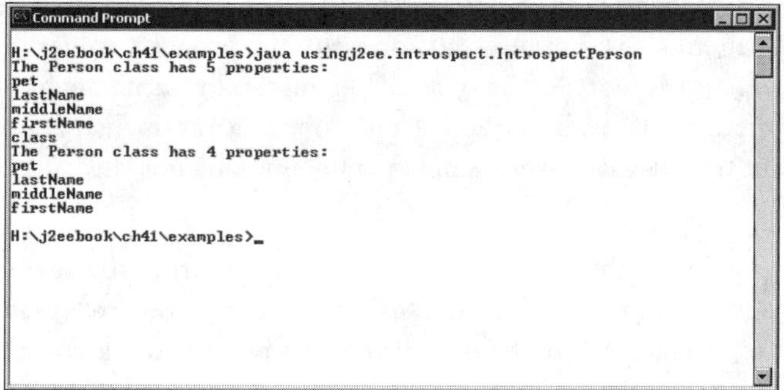

Command Prompt
H:\j2eebook\ch41\examples>java usingj2ee.introspect.IntrospectPerson
The Person class has 5 properties:
pet
lastName
middleName
firstName
class
The Person class has 4 properties:
pet
lastName
middleName
firstName
H:\j2eebook\ch41\examples>_

Figure 41.1
You can control the maximum depth of the introspector's search.

Listing 41.3 shows a utility that searches for the first superclass of a given class that is a member of one of the common Java packages. That way, if you subclass an existing Java class, you can eliminate any properties introduced by the Java packages while keeping ones that you might have inherited from your parent class when you're doing introspection.

LISTING 41.3 SOURCE CODE FOR getRootNonJavaClass ROUTINE

```
public static Class getRootNonJavaClass(Class cl)
{
// Get the parent class of the parameter class
    cl = cl.getSuperclass();
    if (cl == null) return cl;

// Get the name of the superclass
    String rootName = cl.getName();

// Keep looping until you hit one of the common Java classes
    while (!rootName.startsWith("java.") && !rootName.startsWith("javax.")
        && !rootName.startsWith("com.sun.")
        && !rootName.startsWith("org.omg."))
    {
        cl = cl.getSuperclass();
        if (cl == null) return cl;
        rootName = cl.getName();
    }
    return cl;
}
```

THE PropertyDescriptor CLASS

Ultimately, Introspection is really a fancy wrapper around Reflection. Because bean properties function like fields, but have accessor methods, you can't use the `Field` class to update properties, and the `Method` class can only describe a single method. You need an additional class to describe a bean property, and that class is the `PropertyDescriptor` class.

The `PropertyDescriptor` class has two methods called `getReadMethod` and `getWriteMethod` that return the methods you use to read and write the property values. These methods both return a `java.lang.reflect.Method` object. The method returned by `getReadMethod` doesn't take any parameters (that is, pass a zero-length object array as the parameter). The method returned by `getWriteMethod` takes a single parameter, which is the value you want to store in the property.

If a property is indexed, the `PropertyDescriptor` you get from the `BeanInfo` class is actually an `IndexedPropertyDescriptor`. The `getReadMethod` and `getWriteMethod` calls return the methods that store and retrieve the bean properties as an entire array. For example, the `Pet` property in the `Person` class is indexed. The `getReadMethod` call returns the `Method` object for this method:

```
public String[] getPet()
```

If you want to invoke the indexed property methods (that is, the ones that take an index as a parameter), use the `getIndexedReadMethod` and `getIndexedWriteMethod` calls in the `IndexedPropertyDescriptor` class.

Listing 41.4 shows a program that modifies the contents of a bean by using the property descriptors and their underlying `Method` objects.

Listing 41.4 Source Code for ModifyPerson.java

```
package usingj2ee.introspect;

import java.beans.*;
import java.lang.reflect.*;

public class ModifyPerson
{
    public static void main(String[] args)
    {
        try
        {
// Introspect the person class
            BeanInfo info = Introspector.getBeanInfo(Person.class,
                Object.class);

// Create a Person to work with
            Person person = new Person("Samantha", "Lauren", "Tippin");
            person.setPet(new String[] { "Starbuck", "Bunnie" });

// Get the list of properties
            PropertyDescriptor[] props = info.getPropertyDescriptors();

            for (int i=0; i < props.length; i++)
            {
// If this is the first name property, change the value
                if (props[i].getName().equals("firstName"))
                {
                    Method setter = props[i].getWriteMethod();
                    setter.invoke(person, new Object[] { "Kaitlynn" });
                }
// If this is the middle name property, change the value
                else if (props[i].getName().equals("middleName"))
                {
                    Method setter = props[i].getWriteMethod();
                    setter.invoke(person, new Object[] { "Dawn" });
                }
// If this is the pet property, change one of the values
                else if (props[i].getName().equals("pet"))
                {
                    IndexedPropertyDescriptor idx =
                        (IndexedPropertyDescriptor) props[i];

                    Method setter = idx.getIndexedWriteMethod();

                    setter.invoke(person, new Object[]
                        { new Integer(0), "Edward" });
                }
            }

            System.out.println(person.getFirstName()+" "+
                person.getMiddleName()+" "+person.getLastName()+
                " has the following pets:");

            String[] pets = person.getPet();
            for (int i=0; i < pets.length; i++)
```

LISTING 41.4 CONTINUED

```
            {
                System.out.println(pets[i]);
            }
        }
        catch (Exception exc)
        {
            exc.printStackTrace();
        }
    }
}
```

USING INTROSPECTION IN AN APPLICATION

You use Introspection in an application in basically the same places you use Reflection. You typically use Introspection in utility classes that map Java objects onto some other medium (database, XML, network) and in graphical user interfaces.

The JOX library that you saw in Chapter 24, "Using Java-XML Tools," uses Introspection to map Java objects to XML and map XML to Java objects. In fact, the reason that JOX works with JavaBeans instead of any Java object is that JOX uses Reflection.

Introspection makes a lot of sense for GUI applications in which you create an automated tool to copy data between data objects and graphics components. You will see several examples of this technique in the next chapter.

CHOOSING BETWEEN INTROSPECTION AND REFLECTION

Obviously, because Introspection uses Reflection, you can't avoid using Reflection whichever approach you take. There is, however, a good reason to use Introspection for analyzing Java objects rather than just using Reflection.

Introspection works at a higher level than Reflection and filters out a lot of garbage that you don't want to deal with. Bean properties are essentially the data items that a developer has deemed important—the parts of the object that other programs actually want to use. Depending on your application, you might want to work at that level—then again, you might not. Take the JOX library, for example. It deals with XML files and generally works with the public view of the data. In other words, JOX deals with common business entities (people, orders, products) and their data elements (name, ship date, price). These are the kinds of data elements that you expect to see as bean properties. The main reason JOX uses Introspection is that it gets a much smaller view of the data when writing XML. If JOX always used a DTD to write data, it could use Reflection, because the DTD tells it all the elements it needs to write. Because the DTD is optional, JOX assumes that the bean properties represent the data items that are really important and focuses on them.

You tend to see Reflection used more often in database mapping tools because you typically want to slide the data in behind the access methods. In other words, the database contains the persistent state of an object, and when you copy that persistent state back into the object, you don't want to go through the accessor methods that might perform additional operations on the data.

As a general rule, use Introspection when you want a high-level view of the data. Use Reflection when you need to access the underlying fields without going through accessor methods, or when you want to provide scripting capabilities that can invoke any method or modify any fields.

TROUBLESHOOTING

ACCESSING PROPERTIES

Why do I have strange properties like "class" that aren't in my bean?

The introspector is picking up properties and methods from the superclass. Use the optional "stop class" parameter to tell the introspector where to stop. For example, if your class extends `java.lang.Object`, pass `Object.class` as the second parameter of the `getBeanInfo` class.

Why do I get a `NullPointerException` when I access a particular property?

The introspector reports a property if it sees either a `get` or a `set` method; it doesn't need to see both. If you have a `get` method with no corresponding `set` method, the `getWriteMethod` method in the `PropertyDescriptor` object returns `null`. The `getReadMethod` method returns `null` if there is no `get` method for a property.

CHAPTER 42

The Model-View-Controller Paradigm

In this chapter

WHAT IS MODEL-VIEW-CONTROLLER?

The Model-View-Controller (MVC) paradigm is a way to partition your user interface so it's easier to write and maintain. The idea is that you start with a model—a set of classes representing the data you're working with. Next, you construct various views of the data—classes that display the data on the screen. Finally, you create a controller object that accepts user input and updates the model or view.

Figure 42.1 illustrates the idea behind MVC.

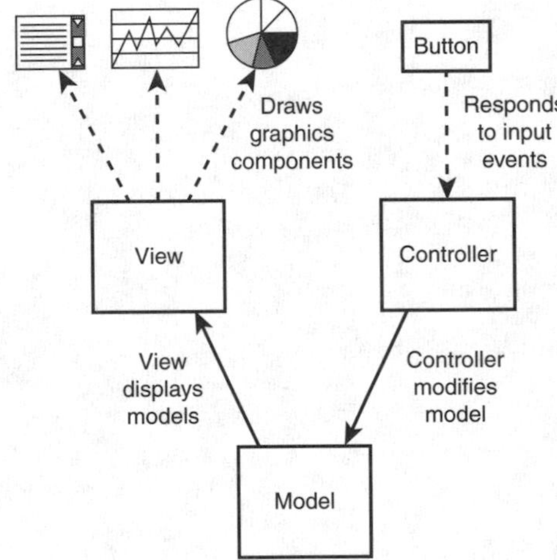

Figure 42.1
A view displays data from the model, and the controller accepts input to change the model.

If you have ever written GUI programs before, you know how convoluted the code can get. You write code to accept a button click and immediately update several classes. If there are different ways to perform the same operation, you might end up duplicating code (unless you're smart enough to use a single method to perform the operation no matter how it is invoked).

MVC takes the approach that the display of the data and the manipulation of the data are both separate from the data itself. If the data changes, the model tells the view that the data has changed, but the view is responsible for updating any of the information it is displaying.

Suppose you make an application that displays stock information. You create an input field for changing the stock symbol and a chart showing the current stock price along with a graph of the stock history over some period of time. If you don't use MVC, you can write a routine that reads the stock symbol value, fetches the stock price and history, and then updates the various onscreen displays. If you add a new representation of the stock price, you must change your routine to refresh the new representation as well as the others.

Now, suppose you do the same application with MVC. The stock symbol input field acts as a controller. When you enter a new symbol, the controller tells the model to update itself with the data for the new stock symbol. After the model updates itself, it notifies the views that the model has changed. The various views then query the model for the updated information.

If you want to add another view of the data, you just create another class that reads data from the model and displays it. You don't need to change the model or the controller. Likewise, if you want to create another way to enter a ticker symbol, maybe by using a combo box or a hyperlink, you can add new controllers that update the model without affecting the views.

Note

Some GUI objects, such as text fields, act as both a view and a controller. The text field displays data from the model, but when you enter a value in the field, it sends an update to the model.

The Java Swing API uses the MVC paradigm to some extent. Specifically, it uses the model-view portion of MVC quite heavily. If you look closely, Swing also uses controllers, but not by name. Many of the event listeners function like controllers. For example, the `ActionListener` interface basically sets up an interface from a controller (a button, for example) to the model, telling the model to perform some action.

USING REFLECTION TO IMPLEMENT MVC

Although Swing has some support for MVC, your model must still understand a lot about Swing. You must either incorporate parts of Swing into your model, or write classes that translate Swing operations into operations for your data model. With a little work, you can write classes that automate some of the repetitive Swing tasks, making it easier to create an MVC-based application.

One of the easiest applications of Reflection for GUI development is in the area of action listeners. When you put a button on the screen, you must create an action listener to handle the button click. To write the listener, you can create an odd-looking anonymous inner class, like this:

```
myButton.addActionListener(new ActionListener() {
    public void actionPerformed(ActionEvent evt)
    {
        // handle the event here
    });
```

Anonymous inner classes tend to make your code harder to read, even if they are a little more convenient. Most developers use inner classes to handle events, setting them up like this:

```
MyButton.addActionListener(new MyClickHandler());
// then later in the class...
class MyClickHandler implements ActionListener
{
```

```
        public void actionPerformed(ActionEvent evt)
        {
            // handle the event here
        };
    }
```

Both of these options result in quite a few extra lines of code just to handle a single event. Some developers even use a technique similar to the ancient JDK 1.0 way of doing things. They create a single action listener and then examine the event source to figure out which button the action came from.

Wouldn't it be nice to simply tell Swing to invoke a specific method in your model whenever someone clicks a button? Using a simple adapter class and the Reflection API, you can do just that!

Listing 42.1 shows a simple class that uses Reflection to intercept an action event and forward it to another method. The other method can either be parameterless or can accept an `ActionEvent` as a parameter.

LISTING 42.1 SOURCE CODE FOR `ActionRelay.java`

```
package usingj2ee.mvc;
import java.awt.event.*;
import java.lang.reflect.*;

/** Listens for an action and then invokes a method to handle the action.
 *  The method to handle the action might take an ActionEvent as a parameter
 *  or take no parameter.
 */
public class ActionRelay implements ActionListener
{
    Method targetMethod;
    Object target;
    boolean parameterless;
    protected static final Object[] NO_PARAMS = new Object[0];

    public ActionRelay(Object theTarget, String targetMethodName)
        throws NoSuchMethodException
    {
        target = theTarget;

        parameterless = false;

        try
        {
// See if the method exists and takes an ActionEvent parameter
            targetMethod = target.getClass().getMethod(
                targetMethodName, new Class[] {
                    ActionEvent.class
                });
        }
        catch (NoSuchMethodException exc)
        {
            parameterless = true;
```

```
// See if the method exists and takes no parameters
            targetMethod = target.getClass().getMethod(
                targetMethodName, new Class[0]);
        }
    }

    public void actionPerformed(ActionEvent evt)
    {
        try
        {
// If the method takes an ActionEvent parameter, pass the event in
            if (!parameterless)
            {
                targetMethod.invoke(target, new Object[] { evt });
            }
            else
            {
// Otherwise, invoke the parameterless method
                targetMethod.invoke(target, NO_PARAMS);
            }
        }
        catch (Exception exc)
        {
// If there's an invocation error, just print the exception
            exc.printStackTrace();
        }
    }
}
```

Using the `ActionRelay` class, you can add an action listener to a button with one line of code. For example

```
myButton.addActionListener(
    new ActionRelay(this, "myButtonHandler"));
```

Listing 42.2 shows a program that uses this technique to recognize button clicks.

LISTING 42.2 SOURCE CODE FOR `ActionTest.java`

```
package usingj2ee.mvc;

import java.awt.*;
import java.awt.event.*;
import javax.swing.*;
import java.util.*;
import javax.rmi.*;
import javax.naming.*;

public class ActionTest extends JPanel
{
    public JButton button1;
    public JButton button2;
    public JLabel infoLabel;

    public ActionTest()
    {
        try
```

LISTING 42.2 CONTINUED

```
        {
            setLayout(new GridLayout(2, 0));

            JPanel buttonPanel = new JPanel();

            button1 = new JButton("Button 1");

// Connect the button to the handleButton1Click method
            button1.addActionListener(
                new ActionRelay(this, "handleButton1Click"));

            buttonPanel.add(button1);

            button2 = new JButton("Button 2");

// Connect the button to the handleButton2Click method
            button2.addActionListener(
                new ActionRelay(this, "handleButton2Click"));

            buttonPanel.add(button2);

            add(buttonPanel);

            infoLabel = new JLabel("");
            add(infoLabel);
        }
        catch (Exception exc)
        {
            exc.printStackTrace();
        }
    }

    public void handleButton1Click()
    {
        infoLabel.setText("You clicked button 1");
    }

    public void handleButton2Click()
    {
        infoLabel.setText("You clicked button 2");
    }

    public static void main(String[] args)
    {
        try
        {
            JFrame actionFrame = new JFrame("Action Test");

            ActionTest test = new ActionTest();

            actionFrame.getContentPane().add(test, BorderLayout.CENTER);
            actionFrame.pack();

// Make the frame exit when closed
            actionFrame.addWindowListener(new ExitOnClose());
```

```
            actionFrame.setVisible(true);
        }
        catch (Exception exc)
        {
            exc.printStackTrace();
        }
    }
}
```

One of the things you might notice about the `ActionTest` class is that it uses a little utility class called `ExitOnClose` to set up a window listener. Many Swing applications, especially simple ones, must add a window listener just to listen for the window-closing event on the main frame so the application can shut down. Again, you usually must create an inner class of some sort. The `ExitOnClose` class, shown here in Listing 42.3, shuts down the application when it receives a window-closing event. Just add it as the window listener for your main frame.

LISTING 42.3 SOURCE CODE FOR `ExitOnClose.java`

```
package usingj2ee.mvc;import java.awt.event.*;
/** Simple utility to exit the program when a window closes.
    You must set up handlers like this so often to close an application's main frame,
   it's easier to just make a class to do it.
 */
public class ExitOnClose extends WindowAdapter
{
    public void windowClosing(WindowEvent e)
    {
        System.exit(0);
    }
}
```

One of the disadvantages of using Reflection this way, of course, is that you lose some compile-time checking. If you mistype a method name, you won't find out until runtime when you use Reflection, because Java doesn't discover the error until to go looking for the named method. This is one of the tradeoffs you must weigh against the simplified coding model you now have.

In addition to using Reflection, you can use Introspection for these GUI utilities. Introspection, of course, makes use of Reflection, but it gives you a higher-level view of the data. Introspection recognizes `get` and `set` methods and works in terms of properties instead of individual fields and methods.

The `ActionRelay` class is a utility that helps you set up the controller side of MVC. That is, it makes it easy for a controller (a button, for example) to invoke a method in the model without the model having to know anything about the GUI framework. You can do a similar thing for the model side of things. You can create a class that acts like a Swing data model but uses Reflection or Introspection to interact with the model.

The `JTable` class has a nice model system set up. You can even use `JTable` with a default model, but you must supply your data as a vector of vectors (the inner vector containing each column value). You don't usually work with a vector of vectors, however. You often work with a vector of Java objects. It would be nice to have a model that could work with objects as they are.

Listing 42.4 shows the `BeanTableModel` class that takes a vector of Java beans and creates a Swing `TableModel` interface for accessing the beans. The model uses Introspection to get information from the beans and can also take an optional list of the properties you want to display and the column headings you want in the table.

LISTING 42.4 SOURCE CODE FOR `BeanTableModel.java`

```
package usingj2ee.mvc;

import javax.swing.*;
import javax.swing.table.*;
import java.beans.*;
import java.lang.reflect.*;
import java.util.*;
public class BeanTableModel extends AbstractTableModel
{
    public static final Object[] NO_PARAMS = new Object[0];

    protected String columnHeaders[];
    protected PropertyDescriptor properties[];
    protected Vector data;

    public BeanTableModel(Vector objects)
    {
        this(objects, null, null, null, null);
    }

    public BeanTableModel(Vector objects, String[] propertyNames)
    {
        this(objects, propertyNames, null, null, null);
    }

    public BeanTableModel(Vector objects, String[] propertyNames,
        String[] colHeaders)
    {
        this(objects, propertyNames, colHeaders, null, null);
    }

    public BeanTableModel(Vector objects, String[] propertyNames,
        String[] colHeaders, Class objectClass, Class stopClass)
    {
        try
        {
            data = objects;

// If the user doesn't specify a class, look at the first object
// in the data vector
            if (objectClass == null)
            {
```

```
// If there are no objects, the model can't function
                if (data.size() == 0) return;    // this is bad

                objectClass = data.elementAt(0).getClass();
            }

            BeanInfo info = null;

// Introspect the object class
            if (stopClass != null)
            {
                info = Introspector.getBeanInfo(objectClass, stopClass);
            }
            else
            {
                info = Introspector.getBeanInfo(objectClass);
            }

            Vector newProps = new Vector();
            Vector newColHeaders = new Vector();

            PropertyDescriptor[] beanProps = info.getPropertyDescriptors();

// If the user specifies a list of property names, look for the
// property descriptors for each property name
            if (propertyNames != null)
            {
                for (int i=0; i < propertyNames.length; i++)
                {
                    for (int j=0; j < beanProps.length; j++)
                    {
                        if (beanProps[j].getName().equals(propertyNames[i]))
                        {
                            newProps.addElement(beanProps[j]);
                            if (colHeaders != null)
                            {
                                newColHeaders.addElement(colHeaders[i]);
                            }
                            else
                            {
                                newColHeaders.addElement(propertyNames[i]);
                            }
                            break;
                        }
                    }
                }
            }
            else
            {
// If the user doesn't specify a set of properties, use all the bean properties
                for (int i=0; i < beanProps.length; i++)
                {
                    newProps.addElement(beanProps[i]);
                    newColHeaders.addElement(beanProps[i].getName());
                }
            }
```

LISTING 42.4 CONTINUED

```
                columnHeaders = new String[newColHeaders.size()];
                newColHeaders.copyInto(columnHeaders);

                properties = new PropertyDescriptor[newProps.size()];
                newProps.copyInto(properties);
            }
            catch (Exception exc)
            {
                exc.printStackTrace();
            }
        }

        public int getRowCount()
        {
            return data.size();
        }

        public int getColumnCount()
        {
            return columnHeaders.length;
        }

        public String getColumnName(int column)
        {
            return columnHeaders[column];
        }

        public Class getColumnClass(int column)
        {
            return properties[column].getPropertyType();
        }

        public Object getValueAt(int row, int column)
        {
            try
            {
                Object ob = data.elementAt(row);

                Method reader = properties[column].getReadMethod();

                if (reader != null)
                {
// Invoke the property's reader method to fetch the object value
                    return reader.invoke(ob, NO_PARAMS);
                }
                else
                {
                    return null;
                }
            }
            catch (Exception exc)
            {
                exc.printStackTrace();
```

```
                return null;
            }
        }

        public void setValueAt(Object value, int row, int column)
        {
            try
            {
                Object ob = data.elementAt(row);

                Method writer = properties[column].getWriteMethod();

                if (writer != null)
                {
// Invoke the property's write method to store the value
                    writer.invoke(ob, new Object[] { value });
                }
            }
            catch (Exception exc)
            {
                exc.printStackTrace();
            }
        }

        public boolean isCellEditable(int row, int column)
        {
// The cell is editable if the property has a write method
            if (properties[column].getWriteMethod() != null)
            {
                return true;
            }
            else
            {
                return false;
            }
        }

        public void setData(Vector newData)
        {
            data = newData;

            fireTableDataChanged();
        }

        public Vector getData()
        {
            return data;
        }
}
```

The BeanTableModel class makes it much easier to put beans in a table. It even allows you to update bean values from the table. Listing 42.5 shows a program that exercises the BeanTableModel class using a simplified person bean.

LISTING 42.5 SOURCE CODE FOR TestBeanTableModel.java

```
package usingj2ee.mvc;

import java.awt.*;
import java.awt.event.*;
import javax.swing.*;
import java.util.*;
import javax.rmi.*;
import javax.naming.*;


public class TestBeanTableModel extends JPanel
{
    SimplePerson[] people = new SimplePerson[] {
        new SimplePerson("Samantha", "Lauren", "Tippin"),
        new SimplePerson("Kaitlynn", "Dawn", "Tippin"),
        new SimplePerson("Edward", "Alexander", "Wutka"),
        new SimplePerson("Norton", "Alexander", "Wutka")
    };

    BeanTableModel model;

    public TestBeanTableModel()
    {
        try
        {
            setLayout(new BorderLayout());

            Vector items = new Vector();
            for (int i=0; i < people.length; i++) items.addElement(people[i]);


            model = new BeanTableModel(
                items,
                new String[] { "firstName", "middleName", "lastName" });

            JTable table = new JTable(model);

            add("Center", table);

            JButton quitButton = new JButton("Quit");
            add("South", quitButton);

            quitButton.addActionListener(
                new ActionRelay(this, "handleQuit"));

        }
        catch (Exception exc)
        {
            exc.printStackTrace();
        }
    }

    public void handleQuit()
    {
        Enumeration e = model.getData().elements();
```

```
        while (e.hasMoreElements())
        {
            System.out.println(e.nextElement());
        }
        System.exit(0);
    }

    public static void main(String[] args)
    {
        try
        {
            JFrame testFrame = new JFrame("Table Test");

            TestBeanTableModel test = new TestBeanTableModel();

            testFrame.getContentPane().add(test, BorderLayout.CENTER);
            testFrame.pack();

// Make the frame exit when closed
            testFrame.addWindowListener(new ExitOnClose());

            testFrame.setVisible(true);
        }
        catch (Exception exc)
        {
            exc.printStackTrace();
        }
    }
}

class SimplePerson
{
    public String firstName;
    public String middleName;
    public String lastName;

    public SimplePerson(String aFirstName, String aMiddleName,
        String aLastName)
    {
        firstName = aFirstName;
        middleName = aMiddleName;
        lastName = aLastName;
    }

    public String getFirstName() { return firstName; }
    public void setFirstName(String fn) { firstName = fn; }
    public String getMiddleName() { return middleName; }
    public void setMiddleName(String mn) { middleName = mn; }
    public String getLastName() { return lastName; }
    public void setLastName(String ln) { lastName = ln; }

    public String toString()
    {
        return firstName+" "+middleName+" "+lastName;
    }
}
```

One of the keys to MVC programming is the Observer-Observable pattern. The `java.util` package contains an `Observable` base class and an `Observer` listener interface. The idea is that an observer registers itself with an observable object and when the observable object changes, it tells all the observers. Typically, a view registers itself as an observer of the model, which is an observable. That way, the views know when the model changes and can update the display appropriately.

Listing 42.6 shows a sample `set` method from an observable class. Notice that the class checks the current value against the new one to see if there is actually a change. If you aren't careful, you can create "update storms" in your program. For example, suppose you change a value in the model and you send out an update message. A text field receives the message, updates its value, and sends out an updated field value. Your model receives the updated value and processes it. If the model doesn't realize that the new value is the same value it already has, it will send out another update. The classes will constantly send each other update messages.

LISTING 42.6 SAMPLE `set` METHOD FOR AN OBSERVABLE OBJECT

```
public void setMobilePhone(String aMobilePhone)
{
    if ((mobilePhone == null) || !mobilePhone.equals(aMobilePhone))
    {
        mobilePhone = aMobilePhone;
        setChanged();
        notifyObservers();
    }
}
```

Suppose you create a whole library of adapter classes to link your views and controllers with your data model. For example, as Figure 42.2 shows, the views act as observers of the model, and through a set of adapters, the model acts as an observer of the controllers.

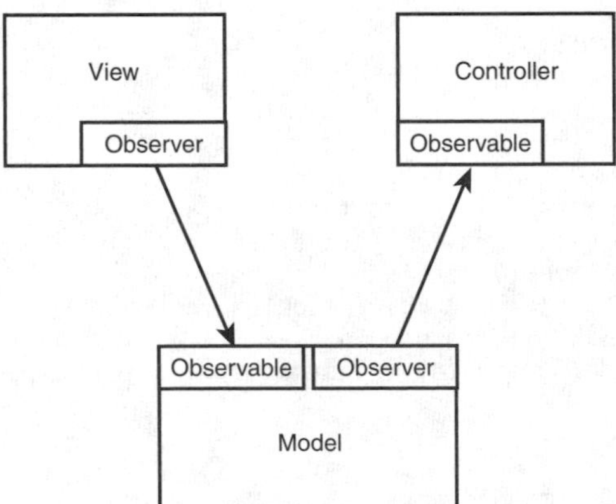

Figure 42.2 The views observe the model; the model observes the controllers.

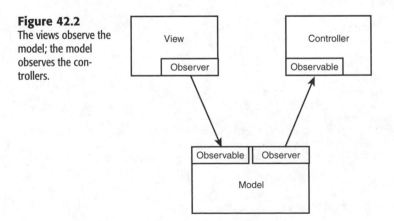

Although this configuration works well when you first set it up, what happens when you want to use a different object? As long as you create a holder class to contain the current model object, you don't need to recreate all the connections between the model and its controllers and views.

Using a holder in an MVC framework, you allow the views and controllers to go through the holder to access the model. That way, you change the current data object by just storing a new object in the holder. The holder has the capability to tell the views and controllers that you've inserted a new object.

Figure 42.3 illustrates the holder's place in an MVC framework.

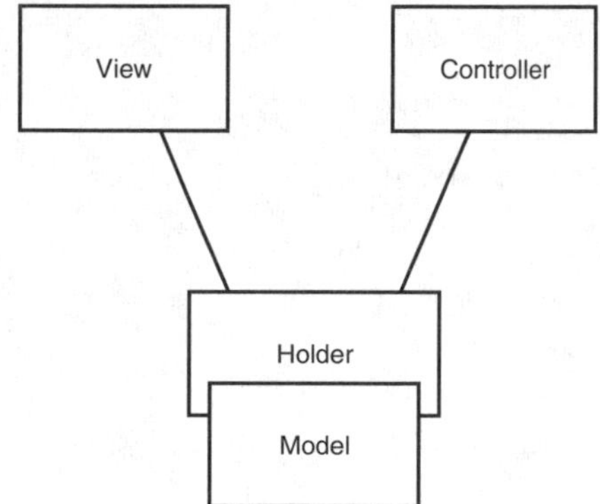

Figure 42.3
The holder acts as a single point of contact for the views and controllers to access the model.

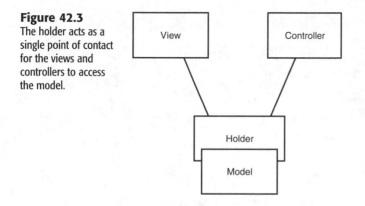

Listing 42.7 shows a simple holder object that acts as an observable. The holder observes the data item it is holding and notifies any observers when the data item changes. This extra level of indirection means that the views don't need to register directly with the data item. When you change the data item, the views automatically observe it. The `HolderChangeListener` interface is similar to the `java.util.Observer` interface. The holder invokes the `holderContentsChanged` to tell any interested listeners that there is a new object in the holder.

LISTING 42.7 SOURCE CODE FOR `Holder.java`

```
package usingj2ee.mvc;import java.util.*;

public class Holder extends Observable implements Observer
{
    protected Observable target;
    protected Vector changeListeners;

    public Holder()
    {
        this(null);
    }

    public Holder(Observable aTarget)
    {
```

LISTING 42.7 CONTINUED

```
        changeListeners = new Vector();

        target = aTarget;

        if (target != null)
        {
            target.addObserver(this);
        }
    }

// Return the actual data item
    public Observable getObject()
    {
        return target;
    }

// Change the data item
    public void setObject(Observable aTarget)
    {
// If there is a previous data item, stop observing it
        if (target != null)
        {
            target.deleteObserver(this);
        }

        target = aTarget;

        Enumeration e = ((Vector) changeListeners.clone()).elements();

// Tell all the change listeners that there is a new object in the holder
        while (e.hasMoreElements())
        {
            ((HolderChangeListener) e.nextElement()).
                holderContentsChanged(target);
        }

// Observe the new data item
        target.addObserver(this);

// Tell all the listeners that the data item has changed (in case
// some don't listen for the holderContentsChanged message)
        setChanged();
        notifyObservers();
    }

// If the data item fires an update (that is, it changed), tell the
// observers that the data item changed
    public void update(Observable obj, Object arg)
    {
        notifyObservers(arg);
    }

    public void addHolderChangeListener(HolderChangeListener listener)
    {
        if (!changeListeners.contains(listener))
        {
```

```
            changeListeners.addElement(listener);
        }
    }

    public void removeHolderChangeListener(HolderChangeListener listener)
    {
        changeListeners.removeElement(listener);
    }
}
```

Listing 42.8 shows a combination view/controller that connects a text field to the model using `get` and `set` methods in the model. It goes through the holder to access the data item and also listens for changes in the holder object so it can locate the `get` and `set` methods again if you store an object in the holder that has a different class than the previous object.

LISTING 42.8 SOURCE CODE FOR `TextFieldController.java`

```
package usingj2ee.mvc;

import java.lang.reflect.*;
import javax.swing.*;
import java.util.*;
import java.awt.event.*;
public class TextFieldController implements ActionListener, Observer,
    HolderChangeListener
{
    protected JTextField field;
    protected Holder holder;
    protected String getMethodName;
    protected String setMethodName;
    protected Method getMethod;
    protected Method setMethod;
    protected Class setArg;

    protected static final Object[] EMPTY_ARGS = new Object[0];

    public TextFieldController(JTextField theField, Holder theHolder,
        String aGetMethodName, String aSetMethodName)
    {
        field = theField;
        holder = theHolder;
        holder.addHolderChangeListener(this);

        getMethodName = aGetMethodName;
        setMethodName = aSetMethodName;

        getTargetMethods();

// Listen for changes in the data
        holder.addObserver(this);

// Listen for changes in the field
        field.addActionListener(this);

// Pretend that the data item has changed
        update(theHolder.getObject(), null);
```

LISTING 42.8 CONTINUED

```
    }

/** Locates the get and set methods for the target object */
    public void getTargetMethods()
    {
        Object target = holder.getObject();

        if (target == null) return;

        Method[] methods = target.getClass().getMethods();

        getMethod = null;
        setMethod = null;

        for (int i=0; i < methods.length; i++)
        {
            if (methods[i].getName().equals(getMethodName) &&
                    (methods[i].getParameterTypes().length == 0))
            {
                getMethod = methods[i];

// If you have both the get and set methods, quit looking
                if (setMethod != null) break;
            }
            else if (methods[i].getName().equals(setMethodName) &&
                    (methods[i].getParameterTypes().length == 1))
            {
                setMethod = methods[i];
                setArg = methods[i].getParameterTypes()[0];

// If you have both the get and set methods, quit looking
                if (getMethod != null) break;
            }
        }
    }

// If the data item changes, invoke the get method and then store
// the result in the text field (use the ValueConverter utility to
// translation numbers to strings if necessary)

    public void update(Observable obj, Object arg)
    {
        if (getMethod != null)
        {
            try
            {
                Object value = getMethod.invoke(holder.getObject(),
                     EMPTY_ARGS);
                field.setText((String) ValueConverter.convert(value,
                    java.lang.String.class));
            }
            catch (Exception exc)
            {
                exc.printStackTrace();
            }
        }
```

```
    }

// If the text field changes, retrieve the value and use the value converter
// to change the string to a number if necessary
    public void actionPerformed(ActionEvent evt)
    {
        if (setMethod != null)
        {
            try
            {
                Object value = ValueConverter.convert(field.getText(), setArg);

                setMethod.invoke(holder.getObject(), new Object[] { value });
            }
            catch (Exception exc)
            {
                exc.printStackTrace();
            }
        }
    }

// If the holder contains a new value, locate the get and set methods
// again in case the object is of a different class
    public void holderContentsChanged(Observable newObject)
    {
        getTargetMethods();
    }
}
```

Using the `TextFieldController` class, you can map a text field to a pair of `get`/`set` methods. For example, the following code fragment creates a text field for a last name and then hooks the field to the `getLastName` and `setLastName` methods:

```
lastNameField = new JTextField(30);
new TextFieldController(lastNameField, dataHolder,
    "getLastName", "setLastName");
```

Now when you enter a value in the last name field, the `TextFieldController` automatically calls the `setLastName` method. If you change the item that's in the holder, or change the last name some other way, the field automatically picks up the changed value.

Listing 42.9 shows a fragment of a GUI program that queries the `Person` EJB for data and the stores the data in the holder.

LISTING 42.9 `searchByLastName` **ROUTINE FROM** `PersonSearch.java`

```
public void searchByLastName()
{
    try
    {
        GUIPersonViewer viewer = (GUIPersonViewer) dataHolder.getObject();

        Collection names = home.findByLastName(viewer.getLastName());

        Iterator iter = names.iterator();
```

LISTING 42.9 CONTINUED

```
            if (iter.hasNext())
            {
                Person person = (Person) iter.next();

                viewer = (GUIPersonViewer) person.getAsView(
                    GUIPersonViewer.class.getName());

                dataHolder.setObject(viewer);
            }
        }
        catch (Exception exc)
        {
            exc.printStackTrace();
        }
    }
```

Figure 42.4 shows the `PersonSearch` program immediately before it calls the `searchByLastName` routine. You enter a last name in the Last Name field and the `searchByLastName` routine picks it up automatically because the `TextFieldController` copies the field value into the `GUIPersonViewer` object.

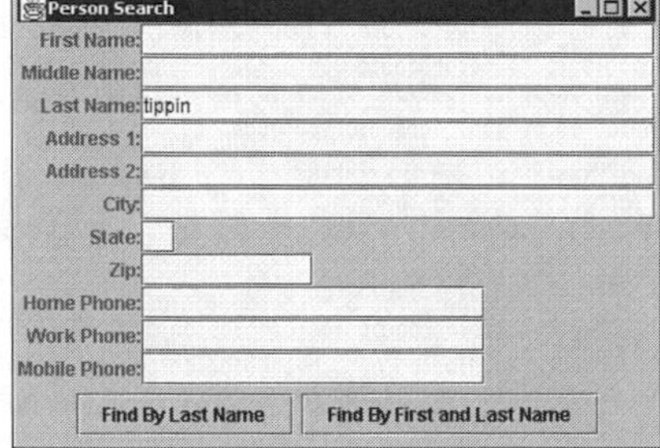

Figure 42.4
The Person Search program appears like this just before you change the value in the holder.

Figure 42.5 shows the `PersonSearch` program immediately after the program places a new value in the holder. Notice that all the fields have been updated to contain new values, but as you saw in the `searchByLastName` routine, the code doesn't update the fields explicitly. Instead, when you store a new value in the holder, all the `TextFieldController` objects see the change and update their respective fields.

Figure 42.5
The combination of the holder and the text field controllers makes it easy to update the onscreen data.

USING MVC IN A WEB APPLICATION

Most developers think of MVC in terms of a graphical user interface because MVC really came from GUI development. With a little imagination, however, you can extend the MVC paradigm to Web development, in terms of servlets and JSP. The idea is that you split your application into three sections. A servlet handles any requests from the browser and acts as a controller. You put your business logic (the model) in Java classes that are neither servlets nor Java Server Pages. Finally, you use Java Server Pages to display the view, a representation of the model.

When applying MVC to a Web application, you have to make some concessions toward the way the Web works. When you use MVC in a GUI application, you can display as many views as you like at any time. You can pop up another window or add some widgets to the screen. Pressing a button might cause only tiny changes in the view.

Because the browser and the Web server spend most of their time disconnected from each other, you can't have that kind of dynamic view or immediate feedback in a Web application. The important thing is that you concentrate on separating the model, view, and controller into distinct pieces.

HOW DOES MODEL-VIEW-CONTROLLER HELP?

Unfortunately, many applications are developed in a piecemeal fashion. Someone comes to a developer and says "Hey, can you write a JSP to display X on a browser." A little while later, that person comes back and says "Great, now can you put X over here, compute Y, and display Z over here." After a few rounds of this, the JSP might look beautiful to the user, but the source code probably looks hideous to the developer.

The sequence of tasks in the JSP can end up looking something like this:

1. Connect to the application server and get some data.
2. Display the data in HTML.
3. Go grab some information from the database.
4. If there's an error in the database, display error information.
5. Display the database information in HTML.
6. Go get the user's profile information from the security server.
7. If the user is a manager, erase the page and redraw it using the special manager's format.

No one ever intends things to be so convoluted; they just get that way sometimes. By applying MVC to this same sequence of events, you get a cleaner picture. The sequence would be something like this:

1. The controller servlet connects to the application server, gets some data, and stores it in the `request` object.
2. The controller servlet grabs some information from the database and stores it in the `request` object.

3. If there is an error fetching data from the database, the controller servlet forwards to an error JSP.
4. The controller servlet fetches the user's profile information from the security server.
5. If the user is a manager, the controller servlet forwards to a JSP that displays the manager's view of the data.
6. If the user is not a manager, the controller servlet forwards to the regular display JSP.
7. The display Java Server Page grabs the information from the `request` object and displays it.

AN EXAMPLE CONTROLLER

Listing 42.10 shows you an example controller that queries a database and then calls a view JSP to show the results. The database access code is not as robust as it should be.

LISTING 42.10 SOURCE CODE FOR `ControllerServlet.java`

```
package usingj2ee;

import java.io.*;
import java.util.*;
import java.sql.*;
import javax.servlet.*;

public class ControllerServlet extends GenericServlet
{
    protected Connection conn;

    public void init()
    {
        try
        {
// Make sure the JdbcOdbcDriver class is loaded
            Class.forName("sun.jdbc.odbc.JdbcOdbcDriver");

// Try to connect to a database via ODBC
            conn = DriverManager.getConnection(
                "jdbc:odbc:usingjsp");
        }
        catch (Exception exc)
        {
// If there's an error, use the servlet logging API
            getServletContext().log(
                "Error making JDBC connection: ", exc);
        }
    }

    public void destroy()
    {
        try
        {
// Only try to close the connection if it's non-null
            if (conn != null)
            {
```

```
                conn.close();
            }
        }
        catch (SQLException exc)
        {
// If there's an error, use the servlet logging API
            getServletContext().log(
                "Error closing JDBC connection: ", exc);
        }
    }

// This servlet isn't doing connection pooling, so just synchronize for
// thread safety.
// For production systems, don't do this, use a connection pool!

    public synchronized void service(ServletRequest request,
        ServletResponse response)
        throws java.io.IOException, ServletException
    {
        Statement stmt = null;

// Parse the minimum and maximum ages and go to an error page if they
// are invalid
        String minimumAgeStr = request.getParameter("minAge");
        int minimumAge = 0;

        try
        {
            minimumAge = Integer.parseInt(minimumAgeStr);
        }
        catch (Exception exc)
        {
            gotoPage("/j2eebook/ch42/examples/BadAge.jsp?"+
                "reason=Invalid+minimum+age",
                request, response);
        }

        String maximumAgeStr = request.getParameter("maxAge");
        int maximumAge = 0;

        try
        {
            maximumAge = Integer.parseInt(maximumAgeStr);
        }
        catch (Exception exc)
        {
            gotoPage("/j2eebook/ch42/examples/BadAge.jsp?"+
                "reason=Invalid+maximum+age",
                request, response);
        }

        try
        {
            stmt = conn.createStatement();

// Get all the people matching the criteria
            ResultSet results = stmt.executeQuery(
                "select * from person where age between "+
```

LISTING 42.10 CONTINUED

```
                    minimumAge+" and "+ maximumAge);

            Vector v = new Vector();

            while (results.next())
            {
// The person class can construct itself from a database row
                v.addElement(new Person(results));
            }

// Store the vector of person objects so the JSP can access it
            request.setAttribute("people", v);

            gotoPage("/j2eebook/ch42/examples/ShowPeople.jsp",
                request, response);
        }
        catch (SQLException exc)
        {
            request.setAttribute("exception", exc.toString());
            gotoPage("/j2eebook/ch42/examples/DatabaseError.jsp",
                request, response);
        }
        finally
        {
            try {
                stmt.close();
            } catch (Exception ignore) {}
        }
    }

// Because the servlet needs to forward to many pages, this method
// comes in handy as a one-liner for forwarding. It should really
// check to make sure it could get the dispatcher and do something
// predictable if it can't.

    public void gotoPage(String pageName,
        ServletRequest request, ServletResponse response)
        throws IOException, ServletException
    {
        RequestDispatcher d = getServletContext().
            getRequestDispatcher(pageName);

        d.forward(request, response);
    }
}
```

AN EXAMPLE VIEW

The controller has done most of the work for this example. The view just needs to display the results. The view uses a `TableServlet` class that uses Reflection to display values in an HTML table. The view just needs to set up the proper parameters for the servlet. In fact, because the controller already stores the data in the `request` object, the view doesn't need to. It just needs to tell `TableServlet` where to find the data. Listing 42.11 shows the example view.

Listing 42.11 Source Code for `ShowPeople.jsp`

```
<HTML>
<BODY bgcolor="#ffffff">

The following people matched your search criteria:
<P>
<%-- Invoke the Table servlet, tell it the name of the attribute
     where the data is stored (data=people), set the border size to 4
     on the <TABLE> tag, and describe each column to display.

     The "people" attribute was sent from the controller servlet
     and contains a vector of people objects. --%>

<jsp:include page="/servlet/usingj2ee.TableServlet" flush="true">
    <jsp:param name="data" value="people"/>

    <jsp:param name="tableOptions" value="BORDER=4"/>

    <jsp:param name="column" value="name"/>
    <jsp:param name="columnType" value="data"/>
    <jsp:param name="columnHeader" value="Name"/>

    <jsp:param name="column" value="age"/>
    <jsp:param name="columnType" value="data"/>
    <jsp:param name="columnHeader" value="Age"/>

    <jsp:param name="column" value="city"/>
    <jsp:param name="columnType" value="data"/>
    <jsp:param name="columnHeader" value="City"/>

    <jsp:param name="column" value="state"/>
    <jsp:param name="columnType" value="data"/>
    <jsp:param name="columnHeader" value="State"/>

    <jsp:param name="column" value="country"/>
    <jsp:param name="columnType" value="data"/>
    <jsp:param name="columnHeader" value="Country"/>

    <jsp:param name="column" value="postalCode"/>
    <jsp:param name="columnType" value="data"/>
    <jsp:param name="columnHeader" value="Postal Code"/>

    <jsp:param name="column" value="email"/>
    <jsp:param name="columnType" value="data"/>
    <jsp:param name="columnHeader" value="E-Mail"/>
</jsp:include>
</BODY>
</HTML>
```

Listing 42.12 shows the `TableServlet` class. The `TableServlet` class uses Reflection to examine the contents of an array or a vector. It creates an HTML table containing an optional header followed by the data items.

LISTING 42.12 SOURCE CODE FOR TableServlet.java

```
package usingj2ee;

import javax.servlet.*;
import java.io.*;
import java.util.*;
import java.lang.reflect.*;

/** This class uses the Reflection API to fetch data from an array or
 *  a vector and put it in a table */

public class TableServlet extends GenericServlet
{
    public static final Class[] NO_PARAMS = new Class[0];

    public void service(ServletRequest request, ServletResponse response)
        throws IOException, ServletException
    {

// First, get the parameters for the TABLE, TR, TD, and TH options
        String tableOptions = request.getParameter("tableOptions");
        if (tableOptions == null) tableOptions = "";

        String trOptions = request.getParameter("trOptions");
        if (trOptions == null) trOptions = "";

        String tdOptions = request.getParameter("tdOptions");
        if (tdOptions == null) tdOptions = "";

        String thOptions = request.getParameter("thOptions");
        if (thOptions == null) thOptions = "";

// Now, get the name of the object that contains the data to display
        String data = request.getParameter("data");

        if (data == null)
        {
            getServletContext().log("No data available");
            throw new ServletException(
                "No data parameter available");
        }

// Get the actual data object
        Object dataOb = request.getAttribute(data);
        if (dataOb == null)
        {
            getServletContext().log("No data object found");
            throw new ServletException(
                "Can't locate the data object named "+
                data);
        }

// Get the list of method/field names to display in each column
        String[] columns = request.getParameterValues("column");

// Get the types of each column field
        String[] columnType = request.getParameterValues("columnType");
```

```
// Get the headers for each column
        String[] columnHeaders = request.getParameterValues(
            "columnHeader");

// Create a table of column names and Fields/Methods for fetching data
        Hashtable columnAccessors =
            getAccessors(dataOb, columns);

// First print the table header
        PrintWriter out = response.getWriter();
        out.println("<TABLE "+tableOptions+">");

// If there are any headers, print them out
        if (columnHeaders != null)
        {
            out.println("<TR "+trOptions+">");
            for (int i=0; i < columnHeaders.length; i++)
            {
                out.print("<TH "+thOptions+">");
                out.println(columnHeaders[i]);
            }
        }

// If the object is a vector, loop through the elements
        if (dataOb instanceof Vector)
        {
            Vector v = (Vector) dataOb;

            Enumeration e = v.elements();

            while (e.hasMoreElements())
            {
// For each row, print out the <TR> tag plus any options
                out.println("<TR "+trOptions+">");

// Print out the column values for the row
                printRow(out, e.nextElement(),
                    columns, columnType,
                    columnAccessors, tdOptions);
            }
        }
// If the object is an array, loop through the objects
        else if (dataOb instanceof Object[])
        {
            Object[] obs = (Object[]) dataOb;

            for (int i=0; i < obs.length; i++)
            {
// For each row, print out the <TR> tag plus any options
                out.println("<TR "+trOptions+">");

// Print out the column values for the row
                printRow(out, obs[i],
                    columns, columnType,
                    columnAccessors, tdOptions);
            }
        }
```

LISTING 42.12 CONTINUED

```
        out.println("</TABLE>");
    }

    protected void printRow(PrintWriter out, Object ob,
        String[] columns, String[] columnTypes,
        Hashtable columnAccessors, String tdOptions)
        throws ServletException
    {

// Loop through all the column names
        for (int i=0; i < columns.length; i++)
        {
// Get the value for this column out of the object
            Object value = getColumnValue(ob, columns[i],
                columnAccessors);

// Print the TD tag
            out.print("<TD "+tdOptions+">");

// If the column type is data, just print the data
            if (columnTypes[i].equalsIgnoreCase("data"))
            {
                out.print(value);
            }
// If the column type is "image", print out an <IMG> tag
            else if (columnTypes[i].equalsIgnoreCase("image"))
            {
                out.print("<IMG src=\""+value+"\">");
            }
        }
    }

/** Fetch a value from an object using either a Field or a Method object */
    protected Object getColumnValue(Object ob, String columnName,
        Hashtable columnAccessors)
        throws ServletException
    {
// Get the object used to fetch this column's value
        Object accessor = columnAccessors.get(columnName);

// If the column is a field...
        if (accessor instanceof Field)
        {
// ... fetch the value using the get method for the field
            try
            {
                Field f = (Field) accessor;

                return f.get(ob);
            }
// Log, then return the IllegalAccessException
            catch (IllegalAccessException exc)
            {
                getServletContext().log(
                    "Error getting column "+
                    columnName, exc);
```

```
                throw new ServletException(
                    "Illegal access exception for column "+
                    columnName);
            }
        }
// If the column is a Method...
        else if (accessor instanceof Method)
        {
// ... invoke the method
            try
            {
                Method m = (Method) accessor;

// The NO_PARAMS value is an empty array of Class defined at the top
// of this class.
                return m.invoke(ob, NO_PARAMS);
            }
// Log, then return any exceptions that come up while invoking the method
            catch (IllegalAccessException exc)
            {
                getServletContext().log(
                    "Error getting column "+
                    columnName, exc);
                throw new ServletException(
                    "Illegal access exception for column "+
                    columnName);
            }
            catch (InvocationTargetException exc)
            {
                getServletContext().log(
                    "Error getting column "+
                    columnName, exc);
                throw new ServletException(
                    "Invocation target exception "+
                    "for column "+columnName);
            }
        }
// If the column is neither a Field nor a Method, return null. You should
// never get to this point.
        return null;
    }

/** Creates a table mapping column-name to Field/Method */
    protected Hashtable getAccessors(Object ob, String[] columns)
        throws ServletException
    {
        Hashtable result = new Hashtable();

// First, get the Class for the kind of object being displayed
        Class obClass = null;

        if (ob instanceof Object[])
        {
// If the objects are in an array, get the first object in the array
            Object[] obs = (Object[]) ob;
// If there are no objects, don't bother filling the table
// it won't be needed
            if (obs.length == 0) return result;
```

LISTING 42.12 CONTINUED

```
            obClass = obs[0].getClass();
        }
        else if (ob instanceof Vector)
        {
// If the objects are in a vector, get the first element of the vector
            Vector v = (Vector) ob;

// If there are no objects, don't bother filling the table
// it won't be needed
            if (v.size() == 0) return result;

            obClass = v.elementAt(0).getClass();
        }

// For each column, look for a field and then a method with the column name
        for (int i=0; i < columns.length; i++)
        {
// First see if there is a field that matches the column name
            try
            {
                Field f = obClass.getField(columns[i]);
// If so, put it in the table and go to the next column name
                result.put(columns[i], f);
                continue;
            }
            catch (Exception ignore)
            {
            }

// Now see if there is a method that matches this column name
            try
            {
// The NO_PARAMS value is an empty array of Class defined at the top
// of this class.
                Method m = obClass.getMethod(columns[i],
                    NO_PARAMS);
// If so, put it in the table
                result.put(columns[i], m);
            }
            catch (Exception exc)
            {
                getServletContext().log(
                    "Exception location field "+
                    columns[i], exc);
                throw new ServletException(
                    "Can't locate field/method for "+
                    columns[i]);
            }
        }

        return result;
    }
}
```

The front end to this Controller-View pairing is a very small HTML page that prompts for the minimum and maximum ages for the query. Listing 42.13 shows the source for the HTML page.

LISTING 42.13 SOURCE CODE FOR PeopleQuery.html

```
<HTML>
<BODY>

Please enter the minimum and maximum ages to view:
<P>
<FORM action="/servlet/usingj2ee.ControllerServlet" method="POST">
Minimum Age: <INPUT type="text" name="minAge"><BR>
Maximum Age: <INPUT type="text" name="maxAge"><BR>
<P>
<INPUT type="submit" value="Perform Query!">
</FORM>
</BODY>
</HTML>
```

Finally, Figure 42.6 shows the output of the view class. Most of the view is actually generated by the `TableServlet` class.

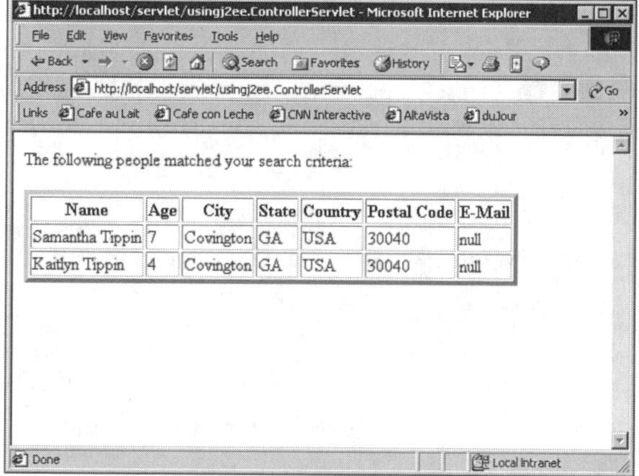

Figure 42.6 The View page is responsible for displaying the data retrieved from the model.

CALLING MULTIPLE CONTROLLERS AND VIEWS

One of the things you will notice in the controller servlet is that it has direct knowledge of the JSP that is handling the view. You should strive to break such dependencies whenever you can. For example, if you wanted to do things exactly the same way in the controller but display a different view of the data, you would have to make a separate version of the controller that displays the alternate view.

The controller should be concerned with sending input information to the model, and the view should be concerned with displaying the output. The only thing that ties the controller to the view at the moment is the fact that the controller contains the logic to forward the request on to the view. The way to completely separate the controller from the view is with a dispatcher servlet.

A dispatcher performs the crucial transition between the controller and the view. Instead of invoking a controller directly, you call the dispatcher and tell it which controller you want to call and which view to display. That way, the controller doesn't have any specific view hard-wired into its code. Likewise, the dispatcher doesn't have a view hard-wired in, either.

Note

This is not the same dispatcher as the `RequestDispatcher` class that is part of the Servlet API. This section of the book refers to a dispatcher in the generic sense.

You can even have the dispatcher call multiple controllers, before calling a view. That way, you can break your business logic down into fine-grained pieces. When the browser sends a request to the server, it might invoke several controllers to update various portions of the model before displaying the view.

One of the traditional problems in designing a Web application is the limited interaction between the browser and the server. You need to do as much as possible within a single request. In the past, this restriction has resulted in large, complicated servlets that perform many different functions. Many times, you would end up with several servlets that were more similar than they were different, because they needed to perform several common functions.

The dispatcher allows you to separate common functions, put them each in their own servlets, and call them when you need them, even if you need to call several of them from a single request.

Listing 42.14 shows the dispatcher servlet. You pass the controllers using parameters (form variables) named `controller`. The pathname for the normal view is passed in the `view` parameter, and the pathname for the error handler view is passed in the `errorView` parameter.

LISTING 42.14 SOURCE CODE FOR `DispatcherServlet.java`

```
package usingj2ee;

import java.io.*;
import java.util.*;
import java.sql.*;
import javax.servlet.*;

public class DispatcherServlet extends GenericServlet
{
    public void service(ServletRequest request,
        ServletResponse response)
        throws java.io.IOException, ServletException
    {
```

```
// Get the list of controllers to call
        String[] controllers =
            request.getParameterValues("controller");

// Get the name of the view to call
        String viewName = request.getParameter("view");

// Get the name of the view to call if there is an error
        String errorViewName = request.getParameter("errorView");

        try
        {
            for (int i=0; i < controllers.length; i++)
            {
                RequestDispatcher d =
                    getServletContext().
                        getRequestDispatcher(
                            controllers[i]);
                if (d != null)
                {
// Invoke the next controller
                    d.include(request, response);
                }
                else
                {
                    getServletContext().log(
                        "No controller named "+
                        controllers[i]);
                }
            }

            RequestDispatcher d = getServletContext().
                getRequestDispatcher(viewName);

// The dispatcher includes the other controllers, but it forwards to the view
            if (d != null)
            {
                d.forward(request, response);
            }
            else
            {
                getServletContext().log(
                    "No view named "+viewName);
            }
        }
        catch (Exception exc)
        {
// If there is an error, forward to the error view

            request.setAttribute("exception", exc.toString());

            RequestDispatcher d = getServletContext().
                getRequestDispatcher(errorViewName);

            if (d != null)
            {
                d.forward(request, response);
```

LISTING 42.14 CONTINUED

```
                }
                else
                {
                    getServletContext().log(
                        "No errorView named "+errorViewName);
                }
            }
        }
}
```

If you want use the dispatcher to call the `ControllerServlet`, you need to strip a few things out of the controller. You no longer need to include the calls to `gotoPage` because the dispatcher is handling that. Instead of calling the error page, make the controller throw a `ServletException` with the reason for the error.

You don't need to change anything in the `ShowPeople.jsp` page to make it work with the dispatcher. The only other thing you need to do is modify the initial HTML form so it passes the controller and view information to the dispatcher. You can insert the information as hidden form variables, so it is automatically passed when the user submits the form. Listing 42.15 shows the modified HTML form.

LISTING 42.15 SOURCE CODE FOR `PeopleQuery2.html`

```
<HTML>
<BODY>

Please enter the minimum and maximum ages to view:
<P>
<FORM action="/servlet/usingj2ee.DispatcherServlet" method="POST">

<INPUT type=hidden name="controller"
    value="/servlet/usingj2ee.ControllerServlet2">
<INPUT type=hidden name="view" value="/j2eebook/ch42/examples/ShowPeople.jsp">
<INPUT type=hidden name="errorView"
    value="/j2eebook/ch42/examples/ErrorHandler.jsp">

Minimum Age: <INPUT type="text" name="minAge"><BR>
Maximum Age: <INPUT type="text" name="maxAge"><BR>
<P>
<INPUT type="submit" value="Perform Query!">
</FORM>
</BODY>
</HTML>
```

CASE STUDY

I have always been fascinated by cryptograms and secret codes. When I work on tough cryptograms, I usually create computer programs to assist me with some of the housekeeping work (counting letter frequencies, for example). While reading the classic book *Cryptanalysis* by Helen Fouché Gaines, I came upon an interesting cipher that screamed for computer assistance.

A *grille cipher* is a cipher in which you take a piece of metal or cardboard and punch holes in various sections. This piece of metal or cardboard is called the grille. You start writing your message in the punched out holes and when you run out of holes, you rotate the piece of metal 90°, but still over the same section of paper. You must take some care in deciding where to punch holes, because you want the holes arranged so that when you rotate the grille by 90°, the holes don't show a place where you have already written a letter.

For example, suppose you create a grille using the pattern shown in Figure 42.7.

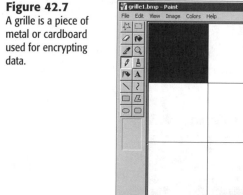

Figure 42.7
A grille is a piece of metal or cardboard used for encrypting data.

To encrypt the message "CRYPTANALYSETHIS," you place the grille on a piece of paper and start writing. Because the grille only has four holes, you can only fit the first four letters of the message into the grille, as shown in Figure 42.8.

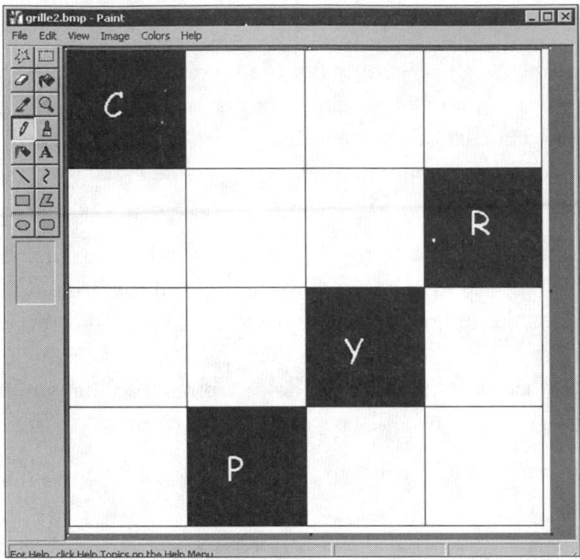

Figure 42.8
You write letters through the holes in the grid until you run out of holes.

Next, you rotate the grille 90° and write the next four letters. Figure 42.9 shows you the next four letters in the grille, with the previous four still present. Notice that the grille holes don't overlap the previous letters.

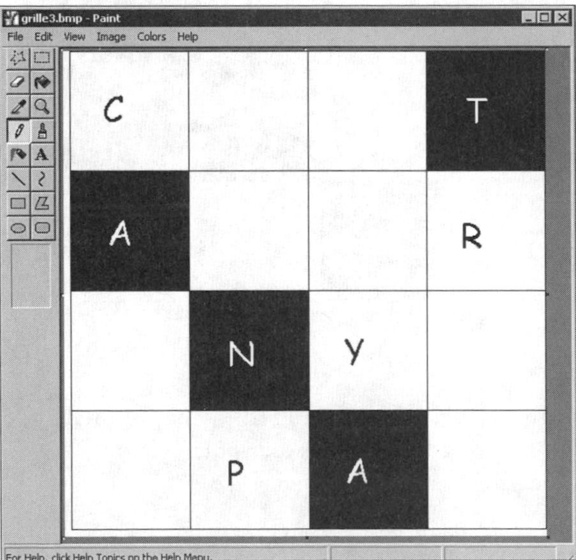

Figure 42.9
The holes in the grille should not overlap when rotated.

If you continue rotating the grille and filling in letters, you eventually end up with a grid that looks like the one shown in Figure 42.10. You can then read off the letters into the cryptogram "CHET ASIR YNYS TPAL."

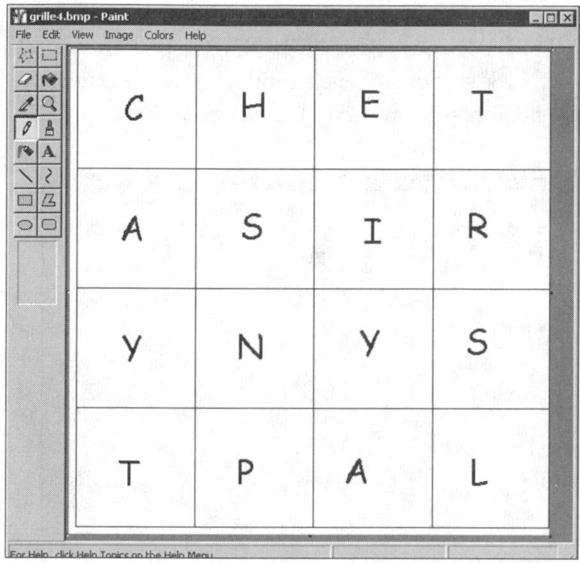

Figure 42.10
When you finish writing the message, you should have a grid containing a scrambled message.

To decode a grille message, you simply arrange the letters back into a square, place the grille over the message, and copy down the letters that appear in the holes. When you've copied all the letters, you rotate the grille 90° and copy the next set of letters. In other words, the decoding procedure is almost identical to the encoding procedure.

The fun of cryptanalysis, of course, is figuring out the original message without knowing the shape of the original grille. I needed a program that would display a grille and let me punch out holes in the grille. The program should show all four rotations of the grille, and show the message text contained in each rotation. Using this program, I could try punching out parts of words and see how it affected other parts of the message. If I saw combinations like FZQ come up, I would know I was on the wrong track.

This kind of application is ideal for a model-view-controller design. The model consists of the encrypted message and the shape of the grille. The view contains the text generated by each rotation of the grille and the shape of each grille. The controller is simply the various grille shapes. I click a location in a grille, and the program either punches a hole in the grille or removes an existing hole.

When I punch out a new hole in the grille, the controller sends a signal to the model telling it to update the current grille setting and the generated text. When the model updates, it sends messages to the text displays and the grille displays telling them to update. The beauty of the program, as with most MVC applications, is that I was able to write each piece individually. The model doesn't know how it is being displayed, and the views and controllers don't worry about maintaining the model.

Figure 42.11 shows the grille application in the middle of solving the cryptogram "TSTHE TTUSH OEDGF RDOEO GRISA AMSNM QEUGI BRIEL NOSTH SICLS ETSWA THABR YPAE." The black sections of each grille display represent the holes. Notice that the text below shows the letters from each black section.

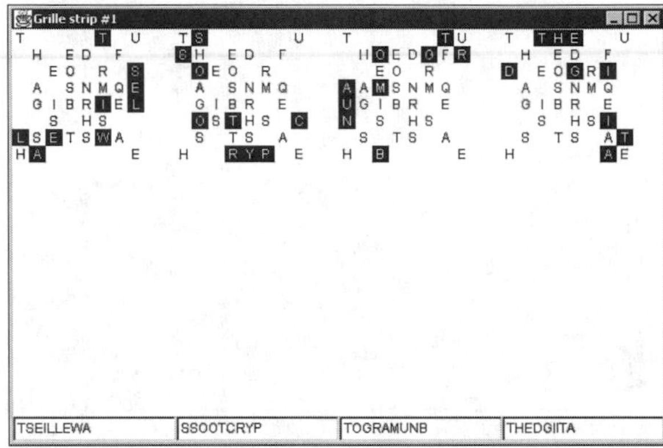

Figure 42.11
The grille application uses the MVC pattern to maintain multiple views of a grille cryptogram.

Whenever you design a graphics application, try to identify the model, views, and controllers before writing your code.

CHAPTER 43

Code Generation

In this chapter

GENERATING CODE AUTOMATICALLY

Some programming is fun, and some is exceedingly boring. Wouldn't it be nice if you could get the computer to write the boring parts? Automatic code generation goes a long way toward helping you with the boring parts.

Java doesn't have any code-generation APIs, but it does have several utilities that perform code generation. The IDL-to-Java compiler generates Java code, the `rmic` RMI interface compiler generates Java class files, the JSP compiler generates servlets, and most EJB deployment tools generate extra classes to make your EJBs work within the container.

Most Java development environments that support drag-and-drop GUI design generate the GUI code automatically. For example, if you use Borland's JBuilder, you can watch it add code as you place items on the screen.

You generally find code generators in three major areas: remote invocation tools (CORBA, RMI), database mapping utilities, and GUI designers. If you use a Computer Aided Software Engineering (CASE) tool such as Rational Rose, you will find that it also generates Java code.

Even though you might not be writing something as complicated as a database mapping layer or a remote invocation library, code generation is still a useful item to have in your toolkit. How many times do you start a new Java class by copying one you already have? You often copy classes that involve a lot of framework setup (making a database connection, initializing your server framework, and so on). Why not make a template with all the setup already done?

Code generation can be an ugly business if you don't have a template-driven program. For example, Listing 43.1 shows a simple Hello World generator program (as if there aren't enough Hello World programs out there). When you write a code generator this way, you must first get the code generator to compile and run, and then you must get the generated code to compile and run. It's a tedious process, but after the generator is done, it saves everyone a lot of time (hopefully more time than it took you to write the program in the first place!)

LISTING 43.1 SOURCE CODE FOR `HelloWorldGenerator.java`

```
package usingj2ee.generate;

import java.io.*;

public class HelloWorldGenerator
{
    public static void main(String[] args)
    {
        try
        {
// Assume the first argument is the class name
            String className = args[0];
```

```
// Create a .java file for the class
            PrintWriter out = new PrintWriter(
                new FileWriter(className+".java"));

// Write out the Hello World program
            out.println("public class "+className);
            out.println("{");
            out.println("    public static void main(String[] args)");
            out.println("    {");

// Print out the command-line arguments as the Hello World message
            out.print("        System.out.print(\"");
            for (int i=1; i < args.length; i++)
            {
                if (i > 1) out.print(" ");
                out.print(args[i]);
            }
            out.println("\");");
            out.println("    }");
            out.println("}");
            out.close();
        }
        catch (Exception exc)
        {
            exc.printStackTrace();
        }
    }
}
```

Listing 43.2 shows an example Hello World program generated by the `HelloWorldGenerator` program.

LISTING 43.2 SOURCE CODE FOR `HiCeal.java`

```
public class HiCeal{
    public static void main(String[] args)
    {
        System.out.print("Hi Ceal!");
    }
}
```

USING XML TO DESCRIBE OBJECTS

XML is handy for describing data for a code generator. XML's capability to handle structured data with ease makes it ideal for generating code.

One of the areas of Java coding that can be particularly tedious is creating JavaBeans—especially when they have a lot of properties. The properties are easy to define, and you typically implement them all the same way—at least until you start adding extra business logic to the getters and setters.

When you generate code, there's no reason you can't edit the generated code. Sometimes a code generator just makes for a good head start.

Now, to generate JavaBeans (for this example, you'll just generate properties and not events), you need a way to represent the parts of the bean you want to generate. The first thing to do is model them in Java. Listing 43.3 shows the `BeanModel` class that represents the bean.

LISTING 43.3—SOURCE CODE FOR `BeanModel.java`

```
package com.wutka.beanmaker;

import java.io.*;
import java.util.*;

/** Represents the class and package names for a Bean and the bean's
 *  properties.
 *
 * @author Mark Wutka
 */

public class BeanModel implements Serializable
{
    protected String className;
    protected String packageName;
    protected Vector propertyVec;
    protected Vector indexedPropertyVec;

/** Creates a new, empty BeanModel */
    public BeanModel()
    {
        propertyVec = new Vector();
        indexedPropertyVec = new Vector();
    }

    public String getClassName() { return className; }
    public void setClassName(String aClassName)
    {
        className = aClassName;
    }

    public String getPackageName() { return packageName; }
    public void setPackageName(String aPackageName)
    {
        packageName = aPackageName;
    }

    public Property[] getProperty()
    {
        Property[] retval = new Property[propertyVec.size()];
        propertyVec.copyInto(retval);
        return retval;
    }

    public void setProperty(Property[] newProperty)
    {
        propertyVec = new Vector(newProperty.length);
        for (int i=0; i < newProperty.length; i++)
        {
            propertyVec.addElement(newProperty[i]);
```

```
        }
    }

    public Property getProperty(int i)
    {
        return (Property) propertyVec.elementAt(i);
    }

    public void setProperty(Property aProperty, int i)
    {
        propertyVec.setElementAt(aProperty, i);
    }

    public Property[] getIndexedProperty()
    {
        Property[] retval = new Property[
            indexedPropertyVec.size()];
        indexedPropertyVec.copyInto(retval);
        return retval;
    }

    public void setIndexedProperty(Property[] newIndexedProperty)
    {
        indexedPropertyVec = new Vector(newIndexedProperty.length);
        for (int i=0; i < newIndexedProperty.length; i++)
        {
            indexedPropertyVec.addElement(newIndexedProperty[i]);
        }
    }

    public Property getIndexedProperty(int i)
    {
        return (Property) indexedPropertyVec.elementAt(i);
    }

    public void setIndexedProperty(Property aIndexedProperty, int i)
    {
        indexedPropertyVec.setElementAt(aIndexedProperty, i);
    }
}
```

The `BeanModel` class uses a `Property` class that describes a bean property. Listing 43.4 shows the `Property` class.

Listing 43.4 Source Code for Property.java

```
package com.wutka.beanmaker;

import java.util.*;

/** Represents a bean property */
public class Property implements java.io.Serializable
{
    protected String propertyName;
    protected String propertyType;
```

LISTING 43.3—CONTINUED

```
    public Property()
    {
    }

    public String getPropertyName() { return propertyName; }
    public void setPropertyName(String aPropertyName)
    {
        propertyName = aPropertyName;
    }

    public String getPropertyType() { return propertyType; }
    public void setPropertyType(String aPropertyType)
    {
        propertyType = aPropertyType;
    }

    public String toString()
    {
        StringBuffer buff = new StringBuffer();
        buff.append("name: ");
        buff.append(propertyName);
        buff.append(",type: ");
        buff.append(propertyType);
        return buff.toString();
    }
}
```

Now, there's a good reason why the `BeanModel` and `Property` classes are implemented as JavaBeans (with `get`/`set` methods for all the attributes). The code generator can use the JOX library to read the model.

Listing 43.5 shows the `BeanMaker` class, which is the class that actually generates the bean code. It uses JOX to read in an XML description of the bean you want to generate, and then it uses a series of print statements to write out the bean.

LISTING 43.5 SOURCE CODE FOR `BeanMaker.java`

```
package com.wutka.beanmaker;

import java.io.*;
import com.wutka.jox.*;

/**
 Creates a JavaBean from a simple XML description.

Here is an example bean description file:
<pre>
&lt;?xml version="1.0"?&gt;
&lt;bean&gt;
    &lt;class-name&gt;Year&lt;/class-name&gt;
    &lt;package-name&gt;com.wutka.jox.test.baseball&lt;/package-name&gt;
    &lt;property&gt;
        &lt;property-name&gt;Year&lt;/property-name&gt;
```

```
        &lt;property-type&gt;String&lt;/property-type&gt;
    &lt;/property&gt;
    &lt;indexed-property&gt;
        &lt;property-name&gt;League&lt;/property-name&gt;
        &lt;property-type&gt;League&lt;/property-type&gt;
    &lt;/indexed-property&gt;
&lt;/bean&gt;
</pre>

 * @author Mark Wutka
 */

public class BeanMaker
{
    public static void main(String[] args)
    {
        if (args.length < 1)
        {
            System.out.println("Please supply an XML file");
        }

        try
        {
// Create a reader to load the XML input file
            JOXBeanReader reader = new JOXBeanReader(
                new FileReader(args[0]));

// Load the XML description into a BeanModel object
            BeanModel model = (BeanModel) reader.readObject(
                BeanModel.class);

// Create a writer for writing out the Java source for the bean
            PrintWriter out = new PrintWriter(new BufferedWriter(
                new FileWriter(model.getClassName()+".java")));

// From here to the end of the method is an ugly mixture of print/println
// spitting out Java code

            if (model.getPackageName() != null)
            {
                out.println("package "+model.getPackageName()+";");
                out.println();
            }
            out.println("import java.util.Vector;");
            out.println();
            out.println("public class "+model.getClassName()+
                " implements java.io.Serializable");
            out.println("{");

            Property[] props = model.getProperty();
            Property[] indexed = model.getIndexedProperty();

            for (int i=0; i < props.length; i++)
            {
                out.println("\tprotected "+props[i].getPropertyType()+
                    " "+uncap(props[i].getPropertyName())+
                    ";");
            }
```

LISTING 43.5 CONTINUED

```
        out.println();

        for (int i=0; i < indexed.length; i++)
        {
            out.println("\tprotected Vector "+
                uncap(indexed[i].getPropertyName())+
                "Vec;");
        }
        out.println();

        out.println("\tpublic "+model.getClassName()+"()");
        out.println("\t{");

        for (int i=0; i < indexed.length; i++)
        {
            out.println("\t\t"+uncap(indexed[i].getPropertyName())+
                "Vec = new Vector();");
        }
        out.println("\t}");
        out.println();


        for (int i=0; i < props.length; i++)
        {
            out.println("\tpublic "+props[i].getPropertyType()+
                " get"+cap(props[i].getPropertyName())+
                "()");
            out.println("\t{");
            out.println("\t\treturn "+uncap(props[i].getPropertyName())+";");
            out.println("\t}");
            out.println();
            out.print("\tpublic void set"+ cap(props[i].getPropertyName())+
                "("+props[i].getPropertyType()+" the"+
                cap(props[i].getPropertyName())+")");
            out.println("\t{");
            out.println("\t\t"+uncap(props[i].getPropertyName())+
                " = the"+cap(props[i].getPropertyName())+";");
            out.println("\t}");
            out.println();
        }

        for (int i=0; i < indexed.length; i++)
        {
            out.println("\tpublic "+indexed[i].getPropertyType()+"[] get"+
                cap(indexed[i].getPropertyName())+"()");
            out.println("\t{");
            out.println("\t\t"+indexed[i].getPropertyType()+
                "[] retval = new "+indexed[i].getPropertyType()+
                "["+uncap(indexed[i].getPropertyName())+
                "Vec.size()];");
            out.println("\t\t"+uncap(indexed[i].getPropertyName())+
                "Vec.copyInto(retval);");
            out.println("\t\treturn retval;");
            out.println("\t}");
            out.println();
            out.println("\tpublic void set"+cap(indexed[i].getPropertyName())+
```

```
                    "("+indexed[i].getPropertyType()+"[] values)");
                out.println("\t{");
                out.println("\t\t"+uncap(indexed[i].getPropertyName())+
                    "Vec = new Vector(values.length);");
                out.println("\t\tfor (int i=0; i < values.length; i++)");
                out.println("\t\t{");
                out.println("\t\t\t"+uncap(indexed[i].getPropertyName())+
                    "Vec.addElement(values[i]);");
                out.println("\t\t}");
                out.println("\t}");
                out.println();
                out.println("\tpublic "+indexed[i].getPropertyType()+
                    " get"+cap(indexed[i].getPropertyName())+"(int i)");
                out.println("\t{");
                out.println("\t\treturn ("+indexed[i].getPropertyType()+
                    ") "+uncap(indexed[i].getPropertyName())+
                    "Vec.elementAt(i);");
                out.println("\t}");
                out.println();
                out.println("\tpublic void set"+cap(indexed[i].getPropertyName())+
                    "(int i, "+indexed[i].getPropertyType()+" value)");
                out.println("\t{");
                out.println("\t\t"+uncap(indexed[i].getPropertyName())+
                    "Vec.setElementAt(value, i);");
                out.println("\t}");
                out.println();
            }
            out.println("}");
            out.close();
        } catch (Exception exc) {
            exc.printStackTrace();
        }
    }

/** Uncapitalizes the first letter in a string
 * @param str The string to uncapitalize
 * @return The uncapitalized version of the string
 */
    public static String uncap(String str)
    {
        if (str == null) return str;
        if (str.length() == 0) return str;

        StringBuffer buff = new StringBuffer(str);

        buff.setCharAt(0, Character.toLowerCase(str.charAt(0)));

        return buff.toString();
    }

/** Capitalizes the first letter in a string
 * @param str The string to uncapitalize
 * @return The uncapitalized version of the string
 */
    public static String cap(String str)
    {
        if (str == null) return str;
        if (str.length() == 0) return str;
```

LISTING 43.5 CONTINUED

```
        StringBuffer buff = new StringBuffer(str);

        buff.setCharAt(0, Character.toUpperCase(str.charAt(0)));

        return buff.toString();
    }
}
```

Obviously, creating the code generator can be more tedious than actually writing the bean. But now that it's written, it's easy to create a new bean. Listing 43.6 shows a sample XML file for generating a bean. Notice that the structure of the XML file matches the structure of the `BeanModel` and `Property` classes.

LISTING 43.6 `DemoBean.xml` SAMPLE FILE

```
<?xml version="1.0"?>
<bean>
    <className>DemoBean</className>
    <packageName>usingj2ee.generate</packageName>
    <property>
        <propertyName>name</propertyName>
        <propertyType>String</propertyType>
    </property>
    <property>
        <propertyName>age</propertyName>
        <propertyType>int</propertyType>
    </property>
    <indexedProperty>
        <propertyName>pet</propertyName>
        <propertyType>String</propertyType>
    </indexedProperty>
</bean>
```

Listing 43.7 shows the bean generated by the `demobean.xml` input file.

LISTING 43.7 SOURCE CODE FOR `DemoBean.java`

```
package usingj2ee.generate;

import java.util.Vector;

public class DemoBean implements java.io.Serializable
{
    protected String name;
    protected int age;

    protected Vector petVec;

    public DemoBean()
    {
        petVec = new Vector();
```

```
    }

    public String getName()
    {
        return name;
    }

    public void setName(String theName)
    {
        name = theName;
    }

    public int getAge()
    {
        return age;
    }

    public void setAge(int theAge)
    {
        age = theAge;
    }

    public String[] getPet()
    {
        String[] retval = new String[petVec.size()];
        petVec.copyInto(retval);
        return retval;
    }

    public void setPet(String[] values)
    {
        petVec = new Vector(values.length);
        for (int i=0; i < values.length; i++)
        {
            petVec.addElement(values[i]);
        }
    }

    public String getPet(int i)
    {
        return (String) petVec.elementAt(i);
    }

    public void setPet(int i, String value)
    {
        petVec.setElementAt(value, i);
    }
}
```

DEALING WITH CHANGES

One of the toughest aspects of code generation is how you deal with regenerating existing classes. The `BeanMaker` program takes the easy way out and just rewrites the class file. Obviously, the `BeanMaker` is meant to be a quick start program just to get a bean going. After that, it's up to you to add additional functionality.

Other code generators take different approaches. Some generators recognize special comment tags that mark off preserved areas of code. For example, you might preserve a method in your generated class with the following:

```
//@PRESERVE
    public String generateUniqueID()
    {
// some code usually goes here
    }
//@END PRESERVE
```

When you run the code generator, it looks for the preserved blocks in the old file and copies them into the new file. Because it might be hard to preserve the order of the original blocks, it's best to preserve whole methods. Of course, it's up to you to write the preservation code when you write the code generator.

Other generators take a much easier approach. All the generated code goes into an abstract base class. The generator also creates a concrete subclass of the base class. If you want to add additional methods, you add them to the concrete subclass. Whenever you regenerate code, the generator looks for the presence of the concrete subclass and if it exists, the generator leaves it alone. The idea is that the abstract base class can only be changed by the code generator (obviously, you can change the code if you want, but you should expect the code to disappear the next time the generator runs). You are the only one allowed to change the concrete base class—the generator won't touch it. Of course, kind code generators do create the initial base class for you, so you don't have to do anything to get started.

When you write your code generator, it's up to you to decide how to handle change. If you must allow users to change the code, it's far easier to write a generator using the two-class method than it is to preserve code blocks.

To Generate or Not to Generate

Although code generators are extremely handy, they also lend themselves to code abuse. There are cases when it's better to make a good class library than it is to generate new classes. For example, you might create a code generator to make a mapping between an SQL database and a Java class. You are probably better off writing a library that does the mapping, however. Many times, you can put all the important information into a file or a small set of files rather than generating it into separate Java classes.

For example, when you deploy the application, you might want to change some of the database mappings. Do you really want to regenerate code when you could just edit a data file? When you use code generation, you must often regenerate a large amount of code just to incorporate a small change.

On the other hand, there are times when you can't replace generated code with a class library. JavaBeans, for example, require rigid class formats. You can't write a class library that makes it look like a particular class has a certain property. The class *must* have the `get` and `set` methods.

CASE STUDY

A software company had a complex and powerful C++ data library. It took developers a long time just to create a C++ class for a single database table just because of the amount of repetitive code required to create a class from scratch. Some developers tried taking shortcuts by copying existing classes, but that introduced errors occasionally because of the different ways the classes were written.

The solution to this problem was a simple code generator written in Java. Given a database table and a list of column-name-to-field-name mappings, the generator created the appropriate C++ classes. After the base class was generated, developers added additional methods to the generated code. The code generator was used as a one-shot time saver.

Applets

CHAPTER 44

Applet Development

In this chapter

WHY AND WHEN TO USE APPLETS

When Java first hit the scene, most developers used it to write applets—graphical Java classes that run inside a browser. Over the past few years, Java development has shifted toward server-side development and standalone graphics applications. Applet usage has diminished as Web developers and users had their fill of nervous text-scrolling marquees. Animated GIF images now provide many of the animation features that applets once provided.

Although applets are generally safe, various security researchers have discovered bugs in various browsers that allow Java applets to wreak havoc on a user's system. Because of these potential security breaches, many companies have installed filters to prevent users from running applets on the company network. Other users disable applets to prevent possible security breaches.

Not only do you need to worry about whether applets are enabled or not, you must also deal with browser-specific differences. Netscape and Internet Explorer use different Java implementations, occasionally causing behavior differences.

Newer versions of Internet Explorer might not support Java at all. Sun and Microsoft have been embroiled in a legal battle revolving around Microsoft's version of Java. Recent versions of Internet Explorer have only included Java as an optional package. Because Internet Explorer now has such a commanding share of the market and because applets aren't as common as they were in the past, IE doesn't necessarily need Java to stay competitive anymore.

Despite the potential problems, there are still several places where applets are still the best choice. Some user interfaces are too complicated to be implemented in HTML—especially when they must display constantly updating data. Applets can communicate with the Web server without redrawing the entire page, making them suitable for displaying news headlines, sports scores, and stock quotes. ESPN has a wonderful Java applet for baseball coverage. The applet displays the base runners, the lineups, a pitch-by-pitch description of the game and updated stats. You can even click player names to get more information about a particular player. Such an application would be much tougher to write as an HTML application because of the number of updates required.

Chat applications are also good candidates for applet development. An applet can listen for messages constantly, while an HTML application must periodically refresh the page to display any new messages. Because the browser doesn't know when a message is available, it must refresh fairly frequently to see whether there are new messages. This can lead to many unnecessary calls to the server, however, because the browser might often discover there are no new messages.

Sometimes, it's just the complexity of the user interface that requires Java. For example, there is an online database of over 2 million chess games. Chess fans around the world can search the database for games with certain openings, certain positions, or certain players. A Java applet allows you to view a game move-by-move and to set up the game positions you want to search for.

Online games are often written in Java. Yahoo! Games, for example, uses Java applets for its online games for two main reasons: Games require frequent and immediate updates (especially in timed games such as chess), and the user interfaces are usually fairly complex. The other advantage of Java is that it is easy to download new code. Whenever Yahoo! adds a new game, it simply adds new Java classes, and users download the classes when they first play the game.

As you can see, two of the main reasons for choosing applets are the need for frequent updates and the complexity of the user interface. You must balance these factors with the knowledge that the browser might not support Java and that an applet might take some time to download initially.

CREATING AN APPLET

There was a time when you could assume that if someone knew Java they also knew how to write an applet. With Java's growing popularity and the diminished use of applets, however, that assumption is no longer valid.

An applet is an AWT component (actually an AWT container—it can contain other graphical objects). Specifically, an applet must be a subclass of `java.applet.Applet`, which is a subclass of `java.awt.Panel`.

Note

If you're into Swing, you can use the `JApplet` class to implement a Swing-based applet. Keep in mind, however, that Swing doesn't work well under Internet Explorer–and because IE doesn't come with the Swing classes built-in, the browser must download them from your Web server.

Every applet is an AWT object. Specifically, every applet is a subclass of the `Panel` class, which means it is not just a `java.awt.Component` but also a `java.awt.Container`. In other words, an applet can contain other AWT objects. Every AWT component contains a `paint` method that is used to draw the component on the screen. Usually, if the component is acting as a container (that is, it contains other components), it doesn't override the `paint` method. On the other hand, if the applet is a simple graphics widget without additional components, the applet redraws itself using the `paint` method.

When the browser first loads the applet, it invokes the applet's `init` method to allow the applet to initialize itself. Next, the browser invokes the applet's `start` method to tell the applet to begin running. You don't often need to override the `start` method unless you need to start a separate execution thread. After the applet has started, the browser will call the `paint` method whenever it needs to repaint the applet or when you explicitly call `repaint`. Finally, when the browser wants to deactivate the applet, it calls the applet's `stop` method.

Listing 44.1 shows the good old "Hello World" program in applet form. It reads a message from the applet's parameter set (you'll see how to set them parameters in just a moment) and then paints the message whenever the browser invokes the `paint` method.

LISTING 44.1 SOURCE CODE FOR `HelloWorldApplet.java`

```
package usingj2ee.applet;

import java.applet.*;
import java.awt.*;

public class HelloWorldApplet extends Applet
{
    protected String messageString;

    public void init()
    {
// Get the message to display from the applet parameters
        messageString = getParameter("message");
        if (messageString == null)
        {
            messageString = "Hello World!";
        }
    }

    public void paint(Graphics g)
    {
// Create a large font
        Font font = new Font("Helvetica", Font.BOLD, 36);

        g.setFont(font);

// Get the measurements for the font
        FontMetrics metrics = g.getFontMetrics();

// Get the font height
        int fontHeight = metrics.getHeight();

// Compute the Y value for a centered message
        int baseY = (getSize().height + fontHeight) / 2;

// Get the font width for the current message
        int fontWidth = metrics.stringWidth(messageString);

// Compute the X value for a centered message
        int baseX = (getSize().width - fontWidth) / 2;

// Display the message
        g.drawString(messageString, baseX, baseY);
    }
}
```

To include the applet in a Web page, you must include an `<applet>` tag specifying the classname (via the `code` attribute), the code base (the location of the class files), and the dimensions of the applet. Within the `<applet>` tag, you can also include `<param>` tags that supply applet parameters. Listing 44.2 shows an HTML file that runs the `HelloWorldApplet` program.

LISTING 44.2 SOURCE CODE FOR HelloWorldApplet.html

```
<html>
<body>
<applet code="usingj2ee.applet.HelloWorldApplet" codebase="."
    width=400, height=100>
    <param name="message" value="Hi There!">
</applet>
</body>
</html>
```


Figure 44.1 shows HelloWorldApplet in action.

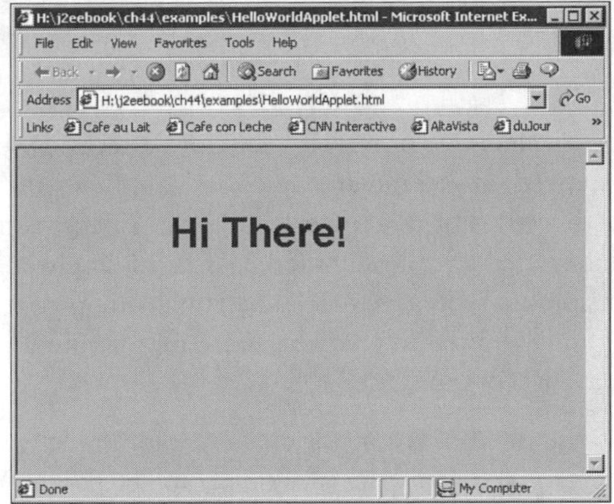

Figure 44.1 An applet is a graphics object that runs in a browser.

You can insert text (including HTML tags) between the `<applet>` and `</applet>` tags. The text only shows up if the browser doesn't support applets. Typically, you display a message indicating that you require applet support.

If you package your applet in a JAR file, you can use the `archive` attribute instead of `codebase`. For example, if you store `HelloWorldApplet.class` in a JAR file called `HelloWorld.jar`, you can run the applet with the HTML file shown in Listing 44.3.

LISTING 44.3 SOURCE CODE FOR HelloWorld2.html

```
<html>
<body>
<applet code="usingj2ee.applet.HelloWorldApplet" archive="HelloWorld.jar"
    width=400, height=100>
    <param name="message" value="Hi There!">
</applet>
</body>
</html>
```

If you want to use multiple JAR files, just list the filenames separated by commas, like this:

```
archive="HelloWorld.jar,OtherFile.jar,ThirdFile.jar"
```

APPLET SECURITY RESTRICTIONS

It's pretty scary to think that a Web site can run code on your machine without your knowledge. Sun realized the potential problems with downloaded code and decided to create an applet *sandbox*—a restricted runtime environment that prevents an applet from corrupting the local system. The sandbox imposes several restrictions on an applet.

Tip

Some browsers relax the security policy for applets that are loaded from files on the local system–that is, files that are loaded with a type of "file:". If you load a file with "http:", even if the file is stored on you local drive, you will be under the full scrutiny of the security manager.

FILE ACCESS RESTRICTIONS

File access is one of the most vulnerable places for malicious attacks. If someone were able to modify files on your system when you ran an applet, he could implant viruses on your system or just destroy data directly. For this reason, no applet is allowed to access the local file system in any way—not even in a read-only mode. After all, you wouldn't want someone implanting invisible applets on his Web page just so he could snoop your hard drive and copy files from it. You might be allowed to read and write files if your applet is loaded from the local file system using a URL of type "file:".

The inability to read and write files poses a major challenge for applet writers. For the moment, the only solution is to read and write files on an applet's home Web server or use digitally signed applets, which you'll learn about in the next chapter.

NETWORK RESTRICTIONS

The network restrictions in Java might seem a little overboard, but they are there for good reason. The general philosophy of network security is that applets can only make network connections back to the Web server they were loaded from. An applet cannot listen for incoming socket connections, nor can it listen for datagrams (connectionless network data) from anywhere but its home server. It also can only send datagrams back to its home server.

These security restrictions are intended to protect organizations that have Internet firewalls set up. In case you are unfamiliar with the intricacies of Internet security, many companies have large internal IP networks (the main networking protocol of the Internet). These networks are connected to the rest of the world through machines called *firewalls*. A firewall's job in life is to protect the internal IP network from prying eyes in the outside world while allowing people on the inside to access data out on the Internet. These firewalls usually render the internal network invisible to the rest of the world. Given the clever ways people have found to attack systems, it is best to not even give out any information about hostnames or addresses on the internal network. See Chapter 26, "Networks and Network Protocols," for a better overview of IP networking and firewalls.

The problem with Java is that applets run inside the firewall on your local machine. This means that without any network restrictions, your entire network is exposed to any malicious applets. You might be thinking that it would be nice if you could just tell your browser the names of hosts that you trust. It would not be difficult for the security system in Java to handle that, but it would keep your poor network administrator on a steady supply of indigestion medication, wondering when someone will trust an untrustworthy host. Keep in mind, also, that Internet Explorer also lets you turn off all security restrictions. Netscape does not support such an option, however.

If your applet is loaded from the local file system, you can get around the networking restrictions. You might have to set the `appletviewer.security.mode` system property to `unrestricted` to completely get around these restrictions when you use `appletviewer`. Because one of the other restrictions on applets is that they cannot change the system properties, you must set this property on the `appletviewer` command line with this option: `Jdappletviewer.security.mode=unrestricted`.

Other Security Restrictions

In addition to the file and network restrictions, most environments also place a few other interesting restrictions.

Nonlocal applets (applets loaded from a Web server) cannot access the system properties. A local applet (one loaded from the local file system) can read and write the system properties. If an applet were able to change the system properties, any applet could change the `appletviewer.security.mode` property, for instance, and throw open a huge security hole. Other system properties contain information about the local machine, which could include the hostname and IP address. If the machine is safe behind a firewall, you might not want this information getting out. Applets can always access "safe" system properties, such as `file.separator`.

Nonlocal applets cannot define their own class loaders. This is really an unfortunate restriction, because the capability to define new ways to add classes to the runtime system is one of Java's neatest features. The problem comes with the fact that when your class refers to another class, the system first goes to the class loader for your class to find the class you are referring to. If you wanted to create an applet that could read and write local files, you could create your own `InputStream` and `OutputStream` classes that did not consult the `SecurityManager` object for permission. When your applet is loaded via your custom class loader, the class loader will be asked if it can load the `InputStream` and `OutputStream` classes. A well-behaved loader would load the system versions of these classes, but an evil class loader will load the nonsecure versions of these.

Applets cannot call native methods. It would be terrible to have all these nice security measures built into Java, only to have an applet come along and bypass them completely by calling the native methods that are used by the system classes. For example, a malicious applet could call the native socket functions directly and snoop around the local network. Unfortunately, this restriction prevents you from using Type 1 and Type 2 JDBC drivers, like the JDBC-ODBC bridge, because these drivers rely on native methods.

Applets cannot execute commands on the local system using the `Runtime.exec` method. Otherwise, a malicious applet could come along and execute commands to delete all your files.

Applets might not be able to define classes that belong to certain packages. Typically, they cannot define classes for the `java` and `sun` packages. Also, Netscape does not permit applets to define classes in the `netscape` package.

When a nonlocal applet opens a top-level frame (a window separate from the browser), the frame contains a warning message indicating that the applet is not trusted.

ACCESSING FILES AND DATA FROM AN APPLET

Without using any special security features, an applet can't access files on a local machine. It can, however, access files on the Web server using a number of different techniques. For example, you can use FTP to access the Web server, possibly using the `FTPSession` class from Chapter 28, "Overview of Internet Protocols." You can also create a custom socket protocol for fetching and storing files. The easiest technique, however, is to use the `HttpURLConnection` class for file access.

RETRIEVING FILES

Using the `URL` and `URLConnection` classes, you can retrieve files directly from the Web server. The advantage of this technique is that you don't need to write any special code on the server side. Essentially, you retrieve files the same way the browser does—using an HTTP GET request.

When you construct a URL for loading or storing a file, you should use the applet's document base URL as the root URL for file access. That is, the applet has a specific URL that it expects to use for loading files. The `getDocumentBase` method returns the document base URL.

Listing 44.4 shows an applet that retrieves a file and displays the contents of the file in a `TextArea` widget.

LISTING 44.4 SOURCE CODE FOR `ShowFile.java`

```
package usingj2ee.applet;

import java.applet.*;
import java.awt.*;
import java.net.*;
import java.io.*;

public class ShowFile extends Applet
{
    public void init()
    {
// Fetch the filename from the applet parameters
        String filename = getParameter("filename");
```

```
// Use a GridLayout to expand the single component to fill the whole area
        setLayout(new GridLayout(1, 0));

// Create the TextArea for displaying the file
        TextArea fileDisplayArea = new TextArea(80, 25);

// Add the TextArea to the applet
        add(fileDisplayArea);

        try
        {
// Create a URL to retrieve the file
            URL fileURL = new URL(getDocumentBase(), filename);

// Open a URLConnection to the file
            URLConnection conn = fileURL.openConnection();

// Create an InputStreamReader to read the file as a stream of
// characters instead of bytes
            InputStreamReader in = new InputStreamReader(
                conn.getInputStream());

// Create a buffer for reading characters
            char[] buffer = new char[4096];

            int len;

// Keep reading until there are no more characters
            while ((len = in.read(buffer)) > 0)
            {
// Add the characters in the buffer to the TextArea
                fileDisplayArea.append(new String(buffer, 0, len));
            }

            in.close();
        }
        catch (Exception exc)
        {
            exc.printStackTrace();
        }
    }
}
```

Listing 44.5 shows the `ShowFile.html` file that invokes the applet.

LISTING 44.5 SOURCE CODE FOR `ShowFile.html`

```
<html>
<body>
<applet code="usingj2ee.applet.ShowFile" codebase="."
    width=640, height=480>
    <param name="filename" value="ShowFile.java">
</applet>
</body>
</html>
```

Figure 44.2 shows the `ShowFile` applet displaying its own source code in a window.

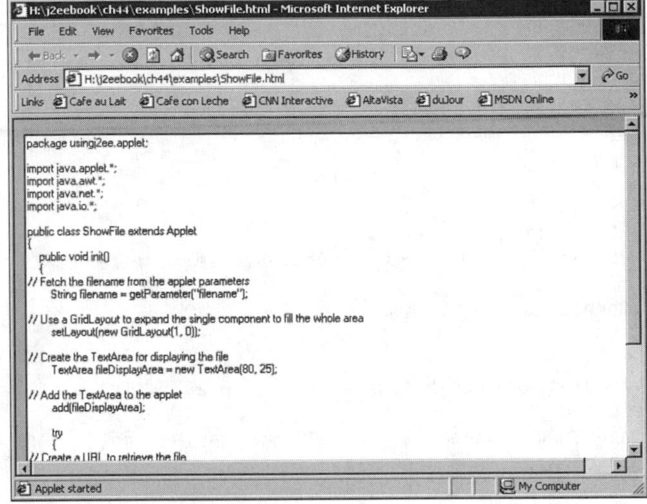

Figure 44.2
An applet can use the `URLConnection` class to read a file.

RETRIEVING IMAGES

Because applets frequently need to access images, the `Applet` class provides a special shortcut for retrieving images. The `getImage` method loads an image from a specific URL (remember, the URL must point to back to the same Web server that the applet itself came from). Listing 44.6 shows a program that retrieves an image and displays it.

LISTING 44.6 SOURCE CODE FOR `ShowImage.java`

```
package usingj2ee.applet;

import java.applet.*;
import java.awt.*;

public class ShowImage extends Applet
{
    protected Image theImage;

    public void init()
    {
// Fetch the image name from the applet parameters
        String imageName = getParameter("image");

// Load the image from the Web server
        theImage = getImage(getDocumentBase(), imageName);
    }

    public void paint(Graphics g)
    {
```

```
// Draw the image
        g.drawImage(theImage, 0, 0, this);
    }
}
```

Figure 44.3 shows the `ShowImage` applet in action.

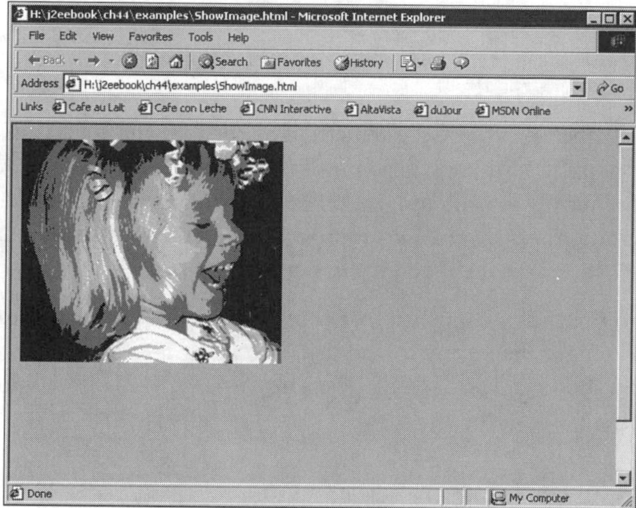

Figure 44.3
An applet can download and display images easily.

Storing Files

The HTTP protocol has a command called PUT that allows you to store files on the Web server. Many Web servers disable PUT by default, but usually allow you to use PUT for certain directories. Consult the documentation for your Web server to determine whether you must do anything special to enable PUT. For example, if you're running Apache, you might need to include the commands in your `httpd.conf` file:

```
LoadModule put_module modules/mod_put.so
AddModule mod_put.c
```

In addition, in the directory where you want to store files, you should include a `.htaccess` file that looks like the one shown in Listing 44.7.

Listing 44.7 Sample `.htaccess` File for PUT Access

```
AuthName "restricted"
AuthType Basic
AuthUserFile /etc/httpd/users
EnablePut on
<Limit PUT>
require valid-user
</Limit>
```

The Apache configuration shown in Listing 44.6 requires you to use username/password validation to perform a PUT into the directory.

In a pure Java environment, using Sun's Java Virtual Machine, you can use the `HttpURLConnection` class to store a file via HTTP PUT. The idea is that you open the connection, cast the `URLConnection` to `HttpURLConnection`, and set the request method, like this:

```
URLConnection conn = myURL.openConnection();
HttpURLConnection httpConn = (HttpURLConnection) conn;
httpConn.setRequestMethod("PUT");
```

You can then use the `getOutputStream` method to get a stream for writing the file. Unfortunately, if your applet is running inside Internet Explorer or Netscape (using the built-in Java Virtual Machine), you can't use this technique. When Netscape and Microsoft created their implementations of the HTTP protocol, they didn't subclass `HttpURLConnection`, so you get a `ClassCastException` if you try to perform the cast.

The solution to this little dilemma is that you must use a socket and connect to the Web server manually rather than using the built-in `URLConnection` class. It's not that hard to do. In fact, the class shown in Listing 44.8 performs an HTTP PUT for you and even supports authentication!

LISTING 44.8 SOURCE CODE FOR HttpPut.java

```
package usingj2ee.applet;

import java.net.*;
import java.io.*;
import usingj2ee.util.*;

/** This class shows you how to open up a socket to an HTTP server
    and send a file to the server using the PUT command. */

public class HttpPut extends Object
{
    public static void put(URL destURL, String data)
        throws IOException
    {
        put(destURL, data, null, null);
    }

    public static void put(URL destURL, String data, String username,
        String password)
        throws IOException
    {
        int port = destURL.getPort();

        if (port < 0) port = 80;

// Open up a socket to the destination host and port
        Socket sock = new Socket(destURL.getHost(), port);
```

```
// Get output stream for the socket connection
        DataInputStream inStream = new DataInputStream(
            sock.getInputStream());
        DataOutputStream outStream = new DataOutputStream(
            sock.getOutputStream());

// Send the PUT request to the server
// The request is of the form: PUT filename HTTP/1.1

        outStream.writeBytes("PUT "+destURL.getFile()+
            " HTTP/1.1\r\n");
        outStream.writeBytes("Host: "+destURL.getHost()+"\r\n");

// If the user specifies a username and password, add an Authorization line
// Notice that the authorization line must be in Base64 format
        if ((username != null) && (password != null))
        {
            outStream.writeBytes("Authorization: Basic "+
                Base64.toBase64(username+":"+password)+"\r\n");
        }

// Next, send the content type (don't forget the \r\n)
        outStream.writeBytes(
            "Content-type: application/octet-stream\r\n");

// Send the length of the request
        outStream.writeBytes(
            "Content-length: "+data.length()+"\r\n");

// Send a \r\n to indicate the end of the header
        outStream.writeBytes("\r\n");

// Now send the information you are saving

        outStream.writeBytes(data);


        String response = inStream.readLine();

        if (!response.startsWith("HTTP/1.1 200"))
        {
            throw new IOException("Error storing file: "+response);
        }

// You're done with the streams, so close them
        inStream.close();
        outStream.close();
    }
}
```

You might recall that Chapter 29, "The HTTP Protocol," showed you how the HTTP protocol works. One of the things that wasn't mentioned at the time, however, was how you do authentication. Although authentication can be a little messy at times, especially if you must send multiple requests, if you just send the username and password in your initial request, authentication is simple.

You need to put the username and password in the form `username:password` and then encode the resulting string using an encoding called Base64. *Base64* is a fairly common encoding and isn't too tough to do. You go through a string and take characters in groups of 3 8-bit bytes, making a 24-bit value. Now, you split the 24-bit value into 4 groups of 6 bits. A 6-bit value can be anywhere from 0 to 63 (hence the term Base-64—there are 64 possible characters). Use A–Z to represent the first 26 6-bit values (that is, 0–25), use a–z to represent the next 26 (26–51), use 0–9 for the next 10 values (52–61), and finally use + and / for the last 2 values. If the characters don't fit evenly (that is, you need to encode 4 characters, which translates into one block of 3 characters and a second block containing only 1), use = to pad out the encoded characters.

For example, the string ABC in hexadecimal is 414243, or in binary 010000010100001001000011. Breaking the string up into four groups of 6 bits, you get 010000 010100 001001 000011, which in decimal is 16 20 9 3. Converting to characters, that's Q U J D, so the Base64 encoding for ABC is QUJD. The letter D represents 3 because A represents 0, B represents 1, and C represents 2. Converting from Base64 back to the original string works using the reverse of the operations. Convert the letters back into their 6-bit values, group every set of four 6-bit values into a 24-bit value and break the 24-bit value back into three 8-bit bytes.

The only place where things get a little strange is at the end of a string when the number of letters isn't divisible by 3. You *always* write out a block of four 6-bit values, so use '=' for any unused positions in the block of four values. For example, to encode AB, a 16-bit value, you need three blocks of 6 bits (which is 18 bytes) so the last byte is unused. The Base64 encoding for AB is QUI=. When you encode a single character, you'll have two pad characters. The Base64 encoding for A is QQ==.

Now that you know how Base64 encoding works, you can easily write a routine to translate to and from Base64. Better yet, just use the class shown in Listing 44.9 (the same one that the `HttpPut` class uses).

LISTING 44.9 SOURCE CODE FOR `Base64.java`

```
package usingj2ee.util;

/** Utility class to convert a string to and from base 64. */

public class Base64
{

/** The characters representing each 6-bit pattern in Base 64 */
    public static final String base64Chars =
        "ABCDEFGHIJKLMNOPQRSTUVWXYZabcdefghijklmnopqrstuvwxyz0123456789+/";

/** Converts a string of characters into a Base 64 string. */
    public static String toBase64(String str)
    {
// Create a buffer to hold the output string
        StringBuffer outBuff = new StringBuffer();
```

```
// Turn the original string into an array of bytes
        byte[] stringBytes = str.getBytes();

// Loop through the string bytes taking 3 at a time
        for (int i=0; i < stringBytes.length; i += 3)
        {
// Holds 3 8-bit characters that will be converted to 4 6-bit characters
            int packed64 = 0;

// Assume that you're writing out 4 full characters each time. At the end
// of the string, you may end up padding with ='s
            int num64Chars = 4;

// Take the first char and stick it in the packing integer
            packed64 = stringBytes[i] << 16;

// If there is another character in the string, add it to the buffer
            if (i+1 < stringBytes.length)
            {
                packed64 = packed64 + (stringBytes[i+1] << 8);
            }
            else
            {
// Otherwise, you need to write out 2 pad characters. Out of 4 6-bit chars,
// you need 2 chars to represent an 8-bit number
                num64Chars = 2;
            }

// If there is still another character available, add it to the buffer
            if (i + 2 < stringBytes.length)
            {
                packed64 = packed64 + stringBytes[i+2];
            }
// Otherwise, if you were still expecting to write out 4 6-bit characters,
// you really only write 3. It's possible to get to this point after already
// setting the number of characters to 2, so you need to make sure you aren't
// accidentally writing one more character than you need to
            else if (num64Chars == 4)
            {
                num64Chars = 3;
            }

// Loop through the packing integer taking 6 bits at a time. Print out the
// character in the base64Chars string that corresponds to each 6-bit
// value.
            for (int j=0; j < num64Chars; j++)
            {
                outBuff.append(base64Chars.charAt(
                    (packed64 >> (6 * (3-j))) & 63));
            }

// If you wrote less than 4 6-bit values, write out pad characters
            for (int j=num64Chars; j < 4; j++)
            {
                outBuff.append('=');
            }
        }
```

LISTING 44.9 CONTINUED

```
// Return the base64 string
        return outBuff.toString();
    }

/** Converts a base64 string to a regular string */
    public static String fromBase64(String str)
    {

// Create a buffer for the regular string
        StringBuffer outBuff = new StringBuffer();

// Convert the base64 string into an array of bytes
        byte[] stringBytes = str.getBytes();

// Loop through the bytes taking 4 at a time
        for (int i=0; i < stringBytes.length; i += 4)
        {
            int currWord = 0;

// Assume that this set of bytes contains 3 whole characters
            int charsInWord = 3;

            for (int j=0; j < 4; j++)
            {
                byte ch = stringBytes[i+j];

// If you hit a pad character, you have fewer than 3 characters encoded
// in this set of 4 bytes. As it turns out, the number of characters
// encoded is equal to the position where you first encounter the '='
                if (ch == '=')
                {
                    charsInWord = j;
                    break;
                }

// Get the 6-bit value that corresponds to this character
                ch = (byte) base64Chars.indexOf(ch);

// Add the 6-bits to the unpacking integer (you build a 24-bit value from
// 4 6-bit values)
                currWord = currWord + (ch << (6 * (3 - j)));
            }

// Pull the characters out of the unpacking integer by taking 8 bits at
// a time.
            for (int j=0; j < charsInWord; j++)
            {
                outBuff.append((char) ((currWord >> (8 * (2-j))) & 255));
            }
        }

// Return the unencoded string
        return outBuff.toString();
    }
```

```
/** A test program to make sure the base64 encoding works. It encodes each
    command-line argument into base64 and then back again.
*/
    public static void main(String args[])
    {
        for (int i=0; i < args.length; i++)
        {
            String base64 = toBase64(args[i]);
            String un64 = fromBase64(base64);

            System.out.println(args[i]+" -> "+base64+" -> "+un64);
        }
    }
}
```


The `Base64` class includes a `main` method that lets you see how various strings convert to Base64. For example, to see the encodings of ABC, AB, and A, just type

```
java usingj2ee.util.Base64 ABC AB A
```

Now that you have a way to store a file, you can write an applet to retrieve a file, edit it, and save the edited file back to the server. Listing 44.10 shows the `EditFile` applet that looks a lot like the `ShowFile` applet except that it can also store the file on the server.

LISTING 44.10 SOURCE CODE FOR `EditFile.java`

```
package usingj2ee.applet;

import java.applet.*;
import java.awt.*;
import java.awt.event.*;
import java.net.*;
import java.io.*;

public class EditFile extends Applet
{
    protected URL fileURL;
    protected TextArea editArea;

    public void init()
    {
// Fetch the filename from the applet parameters
        String filename = getParameter("filename");

// Use a GridLayout to expand the single component to fill the whole area
        setLayout(new BorderLayout());

// Create the TextArea for editing the file
        editArea = new TextArea(80, 25);

// Add the TextArea to the applet
        add("Center", editArea);

// Create a button panel
        Panel buttons = new Panel();
```

LISTING 44.10 CONTINUED

```
// Create a save button
        Button saveButton = new Button("Save");
        saveButton.addActionListener(new SaveHandler());

        buttons.add(saveButton);

// Create a refresh button
        Button refreshButton = new Button("Refresh");
        refreshButton.addActionListener(new RefreshHandler());

        buttons.add(refreshButton);

// Add the button panel to the applet
        add("South", buttons);

        try
        {
// Create a URL to retrieve the file
            fileURL = new URL(getDocumentBase(), filename);
        }
        catch (Exception exc)
        {
            exc.printStackTrace();
        }

        refreshFile();
    }

    public void refreshFile()
    {
        editArea.setText("");

        try
        {
// Open a URLConnection to the file
            URLConnection conn = fileURL.openConnection();

// Create an InputStreamReader to read the file as a stream of
// characters instead of bytes
            InputStreamReader in = new InputStreamReader(
                conn.getInputStream());

// Create a buffer for reading characters
            char[] buffer = new char[4096];

            int len;

// Keep reading until there are no more characters
            while ((len = in.read(buffer)) > 0)
            {
// Add the characters in the buffer to the TextArea
                editArea.append(new String(buffer, 0, len));
            }

            in.close();
        }
```

```
        catch (Exception exc)
        {
            exc.printStackTrace();
        }
    }

    public void saveFile()
    {
        try
        {
// Store the file, use j2eebook as the username and again as the password
            HttpPut.put(fileURL, editArea.getText(), "j2eebook", "j2eebook");
        }
        catch (Exception exc)
        {
            exc.printStackTrace();
        }
    }

    class SaveHandler implements ActionListener
    {
        public void actionPerformed(ActionEvent evt)
        {
            saveFile();
        }
    }

    class RefreshHandler implements ActionListener
    {
        public void actionPerformed(ActionEvent evt)
        {
            refreshFile();
        }
    }
}
```


RETRIEVING DATA FROM A SERVLET

Servlets and Java Server Pages aren't just for serving up Web pages. You can use them to retrieve any kind of data you want. Typically, if you aren't generating a Web page (HTML, XML, WML, and so on), you probably don't need to use a JSP and can stick with a servlet. Keep in mind that although these examples use servlets, they also apply to Java Server Pages.

If you want to invoke a servlet that normally handles Web forms from a Java application, you might need to do a little extra work to pass the form parameters. For an HTTP GET, you pass the form parameters in the URL using a pattern like this:

yourURL?param1=value1¶m2=value2¶m3=value3

The parameter values must be in URL-encoded form. You can encode a string with the `URLEncoder` class. For example, if you want to create a parameter such as `smiley=:-)`, use the following statement:

```
String smileyParam = "smiley="+URLEncoder.encode(":-)");
```

You don't need to encode the parameter names, just the parameter values.

To send parameters for an HTTP POST, you don't put the parameters in the URL. Instead, you must send the parameter list within the request. Basically, use the URL class and call `setDoOutput(true)` to indicate that you want to perform a post. Now, after you open the `URLConnection`, call `getOutputStream` and write out the parameter list (use the same list that you use in a GET: *param1=value1?param2=value2*). You must also set the content type to be `application/x-www-form-urlencoded`.

Listing 44.11 shows a program from Chapter 14, "Java Server Pages," that posts data to the `ShowParametersServlet` class and prints the result. Although the program isn't an applet, you can use the same technique in your applet to send data to a servlet.

LISTING 44.11 SOURCE CODE FOR `URLPost.java`

```
package usingj2ee.applet;

import java.net.*;
import java.io.*;

public class URLPost extends Object
{
    public static void main(String args[])
    {
        try {
            URL destURL = new URL(
                "http://localhost/servlet/usingj2ee.ShowParametersServlet");

// Create a request string
            String request = "moe="+URLEncoder.encode("##Moe##")+
                "&larry="+URLEncoder.encode("%%Larry%%")+"\r\n";

            URLConnection urlConn = destURL.openConnection();

            urlConn.setDoOutput(true);    // you need to write
            urlConn.setDoInput(true);    // just to be safe...
            urlConn.setUseCaches(false);    // get info fresh from server

// Tell the server what kind of data you are sending - in this case,
// just a stream of bytes.

            urlConn.setRequestProperty("Content-type",
                "application/x-www-form-urlencoded");

// Must tell the server the size of the data you are sending. This also
// tells the URLConnection class that you are doing a POST instead
// of a GET.

            urlConn.setRequestProperty("Content-length", ""+request.length());

// Open an output stream so you can send the info you are posting

            DataOutputStream outStream = new DataOutputStream(
                urlConn.getOutputStream());
```

```
// Write out the actual request data

            outStream.writeBytes(request);
            outStream.close();

// Now that you have sent the data, open up an input stream and get
// the response back from the server

            DataInputStream inStream = new DataInputStream(
                urlConn.getInputStream());

            int ch;

// Dump the contents of the request to System.out

            while ((ch = inStream.read()) >= 0) {
                System.out.print((char) ch);
            }

            inStream.close();

        } catch (Exception e) {
            e.printStackTrace();
        }
    }
}
```


Although it might be useful to send and receive the same kind of data that the browser normally does, you can do more interesting things with an applet. For example, you can send a serialized object from a servlet to an applet. Listing 44.12 shows a servlet that returns a serialized `Hashtable`.

LISTING 44.12 SOURCE CODE FOR `GetHashtable.java`

```
package usingj2ee;

import javax.servlet.*;
import javax.servlet.http.*;
import java.io.*;
import java.util.*;

public class GetHashtable extends HttpServlet
{
    public void service(HttpServletRequest request,
        HttpServletResponse response)
        throws IOException
    {
// Tell the Web server that the response is HTML
        response.setContentType("applcation/octet-stream");

        OutputStream out = response.getOutputStream();

// Create a Hashtable and populate it with some data
        Hashtable table = new Hashtable();
        table.put("Moe", "Moe Howard");
        table.put("Larry", "Larry Fine");
```

LISTING 44.12 CONTINUED

```
        Vector others = new Vector();

        others.addElement("Curly");
        others.addElement("Shemp");
        others.addElement("Curly Joe");

        table.put("Others", others);

// Wrap an ObjectOutputStream around the normal output stream
        ObjectOutputStream objOut = new ObjectOutputStream(out);

// Write the Hashtable to the output stream
        objOut.writeObject(table);
    }
}
```

Listing 44.13 shows an applet that reads the serialized object and displays a portion of the content.

LISTING 44.13 SOURCE CODE FOR `ShowHashtable.java`

```
package usingj2ee.applet;

import java.applet.*;
import java.awt.*;
import java.net.*;
import java.io.*;
import java.util.*;

public class ShowHashtable extends Applet
{
    public void init()
    {
// Use a GridLayout to expand the single component to fill the whole area
        setLayout(new GridLayout(1, 0));

// Create the TextArea for displaying information
        TextArea displayArea = new TextArea(80, 25);

// Add the TextArea to the applet
        add(displayArea);

        try
        {
// Create a URL to retrieve the object
            URL fileURL = new URL(getDocumentBase(),
                "/servlet/usingj2ee.GetHashtable");

// Open a URLConnection to the servlet
            URLConnection conn = fileURL.openConnection();

// Create an ObjectInputStream for deserializing the object
            ObjectInputStream in = new ObjectInputStream(
```

```
                new BufferedInputStream(
                    conn.getInputStream()));

// Read the hash table from the stream
            Hashtable table = (Hashtable) in.readObject();

            StringBuffer keyStr = new StringBuffer();

            Enumeration e = table.keys();

// Copy the keys into a string
            while (e.hasMoreElements())
            {
                keyStr.append(e.nextElement());
                keyStr.append(" ");
            }

            in.close();

// Show the string in the display area
            displayArea.append(keyStr.toString());
        }
        catch (Exception exc)
        {
            exc.printStackTrace();
        }
    }
}
```


Note

The `ShowHashtable` applet requires a little extra work because you must load the applet's HTML file from the Web server where the servlet is running. Because almost all servlet engines either plug into a Web server or contain their own Web servers, you should have no problem serving the HTML file from the same server.

Sending Data to a Servlet

Obviously, if you can send serialized data from a servlet to an applet, you should also be able to send serialized data from an applet to a servlet. Listing 44.14 shows an applet that sends a serialized object to a servlet.

Listing 44.14 Source Code for `SendHashtable.java`

```
package usingj2ee.applet;

import java.applet.*;
import java.awt.*;
import java.awt.event.*;
import java.net.*;
import java.io.*;
import java.util.*;
```

LISTING 44.14 CONTINUED

```
public class SendHashtable extends Applet
{
    public void init()
    {
        Button sendButton = new Button("Send Hashtable");

        sendButton.addActionListener(new SendHandler());

        add(sendButton);
    }

    class SendHandler implements ActionListener
    {
        public void actionPerformed(ActionEvent event)
        {
            try
            {
// Create a URL to retrieve the object
                URL fileURL = new URL(getDocumentBase(),
                    "/servlet/usingj2ee.ReceiveHashtable");

// Open a URLConnection to the servlet
                URLConnection conn = fileURL.openConnection();

// Create an ObjectOutputStream for deserializing the object
                ObjectOutputStream out = new ObjectOutputStream(
                    new BufferedOutputStream(
                        conn.getOutputStream()));

// Create a Hashtable and populate it with some data
                Hashtable table = new Hashtable();
                table.put("Moe", "Moe Howard");
                table.put("Larry", "Larry Fine");

                Vector others = new Vector();

                others.addElement("Curly");
                others.addElement("Shemp");
                others.addElement("Curly Joe");

                table.put("Others", others);

                out.writeObject(table);

                out.flush();
                out.close();
            }
            catch (Exception exc)
            {
                exc.printStackTrace();
            }
        }
    }
}
```

Listing 44.15 shows a servlet that reads a serialized object and prints some information about its contents.

LISTING 44.15 SOURCE CODE FOR ReceiveHashtable.java

```
package usingj2ee;

import javax.servlet.*;
import javax.servlet.http.*;
import java.io.*;
import java.util.*;

public class ReceiveHashtable extends HttpServlet
{
    public void service(HttpServletRequest request,
        HttpServletResponse response)
        throws IOException
    {
        try
        {
            ObjectInputStream in = new ObjectInputStream(
                new BufferedInputStream(
                    request.getInputStream()));

            Hashtable table = (Hashtable) in.readObject();

            Enumeration keys = table.keys();

            while (keys.hasMoreElements())
            {
                System.out.println(keys.nextElement());
            }
        }
        catch (ClassNotFoundException exc)
        {
            exc.printStackTrace();
        }
    }
}
```


IMPROVING APPLET DOWNLOADS

Waiting for an applet to finish downloading can be annoying at times, especially for a big applet. A quote like "Great applet, but it takes 5 minutes to download" does not inspire people to run out and try it.

Although there aren't any tricks to shove bits through the network any faster, you can make your applets aware that things might take a while and give the user something to do while he waits.

One of the many nice features of Java is that it can load classes while a program is running. There are some limits on this, however.

If a method references a class, that class must be loaded before the method is executed. Java uses a one-time lookup mechanism for efficiency. The first time an instruction referencing another class is executed, the Java runtime does a lookup on the referenced class. After the class is found, the instruction is changed to refer directly to the referenced class, bypassing the lookup. If you never execute the lookup instruction, the instruction is never changed. You cannot count on this exact behavior, however.

Some Just-In-Time (JIT) compilers resolve all the references when a method is compiled. This means that all the referenced classes must be loaded before the method is called. After a method is compiled, any unresolved references remain unresolved, even if the referenced class is loaded later.

Note

Almost any operations involving an object of a particular class will cause that class to be loaded. If you declare an object of a particular class, that class is not immediately loaded. You can even safely test that object to determine whether it is `null` without causing a load. Almost anything else, however, will trigger a load. Some of the things that require a load are using `instanceof`, invoking a method, and passing the object as a parameter to a method. In the latter case, you might not need to load the class if the parameter type is the same class as the object. If they are different classes, the object's class must be loaded to determine whether that object is an instance of the parameter's class.

Delayed Instantiation

If you know that you won't be needing an object until a certain time, you can delay the instantiation of that object. For example, suppose you have a spreadsheet applet that can create nice graphs of the data. The graphing class might be fairly large.

Someone who just wants to enter data in the spreadsheet doesn't want to wait for the graphing class to be downloaded before they can begin. Rather than instantiating the `graphing` class in the `init` method, you wait until someone really wants to do graphing before downloading the graphing code.

Your applet might look something like this:

```
public class SpreadsheetApplet extends Applet
{
     SpreadsheetGraphing graphing;     // will be loaded later

     public void init()
     {
          // perform setup
     }

     public void createGraph()
     {
          if (graphing == null) {
               graphing = new SpreadsheetGraphing();
          }
          .
          .
          .
```

If the createGraph method is never called, the graphing software is never loaded. Much of the early excitement about Java was over this feature.

The idea that you only grabbed the code you needed as you needed it was a refreshing alternative to the huge pieces of software on the market today, with millions of bytes dedicated to features used only by a small percentage of people.

DOWNLOADING IN THE BACKGROUND

Although delayed instantiation allows an applet to start running quickly, you still have to wait for a class to be instantiated when you use it. You might have saved users the five-minute hit up front by not loading the graphing software. But when they create a graph, then they'll have to wait.

You can alleviate this problem by downloading classes in a background thread. Basically, you create a thread that takes a list of classes and loads them into the runtime environment.

By running this in the background, you can keep your main applet going while loading in extra features that are likely to be needed. You might even keep track of the features a particular user favors and download the code for those features first.

This is an interesting trade-off between a big, do-everything software package and a load-as-you-go system. It starts off as a bare-bones system but gradually grows.

Listing 44.16 shows a class that loads other classes in the background. It uses the Class.forName() method to load the class so it doesn't have to create an instance.

LISTING 44.16 SOURCE CODE FOR BackgroundLoader.java

```
package usingj2ee.applet;

// This class loads other classes in the background so they
// are ready for you when you need them. It supports a callback
// mechanism to let you know when a class has been loaded.

public class BackgroundLoader extends Object implements Runnable
{
    Thread loaderThread;

    String[] classes;    // the classes to load

    LoaderCallback callback;    // who to notify

// This constructor just loads one class with no notification
// The loading doesn't take place until you call the start method.

    public BackgroundLoader(String oneClass)
    {
        this.classes = new String[1];
        this.classes[0] = oneClass;
    }

// This constructor loads a single class, and performs a callback
// when the class is loaded. It doesn't start loading until start is called.
```

LISTING 44.16 CONTINUED

```
    public BackgroundLoader(String oneClass, LoaderCallback callback)
    {
        this.classes = new String[1];
        this.classes[0] = oneClass;
        this.callback = callback;
    }

// This constructor loads a whole set of classes with no callback.
// Again, it doesn't start loading until start is called.

    public BackgroundLoader(String[] classes)
    {
        this.classes = classes;
    }

// This constructor loads a whole set of classes and performs a callback
// It doesn't start loading until start is called.

    public BackgroundLoader(String[] classes, LoaderCallback callback)
    {
        this.classes = classes;
        this.callback = callback;
    }

    public void run()
    {
// If there's nothing to load, we're done
        if (classes == null) return;

        for (int i=0; i < classes.length; i++)
        {

            try
            {

// Class.forName initiates the loading of a class
                Class.forName(classes[i]);

// If there's a callback, call it.
                if (callback != null)
                {
                    callback.classLoaded(classes[i]);
                }
            }
            catch (Exception e)
            {
// Ignore any errors in loading the class. Let the error occur when
// the program tries to instantiate the class. You never know, it
// might not try.
            }
        }
    }

    public void start()
    {
```

```
        loaderThread = new Thread(this);
        loaderThread.start();
    }

    public void stop()
    {
        loaderThread = null;
    }
}
```


Listing 44.17 shows the LoaderCallback interface used by the BackgroundLoader class.

LISTING 44.17 SOURCE CODE FOR LoaderCallback.java

```
package usingj2ee.applet;

public interface LoaderCallback
{
    public void classLoaded(String className);
}
```

RUNNING APPLETS IN A STANDALONE APPLICATION

You can run almost any applet as an application but some are easier than others. If your applet does not use the getDocumentBase, getCodeBase, or any of the AppletContext methods, you might be able to get away with creating a frame and launching the applet in the frame. In these cases, the applet is little more than a typical AWT container (remember, the Applet class is a subclass of java.awt.Panel).

Applets are first initialized by the init method, and then started by the start method. Applications, on the other hand, are initialized and started with a static method called main. Fortunately, these methods can peacefully coexist in the same class.

By adding a main method that automatically creates a frame and adds the applet to the frame, you make your applet run either as an applet or as an application. Listing 44.18 shows a simple applet that will also run as an application.

LISTING 44.18 SOURCE CODE FOR StandaloneApplet.java

```
package usingj2ee.applet;

import java.awt.*;
import java.applet.*;
import java.awt.event.*;

// StandaloneApplet is an applet that runs either as
// an applet or a standalone application. To run
// standalone, it provides a main method that creates
// a frame, then creates an instance of the applet and
// adds it to the frame.
```

LISTING 44.18 CONTINUED

```
public class StandaloneApplet extends Applet
{
    public void init()
    {
        add(new Button("Standalone Applet Button"));
    }

    public static void main(String args[])
    {
// Create the frame this applet will run in
        Frame appletFrame = new Frame("Some applet");

// The frame needs a layout manager, use the GridLayout to maximize
// the applet size to the frame.
        appletFrame.setLayout(new GridLayout(1,0));

// Have to give the frame a size before it is visible
        appletFrame.setSize(300, 200);

        appletFrame.addWindowListener(new WindowAdapter() {
            public void windowClosing(WindowEvent event)
            {
                System.exit(0);
            }
        });

// Make the frame appear on the screen. You should make the frame appear
// before you call the applet's init method. On some Java implementations,
// some of the graphics information is not available until there is a frame.
// If your applet uses certain graphics functions such as getGraphics() in the
// init method, it may fail unless there is a frame already created and
// showing.
        appletFrame.show();

// Create an instance of the applet
        Applet myApplet = new StandaloneApplet();

// Add the applet to the frame
        appletFrame.add(myApplet);

// Initialize and start the applet
        myApplet.init();
        myApplet.start();

        appletFrame.validate();
    }
}
```

Figure 44.4 shows `StandaloneApplet` running within a Web browser, whereas Figure 44.5 shows it running as a standalone application.

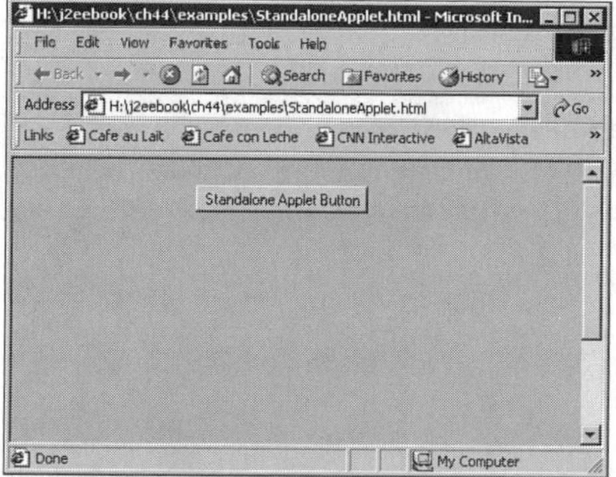

Figure 44.4 Many applets act as simple AWT containers.

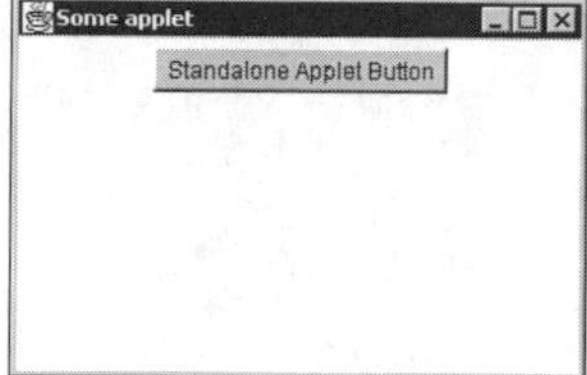

Figure 44.5 Sometimes a simple frame is all you need to run an applet standalone.

USING THE JAVA PLUG-IN

One of the things that really discourages applet developers is the vast difference between the Java Virtual Machines in both Internet Explorer and Netscape. IE's JVM is particularly disheartening because of the many places where it differs from Sun's specifications.

Sun now provides an alternative applet environment called the Java Plug-In. This environment lets you run applets in both Netscape and IE, but using Sun's Java Virtual Machine. You no longer need to worry about odd browser differences. Instead, you use the same JVM that your standalone applications use. With the Java Plug-In, it no longer matters that IE doesn't run Swing very well, or that it doesn't come with built-in RMI support. In fact, it doesn't even matter if your version of IE doesn't have Microsoft's Java support!

One of the few hassles with the Java Plug-In, apart from the fact that it requires the user to download and install a rather large Java VM, is that you must use different tags in IE and Netscape.

Fortunately, the JSP environment provides a special tag for embedding an applet in a Web page that automatically detects the browser type and inserts the appropriate tag in the output. The JSP tag is called `<jsp:plugin>`. Listing 44.19 shows an example usage of `<jsp:plugin>`.

LISTING 44.19 SOURCE CODE FOR ShowApplet.jsp

```
<HTML>
<BODY>
```

LISTING 44.19 CONTINUED

```
Here is the applet:
<BR>

<jsp:plugin type="applet" code="usingj2ee.applet.SwingApplet" codebase="."
    width="500" height="400">
    <jsp:fallback>
        <p>Unable to use Java Plugin</p>
    </jsp:fallback>
</jsp:plugin>

</BODY>
</HTML>
```

The text inside the `<jsp:fallback>` tag is displayed when the browser can't run the Java Plug-in, either because the browser isn't capable or there are problems loading it. If you need to pass parameters to the applet, you can use the `<jsp:params>` tag, which encodes a number of `<jsp:param>` tags like this:

```
<jsp:params>
    <jsp:param name="myParam1" value="param1Value"/>
    <jsp:param name="myParam1" value="param1Value"/>
</jsp:params>
```

The `<jsp:params>` tag should be enclosed within the `<jsp:plugin>` in the same way that `<jsp:fallback>` is enclosed in listing 44.18.

Listing 44.20 shows the generated HTML code when the `ShowParams.jsp` applet is run from within Internet Explorer.

LISTING 44.20 `ShowApplet.jsp` GENERATED HTML FOR INTERNET EXPLORER

```
<HTML>
<BODY>
Here is the applet:
<BR>

<OBJECT classid="clsid:8AD9C840-044E-11D1-B3E9-00805F499D93"
        HEIGHT="400" WIDTH="500"
        CODEBASE="http://java.sun.com/products/plugin
        /1.1/jinstall-11-win32.cab#Version=1,1,0,0">
<PARAM NAME="code" VALUE="usingj2ee.applet.SwingApplet">
<PARAM NAME="codebase" VALUE=".">
<PARAM NAME="type" VALUE="application/x-java-applet;version=1.1">
        <p>Unable to use Java Plugin</p>

</OBJECT>

</BODY>
</HTML>
```

Listing 44.21 shows the code generated when the applet is run under Netscape.

LISTING 44.21 `ShowApplet.jsp` **GENERATED HTML FOR NETSCAPE**

```
<HTML>
<BODY>
Here is the applet:
<BR>

<EMBED JAVA_CODE="usingj2ee.applet.SwingApplet" JAVA_CODEBASE="."
TYPE="application/x-java-applet;version=1.1" HEIGHT="400" WIDTH="500"
PLUGINSPAGE="http://java.sun.com/products/plugin/1.1/plugin-install.html">
<NOEMBED>
<p>Unable to use Java Plugin</p>
</NOEMBED>
</EMBED>


</BODY>
</HTML>
```

The `<jsp:plugin>` tag accepts most of the common `<APPLET>` attributes such as `code`, `codebase`, `archive`, `width`, and `height`.

TROUBLESHOOTING

LOADING AN APPLET

Why do I just get a blank gray box when I load my applet?

There are a number of reasons why this happens. If your browser has a Java console option, turn it on to see whether it shows any exceptions. This usually occurs because you forgot to include a class, the applet encounters an exception while running, or the browser doesn't support applets. Also, check the `codebase` attribute in your `<applet>` tag to make sure it points to the correct directory. As with standalone applications, your directory structure must reflect the package structure of the Java classes.

Why can't I use the JDBC-ODBC bridge from my applet?

Applets can't access native libraries and the JDBC-ODBC bridge uses a native library.

Why does it take so long for my applet to load?

Some browsers may take a long time when starting the Java Virtual Machine. The Java Plug-In is fairly slow when starting up, too. You should also check the size of your applet. If you have a large applet or a large number of class files, consider packaging them in a JAR file to speed up your downloads.

CHAPTER 45

Code Signing

In this chapter

WHY YOU SHOULD DIGITALLY SIGN CODE

When you write Java applets that must execute in a restricted environment, you might have to sign your code to allow it to perform all the functions it needs to. Signing your code is a good practice in general, however, because it verifies the origin of the code. Although it hasn't been a big problem up to now, it's possible for someone to redistribute hacked copies of a popular Java program and wreak havoc on unsuspecting users while giving the original author a bad name.

With Java beginning to appear in smaller devices that require more code to be kept on the servers, there's a good chance you'll have to digitally sign your client-side code more often than you have in the past.

SIGNING CODE FOR THE JAVA PLUG-IN

The Java Plug-In uses the built-in Java security model, so it uses your key store for certificates and your `.java.policy` file to establish the security policy.

Back in Chapter 36, "Java Security Features," you saw how to create a private key and a certificate and then use the two to sign a JAR file. You use the same procedure when you want to sign applet code. Just package the applet code into a JAR file and sign the JAR.

Listing 45.1 shows an example applet that reads a file called `journal` from your home directory (what Java calls `user.home`). You edit the file using the `TextArea` displayed on the screen and click the Save button at the bottom to save the text.

LISTING 45.1 SOURCE CODE FOR `JournalApplet.java`

```
package usingj2ee.applet;

import java.applet.*;
import java.awt.*;
import java.awt.event.*;
import java.io.*;


public class JournalApplet extends Applet
{
    protected TextArea entry;

    public JournalApplet()
    {
    }

    public void init()
    {
        String journalStr = getJournalEntry();

        setLayout(new BorderLayout());

        entry = new TextArea(10, 50);
```

```
        entry.setText(journalStr);

        add("Center", entry);

        Button saveButton = new Button("Save");
        saveButton.addActionListener(new ActionListener() {
            public void actionPerformed(ActionEvent evt) {
                saveJournalEntry(entry.getText());
            }
        });


        add("South", saveButton);
    }

    public File getJournalFile()
        throws IOException
    {
            return new File(System.getProperty("user.home")+
                File.separator+"journal");
    }

    public String getJournalEntry()
    {
        try
        {
            File journalFile = getJournalFile();

            if (journalFile.exists())
            {
                byte[] buffer = new byte[(int) journalFile.length()];
                FileInputStream in = new FileInputStream(journalFile);
                in.read(buffer);
                in.close();

                return new String(buffer);
            }
        }
        catch (Exception exc)
        {
            exc.printStackTrace();
        }
        return "";
    }

    public void saveJournalEntry(String entry)
    {
        try
        {
            File journalFile = getJournalFile();

            FileOutputStream out = new FileOutputStream(journalFile);

            out.write(entry.getBytes());

            out.close();
        }
```

LISTING 45.1 CONTINUED

```
        catch (Exception exc)
        {
            exc.printStackTrace();
        }
    }
}
```

After you compile the applet and put it in a JAR file, sign the JAR file with the following command:

```
jarsigner jarfile.jar certalias
```

For example, if your private key has an alias of `j2eebooksign` and your JAR file is called `journal.jar`, the command is as follows:

```
jarsigner journal.jar j2eebooksign
```

The other thing you need to run the applet is an HTML file or a JSP (if you want to use the `<jsp:plugin>` tag). Rather than using the Java Plug-In to test your applet, you can run it through `AppletViewer` until you're sure you have the security right. It's a little easier to set up the HTML file for `AppletViewer`. After you have everything right, you can use the Java Plug-In to run the applet from a browser.

Listing 45.2 shows the HTML file used to test the applet in `AppletViewer`.

LISTING 45.2 SOURCE CODE FOR `JournalApplet.html`

```
<html>
<body>
<applet code="usingj2ee.applet.JournalApplet" archive="journal.jar"
    width=400 height=400>
</applet>
</body>
</html>
```

The `JournalApplet` class needs to access the `user.home` property and be able to read and write a file called `journal` in the user's home directory. Although the JAR file is signed, the applet can't do anything special yet. You must still create a policy file to grant it access.

> **Note**
>
> The policy file granting the security access for the applet must be on the machine where the applet runs. Every user must configure his own policy file.

You can use a special program called `policytool` to edit your local policy file. Create the policy with a `SignedBy` value of the alias of your digital certificate. Remember, that's the alias of the certificate in the user's certificate database, not necessarily yours. Of course, if you're doing all your testing on the same machine, they are the same file—your key store. If your certificate has an alias of `j2eebooksign`, that's what you use for the `SignedBy` value.

Figure 45.1 shows the policy file entries for the access needed by the `JournalApplet`.

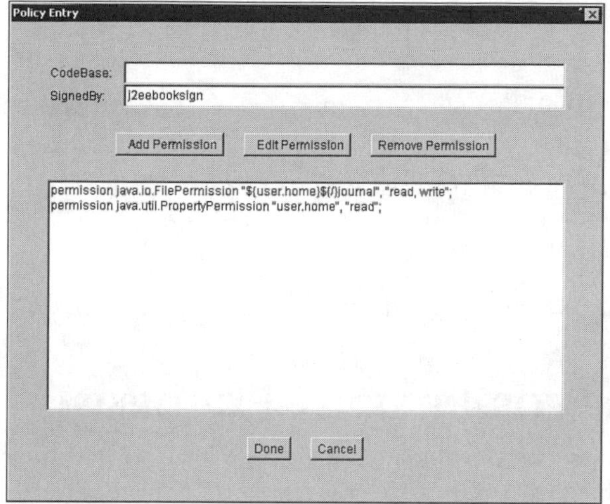

Figure 45.1
The `policytool` program makes it easy to edit policy files.

When you start `policytool` for the first time, it looks for a file called `.java.policy` in your home directory. Remember that filename; it's the name you want to use for your new policy file. After you have created a policy file, you don't need to create a new one. You can specify policies for many classes from the same file.

After you have defined your system policies, test out the applet with `AppletViewer`. Just enter some text and click Save. Figure 45.2 shows the applet running in `AppletViewer`.

Figure 45.2
After the application has permission, it can read and write files.

After you save some data, quit from the `AppletViewer` and start it again to verify that the applet successfully wrote the data and is able to read it again. After you see that it works, you can try loading the applet with the Java Plug-In. Listing 45.3 shows a JSP that uses the `<jsp:plugin>` tag to run the applet.

LISTING 45.3 SOURCE CODE FOR `JournalApplet.jsp`

```
<html>
<body>
<jsp:plugin type="applet" code="usingj2ee.applet.JournalApplet"
    archive="journal.jar" width="500" height="500">
    <jsp:fallback>
        <h1>Unable to load the Java Plug-In</h1>
    </jsp:fallback>
</jsp:plugin>
</body>
</html>
```

SIGNING CODE FOR INTERNET EXPLORER

You have two options when it comes to signing code for Internet Explorer. You can either use the all-or-nothing method, in which the signed code is either trusted or it isn't, or you can use the newer Java Package Manager feature and take advantage of different levels of security.

The Java Package Manager is a bit more complicated than the all-or-nothing method, and given Microsoft's somewhat shaky relationship with Java, it's probably not worth the trouble.

The old style of code signing, in which the file is either fully trusted or not, is easy to use, but you should still consider switching over to the Java Plug-In. Microsoft's Java hasn't kept up with Sun's Java (due to a legal dispute between the two) and Microsoft doesn't support any of the features of Java 1.2. Swing doesn't work well (if at all); you don't get the newer container classes and you have to download RMI as a separate package.

Still, because it's pretty simple to sign a file, and because you don't have to create any additional input files, it's worth exploring the simple code-signing aspect of Microsoft's version of Java. Follow these steps:

1. Download the Microsoft SDK for Java from `www.microsoft.com/java`, which gives you all the tools you need.
2. After you have the SDK installed, you can create a test certificate with the following command:
   `makecert -sv` *`privatekeyfile`*`.pvk -n "CN=`*`Your name`*`"` *`certfile`*`.cer`

   You can specify any name for the private-key file (as long as it ends with .pvk). You must also be sure to keep the private-key file safe. If anyone gets a hold of your private-key file, they can sign code using your name. You can also use any name for the certificate file, as long as it ends with `.cer`.
3. You will be prompted for a key password once or twice when you create the key.
4. Next, create an SPC file (a certificate for signing code) with the following:
   `cert2spc` *`certfile`*`.cer` *`certfile`*`.spc`
5. Initially, your certificate is signed with a test root CA. If you intend to sign production code, you must order a code-signing certificate from a trusted CA. In the mean time,

however, you can tell the system to treat the test certificate as a trusted CA with the following command:

```
setreg 1 true
```

6. When you're done testing, mark the test root CA as untrusted again with the following:

```
setreg 1 false
```

Caution

While you have the test root CA flagged as trusted, make sure you don't visit any internet sites that might try to send you ActiveX controls that might be signed with the test root. The `setreg` command knocks a huge hole in your security. Make *absolutely sure* that you unmark the test root CA when you're done testing!

Now, to package your code, instead of a `JAR` file you must create a `CAB` file. Use the `cabarc` command, specifying `-s 6144` to reserve space for the signature, and `-p` to preserve the subdirectory names. To package the Microsoft Java version of the `JournalApplet`, use the following command:

```
cabarc -s 6144 -p N journal.cab usingj2ee\applet\MSJournal*.class
```

Finally, you must digitally sign the code using the following command:

```
signcode -j javasign.dll -jp LOW -spc certfile.spc journal.cab
```

Notice that the classname for the Microsoft Java version of the applet is different than the normal one. The Microsoft version must use a special call in the `init` method to request permission to read and write to the file system. Listing 45.4 shows the added code.

PART VIII CH 45

LISTING 45.4 ADDITIONAL CODE FOR `MSJournalApplet.java`

```
try
{
// See if the PolicyEngine is available in this JVM
    if (Class.forName("com.ms.security.PolicyEngine") != null)
    {
// If so, request permission to access files
        PolicyEngine.assertPermission(PermissionID.FILEIO);
    }
}
catch (Exception exc)
{
    exc.printStackTrace();
}
```

Note

Because `MsJournalApplet.java` uses Microsoft-specific extensions, you must use the `jvc` command (included in the MS Java SDK) to compile the class.

When you package your classes into CAB files, you specify the CAB filename(s) differently than with JAR files (don't forget that CAB files only work in IE). Listing 45.5 shows the MSJournalApplet.html file that launches the applet in IE.

LISTING 45.5 SOURCE CODE FOR MSJournalApplet.html

```
<html>
<body>
<applet code="usingj2ee.applet.MSJournalApplet" width=400 height=400>
    <param name="cabinets" value="journal.cab">
</applet>
</body>
</html>
```

SIGNING CODE FOR NETSCAPE NAVIGATOR

To digitally sign your code for Netscape Navigator, you'll need Netscape's signing tool, which is available at http://developer.netscape.com.

You must also have the cert7.db and key3.db files available from your Netscape installation. To create a new key, type the following:

```
signtool -G -d dir
```

dir is the directory where your cert7.db and key3.db files are. The signtool program prompts you for the alias of the certificate and also for the information that goes into the certificate.

Netscape uses a capabilities API similar to the one in the standard JDK and in the Microsoft Java implementation. You must ask the security manager to grant you permission to perform a particular operation. It's best to ask before you begin a series of operations because the security is method based. If you ask for a permission from your applet's init method, you won't necessarily have that same permission when you handle a button click.

Listing 45.6 shows the Netscape-specific version of the journal applet.

LISTING 45.6 SOURCE CODE FOR NSJournalApplet.java

```
package usingj2ee.applet;

import java.applet.*;
import java.awt.*;
import java.awt.event.*;
import java.io.*;

import netscape.security.*;

public class NSJournalApplet extends Applet
{
    protected TextArea entry;

    public NSJournalApplet()
```

```
    {
    }

    public void init()
    {
        String journalStr = getJournalEntry();

        setLayout(new BorderLayout());

        entry = new TextArea(10, 50);
        entry.setText(journalStr);

        add("Center", entry);

        Button saveButton = new Button("Save");
        saveButton.addActionListener(new ActionListener() {
            public void actionPerformed(ActionEvent evt) {
                saveJournalEntry(entry.getText());
            }
        });


        add("South", saveButton);
    }

    public File getJournalFile()
        throws IOException
    {
            try
            {
                PrivilegeManager.enablePrivilege("UniversalPropertyRead");
            }
            catch (Exception exc)
            {
                exc.printStackTrace();
            }

            return new File(System.getProperty("user.home")+
                File.separator+"journal");
    }

    public String getJournalEntry()
    {
        try
        {
            PrivilegeManager.enablePrivilege("UniversalFileAccess");

            File journalFile = getJournalFile();

            if (journalFile.exists())
            {
                byte[] buffer = new byte[(int) journalFile.length()];
                FileInputStream in = new FileInputStream(journalFile);
                in.read(buffer);
                in.close();

                return new String(buffer);
            }
```

LISTING 45.6 CONTINUED

```
        }
        catch (Exception exc)
        {
            exc.printStackTrace();
        }
        return "";
    }

    public void saveJournalEntry(String entry)
    {
        try
        {
            PrivilegeManager.enablePrivilege("UniversalFileAccess");

            File journalFile = getJournalFile();

            FileOutputStream out = new FileOutputStream(journalFile);

            out.write(entry.getBytes());

            out.close();
        }
        catch (Exception exc)
        {
            exc.printStackTrace();
        }
    }
}
```

You'll need to download Netscape's Capabilities API class files to compile the `NSJournalApplet` program.

The Netscape code-signing tool is a little quirky. To compile `NSJournalApplet`, put the code files in a separate directory, such as `classes`. Then, run `signtool` this way:

`signtool -k` *`yourcertname`* `-Z` *`newjarfile`*`.jar classes`

The `classes` entry at the end of the command is the name of the directory where `signtool` will look for classes. `signtool` should then create the JAR file for you and you are ready to go.

TROUBLESHOOTING

`AppletViewer` AND PLUG-IN PROBLEMS

Why do I keep getting security violations when I try to perform privileged operations?

Make sure that you have updated your policy file to include the new privileges. Next, make sure that the `SignedBy` name in the policy matches the certificate's alias in the certificate store (or key store). If you still can't figure it out, try running `AppletViewer` with the following extra parameter:

```
-J-Djava.security.debug=policy
```

This option should show you what policy the system is using for your code. You might also try setting the debug level to `java.security.debug=jar` to make sure it's reading your JAR file correctly.

INTERNET EXPLORER PROBLEMS

Why do I keep getting security exceptions with Internet Explorer?

You might not have requested the properties or your file isn't properly signed. Turn on the Java Console (it's in the Internet Options dialog box under Advanced) so you can look for specific exceptions. Make sure that your test root CA is trusted, too.

NETSCAPE PROBLEMS

Why do I keep getting security exceptions with Netscape?

You might not be asking for the right privilege, or you might not be asking often enough. Netscape is more rigid in its security constraints, so you should check with the `PrivilegeManager` before you begin a series of protected operations.

CHAPTER 46

Using Enterprise JavaBeans from an Applet

In this chapter

WHEN APPLETS MAKE SENSE IN AN EJB APPLICATION

As you saw in Chapter 44, "Applet Development," applet use has dwindled since the early days of Java, but still makes a strong showing in a few key areas (interactive programs and data displays). There are times when you might need to use an Enterprise JavaBean (EJB) (almost always a session bean) directly from an applet. Although there are definitely cases in which an applet makes sense, you will probably find that an applet is not always the best choice for front-end development.

When you are deciding whether to use applets for an EJB application, you should consider the following questions:

- Are there any potential firewall issues? EJBs use Remote Method Invocation (RMI), which is notoriously firewall unfriendly.
- Does the application need to run in a browser or can it run standalone?
- Would the code involve a substantial download?
- Is the application highly interactive?
- Does the application have any specific security requirements?

FIREWALL ISSUES

Firewall issues tend to be one of the determining factors in an Internet application. Not only do you have issues in configuring your own firewall, you often encounter problems with firewalls at customer sites. RMI is normally firewall unfriendly. Although you can take various steps to work around firewall issues, it usually makes the development and maintenance of the application a bit more difficult. If you use the RMI-over-HTTP mechanism, you might find that the application is sluggish to respond.

If your applet must run in an environment outside of your control, you should stick to firewall-friendly protocols, such as HTTP. Although HTTPS is also a good choice, it's often difficult to get a good HTTPS library for applets.

You are probably better off using servlets and Java Server Pages if possible. XML-SOAP is another good possibility because it gives you the same basic remote invocation call that you need for an EJB but uses HTTP as the transport protocol so it is firewall-friendly.

BROWSER VERSUS STANDALONE

With the advent of the Java Web Start, which you'll learn about in the next chapter, you have a choice when it comes to downloaded code. Web Start lets you launch Java applications from a Web browser. The applications run outside of the browser. Generally speaking, if your application must run inside the browser (usually because of an artificial user requirement and not a technical one), use an applet. If it's okay to run the application in a separate window, use the Java Web Start.

SUBSTANTIAL DOWNLOAD

One of the problems with applets is that the code is often downloaded every time you start the applet. Some browsers might cache the applet code, but you just don't know when it will download the code again. For a small applet, that's not a problem. If your applet uses a lot of libraries, as it does when it uses J2EE, you must take that into account. If your users are all on a high-speed corporate intranet, a larger download isn't as bad as it is for a user who might be using a modem. Again, the Java Web Start might provide an advantage here because it has built-in caching.

SECURITY REQUIREMENTS

Applets normally run inside of a restricted sandbox that keeps the applet from tampering with the rest of the system. By digitally signing the applet, you can ease the restrictions, but you still require the user to have some knowledge of Java security. If you need to access local files, make network connections to different sites or any of the other things an applet can't normally do, you should consider deploying your code as a standalone application. Java Web Start gives you a few workarounds for common system functions, but it still operates under most of the same restrictions as applets.

CREATING AN APPLET THAT ACCESSES AN EJB

Creating an applet that accesses an EJB is really no different than creating a standalone program that accesses an EJB. In an applet, however, you must identify the JNDI naming factory and provider URL. In a standalone program, you can set the naming factory using a system property, but a downloaded applet doesn't have that same luxury.

If you decide to deploy an EJB-aware applet, you should use the Java Plug-In as your applet environment. You use RMI to communicate with EJBs, and Internet Explorer doesn't come with RMI built-in (you can use RMI with IE, but you must install it separately). The Java Plug-In lets you focus on developing the applet rather than worrying about whose version of Java you might be using. You can also use the AppletViewer program for testing your applet.

Listing 46.1 shows an example applet that accesses the Hello World EJB from Chapter 6, "Creating a Session Bean." It uses the WebLogic EJB server.

LISTING 46.1 SOURCE CODE FOR `TestHelloApplet.java`

```
package usingj2ee.hello;

import java.util.*;
import javax.naming.*;
import java.applet.*;
import java.awt.*;
import java.awt.event.*;

public class TestHelloApplet extends Applet
{
    HelloWorldSession session;
```

LISTING 46.1 CONTINUED

```
    TextField greetingField;
    Label greetingLabel;

    public void init()
    {
        try
        {

            Properties props = new Properties();

// Tell JNDI what class to use as the initial context factory
            props.put(Context.INITIAL_CONTEXT_FACTORY,
                "weblogic.jndi.WLInitialContextFactory");

// Tell JNDI where to find the EJB server
            props.put(Context.PROVIDER_URL, "t3://flamingo:7001");

// Creates a JNDI naming context for location objects
            Context context = new InitialContext(props);

/* Asks the context to locate an object named "HelloWorld" and expects the
 * object to implement the HelloWorldSessionHome interface */

            HelloWorldSessionHome home = (HelloWorldSessionHome)
                context.lookup("HelloWorld");

/* Asks the Home interface to create a new session bean */
            session = (HelloWorldSession) home.create();

// Set the applet's layout manager
            setLayout(new GridLayout(2, 0));

// Create a panel for the input prompt
            Panel greetingInputPanel = new Panel();
            greetingInputPanel.setLayout(new FlowLayout());

// Create a label for the input field
            greetingInputPanel.add(new Label("Enter a new greeting:"));

// Create the input field
            greetingField = new TextField(40);

            greetingInputPanel.add(greetingField);

// Create a button for sending the updated greeting
            Button sendButton = new Button("Send");
            sendButton.addActionListener(new SendHandler());

            greetingInputPanel.add(sendButton);

            add(greetingInputPanel);

// Create a panel for displaying the new greeting
            Panel greetingDisplayPanel = new Panel();

            greetingDisplayPanel.setLayout(new FlowLayout());
```

```
// Create a label to hold the new greeting, initialized with
// the default greeting
            greetingLabel = new Label(session.getGreeting());

            greetingDisplayPanel.add(greetingLabel);

            add(greetingDisplayPanel);
        }
        catch (Exception exc)
        {
            exc.printStackTrace();
        }
    }

    public void destroy()
    {
        try
        {
// Close down the session when the applet is done
            session.remove();
        }
        catch (Exception exc)
        {
            exc.printStackTrace();
        }
    }

    class SendHandler implements ActionListener
    {
        public void actionPerformed(ActionEvent event)
        {
            try
            {
// Get the greeting from the text field, store it in the EJB
                session.setGreeting(greetingField.getText());

// Get the greeting back from the EJB
                greetingLabel.setText(session.getGreeting());
            }
            catch (Exception exc)
            {
                exc.printStackTrace();
            }
        }
    }
}
```

Listing 46.2 shows an HTML file that you can use with AppletViewer to test the applet in Listing 46.1.

LISTING 46.2 SOURCE CODE FOR TestHelloApplet.html

```
<html>
<body>
<applet code="usingj2ee.hello.TestHelloApplet" codebase="classes"
```

LISTING 46.2 CONTINUED

```
   width=400 height=400>
</applet>
</body>
</html>
```

Figure 46.1 shows the applet running inside the AppletViewer program.

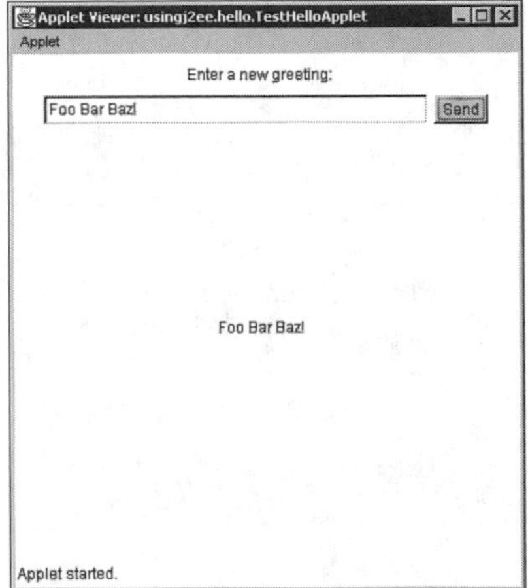

Figure 46.1
The AppletViewer is useful for testing applets that access EJBs.

GETTING TO THE CLASSES YOU NEED

The biggest hassle with using EJBs from an applet is that the Java plug-in doesn't have the EJB classes built-in. If you're using a normal Web server such as Apache to serve up the class files, you might need to unpack all the EJB classes into a directory where the browser can find them. For example, in Listing 46.2, you can see that the codebase for the applet is a directory called `classes`. The `classes` directory contains all the files from the WebLogic `classes` directory, plus the contents of the `weblogicaux.jar` file and the applet classes themselves. You will probably need to perform a similar unpacking routine when you use other EJB servers.

The WebLogic developers realized that you would probably need an easy way to access all the EJB classes, so they created a special servlet that lets you access any of the classes in the WebLogic classpath. That way, you don't need to create a special `classes` directory, you don't need to unpack any JAR files, and you don't need to keep a second copy of the WebLogic class files.

The servlet is called `weblogic.servlet.ClasspathServlet`. You must register it in your `weblogic.properties` file if it isn't there already. Typically, you register it with a root name of `classes` so the servlet handles any pathname beginning with `/classes`. The `weblogic.properties` entry looks like this:

```
weblogic.httpd.register.classes=weblogic.servlet.ClasspathServlet
```

Note

Starting with WebLogic 6.0, you no longer need to register `ClasspathServlet`; the `/classes` directory is already configured into the server.

Now, you change the `TestHelloApplet.html` file to have a codebase of `/classes/` and load the applet from your WebLogic Web server instead of Apache. Listing 46.3 shows the modified file.

LISTING 46.3 `TestHelloApplet.html` FOR WEBLOGIC

```
<html>
<body>
<applet code="usingj2ee.hello.TestHelloApplet" codebase="/classes/"
    width=400 height=400>
</applet>
</body>
</html>
```

You can also use the Java plug-in to run an applet. The easiest way to use the Java plug-in is to use the `<jsp:plugin>` Java Server Pages tag, because it detects the user's browser and inserts the appropriate tags to load the plug-in. Listing 46.4 shows the `TestHelloApplet.jsp` file that loads the Java plug-in and runs the test applet.

LISTING 46.4 SOURCE CODE FOR `TestHelloApplet.jsp`

```
<html>
<body>
<jsp:plugin type="applet" code="usingj2ee.hello.TestHelloApplet"
codebase="/classes/"
    width="400" height="400">
</jsp:plugin>
</body>
</html>
```

TROUBLESHOOTING

LOADING PROBLEMS

Why do I get a `ClassNotFoundException` when I load my applet?

If your applet is in your classpath, you're probably missing some of the EJB classes. If you are using WebLogic, try using `/classes/` as your codebase (make sure you copy your applet into the `WebLogic classes` directory). Otherwise, you should make a directory containing all your EJB classes.

RUNTIME PROBLEMS

Why do I get security exceptions when I run my applet?

Your EJB server might require the applet to do something it's not allowed to do. You can use the code signing technique to sign your code, or just change your security policy to trust classes loaded from the URL where you're loading your servlet.

Why can't my applet find an initial context factory?

Unlike your application, which can take an initial context factory from the command-line, your applet needs to explicitly specify the initial context factory and probably the provider URL in a `Properties` object. See Listing 46.1 earlier in this chapter for an example.

CHAPTER 47

Web Start—An Alternative to Applets

In this chapter

WHAT IS WEB START?

Although applets are useful for many applications, a few drawbacks make applets less palatable for certain applications. For example, you don't have any control over the caching of your applets. For a small applet, you might not care that the user might need to download the applet frequently. On the other hand, if you have a large applet that might take several minutes to download, you definitely want the applet cached. Unfortunately, you're usually at the mercy of the browser when it comes to caching.

A user might want to run your applet as a standalone application without first starting a browser. That certainly isn't possible with an applet. You could, of course, provide the user with a standalone application, but then how would the user know that there is a newer version of the application available for download? Ideally, you want to give the user the option to run the application standalone but still be able to download new versions of the application automatically.

Another hazard in applet programming is the JVM version. You never know what version of the Java Virtual Machine is running in a browser. Even if a user has the Java plug-in installed, you still don't know what version of Java the plug-in uses.

Java Web Start addresses all these problems in an elegant way. First, Web Start integrates with a browser, allowing you to launch applications from a Web server. Second, Web Start can create desktop icons and startup menu options for launching the application without using a browser. Web Start caches application data so you don't need to reload it every time you run the application (unless you specifically want to). You can even specify version numbers for your application JAR files, allowing you to download new versions of the application whenever they become available.

Web Start also provides an expanded "sandbox" model with limited support for printing, accessing the Clipboard, and saving files. These expanded features do not require the JAR files to be digitally signed; they just require the user's approval at the time they are used. If your application needs more capabilities, you can digitally sign the JAR file, which allows the user to grant your application extra capabilities based on the signature.

The Java Network Launching Protocol (JNLP) is the basic foundation of Web Start. The client-side Web Start program reads JNLP data to determine which parts of the application need to be loaded/reloaded. You create a JNLP file and place it on your Web server. When the browser sees the JNLP file, it activates Web Start, which reads the file and determines which application to launch.

CREATING A WEB START APPLICATION

A Web Start application is no different from any standalone application, at least in principle. Some applications that use separate data files might need a little extra work. For example, suppose you have a word-search program that helps you find anagrams and words matching certain patterns. Such tools are popular among avid Scrabble™ players. The word-search program needs a dictionary file of some sort, which can be more than 400KB in size. You don't want to run the word search as an applet because the applet needs to download the 400KB file every time runs. Instead, you can deploy the program using Web Start, allowing the application and the data file to be cached.

Web Start applications that need separate image files and data files should read the files from the application JAR file. In other words, when you package your class files into a JAR file, include any additional data files as well. Your application can use a special method called `getResourceAsStream` to read the data file.

For example, the original word search program used the following statement to open the dictionary file:

```
DataInputStream in = new DataInputStream(
    new BufferedInputStream(
        new FileInputStream("WORDLIST.DAW"))));
```

To read the file out of the JAR file, however, the program must locate its class loader and then call `getResourceAsStream`, like this:

```
DataInputStream in = new DataInputStream(
    new BufferedInputStream(
    getClass().getClassLoader().getResourceAsStream(
        "WORDLIST.DAW")));
```

Rewriting the application to read the data file this way yields two benefits—you can run it with Web Start, and you can create an executable JAR file that doesn't require any additional setup.

To make an executable JAR file, just include a manifest file with a `Main-Class` entry, like this:

```
Main-Class: com.wutka.words.WordSearch
```


Put the entry in a file such as `mainclass` and tell JAR to include the file as part of the manifest by using the `m` option, like this:

```
jar cvfm wordsearch.jar mainclass WORDLIST.DAW com usingj2ee
```

This JAR command creates a file called `wordlist.jar` and adds the contents of `mainclass` to the manifest file. The JAR itself contains the dictionary file (`WORDLIST.DAW`) and all the classes in the `com` and `usingj2ee` directories.

To run the application as a standalone application, just type

```
java -jar wordsearch.jar
```

You don't have to make an executable JAR file to use Web Start, of course, but it never hurts to have multiple ways to run the application.

The real key to Web Start is the JNLP file that describes the application. The JNLP file tells Web Start how to load the program and also how to cache it. You can even specify version numbers for the various application resources, although you need special support on the Web server to support versions.

Listing 47.1 shows the JNLP file that launches the word search application.

LISTING 47.1 SOURCE CODE FOR wordsearch.jnlp

```
<?xml version="1.0" encoding="utf-8"?>
<jnlp spec="1.0" codebase="http://www.wutka.com/usingj2ee"
    href="wordsearch.jnlp">
    <information>
        <title>Word Search</title>
        <vendor>Mark Wutka</vendor>
        <homepage href="wordsearch.html"/>
        <description>Word search and anagramming application
            </description>
        <description kind="short">A word search application
            </description>
        <icon href="wordsearch.gif"/>
        <offline-allowed/>
    </information>
    <security></security>
    <resources>
        <j2se version="1.2"/>
        <j2se version="1.3"/>
        <jar href="wordsearch.jar"/>
    </resources>
    <application-desc main-class="com.wutka.words.WordSearch"/>
</jnlp>
```

The JNLP file is an XML file and the main body tag is the `<jnlp>` tag. The `spec` attribute in the `<jnlp>` tag indicates the version of JNLP that the file is intended for. The `codebase` attribute tells Web Start where to load the application's resources and where the JNLP file itself comes from. The `href` attribute gives the filename of the JNLP file. Web Start might reread the JNLP file when you launch the application to make sure that all the versions are still correct.

The `<information>` contains descriptive information about the application. The `<title>` tag indicates the name of the application, and the `<vendor>` tag indicates the author of the application. The `<homepage>` tag points to a help file for the application. The `<description>` tags give descriptive information about the application. The possible kinds of descriptions are `one-line`, `short`, and `tooltip`.

The `<icon>` tag gives the location of a GIF or JPEG that contains the icon image for the application (which is displayed in the Web Start control panel and possibly on your desktop). The `<offline-allowed>` tag, if present, indicates that you can run the application locally without downloading it from the Web (that is, Web Start can cache it and start it locally).

The `<security>` tag allows you to specify the security requirements of the application. If the application needs all security permissions (the JAR must be signed), include the tag `<all-permissions/>` inside the `<security>` tag. If your application needs the same permissions as a J2EE application client, include the tag `<j2ee-application-client-permissions>`.

The <resources> tag allows you to specify the JAR files that make up the application, and also native libraries, required extensions, properties, and JDK versions. The <j2se> tag lets you require a particular JDK version. You can use multiple <j2se> tags to indicate that your application supports multiple versions. The <jar> tag indicates a JAR file used for the application. You at least need the href attribute to specify the location of the JAR file. You can include a version attribute in the <jar> tag to indicate a required version number for the JAR. Web Start downloads any updated JAR files if it notices a version difference. Unfortunately, versioning requires some special code on the Web server, which might be provided by a CGI script or a servlet.

The <jar> tag can also contain a download attribute whose value can either be eager or lazy. If the attribute is lazy, Web Start won't download the JAR file until your application needs it. You can also tell Web Start that a JAR file contains the main class by setting the main attribute to true.

The <nativelib> tag lets you download native libraries the same way you download JAR files. You use the same attributes for <nativelib> that you do for <jar>.

The <property> tag lets you add system properties for your application. Use the name and value attributes to specify the property name and value.

The <application-desc> tag lets you specify the main class for the application (via the main-class attribute) and also specify the command-line arguments. You specify the command-line arguments with <argument> tags, like this:

```
<application-desc main-class="mymain">
    <argument>Arg1</argument>
    <argument>HereIsArg2</argument>
</application-desc>
```

PART VIII

CH 47

After you create the JNLP file, you put it on your Web server along with any of the files that Web Start might need to download (your JAR file(s), the icon image, and so on). One of the trickier aspects of Web Start is that the Web server must recognize JNLP as a valid file type and have a corresponding MIME type for the file. Each Web server has different ways of specifying MIME types, so you must consult the documentation for your Web server. If you're running Apache, you can include an .htaccess file in the same directory as the JNLP file. To set the MIME type from the .htaccess file, include the following line:

```
AddType application/x-java-jnlp-file JNLP
```

If you're running another kind of Web server, make sure that you associate a file type .jnlp with application/x-java-jnlp-file.

You can point your browser directly at the JNLP file to initiate Web Start (assuming you have already downloaded and installed Web Start from http://java.sun.com). Figure 47.1 shows the word search application after being started by a browser (pointing at http://www.wutka.com/usingj2ee/wordsearch.jnlp).

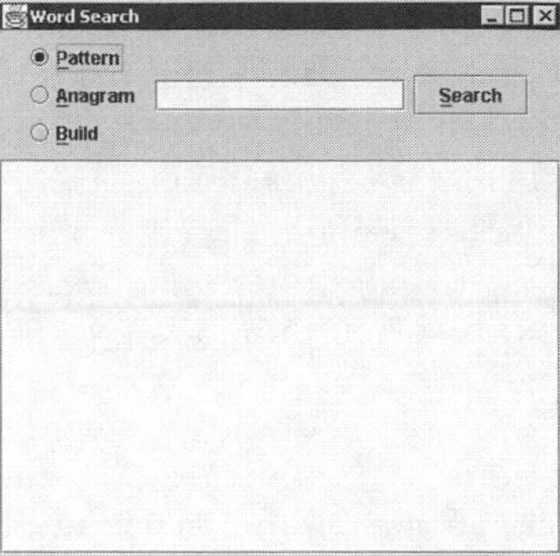

Figure 47.1
Web Start can launch a standalone application from a browser.

After Web Start downloads an application, it stores it in its local cache. You can run the Web Start Application Manager to control the applications that are in the cache. Figure 47.2 shows the Web Start Application Manager in action.

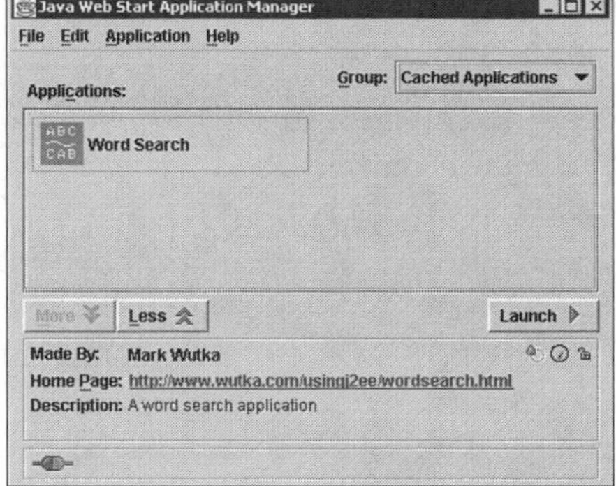

Figure 47.2
The Web Start Application Manager lets you manage the cache and various settings.

Web Start can also create desktop icons and Start menu options for running the application. Figure 47.3 shows the Start menu option for word search as well as the desktop icon. Through the Web Start Application Manager, you can decide when and whether Web Start prompts you to create these shortcuts.

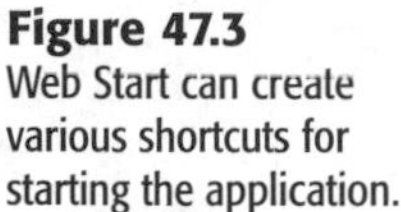

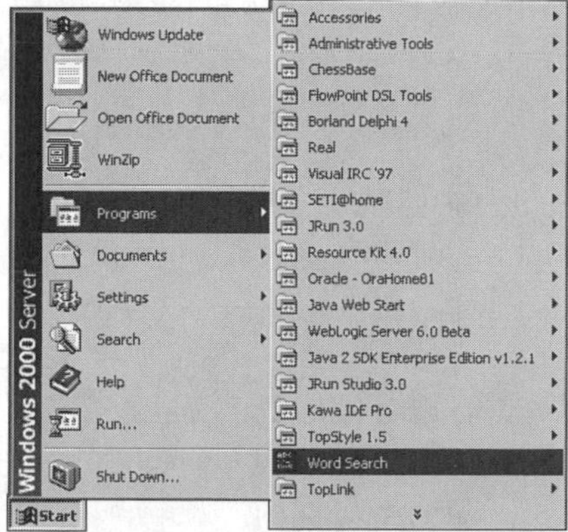

Figure 47.3
Web Start can create various shortcuts for starting the application.

FILE ACCESS AND OTHER USEFUL FEATURES

One of the handy features of Web Start is that it allows you to read and write files. Before you get the impression that Web Start somehow opens your system to hacking, the file access routines in Web Start require the user to select a file for you—giving the user control over what files you can and cannot access.

Web Start has several other useful features to let you perform various other operations that the sandbox security restrictions normally prevent. The `javax.jnlp` package contains interfaces into these various services. You locate the services through a class called `ServiceManager`.

To read to a file, you first use the service manager to locate the `FileOpenService` interface, like this:

```
FileOpenService openService = (FileOpenService)
    ServiceManager.lookup("javax.jnlp.FileOpenService");
```

Next, you ask the open service to open one or more files. To open a single file, call `openFileDialog`, passing a path hint suggesting a possible directory where the file might be located (or `null`) and a string array containing default file extensions (or `null`). To open multiple files at once, call `openMultiFileDialog` using the same parameters that you pass to `openFileDialog`. The `openFileDialog` method returns a `FileContents` object that you can use to read the file. The `openMultiFileDialog` method returns an array of `FileContents` objects.

For example, to open a file, call

```
FileContents contents = openService.openFileDialog(null, null);
```

To get streams for reading or writing file contents, use the `getInputStream` and `getOutputStream` methods in `FileContents`. To determine whether you can read or write a file, call `canRead` or `canWrite`.

To save a file, use the `ServiceManager` class to locate the `FileSaveService`:

```
FileSaveService saveService = (FileSaveService)
    ServiceManager.lookup("javax.jnlp.FileSaveService");
```

If you have a `FileContents` object that you want to save, call `saveFileDialog`, passing the path hint and extensions just as you do for opening a file (use `null` if you don't want to specify either one) and also pass the `FileContents` object you want to save, like this:

```
FileContents saved = saveService.saveAsFileDialog(
    null, null, contentsToSave);
```

You can also call `saveFileDialog` with the path hints and extensions, along with an input stream that will supply the data to save and a suggested filename:

```
FileContents saved = saveService.saveFileDialog(
    null, null, saveInputStream, "saveddata.txt");
```

To treat a `FileContents` object as a random-access file (so you can move to a specific position in the file and read or write), use the `getRandomAccessFile` method, passing either `"r"` for read-only mode or `"rw"` for read/write mode:

```
JNLPRandomAccessFile random = saved.getRandomAccessFile("rw");
```

PRINTING

To print a document, you must first locate the `PrintService` class:

```
PrintService print = (PrintService)
    ServiceManager.lookup("javax.jnlp.PrintService");
```

Get the default page format with

```
PageFormat fmt = print.getDefaultPage();
```

Then, allow the user to modify the page format with

```
PageFormat newFmt = print.showPageFormatDialog(fmt);
```

Finally, print either the `Pageable` object or the `Printable` object (the same kinds of objects you would print using the `PrinterJob` class) using the `print` method:

```
print.print(myPageable);
print.print(myPrintable);
```

ACCESSING THE CLIPBOARD

You can access the Clipboard using `ClipboardService`:

```
ClipboardService clip = (ClipboardService)
    ServiceManager.lookup("javax.jnlp.ClipboardService");
```

Then use `setContents` to store a `Transferable` object (the standard AWT Clipboard object) or use `getContents` to retrieve the current Clipboard contents.

LAUNCHING A BROWSER

You can open up a Web page in a browser from a Web Start application. Just locate the `BasicService` object and call `showDocument`:

```
BasicService basic = (BasicService)
    ServiceManager.lookup("javax.jnlp.BasicService");
basic.showDocument(new URL("http://www.wutka.com"));
```

TROUBLESHOOTING

ACCESSING JNLP FILES

Why does the browser just show the contents of the JNLP file or offer to save the file?

You might not have set up the MIME type properly, or you haven't installed Web Start. You can check the MIME type by fetching the JNLP file using the Telnet program. See Chapter 29, "The HTTP Protocol," for information on how to use Telnet to retrieve a file. Using Telnet, you can examine the MIME type (returned as `Content-Type`) in the HTTP header to determine whether the Web server recognized JNLP files properly.

I have installed Web Start and the MIME type is correct; why does it still fail?

You might have an error in the JNLP file. Also, make sure there is no blank line between the `<?xml?>` tag and the `<jnlp>` tag. Early versions of Web Start would fail if there was a blank line between these tags.

PART IX

PROBLEM SOLVING

CHAPTER 48

Narrowing Down the Problem

In this chapter

THE ART OF DEBUGGING

Debugging can be a chore or it can be an art. Sometimes it's fun, and sometimes it's incredibly boring. Becoming good at debugging is a lot like becoming good at chess. You can read books about it, but it just takes time and experience to get really good. Over time, you'll see common patterns of erroneous behavior that occur over and over. As you become familiar with these patterns, you get better at spotting them.

Some of the most common bug patterns are

- **Development error**—Either a typo or a straightforward error in coding (forgetting to increment a counter, storing the wrong value, and so on).
- **Environmental error**—The program behaves differently on different computers or in different browsers, or the program fails after a system upgrade.
- **Configuration error**—Two different copies of the same program behave differently on the same computer or extremely similar computers.
- **Synchronization error**—Errors crop up when multiple users access the same data at the same time.
- **Resource error**—The program consumes too many resources (or the whole computer is low on resources) and begins to fail.
- **User error**—The program works correctly, but the user thinks it doesn't.
- **Phantom error**—Something strange happens one time and never occurs again.

Most system errors fall into one or more of these categories. Sometimes a particular error is actually an insidious combination of several of these patterns.

PROGRAMMER ERRORS

This category of errors covers a huge number of potential problems and spans from requirements gathering all the way to deployment. Some things reported as errors occur because the user expects the program to behave one way, but the requirements (if there are any) say it should behave differently.

Many of these errors don't require any particular skill in debugging. Often, you can just start up a debugger, step through the code and find the problem in a matter of minutes. Sometimes, you can find these errors before you even get to the debugging stage. You often catch a lot of errors while performing code reviews.

Note

If your organization performs code reviews, make sure you concentrate on finding coding and design errors. Don't use the review as a forum to criticize the developer or to look for nitpicking items, such as misspelled comments. The book *Code Complete* by Steve McConnell (ISBN 1-55615-484-4) has some excellent tips for code reviews and defensive programming.

If you can't find the error with a debugger, you usually must resort to print statements and log files. You can also find problems by reviewing the code.

Pay special attention to compiler warnings, too. Sometimes you ignore a warning because you think it doesn't apply, and then hours later you realize that the warning is there for a reason.

ENVIRONMENTAL ERRORS

Some environmental errors are obvious—something works in one Web browser but fails in another. Some are not quite as obvious. Unix and Windows, for example, use different end-of-line characters. You might find that a program can't read its configuration file correctly on Windows because you copied over the Unix version of the file and the program doesn't pick up the end-of-line characters correctly. Java tends to handle this situation better than other languages, fortunately.

You can also encounter problems caused by different types of CPUs. Intel chips store numbers in memory differently than Sparc chips. If you write a program that writes numbers to a file in binary format, you might have trouble reading the file on another kind of system. You also see this error frequently in networking programs because you typically have different types of machines communicating with each other. Once again, Java tends to be less susceptible to this problem.

Another Unix-Windows glitch that you often find with Web applications is that Windows is not case sensitive when it comes to filenames. If you capitalize a filename in a Web page but use all lowercase when you actually save the file, Windows doesn't care. When you move the application to Unix, however, you suddenly see many errors about missing files because Unix cares about capitalization. Your best bet at preventing this situation is to pick a naming standard and stick with it.

Sometimes the problem is that the system has recently been upgraded and new libraries have caused the failure. It's best to coordinate system upgrades so you are ready to look for problems when the upgrades occur.

CONFIGURATION ERRORS

Configuration is a mixed blessing. It's great that there are so many ways to change the behavior of the program. Unfortunately, there are too many ways to change the behavior of the program. Programs that use many configuration files fall victim to this problem more often than programs that use only a few files.

Unlike an environmental error, a configuration error can occur on identical machines running the same code. A small change in a property file or deployment descriptor on one machine can cause a program to act differently.

SYNCHRONIZATION ERRORS

Synchronization errors are some of the most difficult problems to spot. They usually crop up when you increase the number of people using the system or increase the volume of work the program is doing. Some of the telltale signs are that some users start seeing data from other users. You also see database records and files that look like they contain parts of different records.

Many times, a synchronization error occurs as a result of a design problem, but other times, it's a matter of adding various thread-synchronization statements or reconfiguring the system to be single-threaded. For example, if you have a synchronization problem in a servlet or an EJB, you can mark that servlet or EJB as being single-threaded.

Other times, a synchronization error is a result of improper transaction isolation. You should normally use the highest possible isolation level for your transactions. If you need to reduce the isolation level for performance reasons, you might need to perform extra checking in your code to avoid possible data inconsistencies.

RESOURCE ERRORS

Like synchronization errors, resource errors tend to crop up when you increase the load on the system. You might start seeing errors about having no more file descriptors or being out of memory. When looking for these errors, it often helps to use some of the common system-status tools, such as `netstat`, `top`, `ps`, and the Windows task manager.

USER ERRORS

User errors are frequently not really errors. The user reports an error that turns out to be a mistake by the user and not the program. Sometimes, the user inhibits debugging by providing faulty information. For example, you might know that a particular bug occurs when running Internet Explorer 4, but doesn't occur under IE5. A user might swear up and down that he's running IE5—then after you've wasted hours looking for the problem, you discover that the user is actually running IE4.

Other errors happen because the user just plain makes a mistake. These kinds of problems have various names (mostly provided by frustrated tech support people). One of the interesting terms is an ESU problem—Equipment Superior to User. Calling something an "ESU problem" sounds to the user like it's an equipment failure—so it's something of an inside joke for the developers and support people.

Be careful about blaming problems on the user, however. Sometimes it's poor program design that makes it far too easy for the user to make errors. If your program lets a user do something she shouldn't, that's your problem, not the user's. On the other hand, if the user reports that she entered "Fred" on the keyboard and it came back "Ferd", that sounds more like an ESU problem.

PHANTOM ERRORS

They're pretty rare, but sometimes you get a phantom error—it happens once or twice and never happens again. As a problem solver, even though the error might have vanished, you still want to explain it—otherwise, you can't feel sure it won't happen again. Unfortunately, it's often impossible to figure out why the problem occurred because all the evidence has disappeared. Many times, a phantom error occurs because of a temporary outage or an invalid file. If a file or some other piece of information is invalid, a program might end up correcting it by writing out a corrected file or deleting the offending file.

You can try to duplicate your steps and see if the error happens again, but sometimes you just have to chalk it up to a phantom cause, such as an extreme quantum improbability, or too many neutrinos passing through the system. In other words, you just have to shrug your shoulders and go on to the next problem.

Debugging Techniques

Sometimes you can figure out an error just from the symptoms; other times, you must interact with the program or the system to see what's going on. Some of these techniques just require a little patience, although others require you to exercise an unusual number of brain cells.

Using a Debugger

Obviously, if you're debugging a program, the first thing that leaps to mind is to use a debugger. For small, standalone programs, a debugger is probably the best way to locate a problem. Even for more complicated programs—servlets, EJBs, even Java Server Pages—you can often use a debugger to step through the code. It might be a little tougher to set up the debugger at first, but after you get it going, it can save you many hours of work.

Debuggers aren't as useful for finding synchronization and resource errors because it's hard to locate where the problem is occurring. If the problem happens when 500 users hit the system and it only happens to two users, what are the odds you will be able to catch the situation with a debugger?

Sometimes, the act of using a debugger can fix the problem (or cause a problem). In the C++ world, you often find that a program runs well inside the debugger and crashes without the debugger, or vice-versa. Sometimes these problems are caused by synchronization errors. The debugger changes the speed at which various sections of the program run, so you might expose or hide critical errors when running the debugger.

Logging

In a server application, logging is crucial. You can't rely on being able to trap an error inside a debugger. The system might need to run for hours before an error occurs. The trick is figuring out what to log. Certainly, you want to log exceptions, although you must be careful how often you log them. If you catch an exception, log it, and then throw another exception, you might end up logging that exception, too. You can end up with four or five log messages for the same exception.

When possible, try to rethrow exceptions so they retain the complete stack trace. When you're looking at a stack trace that shows you that the exception originated inside a catch statement, it doesn't tell you where the true error occurred. When you rethrow an exception, call `fillInStackTrace` in the exception before you throw it:

```
try
{
    // do something
}
catch (NullPointerException exc)
{
    exc.printStackTrace();
    throw exc.fillInStackTrace();
}
```

Sometimes when you're logging code, you want to print a stack trace showing how the program got to the current line of code, but you don't really want to throw an exception. For example, if you have a common utility routine that occasionally receives bad data, you want to find out who is calling the routine with the bad data. You can print out a current snapshot of the stack by throwing an exception and immediately printing it:

```
try
{
    throw new RuntimeException();
}
catch (RuntimeException exc)
{
    exc.printStackTrace();
}
```

Sometimes, a Just-In-Time (JIT) compiler causes the stack trace to lose track of the original source code line numbers. You get the routine names, but instead of a line number, you just get "(Compiled Code)". You can turn the JIT off to get line numbers in the stack trace. For JDK 1.2 and above, set the `java.compiler` system property to `NONE`, like this:

```
java -Djava.compiler=NONE mypackage.myclass
```

Keep in mind that the JIT itself might be a culprit in your error—especially in a point-zero release of the JDK (that is, 1.2.0, 1.3.0, and so on) or in a port to a new operating system. You might find that the error no longer occurs when the JIT is off. Of course, the disappearance of the error could be caused by the fact that the program now runs slower with the JIT off. It's always hard to tell.

DETERMINING WHAT HAS CHANGED

Many times, a program stops working because someone changed something in the system—a library, a properties file, a deployment descriptor, a resource bundle, a new user, and so on. The trick is to figure out when and where the change occurred.

For example, if the system stopped working at 3 p.m., start looking for configuration files that changed around 3 p.m. Also check to see if the system was restarted (your log files should indicate when the system starts and maybe when it shuts down). If the system was restarted around the time the error occurred, you might need to look for files changed between the time of the previous restart and the most recent restart. Chances are, if the user restarted the system, the user recently made a change, so you're likely to find that something changed just before the system restarted.

Check for other changes, too. Under Unix, type `uptime` and see how long the system has been up. If it was recently rebooted, someone might have performed an upgrade on the system. Oddly enough, systems that stay up for an extended period of time run the risk of having trouble restarting due to configuration changes. The problem is that someone could make a change to a file that doesn't seem to break anything at first. Then, six months later when the system reboots for the first time since the change, things suddenly break because of the change. Who would suspect that the problem was a change made six months ago?

Examining the System

Sometimes an error isn't generated by your program but by the operating system. The error might still be in your program or it might be caused by another program or even just a system problem. You should examine the system as much as you can to look for anything peculiar. For example, under Windows NT or 2000, bring up the Task Manager (press Ctrl+Alt+Del and select Task Manager). The Task Manager shows you the programs running on the system and the CPU and memory usage for each program and for the whole system. Look for programs that are hogging the CPU—it might indicate an infinite loop. Look for programs that are taking up an enormous amount of memory as well. Also, look at the total system memory usage to make sure you aren't running out of memory. By clicking one of the headings in the task list, you can sort by various criteria. For example, you can sort by CPU usage to find the processes that are using the most CPU time. Likewise, you can sort by memory usage to find the programs using the most memory.

Figure 48.1 shows the Windows Task Manager for Windows 2000.

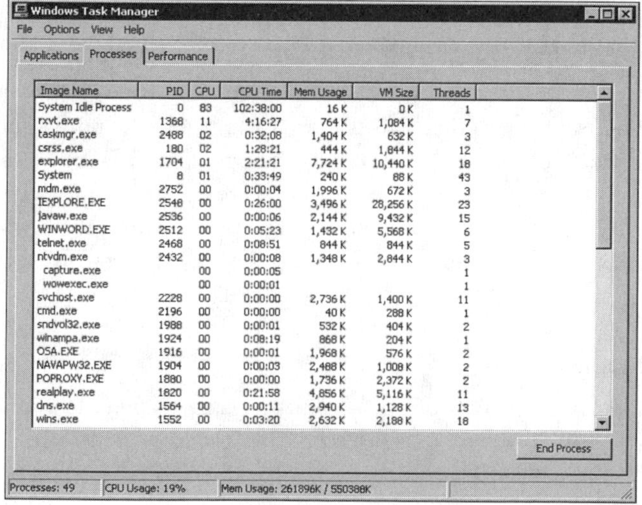

Image Name	PID	CPU	CPU Time	Mem Usage	VM Size	Threads
System Idle Process	0	83	102:38:00	16 K	0 K	1
rxvt.exe	1368	11	4:16:27	764 K	1,084 K	7
taskmgr.exe	2488	02	0:32:08	1,404 K	632 K	3
csrss.exe	180	02	1:28:21	444 K	1,844 K	12
explorer.exe	1704	01	2:21:21	7,724 K	10,440 K	18
System	8	01	0:33:49	240 K	88 K	43
mdm.exe	2752	00	0:00:04	1,996 K	672 K	3
IEXPLORE.EXE	2548	00	0:26:00	3,496 K	28,256 K	23
javaw.exe	2536	00	0:00:06	2,144 K	9,432 K	15
WINWORD.EXE	2512	00	0:05:23	1,432 K	5,568 K	6
telnet.exe	2468	00	0:08:51	844 K	844 K	5
ntvdm.exe	2432	00	0:00:08	1,348 K	2,844 K	3
capture.exe		00	0:00:05			1
wowexec.exe		00	0:00:01			1
svchost.exe	2228	00	0:00:00	2,736 K	1,400 K	11
cmd.exe	2196	00	0:00:00	40 K	288 K	1
sndvol32.exe	1988	00	0:00:01	532 K	404 K	2
winampa.exe	1924	00	0:08:19	868 K	204 K	1
OSA.EXE	1916	00	0:00:01	1,968 K	576 K	2
NAVAPW32.EXE	1904	00	0:00:03	2,488 K	1,008 K	2
POPROXY.EXE	1880	00	0:00:00	1,736 K	2,372 K	2
realplay.exe	1820	00	0:21:58	4,856 K	5,116 K	11
dns.exe	1564	00	0:00:11	2,940 K	1,128 K	13
wins.exe	1552	00	0:03:20	2,632 K	2,188 K	18

Figure 48.1
The Task Manager shows you what's going on in the system.

On some Unix and Linux systems, you can use the `top` command to get the same kind of display. Type `?` to get the various options for `top`—they vary from system to system. As with the Task Manager, look for programs using too much time or consuming too much memory. Also, look at the total system memory to see if you're running out. Figure 48.2 shows top running on a Linux system.

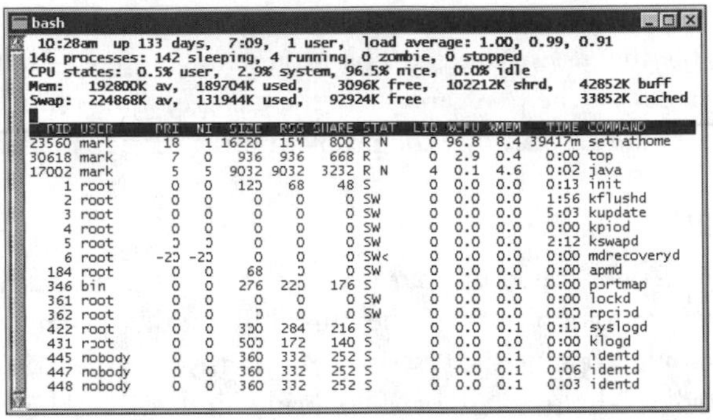

```
bash
 10:28am  up 133 days,  7:09,  1 user,  load average: 1.00, 0.99, 0.91
146 processes: 142 sleeping, 4 running, 0 zombie, 0 stopped
CPU states:  0.5% user,  2.9% system, 96.5% nice,  0.0% idle
Mem:   192800K av,  189704K used,    3096K free,  102212K shrd,   42852K buff
Swap:  224868K av,  131944K used,   92924K free                   33852K cached

  PID USER     PRI  NI  SIZE  RSS SHARE STAT  LIB %CPU %MEM   TIME COMMAND
23560 mark      18   1 16220  15M   800 R N     0 96.8  8.4 39417m setiathome
30618 mark       7   0   936  936   668 R       0  2.9  0.4   0:00 top
17002 mark       5   5  9032 9032  3232 R N     4  0.1  4.6   0:02 java
    1 root       0   0   120   68    48 S       0  0.0  0.0   0:13 init
    2 root       0   0     0    0     0 SW      0  0.0  0.0   1:56 kflushd
    3 root       0   0     0    0     0 SW      0  0.0  0.0   5:03 kupdate
    4 root       0   0     0    0     0 SW      0  0.0  0.0   0:00 kpiod
    5 root       0   0     0    0     0 SW      0  0.0  0.0   2:12 kswapd
    6 root     -20 -20     0    0     0 SW<     0  0.0  0.0   0:00 mdrecoveryd
  184 root       0   0    68    0     0 SW      0  0.0  0.0   0:00 apmd
  346 bin        0   0   276  220   176 S       0  0.0  0.1   0:00 portmap
  361 root       0   0     0    0     0 SW      0  0.0  0.0   0:00 lockd
  362 root       0   0     0    0     0 SW      0  0.0  0.0   0:00 rpciod
  422 root       0   0   300  284   216 S       0  0.0  0.1   0:10 syslogd
  431 root       0   0   500  172   140 S       0  0.0  0.0   0:00 klogd
  445 nobody     0   0   360  332   252 S       0  0.0  0.1   0:00 identd
  447 nobody     0   0   360  332   252 S       0  0.0  0.1   0:06 identd
  448 nobody     0   0   360  332   252 S       0  0.0  0.1   0:03 identd
```

Figure 48.2
The top command shows you what's running on a Unix or Linux system.

If you don't have top and can't locate a version for your operating system, try the ps command. It's not as pretty, but you can see what's running. Type man ps to see the options for ps.

You can also buy commercial tools that provide a wealth of monitoring utilities. Many of these tools can even monitor the system automatically and detect potential problems before they occur.

If you're seeing strange errors trying to write to files, or strange memory errors, your system might be running low on disk space. You can use the Windows Explorer to check the disk space on your Windows machine. On most Unix and Linux systems, you can use the df command to see how much space is available. If you see a file system or drive that's almost out of space, that might be causing your problems.

Another possible problem is that you're using up too many network connections—for example, a Java CORBA program that calls ORB.init over and over might end up creating a huge number of listener sockets. Use the netstat -a command in Windows and Unix to see the open socket connections. You might want to execute the command occasionally when everything's working normally just so you know what a normal configuration looks like. You're likely to see a lot of open connections and listening sockets even when everything is working fine.

NETWORKING PROBLEMS

When you have connectivity problems—someone can't connect to your application—you might have a network problem or there might be an odd protocol problem. You can try the ping command to see whether you can reach the other host:

```
ping otherhost.someplace.com
```

These days, however, you can't always rely on ping because some corporate firewalls block ping requests while allowing other traffic through.

If you're having trouble establishing a connection and you suspect you might have a firewall issue, try telnetting to the particular host and port you are trying to connect to. If Telnet gives you an error, there might be a firewall problem. Of course, you should also do a `netstat -a` from the other machine to make sure there is actually a program listening on the port you are trying to connect to!

Some firewall issues are a bit harder to track. Sometimes, a firewall allows packets in but doesn't let them back out. Other times, you establish a connection but then the connection shuts down suddenly and you need to figure out which side shut it down. Still other times, you might just be getting odd data and you want to see what's going on. For these situations, it might help to do a network trace. Under Linux, there is a program called `tcpdump` that lets you display network traffic. You'll also find this program in various BSD systems. On Solaris 2, the program is called `snoop`, and on older SunOS 4.x machines it was called `etherfind`. You must be the superuser to run any of these programs. They let you see every packet going across the network. You can narrow the trace to just look for traffic between two machines, and even between two ports on two machines.

Although some understanding of networking protocols is necessary to understand the network trace, there are a few simple things to keep in mind for tracing TCP connections. First, if you see a packet labeled SYN, that's a packet for setting up a connection. You should see two SYN packets to set up a connection. A FIN packet shuts down a connection. If you want to see which side closes a connection, see which one sends the FIN packet. All these commands (`tcpdump`, `snoop`, and `etherfind`) let you view the contents of the packets. If you're passing unencrypted data, you might be able to make out the various data items as they go back and forth.

If you notice packets going out but none coming back, that can indicate a firewall problem or a network connectivity problem.

Reviewing the Code

One of the funny things about errors is that they cause you to see your code in a whole new light. You could swear up and down that a routine works perfectly, then someone mentions an odd behavior and, without even looking at the code, you suddenly realize what's wrong with it. When someone reports an odd problem with your system, go back and look at the code with the notion that the problem *is* occurring. Don't try to prove why the error can't happen—it did happen! Instead, try to prove how and why the error occurred.

Narrowing Down the Problem

When someone tells me about a problem—especially one that seems unlikely—my first instinct is to narrow down the situations in which the problem happens. If someone says "the system isn't saving orders," I want to know if it can save any orders at all. If it can save some, what are the circumstances in which it works and in which it fails. The larger the system is, the more important it is to narrow down a problem before you start looking at individual components.

Try to eliminate as many variables as possible. If you're debugging a Web application, does the error happen under all browsers? If you're accessing a particular application server from a Web application, can you also duplicate the error by using a test program (eliminating the Web server as the source of the error).

When you have multiple installations of an application, all hitting different databases, determine whether they all have the error. Maybe it's related to the database or to some external system. Poke and prod at the system. See where it hurts and where it doesn't. The more information you can get about the problem, the easier it is to debug.

When you have eliminated external sources as the cause of the problem, you can then dive into your program and remove sections until you find the offending piece of code. You can often comment out pieces of code until the problem goes away. Just make sure you make careful note of which parts you have commented out. You wouldn't want to uncomment a section of code that had been commented out previously. Many developers leave notes to themselves in the comments so they can keep track the sections that need to be uncommented when the debugging is complete.

After you find a problem, it's important to prevent similar problems in the future. You might want to include extra test cases to check for a common mistake, or add additional checks in your code for particular mistakes. It's amazing how many times the same error occurs because no one takes the time to prevent it from happening again.

TROUBLESHOOTING

THE LACK OF ANYTHING TO TROUBLESHOOT

Why is there no troubleshooting section in this chapter?

Because it's a chapter on troubleshooting.

Isn't the first question a paradox?

Yes.

CHAPTER 49

Decompiling and Patching

In this chapter

DECOMPILING A JAVA CLASS

One of the most interesting aspects of Java is that it maintains quite a bit of information about the class in the compiled files. For example, each class file contains a list of the member variable names and method names, as well as references to other classes.

By mid-1996, Java had only been out for a year and already people were writing Java decompilers. A *decompiler* can take a class file and generate a Java source that performs the same operations as the class file. Not long after the appearance of Java decompilers, of course, came Java code obfuscators. An *obfuscator* changes class, method, and variable names to make it tougher to figure out what the class does.

Many thought that Java decompilers would pose a huge barrier to the acceptance of Java. Because a decompiler can do such a good job of decompiling, it's almost like your sending out the source to your code whenever you distribute a Java program. Although obfuscators can help alleviate the threat of stolen code, they make debugging much more difficult. Whenever you print a stack trace from an obfuscated class, you find that method AA in class XX called method A4 in class QZ and so forth.

Obviously, the fact that you can decompile a Java program hasn't diminished Java's appeal. The Java language and environment is too good to allow something so minor to stand in the way of its success. Although some software vendors use obfuscators as a matter of habit, others use them only for licensing code, and some don't bother to hide anything.

One of the best Java decompilers available is called JAD (JAva Decompiler). You can download JAD for a number of software platforms (ironically, JAD is written in C++) from `http://www.geocities.com/SiliconValley/Bridge/8617/jad.html`. JAD is a simple executable program that requires no special setup. You run JAD on a class file and you get back a `.jad` file containing a Java source approximation of the contents of the class file.

Note

The JAD Web site now offers a graphical front-end for JAD, making it even easier to decompile Java programs.

One of the best ways to get a feel for what JAD can do for you is to decompile a program and compare the results with the original file. Listing 49.1 shows the `HelloWorldSessionImpl.java` file from Chapter 6, "Creating a Session Bean."

LISTING 49.1 SOURCE CODE FOR `HelloWorldSessionImpl.java`

```
package usingj2ee.hello;

import java.rmi.*;
import java.util.*;
import javax.ejb.*;

/** The implementation class for the HelloWorldSession bean */
```

```
public class HelloWorldSessionImpl implements SessionBean
{
/** Holds the session's greeting */
    protected String greeting;

/** The session context provided by the EJB container. A session bean must
    hold on to the context it is given. */

    private SessionContext context;

/** An EJB must have a public, parameterless constructor */

    public HelloWorldSessionImpl()
    {
    }

/** Called by the EJB container to set this session's context */

    public void setSessionContext(SessionContext aContext)
    {
        context = aContext;
    }

/** Called by the EJB container when a client calls the create() method in
    the Home interface */

    public void ejbCreate()
        throws CreateException
    {
        greeting = "Hello World!";
    }

/** Called by the EJB container when a client calls the
    create(String) method in the Home interface */

    public void ejbCreate(String aGreeting)
        throws CreateException
    {
        greeting = aGreeting;
    }

/** Called by the EJB container to wake this session bean up after it
    has been put to sleep with the ejbPassivate method. */

    public void ejbActivate()
    {
    }

/** Called by the EJB container to tell this session bean that it is being
    suspended from use (it's being put to sleep). */

    public void ejbPassivate()
    {
    }

/** Called by the EJB container to tell this session bean that it has been
    removed, either because the client invoked the remove() method or the
    container has timed the session out. */
```

LISTING 49.1 CONTINUED

```
    public void ejbRemove()
    {
    }

/** Returns the session's greeting */

    public String getGreeting()
    {
        return greeting;
    }

/** Changes the session's greeting */

    public void setGreeting(String aGreeting)
    {
        greeting = aGreeting;
    }
}
```

Listing 49.2 shows the decompiled version of the same class.

LISTING 49.2 SOURCE CODE FOR HelloWorldSessinoImpl.jad

```
// Decompiled by Jad v1.5.7d. Copyright 2000 Pavel Kouznetsov.
// Jad home page: http://www.geocities.com/SiliconValley/Bridge/8617/jad.html
// Decompiler options: packimports(3)
// Source File Name:   HelloWorldSessionImpl.java

package usingj2ee.hello;

import javax.ejb.*;

public class HelloWorldSessionImpl
    implements SessionBean
{

    public HelloWorldSessionImpl()
    {
    }

    public void setSessionContext(SessionContext sessioncontext)
    {
        context = sessioncontext;
    }

    public void ejbCreate()
        throws CreateException
    {
        greeting = "Hello World!";
    }

    public void ejbCreate(String s)
        throws CreateException
```

```
    {
        greeting = s;
    }

    public void ejbActivate()
    {
    }

    public void ejbPassivate()
    {
    }

    public void ejbRemove()
    {
    }

    public String getGreeting()
    {
        return greeting;
    }

    public void setGreeting(String s)
    {
        greeting = s;
    }

    protected String greeting;
    private SessionContext context;
}
```

One of the first things you will probably notice in the JAD file is that the comments are gone. That's one of the things that the Java compiler doesn't keep. Another thing is that the class member variables are declared in a different part of the program. Java doesn't necessarily keep the member variables in the same place, so don't be surprised if some of the variables seem to move around.

Another thing you'll find in decompiled files is that the parameter names are gone. Although Java knows the number of parameters and the data types of the parameters, it doesn't save the names. JAD does a reasonable job of generating names, as you can see. Earlier decompilers used symbols such as `p1` and `p2` for parameters, but JAD attempts to make a name that is related to the parameter type—sometimes using the classname, other times using short variables such as `s` or `s1` for strings.

Unless JAD has trouble decompiling the file (it happens occasionally), you should be able to rename the `.jad` file to be a `.java` file and you should be able to compile the file into a Java class.

Tip

You might need to include additional files in your classpath to recompile a decompiled file. JAD doesn't need to see other classes to decompile a file, but the compiler needs to examine additional classes at compile time.

Decompilers are typically associated with hacking into libraries to disable licensing or to steal crucial code. Certainly a decompiler can help you break into a program if you really want to, but with so many libraries available free or for evaluation, why bother? Decompilers do have a legitimate place in a developer's toolkit.

Most commercial software packages carry a license that explicitly forbids decompiling the software, so make sure you check your license to be sure you are permitted to decompile the software.

I once found myself using a software package that was new and very buggy. I decompiled various classes to fix some of the glaring bugs. Because the license forbade decompilation, I negotiated a license that allowed me to decompile the software for the purpose of fixing bugs.

Debugging is typically the most common, legitimate reason for decompilation. You might be running a debugger and need to step into a particular routine. By decompiling some of the libraries, you can possibly step into the other routines, although the decompiler can assign different line numbers to the code. You might need to recompile the decompiled code just to make the line numbers synchronize properly.

Another reason for decompiling is to insert some temporary code to track down an annoying bug. Occasionally, you just can't locate the bug from your own code because it actually occurs deep down in a third-party library. You might need to decompile part of the library to insert some debugging code.

Although some vendors may frown on it, you can learn an awful lot about a library or an application by examining the decompiled code. You can see things that might not be documented, and you might even discover that the documentation doesn't describe the code accurately.

Sometimes, you have a large system installed and you're in an emergency mode because the system is failing. If you have the source code to the system available, that's fine, but if you don't, you at least have a decompiler at your disposal. You can decompile the classes that are causing the error, make an emergency patch to the classes and get the system going again. If you find this procedure to be a regular occurrence, however, you should consider altering your installation procedures to make sure you have the current source code available on the machine—and also work on your QA procedures!

DISASSEMBLING A JAVA CLASS

In rare cases, JAD can't decompile a Java program for a variety of reasons. Some compilers perform optimizations that JAD doesn't understand. Some subtle obfuscators make changes to the code that make decompilation difficult. In these cases, you might need to resort to a Java disassembler. This is really for hard-core Java developers, because you end up with what is essentially an assembly language program.

Obviously, if you disassemble Java code, you must be able to reassemble it back into a Java class. You can't use a Java compiler, you need a Java assembler. One of the most popular Java assemblers is Jasmin, available from `http://www.cat.nyu.edu/meyer/jasmin/`. The Jasmin Web page also lists several disassemblers that work with Jasmin. The D-Java disassembler, available from `http://www.cat.nyu.edu/meyer/jvm/djava/`, is one of the easiest of the Jasmin-compatible disassemblers to use. The Byte Code Engineering Library from `bcel.sourceforge.net` can generate Jasmin-compatible files, and can also patch code without generating intermediate files.

Listing 49.3 shows the disassembled version of the `HelloWorldSessionImpl` class. The command to generate the disassembled listing is

```
d-java -o jasmin HelloWorldSessionImpl.class
```

LISTING 49.3 SOURCE CODE FOR `HelloWorldSessionImpl.jas`

```
;
; Output created by D-Java (mailto:umsilve1@cc.umanitoba.ca)
;

;Classfile version:
;    Major: 45
;    Minor: 3

.source HelloWorldSessionImpl.java
.class  public synchronized usingj2ee/hello/HelloWorldSessionImpl
.super  java/lang/Object
.implements javax/ejb/SessionBean

.field protected greeting Ljava/lang/String;
.field private context Ljavax/ejb/SessionContext;

; >> METHOD 1 <<
.method public <init>()V
    .limit stack 1
    .limit locals 1
.line 22
    aload_0
    invokenonvirtual java/lang/Object/<init>()V
.line 23
    return
.end method

; >> METHOD 2 <<
.method public setSessionContext(Ljavax/ejb/SessionContext;)V
    .limit stack 2
    .limit locals 2
.line 29
    aload_0
    aload_1
    putfield usingj2ee/hello/HelloWorldSessionImpl/context
Ljavax/ejb/SessionContext;
.line 30
    return
.end method
```

LISTING 49.3 CONTINUED

```
; >> METHOD 3 <<
.method public ejbCreate()V
    .throws javax/ejb/CreateException

    .limit stack 2
    .limit locals 1
.line 38
    aload_0
    ldc "Hello World!"
    putfield usingj2ee/hello/HelloWorldSessionImpl/greeting Ljava/lang/String;
.line 39
    return
.end method

; >> METHOD 4 <<
.method public ejbCreate(Ljava/lang/String;)V
    .throws javax/ejb/CreateException

    .limit stack 2
    .limit locals 2
.line 47
    aload_0
    aload_1
    putfield usingj2ee/hello/HelloWorldSessionImpl/greeting Ljava/lang/String;
.line 48
    return
.end method

; >> METHOD 5 <<
.method public ejbActivate()V
    .limit stack 0
    .limit locals 1
.line 55
    return
.end method

; >> METHOD 6 <<
.method public ejbPassivate()V
    .limit stack 0
    .limit locals 1
.line 62
    return
.end method

; >> METHOD 7 <<
.method public ejbRemove()V
    .limit stack 0
    .limit locals 1
.line 70
    return
.end method

; >> METHOD 8 <<
.method public getGreeting()Ljava/lang/String;
    .limit stack 1
```

```
    .limit locals 1
.line 76
    aload_0
    getfield usingj2ee/hello/HelloWorldSessionImpl/greeting Ljava/lang/String;
    areturn
.end method

; >> METHOD 9 <<
.method public setGreeting(Ljava/lang/String;)V
    .limit stack 2
    .limit locals 2
.line 83
    aload_0
    aload_1
    putfield usingj2ee/hello/HelloWorldSessionImpl/greeting Ljava/lang/String;
.line 84
    return
.end method
```

A disassembler is also interesting for exploring the way Java compiles things. For example, Listing 49.4 shows a Java program that performs a few interesting Java operations that look a little more “built-in” than they actually are.

Listing 49.4 Source Code for JavaOps.java

```
public class JavaOps
{
    public static void main(String[] args)
    {
        String str = "Hello";

        String greeting = str + "World!";

        String other = "Hello"+" there"+", Everyone!";
    }
}
```

Most developers think that when you add two strings together, it’s some sort of built-in operation. As Listing 49.5 shows, however, the Java compiler generates code to use a StringBuffer.

Listing 49.5 Source Code for JavaOps.java

```
;
; Output created by D-Java (mailto:umsilve1@cc.umanitoba.ca)
;

;Classfile version:
;    Major: 45
;    Minor: 3

.source JavaOps.java
.class  public synchronized JavaOps
.super  java/lang/Object
```

LISTING 49.5 CONTINUED

```
; >> METHOD 1 <<
.method public <init>()V
    .limit stack 1
    .limit locals 1
.line 1
    aload_0
    invokenonvirtual java/lang/Object/<init>()V
    return
.end method

; >> METHOD 2 <<
.method public static main([Ljava/lang/String;)V
    .limit stack 2
    .limit locals 4
.line 5
    ldc "Hello"
    astore_1
.line 7
    new java/lang/StringBuffer
    dup
    invokenonvirtual java/lang/StringBuffer/<init>()V
    aload_1
    invokevirtual
java/lang/StringBuffer/append(Ljava/lang/String;)Ljava/lang/StringBuffer;
    ldc "World!"
    invokevirtual
java/lang/StringBuffer/append(Ljava/lang/String;)Ljava/lang/StringBuffer;
    invokevirtual java/lang/StringBuffer/toString()Ljava/lang/String;
    astore_2
.line 9
    ldc "Hello there, Everyone!"
    astore_3
.line 10
    return
.end method
```

You're probably not used to reading Java assembly language, but there are a few interesting points here. First, you can see that the assembly language listing calls `new java/lang/StringBuffer`—it obviously uses a string buffer. Furthermore, by examining the `invokevirtual` calls, you see that it calls `append` in the string buffer twice: once to add "Hello" and once to add "World!" Finally, it calls the `toString` method to convert the string buffer back to a string.

The other interesting thing is that when the compiler sees a series of constant strings added together, it puts them together at compile time. Notice that there is no string buffer for the second string assignment. Instead, the compiler has already created the complete string.

Although you might not want to spend every day working with Java at an assembly language level, it's occasionally interesting to see how the compiler is generating code. You'll also find that it's not so hard to read after you get used to it, because you recognize classnames and method names throughout the listing.

PATCHING A JAVA LIBRARY

If you find yourself decompiling a Java class to fix a bug or insert some debugging statements, you might have to insert the class back into the original library. The obvious solution is to unpack the library, copy the class where it belongs, and then use JAR to recreate the library.

Occasionally, the new library doesn't work correctly. Sometimes the process of unpacking and repacking the JAR can lose some information—you might forget a directory, or you might need to force JAR to include the manifest file again. In these situations, it's better to use a ZIP program such as Info-ZIP or WinZIP to update the existing JAR file (after you make a backup copy of the original JAR file!). Because JAR files and ZIP files share the same format, you can use a ZIP tool to manipulate JAR files. It's often much safer and much faster to update a specific file in a JAR than it is to rebuild the entire JAR.

Tip

You can often put the patched files in a separate JAR file and then insert the JAR file into your classpath before the original library.

Although decompiling and patching might be one of those fringe techniques that you might never need to use, it's good to know that it's there when you need it.

TROUBLESHOOTING

DECOMPILATION PROBLEMS

Why does JAD complain that it can't decompile a class completely?

JAD can become confused in some cases, although not very often. If the original class contained inner classes, JAD must be able to locate the class files for the inner classes.

Why can't I compile my decompiled file?

Most of the time, there's something missing from your classpath. In rare cases, the compilation fails because the original class file contained code that wasn't generated by a normal Java compiler and violates some of the normal code generation rules.

DISASSEMBLY PROBLEMS

Why can't I reassemble my disassembled class file?

Most likely, the disassembler generated the file using a format that isn't compatible with your assembler. In some rare cases, if the original class file was tampered with by the vendor (possibly to prevent disassembly/reassembly), you might not be able to reassemble the code at all.

PART X

J2EE IN PRACTICE

CHAPTER 50

A J2EE Web Application

In this chapter

DESIGNING A WEB-BASED EJB APPLICATION

When you design a Web-based EJB application, it's often hard to figure out where to start. Do you start with the Web side or with the EJBs? Looking back at the typical three-tiered application model, your presentation layer depends on its interface to the business layer, and the business layer depends on the interface to the data layer. At some point, then, you need to define the data layer before the business layer, and the business layer before the presentation layer.

You typically find, however, that you jump from layer to layer initially, defining a little bit of each layer until you have a good idea of how your design will look. You then go into depth on each layer, starting with the data layer and working out to the presentation layer. When you gather application requirements, you usually focus on the presentation layer. During requirements gathering, you're concerned with how the system interacts with the user. After you know how the system should behave, you can design it properly.

GATHERING REQUIREMENTS

You often hear developers complain about the lack of requirements for a system. You might never nail down the requirements perfectly up front; users often don't know exactly what they want until they see what's possible. Your task is to try to show the users what is possible as soon as you can.

When you start gathering requirements, the user might say "I want a Web site where people can order our products online." Based on your previous experience with Web applications, you assume that you'll need to create a shopping cart application. There are three main parts of an online ordering system: You present the catalog of available items, you allow people to choose items, and you allow them to submit orders. You must find out how you should accomplish these things.

You sit down with the user and sketch out a possible Web site. You present the catalog of items and allow people to click items to add them to the shopping cart. You must decide how to display the catalog. If you have a small set of items, you might be able to display them all on a single page (the fewer clicks it takes to get to a particular item the better). If you have a large catalog, you might need to add a search capability, or organize the catalog into a series of screens. During requirements gathering, draw these screens on paper or create mockups on a computer. Go through the exact steps a user must take to complete an order. You know the various things that can happen, so go through them with the user to get an idea how the system should respond.

For example, how do you add something to the shopping cart? How do you remove something? How do you place an order? Make sure you go through every mouse click and input field. I worked on a project where the requirements team spent two days designing a search screen, only to end up with a screen that had no search button. There was no way to start the search!

One of the things to consider when creating a shopping cart application is how long to keep items in the cart. Specifically, what happens when the browser closes? Some applications associate items with the browser session. If you close your browser, you lose the items in the cart. Other sites keep the items in a database. Storing items in the database is generally more convenient, but might be slower than using the session.

Do you want to save user preferences? If so, you need a way to track users—perhaps a login mechanism. Do you want the user to log in first thing, or only log in when he performs a user-specific operation? When it comes to placing the order, do you keep credit card information or require the user to re-enter it? If you keep the credit card information, you must take steps to protect the card numbers—that's a big responsibility. You must also consider the potential liability if a hacker gets into your database and steals credit card numbers. You should go over all these issues up front when you establish the system requirements. You might also look at other sites to see how they do things. Amazon, for example, has a nice layout and is easy to use. The ordering system is particularly nice. Amazon's shopping cart keeps items for up to 90 days and also remembers your credit cards, so you can order without reentering your credit card number every time. You protect your personal information with a password.

For the sake of example, suppose you decide on a system in which you present the entire catalog on the main page (it's a small catalog). To order an item, you click the "Add to cart" link. You give a short thumbnail view of the shopping cart on the main page and also allow the user to view the whole cart on a page by itself. The system saves shopping cart entries in a database, so you can close down the browser and come back two days later and still have the same items in your cart. You can also provide an email address and password so the system can remember you. The system should store orders in a database and allow you to get a list of previous orders. When you place an order, you enter a shipping address and a credit card number. After you place an order, your shopping cart becomes empty again.

DESIGNING THE LAYERS

When you design the various parts of your application, it's best to start at the data layer and work your way outward to the presentation layer. You begin by sketching out the objects that you will be working with. You'll need to keep track of customers, so you need a customer object. A customer orders products, so you need a product object as well as an order object. An order has individual line items representing the various items you order, so you need an order line item object. Figure 50.1 shows a simple object model for your application.

These items represent core data items in your application—your entity beans. At this point, you have an idea of what might go into these beans, so go ahead and sketch out the items that belong in these beans.

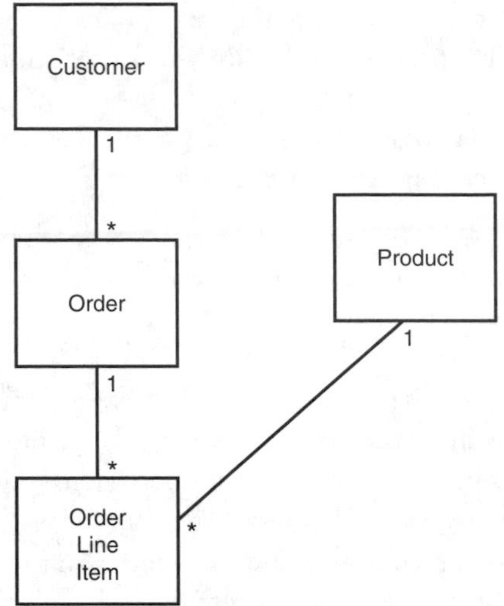

Figure 50.1
For online ordering, you need at least a customer, a product, an order, and an order line item.

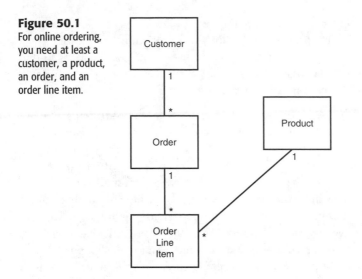

An order must have order line items, a shipping address, and billing information. The shipping address typically contains the customer name, street, city, state, ZIP code (postal code), and country. Depending on the application, you might want to add other values. For billing information, you need a payment method, possibly a credit card number, and of course the various price totals—shipping, tax, grand total.

An order line item contains the product you're ordering, a quantity, and a total price.

A customer must at least have some kind of identifying name—a username or an email address and probably a password so you can keep one customer from accessing another customer's order information. You probably want to keep track of the customer's name and address so you can initialize the shipping data for a new order with the customer's current address.

A product has some kind of identifier, a description and a price. In a typical Web application, you associate many different things with a product—an image, various descriptions, shipping information, customer reviews, and so on.

Now that you have an idea of what the entity beans look like, you start designing your session bean(s) to refine the model to the point where you can create Java code.

For the basic ordering functionality, you must be able to view a list of items somehow, add items to the order, remove items from the order, and complete the order. You must also be able to view a list of your old orders so you can check on the status of an order you placed.

Because you're keeping track of customer data, you need a way for the customer to register with your site, log in, and update any customer data.

After you've identified basic methods in your session bean, start laying out your Web site (on paper or on a white board). Go through a complete ordering sequence looking at how the Web pages interact with the session bean. For example, you want to display products—you have a method in the session bean to display products. What happens if you want to do a search? You might need to add additional search methods to the session bean. How does a customer log in to the site? If the customer is new, does the session bean let you save new customer information?

Make sure you verify that each piece of data you enter on the Web site makes its way to an entity bean (if necessary). By the time you're done with this process, you should know everything the session bean needs to do, everything the entity beans need to do, and everything the Java Server Pages and servlets need to do.

You should also consider going through this process with your user (the person specifying the requirements) to make sure the site does what the user expects. For a more complex application, you might consider creating a user interface prototype and possibly a dummy session bean. If you can go through everything on paper or a white board, however, why waste the time writing code?

As you go through the modeling process, it's tough to resist the urge to start writing code. For smaller applications, you can usually do the modeling in a fairly short amount of time. For larger projects, try breaking the project down into smaller parts. Model a part of the system, implement it, and then model the next part and implement it.

Many organizations don't spend much time modeling the application. Instead, they write code and keep changing the code until it meets the requirements. Part of the problem is that because the code is the end result, they feel the modeling process doesn't accomplish anything. What they often don't realize, however, is you can change something during modeling in a matter of seconds that might take an hour to change in your code.

The other thing to remember about the modeling and design process is that the notation you use to represent your model is *not* the most important thing. The model itself is the important thing. Don't get all bent out of shape because you don't understand all the nuances of UML or another modeling language/notation. Just represent the model the best way you know how. When you have time, study some of the popular notations and see whether they give you a better way to represent something. Using a modeling notation is like using a programming language. You didn't learn everything there was to know about Java before you started using it.

CREATING THE ENTITY BEANS

The first step in defining your entity beans is the creation of the `Remote` interfaces. If you did a thorough job in the design phase, you already know all the methods that you need in the `Remote` interface. If not, you'll probably change the interfaces many times before you get them right. To be honest, even if you modeled the system well, you're probably still going to make changes to the interfaces—but not as many. Listing 50.1 shows the `Remote` interface for the `Customer` bean. In addition to the basic data types, notice that the bean can return itself as a view object.

LISTING 50.1 SOURCE CODE FOR Customer.java

```
package usingj2ee.shopping;

import java.rmi.*;
import javax.ejb.*;
import java.util.Collection;
import java.util.Date;

/** Defines the methods you can call on a Customer object */

public interface Customer extends EJBObject
{
    public String getCustomerId() throws RemoteException;

    public String getFirstName() throws RemoteException;
    public void setFirstName(String aFirstName) throws RemoteException;

    public String getMiddleName() throws RemoteException;
    public void setMiddleName(String aMiddleName) throws RemoteException;

    public String getLastName() throws RemoteException;
    public void setLastName(String aLastName) throws RemoteException;

    public String getAddress1() throws RemoteException;
    public void setAddress1(String anAddress1) throws RemoteException;

    public String getAddress2() throws RemoteException;
    public void setAddress2(String anAddress2) throws RemoteException;

    public String getCity() throws RemoteException;
    public void setCity(String aCity) throws RemoteException;

    public String getState() throws RemoteException;
    public void setState(String aState) throws RemoteException;

    public String getZip() throws RemoteException;
    public void setZip(String aZip) throws RemoteException;

    public String getCountry() throws RemoteException;
    public void setCountry(String aCountry) throws RemoteException;

    public String getEmail() throws RemoteException;
    public void setEmail(String anEmail) throws RemoteException;

    public String getPassword() throws RemoteException;
    public void setPassword(String aPassword) throws RemoteException;

    public Date getLastLogin() throws RemoteException;
    public void setLastLogin(Date lastLogin) throws RemoteException;

    public Collection getOrders() throws RemoteException;
    public void setOrders(Collection orders) throws RemoteException;

    public Order getCurrentOrder() throws RemoteException;
    public void setCurrentOrder(Order aCurrentOrder) throws RemoteException;
```

```
    public CustomerView getView() throws RemoteException;
    public void setFromView(CustomerView aView) throws RemoteException;

    public void register(String email, String password,
        String firstName, String middleName, String lastName)
        throws RemoteException;
}
```

Most of the methods in the Customer interface deal with the customer's name and address. Because a customer might have a number of previous orders, it makes sense to ask the Customer object for a list of previous orders. Also, the customer has a "current order," which is basically the customer's shopping cart.

Listing 50.2 shows the Remote interface for the Order object.

LISTING 50.2 SOURCE CODE FOR Order.java

```
package usingj2ee.shopping;

import java.rmi.*;
import javax.ejb.*;
import java.util.Collection;
import java.util.Date;

/** Defines the methods you can call on an Order object */

public interface Order extends EJBObject
{
    public String getOrderId() throws RemoteException;

    public Customer getCustomer() throws RemoteException;
    public void setCustomer(Customer aCustomer) throws RemoteException;

    public String getAddress1() throws RemoteException;
    public void setAddress1(String anAddress1) throws RemoteException;

    public String getAddress2() throws RemoteException;
    public void setAddress2(String anAddress2) throws RemoteException;

    public String getCity() throws RemoteException;
    public void setCity(String aCity) throws RemoteException;

    public String getState() throws RemoteException;
    public void setState(String aState) throws RemoteException;

    public String getZip() throws RemoteException;
    public void setZip(String aZip) throws RemoteException;

    public String getCountry() throws RemoteException;
    public void setCountry(String aCountry) throws RemoteException;

    public String getCreditCard() throws RemoteException;
    public void setCreditCard(String aCreditCard) throws RemoteException;

    public Date getTimePlaced() throws RemoteException;
```

LISTING 50.2 CONTINUED

```
    public double getSubtotal() throws RemoteException;
    public double getShipping() throws RemoteException;
    public double getTax() throws RemoteException;
    public double getTotalPrice() throws RemoteException;

    public boolean isEmpty() throws RemoteException;

    public int getNextItemNumber() throws RemoteException;
    public void setNextItemNumber(int nextItemNumber) throws RemoteException;

    public String getStatus() throws RemoteException;
    public void setStatus(String aStatus) throws RemoteException;

    public OrderView getView() throws RemoteException;
    public OrderHistoryView getHistoryView() throws RemoteException;
    public void setFromData(OrderData data) throws RemoteException;

    public void addItem(OrderLineItem item) throws RemoteException;
    public void removeItem(OrderLineItem item) throws RemoteException;
    public void removeItem(String productId, int quantity)
        throws RemoteException;

    public String place() throws EJBException, RemoteException;
}
```

Like the `Customer` object, the `Order` object can copy itself into a view object and also initialize itself from a view object. Also notice the `place` method, which places the order. From a shopping cart standpoint, this means that the order is no longer the customer's current order. If the customer adds more items to the cart, they go into a new order.

Listing 50.3 shows the `Remote` interface for the `OrderLineItem` object.

LISTING 50.3 SOURCE CODE FOR `OrderLineItem.java`

```
package usingj2ee.shopping;

import java.rmi.*;
import javax.ejb.*;
import java.util.Collection;

/** Defines the methods you can call on a Customer object */

public interface OrderLineItem extends EJBObject
{
    public String getOrderId() throws RemoteException;

    public int getItemNumber() throws RemoteException;

    public int getQuantity() throws RemoteException;
    public void setQuantity(int aQuantity) throws RemoteException;

    public double getPrice() throws RemoteException;
    public void setPrice(double aPrice) throws RemoteException;
```

```
    public OrderLineItemView getView() throws RemoteException;

    public Order getOrder() throws RemoteException;

    public Product getProduct() throws RemoteException;
    public void setProduct(Product aProduct) throws RemoteException;
}
```


Finally, Listing 50.4 shows the `Remote` interface for the `Product` object.

LISTING 50.4 SOURCE CODE FOR `Product.java`

```
package usingj2ee.shopping;

import java.rmi.*;
import javax.ejb.*;
import java.util.Collection;

/** Defines the methods you can call on a Customer object */

public interface Product extends EJBObject
{
    public String getProductId() throws RemoteException;
    public void setProductId(String aProductId) throws RemoteException;

    public String getName() throws RemoteException;
    public void setName(String aName) throws RemoteException;

    public String getDescription() throws RemoteException;
    public void setDescription(String aDescription) throws RemoteException;

    public double getPrice() throws RemoteException;
    public void setPrice(double aPrice) throws RemoteException;

    public String getCategory() throws RemoteException;
    public void setCategory(String aCategory) throws RemoteException;

    public String getImageURL() throws RemoteException;
    public void setImageURL(String aURL) throws RemoteException;

    public ProductView getView() throws RemoteException;
}
```

In case you've been wondering about `Home` methods and when they might be useful, the `ProductHome` class includes a Home method that returns a list of available product categories. The method doesn't work with a specific bean, so it makes sense as a `Home` method. Don't forget that a `Home` method is a method in the `Home` interface that operates on a set of entity beans, not just a single one. The method is declared as

```
/** Gets a list of available categories */
    public String[] getCategories()
        throws RemoteException;
```

When it comes to implementing the entity beans, it's best to use Container Managed Persistence (CMP) if you have a reasonably efficient implementation available. It's even better if you have a good implementation of EJB 2.0 CMP, because it handles the relationships between the beans automatically.

The `Customer` bean and the `Order` bean both require automatically generated keys (at least for this implementation). Normally, you could use the customer's email address as the key for the `Customer` bean, but because the shopping cart lets you build an order before you log in, you must be able to create a `Customer` before you know the email address.

Listing 50.5 shows the portion of the `CustomerImpl` class that implements the auto-generated key.

LISTING 50.5 EXCERPT FROM `CustomerImpl.java`

```
/** Called by the EJB container when a client calls the create() method in
    the Home interface */

    public String ejbCreate()
        throws CreateException
    {
        try
        {
// compute the new primary key for this object
            setCustomerId(getNextId());

            return null;
        }
        catch (SQLException exc)
        {
            throw new CreateException(
                "Unable to access database: "+exc.toString());
        }
    }

/** Although this class uses CMP, you still need to locate a connection
 *  to generate the primary key (Customer generates its own unique
 *  id automatically using the customer_id_seq table.)
 */
    protected Connection getConnection()
        throws SQLException, NamingException
    {
// Get a reference to the naming service
        InitialContext context = new InitialContext();

// Get the data source for the person database
        DataSource ds = (DataSource) context.lookup(
            "java:comp/env/jdbc/OrderDB");

// Ask the data source to allocate a database connection
        return ds.getConnection();
    }
```

```
/** Uses a separate database table to generate a unique ID number for
    an order. You should perform the update before you read the value
    to make sure you don't have any locking problems.
    */
    protected String getNextId()
        throws SQLException
    {
        Connection conn = null;

        try
        {
            conn = getConnection();

// Increment the next customer ID number
            PreparedStatement ps = conn.prepareStatement(
                "update customer_id_seq set next_customer_id = "+
                    "next_customer_id + 1");

            if (ps.executeUpdate() != 1)
            {
                throw new SQLException("Unable to generate customer id");
            }

            ps.close();

// Read the next customer ID number
            ps = conn.prepareStatement(
                "select next_customer_id from customer_id_seq");

            ResultSet rs = ps.executeQuery();

            if (rs.next())
            {
                return ""+rs.getInt("next_customer_id");
            }
            else
            {
                throw new SQLException("Unable to generate customer id");
            }
        }
        catch (NamingException exc)
        {
            throw new SQLException("Unable to generate customer id: "+
                exc.toString());
        }
        finally
        {
            try
            {
                conn.close();
            }
            catch (Exception ignore) {}
        }
    }
```

CREATING THE SESSION BEAN

There are different schools of thought on whether a client application should be able to access entity beans. Obviously, from a technical perspective, a client might access entity beans—this is more of a design issue. When a client uses the entity beans directly, there is danger that common business logic will move onto the client application making the application harder to maintain. As a general rule of thumb, it's better to have the clients go through session beans to access entity beans.

Some developers question the need for entity beans at all if the client only uses session beans. Although some developers might enjoy writing tedious SQL code, most prefer to concentrate on the real business problems. Entity beans, especially those that use CMP, reduce the amount of database work that the session beans must perform.

The `ShoppingCartSession` bean gives the client application the capability to perform any necessary operations without directly accessing the entity beans. Any time the client needs to see the contents of an entity bean, the `ShoppingCartSession` bean passes back a view of the data instead of a reference to the entity bean itself.

The shopping application is fairly complex when it comes to implementation. It's tough to deal with users who might never have signed in before. You must associate data with an unregistered user, and then when the user registers, you must keep the old data. The real balancing act comes when you try to divide the user interface from the business logic. Should the business logic know about unregistered users? If so, how does it track them? How much work must the front end do in tracking unregistered users?

As it turns out, both the session bean and the front end must do some work to deal with unregistered users (and registered users, for that matter). First, the session bean must allow you to locate data for a previous customer, registered or not. For an unregistered customer, you must use a simple customer ID number. For a registered user, you use the email address and password.

The session bean must also allow the front end to access the product catalog, create orders, and view previous orders. For this application, the session bean simply returns a list of product categories and a list of products within a category (or a list of all products). For more complex applications with hundreds of products, you might need to add additional methods that allow the front end to scroll through the product lists.

To manage an order, you must be able to add items to an order, remove items, display the order, and place the order. Many online shopping applications wait until you are ready to place the order before asking for shipping information, so the `ShoppingCartSession` bean takes the same approach.

Listing 50.6 shows the `Remote` interface for the `ShoppingCartSession` bean.

LISTING 50.6 SOURCE CODE FOR ShoppingCartSession.java

```
package usingj2ee.shopping;

import java.rmi.*;
import javax.ejb.*;

public interface ShoppingCartSession extends EJBObject
{
    public ProductView[] getAllProducts()
        throws EJBException, RemoteException;

    public ProductView[] getProductsByCategory(String category)
        throws EJBException, RemoteException;

    public String[] getProductCategories()
        throws EJBException, RemoteException;

    public void addToShoppingCart(String productId, int quantity)
        throws EJBException, RemoteException;

    public void removeFromShoppingCart(String productId, int quantity)
        throws EJBException, RemoteException;

    public String getCustomerId()
        throws EJBException, RemoteException;

    public String login(String email, String password)
        throws EJBException, RemoteException;

    public String createCustomer()
        throws EJBException, RemoteException;

    public String createCustomer(String email, String password,
        String firstName, String middleName, String lastName)
        throws EJBException, RemoteException;

    public String register(String email, String password,
        String firstName, String middleName, String lastName)
        throws EJBException, RemoteException;

    public boolean customerExists(String email) throws RemoteException;

    public void changePassword(String oldPassword, String newPassword)
        throws EJBException, RemoteException;

    public CustomerView getCustomerData()
        throws EJBException, RemoteException;

    public void updateCustomerData(CustomerView data)
        throws EJBException, RemoteException;

    public OrderView getCurrentOrder()
        throws EJBException, RemoteException;

    public void setOrderData(OrderData data)
        throws EJBException, RemoteException;
```

LISTING 50.6 CONTINUED

```
    public String saveOrder()
        throws EJBException, RemoteException;

    public OrderHistoryView[] getOrderHistory()
        throws EJBException, RemoteException;

    public OrderView getOrder(String orderId)
        throws EJBException, RemoteException;

    public boolean isEmpty()
        throws RemoteException;
}
```

Listing 50.7 shows the implementation of the ShoppingCartSession bean. This bean is really the workhorse of the entire application, and it contains many interesting ideas.

First, when you use other EJBs in your implementation, you must worry about locating the Home interfaces for the other beans. The question is, when do you locate them? If you look for a Home interface just before you use it, you might spend a lot of time searching for the same object over and over. On the other hand, if you locate the Home interface up-front, and for some reason you reconfigure the system and move the Home interface to another server, your old reference isn't valid anymore. This application strikes a reasonable balance. It looks for the Home interfaces whenever it creates a new session. That way, if you do move the Home interfaces to another server, or the server crashes, the old sessions might no longer work, but any new sessions will adapt to the change.

Next, the application addresses the problem of accessing entity bean data in bulk rather than by calling individual methods over and over. When the front end retrieves a list of products, the ShoppingCartSession bean returns a list of ProductView objects containing views of each product. Likewise, when the front end requests an order, it gets a view of the order. Although the views require extra coding, they make a huge difference in performance. The entity beans themselves are responsible for creating the views in this application. Some developers argue that the entity beans should have no concept of views, because the views are more for the front end and they pollute the entity beans. Others argue that because the entity bean has local access to the data, it is best suited for creating the view. In Chapter 42, "The Model-View-Controller Paradigm," you saw a reasonable alternative for creating the views, in which a view object interacts directly with an entity bean using a viewer interface instead of using the Remote interface. This application doesn't use the viewer interface, however. A viewer is necessary when you must create multiple views of the same object. For this simple application, however, there is only one view of each entity bean, so the viewer interface isn't necessary.

Apart from these few issues, the ShoppingCartSessionImpl class simple stores and retrieves entity beans. It doesn't do any database work itself—the entity beans take care of it.

Listing 50.7 Source Code for ShoppingCartSessionImpl.java

```
package usingj2ee.shopping;

import java.io.*;
import java.rmi.*;
import javax.rmi.*;
import javax.ejb.*;
import javax.naming.*;
import javax.sql.*;
import java.util.*;

public class ShoppingCartSessionImpl implements SessionBean
{
// References to the other EJBs used by this class
    protected Customer customer;
    protected ProductHome productHome;
    protected CustomerHome customerHome;
    protected OrderHome orderHome;
    protected OrderLineItemHome orderLineItemHome;

    private SessionContext context;

    public ShoppingCartSessionImpl()
    {
    }

/** Creates a new instance of the shopping cart session */
    public void ejbCreate()
        throws CreateException
    {
        try
        {
            customer = null;

            Context ctx = new InitialContext();

/** Locate the Home interfaces for the other objects this session uses */
            productHome= (ProductHome) PortableRemoteObject.narrow(
                ctx.lookup("java:comp/env/ejb/ProductHome"),
                    ProductHome.class);

            customerHome = (CustomerHome) PortableRemoteObject.narrow(
                ctx.lookup("java:comp/env/ejb/CustomerHome"),
                CustomerHome.class);

            orderHome = (OrderHome) PortableRemoteObject.narrow(
                ctx.lookup("java:comp/env/ejb/OrderHome"),
                OrderHome.class);

            orderLineItemHome = (OrderLineItemHome) PortableRemoteObject.
                narrow(ctx.lookup("java:comp/env/ejb/OrderLineItemHome"),
                OrderLineItemHome.class);
        }
        catch (NamingException exc)
        {
            throw new CreateException("Couldn't create shopping cart: "+
```

LISTING 50.7 CONTINUED

```
                exc.toString());
        }
        catch (EJBException exc)
        {
            throw new CreateException("Couldn't create shopping cart: "+
                exc.toString());
        }
    }

/** Creates a shopping cart session for a particular customer */
    public void ejbCreate(String customerId)
        throws CreateException
    {
        ejbCreate();

        try
        {
            customer = customerHome.findByPrimaryKey(customerId);
        }
        catch (FinderException exc)
        {
        }
        catch (RemoteException exc)
        {
            throw new CreateException("Couldn't create shopping cart: "+
                exc.toString());
        }
    }

    public void setSessionContext(SessionContext aContext)
    {
        context = aContext;
    }

    public void ejbActivate()
    {
    }

    public void ejbPassivate()
    {
    }

    public void ejbRemove()
    {
    }

/** Returns a list of all available products */
    public ProductView[] getAllProducts()
        throws RemoteException, EJBException
    {
        try
        {
            Collection products = productHome.findAll();

            return getProductViews(products);
        }
```

```
        catch (FinderException exc)
        {
            throw new EJBException("Error retrieving products: "+
                exc.toString());
        }
    }

/** Converts a collection of products into an array of product views */
    public ProductView[] getProductViews(Collection products)
        throws RemoteException, EJBException
    {
        ArrayList views = new ArrayList();

        Iterator iter = products.iterator();

// Loop through the collection
        while (iter.hasNext())
        {
            Product prod = (Product) PortableRemoteObject.narrow(
                iter.next(), Product.class);

// Convert the product into a view and add it to the new list
            views.add(prod.getView());
        }

// Convert the new list into an array and return it
        return (ProductView[]) views.toArray(
            new ProductView[views.size()]);
    }

/** Returns an array of products for a specific category */
    public ProductView[] getProductsByCategory(String category)
        throws RemoteException, EJBException
    {
        try
        {
// Get the list of products
            Collection products = productHome.findByCategory(category);

// Turn it into an array of product views
            return getProductViews(products);
        }
        catch (FinderException exc)
        {
            throw new EJBException("Error retrieving products: "+
                exc.toString());
        }
    }

/** Returns a list of the available product categories using a
    Home method in the ProductHome class */
    public String[] getProductCategories()
        throws RemoteException, EJBException
    {
        return productHome.getCategories();
    }
```

LISTING 50.7 CONTINUED

```
/** Adds a product to the current order */
    public void addToShoppingCart(String productId, int quantity)
        throws RemoteException, EJBException
    {
        try
        {
// Locate the product by the product ID
            Product product = (Product) PortableRemoteObject.narrow(
                productHome.findByPrimaryKey(productId), Product.class);

// If there is no current customer, create one
            if (customer == null)
            {
                customer = customerHome.create();
            }

            Order currOrder = customer.getCurrentOrder();

// If there is no current order, create one
            if (currOrder == null)
            {
                currOrder = orderHome.create(customer);
                currOrder.setCustomer(customer);

                customer.setCurrentOrder(currOrder);
            }

// Create a new order line item for this order
            OrderLineItem lineItem = orderLineItemHome.create(currOrder);

            lineItem.setQuantity(quantity);
            lineItem.setProduct(product);
            lineItem.setPrice(product.getPrice() * quantity);

// Add the line item to the order
            currOrder.addItem(lineItem);
        }
        catch (CreateException exc)
        {
            exc.printStackTrace();
            throw new EJBException("Unable to add item to cart: "+
                exc.toString());
        }
        catch (FinderException exc)
        {
            exc.printStackTrace();
            throw new EJBException("Unable to add item to cart: "+
                exc.toString());
        }
    }

/** Removes an item from the cart */
    public void removeFromShoppingCart(String productId, int quantity)
        throws RemoteException, EJBException
    {
```

```
// If there's no customer, there's nothing to remove
        if (customer == null) return;

        Order currOrder = customer.getCurrentOrder();

// If there's no order, there's nothing to remove
        if (currOrder == null)
        {
            return;
        }

// Remove the first item matching this product ID and quantity
        currOrder.removeItem(productId, quantity);
    }

/** Returns the customer ID (primary key) for the current customer */
    public String getCustomerId()
        throws RemoteException, EJBException
    {
        if (customer == null)
        {
            return null;
        }
        else
        {
            return customer.getCustomerId();
        }
    }

/** Logs this session in as a particular customer using the email as the
 *  username. The method returns the customerId of the matching Customer
 *  object or null if the login fails.
 */
    public String login(String email, String password)
        throws RemoteException, EJBException
    {
        try
        {
// See if there is a customer with this email address
            Customer newCustomer = customerHome.findByEmail(email);

// If so, make sure the passwords match
            if (newCustomer.getPassword().equals(password))
            {
                customer = newCustomer;

                return customer.getCustomerId();
            }
            else
            {
                return null;
            }
        }
        catch (FinderException exc)
        {
            return null;
        }
    }
```

LISTING 50.7 CONTINUED

```
/** Creates a new customer object and returns the CustomerId */
    public String createCustomer()
        throws RemoteException, EJBException
    {
        try
        {
            customer = customerHome.create();

            return customer.getCustomerId();
        }
        catch (CreateException exc)
        {
            exc.printStackTrace();
            throw new EJBException("Error creating customer: "
                + exc.toString());
        }
    }

/** Creates a new customer object with some initial values and returns
 *  the CustomerId */
    public String createCustomer(String email, String password,
        String firstName, String middleName, String lastName)
        throws RemoteException, EJBException
    {
        try
        {
            try
            {
                Customer cust = customerHome.findByEmail(email);

                if (cust != null)
                {
                    throw new EJBException("Customer already exists");
                }
            }
            catch (FinderException ignore)
            {
            }

            customer = customerHome.create();
            customer.setEmail(email);
            customer.setPassword(password);
            customer.setFirstName(firstName);
            customer.setMiddleName(middleName);
            customer.setLastName(lastName);

            return customer.getCustomerId();
        }
        catch (CreateException exc)
        {
            exc.printStackTrace();
            throw new EJBException("Error creating customer: "
                + exc.toString());
        }
    }
```

```
/** Registers the current customer with the system (that is, converts an
 *  anonymous customer into a registered customer)
*/
    public String register(String email, String password,
        String firstName, String middleName, String lastName)
        throws RemoteException, EJBException
    {
        try
        {
// Make sure there isn't already a customer registered with this email address
            try
            {
                Customer cust = customerHome.findByEmail(email);

                if (cust != null)
                {
                    throw new EJBException("Customer already exists");
                }
            }
            catch (FinderException ignore)
            {
            }

// If there is no current customer, create one
            if (customer == null)
            {
                customer = customerHome.create();
            }

// Ask the customer object to register itself (mostly just initializes
// the specified fields)
            customer.register(email, password, firstName, middleName, lastName);

            return customer.getCustomerId();
        }
        catch (CreateException exc)
        {
            exc.printStackTrace();
            throw new EJBException("Error creating customer: "
                + exc.toString());
        }
    }

/** Returns true if there is a customer with this email address */
    public boolean customerExists(String email)
    {
        try
        {
            Customer cust = customerHome.findByEmail(email);

            if (cust != null)
            {
                return true;
            }

            return false;
        }
```

LISTING 50.7 CONTINUED

```
        catch (Exception exc)
        {
            return false;
        }
    }

/** Changes the password for the current customer */
    public void changePassword(String oldPassword, String newPassword)
        throws RemoteException, EJBException
    {
        if (customer == null)
        {
            throw new EJBException(
                "Can't change the password - there's no customer!");
        }

        if (!customer.getPassword().equals(oldPassword))
        {
            throw new EJBException(
                "Old password is invalid");
        }

        customer.setPassword(newPassword);
    }

/** Returns a view of the customer data */
    public CustomerView getCustomerData()
        throws RemoteException, EJBException
    {
        if (customer == null)
        {
            return null;
        }
        else
        {
            return customer.getView();
        }
    }

/** Updates a customer from a view */
    public void updateCustomerData(CustomerView data)
        throws RemoteException, EJBException
    {
        if (customer == null)
        {
            return;
        }
        else
        {
            customer.setFromView(data);
        }
    }

/** Returns a view of the current order (that is, the contents of the
 *  shopping cart) */
```

```
    public OrderView getCurrentOrder()
        throws RemoteException
    {
        if (customer == null)
        {
            return null;
        }

        Order order = customer.getCurrentOrder();

        if (order == null)
        {
            return null;
        }

        return order.getView();
    }

/** Stores shipping information into the current order */
    public void setOrderData(OrderData data)
        throws RemoteException, EJBException
    {
        try
        {
// If there's no current customer, create one
            if (customer == null)
            {
                customer = customerHome.create();
            }

            Order order = customer.getCurrentOrder();

// If there's no current order, create one
            if (order == null)
            {
                order = orderHome.create(customer);
                order.setCustomer(customer);

                customer.setCurrentOrder(order);
            }

            order.setFromData(data);
        }
        catch (CreateException exc)
        {
            exc.printStackTrace();

            throw new EJBException("Error updating order: "+exc.toString());
        }
    }

/** Places the current order (that is, saves it in the system and clears
 *  out the shopping cart)
 */
    public String saveOrder()
        throws RemoteException, EJBException
    {
        if (customer == null)
```

LISTING 50.7 CONTINUED

```
        {
            throw new EJBException("No order to save - no customer!");
        }

        Order order = customer.getCurrentOrder();

        if (order == null)
        {
            throw new EJBException("No order to save");
        }

        return order.place();
    }

/** Returns a view of all the customer's previous orders */
    public OrderHistoryView[] getOrderHistory()
        throws RemoteException
    {
// No customer, no history
        if (customer == null)
        {
            return null;
        }

// Get a list of the customer's orders
        Collection orders = customer.getOrders();

        ArrayList viewList = new ArrayList();

        Iterator iter = orders.iterator();

        while (iter.hasNext())
        {
            Order order = (Order) PortableRemoteObject.narrow(
                iter.next(), Order.class);

// If the status is null, it's the shopping cart order - ignore it
            if (order.getStatus() == null) continue;

// Create a view of the order
            viewList.add(order.getHistoryView());
        }

        OrderHistoryView[] views = new OrderHistoryView[viewList.size()];

// Convert the list of views to an array
        return (OrderHistoryView[]) viewList.toArray(views);
    }

/** Returns a detailed view of a specific order */
    public OrderView getOrder(String orderId)
        throws RemoteException
    {
        try
        {
            if (customer == null) return null;
```

```
            Order order = orderHome.findByPrimaryKey(orderId);

            if (order.getCustomer().getCustomerId().equals(
                customer.getCustomerId()))
            {
                return order.getView();
            }

            return null;
        }
        catch (FinderException exc)
        {
            return null;
        }
    }

/** Returns true if the shopping cart is empty */
    public boolean isEmpty()
        throws RemoteException
    {
        if (customer == null) return true;

        if (customer.getCurrentOrder() == null)
        {
            return true;
        }

        return customer.getCurrentOrder().isEmpty();
    }
}
```

CREATING THE WEB INTERFACE

Now that you have the entity and session beans in place, you can create the Web interface for the application. Applying some of the concepts you have seen earlier in this book, the Web application uses a combination of servlets and Java Server Pages. The application uses a simple Model-View-Controller setup in which the servlets act as controllers, translating requests from a browser into changes in the object model. The servlets then forward the request on to a Java Server Page for rendering the view.

Although the application doesn't use custom tags, it does create Java Server Pages that render specific parts of the application. For example, the main page shows information about the user, the product catalog, and a thumbnail sketch of the shopping cart. These three data views are implemented as separate Java Server Pages, however. As you can see in Listing 50.8, the main `Shopping.jsp` page doesn't do much work itself.

LISTING 50.8 SOURCE CODE FOR `Shopping.jsp`

```
<html>
<body bgcolor="#ffffff">
<img src="logo.jpg">
```

Listing 50.8 Continued

```
<table border="0">
<tr>
<td><jsp:include page="CartDisplay.jsp"/></td>
<td>
<h1>Welcome to The Store</h1>
<p>
<jsp:include page="UserInfo.jsp"/>
<p>
<jsp:include page="Catalog.jsp"/>
</td>
</tr>
</table>
</body>
</html>
```

Figure 50.2 shows the main page for the shopping application.

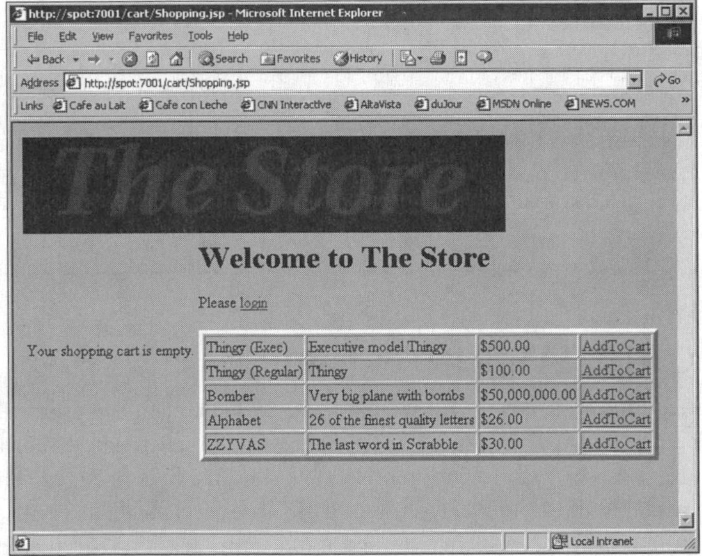

Figure 50.2 The main shopping page includes several other Java Server Pages to assist in displaying information.

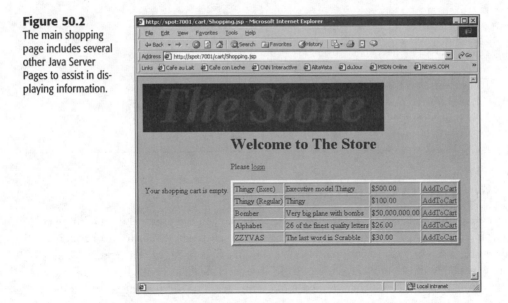

The `CartDisplay.jsp` page, shown in Listing 50.9, displays a reduced version of the shopping cart. The page assumes that it will always be included by another page, so it doesn't contain an `<html>` or a `<body>` tag.

Listing 50.9 Source Code for `CartDisplay.jsp`

```
<%@ page import="usingj2ee.shopping.*" %>
<jsp:useBean id="cart" class="usingj2ee.shopping.CartBean" scope="session"/>
<%
    if (cart.getCart(request).isEmpty())
    {
%>
```

```
<p>Your shopping cart is empty.</p>
<%
    }
    else
    {
        OrderView order = cart.getCart(request).getCurrentOrder();

        out.println("<p>Your shopping cart contains:</p>");
        out.println("<table border=\"0\">");

        for (int i=0; i < order.lineItems.length; i++)
        {
            out.print("<tr><td>"+order.lineItems[i].name+"</td></tr>");
        }
        out.println("</table>");
        out.println("<a href=\"ShoppingCart.jsp\">View Shopping Cart</a>");
    }
%>
```

The `<jsp:useBean>` tag is pretty handy, but unfortunately, it doesn't work very well with Enterprise JavaBeans. Perhaps one day in the future, you might see a `<jsp:useEJB>` or something similar so you can locate an EJB and use it. In the meantime, however, you must create utility beans for locating and using EJBs within a Web application.

Listing 50.10 shows the `CartBean` class that locates the shopping cart servlet. It implements the `HttpSessionBindingListener` interface to detect when it is removed from the current session. One of the other problems you have with EJBs and Web applications is that the client-side stubs have no awareness of the `HttpSession` class (not that they should). When the session goes away, the session bean can continue to exist for some period of time before the EJB container figures out that the client is gone. The `CartBean` class takes care of that problem.

Listing 50.10 Source Code for `CartBean.java`

```
package usingj2ee.shopping;

import java.rmi.*;
import javax.ejb.*;
import javax.rmi.*;
import javax.naming.*;
import javax.servlet.http.*;

public class CartBean implements java.io.Serializable,
    HttpSessionBindingListener
{
    protected ShoppingCartSession cart;

    public CartBean()
    {
    }

    public ShoppingCartSession getCart(HttpServletRequest request)
    {
        if (cart == null)
        {
```

LISTING 50.10 CONTINUED

```
// Make sure this section of code is only executed by one thread at a time
            synchronized(this)
            {
// Check once more to make sure there is no cart yet
                if (cart == null)
                {
                    try
                    {
                        Context ctx = new InitialContext();

// Locate the shopping cart session
                        ShoppingCartSessionHome home =
                            (ShoppingCartSessionHome) PortableRemoteObject.
                            narrow(ctx.lookup("ShoppingCartSessionHome"),
                            ShoppingCartSessionHome.class);

                        String customerId = null;

                        Cookie cookies[] = request.getCookies();

// Look through the browser's cookie list to see if there is an initial
// customer id to use
                        for (int i=0; i < cookies.length; i++)
                        {
                            if (cookies[i].getName().equals(
                                "StoreCustomerId"))
                            {
                                customerId = cookies[i].getValue();
                                break;
                            }
                        }

// If not, create an empty customer
                        if (customerId == null)
                        {
                            cart = home.create();
                        }
                        else
                        {
// Otherwise, create a cart using the existing customer id
                            cart = home.create(customerId);
                        }
                    }
                    catch (NamingException exc)
                    {
                        exc.printStackTrace();
                    }
                    catch (CreateException exc)
                    {
                        exc.printStackTrace();
                    }
                    catch (RemoteException exc)
                    {
                        exc.printStackTrace();
                    }
                }
```

```
            }
        }

        return cart;
    }

    public void valueBound(HttpSessionBindingEvent evt)
    {
    }

    public void valueUnbound(HttpSessionBindingEvent evt)
    {
// When this object disappears from the session object, close
// down the session bean
        if (cart != null)
        {
            try
            {
                cart.remove();
            }
            catch (Exception exc)
            {
                exc.printStackTrace();
            }
        }
    }
}
```

Because the servlets must also access the shopping cart session, they use the same `CartBean` instance as the Java Server Pages. Listing 50.11 shows the servlet that adds a product to the shopping cart.

LISTING 50.11 SOURCE CODE FOR AddToCartServlet.java

```
package usingj2ee.shopping;

import usingj2ee.shopping.*;
import java.io.*;
import java.net.*;
import javax.servlet.*;
import javax.servlet.http.*;

public class AddToCartServlet extends HttpServlet
{
/** Allow the request to come in via GET or POST */
    public void doGet(HttpServletRequest request,
        HttpServletResponse response)
        throws IOException
    {
        processRequest(request, response);
    }

/** Allow the request to come in via GET or POST */
    public void doPost(HttpServletRequest request,
        HttpServletResponse response)
        throws IOException
```

LISTING 50.11 CONTINUED

```
    {
        processRequest(request, response);
    }

/** Processes the incoming request regardless of the HTTP method used */
    public void processRequest(HttpServletRequest request,
        HttpServletResponse response)
        throws IOException
    {
        HttpSession session = request.getSession();

        CartBean cart = (CartBean) session.getAttribute("cart");

// If the cart bean hasn't been created, create it
        if (cart == null)
        {
            cart = new CartBean();
            session.setAttribute("cart", cart);
        }

        String productId = request.getParameter("productId");

        ShoppingCartSession cartSession = cart.getCart(request);

// Add the product to the cart, assume a quantity of 1
        cartSession.addToShoppingCart(productId, 1);

// Make sure the browser has the current customer id saved as a cookie
        Cookie cookie = new Cookie("StoreCustomerId",
            cartSession.getCustomerId());
        cookie.setPath(request.getContextPath());
        cookie.setMaxAge(7776000);

        response.addCookie(cookie);

// Display the main shopping page
        response.sendRedirect(request.getContextPath()+"/Shopping.jsp");
    }
}
```

One of the difficulties in using the Model-View-Controller paradigm with Web applications is that the controller isn't always as separate from the view as it should be. For instance, the `AddToCartServlet` class assumes that it must display the `Shopping.jsp` view page after performing an operation. The controller really shouldn't know what view it needs to display, however. You must be able to reuse a controller in different situations without changing it.

The shopping application encounters such a situation when it deals with logins and registration. When you display your order history or place an order, you must log in. If you don't already have an account, you must register. Suppose a user tries to "check out"—complete the current order. If the user hasn't logged in, you must send the user to the login form. If, on the login form, the user indicates that she is a new user, you must send her to the registration form. After the login or registration is complete, you send the user back to the check out screen.

The shopping application solves this problem by passing a redirect URL to the login or registration servlet, telling it where to send the user when the operation completes. This way, you don't rewrite the login and registration servlets every time you add a new feature that might require a login.

Listing 50.12 shows the `LoginServlet` class. You can see that it automatically detects where to send the user, but defaults to `Shopping.jsp` if no other URL has been provided.

Listing 50.12 Source Code for `LoginServlet.java`

```
package usingj2ee.shopping;

import usingj2ee.shopping.*;
import java.io.*;
import java.net.*;
import javax.servlet.*;
import javax.servlet.http.*;

public class LoginServlet extends HttpServlet
{
    public void doGet(HttpServletRequest request,
        HttpServletResponse response)
        throws IOException, ServletException
    {
        processRequest(request, response);
    }

    public void doPost(HttpServletRequest request,
        HttpServletResponse response)
        throws IOException, ServletException
    {
        processRequest(request, response);
    }

    public void processRequest(HttpServletRequest request,
        HttpServletResponse response)
        throws IOException, ServletException
    {
        String hasAccount = request.getParameter("account");

// If the user indicated that she has no account, let her register
        if ((hasAccount != null) && (hasAccount.equals("no")))
        {
            getServletContext().getRequestDispatcher(
                getContextPath()+"/Register.jsp").
                forward(request, response);
            return;
        }

        String email = request.getParameter("email");
        String password = request.getParameter("password");

        HttpSession session = request.getSession();

        CartBean cart = (CartBean) session.getAttribute("cart");
```

LISTING 50.12 CONTINUED

```
// Create a new cart if necessary
        if (cart == null)
        {
            cart = new CartBean();
            session.setAttribute("cart", cart);
        }

// Log the user in
        String customerId = cart.getCart(request).login(email, password);

        if (customerId == null)
        {
            getServletContext().getRequestDispatcher(
                getContextPath()+"/LoginFailed.html").
                forward(request, response);
            return;
        }

        session.setAttribute("loggedIn", "true");

// Make sure the browser has the most recent customer id
        Cookie cookie = new Cookie("StoreCustomerId",
            cart.getCart(request).getCustomerId());
        cookie.setPath(request.getContextPath());
        cookie.setMaxAge(7776000);

        response.addCookie(cookie);

// Find out where to send the user now
        String redirectURL = request.getParameter("redirectURL");

        if (redirectURL != null)
        {
            response.sendRedirect(request.getContextPath()+redirectURL);
        }
        else
        {
            response.sendRedirect(request.getContextPath()+"/Shopping.jsp");
        }
    }
}
```

DEPLOYING THE APPLICATION

The shopping application requires EJB 2.0, because it uses a `Home` method. The source code on the CD-ROM includes deployment descriptors for deploying the application on BEA WebLogic 6.0. The EJB deployment is reasonably straightforward—the beans don't have any special security requirements or odd transaction boundaries.

The Web application does have one minor requirement: The Java Server Pages and servlets must be deployed as a Web application. Specifically, the Java Server Pages assume that the servlets are part of their application; they don't use the common `/servlet/` prefix to reference a servlet. The benefit to this design is that the servlets don't need to know the complete path to the Java Server Pages; they can assume that they all share the same context path.

Listing 50.13 shows the `web.xml` file for the application. Notice that you don't need to include the Java Server Pages in the file, but you must include all the servlets you use.

Listing 50.13 Source Code for `web.xml`

```
<?xml version="1.0" ?>
<!DOCTYPE web-app PUBLIC "-//Sun Microsystems, Inc.//DTD Web Application 1.2//EN""
"http://java.sun.com/j2ee/dtds/web-app_2_2.dtd">
<web-app>
    <display-name>cart</display-name>
    <servlet>
        <servlet-name>AddToCartServlet</servlet-name>
        <servlet-class>usingj2ee.shopping.AddToCartServlet</servlet-class>
    </servlet>
    <servlet>
        <servlet-name>LoginServlet</servlet-name>
        <servlet-class>usingj2ee.shopping.LoginServlet</servlet-class>
    </servlet>
    <servlet>
        <servlet-name>RegisterServlet</servlet-name>
        <servlet-class>usingj2ee.shopping.RegisterServlet</servlet-class>
    </servlet>
    <servlet>
        <servlet-name>SaveOrderServlet</servlet-name>
        <servlet-class>usingj2ee.shopping.SaveOrderServlet</servlet-class>
    </servlet>
    <servlet-mapping>
        <servlet-name>AddToCartServlet</servlet-name>
        <url-pattern>AddToCartServlet</url-pattern>
    </servlet-mapping>
    <servlet-mapping>
        <servlet-name>LoginServlet</servlet-name>
        <url-pattern>LoginServlet</url-pattern>
    </servlet-mapping>
    <servlet-mapping>
        <servlet-name>RegisterServlet</servlet-name>
        <url-pattern>RegisterServlet</url-pattern>
    </servlet-mapping>
    <servlet-mapping>
        <servlet-name>SaveOrderServlet</servlet-name>
        <url-pattern>SaveOrderServlet</url-pattern>
    </servlet-mapping>
</web-app>
```

The entire application is far too big to include in this chapter. The entire source, along with deployment descriptors for WebLogic, is available on the CD-ROM accompanying this book and also on this book's Web site.

TROUBLESHOOTING

COMPILATION PROBLEMS

Why don't my Java Server Pages see the EJB interfaces?

If you're using a separate JSP container (that is, the EJB container and JSP container aren't running in the same server), you must remember to include the EJB client JAR file in your classpath when you run the JSP container. If you don't have a client JAR file (WebLogic doesn't usually generate one), use the original EJB JAR file.

DEPLOYMENT PROBLEMS

Why doesn't my EJB deployment tool like the `getCategories` method in the `ProductHome` interface?

The `getCategories` method is a `Home` method, which is a feature introduced in the EJB 2.0 specification. Older EJB 1.1 containers don't support Home methods.

How can I deploy the application in an EJB 1.1 server?

You must move the `getCategories` method into a session bean, and then implement all the relationship methods in the various entity beans. You must also create `find` methods in the various `Home` interfaces to locate related object.

CHAPTER 51

Using XML for Data Exchange

In this chapter

WHY XML IS GOOD FOR DATA EXCHANGE

One of the most promising aspects of XML is that it makes it easier for companies to exchange data. In the past, companies had to develop proprietary data formats for exchanging data. Obviously, you must still define a data format when you use XML, but the benefit of XML is that it provides a standard format for defining the data format! Now, instead of working from some free-form text document that describes a proprietary file format, you can read a Document Type Definition (DTD) to understand the format of a document.

Although a DTD lets you convey the overall structure of a document, it doesn't let you specify data types. Another flaw of DTDs is that they aren't valid XML documents. You must use a custom parser to read a DTD file. The new XML Schema language provides a way to specify data types for various XML elements. Not only does XML Schema let you define types, but it also defines a specific format for various data types. In the past, there was no standard for storing date values, for example. When you read a date from one XML file, it might be in a totally different format from the date in another file. XML Schema defines a standard format for dates, eliminating these annoying differences.

The XSL Transformation language is a useful tool for business data exchange. Sometimes, two businesses define data exchange standards that are similar, but not identical. You can use XSLT to transform an XML document from one format into another. For example, you define a standard format for your outgoing XML data. If you get a new client who wants the same data, but in a different format; you write an XSL transformation to change the data from your format into the format required by the client.

You don't need to generate the data over and over for each client; you simply generate the data in your format once and then apply different XSLT transformations for each client.

PARSING XML WITH SAX AND DOM

When a client sends XML to your server, you must be able to parse the XML document. Obviously, you need either a servlet or a Java Server Page to parse the data. Most of the time, you want to parse the data from a servlet and possibly forward to a JSP to generate any XML output. You can use any of several different parsers to turn XML documents into Java data structures.

There are two different approaches for parsing XML in Java: SAX (Simple API for XML) and DOM (Document Object Model). SAX allows you to handle XML tags in the data as the parser encounters them. In other words, when the parser locates an XML tag, it calls a Java method to handle the tag. It's up to you to decide what to do with it. DOM isn't strictly an API; it's an object model describing how an XML document is organized. When you parse an XML document using a DOM parser, the parser reads the entire document and passes you back a `Document` object containing everything that was defined in the XML document.

Each of these approaches has advantages and disadvantages, and you certainly don't need to choose one over the other. You can use whichever one makes sense for your situation. The Java XML API from Sun supports both SAX and DOM.

PARSING XML USING SAX

SAX uses an event-driven model for parsing. The SAX parser reads the XML, and when it finds something interesting, it calls a method in a handler class. The handler class is something that you must write, although there is a skeleton base class that you can start with. SAX tells you when it finds the beginning of a document, the end of a document, an opening tag, a closing tag, or character data within an element. It also tells you when it finds an error.

SAX is most useful when you need to read through a large XML file but you might not need much of the data in the file. If you need to search through a file for a particular tag or data value, SAX is generally much quicker.

Listing 51.1 shows a servlet that reads an XML file sent to it and searches for a particular tag. After it finds the tag, it looks for character data.

LISTING 51.1 SOURCE CODE FOR SaxParseServlet.java

```
package usingj2ee.xml;

import java.io.*;

import javax.servlet.*;
import javax.servlet.http.*;

import javax.xml.parsers.*;
import org.xml.sax.*;

public class SaxParseServlet extends HttpServlet
{
    public void doPost(HttpServletRequest request,
        HttpServletResponse response)
        throws ServletException, IOException
    {
        try
        {
// Create a parser factory
            SAXParserFactory factory = SAXParserFactory.newInstance();

// Ask the parser factory to create a new parser
            SAXParser parser = factory.newSAXParser();

// This servlet just sends a plain text response
            response.setContentType("text/plain");

// Create an input source around the request reader, ask the parser
// to parse the input source and invoke methods in the XMLHandler class
// when it finds XML elements
            parser.parse(new InputSource(request.getReader()),
                new XMLHandler(request, response));
        }
        catch (ParserConfigurationException exc)
        {
            throw new ServletException(exc.toString());
```

LISTING 51.1 CONTINUED

```
        }
        catch (SAXException exc)
        {
            throw new ServletException(exc.toString());
        }
    }

    class XMLHandler extends HandlerBase
    {
        protected HttpServletRequest request;
        protected HttpServletResponse response;

        protected boolean handlingFirstName;
        protected boolean handlingLastName;
        protected boolean inName;

        protected String firstName;
        protected String lastName;

        public XMLHandler(HttpServletRequest aRequest,
            HttpServletResponse aResponse)
        {
            request = aRequest;
            response = aResponse;

            inName = false;
            handlingFirstName = false;
            handlingLastName = false;
        }

        public void startElement(String name, AttributeList attributes)
        {
// Look for a <name> element
            if (name.equals("name"))
            {
                inName = true;
                firstName = null;
                lastName = null;
            }
// If inside a <name> element, look for <first>
            else if (name.equals("first"))
            {
                if (!inName) return;

                handlingFirstName = true;
            }
// If inside a <name> element, look for <last>
            else if (name.equals("last"))
            {
                if (!inName) return;

                handlingLastName = true;
            }
        }
```

```
        public void characters(char[] chars, int start, int length)
        {
// If these characters are occurring inside a <first> element, save them
            if (handlingFirstName)
            {
                firstName = new String(chars, start, length);
            }
// If these characters are occurring inside a <last> element, save them
            else if (handlingLastName)
            {
                lastName = new String(chars, start, length);
            }
            else
            {
                return;
            }
        }

        public void endElement(String name)
            throws SAXException
        {
            if (name.equals("name"))
            {
// After the end of the name element, if there's a first and a last name,
// print them separated by a space
                if ((firstName != null) && (lastName != null))
                {
                    try
                    {
                        PrintWriter out = response.getWriter();

                        out.println(firstName+" "+lastName);
                    }
                    catch (IOException ioExc)
                    {
                        throw new SAXException(ioExc.toString());
                    }
                }
                inName = false;
            }
            else if (name.equals("first"))
            {
                if (!inName) return;
                handlingFirstName = false;
            }
            else if (name.equals("last"))
            {
                if (!inName) return;
                handlingLastName = false;
            }
        }
    }
}
```


Most of the code in Listing 51.1 should look familiar if you look back at the XML parsing code from Chapter 22, "XML—The Extensible Markup Language." The main difference here is that Listing 51.1 contains a servlet. Notice that when the servlet creates the parser, it creates an InputSource object using the getReadergetReader method. In other words, it tells the parser to parse the servlet's input stream directly. Other than this change in the input source, the servlet works just like a standalone XML parsing program.

Listing 51.2 shows a test client program that sends the XML file to the servlet from Listing 51.1.

LISTING 51.2 SOURCE CODE FOR XMLTestClient.java

```
import java.io.*;
import java.net.*;

public class XMLTestClient
{
    public static void main(String[] args)
    {
        try
        {
// args[1] is the name of the file to send
            File f = new File(args[1]);
            int contentLength = (int) f.length();

// args[0] is the URL to send the file to
            URL url = new URL(args[0]);
            URLConnection conn = url.openConnection();

// Tell the URLConnection that this is an XML file
            conn.setDoOutput(true);
            conn.setRequestProperty("content-type", "text/xml");
            conn.setRequestProperty("content-length", ""+contentLength);

            FileInputStream in = new FileInputStream(f);

            byte[] buffer = new byte[4096];
            int len;

            OutputStream out = conn.getOutputStream();

// Send the XML file to the servlet
            while ((len = in.read(buffer)) > 0)
            {
                out.write(buffer, 0, len);
            }

            InputStream resp = conn.getInputStream();

// Read the response back from the servlet
            while ((len = resp.read(buffer)) > 0)
            {
                System.out.write(buffer, 0, len);
            }
        }
        catch (Exception exc)
        {
            exc.printStackTrace();
```

```
        }
    }
}
```

PARSING XML USING DOM

A DOM parser reads an XML file in its entirety before passing any information to you. It creates a representation of the XML contents using a set of Java classes. An XML file is structured like a tree. The main document tag is the base of the tree, and each nested tag is a branch of the tree. The document model used by a DOM parser is also structured like a tree. You receive a `Document` object, which returns a list of `Node` objects.

The `Node` class is really an interface, not a class. DOM has a number of classes that implement the `Node` interface. The one you deal with most often is the `Element` class, which represents a tag or tag pair from an XML document. You might also find `Comment` nodes, `Text` nodes, `CDATASection` nodes, `Character` nodes, and several others. The `Element` class can contain a list of child nodes representing the tags and data contained between the element's opening and closing tags.

Listing 51.3 shows a servlet that uses a DOM parser to parse through the same file as the servlet in Listing 24.9. You can see how different a DOM parser is from a SAX parser. Although SAX is a bit faster, DOM tends to be a bit easier to use when you need to preserve the structure of the document.

LISTING 51.3 SOURCE CODE FOR `DomParseServlet.java`

```
package usingj2ee.xml;

import java.io.*;

import javax.servlet.*;
import javax.servlet.http.*;

import javax.xml.parsers.*;
import org.xml.sax.*;
import org.w3c.dom.*;

public class DomParseServlet extends HttpServlet
{
    public void doPost(HttpServletRequest request,
        HttpServletResponse response)
        throws ServletException, IOException
    {
        try
        {
// Create a parser factory
            DocumentBuilderFactory factory = DocumentBuilderFactory.
                newInstance();

// Ask the parser factory to create a new parser
            DocumentBuilder parser = factory.newDocumentBuilder();
```

LISTING 51.3 CONTINUED

```
// This servlet just sends a plain text response
            response.setContentType("text/plain");

            PrintWriter out = response.getWriter();

// Create an input source around the request reader, ask the parser
// to parse the input source
            Document doc = parser.parse(new InputSource(request.getReader()));

// Get all the Name elements
            NodeList names = doc.getElementsByTagName("name");

            int numNames = names.getLength();

            for (int i=0; i < numNames; i++)
            {
                Element e = (Element) names.item(i);

                String firstName = null;

// See if there is a first name
                NodeList firstNameList = e.getElementsByTagName("first");
                if (firstNameList.getLength() > 0)
                {
                    Element firstNameNode = (Element) firstNameList.item(0);

// Make the really bold assumption that <first> has a child and that
// it is text. You really should check first, however.
                    CharacterData nameText = (CharacterData)
                        firstNameNode.getFirstChild();

                    firstName = nameText.getData();
                }

                String lastName = null;

// See if there is a last name
                NodeList lastNameList = e.getElementsByTagName("last");
                if (lastNameList.getLength() > 0)
                {
                    Element lastNameNode = (Element) lastNameList.item(0);

// Make the really bold assumption that <last> has a child and that
// it is text. You really should check first, however.
                    CharacterData nameText = (CharacterData)
                        lastNameNode.getFirstChild();

                    lastName = nameText.getData();
                }

                if ((firstName != null) && (lastName != null))
                {
                    out.println(firstName+" "+lastName);
                }
            }
```

```
            }
            catch (ParserConfigurationException exc)
            {
                throw new ServletException(exc.toString());
            }
            catch (SAXException exc)
            {
                throw new ServletException(exc.toString());
            }
        }
    }
```

As with the previous SAX parsing servlet, the `DomParseServlet` program in Listing 51.3 creates an `InputSource` object using the servlet's `getReader` method. Again, other than the different input source, the `DomParseServlet` class is similar to a standalone XML parsing program.

In Chapter 22, you saw how to send XML data from a JSP or a servlet. The only thing to remember is that you must change the content type to `text/xml` instead of `text/html`.

TROUBLESHOOTING

USING THE SUN XML LIBRARIES

Why can't the Java compiler find the XML libraries?

You probably forgot to change the content type to `text/xml`.

My program compiles okay, so why does it tell me it can't find the parser?

You must have both `jaxp.jar` and `parser.jar` in your classpath. The `jaxp.jar` file defines the standard interfaces for SAX and DOM but doesn't contain any of the implementation classes. You can compile a program using only `jaxp.jar`, but when you run the program, you need to include an actual XML parser in the classpath.

CHAPTER 52

INTERNATIONALIZATION

In this chapter

The Internet has had a huge impact on software development. Now developers and users from countries around the world can share information almost instantaneously. Oddly enough, developers rarely consider the fact that the people who use their software might be in another country. At least, this is often the case in the United States. In the United States, a large number of Web sites cater mostly to domestic customers and ignore international customers, unfortunately. In other areas, however, like the European Union, many countries participate in open trade and must deal with internationalization issues. As more U.S. companies begin to realize that there is a huge market outside their borders, internationalization will become a greater concern within the United States.

Java provides reasonable support for internationalization, some of which happens behind the scenes. When a Java program starts, it examines the locale configured in the operating system and sets up a default locale. Several Java classes use the locale for formatting dates and currencies. You can also define sets of resources, called *resource bundles*, which are locale-dependent. By confining your locale-specific data to resource bundles, you can support multiple locales in your programs without hard-coding every possible locale variation.

Note

You might have seen "internationalization" abbreviated as I18N. The abbreviation is a clever acknowledgment of the fact that there are 18 letters between the *I* and the *N* in internationalization.

DETECTING THE BROWSER'S PREFERRED LOCALE

As you saw in Chapter 29, "The HTTP Protocol," the browser sends a number of header fields in each request indicating certain preferences. One of these preferences is a list of languages that the browser prefers for Web pages. The `ACCEPT-LANGUAGE` header value contains a list of languages that the browser is prepared to handle. Using this header value, you can locate a locale that you are prepared to support and deliver content targeted toward that locale.

For example, suppose you have a Web site that is in both German and English. Although each version contains links to allow you to change languages at any time, you might want to default the user to the language his browser prefers. For example, if you see `de-DE` as the preferred language, you send the user to the German version of the page, and if you see `en-US` or `en-UK`, you send the user to the English version.

Listing 52.1 shows a JSP that detects the preferred language sent by the browser and chooses one of two possible pages.

LISTING 52.1 SOURCE CODE FOR MyPage.jsp

```
<%
    String lang = request.getHeader("ACCEPT-LANGUAGE");

    String whatPage = "MyPage_En.html";
```

```
    if (lang.startsWith("de"))
    {
        whatPage = "MyPage_De.html";
    }
%><jsp:forward page="<%=whatPage%>"/>
```

Figure 52.1 shows the JSP when viewed from a browser with a preferred language setting of English (en/US), and Figure 52.2 shows the JSP viewed from a browser that prefers German (de/DE).

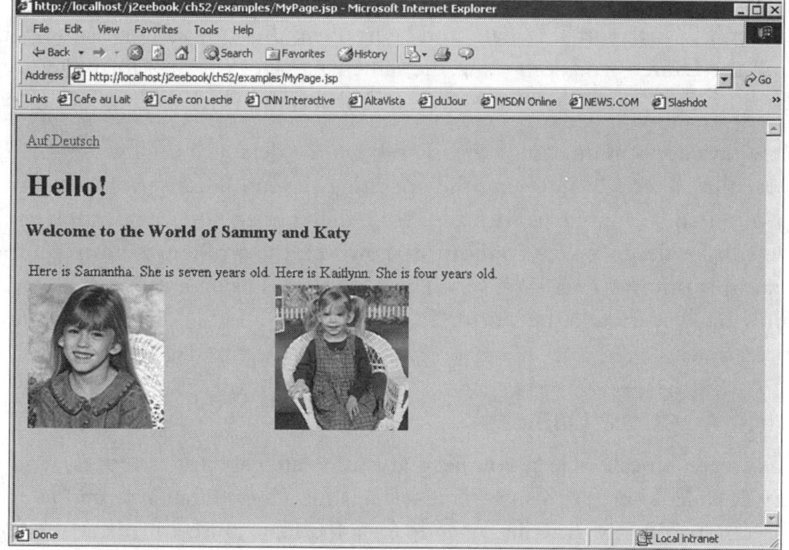

Figure 52.1 You can create a multilingual Web site by detecting the preferred language.

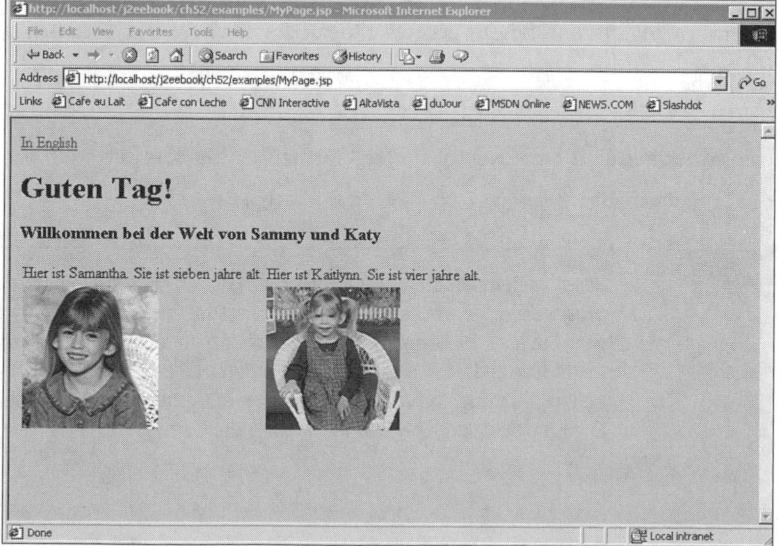

Figure 52.2 When you provide alternate language pages, include links to see the other language versions.

Tip

Both Netscape and Internet Explorer let you set the preferred language for your browser. These settings allow you to view your alternate language pages without changing the language setting for the entire operating system.

USING LOCALE-BASED TEXT FORMATTERS

Java relies on the `java.text` package for providing locale-based formatting. A locale represents both a language and a country, because two countries might share the same language but still format numbers, dates, and currencies differently. For example, the United States and the United Kingdom share the same language, but they format currencies differently because the United States uses a $ symbol and the United Kingdom uses the £ symbol.

In a Java application, you normally rely on the default locale, which the Java Virtual Machine detects by querying the operating system. Because you can assume that users have configured their systems with the locale they prefer, your application can safely rely on the default locale. In a Web application, however, the problem is more complicated. The application is running on a Web server and the user is using a browser on another computer, possibly halfway around the world. You must create a locale object that conforms to the user's preference.

CREATING A LOCALE OBJECT

To create a locale object, you need at least a language for the locale, and preferably a country as well. There are also variant settings for a locale that are vendor- and browser-specific. If you don't know the country code for a locale, just use a blank string. You can still form at dates and numbers without a country, but currencies will not have the correct currency symbol.

The following code fragment creates a locale for French, but does not specify a country code:

```
Locale french = new Locale("fr", "");
```

This code fragment creates a locale for German with a country code for Austria:

```
Locale germanAustria = new Locale("de", "AT");
```

Caution

Resist the temptation to use `Locale.setDefault` to set the current locale to be the browser's locale. You wouldn't need to pass the locale to all the formatting routines that way, but for a Web application, you introduce an ugly threading problem. Two servlets might set the default locale at the same time. One servlet might set the locale to English-US and another might immediately change it to German-Germany. The servlet that wanted English would suddenly find it was using the German format.

FORMATTING DATES

You might have used the SimpleDateFormat class in the java.text package to format dates. Although it might provide an easy way to specify date formats, you lose some of the locale-independence when you use it. When you create an instance of SimpleDateFormat, you must supply a basic pattern for the date. You might pick a format such as MM/dd/yyyy for example. Unfortunately, many countries write dates in the form dd/MM/yyyy.

The DateFormat class doesn't give you the leeway that SimpleDateFormat does, but it does protect you from various locale-dependent formats. The DateFormat class has several factory methods that create a DateFormat object for you. You don't use the constructor. Instead, you call getDateInstance, getDateTimeInstance, or getTimeInstance, depending on whether you want to display only dates, dates and times, or only times.

When you create a DateFormat, you must specify one of four formats: SHORT, MEDIUM, LONG, or FULL. You can also give the locale for the format and if you omit the locale, you'll get the default locale. For getDateInstance and getTimeInstance, you only need to specify one format. For getDateTimeInstance, you must specify SHORT, MEDIUM, LONG, or FULL for both the date and the time. You might choose to write out the date in long format but the time in full format.

Listing 52.2 shows a Java Server Page that displays the date using the four format options. The locale is not included in this example, however. You will see how to include it later in this chapter.

LISTING 52.2 SOURCE CODE FOR ShowDates.jsp

```
<%@ page language="java" import="java.text.*,java.util.*" %>
<%

    DateFormat dtShort = DateFormat.getDateTimeInstance(
        DateFormat.SHORT, DateFormat.SHORT);

    DateFormat dtMedium = DateFormat.getDateTimeInstance(
        DateFormat.MEDIUM, DateFormat.MEDIUM);

    DateFormat dtLong = DateFormat.getDateTimeInstance(
        DateFormat.LONG, DateFormat.LONG);

    DateFormat dtFull = DateFormat.getDateTimeInstance(
        DateFormat.FULL, DateFormat.FULL);
%>
<html>
<body>
A short date/time looks like: <%=dtShort.format(new Date())%><p>
A medium date/time looks like: <%=dtMedium.format(new Date())%><p>
A long date/time looks like: <%=dtLong.format(new Date())%><p>
A full date/time looks like: <%=dtFull.format(new Date())%><p>
</body>
</html>
```

Figure 52.3 shows the output of the ShowDates Java Server page.

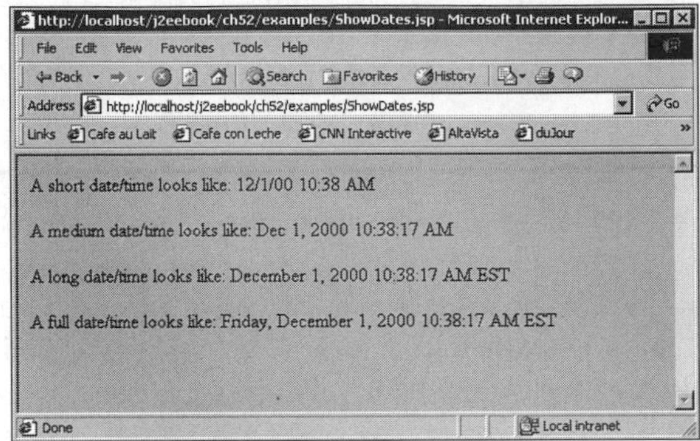

Figure 52.3
You can choose between four basic styles of date and time.

FORMATTING CURRENCY

Formatting currency values is much more involved than formatting dates and times. It's not that there's anything difficult about formatting a currency value; the problem is that you can rarely just switch from one currency to another without performing some sort of conversion. The `NumberFormat` class will format a specific value like 12.34 into dollars as $12.34 or into Deutschmarks as 12,34DM, but 12,34DM is not the same amount of money as $12.34. Java does not provide any way to convert from one currency to another.

When you think about it, it's almost impossible to make a standard API for converting currencies because currencies are traded at various rates. Imagine trying to make an API that lets you get the price of a stock or the price of a car. There would be too many places to go for the information and too many different formats for the data. You have the same problem trying to convert currencies. Perhaps one day all the currency traders will publish rates using a standard XML format and you can perform reasonable conversions. Even so, because the rates fluctuate, you must still worry about how stale the information is. The conversion rate for an unstable currency might plummet over the course of a day or two.

By now, you see that the capability to display currency values for different locales is not such a useful feature. If you do find that you need to display currency values, you can call `NumberFormat.getCurrencyInstance` and pass it the locale whose currency you want to display:

```
NumberFormat currencyFormat =
    NumberFormat.getCurrencyInstance(someLocale);
```

GETTING A LOCALE FOR A BROWSER'S PREFERRED LANGUAGE

When you examine the `ACCEPT-LANGUAGE` header value, you will find a list of locale codes consisting of a two-letter language code, possibly a country code, and even variant options after the country code. Each locale code is separated by a comma. When you just want the preferred language (the browser sends the locales in order of preference), you need to grab the first one in the list.

Listing 52.3 shows a Java Server Page that parses the ACCEPT-LANGUAGE header value and gets a locale value for the preferred locale.

Listing 52.3 Source Code for TestLocale.jsp

```
<%@ page language="java" import="java.text.*,java.util.*" %>
<%

// Get the default locale in case you can't determine the
// user's locale
    Locale locale = Locale.getDefault();

// Get the browser's preferred language
    String acceptLangString = request.getHeader("ACCEPT-LANGUAGE");

// If there is an ACCEPT-LANGUAGE header, parse it
    if (acceptLangString != null)
    {

// The accepted languages should be separated by commas, but also
// add space as a separator to eliminate whitespace
        StringTokenizer localeParser = new StringTokenizer(
            acceptLangString, " ,");

// See if there is a language in the list (you only need the first one)
        if (localeParser.hasMoreTokens())
        {
// Get the locale
            String localeStr = localeParser.nextToken();

// The locale should be in the format ll-CC where ll is the language
// and CC is the country, such as en-US for English in the U.S. and
// de-DE for German in Germany. Allow the browser to use _ instead
// of -, too.
            StringTokenizer localeSplitter = new StringTokenizer(
                localeStr, "_-");

// Assume both values are blank
            String language = "";
            String country = "";

// See if there is a language specified
            if (localeSplitter.hasMoreTokens())
            {
                language = localeSplitter.nextToken();
            }

// See if there is a country specified (there won't always be one)
            if (localeSplitter.hasMoreTokens())
            {
                country = localeSplitter.nextToken();

            }

// Create a locale based on this language and country (if country is
// blank, you'll still get locale-based text, but currencies won't
```

LISTING 52.3 CONTINUED

```
// display correctly.
            locale = new Locale(language, country);
        }
    }
%>
<html>
<body>
Your locale language is <%=locale.getLanguage()%>.<p>
Your locale country is <%=locale.getCountry()%>.<p>
<%
// Get a formatter to display currency
    NumberFormat currencyFormatter =
        NumberFormat.getCurrencyInstance(locale);

// Get a formatter to display dates and times
    DateFormat dateFormatter =
        DateFormat.getDateTimeInstance(
            DateFormat.FULL, DateFormat.FULL, locale);
%>
A currency in your locale looks like this:
    <%= currencyFormatter.format(12.34) %><p>
A date in your locale looks like this:
    <%= dateFormatter.format(new Date()) %><p>
</body>
</html>
```

Figure 52.4 shows the `TestLocale` Java Server Page running with a locale of en-US (English - U.S.).

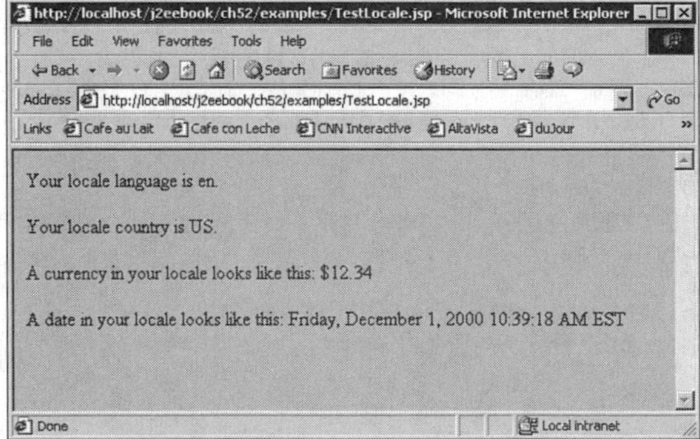

Figure 52.4
The `java.text` package can format dates and currencies.

Figure 52.5 shows the TestLocale Java Server Page running with a locale of de (German) and no country code. Notice the odd looking character in the currency. If you don't specify a country, you'll see this odd symbol. Also notice that the currency formatter still uses the German convention of using a comma where English text uses a period. Although the currency formatter doesn't know the currency symbol, it uses the number formatter to format the currency value, and the number formatter doesn't need to know the country.

Figure 52.5
If you don't specify a country for a locale, the currency symbol isn't correct.

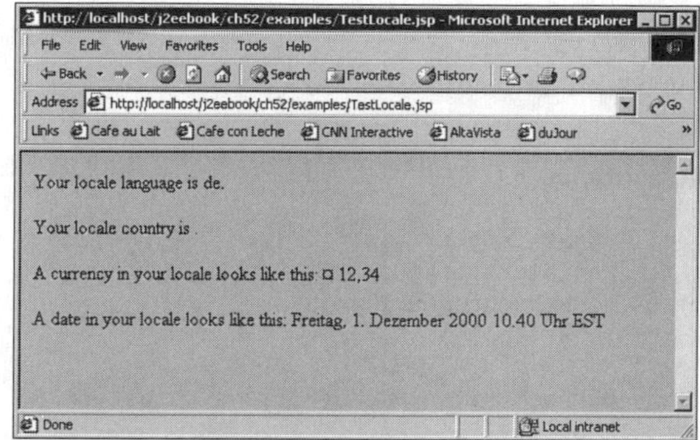

Using Resource Bundles

The Java's i18n support includes objects known as *resource bundles*. When you create a multilingual application or Web site, you don't always want to make separate screens or pages for each language. For example, when you create an HTML form, the prompt strings can be in different languages, but the HTML for defining the form itself is the same no matter what language you use.

By using resource bundles, you can group various prompt strings and other objects that are locale-dependent. When you create a resource bundle class, you decide on a base classname and then define each locale's resources in a class whose name is formed by adding the locale to the end of the classname.

For example, you might store some resources in a class called `SomeResources`. The French version of the resources would be in a class called `SomeResources_fr`, and the German version would be in a class called `SomeResources_de`. If you need to make a special German version of the resources tailored to Austria, you can put them in a class called `SomeResources_de_AT`.

Because writing resource bundles can be tedious, Java gives you some prebuilt framework classes. The `ListResourceBundle` class allows you to store the resources in an array of objects. Listing 52.4 shows an example `ListResourceBundle`. Notice that there is no locale at the end of the classname. That makes this class the default bundle if there is no bundle for the browser's locale.

Listing 52.4 Source Code for `TestResources.java`

```
package usingj2ee.i18n;

import java.text.*;
import java.util.*;

public class TestResources extends ListResourceBundle
{
    public Object[][] getContents()
    {
```

LISTING 52.4 CONTINUED

```
        return contents;
    }

    final Object[][] contents =
    {
        { "namePrompt", "What is your name: " },
        { "agePrompt", "How old are you: " },
        { "placePrompt", "Where do you live: " },
        { "greetHeading", "Hello!" },
        { "welcomeText",
            "Welcome to our web site. Please take a moment to "+
            "fill out our survey" },
        { "submitButtonText", "Submit" }
    };
}
```

Listing 52.5 shows the German version of the `TestRsources` resource bundle.

LISTING 52.5 SOURCE CODE FOR `TestResources_de.java`

```
package usingj2ee.i18n;

import java.util.*;
import java.text.*;

public class TestResources_de extends ListResourceBundle
{
    public Object[][] getContents()
    {
        return contents;
    }

    final Object[][] contents =
    {
        { "namePrompt", "Wie hei[gb]en Sie" },
        { "agePrompt", "Wie alt sind Sie: " },
        { "placePrompt", "Wo wohnen Sie: " },
        { "greetHeading", "Guten Tag!" },
        { "welcomeText",
            "Willkommen bei unserer Web-Site. Bitte, dauern Sie einen "+
            "Moment Um unsere Umfrage auszufüllen" },
        { "submitButtonText", "Senden" }
    };
}
```

Listing 52.6 shows a Java Server Page that displays an HTML form using the prompts from the `TestResources` resource bundle. Notice that you don't need separate pages for each language. Only the prompts need to change.

LISTING 52.6 SOURCE CODE FOR `ResourceBundles.jsp`

```
<%@ page language="java" import="java.text.*,java.util.*" %>
<%
```

```
// Get the default locale in case you can't determine the
// user's locale
    Locale locale = Locale.getDefault();

// Get the browser's preferred language
    String acceptLangString = request.getHeader("ACCEPT-LANGUAGE");

// Allow the user to override the browser's language setting. This
// lets you test with tools such as Babelfish (which isn't that great
// at translating to begin with).
    String override = request.getParameter("langOverride");

    if (override != null)
    {
        acceptLangString = override;
    }

// If there is an ACCEPT-LANGUAGE header, parse it
    if (acceptLangString != null)
    {

// The accepted languages should be separated by commas, but also
// add space as a separator to eliminate whitespace
        StringTokenizer localeParser = new StringTokenizer(
            acceptLangString, " ,");

// See if there is a language in the list (you only need the first one)
        if (localeParser.hasMoreTokens())
        {
// Get the locale
            String localeStr = localeParser.nextToken();

// The locale should be in the format ll-CC where ll is the language
// and CC is the country, such as en-US for English in the U.S. and
// de-DE for German in Germany. Allow the browser to use _ instead
// of -, too.
            StringTokenizer localeSplitter = new StringTokenizer(
                localeStr, "_-");

// Assume both values are blank
            String language = "";
            String country = "";

// See if there is a language specified
            if (localeSplitter.hasMoreTokens())
            {
                language = localeSplitter.nextToken();
            }

// See if there is a country specified (there won't always be one)
            if (localeSplitter.hasMoreTokens())
            {
                country = localeSplitter.nextToken();

            }
```

LISTING 52.6 CONTINUED

```
// Create a locale based on this language and country (if country is
// blank, you'll still get locale-based text, but currencies won't
// display correctly).

            locale = new Locale(language, country);
        }
    }

// Get the bundle of resource strings for this locale
    ResourceBundle resources = ResourceBundle.getBundle(
        "usingj2ee.i18n.TestResources", locale);
%>
<html>
<body>
<h1><%= resources.getString("greetHeading")%></h1>
<p>
<%= resources.getString("welcomeText")%>:
<p>
<form action="your_form_handler_here" method="post">

<%=resources.getString("namePrompt")%>
<input type="text" name="name"><br>

<%=resources.getString("agePrompt")%>
<input type="text" name="age"><br>

<%=resources.getString("placePrompt")%>
<input type="text" name="place"><br>

<p>
<input type="submit" value="<%=resources.getString("submitButtonText")%>">
</form>
</body>
</html>
```

Figure 52.6 shows the `ResourceBundles` JSP running in a browser with a preferred language of English.

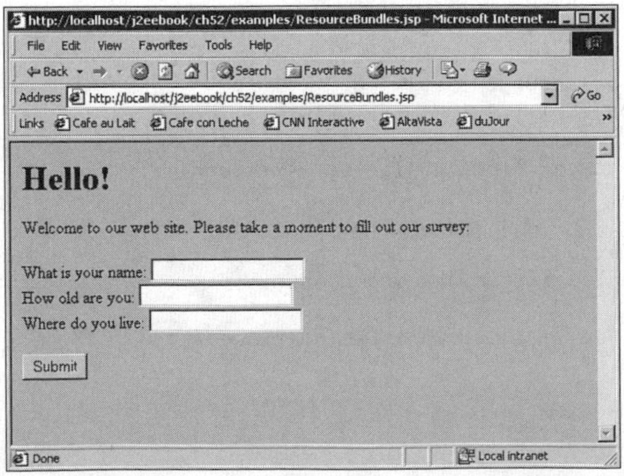

Figure 52.6
Resource bundles let you customize parts of a JSP or servlet.

Figure 52.7 shows the `ResourceBundles` JSP running in a browser with a preferred language of German.

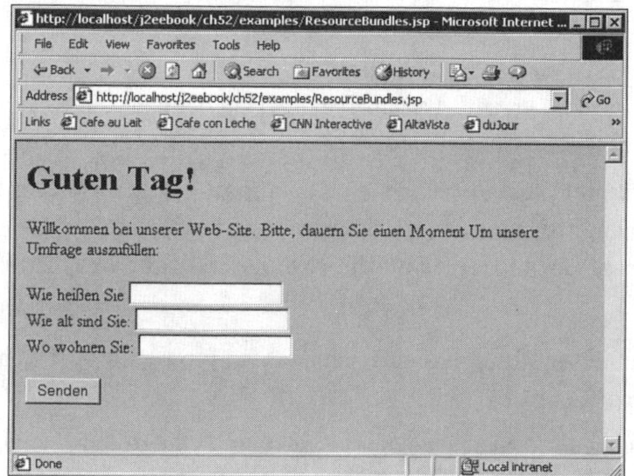

Figure 52.7
The `ResourceBundle` class locates a resource bundle for a particular locale.

Although the `ListResourceBundle` class makes it easy to customize various items in a Web page, the `PropertyResourceBundle` class makes it even easier. The `PropertyResourceBundle` class lets you store locale-specific strings in a properties file instead of a Java class, making it much easier to customize the resources. All you need to do to use the `PropertyResourceBundle` class is to create a properties file with lines of the form `name=value`. Listing 52.7 shows a properties file defining the same resource names as `TestResources.java`. Make sure the properties file ends with `.properties`. The `ResourceBundle` class specifically looks for files with the `.properties` extension.

Note

Some EJB developers worry that they can't use resource bundles in their EJBs because accessing a properties file seems to violate the rule against using `java.io` to access files. Because the `PropertyResourceBundle` class uses the Java class loader to load the resources, this isn't against the EJB rules.

Listing 52.7 Source Code for `TestResourceProps.properties`

```
namePrompt=What is your name:
agePrompt=How old are you:
placePrompt=Where do you live:
greetHeading=Hello!
welcomeText=Welcome to our Web site.
➥Please take a moment to fill out our survey.
submitButtonText=Submit
```

Listing 52.8 shows the German version of the properties file. Notice that you just need to append the language to the end of the name of the properties file, right before the `.properties` extension.

LISTING 52.8 SOURCE CODE FOR TestResourceProps_de.properties

```
namePrompt=Wie hei[gb]en Sie:
agePrompt=Wie alt sind Sie:
placePrompt=Wo wohnen Sie:
greetHeading=Guten Tag!
welcomeText= Willkommen bei unserer Web-Site.
➥Bitte, dauern Sie einen Moment Um unsere Umfrage auszufüllen
submitButtonText=Senden
```

The beauty of the `PropertyResourceBundle` class is that it treats the files as if they were classnames. That is, you just need to put the properties files somewhere in your classpath and call `ResourceBundle.getBundle` using the base name of the properties file (such as `TestResourceProps`).

You only need to change one line in `ResourceBundles.jsp` to support properties files instead of using the `TestResources` class:

```
ResourceBundle resources = ResourceBundle.getBundle(
    "TestResourceProps", locale);
```

Note

If you have a properties file named `TestResourceProps.properties` and a class named `TestResourceProps`, the class takes precedence over the properties file. The `ResourceBundle` class loads the `TestResourceProps` class instead of the properties file.

TROUBLESHOOTING

TESTING MULTILINGUAL WEB SITES

How can I tell if my Web site actually works for other languages?

You can change the language setting for your browser to specify a different preferred language.

LOCATING RESOURCE BUNDLES

Why can't the resource bundle find my properties file?

Treat the properties file like a `.class` file. It must be visible somewhere along your classpath. Also, make sure that the browser is requesting a language that you support. If not, make sure you have a default properties file (one without a language on the end).

CHAPTER 53

Creating a Wireless Web Application

In this chapter

Over the past few years, mobile phone networks have been switching from analog to digital transmission. In addition to getting better reception, digital Personal Communication System (PCS) phone users are finding that their little phone is more than just a glorified walkie-talkie. Digital transmission makes it much easier for the phone network to pass data as well as voice traffic through the airwaves. Although this was possible with an analog system, it was much more complicated.

PCS phones now come with tiny Web browsers that work over a "wireless Web". This wireless Web is not quite the same as the Web you use from your home computer. Although there are gateways bridging the two Webs together, the data traffic on the wireless Web uses the Wireless Application Protocol (WAP) to transmit data. Without getting bogged down in the details, the wireless networks don't have the same data capacity as the rest of the Internet. WAP was designed to accommodate the low bandwidth and reduced connectivity restrictions of wireless networks.

Figure 53.1 shows how a typical Web browser interacts with a Web server. By now, you can probably draw this picture in your sleep.

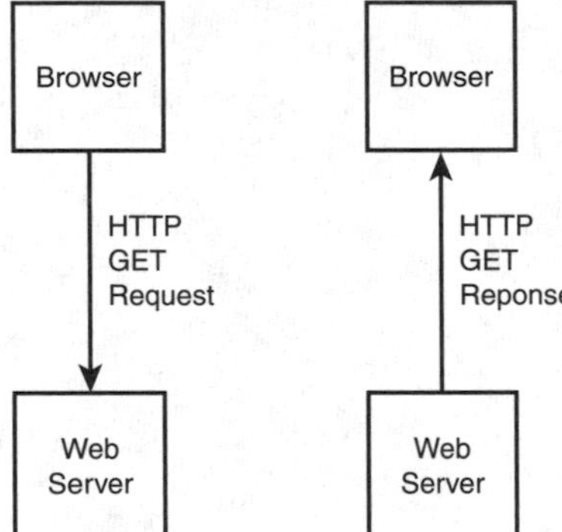

Figure 53.1
A Web browser uses the TCP/IP to communicate with a Web server.

Figure 53.2 shows the path that a PCS phone takes to get to that same Web server. The WAP gateway sits between the wireless network and the TCP/IP network and serves as the bridge between the two networks.

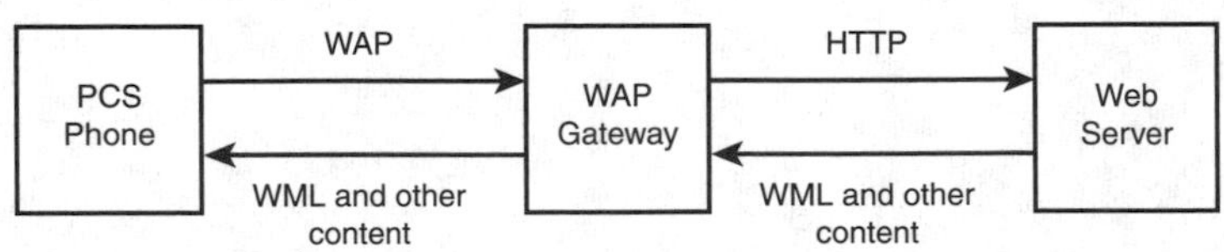

Figure 53.2
The WAP gateway passes requests between a wireless network and a TCP/IP network.

Most wireless Web sites use the Wireless Markup Language (WML) which is a form of XML. That is, WML is defined using an XML Document Type Definition (DTD) and is specifically designed to accommodate the small browsers embedded inside PCS phones.

Because many Web providers aren't yet willing to take the time to create a WML version of their sites, it is possible to create an HTML-WML translator to make most of the Web available to PCS phones. Unfortunately, although this idea sounds good, few Web sites translate well because of their layout. It is better to create a scaled-down version with WML.

One of the disadvantages of the gateway approach is that the WAP gateway can become a huge bottleneck. All the requests from the wireless network must funnel through the WAP gateway, which must keep track of connections on both networks. It is possible to create a WAP server that serves WML directly to the wireless network without using a TCP/IP network, as shown in Figure 53.3.

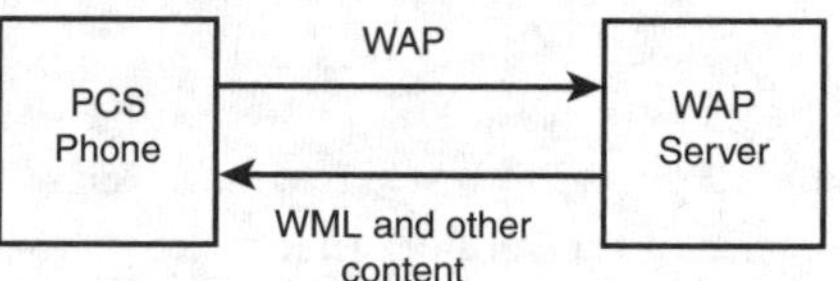

Figure 53.3
A WAP server provides content straight to the wireless network.

Although no WAP servers provide a servlet API yet, you might soon be able to write servlets and JSPs specifically for wireless networks. In the meantime, however, you can use JSP and servlets to create WML content that is accessed through a WAP gateway.

A WIRELESS "HELLO WORLD" PAGE

Listing 53.1 shows the ubiquitous "Hello World" application for a wireless device.

LISTING 53.1 SOURCE CODE FOR `WirelessHello.jsp`

```
<%@ page language="java" contentType="text/vnd.wap.wml" %>
<?xml version="1.0"?>
<!DOCTYPE wml PUBLIC "-//WAPFORUM//DTD WML 1.1//EN"
    "http://www.wapforum.org/DTD/wml_1.1.xml">


<wml>
<card id="hello">
<p>
Hello Wireless World!
</p>
</card>
</wml>
```

The first thing you might notice in `WirelessHello.jsp` is that the content type is not `text/html`. Of course, it isn't `text/wml` either, which would probably make a lot more sense than `text/vnd.wap.wml`, but that's the way it is.

After you get past the `<%@page` line, the file looks like a typical XML file. You must always have the `<?xml` header. The `<!DOCTYPE` tag isn't strictly necessary for all XML pages, but if a DTD is defined for the XML you are generating, you should include it.

Now you get into the actual WML code. The `<wml>` tag is the root tag of a WML document. Everything else must be enclosed within it. As you will see in a moment, a WML page consists of a number of cards, which are really like little pages. The `WirelessHello` page contains a single card named `hello`. The one tag that is familiar from the HTML world is the `<p>` tag defining a paragraph.

Tip

Remember that because WML is an XML-based markup language, a tag must always have a closing tag or end with `/>`. You must remember to use a closing `</p>` tag for paragraphs, and put a `/` in the `<br/>` tag to insert a line break.

VIEWING THE WIRELESS HELLO PAGE

You don't need a wireless Web-enabled phone to test out your wireless Web pages. You can get a WAP phone simulator from some of the vendors that make phones and phone software. Openwave.com (formerly Phone.com) provides the wireless Web browser software for a number of phone manufacturers and makes a WAP gateway. You can download their UP.SDK development kit that includes a nice phone simulator from `http://developer.openwave.com`.

Follow the link for developers and you will see what Phone.com has to offer.

Figure 53.4 shows the `WirelessHello` page running in the Phone.com simulator.

Figure 53.4
A phone simulator lets you debug wireless Web pages without paying for wireless Web time.

Note

In case you're wondering why Phone.com's SDK is called UP.SDK, the company was once called Unwired Planet—thus the UP in UP.SDK.

Nokia, the well-known phone manufacturer, also has a phone simulator. Go to `http://www.forum.nokia.com`, then follow the link for WAP developers. The Nokia phone simulator is in the Nokia WAP toolkit. Figure 53.5 shows the `WirelessHello` page running in the Nokia phone simulator.

Figure 53.5
Nokia's phone simulator will show you the WML it is displaying.

A BRIEF INTRODUCTION TO WML

As you now know, WML is based on XML and is optimized for low-bandwidth transactions. One of the optimizations in WAP and WML is that a server can return multiple display pages in a single request. These display pages are referred to as *cards*. When you return a response to a WAP phone (or other device), the response can contain a series of `<card>` tags. The phone displays the first card in the response and it is up to you to provide navigation to the other cards. Figure 53.6 illustrates the layout of a response.

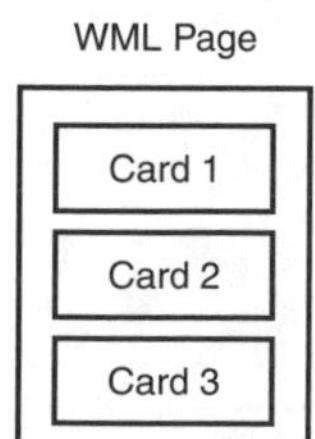

Figure 53.6
A response can contain multiple "pages" organized into cards.

NAVIGATING BETWEEN CARDS

There are two main ways to navigate between cards. You can use the `<a>` tag, which creates a hyperlink just like in HTML, or you can use the `<do>` tag, which lets you perform an action when the user presses a particular key or activates some other feature of the device.

Listing 53.2 shows an example page with four cards. The main card contains three hyperlinks to the other cards. In a WML hyperlink, the text after the # in a URL indicates the card name. For example, `href="#moe"` refers to the card with an ID of `moe`.

LISTING 53.2 SOURCE CODE FOR Hyperlinks.jsp

```
<%@ page language="java" contentType="text/vnd.wap.wml" %>
<?xml version="1.0"?>
<!DOCTYPE wml PUBLIC "-//WAPFORUM//DTD WML 1.1//EN"
    "http://www.wapforum.org/DTD/wml_1.1.xml">

<wml>

<card id="main">
    <p>
        <a href="#moe" title="Moe">Moe Howard</a>
        <a href="#larry" title="Larry">Larry Fine</a>
        <a href="#curly" title="Curly">Curly Howard</a>
    </p>
</card>

<card id="moe">
    <p>
        Moe Howard<br/>
        Why I oughta...
    </p>
</card>

<card id="larry">
    <p>
        Larry Fine<br/>
        Ow! Ow! Ow!
    </p>
</card>

<card id="curly">
    <p>
        Curly Howard<br/>
        Woob woob woob woob<br/>
        Nyuk nyuk nyuk
    </p>
</card >
</wml>
```

Figure 53.7 shows the main menu running in the Phone.com simulator.

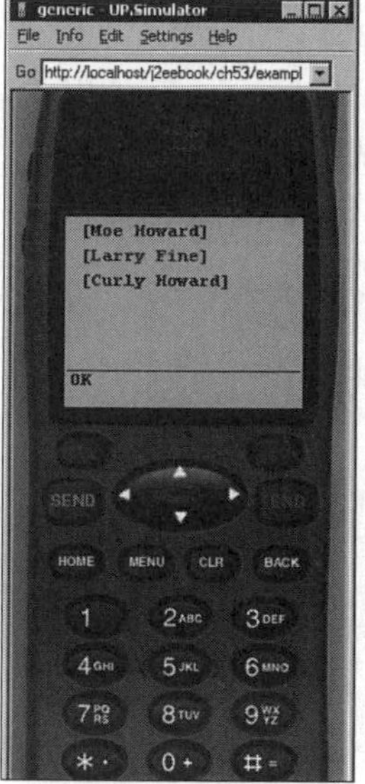

Figure 53.7
The phone only displays the first card. You must navigate to the others.

In addition to hyperlinks, you can control navigation based on the keys the user presses. When you control navigation by key presses, you can look for the keys either within a particular card, or within the entire deck.

Tip

A WML page is referred to as a *deck* because it usually consists of a number of cards.

Listing 53.3 shows a Web page similar to `Hyperlinks.jsp`, except that you use the `Accept` keys to navigate forwards through the list.

Listing 53.3 Source Code for `Next.jsp`

```
<%@ page language="java" contentType="text/vnd.wap.wml" %>
<?xml version="1.0"?>
<!DOCTYPE wml PUBLIC "-//WAPFORUM//DTD WML 1.1//EN"
    "http://www.wapforum.org/DTD/wml_1.1.xml">

<wml>

<card id="moe">
    <!-- If the user presses Accept, display the Larry card -->
    <do type="accept" label="Larry">
        <go href="#larry"/>
    </do>
    <p>
        Moe Howard<br/>
        Why I oughta...
```

Listing 53.3 Continued

```
    </p>
</card>

<card id="larry">
    <!-- If the user presses Accept, display the Curly card -->
    <do type="accept" label="Curly">
        <go href="#curly"/>
    </do>

    <p>
        Larry Fine<br/>
        Ow! Ow! Ow!
    </p>
</card>

<card id="curly">
    <!-- If the user presses Accept, display the Moe card -->
    <do type="accept" label="Moe">
        <go href="#moe"/>
    </do>
    <p>
        Curly Howard<br/>
        Woob woob woob woob<br/>
        Nyuk nyuk nyuk
    </p>
</card >
</wml>
```

Note

The `Accept` key is usually directly below the display. On some phones (and simulators) it's on the right, and on others it's on the left. The phone usually gives you a clue by placing the label string on the side where the `Accept` key is.

Remember, too, that not all phones have a `Back` key. You need to make sure that the user can navigate around from whatever card they are on. For example, in the Hyperlinks example, you can't get back from any of the specific cards unless you have a back key. Figure 53.8 shows the Curly card running in the Nokia phone simulator. There's no way out!

Figure 53.8
Watch your navigation! Don't leave any dead-ends for people with no back button.

Creating Input Forms

Although WML doesn't have a `<form>` tag like HTML, you can still create input forms and process them as if they were HTML forms. The `<input>` tag creates an input field much like its HTML equivalent. When you create an input field, you must give the field a name, but all other attributes of the tag are optional. You can specify `size` and `maxlength` just like in HTML. The `type` attribute can be `text` or `password`, with `text` being the default. One of the interesting options is that you can specify a format.

The format is a list of characters indicating what kinds of values can be entered at each position in the field. The format characters are `A`, `a`, `M`, `m`, `N`, `X`, and `x`:

- `A` permits any uppercase character except a number.
- `a` allows any lowercase character except a number.
- `M` allows any character (including symbols and numbers) and defaults the first character to uppercase.
- `m` allows any character and defaults the first character to lowercase.
- `N` allows only numbers.
- `X` allows any uppercase characters, plus any symbols or numbers.
- `x` allows any lowercase characters plus any symbols or numbers.

Normally, a format character represents a single position in the field. For example, if you specify a format of `NANA`, you require the first and third characters to be numbers and the second and fourth to be letters.

If you put an asterisk before a character, you allow any number of those characters. For example, if you want a format that allows a single letter followed by any number of digits, use `A*N`. If you want a format that allows any character but requires at least one, use `M*M`. Remember, the `*` can represent 0 characters.

Tip

When creating format strings for an input field, remember that the * is associated with the character to its right, not its left. In most other wildcard formats, the * is associated with the character to its left.

You can also use a specific count instead of the *. For example, if you want to require exactly four letters, you could use either `AAAA` as a format or `4A`.

Note

The * and the count format options can only be applied to the last format character. In other words, you can't do something like `A*AN`.

The following `<input>` tag allows only letters and requires at least two letters:

```
<input name="atleasttwo" format="AA*A">
```

You can also insert fixed characters in the format text by preceding that character with a `\`. For example, a field that allows you to enter a Social Security number looks like this:

```
<input name="ssn" format="NNN\-NN\-NNNN">
```

You can also create select lists using the `<select>` and `<option>` tags like you do in HTML. Here is a select list that allows you to pick a color:

```
<select name="color">
    <option value="r">Red</option>
    <option value="g">Green</option>
    <option value="b">Blue</option>
</select>
```

PROCESSING FORM INPUT

One of the unique things about WML is that it makes the values of input and select fields available within the deck. You can reference the value of a field by putting a $ in front of the field name. Listing 53.4 shows a single-card deck with a text-input field and a select list. In between the input field and the select list, it prints out the value from the input field.

LISTING 53.4 SOURCE CODE FOR `Input.jsp`

```
<%@ page language="java" contentType="text/vnd.wap.wml" %>
<?xml version="1.0"?>
<!DOCTYPE wml PUBLIC "-//WAPFORUM//DTD WML 1.1//EN"
    "http://www.wapforum.org/DTD/wml_1.1.xml">

<wml>
```

```
<card id="fieldfun">
<p>Type something:
    <input name="ssn" format="NNN\-NN\-NNNN"/>
    $ssn
    <select name="colors">
        <option value="r">Red</option>
        <option value="g">Green</option>
        <option value="b">Blue</option>
    </select>
</p>
</card>
</wml>
```

The $ssn symbol right before the <select> tag inserts the value from the text field into the output from the card. In the Phone.com simulator, it displays the value right above the select field, as shown in Figure 53.9.

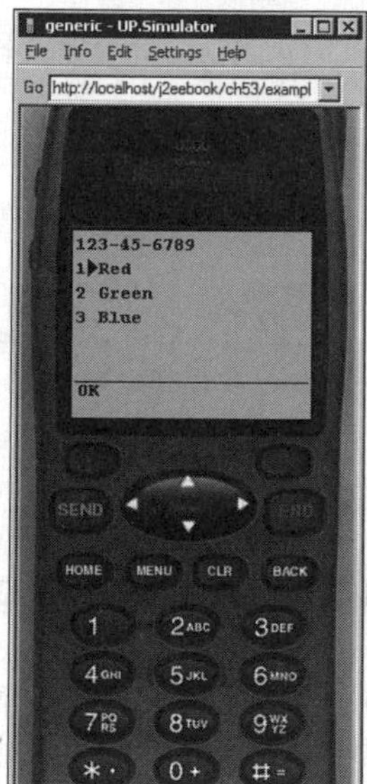

Figure 53.9
You can display input values in other parts of the deck.

Note

Notice that the phone image in the Phone.com simulator is different than the one you saw before. The Phone.com simulator comes with different configurations so you can see what a page would look like in several different phones.

To post a form to a Web server, use the <do> tag to define an action for a keypress and a <go> tag to define the action to be taken. Within the <go> tag, you use <postfield> tags to specify the values you want to send. Listing 53.5 shows how you would post the values from `Input.jsp` back to a Web page called `HandleInput.jsp`.

LISTING 53.5 SOURCE CODE FOR Input2.jsp

```
<%@ page language="java" contentType="text/vnd.wap.wml" %>
<?xml version="1.0"?>
<!DOCTYPE wml PUBLIC "-//WAPFORUM//DTD WML 1.1//EN"
    "http://www.wapforum.org/DTD/wml_1.1.xml">

<wml>

<card id="fieldfun">
<do type="accept">
    <go href="HandleInput.jsp" method="post">
       <postfield name="ssn" value="$(ssn)"/>
       <postfield name="colors" value="$(colors)"/>
    </go>
</do>

<p>Type something:
    <input name="ssn" format="NNN\-NN\-NNNN"/>
    $ssn
    <select name="colors">
        <option value="r">Red</option>
        <option value="g">Green</option>
        <option value="b">Blue</option>
    </select>
</p>
</card>
</wml>
```

The form input is delivered to your servlet or JSP exactly the same way it is when it comes from a browser.

DETECTING WIRELESS CLIENTS IN A JSP OR SERVLET

You can write a JSP or servlet that services requests from wireless phones and Web browsers at the same time, especially when you are handling form input. When you send a response back, of course, you want to know whether you should send HTML or WML. When the browser or the phone makes a request, it passes the Web server a list of the kinds of content it will accept. You can retrieve the list by making the following method call:

```
String accept = request.getHeader("Accept");
```

For a wireless client, you should see `text/vnd.wap.wml` somewhere in the accept string. You can test for it this way:

```
if (accept.indexOf("text/vnd.wap.wml") >= 0)
{
    // handle a wireless client
}
else
{
    // handle a regular Web client
}
```

A Wireless Score Entry and Reporting System

As an avid Scrabble player, I go to several tournaments a year. Scrabble is not exactly a spectator sport, so the only way my family knows how I'm doing is when I call. Wouldn't it be nice to enter the results using a wireless phone and post them on a Web page for all to see? That sounds like a good application for JSP and servlets!

The winner of a Scrabble tournament is the person with the most wins. In case of a tie, the winner is the one whose cumulative win-loss spread is the highest. In other words, you take the total number of points you won by in all your games and subtract the total number of points you lost by and that's the cumulative spread. Winning 500 to 400 is the same as winning 350 to 250. You get a win and add 100 points to your cumulative spread.

The five core elements you need to represent a result from a Scrabble tournament game are

- The round the game was played in
- The player's name
- The player's score
- The opponent's name
- The opponent's score

You can compute a won-lost record and a cumulative spread from the results so there's no need to store them. You can represent these items in a database with a SQL table like this:

```
create table scores
    ( round int not null,
      player varchar(30) not null,
      opponent varchar(30) not null,
      player_score int not null,
      opponent_score int not null,
      primary key (round, player) );
```

Note

This application makes the assumption that you are tracking the performance of a single player, thus the "player" column in the table is the player you are tracking. For a more general application, you would need to do a little more work.

Listing 53.6 shows a database object that represents a score in the database.

Listing 53.6 Source Code for `Score.java`

```
package usingj2ee.scores;

import usingj2ee.DatabaseObject;
import java.sql.*;
import java.io.*;
import java.util.*;
```

LISTING 53.6 CONTINUED

```
/** A class to contain scores */
public class Score extends DatabaseObject
    implements java.io.Serializable
{
    public int round;
    public String player;
    public String opponent;
    public int playerScore;
    public int opponentScore;

    public Score()
    {
    }

    public Score(ResultSet results)
        throws SQLException
    {
        round = results.getInt("round");
        player = results.getString("player");
        opponent = results.getString("opponent");
        playerScore = results.getInt("player_score");
        opponentScore = results.getInt("opponent_score");
    }

    public int getRound() { return round; }
    public void setRound(int aRound) { round = aRound; }

    public String getPlayer() { return player; }
    public void setPlayer(String aPlayer) { player = aPlayer; }

    public String getOpponent() { return opponent; }
    public void setOpponent(String aOpponent)
        { opponent = aOpponent; }

    public int getPlayerScore() { return playerScore; }
    public void setPlayerScore(int aPlayerScore)
        { playerScore = aPlayerScore; }

    public int getOpponentScore() { return opponentScore; }
    public void setOpponentScore(int aOpponentScore)
        { opponentScore = aOpponentScore; }

/** Returns the name of the table containing scores */
    public String getTableName() { return "scores"; }

/** Returns a list of the table fields this class uses */
    public String getFieldList()
    {
        return "round,player,opponent,player_score,opponent_score";
    }

/** Creates a new instance of this object from a database row */
    public DatabaseObject createInstance(ResultSet results)
        throws SQLException
    {
```

```
        return new Score(results);
    }

/** Returns the SQL statement used to insert this object into
 *  the database */
    public String getInsertStatement()
    {
        return "insert into scores "+
            "(round,player,opponent,player_score,opponent_score) "+
            " values (?,?,?,?,?)";
    }

/** Populates an insert statement with this object's data */
    public void prepareInsertStatement(PreparedStatement s)
        throws SQLException
    {
        s.setInt(1, round);
        s.setString(2, player);
        s.setString(3, opponent);
        s.setInt(4, playerScore);
        s.setInt(5, opponentScore);
    }

/** Returns the SQL statement used to update this object in
 *  the database */
    public String getUpdateStatement()
    {
        return "update scores set "+
            "opponent=?,player_score=?,opponent_score=? "+
            " where round=? and player=?";
    }

/** Populates an update statement with this object's data */
    public void prepareUpdateStatement(PreparedStatement s)
        throws SQLException
    {
        s.setString(1, opponent);
        s.setInt(2, playerScore);
        s.setInt(3, opponentScore);
        s.setInt(4, round);
        s.setString(5, player);
    }

/** Returns the SQL statement used to delete this object from
 *  the database */
    public String getDeleteStatement()
    {
        return "delete from scores where round=? and player=?";
    }

/** Populates a delete statement with this object's data */
    public void prepareDeleteStatement(PreparedStatement s)
        throws SQLException
    {
        s.setInt(1, round);
        s.setString(2, player);
    }
}
```

When you break it down, there are three main functions this application needs to perform:

- Insert new scores into the database
- Compute the player's won-lost record and cumulative point spread
- List the results from each game

Inserting a score in the database should work the same way whether the data was entered from a browser or from a phone. Computing the player's record and fetching the scores are also display-independent tasks. Using the notion of handling display tasks in JSPs and nondisplay tasks in servlets, it makes sense to use servlets to perform the major system tasks and then use JSPs to display the results.

Listing 53.7 shows the servlet that receives a score and inserts it into the database.

LISTING 53.7 SOURCE CODE FOR RegisterScoreServlet.java

```
package usingj2ee.scores;

import javax.servlet.*;
import javax.servlet.http.*;
import java.io.*;
import java.sql.*;

import usingj2ee.*;

public class RegisterScoreServlet extends HttpServlet
{
    public void service(HttpServletRequest request,
        HttpServletResponse response)
        throws IOException, ServletException
    {
        Connection conn = null;
        IConnectionPool pool = null;

        try
        {
// Require the user to enter a secret numeric code just to keep
// other people from entering fake scores
            String passCode = request.getParameter("passcode");

            if (!passCode.equals("12345")) // same code as my luggage!
            {
                throw new RuntimeException("Invalid passcode!");
            }

// Get a reference to the connection pool
            pool = ScoreSupport.getConnectionPool(getServletContext());

// Allocate a database connection
            conn = pool.getConnection();

// Create a new score object and populate its fields
            Score score = new Score();
            score.round = Integer.parseInt(
```

```
                request.getParameter("round"));
            score.player = request.getParameter("player");
            score.playerScore = Integer.parseInt(
                request.getParameter("score"));
            score.opponent = request.getParameter("opponent");
            score.opponentScore = Integer.parseInt(
                request.getParameter("opponentscore"));

// Insert the score into the database
            score.insert(conn);

// Assume that the client is using HTML
            String destPage = "/ScoreMenuHTML.jsp";

// If the client is using WML, send them to a different page
            if (ScoreSupport.isWML(request))
            {
                destPage = "/ScoreMenuWML.jsp";
            }

            getServletContext().getRequestDispatcher(destPage).forward(
                request, response);
        }
        catch (Exception exc)
        {
            String errorPage = "/ErrorHTML.jsp";

            if (ScoreSupport.isWML(request))
            {
                errorPage = "/ErrorWML.jsp";
            }

            request.setAttribute("exception", exc);

            exc.printStackTrace();

            getServletContext().getRequestDispatcher(errorPage).forward(
                request, response);
        }
        finally
        {
            if (conn != null)
            {
                try
                {
                    pool.releaseConnection(conn);
                } catch (Exception ignore) {}
            }
        }
    }
}
```


All the core servlets need to use the database pool, and there is no way to know which one will be called first. Each servlet needs to determine whether the pool has been created, and if not, create it. Rather than duplicate the code, you just put it into a utility class. Likewise, each servlet needs to figure out whether the client supports HTML or WML. Again, the utility class is the way to go.

Listing 53.8 shows the ScoreSupport utility class that performs some commonly used functions.

LISTING 53.8 SOURCE CODE FOR ScoreSupport.java

```
package usingj2ee.scores;

import javax.servlet.*;
import javax.servlet.http.*;
import java.sql.*;
import usingj2ee.*;

public class ScoreSupport
{
    public static IConnectionPool getConnectionPool(
        ServletContext application)
        throws SQLException
    {
        IConnectionPool pool =
            (IConnectionPool) application.getAttribute(
                "ScoresConnectionPool");

        if (pool == null)
        {
            synchronized (application)
            {
                pool = (IConnectionPool) application.getAttribute(
                        "ScoresConnectionPool");
                if (pool == null)
                {
                    try
                    {
                        Class.forName("org.gjt.mm.mysql.Driver").
                            newInstance();
                    }
                    catch (Exception exc)
                    {
                        application.log("Error loading JDBC driver", exc);
                    }

                    pool = new ConnectionPool(
                        "jdbc:mysql://localhost/usingj2ee", "", "", 3);

                    application.setAttribute("ScoresConnectionPool",
                        pool);
                }
            }
        }

        return pool;
    }

    public static boolean isWML(HttpServletRequest request)
    {
        String accept = request.getHeader("Accept");
        if (accept == null) return false;

        if (accept.indexOf("text/vnd.wap.wml") >= 0)
        {
```

```
            return true;
        }

        return false;
    }
}
```

The score-input form for a Web browser is rather mundane and you could certainly write one in a matter of minutes. The input form for a wireless phone is much more interesting.

You really only need six input fields for entering a score and sending it to `RegisterScoreServlet`. The input form isn't too different from `Input2.jsp`, just a few more fields. Listing 53.9 shows the WML version of the score input form.

LISTING 53.9 SOURCE CODE FOR `RegisterScoreWML.jsp`

```
<%@ page language="java" contentType="text/vnd.wap.wml" %>

<?xml version="1.0"?>
<!DOCTYPE wml PUBLIC "-//WAPFORUM//DTD WML 1.1//EN"
    "http://www.wapforum.org/DTD/wml_1.1.xml">

<wml>
<card id="regscore">
<do type="accept">
    <go href="RegisterScoreServlet"
        method="post">
        <postfield name="passcode" value="$(passcode)"/>
        <postfield name="round" value="$(round)"/>
        <postfield name="player" value="$(player)"/>
        <postfield name="score" value="$(score)"/>
        <postfield name="opponent" value="$(opponent)"/>
        <postfield name="opponentscore" value="$(opponentscore)"/>
    </go>
</do>
<p>Passcode:
<input type="text" name="passcode" maxlength="6" format="N*N"/>
</p>
<p>Round:
<input type="text" name="round" maxlength="2" format="N*N"/>
</p>
<p>Player:
<input type="text" name="player" maxlength="20" format="*m" value="Mark"/>
</p>
<p>Score:
<input type="text" name="score" maxlength="4" format="N*N"/>
</p>
<p>Opponent:
<input type="text" name="opponent" maxlength="20" format="*m"/>
</p>
<p>Opp. Score:
<input type="text" name="opponentscore" maxlength="4" format="N*N"/>
</p>
</card>
</wml>
```

Now, you have everything you need to enter a score. The next thing you need to do is display the won-lost record. Because the database object takes much of the pain out of database queries, the `ShowScoresServlet` class doesn't need to do much work.

Listing 53.10 shows the `ShowScoresServlet` class, which fetches the list of scores for all players or a particular player and calls the appropriate display JSP.

LISTING 53.10 SOURCE CODE FOR `ShowScoresServlet.java`

```
package usingj2ee.scores;

import javax.servlet.*;
import javax.servlet.http.*;
import java.io.*;
import java.sql.*;
import java.util.*;

import usingj2ee.*;

public class ShowScoresServlet extends HttpServlet
{
    public void service(HttpServletRequest request,
        HttpServletResponse response)
        throws IOException, ServletException
    {
        Connection conn = null;
        IConnectionPool pool = null;

// See if there is a specific player whose scores should be shown
        String whichPlayer = request.getParameter("player");

        try
        {
            pool = ScoreSupport.getConnectionPool(getServletContext());

            conn = pool.getConnection();

            Score query = new Score();

// By default, use a dummy where clause that would retrieve all scores
            String whereClause = "round > 0";

// If the query should search for a specific player, change the where clause
            if (whichPlayer != null)
            {
                whereClause = "player = '"+whichPlayer+"'";
            }

// Do the query and add an "order by" clause to make display easier
            Vector v = query.getAll(conn,
                whereClause + " order by round, player");

// Put the list in the request so the JSP can get at it
            request.setAttribute("scoreList", v);

            String destPage = "/ShowScoresHTML.jsp";
```

```
                if (ScoreSupport.isWML(request))
                {
                    destPage = "/ShowScoresWML.jsp";
                }

                getServletContext().getRequestDispatcher(destPage).forward(
                    request, response);
            }
            catch (Exception exc)
            {
                String errorPage = "/ErrorHTML.jsp";

                if (ScoreSupport.isWML(request))
                {
                    errorPage = "/ErrorWML.jsp";
                }

                request.setAttribute("exception", exc);

                exc.printStackTrace();

                getServletContext().getRequestDispatcher(errorPage).forward(
                    request, response);
            }
            finally
            {
                if (conn != null)
                {
                    try
                    {
                        pool.releaseConnection(conn);
                    } catch (Exception ignore) {}
                }
            }
        }
}
```


Although there are many ways to arrange the output, it makes sense to put the results from a particular round into a card. The deck of cards from ShowScoresWML would represent all the scores from the tournament. Listing 53.11 shows the ShowScoresWML Java Server Page that displays the list of scores.

Listing 53.11 Source Code for ShowScoresWML.jsp

```
<%@ page language="java" contentType="text/vnd.wap.wml" %>
<%@ page import="java.net.*,java.util.*,usingj2ee.scores.*" %>

<?xml version="1.0"?>
<!DOCTYPE wml PUBLIC "-//WAPFORUM//DTD WML 1.1//EN"
    "http://www.wapforum.org/DTD/wml_1.1.xml">

<wml>
<%
    Vector scoreList = (Vector) request.getAttribute("scoreList");
```

LISTING 53.11 CONTINUED

```
    int currRound = 0;
    int numElements = scoreList.size();
    int maxRound = 0;

// Figure out which round is the last one
    for (int i=0; i < numElements; i++)
    {
        Score s = (Score) scoreList.elementAt(i);

        if (s.round > maxRound) maxRound = s.round;
    }

    for (int i=0; i < numElements; i++)
    {
        Score s = (Score) scoreList.elementAt(i);

// If this score starts a new round, start a new card
        if (s.round != currRound)
        {
            if (currRound != 0) out.println("</card>");
            out.println("<card id=\"round"+s.round+"\">");
            currRound = s.round;
        }

// By default, the next link goes back to the main menu
        String dest="Scores.jsp";

// If there are more rounds to go, make the next link go to the next round
        if (s.round < maxRound)
        {
            dest="#round"+(s.round+1);
        }
%>
<do type="accept" label="Next">
    <go href="<%=dest%>"/>
</do>
<p>
Round: <%= s.round %><br/>
<%= s.player %>: <%= s.playerScore %>
    (<%= s.playerScore > s.opponentScore ? "W" : "L"%>)<br/>
<%= s.opponent %>: <%= s.opponentScore %>
    (<%= s.opponentScore > s.playerScore ? "W" : "L"%>)<br/>
Spread: <%= s.playerScore - s.opponentScore %>

</p>
<%
    }
%>
</card>
</wml>
```

Figure 53.10 shows a card generated by the `ShowScoresWML` JSP.

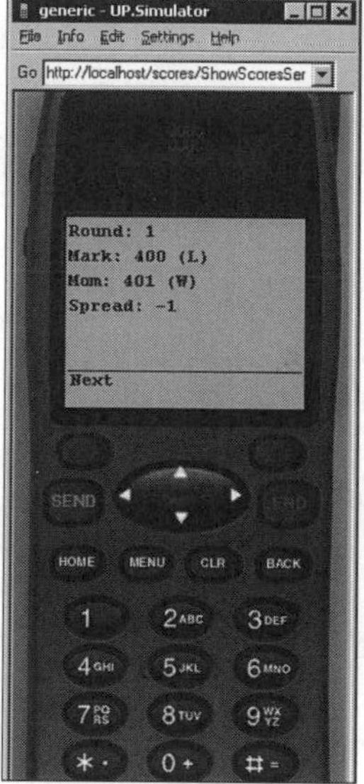

Figure 53.10 Cards usually display a logical grouping of your data.

The ShowScoresServlet has the capability to filter on a particular player. If you do enter scores for all the players in the tournament, you would have a tough time scanning through them all on your phone. From a Web browser, it's easy to see the entire list. To reduce the clutter on a phone, this application lets you list the records for each player, and then examine the list of scores for that player. If you're on a Web browser, you can get the complete list of scores directly.

Listing 53.11 shows the final of the three core servlets: ShowRecordsServlet. Like ShowScoresServlet, it fetches data and then calls an appropriate JSP to render the output.

Listing 53.11 Source Code for ShowRecordsServlet.java

```
package usingj2ee.scores;

import javax.servlet.*;
import javax.servlet.http.*;
import java.io.*;
import java.sql.*;
import java.util.*;

import usingj2ee.*;

public class ShowRecordsServlet extends HttpServlet
{
    public void service(HttpServletRequest request,
        HttpServletResponse response)
        throws IOException, ServletException
    {
        Connection conn = null;
        IConnectionPool pool = null;
```

Listing 53.11 Continued

```
        try
        {
            pool = ScoreSupport.getConnectionPool(getServletContext());

            conn = pool.getConnection();

            Score query = new Score();

// Get all the scores
            Vector v = query.getAll(conn);

// Create a table to keep track of each player
            Hashtable playerRecords = new Hashtable();

            Enumeration e = v.elements();

            while (e.hasMoreElements())
            {
                Score s = (Score) e.nextElement();

// Get the player's wins, losses, and cumulative spread
                int[] playerRecord = (int[]) playerRecords.get(
                    s.player);

// If this player isn't in the table, create a blank entry
                if (playerRecord == null)
                {
                    playerRecord = new int[] { 0, 0, 0 };
                    playerRecords.put(s.player, playerRecord);
                }

// If the player won this game, increment the wins
                if (s.playerScore > s.opponentScore)
                {
                    playerRecord[0]++;
                }
                else
                {
// Otherwise, increment the losses (a bug here: a tie shows up as a loss)
                    playerRecord[1]++;
                }
// Update the cumulative spread
                playerRecord[2] += (s.playerScore - s.opponentScore);
            }

// Put the table in the request so the JSP can get at it
            request.setAttribute("recordTable", playerRecords);

            String destPage = "/ShowRecordsHTML.jsp";

            if (ScoreSupport.isWML(request))
            {
                destPage = "/ShowRecordsWML.jsp";
            }
```

```
            getServletContext().getRequestDispatcher(destPage).forward(
                request, response);
        }
        catch (Exception exc)
        {
            String errorPage = "/ErrorHTML.jsp";

            if (ScoreSupport.isWML(request))
            {
                errorPage = "/ErrorWML.jsp";
            }

            request.setAttribute("exception", exc);

            exc.printStackTrace();

            getServletContext().getRequestDispatcher(errorPage).forward(
                request, response);
        }
        finally
        {
            if (conn != null)
            {
                try
                {
                    pool.releaseConnection(conn);
                } catch (Exception ignore) {}
            }
        }
    }
}
```


Listing 53.12 shows the Java Server Page that shows the various player records. Each player is displayed on a separate card and each card contains a link to the `ShowScoresServlet` to show that player's scores.

Listing 53.12 Source Code for `ShowRecordsWML.jsp`

```
<%@ page language="java" contentType="text/vnd.wap.wml" %>
<%@ page import="java.net.*,java.util.*,usingj2ee.scores.*" %>

<?xml version="1.0"?>
<!DOCTYPE wml PUBLIC "-//WAPFORUM//DTD WML 1.1//EN"
    "http://www.wapforum.org/DTD/wml_1.1.xml">

<wml>
<%
    Hashtable recordTable = (Hashtable) request.getAttribute(
        "recordTable");

    Enumeration keys = recordTable.keys();

    int playerNumber = 0;
```

Listing 53.12 Continued

```
    while (keys.hasMoreElements())
    {
        String playerName = (String) keys.nextElement();

        int[] playerRecord = (int[]) recordTable.get(playerName);

        playerNumber++;
%>
<card id="ply<%=playerNumber%>">
<p><%=playerName%><br/>
W: <%=playerRecord[0]%><br/>
L: <%=playerRecord[1]%><br/>
Cume: <%=playerRecord[2]%><br/>
<a href="ShowScoresServlet?player=<%=URLEncoder.encode(playerName)%>"
    title="Scores">Scores</a>
</p>
</card>
<%
    }
%>
</wml>
```

Figure 53.11 shows a card generated by `ShowRecordsWML.jsp`.

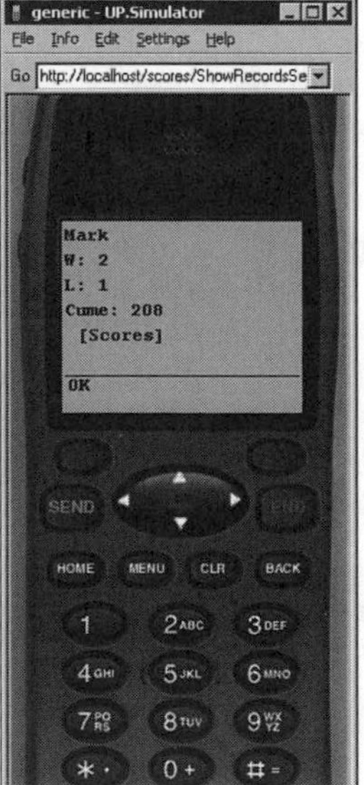

Figure 53.11
A card can link to a JSP or servlet to retrieve additional data.

Last, but not least, Listing 53.13 shows the main menu page for the WML version of the application.

Listing 53.13 Source Code for ScoreMenuWML.jsp

```
<%@ page language="java" contentType="text/vnd.wap.wml" %>

<?xml version="1.0"?>
<!DOCTYPE wml PUBLIC "-//WAPFORUM//DTD WML 1.1//EN"
    "http://www.wapforum.org/DTD/wml_1.1.xml">

<wml>
<card id="scoremenu">
<p>
<a href="ShowRecordsServlet" title="Show Records">Show Records</a><br/>
<a href="RegisterScoreWML.jsp" title="Enter Score">Enter Score</a>
</p>
</card>
</wml>
```

Figure 53.12 shows the main menu running in a simulator.

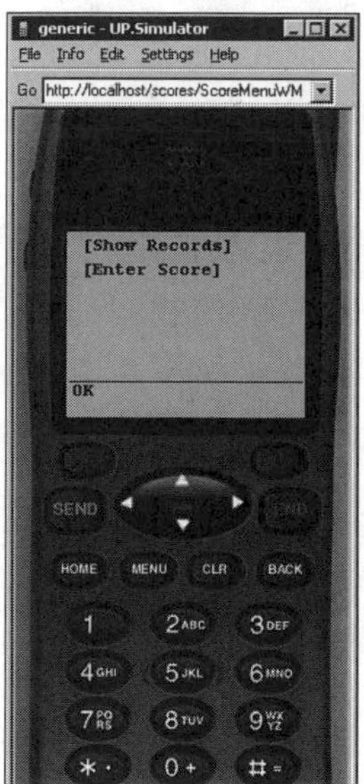

Figure 53.12 The main menu for the Scores application appears in the simulator.

Deploying the Scores Application

The Scores application strives to be a reasonably well structured servlet/JSP application. It delegates display functions to Java Server Pages and performs nondisplay work in servlets. The final piece to make the application complete is a Web Archive (WAR) file that contains all the pieces of the application.

The WAR file contains all the JSPs at the root level, a WEB-INF directory containing the web.xml deployment descriptor, and a directory containing all the compiled Java classes. To create the WAR file, assuming you have all the JSP and Java files in your current directory, you would enter the following two commands:

```
javac -d WEB-INF\classes *.java
jar cvf scores.war *.jsp WEB-INF
```

You should also make sure that the `web.xml` file is in the `WEB-INF` directory before you create the WAR file.

Listing 53.14 shows the `web.xml` file for the Scores application.

LISTING 53.14 SOURCE CODE FOR web.xml

```
<web-app>
    <display-name>Scores Application</display-name>
    <description>An application for entering and displaying scores</description>
    <servlet>
        <servlet-name>RegisterScoreServlet</servlet-name>
        <servlet-class>usingj2ee.scores.RegisterScoreServlet</servlet-class>
    </servlet>
    <servlet>
        <servlet-name>ShowScoresServlet</servlet-name>
        <servlet-class>usingj2ee.scores.ShowScoresServlet</servlet-class>
    </servlet>
    <servlet>
        <servlet-name>ShowRecordsServlet</servlet-name>
        <servlet-class>usingj2ee.scores.ShowRecordsServlet</servlet-class>
    </servlet>
    <servlet-mapping>
        <servlet-name>RegisterScoreServlet</servlet-name>
        <url-pattern>/RegisterScoreServlet</url-pattern>
    </servlet-mapping>
    <servlet-mapping>
        <servlet-name>ShowScoresServlet</servlet-name>
        <url-pattern>/ShowScoresServlet</url-pattern>
    </servlet-mapping>
    <servlet-mapping>
        <servlet-name>ShowRecordsServlet</servlet-name>
        <url-pattern>/ShowRecordsServlet</url-pattern>
    </servlet-mapping>
    <welcome-file-list>
        <welcome-file>Scores.jsp</welcome-file>
    </welcome-file-list>
</web-app>
```

After the WAR file is created, you can deploy it in your Web server using whatever management tools the Web server provides.

After you have installed the WAR file, you can access the `Scores.jsp` file to see the main menu. From the main menu, you can enter scores and view other scores. Because the `Scores.jsp` file detects both phones and browsers, you use the same URL whether you're using a phone or a browser.

TROUBLESHOOTING

RUNNING WITH THE SIMULATOR

Why does the simulator report an error when reading my WML files?

There are four major possibilities for this. First, your JSP or servlet may be reporting an error. You can test this by pointing your browser to the same URL you are trying to access from the phone simulator. If the browser doesn't report an error, you're probably okay there. The next possibility is that you forgot to set the content type to "text/vnd.wap.wml". The third possibility is that your WML contains an error. The phone.com simulator has a separate window that shows any error messages that occur as a result of parsing the WML output. Likewise, the Nokia simulator shows you any parsing errors in a source-code window. The last possibility is that the WML file is too large. Some phones and simulators may only accept about 1,500 bytes of data.

RUNNING WITH A REAL PHONE

Why does my phone report an error when the simulator had no problem?

Unfortunately, the simulators are not 100% accurate. They often handle errors that the phones do not. Also, the simulators usually support the most recent additions to the WML specification. Because the browser is embedded into the phone's firmware, it can't be changed easily and lags behind the standard.

CHAPTER 54

Creating a Business-to-Business Application

In this chapter

WHAT DOES BUSINESS-TO-BUSINESS MEAN?

Most of the e-commerce Web sites you see on the Internet are *Business-to-Consumer* (B2C) applications—a business and a consumer take part in a transaction. A typical B2C application presents a consumer with a variety of products and allows the consumer to make a purchase. *Business-to-Business* (B2B) applications take place between two businesses and are often invisible to Web users.

B2C applications are human-oriented—they assume that the end user is a person, perhaps using a Web browser. A B2B application, on the other hand, usually expects to talk to another application. A typical B2C application might need to "sell" the product to a consumer; it might need to present products in various formats with different options that might convince the consumer to make a purchase. Businesses that participate in a B2B transaction usually know what products they need ahead of time. For example, a manufacturing system might use a B2B application to order parts when the current inventory drops below a certain level.

B2B applications tend to have fewer users than B2C applications. After all, there are far more consumers than there are businesses. Businesses also tend to have better Internet access than typical consumers, so B2B applications might occasionally require high-speed connections or even private connections between participants. As a general rule, however, you should try to minimize these requirements to allow more businesses to interact with your application.

B2B applications can require more initial setup. Where a B2C application must be able to accept new users at any time, a B2B application might require more setup and might require new users to install additional software. For example, when two banks need to exchange data, they might use encryption and digital certificates to verify each other's identities. To insure security, the banks might exchange and store each other's certificates in addition to using a third-party certificate authority.

USING DIFFERENT METHODS OF COMMUNICATION

B2B applications generally have greater flexibility in choosing a communication method. Although most B2C applications must assume that the user only has a Web browser, a B2B application might require its users to support CORBA, RMI, or other protocols.

Your choice of protocol for a B2B application depends on your potential users. Each protocol has distinct advantages and disadvantages.

RMI

From a Java standpoint, RMI is one of the easiest communication mechanisms. You define a remote interface and then create stubs and skeletons. For B2B applications, however, you must consider some of RMI's limitations. First and foremost, RMI is a Java-only solution. If RMI is the only way to access the application, you can't support customers that don't use Java.

Second, RMI is not firewall-friendly. Although there are some ways to use RMI with a firewall (including RMI over HTTP), it's not always easy to set up. You should also strongly consider using SSL with RMI to provide additional security.

RMI is useful when your application requires a lot of two-way communications and you don't need to support other programming languages.

CORBA

If you need to allow non-Java clients to access your application, you should consider using CORBA. Although CORBA allows your customers to write client applications in different languages, the clients are still restricted to languages that CORBA supports. As with RMI, you still have firewall issues and you should also use SSL to secure the application.

You can also use RMI-IIOP as a hybrid solution—you allow clients to access your application via CORBA, but you write the application as an RMI application. You don't need to write any IDL this way, but you still get the cross-language support.

CUSTOM SOCKETS

Some B2B applications use a custom socket protocol for communications. A custom socket protocol is usually your last choice for a solution because it requires so much extra work. You usually need to supply a communication library to your customers; otherwise, your customers must write software to use your custom protocol.

HTTP

HTTP is the most customer-friendly solution for your B2B application. Customers can use just about any language to access your application, and because most companies use HTTP anyway, you usually don't encounter any firewall issues.

If you use HTTP, remember that the common session mechanism—cookies—might not work well for custom clients. Cookies are a function of the browser. When you write a custom client application, even in Java, the HTTP libraries don't understand cookies. You might not be able to use the `HttpSession` class as easily in a B2B application.

DATA FORMATTING ISSUES

If you use HTTP or a custom socket protocol, you must also consider how to format data. B2B applications are one of the places where XML is the most useful. You can use a Document Type Definition (DTD) to specify the format of the XML documents you will accept. As XML Schema becomes more popular, you will be able to provide a more accurate description of your data format.

When you use XML for B2B data exchange, you also gain the ability to use XSL to reformat the data for various customers. Depending on your application (and your customers) you might need to format data different ways for different customers. To minimize the amount of custom work you need to do, you can create different XSL transformations for different customers. When you send data to a particular customer, you retrieve the XSL transformation for that customer and apply it to the data. That way, you can add new transformations without changing your application.

CREATING A B2B APPLICATION

Creating a B2B application isn't very different from creating a B2C application—the presentation layer is the only real difference. The presentation layer for a B2B application focuses on the quick, simple exchange of data. Because the two participants in a B2B transaction are usually programs, the presentation layer can assume that the user is an expert.

Digital signatures become very useful in B2B applications. You can use them to verify the identity of a client. In fact, you can often use the signature as the authentication mechanism for a user, eliminating the standard username/password combination. You can use digital signatures and certificates in several ways. The easiest way, from a programming standpoint, is to use SSL with client authentication. In this scenario, SSL requires the client to provide a certificate (usually the server is the only participant required to have a certificate). The server can then examine the client's certificate to identify the client.

The advantage of client authentication is that you don't need to sign the actual data; you just pass data over the SSL connection as you normally would. In a servlet, you can access the certificate by examining the `javax.servlet.request.X509Certificate` attribute in the request. Unfortunately, not all servlet engines support client certificates. Even when you find a servlet engine that does support client certificates and can pass you the certificate in an attribute, you might still have problems if you run the servlet engine underneath a standard Web server, such as Netscape or Apache. The Web server might not pass the certificate information to the servlet.

You can also digitally sign the data manually and pass the data and the signature as part of an HTTP request. Although this method is a little more cumbersome, you can be sure that it will work with any servlet engine and any Web server.

Listing 54.1 shows a servlet that reads a digitally signed XML request and then creates a new order in the database using the XML data. Both the servlet and its client program use JOX to convert a Java object into XML and read it back out again. The servlet expects the digital signature to be in Base64 format. When you pass binary data to a servlet using form variables, you must encode the data into a text-only form. Base64 is a reasonably fast and efficient way to perform the conversion.

The servlet must perform a few initialization steps before it is ready to accept requests. First, it locates the `Home` interfaces for the various EJBs it uses. Although this is an efficient way to locate the `Home` interfaces, you might run into problems if the EJB server crashes and restarts. The `Home` interface references might no longer be valid. When this happens, you must restart the servlet engine. You have other alternatives, of course. You could search for the `Home` interfaces when you handle a request, but that can be pretty inefficient. You can also add code to detect when the `Home` interface is no longer valid and then reestablish the connection, but that can be a cumbersome task.

The servlet also locates the Java key store during initialization. For some installations, you may need to hard-code the key store location, or at least make it a configuration parameter. Because the servlet uses the `user.home` environment variable to locate the key store, you must run the servlet engine using the user ID that owns the key store. For some servlet engines that plug directly into the Web server, this might not be possible.

When processing an incoming order, the servlet first decodes the data and then verifies the digital signature of the data. Next, it uses entity beans to insert the order information into the database. Some developers argue that you should never use entity beans directly—you should create a session bean to perform these tasks. Because this is such a simple operation, however, using a session bean doesn't really buy you anything.

LISTING 54.1 SOURCE CODE FOR `SubmitOrderServlet.java`

```
package usingj2ee.b2b;

import javax.servlet.*;
import javax.servlet.http.*;
import java.security.*;
import java.security.cert.*;
import java.security.cert.Certificate;
import java.io.*;
import com.wutka.jox.*;
import javax.naming.*;
import javax.rmi.*;
import usingj2ee.util.*;

public class SubmitOrderServlet extends HttpServlet
{
    protected CustomerHome custHome;
    protected OrderHome orderHome;
    protected KeyStore keystore;

    public void init()
        throws ServletException
    {
        try
        {
            Context context = new InitialContext();

// Locate the various home objects
            custHome = (CustomerHome) PortableRemoteObject.narrow(
                context.lookup("CustomerHome"), CustomerHome.class);

            orderHome = (OrderHome) PortableRemoteObject.narrow(
                context.lookup("OrderHome"), OrderHome.class);

            keystore = KeyStore.getInstance("JKS");

// Hard code the location of the key store - this is better
// implemented as a servlet parameter

// Figure out where the user's key store is located
            String keystoreFilename = System.getProperty("user.home")+
                File.separator+".keystore";
```

LISTING 54.1 CONTINUED

```
// Load the key store from the key store file (hard code the password)
                keystore.load(new FileInputStream(keystoreFilename),
                    "kspass".toCharArray());

            }
            catch (Exception exc)
            {
                exc.printStackTrace();
                throw new ServletException(exc.toString());
            }
        }

        public void doPost(HttpServletRequest request,
            HttpServletResponse response)
            throws IOException, ServletException
        {
            try
            {
// Read the order from the request
                String orderString = request.getParameter("order");

// Read the signature from the request
                String signatureString = request.getParameter("signature");

// Convert the signature back from base64 to a byte array
                byte[] sigBytes = Base64.fromBase64Bytes(signatureString);

// Use JOX to convert the XML order string into an OrderView object
                JOXBeanInputStream in = new JOXBeanInputStream(
                    new ByteArrayInputStream(orderString.getBytes()));

                OrderView order = (OrderView) in.readObject(OrderView.class);

                in.close();

// Locate the customer that the order belongs to
                Customer cust = custHome.findByPrimaryKey(
                    order.getCustomerId());

// Locate the customer's certificate in the key store
                Certificate cert = keystore.getCertificate(cust.getCertificate());

                Signature signature = Signature.getInstance("MD5withRSA");

                signature.initVerify(cert);

                byte[] orderBytes = orderString.getBytes();

                signature.update(orderString.getBytes());

// Verify that the data was signed with this customer's certificate
                if (!signature.verify(sigBytes))
                {
                    sendError("Invalid Signature", response);
```

```
                return;
            }

// Place the order
            Order newOrder = orderHome.create();
            newOrder.setFromView(order);
            newOrder.setCustomer(cust);

            String confirmation = newOrder.getOrderId();

// Send back the order ID as a confirmation number
            sendOK(confirmation, response);
        }
        catch (Exception exc)
        {
            exc.printStackTrace();

            sendError("Error processing request: "+exc.toString(), response);
        }
    }

    public void sendOK(String confirmation, HttpServletResponse response)
        throws IOException
    {
        response.setContentType("text/xml");
        PrintWriter out = response.getWriter();

        out.println("<?xml version=\"1.0\"?>");
        out.println("<confirmation>"+confirmation+"</confirmation>");
    }

    public void sendError(String error, HttpServletResponse response)
        throws IOException
    {
        response.setContentType("text/xml");
        PrintWriter out = response.getWriter();

        out.println("<?xml version=\"1.0\"?>");
        out.println("<error>"+error+"</error>");
    }
}
```


Listing 54.2 shows an example client program that connects to the servlet and submits an order.

LISTING 54.2 SOURCE CODE FOR `SendOrder.java`

```
package usingj2ee.b2b;

import java.io.*;
import java.net.*;
import com.wutka.jox.*;
import java.security.*;
import java.security.cert.*;
import java.security.interfaces.*;
import java.security.cert.Certificate;
```

LISTING 54.2 CONTINUED

```
import javax.xml.parsers.*;
import org.w3c.dom.*;
import org.xml.sax.*;
import usingj2ee.util.*;

public class SendOrder
{
    public static void main(String[] args)
    {
        try
        {
// Get the URL for the ordering servlet
            String urlStr = args[0];

            String keystorePassword = System.getProperty("kspass", "kspass");
            String keyAlias = System.getProperty("key", "testkey");
            String keyPassword = System.getProperty("keypass", "testkey");

// Create a dummy order
            OrderView order = new OrderView();
            order.setCustomerId("2");
            order.setProductId("TK421");
            order.setQuantity(10);

            URL url = new URL(urlStr);

// Create a connection to the ordering servlet
            URLConnection conn = url.openConnection();

// Setting doOutput to true makes this a POST request
            conn.setDoOutput(true);
            conn.setDoInput(true);

            ByteArrayOutputStream xmlOut = new ByteArrayOutputStream();

// Use JOX to write the OrderView object out to a byte array stream
            JOXBeanOutputStream out = new JOXBeanOutputStream(xmlOut);
            out.writeObject("order", order);
            out.close();

// Convert the stream into a byte array
            byte[] xmlBytes = xmlOut.toByteArray();

            KeyStore keystore = KeyStore.getInstance("JKS");

// Figure out where the user's key store is located
            String keystoreFilename = System.getProperty("user.home")+
                File.separator+".keystore";

// Load the key store from the key store file
            keystore.load(new FileInputStream(keystoreFilename),
                keystorePassword.toCharArray());

// Locate the key with the specified alias and password
            Key signingKey = keystore.getKey(keyAlias,
                keyPassword.toCharArray());
```

```
            RSAPrivateKey pvtKey = (RSAPrivateKey) signingKey;

            Signature signer = Signature.getInstance("MD5withRSA");

            signer.initSign(pvtKey);

            signer.update(xmlBytes);

// Sign the data
            byte[] signatureBytes = signer.sign();

// Create the HTTP data string
            String requestString = "order="+
                URLEncoder.encode(new String(xmlBytes))+"&signature="+
                URLEncoder.encode(Base64.toBase64(signatureBytes));

// Make this request look like a form submission
            conn.setRequestProperty("content-type",
                "application/x-www-form-urlencoded");

            conn.setRequestProperty("content-length", ""+
                requestString.length());

// Write out the data
            OutputStream connOut = conn.getOutputStream();
            connOut.write(requestString.getBytes());
            connOut.close();


// Create an XML parser to read the response
            DocumentBuilderFactory factory =
                DocumentBuilderFactory.newInstance();

            DocumentBuilder builder = factory.newDocumentBuilder();

            Document doc = builder.parse(new InputSource(
                conn.getInputStream()));

            Element element = doc.getDocumentElement();

// Look at the document element and see if it is a confirmation or an error
            if (element.getTagName().equals("confirmation"))
            {
                String confirmationNumber = getElementString(element);

                System.out.println("Confirmation number: "+
                    confirmationNumber);
            }
            else if (element.getTagName().equals("error"))
            {
                String errorMessage = getElementString(element);

                System.out.println("Error: "+errorMessage);
            }
            else
            {
                System.out.println("Unknown tag in reply: "+
```

LISTING 54.2 CONTINUED

```
                    element.getTagName());
            }
        }
        catch (Exception exc)
        {
            exc.printStackTrace();
        }
    }

/** Searches the children of an element looking for a Text node. If
 * it finds one, it returns it.
 * @param element The element whose children will be searched
 * @return The text for the element, or null if there is none
 */
    public static String getElementString(Element element)
    {
        NodeList nodes = element.getChildNodes();

        int numNodes = nodes.getLength();

        for (int i=0; i < numNodes; i++)
        {
            Node node = nodes.item(i);

            if (node instanceof Text)
            {
                return ((Text) node).getData();
            }
        }

        return null;
    }
}
```

In many EJB applications, you might find that you need to automatically generate the primary key for an object. If you use a simple sequence number, it gets monotonous writing the same key-generation code over and over. Listing 54.3 shows a base class that you can use for implementing entity beans with automatically generated keys.

LISTING 54.3 SOURCE CODE FOR AutoGenerate.java

```
package usingj2ee.b2b;

import java.rmi.*;
import java.util.*;
import javax.ejb.*;
import java.sql.*;
import javax.sql.*;
import javax.naming.*;
import java.util.Date;

public abstract class AutoGenerate
{
```

```
/** The database connection used by this entity bean */
    private Connection conn;

    protected String dataSource;
    protected String sequenceTable;
    protected String sequenceColumn;

    public AutoGenerate(String aDataSource, String aSequenceTable,
        String aSequenceColumn)
    {
        dataSource = aDataSource;
        sequenceTable = aSequenceTable;
        sequenceColumn = aSequenceColumn;
    }

    protected Connection getConnection()
        throws SQLException, NamingException
    {
// Get a reference to the naming service
        InitialContext context = new InitialContext();

// Get the data source for the person database
        DataSource ds = (DataSource) context.lookup(
            "java:comp/env/jdbc/"+dataSource);

// Ask the data source to allocate a database connection
        return ds.getConnection();
    }

/** Uses a separate database table to generate a unique ID number for
    an order. You should perform the update before you read the value
    to make sure you don't have any locking problems.
    */
    protected String getNextId()
        throws SQLException
    {
        Connection conn = null;

        try
        {
            conn = getConnection();

// Increment the next customer ID number
            PreparedStatement ps = conn.prepareStatement(
                "update "+sequenceTable+" set "+sequenceColumn+" = "+
                    sequenceColumn+"+ 1");

            if (ps.executeUpdate() != 1)
            {
                throw new SQLException("Unable to generate "+sequenceColumn);
            }

            ps.close();

// Read the next customer ID number
            ps = conn.prepareStatement(
                "select "+sequenceColumn+" from "+sequenceTable);
```

LISTING 54.3 CONTINUED

```
            ResultSet rs = ps.executeQuery();

            if (rs.next())
            {
                return ""+rs.getInt(sequenceColumn);
            }
            else
            {
                throw new SQLException("Unable to generate "+sequenceColumn);
            }
        }
        catch (NamingException exc)
        {
            throw new SQLException("Unable to generate "+sequenceColumn+" : "+
                exc.toString());
        }
        finally
        {
            try
            {
                conn.close();
            }
            catch (Exception ignore) {}
        }
    }
}
```

Finally, Listing 54.4 shows the implementation for the Customer object used in the ordering system. Because customers have automatically generated keys, the `CustomerImpl` class is a subclass of `AutoGenerate`. Notice that the constructor calls the `AutoGenerate` constructor with the data source, table name, and column name for the sequence value.

LISTING 54.4 SOURCE CODE FOR `CustomerImpl.java`

```
package usingj2ee.b2b;

import java.rmi.*;
import java.util.*;
import javax.ejb.*;
import java.sql.*;
import javax.sql.*;
import javax.naming.*;
import java.util.Date;
import java.security.cert.Certificate;

public abstract class CustomerImpl extends AutoGenerate implements EntityBean
{
/** The entity context provided by the EJB container. An entity bean must
    hold on to the context it is given. */

    private EntityContext context;
```

```
/** An EJB must have a public, parameterless constructor */

    public CustomerImpl()
    {
        super("OrderDB", "customer_id_seq", "next_customer_id");
    }

/** Called by the EJB container to set this entity's context */

    public void setEntityContext(EntityContext aContext)
    {
        context = aContext;
    }

/** Called by the EJB container to clear this entity's context */

    public void unsetEntityContext()
    {
        context = null;
    }

/** Called by the EJB container when a client calls the create() method in
    the Home interface */

    public String ejbCreate()
        throws CreateException
    {
        try
        {
// compute the new primary key for this object
            setCustomerId(getNextId());

            return null;
        }
        catch (SQLException exc)
        {
            throw new CreateException(
                "Unable to access database: "+exc.toString());
        }
    }

/** Called by the EJB container after ejbCreate to allow the bean to do
    any additional setup that might be required. */
    public void ejbPostCreate()
        throws CreateException
    {
    }

/** Called by the EJB container to put the bean into active mode */

    public void ejbActivate()
        throws EJBException
    {
    }

/** Called by the EJB container to tell this bean that it is being
    deactivated and placed back into the pool */
```

LISTING 54.4 CONTINUED

```
    public void ejbPassivate()
        throws EJBException
    {
    }

/** Called by the container to tell the entity bean to read its data from
    the database */

    public void ejbLoad()
        throws EJBException
    {
    }

/** Called by the EJB container to tell the entity bean to
    write its data out to the database */
    public void ejbStore()
        throws EJBException
    {
    }

/** Called by the EJB container to tell this bean that it has been
    removed. */

    public void ejbRemove()
        throws EJBException
    {
    }

// Implement the get/set methods for all the data elements
    public abstract String getCustomerId();
    public abstract void setCustomerId(String aCustomerId);

    public abstract Collection getOrders();
    public abstract void setOrders(Collection orders);

    public abstract String getName();
    public abstract void setName(String aName);

    public abstract String getCertificate();
    public abstract void setCertificate(String aCert);
}
```

As you can see, a B2B application is just another form of EJB application. The importance of B2B applications is huge. Companies can automate their ordering systems to speed up the manufacturing process. Companies can create auction systems where you submit an order for an item and have various companies bid to fulfill your order at the lowest price or in the fastest time.

Throughout this book, you have seen many different Java technologies, some of them are part of Java 2 Enterprise Edition, and some are separate technologies. Hopefully, you now have a better understanding of how these technologies fit together and how to apply them to business applications. Whether you use J2EE or not, you can still use many of these concepts when you develop applications.

As you learn to use more and more technologies, you'll become better at learning new things. Many hot new technologies are really just variations on old ideas. The UCSD Pascal Compiler, available on the old Apple][and Commodore 64 machines compiled Pascal programs into P-code, which it then interpreted. You could take the P-code from one machine and execute it on another machine without recompiling—much like Java code. Understanding concepts is much more important than knowing the nuts and bolts of a particular API, although the latter is convenient.

As you experiment with the concepts and examples you find in this book, don't be afraid to experiment. That's the best way to learn. Good luck!

INDEX

D

F

M

N

Q-R

S

T

U

X-Z

Other Related Titles

Java 2 From Scratch
Steven Haines
ISBN: 0-7897-2173-2
$39.95 US/$59.95 CAN

Java Server Pages From Scratch
Maneesh Sahu
ISBN: 0-7897-2459-6
$39.95 US/$59.95 CAN

Java 2 by Example
Geoff Friesen
ISBN: 0-7897-2266-6
$24.99 US/$37.95 CAN

XML by Example, Second Edition
Benoît Marchal
ISBN: 0-7897-2504-5
$29.99 US/$44.95 CAN

XML and Java From Scratch
Nicholas Chase
ISBN: 0-7897-2476-6
$39.99 US/$59.95 CAN

Applied XML Solutions
Benoît Marchal
ISBN: 0-672-32054-1
$44.99 US/$67.95 CAN

Special Edition Using Java Server Pages and Servlets
Mark Wutka
ISBN: 0-7897-2441-3
$39.99 US/
$59.95 CAN

Special Edition Using Enterprise JavaBeans 2.0
Chuck Cavaness and Brian Keeton
ISBN: 0-7897-2567-3
$39.99 US/
$59.95 CAN

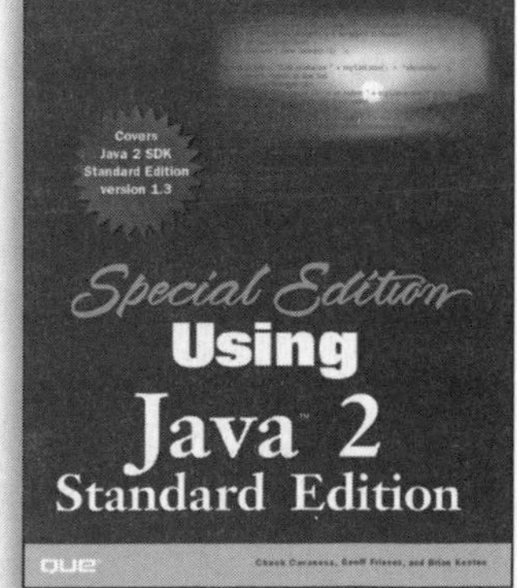

Special Edition Using Java 2 Standard Edition
Chuck Cavaness, Geoff Friesen, and Brian Keeton
ISBN: 0-7897-2468-5
$39.99 US/
$59.95 CAN

www.quecorp.com

All prices are subject to change.

What's on the Disc

The companion CD-ROM contains all of the author's source code, samples from the book, many third-party software products, and Appendixes A–H, which reference various APIs.

Windows 95 Installation Instructions

1. Insert the CD-ROM disc into your CD-ROM drive.
2. From the Windows 95 desktop, double-click the My Computer icon.
3. Double-click the icon representing your CD-ROM drive.
4. Double-click the icon titled START.EXE to run the installation program.

Note

If Windows 95 is installed on your computer and you have the AutoPlay feature enabled, the START.EXE program starts automatically whenever you insert the disc into your CD-ROM drive.